2

Contemporary
Clinical
Psychology

CONTEMPORARY CLINICAL PSYCHOLOGY

Third Edition

Thomas G. Plante
Santa Clara University and
Stanford University

WILEY

JOHN WILEY & SONS, INC.

Copyright © 2011 by John Wiley & Sons, Inc. All rights reserved.

Published by John Wiley & Sons, Inc., Hoboken, New Jersey.

Published simultaneously in Canada.

Library of Congress Cataloging-in-Publication Data:

Plante, Thomas G.
   Contemporary clinical psychology / Thomas G. Plante. -- 3rd ed.
       p. ; cm.
   Includes bibliographical references and indexes.
   ISBN 978-0-470-58739-3 (cloth : alk. paper)
   1. Clinical psychology. 2. Psychotherapy. I. Title.
   [DNLM: 1. Psychology, Clinical. 2. Mental Disorders--therapy. 3.
Psychotherapy. WM 105 P713c 2011]
   RC467.P56 2011
   616.89--dc22   2010010871

Printed in the United States of America

10 9 8 7 6 5 4 3 2 1

For Lori and Zach,
who make everything worthwhile and meaningful

Chapter 3

Recent History of Clinical Psychology   49

Chapter 4

Research: Design and Outcome   73

Chapter 5

The Major Theoretical Models: Psychodynamic, Cognitive-Behavioral, Humanistic, and Family Systems   **111**

Chapter 6

Integrative and Biopsychosocial Approaches in Contemporary Clinical Psychology   **135**

PART TWO
Roles and Responsibilities   167

Chapter 7
Contemporary Psychological Assessment I: Interviewing and Observing Behavior   169

Chapter 8
Contemporary Psychological Assessment II: Cognitive and Personality Assessment **201**

Chapter 9

Psychotherapeutic Interventions   **247**

Chapter 10

Psychotherapeutic Issues   **279**

Chapter 11

Areas of Specialization   303

Chapter 12

Chapter 13

The goals, activities, and contributions of contemporary clinical psychology are very appealing to many who are fascinated by human behavior and relationships. The enormous popularity of psychology as an undergraduate major; of clinical psychology as a career path; and of popular psychology books, movies, television shows, web sites, and blogs is a testament to the inherent interest of clinical psychology and of human behavior at its best and at its worst. The goal of clinical psychology is noble: to use the principles of psychology and our understanding of human behavior to promote health, happiness, satisfaction with and improvement of self and others, and an enhanced quality of life.

Like so many other professional disciplines, contemporary clinical psychology is changing and growing at a rapid pace. The changing needs of a multicultural society, technological and other scientific advances, the changing health-care and mental health-care landscape, as well as complex problems in today's culture, have all greatly impacted both the science and practice of contemporary clinical psychology. Some of these changes are positive; others are negative. Despite the challenges confronting clinical psychology, the field remains a fascinating and exciting endeavor with tremendous potential to help individuals, groups, and society.

As more research evidence emerges concerning the interplay of biological, psychological, and social influences on behavior, contemporary clinical psychologists must incorporate new knowledge to develop better applications in their efforts to understand and help others. Biopsychosocial integration in many ways best reflects contemporary clinical psychology, expanding the range and usefulness of its efforts.

This book provides students an overview of contemporary clinical psychology from an integrative biopsychosocial perspective. The book highlights the various activities, roles, and responsibilities of the contemporary clinical psychologist as well as provides a foundation of the discipline through a detailed review of its history, scientific underpinnings, and theoretical orientations. An overview of contemporary issues in clinical psychology serves as a roadmap for those interested in pursuing clinical psychology as a career.

Each chapter includes a highlight of a contemporary clinical psychologist who provides a frank reflection on the pros and cons of contemporary clinical psychology as well as his or her view of the future of the field. A typical schedule is also provided so that you get a sense of what a day in the life of a contemporary clinical psychologist might be like. The psychologists were chosen to reflect the broad range and diversity of people who are clinical psychologists. Some of the psychologists are well known; others are not. Several work in colleges and universities conducting research and teaching. Several work in solo or group private practice. Some work in hospitals, government agencies, or university counseling clinics. One works in the United States Senate. Several work overseas. Some combine work in several diverse settings. Some work part-time while raising a family. Psychologists from diverse training programs, from both genders, a variety of ethnic groups, from locations across the United States and elsewhere, and with disabilities are represented. The range of activities, roles, and responsibilities of these psychologists reflects the diversity of careers open to the contemporary clinical psychologist.

Each chapter includes a detailed list of key points and terms to help enhance understanding. Each chapter also includes a section entitled The Big Picture, which provides a bottom-line or "take-home message" summary of the chapter as well as a look toward the future of the topic covered in that particular chapter. Each chapter also provides several questions readers have had after reading each chapter. Most chapters include one or more Spotlights on a contemporary issue in clinical psychology. A great deal of clinical case material is presented throughout the book as well. Several cases, such as Mary, a 65-year-old woman with a long history of panic attacks, are discussed in several chapters for the reader to trace the theoretical conceptualization, assessment, and treatment of one case in some detail. All of the patients presented are based on actual clinical cases. All of the examples from testing, therapy, consultation, and ethics are also based on actual cases. However, the details have been altered to protect patient and psychologist confidentiality.

This book uses an integrative biopsychosocial approach throughout. This approach best reflects the perspective of most contemporary clinical psychologists. Less emphasis is placed on traditional theoretical models such as behavioral, psychodynamic, and humanistic approaches since most contemporary clinical psychologists integrate these and other approaches and orientations rather than exclusively using one. An emphasis is placed on the real world of clinical psychology to provide a window into how the science and practice of clinical psychology is actually conducted. I have attempted to provide the reader with a realistic, practical, and current portrayal of the contemporary clinical psychology field in many different settings. Finally, this book provides a separate chapter on ethics and a separate chapter on the consultation, administration, and teaching responsibilities of clinical psychologists. Emphasis is placed on contemporary issues in clinical psychology such as diversity, empirically supported and evidence-based treatments, managed health care and health-care reform, and other hot topics.

I have updated this third edition of the book with hundreds of new references published since 2005, when the second edition was published. Sections on evidence-based practice and empirically supported treatments have been expanded as well as the sections on neuropsychology. The assessment chapters have been updated to incorporate the most recent versions of common psychological testing instruments (e.g., WAIS-IV, MMPI-2-RF, Roberts-2). In order to make the textbook more approachable and hopefully more interesting for students, some of the psychologists highlighted in chapters have been replaced with other psychologists from more diverse backgrounds, careers overseas, and several who work in counseling centers on college campuses.

The book assumes that students have already completed undergraduate courses in introductory and abnormal psychology. The book is appropriate for upper-division college students who are likely to be psychology majors or first-year graduate students in clinical psychology. The book might also be a helpful reference for those who provide career guidance for students potentially interested in a career in psychology or related fields.

The instructor's guide that accompanies this book provides faculty with a detailed book outline, multiple choice and essay examination questions, Power Point slides for class use, a list of references, web sites, popular and educational films, class activities, and a sample course syllabus. The instructor's guide is available online.

I welcome comments about the book from both students and faculty. These comments will be used to create improved future editions.

In fact, many of the changes made to this edition were based on comments provided to me by students and instructors using the book.

You can contact me at tplante@scu.edu or check my web site at www.scu.edu/tplante.

Thank you for reading this book and welcome to the exciting, fascinating, and ever-changing world of contemporary clinical psychology.

Acknowledgments

Numerous people other than the author assist in the development and completion of a book. Some provide help in a direct and concrete manner while others provide help in less direct and more supportive ways. I would like to acknowledge the assistance of the many people who have helped in both ways and have contributed to the development of the book and of myself.

First, I would like to thank the many wonderful people at John Wiley & Sons who have enthusiastically worked to publish this book. I'd like to thank my editor, Patricia Rossi, and her assistant, Fiona Brown, for their interest, dedication, and enthusiasm with the project as well as their high level of professionalism. I would like to thank the production staff as well. I thank the anonymous patients referred to in this book for allowing their life experiences and challenges to be an instrument of learning for others. I would like to thank the reviewers for offering their helpful suggestions and perspectives on earlier editions of the book, which I have now incorporated into this third edition.

I would also like to thank my many students for helping me better understand what is useful, interesting, and helpful for them to learn and for providing me with inspiration. Their passion and curiosity for clinical psychology is inspiring. I'd like to especially thank the students who provided the questions at the end of each chapter in the Real Students, Real Questions sections. Finally, I would like to thank my wife, Lori, and son, Zach, for their love and support, and for making everything worthwhile and meaningful. Additionally, my son provided many of the new photos in this edition.

Thomas G. Plante is a Professor of Psychology and Director of the Spirituality and Health Institute at Santa Clara University. He is also an Adjunct Clinical Professor of Psychiatry at Stanford University School of Medicine. He teaches undergraduate courses in Introductory, Abnormal, Clinical, Ethics, and Health Psychology at Santa Clara as well as Professional Issues and Ethics for clinical psychology interns and postdoctoral fellows at Stanford. He is a licensed psychologist in California and a Diplomate of the American Board of Professional Psychology in Clinical Psychology, also maintaining a private practice. He is a fellow of the Academy of Clinical Psychology, the American Psychological Association (Divisions 12, 36, 38, 46, and 47), and the Society of Behavioral Medicine. He currently serves as Vice-Chair of the National Review Board for the Protection of Children and Youth for the United States Council of Catholic Bishops and is President of Division 36 (Psychology and Religion) of the American Psychological Association.

Dr. Plante was born and raised in Rhode Island and received his ScB degree in psychology from Brown University, his MA and PhD degrees in clinical psychology from the University of Kansas, and his clinical internship and postdoctoral fellowship in clinical and health psychology from Yale University. He is the former chief psychologist and mental health director of the Children's Health Council, as well as a former staff psychologist and medical staff member at Stanford University Hospital.

He has published over 150 professional journal articles and chapters on topics such as clinical psychology training and professional issues, psychological benefits of exercise, personality and stress, spirituality and health, and psychological issues among Catholic clergy. He has published 14 books, including *Faith and Health: Psychological Perspectives* (2001, Guilford), *Do the Right Thing: Living Ethically in an Unethical World* (2004, New Harbinger), *Mental Disorders of the New Millennium* (Vols. I, II, and III, 2006, Greenwood), *Spirit, Science and Health: How the Spiritual Mind Fuels Physical Wellness* (2007, Greenwood), and most recently, *Spiritual Practices in Psychotherapy: Thirteen Tools for Enhancing Psychological Health* (2009, American Psychological Association) and *Contemplative Practices in Action: Spirituality, Meditation, and Health* (2010, Greenwood).

He has been featured in numerous media outlets, including *Time* magazine, *CNN, NBC Nightly News, The PBS News Hour, New York Times, USA Today, British Broadcasting Company,* and *National Public Radio,* among many others. He has evaluated or treated more than 600 priests and applicants to the priesthood and diaconate and has served as a consultant for a number of Roman Catholic and Episcopal Church dioceses and religious orders. *Time* magazine referred to him (April 1, 2002) as one of "three leading (American) Catholics."

Part One

FOUNDATIONS AND FUNDAMENTALS

Photo: Courtesy Zach Plante.

What Is Contemporary Clinical Psychology?

1

Chapter

Case Study: Carlos

Carlos experiences depression, substance abuse, attentional problems, learning disabilities, diabetes, and family stress.

Carlos is a biracial (part Latino and part Caucasian) 14-year-old boy who feels isolated, depressed, and hopeless. He has few friends, his schoolwork is poor, and he feels uncomfortable in his predominantly Caucasian high school. He is new at school, having recently moved to a new town from out of state. He complains that he doesn't fit in and misses his old middle school, which had predominantly Latino and African American students. He was evaluated by a psychologist at school when he was 9 years old and was found to experience an attentional problem as well as a learning disability that makes reading difficult. He has taken medication in the past for his attentional problem and he also takes insulin for his diabetes.

Carlos' mother is Latina and works as a social worker at a local hospital. She was recently diagnosed with breast cancer. His father is Caucasian of German descent and works as a clerk at a large computer company. His mother is Roman Catholic and very active in her church, whereas his father was raised Lutheran but describes himself as an atheist. His father has had an alcohol problem for many years and has suffered from depression as well. He has been fired from several jobs due to his alcohol troubles and temper. He also had attentional and learning difficulties in school but coped fairly

continued

Case Study (Continued)

well with these problems and graduated from community college with good grades.

Carlos' parents have had a great deal of marital conflict and have separated on several occasions. Their differences in faith, ethnic background, financial concerns, and his father's alcohol abuse, depression, and temper have taken a toll on the family. Carlos' younger sister is a "star" student, has lots of friends, and seems to cope very well with the stress in the family. Carlos feels that his sister makes him "look bad."

Carlos' mother felt that Carlos should see a clinical psychologist about his depressive mood. Her managed care health insurance will allow Carlos and his family up to six sessions with a local clinical psychologist who is on the company's list of preferred providers. Carlos is willing to get help but feels that there is little anyone can do for him. He also worries about confidentiality

because he does not want his parents to know that he has been sexually active and has used alcohol and drugs on occasion. He would like to see a Latino psychologist but the managed care company does not have one on its local panel of providers.

If you were the clinical psychologist Carlos and his family came to, how would you help them during the allotted six sessions? How would you further evaluate Carlos and his family? What would you suggest they do to help themselves and each other? How would you manage confidentiality arrangements? What research is available to guide you in your work? How much can you accomplish in six sessions? What do you do if after six sessions Carlos and his family still need your help? How do you evaluate if your work has been helpful? What do you do if Carlos becomes in danger of hurting himself?

As you can tell from this example, clinical psychology is a complex field that parallels the complexity of human behavior and emotion. Just as we are defined by more than blood and tissue, emotions and ideas, or our relationships to others, the field of clinical psychology is, by necessity, an integrative effort to understand the interaction of the biological, psychological, and social factors that make each of us "tick." Furthermore, modern clinical psychology must respond to contemporary issues that impact all of our lives. For example, the importance of ethnicity, culture, and gender in today's society informs and enriches the field of contemporary clinical psychology as do current issues related to economics, technology, ethics, and popular culture.

As with medicine and other fields, the roots of clinical psychology are viewed as simplistic and narrowly conceived. However, with scientific advancements and collaboration between various fields and schools of

thought, contemporary clinical psychology champions a sophisticated integration that pulls together the best of these models for optimal treatment, assessment, consultation, and research.

Before describing the historical evolution of clinical psychology into its contemporary form, this chapter defines clinical psychology and the varied roles and activities of today's clinical psychologist. In addition, the integrative and evidence-based nature of contemporary clinical psychology will be highlighted. The purpose of this chapter is to examine exactly what clinical psychology is all about. I will define clinical psychology as well as outline the educational process for clinical psychologists, detail their typical roles and professional activities, list the usual employment settings, the various subspecialties within clinical psychology, the professional organizations of clinical psychology, and the similarities and differences between clinical psychology and related fields. Subsequent chapters will highlight these issues (and others) in much more detail. In doing so, a comprehensive and realistic view of the field of clinical psychology will be presented.

Throughout the course of this book, I discuss the field of clinical psychology as understood and practiced in the United States. However, clinical psychology is recognized and practiced in many other countries. The American Psychological Association (APA), the Canadian Psychological Association, and the British Psychological Society, for example, have more similarities than differences and often host joint meetings and other professional activities. The doctorate is the expected level of training for psychologists in the United States, Canada, and the United Kingdom. Much of Europe and elsewhere do not require doctoral training for clinical psychologists. Unfortunately, it is beyond the scope of this book to detail the training, history, and activities of clinical psychologists in other countries. However, much of the information presented is universally relevant to clinical psychologists.

Definition and Inherent Intrigue

What could be more intriguing than human behavior and interpersonal relationships in all their complexity? A visit to any major bookstore or a Google search of "psychology" reveals that topics such as clinical psychology, self-help, and the general use of psychological principles in understanding our lives are enormously popular and pervasive. Hundreds if not thousands of books are published each year that focus on ways to better understand human behavior, replete with methods to improve psychological functioning as it interacts with physical wellbeing, emotions, and interpersonal relationships. Furthermore, a popular television program during recent years has been *The Dr. Phil Show,* a clinical psychologist offering advice on numerous wide-ranging topics for willing participants and a national audience.

Although the independent discipline of psychology is only about 100 years old, psychology is one of the most popular current undergraduate majors in most colleges and universities. Furthermore, clinical psychology is the most popular specialty area within psychology (APA, 2009a, b; Norcross, Sayette, & Mayne, 2008). Doctorates in psychology are more common than any other doctoral degree awarded in the United States with the majority of psychology doctorates being awarded in clinical psychology (APA, 2009a, b; Norcross et al., 2008). The majority of members of the APA list clinical psychology as their area of specialization (APA, 2010a). Additionally, being a clinical psychologist has also made recent lists of "hottest jobs" by *Money* magazine and other popular national publications.

How is clinical psychology defined? Clinical psychology focuses on the *assessment, treatment,* and understanding of psychological and behavioral problems and disorders. In fact, clinical psychology focuses its efforts on the ways in which the human psyche interacts with physical, emotional, and social aspects of health and dysfunction. According to the APA, **clinical psychology** attempts to use the principles of psychology to better understand, predict, and alleviate "intellectual, emotional, biological, psychological, social, and behavioral aspects of human functioning" (APA, 2009a). Clinical psychology is "the aspect of psychological science and practice concerned with the analysis, treatment, and prevention of human psychological disabilities and with the enhancing of personal adjustment and effectiveness" (Rodnick, 1985, p. 1929). Thus, clinical psychology uses what is known about the principles of human behavior to help people with the numerous troubles and concerns they experience during the course of life in their relationships, emotions, and physical selves. For example, a clinical psychologist might evaluate a child using intellectual and educational tests to determine if the child has a learning disability or an attentional problem that might contribute to poor school performance. Another example includes a psychologist who treats an adult experiencing severe depression following a recent divorce. People experiencing substance and other addictions, hallucinations, compulsive eating, sexual dysfunction, physical abuse, suicidal impulses, and head injuries are a few of the many problem areas that are of interest to clinical psychologists.

Who is a clinical psychologist? Many people with different types of training and experience are involved with helping understand, assess, and treat people with problems in living. Counselors, nurses, psychiatrists, peer helpers, and others are involved with the areas of concern already listed. Clinical psychologists "have a doctoral degree from a regionally accredited university or professional school providing an organized, sequential clinical psychology program in a department of psychology" (APA, 1981, p. 641). Although many universities offer master's degree training programs in clinical psychology, the doctorate is assumed to be the minimal level of training to be considered a clinical psychologist. Clinical psychology is not so much a specialty separate from psychology, but is more a unique application of psychology to the realm of emotional and behavioral problems (APA 1987a, 2009a; Matarazzo, 1987; Norcross et al., 2008).

Perspective and Philosophy

Clinical psychology uses the scientific method to approach and understand human problems in behavior, emotions, thinking, relationships, and health. Rigorous scientific inquiry is used to select and evaluate assessment and treatment approaches and activities. Treatment outcome research helps to determine which treatments might be most effective for people seeking help with particular clinical problems. However, clinical psychology is both a science and an art. Findings from scientific investigations must be applied to the unique and special needs of an individual, group, or organization. What might be helpful to one person may not be to another even if they both experience the same diagnosis or problems. The science of clinical psychology informs the art while

the art also informs the science. For example, research findings from experiments on psychotherapy outcomes are used to determine which type of psychotherapy is most useful with people experiencing depression, whereas clinical experience working with people struggling with depression is used to better design and implement psychotherapy outcome research.

Contemporary clinical psychology uses integrative evidence-based approaches to understand and address problems in human behavior. While a wealth of individual perspectives contribute important pieces of understanding to the puzzle of human behavior, these pieces must often be joined in novel ways to provide the most complete and holistic perspective. For example, advances in biology have provided important knowledge about the role of neurotransmitters in depression. Similarly, personal variables such as history of loss and trauma, as well as sociocultural factors such as poverty, discrimination, and community support in depression, are well appreciated. Ultimately, an intelligent melding of these biological, psychological, and social factors leads to intervention strategies that best address the complex needs of depressed individuals. Therefore, this book emphasizes integrative efforts to address human behavior, referring to biopsychosocial factors throughout.

Although individual clinical psychologists may be closely aligned with particular theoretical perspectives on human behavior, most contemporary clinical psychologists also appreciate the integral roles of biopsychological factors in health and illness. The biopsychosocial perspective, an example of an integrative approach, will be more fully described in Chapter 6. To understand psychology's roots and gradual development into its present form as an integrative endeavor, it is important to keep in mind the impact of biopsychosocial issues simply as the interplay of relevant biological, psychological, and social factors in human behavior.

Research and practice in clinical psychology has found that certain approaches to understanding and treating problems may be especially useful for certain people and problems while different approaches might be most helpful for others. For example, some people who experience depression respond well to medication while others respond to cognitive-behavioral psychotherapy. Others respond well to supportive therapies such as the humanistic approach. Still others respond to a combination of these and other approaches. Although medication might be useful to treat someone with depression, family therapy, vocational counseling, and group social skills training may enhance treatment success.

Many people who seek the services of a clinical psychologist often have several problems or diagnoses occurring at the same time. For example, the person who experiences depression may also suffer from a chronic illness, a personality disorder, a learning disability, alcohol troubles, and marital discord. Furthermore, stressful life events, intellectual functioning, ethnic background, religious orientation, and other factors contribute to the manifestation of the depressive disorder and other problems. One theoretical orientation alone may not address the complexity of the person seeking help. Although various clinical psychologists may be closely aligned with one particular theoretical or philosophical orientation, most contemporary clinical psychologists believe that problems in human behavior are multidimensional. They use an integrative and evidence-based approach that suggests that interacting causal factors generally contribute to human problems and that a multidimensional approach is usually needed to tackle these issues. Thus, many factors may contribute to human problems and a selection of factors must be utilized to help alleviate these concerns. Today, many clinical psychologists use an integrative evidence-based perspective that maintains a biopsychosocial orientation.

The **biopsychosocial perspective** emphasizes the interaction of biological, psychological, and social influences on behavior and psychological functioning. Each must be carefully considered and the individual viewed in a broader biopsychosocial context in order to best understand the complexities of human behavior and the most effective means of intervention (Borrell-Carrió, Suchman, & Epstein, 2004; Engel, 1977, 1980; N. Johnson, 2003; G. E. Schwartz, 1982, 1984). Although clinical psychologists may not be able to intervene at the biological, psychological, or social level, they must take into consideration these influencing factors in understanding and treating people who seek their services. For example, psychologists cannot prescribe medication in most states, conduct physical examinations, or offer surgery to their patients. They cannot alter ethnic, religious, socioeconomic, or cultural backgrounds. However, clinical psychologists can work to understand these influences on behavior and clinical problems and can consult with others who can provide additional services such as medication management, surgery, and spiritual and religious direction.

The biopsychosocial approach is a systemic perspective (Borrell-Carrió et al., 2004; Schwartz, 1982, 1984); that is, changes in one area of functioning will likely impact functioning in other areas. The fluid and systemic nature of the biopsychosocial approach highlights the mutual interdependence of each system on each of the other systems. For example, feelings of depression may be associated with brain neurochemicals, interpersonal conflicts, disappointments in life, stresses at home and at work, unrealistic expectations, cultural context, and many other interacting factors. Someone might be genetically or biologically vulnerable to depression due to brain chemistry. Stressful life events such as a divorce, illness, or job loss may trigger a depressive episode. Feelings of depression may result in poor work performance, social isolation, feelings of hopelessness, and lower self-esteem, which may deepen the depression as well as trigger brain chemistry that in turn further worsens the depression. Educational, cultural, socioeconomic, and other factors might influence whatever treatment, if any, is pursued by the depressed person. Treatment success may be influenced by both patient and therapist motivation, expectations, and comfort with the treatment plan. The biopsychosocial model has been endorsed as the preferred approach to understanding and treating health-related problems and issues by the APA (Borrell-Carrió et al., 2004; Fava & Sonino, 2008; Johnson, 2003) and other organizations (Institute for the Future, 2000).

Details on theoretical orientations and the biopsychosocial perspective will be discussed more fully in Chapters 5 and 6.

Education and Training

Few people are aware of the long and intensive training process that is involved in becoming a clinical psychologist. Most do not realize that the training process includes experimental research as well as clinical training in psychological testing and psychotherapy. Although master's degrees are awarded in clinical psychology as well as other areas of applied psychology (e.g., school psychology), the doctorate is considered the minimal educational requirement to become a clnical psychologist (APA, 1987b). Finally, mandatory training continues even beyond the doctorate. The road to becoming a clinical psychologist is a long one divided by a number of distinct stages and phases that include college, graduate school, clinical internship, postdoctoral fellowship, licensure, and finally employment, continuing education, and advanced certification. Although a brief overview of the training process is presented here, details of the training of clinical psychologists are outlined in Chapter 15.

Students interested in becoming clinical psychologists and gaining admission to quality graduate programs must take their college experience very seriously. Completing courses in psychology, research design, and statistics as well as having excellent grades, Graduate Record Examination (GRE) scores, and high-quality research and clinical experience during the college years are important.

Graduate training in clinical psychology involves coursework as well as clinical and research experiences and training. Graduate school in clinical psychology takes at least five years to complete, including a one-year clinical internship. However, many students find that they need more than five years to complete their graduate education. Dissertation projects and other factors often extend the training process to an average of six to eight years. A student interested in obtaining a doctorate in clinical psychology can choose between two types of degrees: the traditional **PhD (Doctor of Philosophy)** or the **PsyD (Doctor of Psychology)**. Although the APA recommends a core curriculum of courses and activities (APA, 1987b, 2009a; Norcross et al., 2008), each program maintains its own unique orientation based on the faculty and traditions of the program. In researching graduate programs, you will find that each program has its own unique balance on emphasizing the roles of biological, psychological, and social factors in human behavior.

Almost all graduate training programs in clinical psychology require that students complete a one-year, full-time (or two-year, part-time) clinical internship prior to being awarded the doctorate. The internship is the most focused clinical training experience generally available during graduate training. The training usually occurs in hospitals, clinics, or various clinical settings throughout the United States and Canada. The activities during the clinical internship focus specifically on clinical training, such as the practice of psychotherapy, psychological testing, and consultation activities with a variety of patient or client populations.

Most states now require one to two years of postdoctoral training and supervision before you are eligible to take the national and state licensing examinations. However, nine states (e.g., Washington, Ohio, Arizona, Connecticut) allow students who have already secured two years of supervised training to obtain their license without a postdoctoral fellowship year. Postdoctoral training occurs in a wide variety of settings, including hospitals, clinics, counseling centers, universities, and even private practices. Postdoctoral training can include clinical work as well as research, teaching, and other professional activities.

Dr. Phil, Dr. Laura, Dr. Drew, and Other "Psychology" Celebrity Personalities

Phillip McGraw (aka Dr. Phil) has received a great deal of attention during the past decade due to his highly successful television show. Started in September 2002, it quickly became the highest rating new syndicated television show in 16 years. Prior to *The Dr. Phil Show*, he regularly appeared on the *Oprah Winfrey Show* starting in 1998, acting as an expert on relationships, life strategies, and behavior. Dr. Phil is, unlike many other well-known "psychology" celebrity personalities such as Dr. Laura (Schlessinger), Dr. John Gray, and Dr. Drew (Pinsky), a clinical psychologist and was licensed as a psychologist in Texas. He obtained his PhD in clinical psychology from the University of North Texas and opened a clinical practice in 1979. Dr. Phil is a clinical psychologist who uses his professional training and skill to host his popular television show and write popular books on relationship issues, weight loss, and so forth.

Unlike Dr. Phil, Dr. Laura (Laura Schlessinger) is not a clinical psychologist or a psychologist at all. Her PhD degree is in physiology from Columbia University. Although she has received training in marriage and family therapy at the University of Southern California, she is not a licensed psychologist. The same is true for John Gray, PhD. He is the well-known author of the popular *Men Are from Mars and Women Are from Venus* books published by HarperCollins. He is neither a clinical psychologist, nor a licensed psychologist. Dr. Drew Pinsky is an internal medicine physician (neither a psychologist, nor a psychiatrist) and is a frequent guest on television news and entertainment shows as well as hosting the popular shows, *Celebrity Rehab with Dr. Drew* and the radio and television advice show, *Loveline*. Many other "psychology" celebrities frequently seen in television and print media, such as Cooper Lawrence and Dr. Jenn Berman, are also neither licensed psychologists nor clinical psychologists.

Regardless of what you think about these well-known psychology personalities, their popularity speaks to the remarkable interest the general population has in the use of applied psychology to help people solve life problems, improve relationships, and live better lives.

Each state offers appropriately trained psychologists an opportunity to acquire a license to practice psychology and offer professional services to the public. Licensing attempts to protect the public from untrained or unethical practitioners helps to protect the integrity of the profession by offering minimum standards of care. All states use the same national written examination for licensing (i.e., the Examination for Professional Practice in Psychology, EPPP). After successful completion of the written examination, many states then require an oral (or sometimes an essay) examination before obtaining the license. Following licensure, most states require continuing education in order to renew the psychology license.

After being awarded the doctorate, a clinical psychologist is eligible to become a *diplomate*, an advanced level of certification. This diploma is an optional post-licensing certification that reflects advanced competency in a subspecialty area of professional practice. The American Board of Professional Psychology (ABPP) acts as the credentialing agency for psychology diplomates in a variety of specialty areas (e.g., clinical psychology, counseling psychology, neuropsychology, school psychology, health psychology).

Activities

Clinical psychologists certainly do more than talk to people who are distressed about personal matters. Clinical psychologists often do vastly different types of activities, from teaching to psychotherapy to laboratory research.

Clinical psychologists also may be involved in a wide range of professional activities including teaching at the college or university level, conducting independent and/or collaborative research, providing consultation to a variety of professionals and organizations, conducting psychotherapy, and providing psychological assessment and diagnostic services. Clinical psychologists work in a plethora of environments such as universities, hospitals, clinics, schools, businesses, government agencies, military institutions, and private or group practices. These varied roles and settings often assist the clinical psychologist in appreciating multidimensional factors and integrating key approaches into his or her work.

Research

Research is at the foundation of all clinical psychology activities. Research conducted by psychologists or others in the behavioral sciences provides the basis and direction for all professional activities. Clinical psychologists often conduct and publish a wide variety of research studies. **Research programs** help to determine which assessment or treatment approach might be most effective for a particular clinical problem such as depression, anxiety, eating disorders, or substance abuse problems. Projects may help identify those at risk

for the development of certain psychological problems. Other projects might evaluate methods to better determine clinical diagnoses. The types of research activities conducted by clinical psychologists are extremely diverse.

Most psychologists who are actively engaged in research are faculty members at colleges, universities, or medical schools. They, like faculty in other academic disciplines, may conduct research on a wide range of subject areas, publish their findings in professional journals, and present their research at international, national, and regional professional conferences. Psychologists who are not academic faculty members at colleges or universities might also conduct research at their hospitals, clinics, government agencies (e.g., National Institute of Mental Health), industry (e.g., pharmaceutical companies, psychological testing companies, managed care insurance companies), or private practices. Research in clinical psychology encompasses biological, psychological, and social aspects of human behavior, from research exploring neuroimaging techniques, to ethnic factors in hypertension, to spiritual aspects of love and intimacy.

Although not all clinical psychologists conduct and publish their own research, all are expected to be constant consumers of research in order to inform their professional activities. Clinical psychologists must understand the research findings of others in order to improve their own professional activities. Many regularly read professional journals that cover research topics of special interest.

Assessment

Many clinical psychologists use psychological tests and procedures to assess or diagnose various psychiatric (e.g., depression, psychosis, personality disorders, dementia) as well as non-psychiatric issues (e.g., relationship conflicts, learning differences, educational potential, career interests, and skills). Generally, psychologists are the only mental health professionals who administer psychological tests. In fact, clinical psychologists not only conduct

Terrorism and Its Aftermath

The horrific terrorist events of September 11, 2001, in the United States that claimed the lives of approximately 3,000 people have had enormous implications for life in America and elsewhere. In many ways, life in the United States is very different after September 11 than it was before that fateful day. The new U.S. Department of Homeland Security and Congress altered the way foreign students and visitors to the United States are screened and evaluated. Laws and transportation policies and procedures have been greatly changed in an attempt to increase security. Air travel security procedures, for example, have changed dramatically following September 11. Wars in Afghanistan and Iraq commenced with thousands of military young people being shipped overseas and, tragically, many did not return home. Many people from Islamic countries or religious traditions have experienced prejudice and suspicion.

Clinical psychology has been involved with the response to terrorism in the United States in a number of different ways. Immediately following the terrorism events and since, psychologists have counseled those who lost loved ones in the tragedy as well as those terribly stressed by the events. For example, airplane phobias have always been treated by clinical psychologists. Yet, following the terrorism events, the need for this type of specialized counseling increased a great deal. Children and others in the New York and Washington areas (as well as elsewhere) experienced posttraumatic stress symptoms, such as anxiety and sleep disturbances, that needed treatment and consultation (Cormer & Kendall, 2007). Furthermore, clinical psychologists and others have been involved in research to help better understand the causes and risk factors for terrorist acts as well as the psychological consequences for those impacted by these events (e.g., Eidelson & Eidelson, 2003; La Greca, 2007; Moghaddam & Marsella, 2004; Post, 2007; Pyszczynski, Solomon, & Greenberg, 2003).

For example, Eidelson and Eidelson (2003) have examined research on what propels groups toward conflict and violence that has many useful implications for understanding and hopefully preventing terrorism. They have highlighted five "dangerous ideas [that include] superiority, injustice, vulnerability, distrust, and helplessness" (p. 182) that act as risk factors for conflict and violence.

Superiority refers to the belief and conviction that a person or group is better than everyone else in a variety of important ways. For example, someone might believe that they or their group are the only ones who have a clear understanding of God's will and plan. This belief has certainly caused wars, terrorism, mass killings, and so forth for thousands of years. This perspective is rather narcissistic in that someone or a group believes that they have some special information, entitlement, or gifts that others do not have or can't have access to obtain. *Injustice* and victimization refer to the belief that the person or group has been badly mistreated by specific

(continued)

others or the world in general. Although injustice and victimization have been common human experiences since the dawn of time, this perspective can lead (and has led) to retaliatory acts and rage against others. *Vulnerability* refers to the notion that a person or group is highly likely to experience danger or further victimization and that hypervigilance and preemptive acts are needed to reduce the risk of further harm. *Distrust* refers to the belief that very few people can be trusted and that only the inner circle of true believers can be considered appropriate and trustworthy group members. This point of view leads to paranoia and potential misunderstandings attributing benign others as hostile and malevolent. Finally, *helplessness* refers to feelings of powerlessness and dependency that often become overly pessimistic and negative. This perspective can lead to extreme measures to help feel more in control and more powerful. These five dangerous beliefs can be applied to the actions of many conflicts between nations and peoples as well as to the terrorism experienced in America on September 11, 2001, and elsewhere. Many countries have been dealing with terrorism for a long time. For example, Ireland, the United Kingdom, Israel, and many other areas of the world have regularly had to deal with terrorism for many years. Lessons learned from these countries can be applied to the current concerns in the United States. Psychologists in these other locations have studied and counseled those affected by terrorism for many years.

Clinical psychology has much to offer in our efforts to help those touched by terrorism as well as to help us better understand the factors that contribute to such horrific violence perpetrated against others (Cormer & Kendall, 2007).

---

psychological evaluations with individuals to assess intellectual, educational, personality, and neuropsychological functioning, but also assess groups of people (e.g., families) and even organizations.

There are numerous components to psychological **assessment,** including cognitive, personality, behavioral, neuropsychological, and observational measures. For example, a neuropsychologist may be called on to evaluate an urban Latino adolescent boy for temporal lobe epilepsy, which often results in impulsive behavior and aggression. Neuroimaging techniques conducted by a physician will augment the findings, as well as a developmental history, to rule out personality or environmental factors such as trauma as causal in the behavioral manifestations of the disorder. Thus, while focusing on neuropsychological

measures, the psychologist needs to be keenly aware of medical, psychological, and social factors that may contribute to or otherwise explain "seizure-like" symptomology.

Integration in assessment will be more fully explored in conjunction with its component elements in Chapters 7 and 8. An extremely challenging and exciting area of clinical psychology, assessment requires the psychologist to be something of a psychological sleuth, utilizing an arsenal of tools in determining subtle and often hidden problems and syndromes in the context of biological, psychological, and sociocultural factors.

Treatment

Contemporary psychological interventions address a tremendous range of human problems through a diversity of approaches. Psychotherapy may involve individuals, couples, families, and groups, and address an endless array of target problems. Anxiety, phobias, depression, shyness, physical illness, loss, trauma, drug addiction, eating difficulties, sexuality concerns, hallucinations, relationship problems, and work difficulties may all prompt individuals to seek psychological **treatment.** Furthermore, it has become increasingly incumbent upon psychologists to become educated and sensitized to cultural factors in treating clients, as well as the entire spectrum of individual differences (e.g., sexual preference, religious faith, disabilities, ethnic identities, economic status) that comprise today's mosaic society. Various treatment approaches and theoretical models are utilized to treat psychological and behavioral problems. Most psychologists use an eclectic strategy, defined as integrating a variety of perspectives and clinical approaches in their treatment (Norcross, 2009; Norcross & Goldfried, 2005; Norcross, Karg, & Prochaska, 1997a, b; Weston, 2000). Others tend to specialize in one of a number of treatment approaches, such as psychoanalysis, family therapy, or hypnosis. The major theoretical schools of thought in psychology are psychodynamic, cognitive behavioral, humanistic/existential, and family systems. Each of these theoretical orientations or perspectives is discussed in detail in Chapter 4, leading to our current understanding of integrative models.

Efforts to develop *empirically supported* or *evidence-based* treatments to assist clinicians and researchers in providing structured treatments and the use of treatment manuals that are based on treatment outcome research findings have received a great deal of attention and support from the APA and others (Addis, 2002; APA Presidential Task Force on Evidence-Based Practice, 2006; Becker, Stice, Shaw, & Woda, 2009; Chambless & Ollendick, 2001; Crits-Christoph, Chambless, Brody, & Karp, 1995; Lamberg, 2008; Sanderson & Woody, 1995). Empirically supported treatments hinge on the notion that psychological treatment approaches should always be based on solid empirical research data and supported by professional organizations such as the APA (APA Presidential Task Force on Evidence-Based Practice, 2006; Chambless & Hollon, 1998). Empirically supported treatment approaches are manualized treatments and have been developed for a variety of clinical problems such as depression (Cornes & Frank, 1994; Cuipers, van Straten, & Warmerdam, 2007; Hollon & Beck, 1994; Lamberg, 2008), anxiety (Landon & Barlow, 2004; Newman & Borkovec, 1995), conduct disordered children (Feldman & Kazdin, 1995; Schmidt & Taylor, 2002), and pain control (Chou & Huffman, 2007; Hawkins, 2001). The Clinical Psychology Division of the American Psychological Association (The Society of Clinical Psychology, Division 12) maintains a web site (www.PsychologyTreatments.org) that keeps updated information including clinical and research references for state-of-the-art empirically supported treatments. For example, cognitive and interpersonal psychotherapy have been determined to be empirically supported treatments for both depression and bulimia while exposure and response prevention have been found to be an empirically supported treatment for obsessive-compulsive disorder (APA Presidential Task Force on Evidence-Based Practice, 2006; Chambless & Ollendick, 2001; Crits-Christoph et al., 1995). While many treatment approaches are based on research support, the concept of empirically supported treatments and evidence-based practice is the most recent effort to systematize service delivery to carefully studied populations and problems (APA Presidential Task Force on Evidence-Based Practice, 2006; Chambless & Hollon, 1998; Nathan & Gorman, 2007). Controversy exists over the development of "approved" treatment approaches for various clinical problems, with critics usually highlighting the challenges of applying research findings to complex clinical situations (APA Presidential Task Force on Evidence-Based Practice, 2006; Cooper, 2003; Ingram, Hayes, & Scott, 2000; Messer, 2004). These issues will be further discussed in detail in Chapter 14.

Teaching

Clinical psychologists teach in a variety of settings. Some are full-time professors in colleges and universities across the United States and elsewhere. These professionals teach undergraduates, graduate students, and/or postgraduate students. Other psychologists might teach on a part-time basis at local colleges and universities as adjunct professors or lecturers. Still others might teach by providing one-on-one clinical supervision of graduate students, interns, or postdoctoral fellows. During supervision, psychologists discuss the trainees' clinical cases in depth while providing therapeutic guidance as they learn psychotherapy, psychological evaluation, and consultation skills. **Teaching** may occur in hospitals, clinics, or business environments as well. For example, a clinical psychologist might offer a stress management course for attorneys, business executives, nurses, clergy, police officers, or others. A psychologist might also teach a workshop on intimate relationships to young couples about to be married. A psychologist might teach other professionals such as doctors or clergy how to better maintain professional boundaries or understand psychopathology among the persons they counsel. As in psychological treatment facilities, there are numerous examples and opportunities for psychologists to teach in a wide variety of professional settings.

Highlight of a Contemporary Clinical Psychologist

Patrick H. DeLeon, PhD, ABPP

Photo: Courtesy Patrick
H. DeLeon

Dr. DeLeon uses his training and skills as a clinical psychologist by working on Capitol Hill. He helps shape policy and legislation that best reflects both the science and application of clinical psychology. He is a former president of the American Psychological Association.

Birth Date: January 6, 1943

College: Amherst College (BA, Liberal Arts), 1964

Graduate Program: Purdue University (MS, Psychology), 1966; Purdue University (PhD, Clinical Psychology), 1969; University of Hawaii (MPH, Health Services Administration), 1973; Catholic University, Columbus School of Law (JD), 1980

Clinical Internship: Fort Logan Mental Health Center, Denver, Colorado

Current Job: Chief of Staff, U.S. Senator D. K. Inouye, United States Senate

Pros and Cons of Being a Clinical Psychologist:
Pros: "Substantive knowledge about people, systems, health care, etc."

Cons: "Most psychologists or psychology colleagues do not appreciate how little they know about public policy and national trends."

Future of Clinical Psychology: "The knowledge base will continue to expand; whether services are provided by psychologists or other professionals is an open question. Psychology controls its own destiny—to not seek new agendas and to not address society's needs means to be replaced by other professions."

Changes during the Past 5 to 7 Years: "We have developed a significantly broader focus and thus have brought the behavioral sciences to a wider range of activities, especially within the generic health-care arena. As our numbers have increased, we have developed a greater presence (i.e., influence) in defining quality care and health-care priorities. Significantly more colleagues are now personally active within the public policy and political process, thus ensuring that psychology's voice (and values) will be heard. The development of postdoctoral training positions has resulted in society developing a greater appreciation for the importance of the psychosocial aspects of health care. Clearly, the prescription privileges agenda and advances in communications technology will revolutionize all of mental health care delivery."

What do you think will be the major changes in clinical psychology during the next several years? "The prescription privilege agenda will continue to expand and thereby absolutely redefine quality mental health care. Advances in the technology and communications fields will be found to have direct applicability to health care and psychology will play a major role in addressing this challenge. Health care will become more patient-centered and interdisciplinary in nature. No longer will any of the health-care professions be allowed to foster isolated or 'silo-oriented' training modules. The percentage of women in the field will continue to increase. And, clinical protocols will focus concretely on special populations (such as the elderly, children, and various ethnic minority clients). Health care will become more accountable and data driven. Distance learning and virtual training programs will become the norm."

Typical Schedule: "Every day brings new and unexpected challenges and opportunities. One tries to visit with a committee staff person each day or with a colleague in another senate office or from the administration. The key to legislative success is to anticipate which bills will be moving long before they do and to convince relevant committee staff (or administration, including house aides) to incorporate provisions addressing one's vision. Listening to and interacting with Hawaii constituents and professional lobbyists provides an excellent opportunity to develop legislative agendas. For Hawaii, expanding the resources for federally qualified community health centers provides an excellent vehicle for expanding psychology's agenda."

Consultation

Many clinical psychologists provide **consultation** to churches, health-care professionals, businesspersons, schools, lawmakers, organizations, and even to other mental health professionals. Consultation might involve an informal discussion, a brief report, or a more ongoing and formal consultation arrangement. For example, companies might consult with a psychologist to help reduce coworker conflicts or provide stress management strategies for high-stress employees such as business executives, firefighters, police officers, or prison guards. Consultation might involve helping a physician to better manage patient noncompliance with unpleasant medical procedures. Consultation could include working with a religious superior in helping to better select applicants who wish to enter a religious order or become a clergy member. Consultation might include working with law enforcement professionals on violence prevention or screening applications for the police academy. Clinical psychologists provide professional consultation in a wide variety of settings using a range of techniques. Consultation might also include assessment, teaching, research, and brief psychotherapy activities.

Administration

Many clinical psychologists find themselves (intentionally or unintentionally) in administrative positions. Administrative duties might include serving as chairperson of a psychology department, or dean, provost, or even president of a college or university. Other psychologists might hold administrative positions in hospitals, mental health clinics, or other agencies. They may act as a unit chief directing a psychiatric hospital unit or ward, or directing mental health services for a community mental health clinic. They may act as directors of training in numerous clinical settings. Some psychologists have become members of Congress and even state governors (e.g., Ted Strickland in Ohio). In **administration,** these psychologists generally manage a budget, lead a multidisciplinary professional and support staff, make hiring and firing decisions, develop policies and procedures for clinical, research, or other operations, and manage a large and populous state such as Ohio.

Employment Settings

Clinical psychologists work in many different employment settings including hospitals, medical schools, outpatient clinics, colleges and universities, businesses and industry, and private or group practices. Many clinical psychologists work in some type of part-time or full-time private practice as well (Norcross et al., 2008; Norcross, Hedges, & Castle, 2002). Following private practice, teaching in colleges and universities is the second most common employment choice for clinical psychologists (APA, 2000a, 2009b, 2010a, b; Norcross et al., 2002, 2008). Many psychologists work in more than one setting, combining various positions and activities. For example, it is common for a clinical psychologist to work at a hospital or clinic several days a week, teach a course or two at a local college or university, and conduct a private practice one or more days each week. A clinical psychologist may be a full-time professor teaching and conducting research while also operating a small private practice and offering consultation services to various clinics, hospitals, or businesses. The diversity of experiences available

to psychologists is quite appealing and offers tremendous flexibility and options.

Private or Group Practices

About 35% of clinical psychologists primarily work in solo or group private practices (APA, 2010a, b; Norcross et al., 2008; Norcross, Karpiak, & Santoro, 2005; Norcross, Prochaska, & Gallagher, 1989). Professionals in private practice may provide clinical services in their own solo practice or in conjunction with other mental health or health-care practitioners in a multidisciplinary setting. However, clinical psychologists who offer psychotherapy service tend to do so in private practice environments (Norcross et al., 2005, 2008). Many psychologists are drawn to independently providing direct clinical, consultation, and other professional services to their own patients and clients and enjoy being their own boss and setting their own hours and policies. In fact, private practitioners report more job satisfaction (Norcross et al., 1997, 2005, 2008; Norcross & Prochaska, 1988) and less job stress than psychologists employed in other settings such as academia (e.g., Boice & Myers, 1987). However, significant changes in health-care reform, managed health care, and insurance reimbursement for psychological services are likely to alter this rosy view of private practice for many professionals in the future. Many private practice psychologists, along with other mental health and health-care professionals operating practices, have experienced reductions in profits and freedoms as a result of the changing health-care industry.

In fact, some authors have predicted for quite some time that solo private practice may no longer exist in the future (Cummings, 1995). Cummings predicted that these clinicians will be employed primarily in multidisciplinary health settings such as health maintenance organizations (HMOs) or very large and comprehensive medical group practices. Others disagree with Cummings' pessimistic view concerning the future of private practice, stating that managed care accounts for a minority of the fees collected by private practitioners. Furthermore, the percentage of psychologists engaged in at least part-time private practice has not decreased even several decades after the onset of managed health care and other health-care changes and, as of this writing in 2010, private practice is still alive and well for many professionals (APA, 2000a, 2009b, 2010a, b; Norcross et al., 2002, 2005, 2008).

Colleges and Universities

About 20% of clinical psychologists are employed in academic environments (APA, 1993a, 1997, 2000a, 2010a, b; Norcross et al., 1997a, b, 2002, 2005, 2008). Most of these psychologists work as professors at colleges and universities across the United States and Canada. They generally teach psychology courses, supervise the clinical and/or research work of psychology students, and conduct both independent and collaborative research. They also typically serve on various college or university committees, providing leadership and assistance with the academic community. Some clinical psychologists work in academic clinical settings, such as student counseling centers, providing direct clinical services to students.

Hospitals

Many clinical psychologists work in hospital settings (APA, 2009b, 2010). They may conduct psychological testing; provide individual, family, or group psychotherapy; act as a consultant to other mental health or medical professionals on psychiatric or general medical hospital units; and may serve in administrative roles, such as unit chief, on a psychiatric ward. Many states now allow psychologists to become full members of the medical staff of hospitals. The *CAPP v. Rank* decision in California, for example, allowed psychologists to have full admitting, discharge, and treatment privileges at appropriate California hospitals. Full medical staff privileges allow psychologists to treat their patients when they are hospitalized and allow psychologists to participate in hospital committees, including holding elected positions. The majority of psychologists working in hospital settings are affiliated with Veterans Administration (VA) hospitals. In fact, the majority of internship training sites are located in VA hospitals (Association of Psychology Postdoctoral and Internship Centers, 2009).

Medical Schools

Some hospitals and medical centers are affiliated with medical schools. In addition to the professional hospital activities mentioned previously, clinical psychologists serve on the faculties of many medical schools. They typically act as "clinical faculty," which generally involves several hours (i.e., two to four) per week of pro bono time contributed to training medical center trainees. These trainees might include psychiatry residents, other medical residents and fellows (e.g., pediatric residents), medical students, nursing students, or nonmedical hospital trainees such as psychology interns or postdoctoral fellows, social work interns, nursing students, or chaplaincy interns. These psychologists might teach a seminar or provide individual case supervision and consultation. Psychologists may also serve as academic or research faculty at medical schools. In fact, approximately 3,000 psychologists are employed as faculty in medical schools (APA, 2009b; Pate, 2004; Sweet, Rozensky, & Tovian, 1991). These psychologists tend to primarily conduct research and are often funded by national grants (e.g., National Institute of Mental Health, National Science Foundation, American Heart Association) to pay their salaries, thus allowing them to conduct their research. Finally, many psychologists employed in medical school settings evaluate, treat, and consult on patient care, and others teach and train both medical and nonmedical students.

Outpatient Clinics

Many clinical psychologists work in various outpatient clinics such as community mental health centers (APA, 2009b). These psychologists often provide a range of clinical services to other professionals and organizations. For example, these psychologists might provide psychotherapy for children who have been abused or group therapy for adult substance abusers. They might also provide parent education classes. While psychologists in these settings may conduct research, direct clinical service is often the primary activity and priority of these settings.

Business and Industry

Many clinical psychologists working in business and industry settings offer consultation services to management and assessment and brief psychotherapy to employees, and conduct research on various psychosocial issues important to company functioning and performance (APA, 2009b). For example, these psychologists might consult with the human resources department, provide stress management workshops, or conduct interpersonal skills–building workshops. Psychologists might help managers learn to improve their ability to motivate and supervise their employees. They may also assist in developing strategies for interviewing and hiring job applicants. They may help groups develop mission, value, and strategic plans.

Military

Many clinical psychologists are employed by one of the branches of the U.S. military such as the navy, air force, or army (APA, 2009b). They often provide direct clinical services. Some conduct research while others act as administrators in military hospitals and clinics. Typically, psychologists working in the military hold an officer rank such as captain. Other psychologists are civilians working in military hospitals such as VA hospitals. In fact, since World War II, VA hospitals have been among the largest employers of clinical psychologists.

Other Locations

Clinical psychologists are also employed in a variety of other settings, such as police departments, prisons, juvenile halls and detention centers, rehabilitation centers for disabled children and/or adults, substance abuse and/or mental illness halfway houses, battered women's shelters, seminaries, schools, and many other work environments. These psychologists provide a wide range of professional services such as psychological assessment, consultation, and counseling.

Subspecialties

Most clinical psychologists are trained in the research, assessment, and treatment of a variety of clinical issues pertaining to a diverse set of client populations. The core curriculum for all clinical psychologists includes coursework on the biological, social, cognitive, and individual influences on behavior as well as classes on research, statistics, ethics, assessment, and treatment. The core curriculum can then be applied, with additional specialty training, to various populations such as children and adults. Further training may be offered in many subspecialty areas. Although a core set of competencies are expected from all clinical psychologists, not all clinical psychologists are trained exactly alike. Many clinical psychologists ultimately specialize in one or more areas of research or practice. Just as medicine offers doctors various specialties such as pediatrics, oncology, psychiatry, internal medicine, and cardiology, there are many clinical psychology subspecialties. Some of the most common specialties include child clinical psychology, clinical health psychology, clinical neuropsychology, forensic psychology, and geropsychology. Furthermore, each specialty includes a variety of subspecialties. For example, child clinical psychologists might specialize in working with very young children or adolescents. Clinical health psychologists might choose to specialize in eating disorders, anxiety disorders, or pain disorders.

Child Clinical Psychology

Of the 307 million Americans, there are 74 million children under the age of 18 in the

United States (U.S. Census Bureau, 2009). Many of these children and families are in need of professional services offered by a psychologist specially trained to work with this population. Child clinical psychologists specialize in working with both children and families. A recent survey by the APA revealed that about 2,000 APA members (about 3%) identify themselves as specializing in **child clinical psychology** (APA, 2010a, b). A child and family focus in clinical training has become enormously popular within graduate training programs (Norcross et al., 2008). In addition to standard training in general clinical psychology, these psychologists obtain in-depth training in developmental psychology and child assessment (e.g., behavioral disorders, learning disabilities, and motor developmental delays) and treatment (e.g., family therapy, parent consultation). They commonly work in schools, children's hospitals, community clinics, and in private practices. Child clinical psychologists may work with children who have experienced physical and/or sexual abuse or who experience attention deficit/hyperactivity disorder, conduct disorders, autism, enuresis (bed wetting), learning disabilities, serious medical illnesses, school phobia, posttraumatic stress disorder, or a host of other emotional, behavioral, or medical problems. These psychologists may provide consultation to teachers, school counselors, pediatricians, day-care workers, parents, and others. They may assist teachers in classroom behavior management or parents in developing better parenting skills.

Pediatric psychologists are child clinical psychologists who generally work with children and families in hospital settings where the child has a significant medical disorder (Brown, 2003). These medical problems might include cancer, epilepsy, diabetes, cystic fibrosis, and neurological disorders and disabilities. The pediatric psychologist might offer pain management strategies to a child while helping the family cope more effectively with and locate community resources. He or she may act as a consultant to various medical units and departments to help physicians, nurses, and others deal with the emotional and behavioral consequences of severe medical illnesses in children. For example, a pediatric psychologist might consult with a physician about an adolescent with diabetes who refuses to monitor his or her blood sugar level due to concerns about being different relative to peers. A pediatric psychologist might consult with nurses about a child who is hospitalized with cystic fibrosis and struggling with significant depression and social isolation.

Clinical Health Psychology

The field of clinical **health psychology** formally began around 1980 (Matarazzo, 1980) and has been defined as:

> ... the aggregate of the specific educational, scientific, and professional contributions of the discipline of psychology to the promotion and maintenance of health, the prevention and treatment of illness, the identification of etiologic and diagnostic correlates of health, illness, and related dysfunction, and to the analysis and improvement of the health care system and health policy formation. (Matarazzo, 1982, p. 4)

Since its inception during the early 1980s, health psychology has become one of the fastest growing areas of clinical psychology and one of the most popular areas of research in graduate training programs (Norcross et al., 2008). This subspecialty serves as an excellent example of integrative trends in the field (Johnson, 2003; Taylor, 2009).

It has been estimated that 50% of all deaths are caused by lifestyle factors such as smoking cigarettes, drinking too much alcohol, eating high fat foods, not exercising, and refusing to wear seatbelts (Centers for Disease Control, 2009). Furthermore, over 15% of the gross national product is devoted to health care (Centers for Disease Control, 2009). Health psychologists work to help healthy people stay healthy and assist people with various illnesses or risk factors to cope more effectively with their symptoms. Health psychologists work toward helping others develop health-enhancing lifestyles, which can be a surprisingly difficult task. For example, about 95% of those who lose weight tend to regain all their lost weight within 5 years (Brownell, 1993; Wadden, Sternberg, Letizia, Stunkard, & Foster, 1989). Over 50% of those who start an exercise program drop it within 6 months, while 75% drop it within nine months (Dishman, 1982). About a half-million people die in the United States each year due to smoking tobacco (Centers for Disease Control, 2008). Health psychologists work with individuals and groups in order to maximize health-enhancing behaviors (e.g., exercise, low-fat-food consumption, smoking cessation) and minimize health-damaging behaviors (e.g., smoking, stress, drinking alcohol). They also help in the treatment of chronic pain, panic disorders, and migraine headaches, and other physical conditions with prominent biopsychosocial features (S. Taylor, 2009).

Health psychologists are often trained in clinical psychology, counseling psychology, social psychology, or child clinical psychology but specialize in health-related problems and interventions. Health psychologists typically work in hospital settings; however, many also work in academic, business, and outpatient clinic settings. Health psychologists often utilize specialized techniques such as biofeedback, hypnosis, relaxation training, and self-management strategies in addition to general psychotherapy in the course of the overall treatment process.

Clinical Neuropsychology

Neuropsychology focuses on brain–behavior relationships. These are defined as how brain functioning impacts behavior and behavioral problems. Neuropsychologists assess brain and behavioral functioning and offer strategies for patients suffering from brain impairment due to a large range of problems such as dementia, head injuries, tumors, autism, stroke,

AIDS, Alzheimer's disease, epilepsy, and other problems that result in cognitive and neurological dysfunction. Neuropsychologists are well trained in assessing a range of cognitive abilities, including executive or higher order cognitive functioning (i.e., planning, judgment, problem solving), sensory and motor functioning, and memory skills and abstract reasoning, and use a variety of specialized tests to assess these brain–behavior relationships. Many psychologists who specialize in neuropsychology are trained as clinical or counseling psychologists or they may be trained in cognitive science or neuroscience. Most neuropsychologists work in hospital, rehabilitation, or clinic settings. Some specialize in working with children. Many also work in private or group practice environments.

Forensic Psychology

Forensic psychology is usually defined as the "application of psychology to legal issues" (Cooke, 1984, p. 29). Forensic psychologists specialize in using principles of human behavior in the judicial and legal systems (Otto & Heilbrun, 2002). They are often trained as clinical or counseling psychologists with a specialty in forensic work. Forensic psychologists may conduct psychological evaluations with defendants and present their findings as an expert witness in court. They may also provide evaluations for child custody arrangements, or be asked to predict dangerousness or competency to stand trial. They may be asked to participate in worker's compensation claims, or serve as consultants to attorneys who are selecting a jury.

Geropsychology

Psychologists who specialize in **geropsychology** provide a range of psychological services to elderly members of society. The elderly are the largest growing segment of today's society and are often in need of professional psychological services. In fact, the number of elderly Americans has increased from 3.1 million to

35 million during the twentieth century, now representing 1 in 8 Americans, and will likely grow to more than 15% of all Americans by 2020 (U.S. Census Bureau, 2008). Geropsychologists might consult with senior centers, convalescent or nursing homes, and hospital medical units that serve elderly patients. These psychologists might provide psychological or neuropsychological testing, and brief individual or family psychotherapy, and consult on strategies to maximize independence and self-care. These psychologists might develop activities to enhance self-esteem and control and alleviate depression among elderly patients.

Organizations

As in most professions, clinical psychology boasts a variety of professional organizations. These organizations provide an opportunity for their members to meet and collaborate, attend yearly conventions and learn about new advances in the field, and participate in a number of activities that help psychologists as well as the public. These organizations are international, national, regional, and local.

American Psychological Association

Clinical psychologists are usually members of several professional organizations. Most are members of the **American Psychological Association** (APA). The APA was founded in 1892 and is the largest organization of psychologists anywhere in the world. There are 150,000 members of the organization (APA, 2010a, b) representing all specialties within psychology (e.g., clinical psychology, social psychology, school psychology, experimental psychology). Students of psychology and associates of psychology (e.g., high school psychology teachers) are also included in the APA. In recent surveys, approximately half of APA members identified themselves within clinical psychology (APA, 2000a, 2009) and about half have a license to practice in one or more states (APA, 2000a, 2009, 2010a, b). The APA was incorporated in 1925 and is located in Washington, DC. Since the first meeting in Philadelphia in 1892, the APA holds a yearly national convention each August in a large American or Canadian city. The APA is divided into four directorates focusing on professional practice, education, public policy, and science.

The APA is also home to 56 topic interest divisions (e.g., Division 2 is Teaching of Psychology; Division 12 is Clinical Psychology). About 6,000 psychologists are members of the APA's Division 12 (Clinical Psychology). The APA publishes numerous professional journals (e.g., *American Psychologist, Professional Psychology: Research and Practice, Journal of Consulting and Clinical Psychology, Journal of Abnormal Psychology*) as well as many books. The APA acts as a lobbying force in Washington, DC, promoting legislation that will be favorable to psychology as a profession and to consumers of psychological services. The APA also provides standards for the education, certification, and ethical conduct of psychologists.

American Psychological Society

In 1988, the **American Psychological Society** (APS) was founded. Many of the psychologists in the APA who regarded themselves as academically and scientifically focused felt that the APA no longer adequately represented their interests. Founding members of the APS felt that the APA had become too focused on professional practice and was becoming neglectful of the science of psychology. A proposal was considered to either reorganize the APA to reflect these concerns or start a new organization dedicated to the science of psychology only. Clinical psychologists who were especially interested in the science of psychology joined APS. Many psychologists belong to both organizations while others resigned from the APA to join the APS.

State and County Psychological Associations

Each state and most counties maintain psychological associations. Many practicing clinical psychologists join their state psychological association and may also join their county psychology association. Approximately 40% of APA members (both clinical and other psychologists) are also members of their state psychological association (APA, 2000a, 2010a). These organizations provide networking opportunities for psychologists as well as assistance in lobbying state legislatures regarding issues important to psychologists and the public's psychological welfare. Most state and county psychological associations provide workshops and conferences for their members that address various clinical and research topics. The state psychological associations frequently work closely with the state boards of psychology to assist in the policing of unethical and illegal conduct of psychologists as well as in developing licensing laws and criteria for acceptable professional practice.

American Board of Professional Psychology

The **American Board of Professional Psychology** (ABPP) was founded in 1947 as an agency that would certify psychologists in several specialty areas. The ABPP diploma is considered an advanced level of accomplishment beyond a state license to practice as a psychologist. The ABPP is an independent organization closely associated with the APA. The ABPP diploma is offered in a number of specialty areas: The majority of diplomas are in clinical psychology. Approximately 1,000 psychologists hold the ABPP diploma in clinical psychology (APA, 2010a).

Other Organizations

There are a number of other international, national, and regional organizations that many clinical psychologists may join depending on their specialty interests. For example, many clinical psychologists are members of the Society of Behavioral Medicine (SBM), the Society of Pediatric Psychology, the International Neuropsychology Society (INS), the Association of Behavior Analysis (ABA), the International

Society of Clinical Psychology (ISCP), or many other organizations. Most of these organizations sponsor a yearly national conference, publish one or more professional journals, are involved in lobbying efforts of interest to their membership, and provide members with a range of services.

Many other countries also maintain psychological associations. The Canadian Psychological Association (CPA), for example, has a long and distinguished history providing yearly conventions, maintaining an ethics code, and accrediting programs throughout Canada, among other activities. This is also true for the British Psychological Society (BPS). Chapter 15 lists the contact information for many of these organizations.

How Does Clinical Psychology Differ from Related Fields?

Many people are unaware of the similarities and differences between clinical psychology and related fields. For example, a popular question is, "What is the difference between a psychologist and a psychiatrist?" It can be confusing to the public (and even to many professionals in the field) to understand the similarities and differences between mental health disciplines. Since almost all of the mental health disciplines share certain activities such as conducting psychotherapy, understanding differences between these fields can be very challenging.

Many professionals and members of the public wonder how clinical psychology differs from related mental health fields such as counseling psychology, school psychology, psychiatry, nursing, social work, and counseling. A brief overview of these disciplines will be provided in Table 1.1.

Counseling Psychologists (PhD)

Of all the different mental health professionals, **counseling psychologists** are perhaps the most similar to clinical psychologists in actual

Table 1.1   **Mental Health Professionals**

Degree	Program	Years of Training Prior to Degree*	Years of Postdegree Training	License
PhD	Clinical Psych	4–5	1–2	Psychologist
PhD	Counseling Psych	4–5	1–2	Psychologist
PhD	School Psych	4	1–2	School Psychologist
PsyD	Clinical Psych	4–5	1–2	Psychologist
MA/MS	Clinical Psych	2	1–2	MFT
MA/MS	Counseling Psych	2	1–2	MFT
MA/MS	School Psych	2	1	School Psychologist
MSW	Social Work	2	1–2	Social Worker
MD	Medicine	4	3–4	Physician (e.g., Psychiatrist)

*While graduate school can take 4 to 5 years to complete, this is highly variable. Research projects such as dissertations as well as practicum experiences often result in a longer period of time to complete training.

practice. While there are generally differences in philosophy, training emphases, and curriculum between clinical and counseling graduate programs, differences between clinical and counseling psychologists are subtle. Like clinical psychologists, counseling psychologists generally major in psychology as undergraduates, attend a four-year graduate training program (however, in counseling psychology rather than clinical psychology), complete a one-year clinical internship, and complete postdoctoral training prior to obtaining their license as a psychologist. The differences between clinical and counseling psychology were more dramatic several decades ago in comparison to current times.

Historically, counseling psychologists worked in outpatient, college, and vocational settings with people who did not experience major psychiatric difficulties. They often provided educational and occupational counseling to students and employees. Testing conducted by counseling psychologists generally involved career and vocational interests and skills. Today, counseling psychologists can be found in hospital, clinic, industry, and private practice settings. In fact, in most states, counseling psychologists practice under the same license as clinical psychologists. Some authors have argued that distinctions between clinical and counseling psychology, along with separate training programs, may no longer be warranted (e.g., Beutler & Fisher, 1994). There are about three times more clinical psychologists than counseling psychologists in the United States. For example, while 1,185 doctorates were awarded in clinical psychology in 1999, 367 were awarded in counseling psychology (APA, 2000a). According to surveys conducted by the APA (2000a, 2009b), about 11% of APA members identify themselves as counseling psychologists and about 15% of all doctorates awarded in psychology are awarded in counseling psychology.

School Psychologists (MA or PhD)

While doctorates in school psychology are available (e.g., 130 were awarded in 1999; APA, 2000b), a master's degree is generally the degree of choice for school psychologists. Surveys by the APA (2000a, 2009b) revealed that about 4% identify themselves as working in the field of school psychology and about 3% of all doctorates awarded in psychology are awarded in school psychology. **School psychologists** typically work in elementary, secondary, or special education schools providing cognitive testing, brief counseling, and consultation to schoolteachers, administrators, parents, and students. Some school psychologists also provide tutoring help and some maintain private practices. School psychologists often work with children receiving special education services for problems such as attention deficit/hyperactivity disorder, learning disabilities, or mental retardation. These professionals often provide guidance to both children and their families concerning educational and psychological concerns. School psychologists interested in careers in research, academics, or administration usually choose PhD programs while those most interested in practice with children and families generally choose MA programs.

Psychiatry (MD)

Psychiatrists are physicians who earn a medical degree (MD) and complete residency training in **psychiatry.** The American Psychiatric Association reports that there are approximately 40,000 psychiatrists who are members of the association (American Psychiatric Association, 2010). Approximately 40% of psychiatrists work in solo private practices (American Psychiatric Association, 2010). Typically, psychiatrists receive their bachelor's degrees in premedical related fields (e.g., biology, chemistry), and then complete 4 years of medical school to obtain an MD degree. Subsequently, a one-year medical clinical internship is completed, prior to a residency (usually three years) in psychiatry. Unlike the internship completed in clinical psychology, the medical internship focuses on general medical (not psychiatric) training. While the residency training years may include some training activities similar to that obtained by clinical psychology interns (e.g., psychotherapy), most programs focus on medication management and other pharmaceutical approaches to psychiatric disorders. The residency is usually completed in a hospital or medical center environment. However, residency training can also occur in outpatient settings such as community mental health clinics. These physicians obtain their medical license following medical school and often take their boards to become board certified in a specialty area (e.g., child psychiatry) when they complete their residency program.

Because psychiatrists are physicians, they use their medical training to diagnose and treat a wide spectrum of mental illnesses. Psychiatrists, as MDs, can prescribe medication, treat physical illnesses, and may utilize other biological interventions (e.g., electroconvulsive therapy). Although there are exceptions, psychiatric training generally focuses on clinical diagnoses and treatment of major psychopathology (i.e., affective or mood disorders, such as bipolar disorder, and psychotic disorders, such as schizophrenia). Training in general human behavior and research is usually minimal.

Relative to other mental health disciplines, there are a variety of pros and cons to being a psychiatrist. Advantages include several factors. First, as physicians, psychiatrists have extensive training in the biological basis of behavior and behavioral problems. They are able to use this expertise to understand and treat a wide range of medical and psychiatric problems. Psychiatrists have superior knowledge of medical aspects of certain disorders, and have been trained to take a leadership role vis-à-vis these patients. Thus, they can prescribe medication and other biological treatments for their patients, whereas most other clinicians must refer patients to an MD if medication or other biological interventions are indicated. However, psychologists are able to prescribe medication in several states (e.g., New Mexico, Louisiana; Beutler, 2002). Second, psychiatrists have a much higher earning potential than any other mental health professional. Starting salaries typically are over $100,000, with average salaries about $150,000 depending on the work setting. In comparison, the average starting salary for practicing psychologists is about two-thirds of psychiatrists at about $70,000 (American Psychological Association, 2008). Third, as physicians, psychiatrists generally hold greater status and positions of greater authority, especially in hospital or other medical settings. Higher salaries and prestige are due to the costs and competitiveness of medical education as well as society's admiration of physicians in general.

There are several important disadvantages to becoming a psychiatrist. First, the costs of medical training are extremely high compared with the training costs of other mental health professionals. Second, psychiatrists tend to have much less training in general human behavior and psychotherapy than most other mental health professionals. For example, while most psychologists spend four undergraduate, five graduate, and one to two postdoctoral years focusing specifically on psychology and psychotherapy, psychiatrists only spend the three residency years focused on psychiatry, which tends to primarily train these professionals on using medications for behavioral and emotional problems. Thus, many first-year psychiatry residents are far "greener," for example, than most advanced psychology graduate students or predoctoral psychology interns. Third, psychiatrists also are not trained in psychological testing and assessment, and must defer to clinical psychologists in order to acquire this often-critical information. Fourth, psychiatrists are rarely trained as extensively as clinical psychologists in rigorous research methodology. Finally, fewer and fewer medical students choose psychiatry as a specialty, in fact dropping by 40% since the 1980s alone (Tamaskar & McGinnis, 2002). Psychiatric salaries, although high in comparison to non-MD mental health professionals, are very low compared with other physicians. In recent decades, traditional psychodynamic and interpersonal relational approaches to psychiatry have given way to more biological approaches, partially due to new discoveries in the neurosciences, psychopharmacology, genetics, and other medical areas (e.g., Fleck, 1995; Glasser, 2003; Michels, 1995), as well as the demand by managed care insurance companies and patients for quicker acting treatment approaches (e.g., Cummings, 1995). Finally, the lobbying efforts of the pharmaceutical industry have also influenced the reliance on medications to treat all sorts of behavioral and emotional concerns (Glasser, 2003).

Social Work (MSW)

There are approximately 150,000 members of the National Association of Social Workers (NASW, 2010). Social workers have typically obtained a bachelor's degree in a social science such as psychology or sociology and subsequently entered a two-year graduate program to attain their master's degree in social work (MSW). Next, they must complete up to two years of supervised clinical experience (depending on the state) to become a Licensed Clinical Social Worker (LCSW). Similar to the clinical psychology internship, many social workers receive training in psychotherapy and psychiatric diagnoses during their year or years of supervised clinical experience. Unlike in psychology, they generally do not obtain extensive training in conducting research or using psychological testing instruments. However, those who earn a doctorate degree in **social work** (DSW) often are interested in research and academic careers.

Historically, social workers focused on patient case management (i.e., helping the patient get the most out of his or her inpatient or outpatient treatment and helping patients transition to work or further treatment following discharge), patient advocacy, and a liaison to optimal social service agencies and benefits. Whereas psychiatrists have historically focused on biological theories and interventions and psychologists have focused on psychological theories and intervention, social workers have focused on social theories and interventions. Today, social workers can conduct psychotherapy with individuals, families, or groups, or undertake administrative roles within agencies, hospitals, or social service settings. Providing direct clinical services to clients and patients is the most frequently reported activity of social workers (National

Association of Social Workers, 2010). Social workers can be employed in numerous settings including schools, hospitals, clinics, and private practice. Employment in social service agencies and both inpatient and outpatient health facilities are the most common settings for social workers while about 12% are engaged in private practice (National Association of Social Workers, 2010). Social workers also may act as patient case managers and advocates, securing necessary follow-up care and social services following hospital discharge, for example.

Advantages to becoming a social worker include first a shorter (and, thus, less expensive) length of graduate training (i.e., two years as opposed to the minimum five years necessary for a PhD degree in clinical psychology). Second, training in social work tends to highlight social factors such as poverty, crime, racism, and oppression that influence individual, group, and organizational behavior as well as emphasizing advocacy for the rights of others. Third, no dissertation or large research study master's thesis is required for those who are not interested in conducting these types of large-scale research projects. Disadvantages include less training and emphasis on the biological influences on behavior and less attention on research. Additional disadvantages include lower earning ability than psychologists and psychiatrists. Average salaries tend to be about $50,000 depending on the position and location. Social workers, like any clinician, can specialize and become expert in any nonprescribing or nonpsychological assessment enterprise.

Psychiatric Nursing (RN)

There are over 11,000 **psychiatric nurses** who have specialty training in psychiatric illnesses and treatment (American Psychiatric Nurses Association, 2009). They usually obtain both an undergraduate and master's degree in nursing. They are licensed as registered nurses (RN) following the completion of their undergraduate degree. During their training, they, like other mental health professionals, learn about psychiatric diagnosis and treatment. However, they also learn about psychopharmacology and are often involved in the dispensing of psychotropic medications to patients. Psychiatric nurses provide psychotherapy to individuals, families, and groups as well as assisting in medical management of psychotropic medications. Many psychiatric nurses are employed in hospitals and clinics; however, many maintain private practices as well.

Marriage and Family Therapists (MFT)

The mental health discipline of **marriage and family therapists** is very popular in California and several other states. There are approximately 25,000 MFTs in California alone and about 50,000 nationally. The Association of Marriage and Family Therapists has about 25,000 members nationally. MFTs typically complete a bachelor's degree in any field (typically a social science discipline such as psychology, sociology, or education), and later pursue a master's degree in a terminal master's counseling or psychology program. Following up to two years of supervised experience, MFTs can be licensed to practice independently in most but not all states. Despite the title, MFTs are not necessarily experts solely in marriage and family counseling. Often, they treat adults in individual therapy, as well. Advantages to becoming an MFT include the ease of acceptance into programs and the one to two years necessary to obtain a master's degree. Disadvantages include the general mixed quality and training of professionals in this field.

Many states offer licensure as a Licensed Professional Counselor (LPC) designed for master's-level practitioners. The training and experience for this profession tends to be similar to those outlined for MFTs.

Other Counselors

Many hospitals and clinics employ a variety of counselors such as occupational therapists, activity therapists, alcohol counselors, art therapists, psychiatric technicians, and others. These professionals provide a wide variety of services to patients including individual, family, and group counseling, and therapeutic activities such as art, dance, and music groups. Some of these professionals obtain a license or certification to practice (e.g., occupational therapists) while others do not (e.g., psychiatric technicians). Legislation in many states, such as Missouri, has been proposed or passed allowing occupational therapists, for example, to be licensed as "mental health professionals."

Other Psychologists

There are many different types of psychologists besides the clinical, counseling, and school psychologists previously described. Cognitive, developmental, experimental, social, personality, industrial-organizational, physiological, and other types of psychologists are represented in the field. They complete a doctoral degree in psychology with specialization in one or more of the areas already listed. Unlike clinical psychologists, they are not mandated to complete an internship or postdoctoral fellowship. These psychologists work in educational settings such as colleges and universities as well as in business, government, and the military. They conduct research, consult with individuals and groups, and develop policies. They have different areas of expertise and skill but generally do not assess or treat patients experiencing emotional, behavioral, interpersonal, or other clinical problems. They are not considered mental health professionals and may not even be interested in human behavior. For example, an experimental psychologist might conduct research on the memory functioning of rats or the visual functioning of cats. A social psychologist might be interested in the social functioning of groups of primates. A physiological psychologist might be interested in how organisms such as birds learn new behaviors. These psychologists might be interested in human behavior but not in abnormal or clinical problems. For example, an industrial-organizational psychologist might help an executive interact with employees to improve performance or morale. A cognitive psychologist might study how medications impact attentional processes and sleeping behavior. A developmental psychologist might be interested in how children who are in full-time day care that starts during the first weeks of life bond with their mothers. With the exception of industrial-organizational psychologists, these psychologists do not obtain a license to practice psychology and therefore do not treat clinical problems.

The Big Picture

The goals, activities, and contributions of clinical psychologists are very appealing to many who are fascinated by human behavior and relationships. Contemporary clinical psychology can be defined as the assessment, treatment, and study of human behavior in the context of biological, psychological, and social factors. Thus, integration as well as awareness of such individual differences such as culture, ethnicity, and gender is part and parcel of the state of this current art and science. The enormous popularity of psychology as an undergraduate major, of clinical psychology as a career path, and of popular psychology books, shows, web sites, and blogs are a testament to the inherent interest of clinical psychology. Most psychologists report a high degree of satisfaction with their career choice, and enjoy the tremendous flexibility and diversity of potential employment settings, the opportunity to work with people from diverse backgrounds, and participation in the rapid scientific advances impacting the field. However, changes in health-care delivery and reimbursement, the large number of degrees being awarded in clinical psychology and other mental health disciplines, and the modest salaries of most psychologists must be viewed realistically along with the many advantages of clinical psychology as a career. The goals and activities of clinical psychology are noble: to use the principles of psychology and our understanding of human behavior to promote health, happiness, and enhanced quality of life.

Key Points

1. Clinical psychology focuses on the diagnosis, treatment, and study of psychological and behavioral problems and disorders. Clinical psychology attempts to use the principles of psychology to better understand, predict, and alleviate "intellectual, emotional, biological, psychological, social, and behavioral aspects of human functioning" (APA, 2009).

2. The road to becoming a clinical psychologist is a long one divided by a number of distinct stages and phases, which include college, graduate school, clinical internship, postdoctoral fellowship, licensure, and finally employment. However, academic positions are usually available following receipt of a doctorate degree and prior to licensure.

3. One of the great advantages of being a clinical psychologist is that there are a wide variety of activities and employment settings in which to work. Becoming a clinical psychologist allows one to teach at the university level, conduct research, provide consultation to a wide variety of professionals and organizations, and conduct psychotherapy and psychological testing with a wide range of populations.

4. Clinical psychologists work in many different employment settings including hospitals, medical schools, outpatient clinics, colleges and universities, business and industry settings, and private or group practices. The majority of clinical psychologists work in some type of part-time or full-time private practice. Following private practice, educational settings, such as academic careers in colleges and universities, are the second most common employment setting for clinical psychologists.

5. Many clinical psychologists ultimately specialize in one or more areas of research or practice. While there are many types of clinical psychology subspecialties, the most common include child clinical psychology, health psychology, neuropsychology, and forensic psychology.

6. Clinical psychologists are organized into a wide variety of professional organizations. Most psychologists are members of the APA. The APA is also divided into 56 topic interest divisions. About 6,000 psychologists are members of the APA Division 12 (Clinical Psychology).

7. In 1988, the American Psychological Society (APS) was founded by many of the academic or science-minded psychologists in the APA who felt that the APA no longer adequately represented their interests. Founding members of the APS felt that the APA had become too focused on professional practice and was becoming less and less attuned to the science of psychology.

8. Each state and most counties maintain psychological associations. Most clinical psychologists join their state psychological association and may also join their county psychology association.

9. The American Board of Professional Psychology (ABPP) was founded in 1947 as an agency that would certify psychologists in several specialty areas. The ABPP diploma is considered an advanced level of recognition and is certification beyond a state license to practice as a psychologist.

10. Clinical psychology maintains both similarities and differences with other mental health–related fields such as counseling psychology, school psychology, psychiatry, social work, nursing, and marriage, family, and child counseling.

11. Changes in health-care delivery and reimbursement, the large number of degrees being awarded in clinical psychology and other mental health disciplines, and the moderate salaries of most psychologists can be viewed as some disadvantages of clinical psychology as a career option.

12. The field of clinical psychology is dedicated to humanitarian concerns. Clinical psychology seeks to use the principles of human behavior to minimize or eliminate human suffering and enhance and improve

human quality of life. Clinical psychology attempts to help individuals, couples, families, groups, organizations, and society achieve healthier, happier, and more effective functioning.

Key Terms

Administration
American Board of Professional Psychology
American Psychological Association
American Psychological Society
Assessment
Biopsychosocial perspective
Child clinical psychology
Clinical psychology
Consultation
Counseling psychologists
Doctor of Philosophy (PhD)
Doctor of Psychology (PsyD)
Forensic psychology
Geropsychology
Health psychology
Marriage and family therapists
Neuropsychology
Psychiatric nurses
Psychiatry
Research program
School psychologists
Social work
Teaching
Treatment

For Reflection

1. Define clinical psychology.
2. Why do you think clinical psychology is so popular?
3. Outline the major stages of clinical psychology training.
4. Outline the six major activities of clinical psychology.
5. Where do most clinical psychologists work?
6. Discuss the major subspecialties in clinical psychology.
7. Outline the major professional organizations associated with clinical psychology.
8. How do clinical psychologists differ from other psychologists?

9. How do clinical psychologists differ from other mental health professionals?

Real Students, Real Questions

1. Are the requirements to be a clinical psychologist very different outside of the United States and Canada?
2. How can treatment be based on solid research data when people are so different in their coping and healing patterns?
3. If clinical and counseling psychologists do similar things, then why the need for any distinction?
4. Do people like Dr. Phil, Dr. Laura, Dr. Drew and others discourage or encourage people from seeking help?
5. Other than prescribing medications, are there any significant differences between a psychologist and a psychiatrist?

Web Resources

http://www.apa.org
Learn more about the American Psychological Association.

http://www.aamft.org
Learn more about the American Association for Marriage and Family Therapy.

www.psych.org
Learn more about the National Association of Social Workers.

http://www.socialworkers.org/
Learn about the American Psychiatric Association.

http://www.apa.org/divisions/div12/aboutcp.html
Learn more about the Society of Clinical Psychology, Division 12 of APA.

http://www.guidetopsychology.com/cln_cns.htm
Learn more about clinical psychology licensing.

Foundations and Early History of Clinical Psychology

2

Chapter

Today, clinical psychology is a complex and diverse field encompassing numerous subspecialties and a continuum of scientific and practitioner-focused enterprises. In seeking to alleviate human suffering in emotional, behavioral, and physical realms, clinical psychology has borrowed from philosophical, medical, and scientific advances throughout the centuries. Chapters 2 and 3 highlight the seminal historical influences and fundamental contributors to the ever-evolving science and practice of today's clinical psychology. First, the evolution of Western medicine from a nonscientific endeavor to today's high-tech standard of practice is traced. Central to this evolution has been the titanic human struggle to understand abnormal behavior in the context of the mind and the body. As you will see, an integration between the forces of mind and

body has been long in coming, developing in fits and starts throughout the ages into today's biopsychosocial appreciation for the dynamic forces that join to create behavior. And just as this mind–body integration has developed, the practice and training of clinical psychologists have mirrored landmark scientific changes in this evolving field of study.

This chapter highlights the early influences and foundations that led to the development of clinical psychology as an independent science and profession. It traces the history and development of issues relevant to contemporary clinical psychology, from ancient times until World War I. Ideas, events, institutions, and people associated with this history are highlighted. Also, Table 2.1 provides an outline of significant events in the field prior to World War II. The influence of biological, psychological, and social factors and the roots of

Table 2.1   **Significant Events in Clinical Psychology Prior to World War II**

Before Psychology Was Founded as a Field

2500–500 B.C.	Supernatural, magic, herbs, and reason was the approach to mental and physical illness.
470–322 B.C.	Greeks use holistic approach to illness, which is attentive to biological, psychological, and social influences.
130–200 A.D.	Galen develops foundation of Western medicine based on the influence of the Greeks, which lasts 1,000 years.
500–1450	Middle Ages believe supernatural forces influence health and illness.
1225–1274	Saint Thomas Aquinas uses scientific thinking to help explain health and illness.
1490–1541	Paracelsus suggests that the movements of the stars, moon, sun, and planets influence behavior.
1500–1700	Renaissance witnesses numerous scientific discoveries suggesting that biological factors influence health and illness.
1596–1650	René Descartes develops mind/body dualism.
1745–1826	Pinel, in France, develops humane moral therapy to treat mentally ill.
1802–1887	Dorothea Dix advocates for humane treatment of mentally ill in America.
1848	New Jersey becomes first state to build a hospital for mentally ill patients.

After Psychology Was Founded as a Field and until World War II

1879	Wilhelm Wundt develops first laboratory in psychology.
1879	William James develops first American psychology laboratory at Harvard.
1883	G. Stanley Hall develops second psychology laboratory at Johns Hopkins.
1888	James McKean Cattell develops third American psychology laboratory.
1890	James publishes *Principles of Psychology*.
1890	Cattell defines *mental test*.
1892	American Psychological Association founded.
1896	Lightner Witmer establishes first psychology clinic at the University of Pennsylvania.
1900	Freud publishes *The Interpretation of Dreams*.
1904	Alfred Binet begins developing an intelligence test.
1905	Binet and Theodore Simon offer Binet-Simon scale of intelligence.
1905	Carl Jung creates a word association test.
1907	*Psychological Clinic*, first clinical journal, is published.
1908	Clifford Beers begins mental hygiene movement.
1909	Clinical psychology section formed at APA.
1909	Freud's only visit to America at Clark University.
1909	William Healy develops child guidance clinic in Chicago.
1916	Lewis Terman develops Stanford-Binet Intelligence Test.
1917	Clinicians of APA leave to form American Association of Clinical Psychologists (AACP).
1917	Robert Yerkes and committee develop Army Alpha test.

(continued)

Table 2.1   *Continued*

After Psychology Was Founded as a Field and until World War II	
1919	AACP rejoins APA.
1921	Cattell develops Psychological Corporation.
1921	Hermann Rorschach presents his inkblot test.
1924	Mary Cover Jones uses learning principles to treat children's fears.
1935	APA Committee on Standards and Training define clinical psychology.
1936	Louttit publishes first clinical psychology textbook.
1937	Clinicians leave APA again to form American Association of Applied Psychology (AAAP).
1937	*Journal of Consulting Psychology* begins.
1939	The Wechsler-Bellevue Intelligence Scale is published.
1945	AAAP rejoins APA.
1945	Connecticut passes first certification law for psychology.

integration of perspectives are noted. It is unlikely that the people associated with these ideas and events could have predicted how they might influence further generations to derive the perspectives of today. Chapter 3 examines the more recent developments in the field, from World War II until the present. A full understanding of contemporary clinical psychology hinges on a sound appreciation and understanding of its foundation and history.

Early Conceptions of Mental Illness: Mind and Body Paradigms

The Greeks

Several Greek thinkers were pivotal in the early development of integrative approaches to illness, and, thus, were precursors to a biopsychosocial perspective. Although the ancient Greeks felt that the gods ultimately controlled both health and illness, they looked beyond supernatural influences and explored biological, psychological, and social influences on illness (Maher & Maher, 1985a). The Greeks believed that the mind and body were closely interconnected. Somewhat similar to today's health resorts, ailing Greeks often would spend a few days at a temple where they would engage in treatments that might include prayer, special foods, bathing, dream analysis, and animal sacrifice. The doctor-priest who conducted these treatments believed that healing could occur through activation of a life force stimulated by the treatment protocols (Mora, 1985).

The famous Greek physician, Hippocrates (460–377 B.C.), who led the writing of the *Hippocratic Corpus*, felt that disease was primarily the result of an imbalance in four bodily fluids or *humors*, rather than of spiritual factors (Maher & Maher, 1985a). These fluids were black bile, yellow bile, phlegm, and blood. Furthermore, Hippocrates felt that the relationship between these bodily fluids also determined temperament and personality. For example, too much yellow bile resulted in a *choleric* (angry, irritable) temperament, whereas too much black bile resulted in a *melancholic* (sadness, hopelessness) personality. Hippocrates felt that these imbalances might originate in the patient's environment. For example, it was believed that water quality, altitude, wind, and time of year were important considerations in the etiology of illness. Hippocrates encouraged fellow doctors to be gentle and patient with their patients because various stressors were viewed as capable of preventing healing.

Hippocrates maintained a holistic approach to health and illness reflected in his statement: "In order to cure the human body, it is necessary to have a knowledge of the whole of things." He felt that head trauma and heredity could also account for abnormal behavior and illness. He was sensitive to interpersonal, psychological, and stress factors that contribute to problem behavior. The thinking and writing of Hippocrates helped to move from a spiritualistic toward a more naturalistic view or model of health and illness. Hippocrates suggested that biological, psychological, and social factors all contribute to both physical and emotional illness. This early biopsychosocial perspective was further championed by Plato, Aristotle, and Galen until its temporary demise in the Middle Ages.

Plato (427–347 B.C.) saw the spirit or soul as being in charge of the body and that problems residing in the soul could result in physical illness (Mora, 1985). Plato quoted Socrates (470–399 B.C.) as stating: "As it is not proper to cure the eyes without the head, nor the head without the body, so neither is it proper to cure the body without the soul." Plato felt that mental illness resulted from sickness in the *logistikon* or the part of the soul that operates in the head, controlling reason. He felt that personality, a lack of harmony, and ignorance about the self were responsible for mental illness symptoms. Aristotle (384–322 B.C.) maintained a scientific emphasis and felt that certain distinct emotional states including joy, anger, fear, and courage impacted the functioning of the human body. Aristotle felt that treatment for mental problems should include talking and the use of logic to influence the soul and psyche (Maher & Maher, 1985a). The use of logic and reason to influence emotional and behavioral problems is one of the major principles behind today's cognitive therapy. These Greek philosophers and physicians viewed health, illness, personality, and behavior as being intimately interconnected.

Galen (A.D. 130–200) was a Greek physician who integrated the work and perspectives outlined by Hippocrates, Plato, Aristotle, and others and developed a holistic program of medical practice that became the foundation of medicine in Europe for 1,000 years (Maher & Maher, 1985a; Mora, 1985). Like his Greek colleagues, Galen also used the humoral theory of balance between the four bodily fluids discussed previously as a foundation for treatments. Induced vomiting to treat depression as well as induced bleeding or *bloodletting* to treat a variety of ailments were common treatments used for centuries (Burton, 1621/1977; Kemp, 1990). Galen also felt that the brain was the rational soul and the center of sensation and reason. Additionally, he thought that humans experienced one of two irrational subsouls, one for males and one for females. The male subsoul was thought to be located in the heart, whereas the female subsoul was thought to be located in the liver. Unlike Plato, Galen felt that the soul was the slave and not the master of the body, and that wishes of the soul in the body resulted in health and illness.

Together, the Greeks developed a remarkably holistic perspective in which we can see many of the roots of our current beliefs on mind and body interactions in mental and physical illness. However, the ensuing Middle Ages would temporarily derail from this line of reasoning, instead embracing largely supernatural views of illness.

The Middle Ages

During the Middle Ages (A.D. 500–1450), earlier notions regarding the relationship among health, illness, mind, and body reemerged (Kemp, 1990). Perhaps as a response to the highly turbulent, frightening, and stressful times during the Black Plague, numerous wars, and the split within the Roman Catholic Church resulting in two Catholic centers and popes, the focus on supernatural influences to explain events became commonplace. Disease and "insanity," many believed, were caused by spiritual matters such as the influence of demons, witches, and sin. Therefore, healing and treatment became, once more, a spiritual rather than a medical issue using integrative biopsychosocial strategies. Those who were ill would consult with priests or other clergy, and atonement for sins would likely be prescribed as the road to recovery. People who were "insane" would often be treated by exorcism. Some were chained to church walls in order to benefit from prayers; some were tortured and killed. In 1484, Pope Innocent VIII issued a papal statement approving of the persecution of "witches." Although the mentally ill were certainly not the only people targeted, it has been estimated that 150,000 people were executed in the name of religion during this time period (Kemp, 1990).

Although most modern people would disagree with the supernatural emphasis and inhumane treatments during the Middle Ages, some of the same type of thinking and blaming of the victim is found today. For example, many of the problems of the Germans during the 1930s and early 1940s were blamed on the Jews. During the 1980s, many (including several U.S. senators) suggested that AIDS was a plague from God for "immoral" homosexual behavior. Today, many blame illegal immigration as a critical factor in many societal ills, including problems such as economic woes, violence, and youth crime.

Not everyone during the Middle Ages believed that good and evil, spirits and demons, sorcery and witchcraft contributed to mental illness (Kemp, 1990; Maher & Maher, 1985a). Some, such as Saint Thomas Aquinas (1225–1274), felt that there was both theological truth and scientific truth. For example, Aquinas reasoned that the soul was unable to become "sick" and, therefore, **mental illness** must have a physical cause or be due to problems in reason or passion (Aglioni, 1982). The late fourteenth-century French bishop Nicholas Oresme felt that abnormal behavior and mental illness were due to diseases such as melancholy (today's depression). Furthermore, the insane were sometimes humanely and compassionately cared for by people living in rural villages.

Another model to explain abnormal behavior, which became especially popular during the sixteenth century, was the influence of the moon, stars, and alignment of the planets.

A Swiss physician, Paracelsus (1490–1541), popularized the notion that various movements of the stars, moon, and planets influenced mood and behavior. Paracelsus also focused on the biological foundations of mental illness and developed humane treatments. Juan Luis Vives (1492–1540) and Johann Weyer (1515–1588) helped to shift theories of mental illness from a focus on the soul to an emphasis on behavior and promoted humane treatments of the mentally ill. During the Middle Ages, the biological, psychological, social, astrological, and supernatural influences on behavior were believed to be responsible for mental illness and abnormal behavior. Different institutions, groups, and individuals maintained different opinions concerning which of these factors could explain behavior the best. Sadly, some of these beliefs resulted in poor or no treatment as well as inhumane behavior toward others.

The Renaissance

During the Renaissance, renewed interest in the physical and medical worlds emerged, overshadowing supernatural and religious viewpoints. Interest in the mind and soul were considered unscientific and thus relegated to the philosophers and clergy. New discoveries in chemistry, physics, biology, and mathematics unfolded rapidly and were met with great enthusiasm (Mora, 1985). Giovanni Battista Morgagni (1682–1771), for example, discovered through autopsy that a diseased organ in the body could cause illness and death. Andreas Vesalius (1514–1564), a Dutch physician, published an anatomy textbook in 1543 delineating dissection of the human body. The emphasis on scientific observation and experimentation rather than reason, mythology, religious beliefs, and dogma provided a model for future research and teaching. When William Harvey, an English physician, used the scientific method in 1628 to determine that blood circulated through the body because of the function of the heart, the Greek notion of imbalance of bodily fluids vanished from medical thinking.

New medical discoveries during the Renaissance resulted in biomedical reductionism in that disease, including mental illness, could be understood by scientific observation and experimentation rather than beliefs about mind and soul. The biological side of the integrative biopsychosocial perspective was emphasized. René Descartes (1596–1650), a French philosopher, argued that the mind and body were separate. This dualism of mind and body became the basis for Western medicine until recently. The mind and body were viewed historically as split, in that diseases of the body were studied by the medical sciences while problems with the mind or emotional life were delegated to the philosophers and clergy. However, mental illness was often considered a disease of the brain, and thus the insane were treated using the medical orientation of the time.

Treatment of mental illness, however, lagged behind these medical developments. During this period, physicians treated people who were considered deviant or abnormal by confining them to hospitals and asylums. Little treatment, other than custodial care, was provided to these patients and thus these asylums were renowned for their prison-like environments. The term *bedlam* (a variant of *Bethlehem*), connoting chaos and hellish circumstances, originated when St. Mary's of Bethlehem was opened in London during 1547. Active treatments, besides custodial care, included restrictive cribs, hunger cures, bloodletting, cold-water dunking or *hydrotherapy*, and other painful treatments (Kemp, 1990; Mora, 1985).

The Nineteenth Century

In the nineteenth century, numerous advances in understanding mental and physical illness allowed for a more sophisticated understanding of the relationship between body and mind in both health and illness. A breakthrough of the nineteenth century involved the discovery by Rudolf Virchow (1821–1902), Louis Pasteur (1822–1895), and others that disease and illness could be attributed to dysfunction at the cellular level (Maher & Maher, 1985a). For example, the discovery that syphilis was caused by microorganisms entering the brain following sexual activity helped to support the biological model of mental illness. The laboratory thus took center stage as the arena for the investigation of disease. The nineteenth-century discovery that *germs* or microorganisms can cause disease, along with the twentieth-century advances in medical, genetic, and technological discoveries, have continued to support the "Cartesian dualism" perspective of Descartes in the seventeenth century.

However, **dualism** was tempered in the last part of the eighteenth century and during the nineteenth century due to the work and influence of a variety of physicians who believed that the mind and body were connected, not separate. Benjamin Rush (1745–1813) authored the first American text in psychiatry, positing that the mind could cause a variety of diseases. Franz Mesmer (1733–1815), an Austrian physician, and others noticed that many people experiencing paralysis, deafness, and blindness had no biomedical pathology, leaving psychological causes suspect. Claude Bernard (1813–1878) was a prominent physician who argued for recognition of the role of psychological factors in physical illness. Jean Martin Charcot (1825–1893), a French physician, used hypnosis to treat a wide variety of conversion disorders (i.e., physical symptoms such as paralysis, blindness, deafness without apparent physical cause). Thus, many nineteenth-century physicians laid the groundwork for today's current theories and practices integrating the influences of physical, psychological, and social factors on health and well-being.

These advances lead to greater sensitivity and sophistication regarding the treatment of individuals with mental illness. A psychosocial approach to mental illness called **moral therapy** emerged during this time. Moral therapy sought to treat patients as humanely as possible and encouraged the nurturance of interpersonal relationships. Its founder, French physician Philippe Pinel (1745–1826), did much to improve the living conditions and treatment approaches used by mental hospitals during the nineteenth century. He became director of several mental hospitals in France and altered the treatment facilities to maximize patient welfare and humane forms of treatment. Using the same principles in the United States, Eli Todd (1769–1833) developed a retreat-like program for the treatment of the mentally ill in Hartford, Connecticut. This program is still in operation today and is called the Institute of Living. William Tuke (1732–1822) also developed more humane treatment approaches in English mental hospitals. Dorothea Dix (1802–1887), a Massachusetts school teacher, worked heroically for 40 years to improve treatment conditions for the mentally ill in the United States. During the Civil War, she acted as the head nurse for the Union Military. Due to her efforts, New Jersey became the first state to build a hospital for the mentally ill in 1848. Many states quickly followed suit.

Significant improvements in the diagnosis of mental illness emerged during this time as well. Efforts to apply scientific methodology to better classify and diagnose abnormal behavior were implemented. For example, influential German physician Emil Kraeplin (1856–1926) defined the term *dementia praecox* to describe the constellation of behaviors we generally now consider *schizophrenia* [named by Eugen Bleuler (1857–1930)]. Kraeplin also asserted that mental disorders were brain disorders, and mental illness could be classified as rising from either exogenous or endogenous influences. The thinking and work of Kraeplin, Bleuler, and others during this period not only helped to clarify mental disorders as medical problems but also assisted in developing a classification system for understanding and categorizing many mental disorders.

Franz Alexander (1891–1964) also studied the association between psychological factors and both physical and mental illnesses (Mora, 1985). He proposed that as a specific stressor occurred, a genetically predetermined organ system of the body responded. By repressing conflict, for example, Alexander felt that psychic energy could be channeled into the sympathetic division of the autonomic nervous system, thus overstimulating this system and producing disease. Therefore, while one person might repress conflict and eventually develop an ulcer (due to gastric acid secretion), another person might develop colitis, headache, or asthma. Alexander argued that specific personality styles, as opposed to unconscious conflicts, resulted in specific disease. For example, he felt that dependence would typically result in the development of ulcers while repressed rage would result in hypertension. Research continues to reveal biological, psychological, and social influences in the development of ulcers, hypertension, and other diseases.

A confluence of factors thus led to the birth of psychology as an independent discipline and science separate from, but related to, philosophy, medicine, and theology. We can see the roots of today's mind–body integrative and biopsychosocial perspective. The evolution of the Western view of medicine and of abnormal behavior; the use of the scientific method to make new discoveries in biology, chemistry, physics, and math; the emergence of psychoanalytic thinking; and the interest in individual differences in behavior together combined to set the stage for the subsequent emergence of the science and practice of psychology.

The Birth of Psychology

In 1860, Theodor Fechner (1801–1887) published *The Elements of Psychophysics* while Wilhelm Wundt (1832–1920) published the *Principles of Physiological Psychology* in 1874. These publications were the first to indicate clearly that techniques of physiology and physics could be used to answer psychological questions. The first laboratory of psychology was subsequently developed by Wundt at the University of Leipzig, Germany, in 1879, and psychology was born. Wundt was especially interested in individual and group differences in sensation and perception, studying human reaction times in various laboratory experiments. He was also interested in using both the scientific method and introspection to better understand the structure and components of the mind. William James also established a psychology laboratory at Harvard University at about the same time that Wundt was developing his laboratory. Whereas Yale University offered the first formal PhD in "Philosophy and Psychology" in 1861, Harvard University offered the first American PhD in psychology in 1878. G. Stanley Hall established the second American psychology laboratory at Johns Hopkins University in 1883 while James McKeen Cattell established the third American laboratory in 1888. Hall also established the first independent psychology department at Clark University in 1887.

In 1890, James published *Principles of Psychology,* which became the first classic psychology text. In 1891, James Baldwin established the first psychology laboratory in Canada at the University of Toronto. In 1892, the **American Psychological Association** (APA) was founded, and G. Stanley Hall was elected its first president. During the beginning months and years of this new field, American psychology nurtured its roots in experimental psychology and was less interested in clinical or applied psychology. The early members of the APA tended to be academics in universities conducting empirical research.

In addition to sensation, perception, and understanding the dimensions of the mind through experimentation, the early psychologists were interested in the development and use of mental tests. Although not a psychologist, Francis Galton, a relative of Charles Darwin, was interested in statistical analysis of differences among people in reaction time, sensory experiences, and motor behavior. He developed a laboratory in England to study these issues in 1882. In the United States, James McKeen Cattell (1860–1944) also studied reaction time and other differences in human behavior. Cattell coined the term *mental test* in 1890 to refer to measures that he developed in the hopes of tapping intellectual abilities. At the University of Freiburg, Germany, Hugo Münsterberg also developed a series of tests to investigate the mental abilities of children in 1891. This emerging interest in testing later grew into one of the fundamental cornerstones and contributions of the discipline of clinical psychology.

Thus, psychology was founded, and its early years were launched by academic psychologists interested in empirically measuring various aspects of human behavior to better understand the components of the mind. They had very little interest in applying their findings to assist people with emotional, behavioral, or intellectual problems or disorders. The desire to apply these newly developed methods and principles of psychology to people in need was soon to result in the birth of clinical psychology (Maher & Maher, 1985b).

The Founding of Clinical Psychology

While psychology was born as a distinct discipline with the founding of the APA in 1892, the birth of clinical psychology as a specialty area occurred four years later in 1896 with the opening of the first psychological clinic at the University of Pennsylvania by Lightner Witmer (1867–1956). Witmer completed his undergraduate studies at the University of Pennsylvania in 1888 and earned his PhD in psychology at the University of Leipzig under Wilhelm Wundt in 1892. Following his doctoral studies, Witmer returned to the University of Pennsylvania to become director of their psychology laboratory.

Witmer became the first psychologist to use his understanding of the principles of human behavior to help an individual with a particular problem. He was asked by a teacher to help one of her students who was not performing well in school. After assessing the child's problem, Witmer developed a specific treatment program. He found that the child had difficulty in spelling, reading, and memory, and recommended tutoring, which later proved to be a successful intervention (McReynolds, 1987).

In 1896, Witmer described his methods of diagnosis and treatment to members of the newly formed APA. He proposed that a psychological clinic could be devoted to diagnosis and evaluation, individual treatment, public service, research, and the training of students. Apparently, his thoughts were not well received by his professional colleagues at the time (Brotemarkle, 1947; Reisman, 1976). His colleagues disliked the notion that psychology as a science should be applied to actual clinical problems. It is important to note that during this time, psychology was considered a science and its purpose was to better understand general (not abnormal or dysfunctional) human behavior. Despite the lukewarm reception, Witmer independently developed his psychological clinic at the University of Pennsylvania along with programs to assist children with primarily school-related difficulties and challenges.

Many of the principles that Witmer developed in his psychological clinic are still used today. For example, he favored a diagnostic evaluation prior to offering treatment procedures and services. He favored a multidisciplinary team approach as opposed to individual consultation. He used interventions and diagnostic strategies based on research evidence. Finally, he was interested in preventing problems before they emerged.

Highlight of a Contemporary Clinical Psychologist

Rev. Gerdenio "Sonny" Manuel, SJ, PhD

Photo: Courtesy Rev. Gerdenio Manuel

As a clinical psychologist, Catholic priest, and university professor, Fr. Manuel's general area of interest is higher education, particularly curricular and co-curricular programs that enable faculty and students to develop the habits of mind and heart that lead them to reflective engagement with the world and that deepen their commitment to fashioning a more humane and just world, especially for those in greatest need.

Birth Date: June 8, 1951

College: University of San Francisco (BA, Political Science), 1971

Graduate Program: Duke University (MA, PhD, Clinical Psychology), 1985

Clinical Internship: Cambridge Hospital/Harvard University School of Medicine (1984–1985)

Postdoctoral Fellowship: Cambridge Hospital/Harvard University School of Medicine (1985–1986)

Current Job: Rector, Santa Clara University Jesuit Community

Pros and Cons of Being a Clinical Psychologist:

Pros: "Insight into life and life's meaning, an appreciation of the lights, shadows, and dreams of human life."

Cons: "Allowing oneself spontaneity in nonclinical situations; it's hard to give up the therapist role in off hours."

Future of Clinical Psychology: "The role of clinical psychology will be enhanced as we continue to strive for ways to stay in touch with our humanity and deepest desires in an increasingly technological and stress- and strife-filled world."

Typical Schedule:

8:00	E-mail correspondence
9:00	University or Jesuit Community meetings
11:00	Clinical consultation–individual and groups
12:00	Working lunch—University trustees, faculty groups, etc.
2:00	Teaching Clinical Foundations of Pastoral Counseling
3:00	Writing and research
5:30	Liturgy, prayer
8:00	Pastoral counseling, spiritual direction

By 1904, the University of Pennsylvania began offering formal courses in clinical psychology. In 1906, Morton Price published the first edition of the *Journal of Abnormal Psychology*. By 1907, Witmer began the first professional journal dedicated to the field of clinical psychology, entitled *The Psychological Clinic.* Through these activities and landmark events clinical psychology was born. However, while Witmer helped launch the clinical psychology specialty, a variety of other people and events further molded clinical psychology into its current form.

The Influence of Binet's Intelligence Test

In 1885, Alfred Binet, a French scientist and attorney, founded (along with Henri Beaunis) the first psychology laboratory in France. Binet and his colleagues were especially interested in developing tests to investigate mental abilities in children. In 1904, a French commission invited Binet and his colleague, Theodore Simon, to develop a method to assist in providing mentally disabled children with appropriate educational services. Binet and Simon developed an intelligence test that could be used with children in order to assist teachers and schools in identifying children whose mental abilities prevented them from benefiting from regular classroom instruction. The Binet-Simon scale was then developed in 1908 specifically for school use. Binet felt that the test did not provide a comprehensive and objective index of intellectual functioning and highlighted the limitations of his testing methods for use beyond the classroom.

Henry Goddard, who had developed a clinic for children at the Vineland Training School in New Jersey, learned about the Binet-Simon scale while in Europe during 1908. He was impressed with the scale and brought it back to the United States for translation and use. In 1916, Stanford University psychologist Lewis Terman revised the scale and renamed it the Stanford-Binet. The Binet approach to testing became remarkably popular in the United States, as various institutions throughout the country adopted the Binet-Simon and later the Stanford-Binet tests to assess children. By 1914, over 20 university psychology clinics were utilizing the Binet approach. Measuring the intellectual abilities of children quickly became a major activity of clinical psychologists during the early days of the field.

The Influence of the Mental Health and Child Guidance Movement

The momentum achieved through the emergence of psychological clinics and psychological testing soon progressed into the realm of mental illness and problematic behavior. A former mental patient, Clifford Beers, who may be credited with the expansion, founded the National Committee for Mental Hygiene, which later became known as the National Association for Mental Health. Beers was hospitalized with severe depression that also included episodes of mania. Today, he would have likely been diagnosed with bipolar disorder (manic depression). His treatment, from a contemporary viewpoint, would be considered inhumane although it was common at the time. Once he was released from the hospital, he wrote a book entitled *A Mind That Found Itself*, published in 1908. The book focused on the inhumane treatment he experienced while hospitalized. The mission of his post-hospitalization life and his newly founded association was to improve the treatment of those suffering from mental illness.

Beers and his organization were successful due in part to the support of prominent psychologist and Harvard professor William James and prominent psychiatrist Adolf Meyer. This success led to the opening of William Healy's Juvenile Psychopathic Institute in 1909 and to the subsequent establishment of child guidance clinics throughout the country. Unlike Witmer's focus on learning differences and educational challenges, the child guidance clinics, such as the one developed by Healy, focused on disruptive behaviors of children interacting with schools, police, and the courts. The philosophy of these clinics was based on the view that disruptive behavior in children was due to mental illness and that intervention should occur early before significant problems such as stealing, fire setting, and robbery began. In 1917, Healy founded the influential Judge Baker Foundation in Boston, Massachusetts. The child guidance movement applied the new principles of psychology to the treatment of children and their families encountering mental illness and problem behaviors. Thus, the child guidance perspective helped to emphasize the psychological and social influences of behavior and mental illness.

The Influence of Sigmund Freud in America

The work and writings of Sigmund Freud (1856–1939) and his colleagues were highly influential in further understanding the connection between the mind and body. Freud proposed that unconscious conflicts and emotional influences could bring about mental and physical illness. Freud reawakened earlier Greek notions that a more holistic view of health and illness including the study of emotional experience was necessary for a fuller understanding of health, illness, and abnormal behavior. Freud's 1900 publication of *The Interpretation of Dreams* resulted in mainstream acceptance of the psychoanalytic perspective.

Freud had little influence on the development of clinical psychology in the United States until September 1909. At that time, Freud made his landmark and only trip to the United States in response to an invitation by G. Stanley Hall (the APA's first president and president of Clark University in Worcester, Massachusetts). Clark University was celebrating its twentieth anniversary as an institution and Hall invited a large number of prominent psychologists, psychiatrists, and academics for a series of lectures. In addition to Sigmund Freud, Carl Jung, Otto Rank, Sandor Ferenczi, James McKeen Cattell, E. B. Titchener, and William James were also in attendance—a veritable "who's who" of influential names at the time. This conference stimulated the widespread acceptance of Freud's psychoanalytic theories in the United States. The psychological and child guidance clinics, quickly growing in the United States at the time, tended to adopt Freud's orientation to mental illness and treatment after the 1909 lectures.

Thus, the psychoanalytic perspective to behavioral and mental problems was highlighted in these clinics. Furthermore, the enthusiasm afforded psychological testing in the wake of the Binet-Simon scale grew dramatically during this period as well. 1900's

The American Psychological Association and Early Clinical Psychology
1900-1920

The first two decades of the twentieth century witnessed tremendous growth in the field of clinical psychology. During this time, the APA was interested primarily in scientific research in academic settings and was largely disinterested in clinical applications in the field. Therefore, these rapid developments in the provision of psychological services in psychological clinics and child

Sigmund Freud

Sigmund Freud was born in what is now Austria on May 6, 1856, and spent most of his childhood in Vienna. He came from a large family and was the oldest of seven children. He appeared to have been the favorite child, getting attention and perks that other children in the family didn't get. Like many Jews at the time, he experienced discrimination that led him to make certain life sacrifices. For example, he wanted to become a university professor but, as a Jew, he was unable to pursue this desire since Jews were not allowed these types of positions at the time. He chose medicine as an alternative and completed his medical degree at the University of Vienna in 1881. He initially was attracted to research endeavors and published several medical articles but eventually switched to private practice. Freud was not a psychologist or a psychiatrist; he was a neurologist. He married Martha Bernays and had six children; one, Anna, became a well-known psychoanalyst.

Freud's most notable books include *Studies on Hysteria* (published in 1895) and *The Interpretation of Dreams* (published in 1900). His influence grew and by the early 1900s he was highly respected. The influence of his thinking, writing, and theories had grown enormously in the professional community. He made one trip to the United States in 1909 to give a series of lectures at Clark University in Wooster, Massachusetts. Curiously, it was a trip he later regretted due to the hassles of such travel with few rewards.

Freud had two great loves: antiquities and cigars. His office was full of small antiquities and he spent a great deal of time (and money) on his hobby. Although his love of cigars resulted in throat cancer and a number of years of pain and surgeries, he found it impossible to give up the unhealthy habit that ultimately killed him. Due to Nazi persecution, he fled Austria in 1938 and moved to a residential neighborhood in north London where he continued writing and seeing patients until just a few days before his death in September 1939. His London home is now a museum where many of his antiquities as well as his famous couch and desk can still be viewed.

guidance clinics were generally ignored by the association.

The growth of clinical psychology therefore occurred not because of the APA but in spite of it. Clinicians frustrated with the lack of interest and support by the APA decided to leave the organization and form the American Association of Clinical Psychologists (AACP) in 1917. This separation did not last and in 1919, the AACP and APA agreed to a reconciliation

of sorts and the AACP rejoined the APA as a clinical section.

The Influence of World War I

When the United States entered World War I in 1917, a large number of recruits needed to be classified based on their intellectual and psychological functioning. The U.S. Army

Medical Department contacted the current president of the APA (Robert Yerkes) to assist in developing an appropriate test for the military recruits. A committee was formed that included Henry Goddard, Lewis Terman, and Guy Whipple (who had published a book entitled *Manual of Mental and Physical Tests* in 1910). The committee developed what became known as the Army Alpha and Army Beta intelligence tests. The Army Alpha was a verbal test while the Army Beta was a nonverbal test. Unlike intelligence tests such as the Stanford-Binet that could be administered to only one subject at a time, the Army Alpha and Army Beta tests could be administered to very large groups of people. Furthermore, the tests could be used for both literate and nonliterate adults. To assess psychological functioning, the committee suggested that the Psychoneurotic Inventory (developed by Robert Woodworth in 1917) also be used. Approximately two million people were evaluated using these tests by 1918. This opportunity for psychology to contribute to the war effort through the application of psychological tests increased the status and visibility of psychologists and of psychological testing.

Clinical Psychology between the World Wars

Psychological Testing

Following World War I, psychologists became well known for their testing skills (Kiesler & Zaro, 1981; B. A. Maher & W. B. Maher, 1985b). A testing development explosion occurred, such that by 1940 over 500 psychological tests had been produced. These tests included both verbal and nonverbal intelligence tests, personality and psychological functioning tests, and career interest and vocational skill tests. Tests were available for children of all ages and abilities as well as for adults. The more popular and well-known tests included the Rorschach Inkblot Test (1921), the Miller Analogies Test (1927), the Word Association Test developed by Carl Jung (1919), the Goodenough Draw-A-Man Test (1926), the Thematic Apperception Test (1935), and the Wechsler-Bellevue Intelligence Scale (1939). In fact, testing boomed to such an extent that in 1921, James McKeen Cattell founded the Psychological Corporation to sell psychological tests to various organizations and professionals.

Projective testing became very popular with the 1921 publication of Hermann Rorschach's *Psychodiagnostik,* the famous inkblot test. Rorschach was a Swiss psychiatrist who died shortly after the publication of his famous test. In 1937, S. J. Beck and Bruno Klopfer both published comprehensive scoring procedures for the Rorschach Inkblot Test that facilitated much more research to be conducted using the instrument. In 1939, David Wechsler developed the first comprehensive and individually administered intelligence test for adults. The Wechsler-Bellevue (and subsequent revisions) quickly became the standard measure with which to assess adult intellectual abilities.

By the 1930s, 50 psychological clinics and about 12 child guidance clinics were operating in the United States. By the end of the 1930s, some clinical psychologists began to offer their professional services to clients and patients in private practice.

Psychotherapy

The early work of clinical psychologists involved primarily psychological and intellectual testing. Psychotherapy and other treatment services for those suffering from mental illness were conducted primarily by psychiatrists. Most psychotherapy during this time utilized Freud's psychoanalytic principles and techniques. Although Freud disagreed (Freud, 1959), psychiatrists in the United States believed that only physicians could adequately provide psychotherapy, thus preventing clinical psychologists and other nonphysicians from conducting psychotherapy services. In fact, it wasn't until a major lawsuit in the late 1980s that psychologists won the right to be admitted as full members of American psycho-analytic institutes, resulting in their current ability to conduct psychoanalysis with patients (De Angelis, 1989). Prior to the lawsuit, most psychoanalytic institutes admitting psychologists required that they use their training for research rather than clinical purposes.

Despite this initial prohibition, clinical psychologists gradually began providing consultation as an outgrowth of their assessment work with children. Consultation as well as treatment evolved naturally from the testing process. Consultation with teachers, children, and parents eventually led to the provision of a full range of psychotherapy and other intervention services. Unlike the psychoanalytic treatment provided by psychiatrists at the time, psychological treatment was more behavioral in orientation, reflecting the research developments in academic laboratories. For example, in 1920, John Watson detailed the well-known case of little Albert who was conditioned to be fearful of white furry objects (Watson & Rayner, 1920), while Mary Cover Jones (1924) demonstrated how these types of fears could be removed using conditioning techniques.

Training

By the early 1940s, there were no official training programs or policies regulating the field of clinical psychology. Though the majority of clinical psychologists had earned BA degrees, very few had earned PhD or even MA degrees. To be employed as a clinical psychologist, one merely needed to have a few courses in psychological testing, child development, and abnormal psychology. The APA was of little help because of their discomfort with "applied" psychology. The vast majority of the APA membership still consisted of academics primarily interested in research rather than practice applications. However, in 1935, the APA Committee on Standards of Training in Clinical Psychology recommended that a PhD and one year of supervised clinical experience be required to become a clinical psychologist.

The recommendation was largely ignored because the APA did nothing to enforce their recommendation at that time (Shakow, 1947).

Organizational Split and New Publications

As in 1917, a large group of clinicians again left the APA in frustration during 1937 to form a new organization, the American Association of Applied Psychology (AAAP). History repeated itself when this new organization rejoined the APA, this time eight years later in 1945. The split between basic experimentalists and those interested in applied areas of psychology has ebbed and flowed throughout psychology's history. Nonetheless, clinical psychology continued to develop and define itself. The first clinical psychology textbook was published in 1936 by Chauncey Louttit while the *Journal of Consulting Psychology* (now called the *Journal of Consulting and Clinical Psychology*) was first published in 1937.

The Influence of World War II

With U.S. involvement in World War II, the need to assess military recruits again became pressing. As during World War I, a committee of psychologists was formed to develop an assessment procedure to efficiently evaluate intellectual and psychological functioning as well as other skills of potential soldiers (Maher & Maher, 1985b). Reflecting the rapid development in psychological testing since World War I, the testing conducted during World War II was much more extensive and sophisticated than the Army Alpha and Army Beta used earlier. The committee developed a group-administered intelligence test called the Army General Classification Test. The committee also recommended several other tests, such as the Personal Inventory, which assessed psychiatric problems, and brief versions of the Rorschach Inkblot Test and the Thematic Apperception Test to assess personality. Additionally, various ability tests were used to assess military officers and certain specialty military groups.

These tests were given to over 20 million people during World War II (Reisman, 1976). Due to the military's desperate need for psychological services beyond testing, psychologists were called upon to provide other clinical services such as psychotherapy and consultation (Maher & Maher, 1985b; J. Miller, 1946).

In addition to the enormous needs of the military during the war effort, additional advances and developments were associated with the growth of clinical psychology. For example, new tests were developed such as the Minnesota Multiphasic Personality Inventory (MMPI; Hathaway, 1943). The MMPI was developed as an objective personality inventory geared toward assessing psychiatric problems. The MMPI and current revisions (MMPI-2, MMPI-A) are among the most widely used psychological tests today. In 1949, David Wechsler published the Wechsler Intelligence Scale for Children (WISC), which became the first significant alternative to the well-known and most often used Stanford-Binet. The current version of the WISC (the WISC-IV) is the most commonly used intelligence test for children ages 6 to 16 given today.

In 1945, Connecticut became the first of many states to pass a certification law for psychologists, thereby launching the regulation of the practice of clinical psychology among qualified professionals. Thus, only those deemed qualified by training and experience could call themselves "psychologists" and offer services to the public for a fee. In 1946, the first edition of the *American Psychologist* was published, and the American Board of Examiners in Professional Psychology (ABEPP) was created to certify psychologists. The ABEPP developed a national examination for all clinical psychologists seeking licensure. This frequently revised examination is now used in every state.

The Big Picture

Although clinical psychology did not become a specialty within psychology until 1896, the many perspectives in understanding, assessing, and treating emotional and behavioral problems during the preceding centuries set the stage for its development. Understanding the influences of biological, psychological, and social factors in the development and maintenance of problem behavior and emotional distress evolved over many years. Each generation grappled with trying to best understand the influences of various factors on behavior. As more and more scientific discoveries were revealed, theories about the relative importance of biological, psychological, and social factors in behavior and emotions were altered to accommodate the most up-to-date discoveries and thinking. However, historical events, influential people, and social perspectives influenced past and current thinking about topics of interest to clinical psychology.

Prior to World War II, clinical psychology was essentially defining itself, struggling with its relationship with the APA, and making scientific and clinical inroads. However, World War II and especially the aftermath of the war changed clinical psychology significantly. Chapter 3 chronicles the history and development of clinical psychology in modern times following World War II.

Humankind has struggled inexorably to make sense of human behavior in the context of changing social, theological, and political times. Changing notions of how the mind, body, and environment interact to create mental health and illness has developed through fits and starts into the roots of our current integrative appreciation for the dynamic interplay of biological, psychological, and social factors. Psychology as a science and clinical psychology as a discipline emerged in these early eras through experimentation, testing, and, eventually, consultation and treatment. Yet to come, however, is the modern era of clinical psychology, and the exciting explosion of ideas, methods, and practices applied to human problems in our contemporary world.

Key Points

1. Before Lightner Witmer opened the first psychological clinic at the University of

Pennsylvania and coined the term *clinical psychology* in 1896, a number of events during the course of history set the stage for the development of clinical psychology as a profession.

2. The ancient Greeks felt that the gods were the cause of both health and illness and that the mind and body were closely interconnected. The famous Greek physician, Hippocrates (460–370 B.C.), believed that disease was primarily the result of an imbalance of four bodily fluids or *humors* rather than of spiritual factors.

3. During the Middle Ages (A.D. 500–1450), the early notions of the relationship between health, illness, mind, and body returned. Disease and insanity, it was believed, were caused by spiritual matters such as the influence of demons and witches and the results of sin.

4. During the Renaissance, renewed interest in the physical and medical world emerged once again with diminishing influences of the supernatural or religious viewpoints. New medical discoveries during the Renaissance resulted in biomedical reductionism in that disease, including mental illness, could be understood by scientific observation and experimentation rather than beliefs about mind and soul.

5. It wasn't until the work of Sigmund Freud (1856–1939) and colleagues that the connection between mind and body reemerged. Freud demonstrated that unconscious conflicts and emotional influences could bring about diseases. As the ancient Greeks believed, Freud reawakened the notion that a more holistic view of health, which included the role of emotional life, was necessary to a fuller understanding of health, illness, and abnormal behavior.

6. Psychology was born when the first laboratory of psychology was developed by Wilhelm Wundt at the University of Leipzig, Germany, in 1879. In 1890, William James published *Principles of Psychology*, which became the first classic psychology text, and in 1892, the APA was founded and elected G. Stanley Hall as its president.

7. The birth of clinical psychology occurred in 1896 with the opening of the first psychological clinic at the University of Pennsylvania by Lightner Witmer (1867–1956). Witmer became the first psychologist to use his understanding of the principles of human behavior to help an individual with a particular problem: He was asked by a teacher to help one of her students who was not performing well in school.

8. Alfred Binet and Theodore Simon developed an intelligence test that could be used with children in order to assist teachers and schools identify children whose mental abilities prevented them benefitting from regular classroom instruction. The Binet-Simon scale was developed in 1908 specifically for school use. In 1916, Stanford University psychologist Lewis Terman revised the scale and renamed it the Stanford-Binet. The Binet approach to testing became remarkably popular in the United States. Various institutions throughout the country adopted the Binet-Simon and later the Stanford-Binet approach to assess children.

9. Former mental patient Clifford Beers founded the National Committee for Mental Hygiene, which was concerned about the inhumane treatment mental patients experience while hospitalized. The mission of Beers' post-hospitalization life and his newly founded association was to improve treatment for those suffering from mental illness as well as assist in the prevention of mental disorders. Beers and his association founded the child guidance movement, which used the new principles of psychology to help children and their families deal with mental illness and problem behaviors.

10. During World War I and World War II, millions of recruits needed to be evaluated for psychological and intellectual functioning. The military turned to psychology to provide them with testing to evaluate the troops.

Key Terms

American Psychological Association
Dementia praecox
Dualism
Mental illness
Moral therapy

For Reflection

1. What influence did the Greeks have on clinical psychology?
2. Explain how the Greeks combined several perspectives on health and illness.
3. Why did the Middle Ages represent a step backward in mind and body understanding?
4. What factors contributed to the rise of supernatural beliefs regarding mental illness during the Middle Ages?
5. What was the seventeenth century's influence on medicine and, ultimately, clinical psychology?
6. Why did clinical psychology and the APA often have significant differences of opinion?
7. What happened at Clark University in 1909 that shaped clinical psychology?
8. What causal themes continue to exist in our understanding of the factors that contribute to health and illness?
9. How did World Wars I and II influence the formation of clinical psychology?

Real Students, Real Questions

1. What kinds of questions were included in the Army Alpha and Army Beta tests?
2. Are the IQ test items of the past valid questions today?
3. What direction might psychology have gone in if World Wars I and II hadn't happened?

Web Resources

http://www.apa.org/archives/apa-history.html
www.cop.es/English/docs/brief.htm
Learn more about the history of clinical psychology.

Recent History of Clinical Psychology

Chapter Objectives

1. To highlight the history of clinical psychology from World War II until the present time.
2. To outline the development of theoretical approaches used in clinical psychology.

Chapter Outline

Clinical Psychology Immediately after World War II

The Rise of Alternatives to the Psychodynamic Approach

Highlight of a Contemporary Clinical Psychologist: Nadine J. Kaslow, PhD, ABPP

A New Training Model Emerges

The Rise of Empirically Supported Treatments and Resurgence of Cognitive Behavioral Models

Present Status

3
Chapter

The past 60 years have shaped clinical psychology every bit as significantly as the previous 2,000 years. Since World War II, clinical psychology has defined, refined, and expanded itself in concert with contemporary issues and demands. New theories, medications, and integrative views have led to today's field of clinical psychology. Similarly, current compelling issues related to gender, culture, ethnicity, other individual differences, and the changing economic climate of health care, have demanded an up-to-date awareness and sensitivity for today's psychologists. This chapter details the major developments in clinical psychology from immediately after World War II to the present (Table 3.1). The conclusion contains a description of contemporary factors in training, sensitivity to individual differences, and health care.

Clinical Psychology Immediately after World War II

Following the war, over 40,000 veterans were hospitalized in **Veterans' Administration** (VA) hospitals for psychiatric reasons, representing about 60% of the total VA hospital patient population (Miller, 1946). Psychiatrists and other physicians were unable to meet the treatment demands of these enormous numbers of veterans. Therefore, the overwhelming need for clinical services resulted in a huge increase in the number of clinical psychologists who could provide a full range of comprehensive psychological services, including psychological testing, psychotherapy, consultation, and research. In 1946, the VA requested 4,700 clinical psychologists be employed in the VA system. The chief medical director of

Table 3.1   **Significant Events in Clinical Psychology after World War II**

1940s	
1946	VA and NIMH fund clinical psychology training.
1947	ABEPP is founded to certify clinicians.
1949	Halstead presents neuropsychological testing battery.
1949	Boulder Conference defines scientist-practitioner model of training.

1950s	
1950	Dollard and Miller publish *Personality and Psychotherapy: An Analysis in Terms of Learning, Thinking, and Culture*.
1951	Rogers publishes *Client-Centered Therapy*.
1952	Eysenck publishes *The Effects of Psychotherapy: An Evaluation*.
1952	American Psychiatric Association publishes diagnostic categories in the *Diagnostic and Statistical Manual* (*DSM-I*).
1953	APA publishes *Ethical Standards*.
1953	Skinner presents operant principles.
1955	Joint Commission on Mental Health and Illness founded.
1956	Stanford University training conference.
1958	Wolpe publishes *Psychotherapy by Reciprocal Inhibition*.
1958	Miami training conference.
1959	Mental Research Institute (MRI) founded.

1960s	
1960	Eysenck publishes *Handbook of Abnormal Psychology: An Experimental Approach*.
1963	Congress passes legislation creating community mental health centers.
1965	Chicago training conference.
1965	Conference at Swamscott, MA, starts community psychology movement.
1967	Association for Advancement in Behavior Therapy founded.
1968	First PsyD program founded at the University of Illinois.
1969	First freestanding professional school of psychology founded at California School of Professional Psychology.

1970s	
1970	*DSM II* published.
1973	Vail training conference.
1976	National Council of Schools of Professional Psychology (NCSPP) founded.
1977	George Engel publishes paper in *Science* defining biopsychosocial model.
1977	Wachtel publishes *Psychoanalysis and Behavior Therapy: Toward an Integration*.

1980s	
1980	*DSM-III* published.
1981	APA ethical standards revised.

Table 3.1   **Continued**

1982	Health psychology defined.
1986	NCSPP Mission Bay training conference.
1987	Salt Lake City training conference.
1987	*DSM-III-R* published.
1988	American Psychological Society founded.
1989	NCSPP San Juan training conference.

1990s

1990	NCSPP Gainesville training conference.
1991	NCSPP San Antonio training conference.
1992	Michigan Conference on postdoctoral training.
1994	*DMS-IV* published.
1994	Academy of Psychological Clinical Science founded at Indiana University.
1995	APA publishes a list of empirically validated treatments.
1998	International Society of Clinical Psychology founded in San Francisco.
1999	Guam authorizes psychologists to prescribe psychotropic medication.

2000s

2001	APA alters its mission statement to reflect psychology as a health-care discipline.
2002	APA ethics code revised.
2002	New Mexico and Guam allows psychologists medication prescription authority.
2003	Health Insurance Portability and Accountability Act (HIPAA) becomes law.
2004	Louisiana allows psychologists prescription authority.
2006	APA publishes findings from a Presidential Task force on guidelines for evidence-based practice.
2008	The U.S. Congress passes the Paul Wellstone Mental Health and Addiction Equity Act of 2007, allowing mental health parity in health care.

the VA system met with officials from a group of major universities to request that formal training programs in clinical psychology be developed. By later that year, 200 graduate students in clinical psychology were being trained at 22 VA institutions (Peck & Ash, 1964). VA hospitals offered clinical psychologists secure job positions, attractive salaries, and the freedom to provide a full range of professional services. By the early 1950s, the VA hospitals became the largest single employer of clinical psychologists in the United States (Maher & Maher, 1985b; Peck & Ash, 1964).

Academic psychologists had mixed feelings about the tremendous boom in clinical psychology due to the needs of the VA hospitals. Many thought that this was an opportunity to increase the activities, prestige, and influence of clinical psychology. Many others were disinterested in the applied aspects of psychology, preferring to focus solely on the science of psychology in academic environments. This division between science and practice has remained an area of contention within psychology from the very earliest days of the discipline until the present.

Training

The need for qualified mental health professionals after World War II resulted in the National Institute of Mental Health (NIMH) developing grant programs to help train clinical psychologists (as well as psychiatrists, nurses, and social workers). The grant program started with $212,000 in 1948 and rose to $10 million in 1980 (Kiesler & Zaro, 1981). These monies attracted more and more students to the mental health fields, necessitating both new training programs and new guidelines quickly.

The APA Committee on Training in Clinical Psychology under the leadership of David Shakow sought to develop training standards and guidelines for graduate and internship training in clinical psychology (Shakow, 1947). Ultimately, the committee's guidelines not only became the gold standard for clinical training but were used to determine whether federal monies would be used to support these graduate training programs. The guidelines included the central admonishment that clinical psychologists be trained rigorously in a four-year doctoral program along with a one-year clinical internship. The guidelines also created the standard that training include several different content areas such as biological, cognitive, individual difference, and social aspects of behavior (Shakow, 1947, 1976, 1978). In addition, psychologists were to be trained as both scientists *and* clinicians. The committee recommended that training be comprehensive in research, treatment, and assessment. In 1948, the American Psychological Association (APA) began to carefully evaluate, critique, and accredit doctoral training programs. These guidelines led to the most influential training conference in the history of clinical psychology: the 1949 Boulder Conference.

The Boulder Conference

Two years after the training report was released, a committee met in Boulder, Colorado, and formally adopted the advised model of clinical training. The Conference was financially supported by the Veterans' Administration as well as the U.S. Public Health Service via the NIMH. The financial support provided by these government agencies reflected the enormous interest and stake the U.S. government had in the field of clinical psychology. Clinical psychology had come a long way since its humble beginnings in Witmer's clinic in 1886. The **Boulder model** also became known as the **scientist-practitioner model,** and emphasized that clinical psychologists should be competent in both conducting research and providing professional psychological services such as psychotherapy and assessment. This training model stated that a PhD degree in psychology from a university-based training program plus a one-year clinical internship were necessary for adequate preparation. This model has been the predominant training approach since then (Norcross et al., 1997a, b, 2005, 2008; Norcross, Hedges, & Castle, 2002; Shakow, 1978). In 1995, the Academy of Psychological Clinical Science (APCS) was formed to reinvigorate the Boulder model and recommit to the scientific approaches in clinical psychology (Norcross, Hedges et al., 2002). By 1948, there were 22 APA-accredited clinical psychology training programs in universities and by 1949, 42 schools offered accredited doctoral training in clinical psychology, almost doubling the number in just one year.

Post–Boulder Conference Events

Not everyone was pleased with the results and recommendations of the Boulder Conference (Frank, 1984; Korman, 1976; Strother, 1956). Additional conferences convened to discuss the pros and cons of the clinical psychology training model. Conferences occurred at Stanford University in 1955 (Strother, 1956), Miami Beach in 1958 (Roe, Gustad, Moore, Ross, & Skodak, 1959), Chicago in 1965 (Zimet & Throne, 1965), Vail in 1973 (Korman, 1976), and Salt Lake City in 1987 (Bickman, 1987). The Chicago Conference was the first to question seriously the wisdom of the Boulder model. Some Conference participants

The Boulder Conference

Curiously, doctoral training in psychology had been going on for more than 60 years before a national conference was called to discuss guidelines for training graduate students. Prior to 1949, individual psychology departments in universities across the country had a great deal of freedom to determine how they should run their training programs. The Boulder Conference was the first national meeting to discuss standards for doctoral training in psychology. Seventy-three people were invited to attend the two-week-long conference at the University of Colorado at Boulder during the summer of 1949 (see pages [54–55]). Part of the impetus for the Conference was related to the federal government's desire to provide adequate mental health services to the many veterans following World War II. They teamed with academic psychology and the VA hospital network to develop strategies to best train psychologists who could apply their skills to the assessment, psychotherapy, and consultation needs of returning World War II veterans.

The resulting recommendations from the Conference were published in a book entitled, *Training in Clinical Psychology,* edited by Victor Raimy in 1950. The *American Psychologist* (Vol. 55, No. 2, 2000) published a series of articles reflecting on the 50 years following the now-famous Boulder Conference.

After two grueling weeks, the Conference participants reached consensus on 70 resolutions regarding training clinical psychologists. They coined the notion of the *scientist-practitioner model* that included extensive training in both research and clinical practice. They agreed on standards for a graduate core curriculum, clinical specialties, ethics training, funding issues, pre- and postdoctoral internship training, and a host of other aspects of doctoral training. Remarkably, the consensus reached by these 73 people from across the country at the 1949 conference still reflects the training model used today in most graduate training programs in clinical psychology. Although many people criticize aspects of the Boulder model, the results of the Conference have stood the test of time.

felt that because only about 10% of psychologists actually publish research, too much emphasis and energy were being spent teaching graduate students how to conduct psychological research (Brems, Johnson, & Gallucci, 1996; Frank, 1984; Levy, 1962). Although this concern has continued to be expressed over the years, no resolution regarding this conflict has occurred in university-based training programs. The advent of the PsyD degree and freestanding professional schools of psychology have attempted to deal with this issue by offering more practiced-based (and less research-based) training.

By the early 1950s, over 1,000 members of the APA were members of the Clinical Division. The growth of clinical psychology during the 1950s was enormous. APA membership more than doubled during the 1950s and federal research grants supporting psychology training and research tripled during the same time period.

1. Isabelle V. Kendig, St. Elizabeth's Hospital, Washington, DC
2. Robert A. Brotemarkle, University of Pennsylvania
3. Robert G. Bernreuter, Pennsylvania State College
4. Nicholas Hobbs, Columbia University
5. Edward S. Bordin, University of Michigan
6. C. Roger Myers, University of Toronto
7. Joseph E. Brewer, Wichita Guidance Center
8. Arthur L. Benton, University of Iowa
9. Graham B. Dimmick, Duke University
10. Eston J. Asher, Purdue University
11. Delton C. Beier, Indiana University
12. Robert E. Harris, University of California Medical School
13. Earl E. Swartzlander, Veterans Administration Hospital, Long Island, NY
14. George F. J. Lehner, University of California, Los Angeles
15. Harold M. Hildreth, Veterans Administration, Washington, DC
16. Jane Hildreth, American Psychological Association Staff (guest)
17. Robert R. Blake, University of Texas
18. Cecil W. Mann, Tulane University
19. Lyle H. Lanier, University of Illinois
20. Albert I. Rabin, Michigan State College
21. John Gray Peatman, City College of New York
22. Jerry W. Carter, Jr., National Institute of Mental Health
23. Donald K. Adams, Duke University
24. George E. Levinrew, American Association of Psychiatric Social Workers
25. Robert C. Challman, Menninger Foundation, Topeka, KS
26. Julian B. Rotter, Ohio State University
27. Chester C. Bennett, Boston University
28. John W. Stafford, Catholic University
29. Bertha M. Luckey, Cleveland Public Schools
30. William R. Grove, Phoenix Elementary Schools

31. Carroll A. Whitmer, University of Pittsburgh
32. Howard F. Hunt, University of Chicago
33. T. Ernest Newland, University of Tennessee
34. Marion E. Bunch, Washington University
35. Starke R. Hathaway, University of Minnesota
36. Howard P. Longstaff, University of Minnesota
37. Brian E. Tomlinson, New York University
38. Paul Henry Mussen, University of Wisconsin
39. Carlyle Jacobsen, University of Iowa
40. Marshall R. Jones, University of Nebraska
41. Clarence L. Winder, Stanford University
42. Helen M. Wolfle, Managing Editor, American Psychologist
43. Rex M. Collier, University of Illinois
44. Dael Wolfle, American Psychological Association, Executive Secretary
45. Dorothy Randall, University of Colorado (Conference Assistant)
46. James W. Layman, University of North Carolina
47. David B. Klein, University of Southern California
48. Laurance F. Shaffer, Columbia University
49. Paul E. Huston, University of Iowa
50. Mary Schmitt, National League of Nursing Education
51. Virginia T. Graham, University of Cincinnati
52. O. Hobart Mowrer, University of Illinois
53. Eliot H. Rodnick, Worcester State Hospital, MA
54. Max L. Hutt, University of Michigan
55. Martin Scheerer, University of Kansas
56. David Shakow, University of Illinois Medical School, Chicago
57. Jean W. Macfarlane, University of California, Berkeley
58. Bert Kaplan, Harvard University
59. Thelma G. Alper, Clark University
60. Charles S. Gersoni, United States Army
61. Joseph M. Bobbitt, National Institute of Mental Health

62. Charles R. Strother, University of Washington
63. James G. Miller, University of Chicago
64. Wayne Dennis, University of Pittsburgh
65. John C. Eberhart, National Institute of Mental Health
66. E. Lowell Kelly, University of Michigan
67. Karl F. Heiser, American Psychological Association, Associate Executive Secretary
68. William A. Hunt, Northwestern University
69. Victor C. Raimy, University of Colorado
70. Dorothea A. McCarthy, Fordham University
71. Seymour B. Sarason, Yale University
72. Robert H. Felix, National Institute of Mental Health
73. George Richard Wendt, University of Rochester

Not pictured: Dwight W. Miles, Western Reserve University; Ruth S. Tolman, Veterans Administration Hospital, Los Angeles, CA.

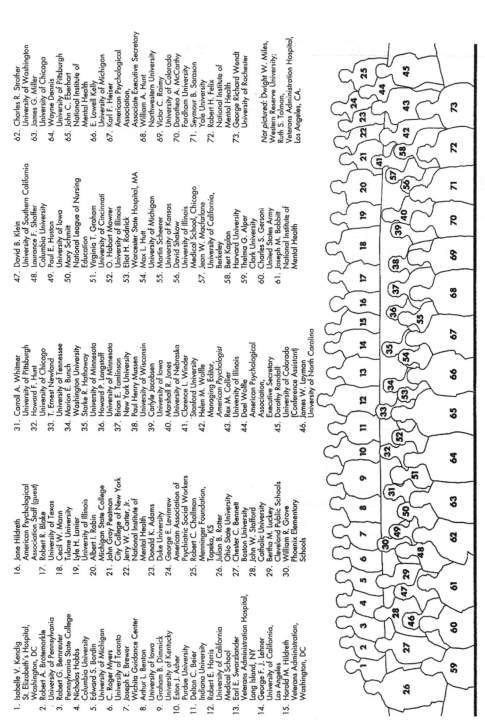

Participants in the Conference on Graduate Education in Clinical Psychology. Boulder Colorado, August/September 1949.

In 1953, the first attempt to outline ethical principles for psychologists was published. The ethical principles have been revised nine times since then and as recently as 2002. The Ethics Code outlines expected behavior among all psychologists including those involved with clinical, research, teaching, forensic, and administrative activities and is discussed in detail in Chapter 13.

The Rise of Alternatives to the Psychodynamic Approach

During the first half of the twentieth century, the psychoanalytic approach founded by Freud and, to a much lesser extent, the behavioral conditioning approach founded by John Watson served as the preeminent theoretical and treatment approaches to mental illness. During the 1950s, 1960s, and 1970s, many new approaches were developed as alternatives to the traditional psychodynamic approach. Psychologists were becoming well established in psychotherapy, augmenting their already acknowledged testing services. The humanistic, behavioral, cognitive-behavioral, and family systems approaches to treatment emerged as compelling and popular alternatives to the more traditional theories and interventions. Furthermore, the rise of the community mental health movement in the 1960s as well as the introduction of psychotropic medication in treating mental illness had powerful influences on clinical psychology. During the turbulent yet optimistic 1960s and early 1970s, clinical psychology continued to expand with increasing knowledge, tools, and professional resources. Finally, integrative approaches such as the biopsychosocial perspective emerged, adding to the sophistication of thought and practice in the field. This chapter examines these alternatives to the psychodynamic viewpoint from a historical perspective. I introduce the persons responsible for these theories and how they emerged over time. The next two chapters highlight these perspectives in more detail, focusing on how the theories and principles are applied to issues of concern in clinical psychology.

The Behavioral Approach

The behavioral approach applies theories of learning and conditioning to the understanding of human behavior and the treatment of behavioral and psychological problems. Rooted in the conditioning research of Ivan Pavlov (1849–1936) in Russia as well as the American research on behaviorism and learning theory conducted by John Watson, Edward Thorndike, Clark Hull, John Dollard, Neal Miller, and B. F. Skinner, **behavioral** principles in psychological treatment became an attractive alternative to medical and psychodynamic strategies during the 1950s and 1960s. Many psychologists were unimpressed with both the methods and outcomes of the medical or psychodynamic approaches practiced by psychiatrists and other professionals. For example, the review article by Eysenck (1952) examining psychotherapy treatment results was not favorable to psychoanalytic techniques. The behavioral platform was especially attractive to research-oriented clinicians who felt that behavior therapy approaches proved more effective in empirical research trials relative to traditional theories and methods such as psychoanalysis. Therefore, the behavioral approach to understanding human behavior, diagnosis, and treatment of mental illness was viewed by many as more scientifically based, and thus justified, than the psychodynamic approach. Furthermore, behavior therapy approaches were advanced by researchers because, more than other treatment modalities, behavioral techniques were more readily operationalized to allow for research. For example, it was easier to measure the number of times a child had a temper tantrum or a person had a panic attack than measuring constructs such as the id, transference, or unconscious conflicts. Behavioral approaches allowed for greater ease of measuring outcome data, defining concepts, and statistical analysis.

Behavior therapy approaches to treatment were being developed in South Africa by Joseph Wolpe and colleagues and in England by Hans Eysenck, M. B. Shapiro, and Stanley Rachman, among others. Wolpe (1958) had developed systematic desensitization to treat a variety of anxiety-based disorders such as phobias. Eysenck and colleagues at the University of London Institute of Psychiatry and the Maudsley Hospital used research-supported techniques guided by learning theory to treat a number of psychiatric complaints (Eysenck, 1960). These later researchers were applying the principles of conditioning and learning theory to treat a variety of clinical problems including phobia, obsessive-compulsive behavior, anxiety, and disruptive behavior in children. The publication of several books by these professionals set the stage for behavior therapy to be widely accepted and practiced in the United States (e.g., Eysenck, 1960; Krasner & Ulmann, 1965; Skinner, 1953; Wolpe, 1958; Wolpe & Lazarus, 1966).

Behavior therapy was also well suited to the Boulder model because clinical psychology training was designed to emphasize both the science and practice of psychology. The behavioral approach also was well suited to the social and political influences of the time that included the optimistic notion that we could create a more perfect society using social engineering and conditioning techniques (Skinner, 1948).

Although there are various types of behavior therapy such as applied behavioral analysis (Wilson & Frank, 1982), social learning theory–based treatment (Bandura, 1969, 1982), and cognitive-behavioral therapy (Kendall & Bemis, 1983), there are also several commonalities to the behavior therapies in terms of their understanding of human behavior and approach to assisting those who experience emotional and behavioral problems. These include the notion that most problematic behavior is learned and can be altered through the use of learning principles. Furthermore, treatment methods are based on scientifically derived procedures and can be objectively used and evaluated. Finally, behavior therapy is not imposed on others but is agreed to by clients through a collaborative and contractual relationship (O'Leary & Wilson, 1987). In 1967, the Association for Advancement of Behavior Therapy (AABT) was founded and remains as one of the major professional organizations for clinical psychologists who not only conduct behavior therapy but are broadly interested in the application of scientifically derived data.

The Cognitive-Behavioral Approach

Although the cognitive approach became popular during the 1970s after the rise of several other methods that will be discussed later in this chapter, since it is closely related, the cognitive approach is presented here following the behavioral discussion. During the 1970s, many researchers and clinicians adhering to the behavioral approach to research and treatment acknowledged a number of significant limitations in their model. Primarily, a strict focus on overt behavior neglected the contributions of thinking and attitudes in human behavior. The work of Albert Ellis (Ellis, 1962; Ellis & Grieger, 1977) using Rational-Emotive Therapy (RET; now called Rational-Emotive Behavior Therapy, REBT); Aaron Beck (1976) using cognitive treatments for depression; the cognitive restructuring work of Mahoney (1974); the stress inoculation work of Meichenbaum (1977); and the self-efficacy work of Bandura (1969, 1982) led the charge in integrating cognitive approaches with behavioral approaches. Treatment focusing on changing thinking, feeling, and expectations became as important as the goal of changing overt behavior.

For example, Ellis' REBT attempts to alter the patient's irrational beliefs concerning the "shoulds" and "oughts" about themselves and others. Beck's cognitive approach focuses on the notion that depressed people tend to view themselves, others, and the world as more negative than non-depressed persons. Altering maladaptive thought patterns and developing more adaptive ways of thinking are central to Beck's approach. Meichenbaum's self-instructional approach uses *self-talk* to guide and alter problematic thinking and behavior. While there are a number of different cognitive therapies, commonalities include the notion that learning and behavior are cognitively mediated by attitudes and attributions and that the role of the therapist is to serve as a coach, educator, or consultant in assisting the alteration of maladaptive cognitive processes and behavior (Ingram & Scott, 1990; Kendall & Bemis, 1983). The cognitive approach has become so popular that by 1990 the majority of AABT members (69%) identified themselves as being **cognitive-behavioral** while only 27% reported being strictly behavioral in orientation (Craighead, 1990). By 2005, AABT actually changed their organization name to the Association of Behavioral and Cognitive Therapies, reflecting the strong influence of cognitive approaches to behavioral research, assessment, and interventions. Furthermore, while only 2% of clinical psychologists in the APA identified themselves as being cognitive in their theoretical orientation in 1973, 28% identify themselves as cognitive in 2003 (Norcross et al., 2005).

The Humanistic Approach

The **humanistic** approach employed philosophy, existentialism, and theories of human growth and potential to understand human behavior and offer strategies for psychological treatment. The humanistic approach focused on the patient's experience or phenomenology of their concerns and offered warmth, empathy, and unconditional positive regard in psychotherapeutic interactions. During the 1950s and 1960s (an age of anxiety following World War II and during the Cold War), the humanistic approach to psychological treatment gained widespread acceptance. Frustrated with the limitations of the psychodynamic and behavioral approaches regarding treatment process, outcome, and both client and therapist satisfaction, as well as

the perceived negative psychodynamic and behavioral views of human nature (e.g., the psychodynamic emphasis on neuroses as well as infantile and primitive needs; the behavioral focus on governing behavior through external reinforcement), many mental health professionals began to incorporate the more optimistic and embracing views purported by the humanistic school of thought. The humanistic approach became known as the *third force* in psychology following the psychodynamic and behavioral approaches.

The humanistic approach was strongly influenced by philosophy as well as the existential approach to psychotherapy. The existential approach became especially popular after the atrocities of World War I and most especially in response to Nazi Germany during World War II (Frankl, 1963, 1965). The existential approach had its roots in European philosophy in the works of Kierkegaard, Nietzsche, Sartre, Buber, and Heidegger among others. This approach focused, for example, on the human need to seek and define meaning in life. American writers such as psychologist Rollo May (May, 1977; May, Angel, & Ellenberger, 1958) and psychiatrist Irvin Yalom (1980) helped to delineate and popularize the existential approach to humanistic therapy in the United States. Psychoanalytic writers such as Hans Kohut, Otto Kernberg, and Merton Gil have integrated some of the humanistic perspective into their writing as well.

Leading humanistic psychotherapists and theorists such as Carl Rogers, Abraham Maslow, Frederick Perls, Victor Frankl, and others all uniquely contributed to the development of the humanistic approaches to professional psychotherapy. Whereas each offered a somewhat different approach, their commonalities are notable and together comprise the humanistic school. These commonalities include the commitment to the phenomenological model that emphasizes that humans are able to be consciously reflective and have the ability to experience self-determination and freedom. Thus, therapists must be able to fully understand a person's perception of internal and external reality in order to not only better understand their feelings and behavior but also offer assistance. Another commonality included the notion that humans strive toward growth and are not, for example, trying to maintain homeostasis by satisfying various primitive needs and conflicts. The humanistic approach also championed a belief in free will and regarded human behavior as more than just a by-product of early childhood experiences or merely conditioned responses to the external environment. Finally, the humanistic approach is person-centered, with maximum respect for the individual and his or her experiences (Tageson, 1982).

The client-centered and phenomenological approach of Carl Rogers became the most influential humanistic therapy. While Rogers was trained in the more traditional psychodynamic approach, he rejected it to provide a compelling alternative with the client-centered approach. The approach emphasizes therapist empathy, unconditional positive regard, congruence, intensive active listening, and support to help individuals and groups reach their full human potential (Rogers, 1951, 1954, 1961). Rogers felt that humans naturally strive toward their potential and that psychotherapy was a catalyst that could assist them in this endeavor.

The Family Systems Approaches

Unlike the psychodynamic, behavioral, and humanistic approaches already outlined, the **family systems** approaches tend to utilize the entire family in understanding and treating problematic feelings and behavior. Rather than working with an individual patient who reports problematic symptoms, the family approaches generally work with the entire (or a subset of the) family. Prior to the 1950s, most psychological treatment focused on the *identified patient* defined as the person regarded within the family as manifesting problematic symptoms, behaviors, or attitudes. The family members of the identified patient were generally left out of the treatment and not viewed as potentially active agents of dysfunction and

potential recovery. During the 1950s, 1960s, and especially the 1970s, the family systems approach to treatment became popular among clinical psychologists and other mental health professionals (Haley, 1976; Minuchin, 1974). The systems approach took exception to the notion that only the identified patient was in need of intervention services. In fact, the systems approach asserted that the dysfunction resided in the family as an interrelated system and not only in one family member. For example, therapists observed that patient functioning often deteriorated when he or she interacted with family members. Therefore, all family members were treated together—a radical departure from traditional treatment modalities. Family therapy became a very common intervention strategy for numerous problems.

The family systems approach emerged from the Bateson Project during the 1950s in California. Gregory Bateson, an anthropologist, was especially interested in communication styles, collaborating with Jay Haley (an expert in communications), John Weakland (an engineer), and Don Jackson (a psychiatrist) to examine communication styles such as *double-bind communication* and *meta-messages* in psychiatric patients (especially schizophrenic patients) at the Palo Alto Veterans Hospital (Bateson, Jackson, Haley, & Weakland, 1956). Double-bind messages include impossible-to-satisfy requests (e.g., someone ordering another person to be spontaneous) while meta-messages involve what someone really means rather than what he or she actually says (e.g., someone may report deeply loving someone but never show any actions or sincere statements that support the claim). Jackson later founded the Mental Research Institute (MRI) in Palo Alto, California, in 1959 in conjunction with another well-known family therapist, Virginia Satir.

Jay Haley later left the Bateson Project and joined forces with Salvador Minuchin to develop the structural family therapy model at the Philadelphia Child Guidance Clinic. Haley later moved to Washington, DC, in the

1970s and founded the Washington Family Institute, where his wife, Cloe Madanes, developed the strategic therapy model (Haley, 1976). Strategic therapy uses paradoxical intention, or *reverse psychology,* and techniques to effect behavioral change. This model of family therapy prescribes the symptom in order to cope with resistance in treatment. Further details regarding this and other family therapy approaches will be provided in the next chapter.

During the 1960s and 1970s, a variety of models of family therapy emerged in various parts of the United States and Europe. For example, Maria Selvini-Palazoli and colleagues founded the Milan Associates in the late 1960s to treat families confronted with anorexia nervosa in a family member. The Milan group sought to use the family systems theory to better understand family rules and to avoid getting trapped into family alliances and coalitions. Being trapped or manipulated into family alliances (e.g., joining or agreeing with the parents that all of the problems in the family are due to the child's aggressive behavior or the spouse's infidelity) may prevent effective therapy for the whole family. Watzlawick, Weakland, and Fisch (1974) developed the Brief Therapy Project at the Mental Research Institute. The program focused on repetitive cycles of interpersonal behavior that often tend to reinforce problems rather than solve them. Some family theorists (such as John Bell, Ivan Nagy, James Framo, Lyman Wynne, and Murray Bowen) used psychoanalytic theory in their application of family therapy (J. Bell, 1961; Bowen, 1978). Others, such as Carl Whitaker and Virginia Satir, focused on experiential models with an emphasis on intuition and feelings (Satir, 1967, 1972; Whitaker & Keith, 1981). Still others, such as Nathan Ackerman and Salvador Minuchin, developed structural family therapy and focused on family boundaries and generational hierarchies, especially among child-focused families.

While a wide variety of family therapy approaches and strategies emerged following the Bateson Project throughout the latter part of the twentieth century (especially during the 1960s and 1970s), commonalities primarily included a focus on the role of the entire family system in producing and maintaining problematic behavior, communication patterns associated with family problems, and ongoing maladaptive relationship patterns among family members. Intervention at the family level rather than at the individual level became the goal of each of these treatment strategies.

Psychotropic Medication

Although biological treatments and medications such as opium, insulin, bromides, and electric convulsive therapy (ECT) were used to treat mental illnesses during the early and middle part of the twentieth century, it was not until the 1950s that effective medications were developed to treat severe disorders such as schizophrenia and bipolar illness. Typical of many discoveries, it was by accident that these **psychotropic medications** were found to be effective in the treatment of mental illness.

Australian psychiatrist, John Cade, noticed that guinea pigs became calm when they were given lithium chloride, a natural salt. Cade then gave lithium to psychotic patients and found that it had the same calming effect as discovered in the guinea pigs. French physician, Henri Laborit, used the medication in an attempt to lower blood pressure prior to surgery and found that it lowered patient anxiety. In 1952, two French psychiatrists (Pierre Deniker and Jean Delay) gave the medication (chlorpromazine or Thorazine) to psychiatric patients. They found that patients were less anxious and that schizophrenic patients experienced fewer hallucinations and delusions. Thus, the discovery of rauwolfia serpentona (or reserpine) and the neuroleptics (such as Thorazine and Haldol) proved helpful in reducing the hallucinations, delusions, and agitation of psychotic patients. Furthermore, benzodiazepines (such as Valium) were found in the early 1960s to be effective in reducing profound symptoms of anxiety.

The initial response to the discovery of these medications was marked by tremendous enthusiasm in the professional and lay communities. Later, however, problematic side effects and treatment limitations tempered the initial enthusiasm. Nonetheless, the effectiveness of these treatments ultimately enabled patients to leave mental hospitals in droves. For example, in 1950 there were approximately 500,000 patients hospitalized in state and county mental hospitals in the United States. This number dropped to only 57,000 by 1998 (Lamb & Weinberger, 2001). This number continues to decrease with an even larger population. These medications also created a new role for psychiatrists who were generally providing only psychoanalytic, limited biological (e.g., electroconvulsive therapy), and custodial treatments for their patients. The effectiveness of medication further solidified the notion that many mental illnesses were brain diseases and thus did not emerge from unconscious conflicts alone. The increasing use of medication to treat psychiatric problems also promulgated the frequent leadership role physicians currently take in treating mental illness. Today, about 20% to 30% of all medications prescribed are intended to impact emotional or behavioral factors such as depression, anxiety, and impulsive behavior (Glasser, 2003). In recent years, psychologists have secured prescription privileges in several locations such as Louisiana, New Mexico, Guam, and in the military.

Community Mental Health Movement

During the 1950s, psychotropic medication allowed many psychiatric patients to leave the institutional setting of mental hospitals and reenter society. Furthermore, reflecting the sociopolitical climate of the time, the "warehousing" of patients in mental hospitals was replaced by more humane community-based treatments. During this period of deinstitutionalization, psychiatric patients needed outpatient services to readjust to society, obtain gainful employment, and cope with the stresses of life and increased social demands and opportunities. Furthermore, interest in the prevention of mental illness as well as the social factors that contribute to mental illness—such as poverty, homelessness, racism, unemployment, and divorce—developed a more prominent role in the theories and interventions associated with mental illness. This resulted in the rise of the **community mental health movement.** Congress passed legislation in 1955 to create the Joint Commission on Mental Health and Illness, which sought to develop community mental health services outside of the inpatient mental hospital setting. In 1963, legislation was passed to use federal monies to create community mental health centers throughout the United States. In 1965, a group of psychologists met in Swampscott, Massachusetts, to plan for the unique role psychology would play in this movement. The mission of the community mental health movement was to provide affordable mental health services to all aspects of society on an outpatient basis, as well as to use early intervention and detection programs to prevent mental illness from developing. The community mental health clinics that opened throughout the United States were typically funded by state and federal grant monies. The movement resulted in opportunities for psychologists to provide a wide range of professional services including psychological testing, consultation, treatment, crisis intervention, and services focused on the prevention of mental illness (e.g., education). However, within 20 years of passing the legislation that created the community mental health movement, the federal and state governments significantly reduced funding and most of the programs closed, reduced services, or were incorporated into private clinics.

The Integrative Approaches

After the explosion of new theories and approaches during the 1950s, 1960s, and 1970s, many researchers and clinicians felt dissatisfied with strict adherence to one particular theory or theoretical orientation. Each school of thought (behavioral, cognitive-behavioral, humanistic, family systems, psychodynamic) developed its own philosophy or worldview of human behavior and translated these views into strategies for effecting positive change in feelings, behavior, and relationships. During the late 1970s and early 1980s, many professionals sought to integrate the best that the various schools of thought had to offer on a case-by-case basis. Rather than focusing on the differences in these approaches, an emphasis was placed on common factors. The fact that research was unable to demonstrate that any one treatment approach or theoretical orientation was superior relative to the others (Smith, Glass, & Miller, 1980) and the finding that the majority of practicing clinicians identified themselves as being eclectic or **integrative** (Garfield & Kurtz, 1976; Messer, 2001, 2008; Norcross & Prochaska, 1988; Norcross et al., 2002, 2005, 2008) further motivated the professional community to consider integrative approaches to theory, research, and practice (O'Brien & Houston, 2000).

In the 1950s, Dollard and Miller (1950) attempted to understand psychodynamic concepts through behavioral or learning theory language. Other authors, especially during the 1970s, took an interest in integrating psychodynamic and behavioral concepts and techniques (Feather & Rhoads, 1972; Wachtel, 1975, 1977, 1984). The most notable work in this area was the work of Paul Wachtel. Wachtel sought to take the strengths of each approach by incorporating elements of both in a logical and consistent manner. He focused on the importance of unconscious influences, meaning, and fantasies as well as the importance of empirical evidence, the patient's goals of treatment, and respect for the environmental influences and context of behavior.

Jerome Frank (1961, 1982) examined the commonalities of various treatment methods (as well as placebo effects and faith healing) and found that they all include instilling hope and emotional arousal in the patient, encouraging improved morale and understanding of self and others, a healing setting (e.g., psychotherapy office), and supporting change

outside of the treatment environment. Other authors focused on the nature of the professional relationship as being a common curative factor in all types of therapies (Rogers, 1954; Schofield, 1964; Truax & Mitchell, 1971).

Other, more recent, authors have focused on eclecticism and the integrative use of techniques from various theoretical orientations without specific allegiance to the theoretical underpinnings of these techniques (Brooks-Harris, 2008; Norcross & Goldfried, 2005; Norcross et al., 2002; Stern, 2003). These approaches focus on a more functional and pragmatic approach to incorporating various treatment strategies to fit the needs of the individual patient (Brooks-Harris, 2008; O'Brien & Houston, 2000).

The Biopsychosocial Approach

Ever since the seventeenth century and the influence of Descartes and Newton, theories of health and illness have tended to separate the mind from the body. Thus, Western medicine often tends to view illness, including mental illness, as being influenced *either* by biology, such as genetics and neurochemical imbalances, *or* by the mind, such as personality and interpersonal conflicts. Advances in medicine, science, psychology, sociology, ethnic and minority studies, and other fields during the last half of the twentieth century have provided evidence for interactive multidimensional influences on health and illness, including mental illness. New discoveries in genetics and neurochemistry, along with new techniques to investigate the brain such as neuroimaging, have solidified the contribution of biology to emotion and behavior. The effectiveness of psychotropic medications further provided clues to the profound biological influences impacting behavior. The new theories and supporting research proposed by the behavioral, cognitive-behavioral, humanistic, and family systems perspectives provided further evidence and credence for psychological and social factors influencing health, illness,

George Engel

George Engel, MD, is the father of the biopsychosocial model. He coined the term *biopsychosocial model* in a landmark 1977 article in *Science*. George Engel was born and raised in New York City. He began college at the age of 16 in 1930, majoring in chemistry at Dartmouth College in New Hampshire. During the summer of his junior year, he worked at the well-known Woods Hole Marine Biological Laboratory in Massachusetts, which led to his first published paper in 1935 at the age of 21. After graduation from college, he attended Johns Hopkins Medical School and graduated in 1938. He completed his residency training at Mount Sinai Hospital in New York City. He then moved to the University of Cincinnati College of Medicine in 1942, with positions in both medicine and psychiatry departments, and then to the University of Rochester in 1946. At both Cincinnati and Rochester, Engel worked closely with Dr. John Romano. Together, they published a variety of papers on the biopsychosocial model and emphasized multidisciplinary training in medicine, developing a progressive and unique curriculum for medical education. Dr. Engel retired in 1979 from the University of Rochester but remained active as a professor emeritus until his death at 85 in December 1999.

Highlight of a Contemporary Clinical Psychologist

Nadine J. Kaslow, PhD, ABPP

Photo: Courtesy Nadine J. Kaslow

Birth Date: 5/29/57

College: University of Pennsylvania, BA, 1978

Graduate Program: University of Houston, PhD, 1983

Clinical Internship: University of Wisconsin–Madison, Department of Psychiatry, July 1, 1982–June 30, 1983

Current Job: Professor, Chief Psychologist, and Vice Chair for Faculty Development, Emory Department of Psychiatry and Behavioral Sciences, Atlanta Georgia. I also am the President of the American Board of Clinical Psychology and President Elect of the American Board of Professional Psychology. Further, I am the President of the Division of Psychotherapy of the American Psychological Association and next year begin a three-year term on the Board of Directors of the American Psychological Association. In addition, I am the Incoming Editor of the *Journal of Family Psychology*.

Pros and Cons of Being a Clinical Psychologist:

Pros: ''(1) Can have a very varied job that includes clinical work, research, education/supervision, administration, and advocacy; (2) have the opportunity to help people deal with the stresses and challenges of their lives and to cope more effectively and have more meaningful and satisfying lives; (3) advance knowledge that helps us better understand people from a biopsychosocial perspective and therefore be more effective at intervening in their lives; (4) inspire the next generation of clinical psychologists through creative and innovative approaches to teaching and supervision; and (5) advocate on behalf of the mental health needs of people in our nation."

Cons: "(1) There is not sufficient parity for mental health services and thus many people are not able to receive our services adequately; (2) there remains stigma about mental health, which makes some people feel uncomfortable receiving the psychological care that they need; (3) there is a supply–demand imbalance, such that there are more graduate students than available internship positions, and I worry that with the economic downturn in our country, there will be more clinical psychologists who struggle to find meaningful employment."

Your Specialty and How You Chose It: "I chose to be a clinical psychologist in part because my mother is a clinical psychologist. Further, even as a child, I was drawn to books about psychological problems and their treatment. I was fascinated in college by my psychology courses, particularly those related to abnormal psychology, child psychology, personality theory, and various psychological disorders (depression, schizophrenia). I realized that I truly wanted a balanced career where I could engage in psychotherapy, conduct research on psychological interventions, train psychotherapists, and advocate for various mental health causes, and I believed and still believe that clinical psychology allows me to do so."

Future of Clinical Psychology: "The future of clinical psychology is very bright. We are making progress toward the development and dissemination of effective, culturally competent, developmentally informed, gender-sensitive, and evidence-based assessment and intervention approaches. We recognize that these approaches need to be conducted in the context of a strong and collaborative working alliance. Clinical psychologists are expanding their research horizons, so that they pay more attention to integrating biological, psychological, and social variables. I hope that there will be a greater emphasis placed on prevention efforts. There continues to be debate about clinical psychologists securing prescription privileges in more states, as legislation to make this possible has been slow in coming. I believe that more clinical psychologists will become board certified through the American Board of Professional Psychology. There also is likely to be some level of re-credentialing in terms of state licensure for clinical psychologists."

Thoughts about Clinical Psychology Graduate and Postgraduate Training in the Future: "There has been a burgeoning interest in a competency-based approach to psychology education, training, and credentialing, and I believe that this shift will continue to be of relevance. Students will be trained more systematically in the core foundational and functional competencies and state-of-the-art assessment approaches will be used to assess their attainment of these competencies. Strategies will need to be put into place to resolve the supply–demand imbalance problem. There is much debate about the postdoctoral requirement for licensure that needs to be resolved and this influences the training and credentialing sequence in clinical psychology. There are, however, many exciting opportunities for postdoctoral training in new settings for clinical psychologists. There is a growing emphasis on lifelong learning."

Thoughts about Current Trends in Clinical Psychology: "There is considerable competition for individuals interested in clinical psychology to gain admission to graduate programs and to secure predoctoral internship programs. There are a lot of concerns about decreasing reimbursement for psychological services, despite the growth in innovative, evidence-based clinical programs. Public health perspectives are increasingly being integrated within clinical psychology. There is much greater awareness of the necessity of integrating diversity considerations in all activities performed by clinical psychologists. The settings in which clinical psychologists find themselves in have expanded dramatically and hopefully there will be continued growth in the diversity of contexts in which clinical psychologists will have roles. Further, settings in which clinical psychologists have practiced historically are continuing to evolve and more evolution is likely if health-care reform occurs.''

Typical Schedule:

7:00	My own psychotherapy
8:00	E-mail
9:00	Team meeting on inpatient unit with my interns and postdoctoral fellows present
10:00	Administrative meeting related to faculty development
11:00	Supervision of a psychology postdoctoral fellow
12:00	Supervision of a psychology intern, which includes seeing a patient and his/her family on the inpatient unit
1:00	Research team meeting
2:00	Write an article
3:00	Conference call related to national professional psychology organizational work
4:00	*Journal of Family Psychology* editorial responsibilities
5:00	E-mail
6:00	Private practice patient
7:00	Private practice patient
8:00	Private practice patient
9:00	Private practice patient

emotions, and behavior. Finally, the community mental health movement beginning in the 1960s demonstrated the influence of social, cultural, and economic factors in mental illness. The confluence of these new discoveries and perspectives allowed a **biopsychosocial** orientation to emerge during the late 1970s.

In 1977, George Engel published a paper in the journal *Science* that proposed the biopsychosocial approach as the optimal model of understanding and treating illness. The approach, with its roots in the ancient Greek notions of Hippocrates discussed earlier, suggests that physical and psychological problems are likely to have a biological, psychological, and social element that should be understood in order to provide effective intervention strategies. Thus, rather than a unidimensional causal approach to problems, the biopsychosocial perspective utilizes a multidimensional and interactive approach. The biopsychosocial framework suggests that the biological, psychological, and social aspects of health and illness intimately influence each other.

The biopsychosocial perspective is not new. As was discussed in the previous chapter, the appreciation for biological, psychological, and social influences on behavior, emotions, and health was recognized centuries ago. However, over the years, emphasis has been placed on different elements of the perspective, which has sometimes excluded other elements. Furthermore, scientific discoveries, influential people, and social thinking of the time have tended to highlight either biological, psychological, or social influences.

The biopsychosocial approach has been accepted in both medicine and psychology with research support to demonstrate its usefulness (Fava & Sonino, 2008; Institute for the Future, 2000; Institute of Medicine, 2001, 2008; Johnson, 2003; McDaniel, 1995; Melchert, 2007). For example, research has indicated that many diverse problems such as obesity, alcoholism, learning disabilities, anxiety, and depressive disorders all involve a complex interaction between biological, psychological, and social influences. An understanding of and appreciation for these interactions should be taken into consideration when designing treatment and prevention interventions. The biopsychosocial approach became the foundation for the field of health psychology in the early 1980s (Schwartz, 1982). It has become an influential perspective in clinical psychology as well. The APA endorsed this model when it changed its mission statement and other policy statements (see Johnson, 2003, for a review). The Institute of Medicine

(2001) also stated that "health and disease are determined by dynamic interactions among biological, psychological, behavioral, and social factors. . . . Cooperation and interaction of multiple disciplines are necessary for understanding and influencing health and behaviors" (p. 348). Therefore, psychologists must be aware of multidimensional biopsychosocial influences to understand and treat others (Fava & Sonino, 2008; Johnson, 2003; Melchert, 2007).

A New Training Model Emerges

The Vail Conference

A turning point in the philosophy of clinical psychology training occurred during the 1973 Vail Conference held in Vail, Colorado (Korman, 1976). The Conference was held to discuss how training could be altered to accommodate the changing needs of both clinical psychology students and society. The National Conference on Levels and Patterns of Professional Training in Psychology received financial support from NIMH. The most significant outcome of the Conference was the acceptance of a new training model for clinical psychology. In addition to the Boulder or scientist-practitioner model, the Vail or **scholar-practitioner model** was endorsed as an appropriate alternative. This model suggested that clinical training could emphasize the delivery of professional psychological services while minimizing research training. Furthermore, the Conference endorsed the notion that graduate training need not occur only in university psychology departments but could also occur in freestanding professional schools of psychology. Freestanding schools were developed independent of university affiliation. One of the first and largest schools is the California School of Professional Psychology with four campuses and over 5,000 students enrolled. Following the Conference in 1973, the National Council of Schools of Professional Psychology was formed to address issues

unique to these new schools and programs. Finally, the Conference endorsed the PsyD (or doctor of psychology) degree as an alternative to the PhD degree. The PsyD degree would be given to clinicians trained in the **Vail model** who were more practitioner oriented than those trained in the traditional Boulder model, which emphasized both research and clinical training. This new model allowed students to choose the type of emphasis they wanted in their graduate education. Vail model programs have become very popular. Students trained in Vail model programs outnumber those in Boulder model programs by a ratio of approximately 4 to 1 (Norcross et al., 2002, 2005, 2008). These choices are still available for current students seeking graduate training. The first PsyD program developed in 1968 at the University of Illinois (Peterson, 1968) is no longer in existence.

For the first time ever, the Vail Conference also endorsed the notion that recipients of a terminal master's degree be considered professional psychologists rather than merely prospective recipients of a doctoral degree. However, in 1977, the APA stated that a doctorate was needed for the title *psychologist*, thereby diminishing the role of the terminal master's degree supported by the Vail Conference. Although numerous graduate programs across the United States and Canada offer terminal master's degree programs in clinical psychology and many states license master's-level professionals as counselors, the APA has chosen not to support terminal master's degree education as adequate for the independent practice of psychology. In practice, professionals with master's degrees often provide independent professional services under the title *counselor* or marriage and family *therapist* but not *psychologist*.

Salt Lake City Conference

During 1987, the National Conference held yet another meeting to examine how training models best fit the needs of students, society, and the profession. This Conference endorsed the notion that all graduate training in clinical psychology, regardless of the degree (PhD or PsyD) or setting (university or free-standing professional school), should include a core curriculum containing courses such as research methods, statistics, professional ethics, history and systems, and psychological assessment, and on the biological, social, cognitive, and individual difference bases of behavior. However, the Salt Lake City Conference tempered the Vail Conference's enthusiasm for freestanding professional school training of clinical psychologists. Most notably, the Conference stated that by 1995, all APA-accredited programs should at least be affiliated with a regionally accredited university. This measure was passed in order to maintain better control over the training conducted at the rapidly proliferating freestanding professional schools (Bickman, 1987). However, this recommendation has largely been ignored to the extent that, by 2010, the majority of freestanding professional schools of psychology are still not associated with any universities. In fact, about 50% of all doctorates in clinical psychology are now awarded from these freestanding professional schools not associated with universities, with the vast majority being located in California.

Additional Conferences

The National Council of Schools in Professional Psychology held several national meetings: Mission Bay in 1986, San Juan in 1989, Gainesville in 1990, and San Antonio in 1991. These meetings led to a refinement of the mission of Professional Schools of Psychology. New goals included an emphasis on adequate training in service to ethnic minorities and underserved groups as well as a recommitment to integrating science and practice into clinical training.

In the 1990s, a movement emerged to develop a **clinical scientist model** that sought to develop a more research-oriented and scientific approach to training relative to the earlier more clinically oriented training models (i.e., Boulder and Vail models). Following a professional conference at Indiana University in 1994, the **Academy of Psychological Clinical Science** (APCS) was developed and Richard McFall served at the first president (McFall, 1991; Academy of Psychological Clinical Science, 2009).

Michigan Conference on Postdoctoral Training

In October 1992, the National Conference on Postdoctoral Training in Professional Psychology was held at the University of Michigan to specifically address postdoctoral training issues in psychology (Larsen et al., 1993). While the APA accredits and provides detailed guidelines for graduate and internship training, no comprehensive APA guidelines have been provided for postdoctoral training. Since most states require postdoctoral training prior to licensure, almost all clinical psychologists had been participating in postdoctoral training programs without APA guidance. Many professionals have called for national standards for postdoctoral training (Belar et al., 1989; Plante, 1988). The Michigan Conference developed guidelines and plans for further control and regulation of postdoctoral training in clinical psychology. For example, recommendations included the completion of APA-accredited doctoral and internship training programs prior to admission to accredited postdoctoral training programs; at least two hours per week of face-to-face supervision by a licensed psychologist; and a systematic evaluation mechanism for examining the trainees and program, among others.

The Rise of Empirically Supported Treatments and Resurgence of Cognitive Behavioral Models

In recent years, clinical psychology has moved to treatment models that highlight empirically supported and evidence-based practices that more often than not use cognitive behavioral approaches to intervention. The Task Force on Promotion and Dissemination of Psychological Procedures (1995) of the APA Division of Clinical Psychology (Division 12) has developed guidelines for psychotherapy treatments based on solid research findings (Chambless et al., 1996). **Empirically supported treatments** are well-established treatment approaches that have received significant research support demonstrating their efficacy (Beutler, 2009; Chambless & Ollendick, 2001; Rehm, 1997; Sanderson, 1994; Sanderson & Woody, 1995). Criteria for acceptance as empirically supported treatments include the demonstration of efficacy using well-designed between-group and/or a large series of single-case design experiments. Results from these experiments must have demonstrated treatment superiority to placebo or other treatments as well as having used enough subjects to have adequate statistical power. Furthermore, the experiments must be conducted using treatment manuals and the characteristics of the clients must be very clearly specified. Finally, the effects must be found by at least two independent researchers or research teams. These standards have been applied to the numerous treatment approaches that have been used to treat a large range of problems.

Empirically supported treatments have been developed for the treatment of chemical abuse and dependency, anxiety, depressive, sexual, eating, and health problems. Examples of empirically supported treatments include exposure treatment for phobias and post-traumatic stress disorder, cognitive-behavior therapy for headache, panic, irritable bowel syndrome, and bulimia, and insight-oriented dynamic therapy for depression and marital discord. Many contemporary clinical psychologists argue that only empirically validated treatments should be used in clinical practice (Chambless, 1996; Chambless & Ollendick, 2001; Crits-Christoph, 1996; Meehl, 1997; Nathan & Gorman, 2002, 2007; Rehm, 1997).

Others are more skeptical of empirically supported approaches, citing limitations to these approaches (Cooper, 2003; Garfield,

1996; Havik & VandenBos, 1996; Ingram et al., 2000; La Roche & Christopher, 2008). Skeptics often cite problems such as the difficulty making the generalization from research findings to actual clinical practice and the complexity of each unique individual as reasons for being less enthusiastic about the development of these treatment approaches (Norcross, Beutler, & Levant, 2006). These concerns led to a 2005 APA Presidential Task Force that addressed many of the concerns articulated about empirically supported treatments and proposed an emphasis on **evidence-based practice** (EBP) (APA Presidential Task Force on Evidence-Based Practice, 2006; Levant & Hasan, 2008).

Evidence-based practice attempts to integrate the best available clinical research with quality clinical expertise to help the unique individual seeking professional psychological services get his or her needs met. Contemporary clinical psychology focuses on developing empirically supported treatments and using them in many research and clinical investigations to support evidence-based practice. For example, Barry Duncan, Scott Miller, and colleagues offer useful books and articles that well articulate treatments that work based on quality evidence (e.g., Duncan, Miller, Wampold, & Hubble, 2009). Nathan and Gorman (2007) do the same and provide a hierarchy of evidence to help determine which treatment approaches have the most solid research support. In reviewing their list of quality research support, cognitive behavioral approaches tend to be predominantly represented.

In addition to evidence-based practices, some researchers have discussed empirically supported therapy relationships (Norcross, 2001, 2002) and empirically supported therapy principles (Castonguay & Beutler, 2006) to further address the challenges and limitations of empirically supported and manual-based treatments. Others have closely examined the pros and cons and have tried to expand the more narrow views sometimes presented for empirically supported treatments (Beutler, 2009; Levant & Hasan, 2008). Still others, especially in the United Kingdom, have developed and implemented **clinical practice guidelines** that provide specific step-by-step recommendations for assessing and treating particular problems (Institute of Medicine, 2008; United Kingdom Department of Health, 2001).

Although developing empirically supported treatments has been of interest to clinical psychologists for several decades, changes in health-care reimbursement systems and the advent of managed health care have resulted in a great deal of financial impetus to the research and development of validated treatments. Funding sources are in increasingly shorter supply, and require increasing assurance of cost-effectiveness prior to committing resources.

Additionally, litigation against providers who do not provide empirically supported services in malpractice lawsuits also helps to encourage more emphasis on providing evidence-based practice and using clinical practice guidelines in contemporary professional practice. While managed health care will be discussed in detail in Chapter 14, the increased demand for accountability in both cost-effective and validated treatments has been of interest to contemporary mental health professionals, managed care companies, politicians, and the public (Institute of Medicine, 2008; Levant & Hasan, 2008; Lilienfeld, Lynn, & Lohr, 2004).

Contemporary clinical psychology students are more likely to be trained in evidence-based practice and clinical practice guidelines that tend to focus on cognitive-behavioral interventions since these approaches tend to have the most research support using quality randomized trial research methodologies (Beutler, 2009; Duncan et al., 2009; Institute of Medicine, 2008; Nathan & Gorman, 2007; Norcross et al., 2008).

Present Status

Contemporary clinical psychology, ever evolving, is currently adapting to numerous changes

and challenges. While a detailed discussion addresses these current issues in Chapter 14, brief mention is warranted at this point regarding clinical psychology's response to increasing imperatives regarding diversity and cultural sensitivity, changing trends in professional training, and ongoing economic and privacy issues affecting the study and practice of clinical psychology.

The United States is both blessed and challenged with tremendous diversity. Diversity in gender, culture, ethnicity, language, religious faith, sexual orientation, physical ability and disability, and the entire spectrum of individual differences has necessarily informed and enriched the practice and study of psychology. No longer can researchers, educators, or clinicians assume a white, male, English-speaking, heterosexual population. For example, of the approximately 307 million Americans, according to the U.S. Census Bureau (2010), approximately 37 million are African American (12%); 44 million are Latino or Hispanic (15%); and 13 million (5%) are of Asian descent. The number of mixed racial groups is difficult to quantify. Increasingly, it has become incumbent upon clinical psychologists to acquire the education and insight necessary to develop important sensitivities in their work with diverse individuals and populations (APA, 2003b). The contribution of diversity to the field is more fully explored in Chapter 14, but can be seen throughout this book given its contemporary emphasis. Training itself is undergoing significant changes. First, more than half of all clinical psychologists now train in freestanding professional schools of psychology rather than in traditional university programs. This has resulted in many more psychologists seeking employment, as well as many more being trained within the Vail (i.e., scholar-practitioner), rather than the Boulder (i.e., scientist-practitioner), model. Second, after being predominantly a male profession, the gender distribution of students and new graduates in clinical psychology has changed from being mostly men to being mostly women. While about 60% of the APA members are men (representing all areas of psychology), the majority of new doctorates in clinical psychology are now awarded to women (APA, 2003a, 2009a; Norcross et al., 2005, 2008; Snyder, McDermott, Leibowitz, & Cheavens, 2000). For example, between 1973 and 1991, the number of men who entered the field of psychology rose by 130% while the number of women choosing psychology as a career increased by 530% (APA, 1995c). The feminization of psychology in general and clinical psychology in particular has significantly altered the face of the field.

Economic factors in health care are also significantly altering the landscape for psychologists. Significant reductions in federal grant funding have resulted in far less federal dollars available for clinical psychology research and training. This has resulted in more competition for limited research funding. While the number of clinical psychologists choosing full-time private practice as their career choice has grown steadily over the past several decades, the trend could change due to significant and sweeping changes in health care. Thus, solo independent practice may become less attractive as a career option for psychologists in the future. Clinical psychology has expanded beyond the mental health field into the general health-care and preventative health-care fields. Therefore, clinical psychology has found its way into general health care with applications to numerous medical problems and issues (Fava & Sonino, 2008; Johnson, 2003; S. Taylor, 2009). Clinical psychology has also secured more independence, for example, gaining hospital admitting privileges in most states, as well as the ability to prescribe medication in certain settings, such as in the military and in New Mexico, Louisiana, and Guam (Beutler, 2002). This has expanded the types of professional activities and roles available to clinical psychologists. Finally, changes in the health-care delivery and reimbursement systems in the United States have posed one of the biggest challenges to clinical psychology and other health-related fields. Limited services and monies are available from insurance companies to treat mental and physical problems. Challenging new laws regarding managing privacy issues (e.g., HIPAA) have altered the way clinical psychology is practiced. Each of these current issues is discussed in more detail in Chapter 14.

The Big Picture

Clinical psychology has come a long way since Witmer founded the specialty by opening the first psychological clinic in 1886. It is hard to imagine that about 50 years ago there were no psychology licensing laws in any state and no comprehensive clinical psychology training guidelines, accreditation standards, or models of training. Furthermore, it is astonishing that 50 years ago, clinical psychologists were often not allowed to conduct psychotherapy since it was the exclusive domain of psychiatrists. Today, clinical psychology is a thriving field, utilizing the integrated resources of numerous perspectives and interventions. Clinical psychology is now practiced in a wide variety of hospitals, clinics, businesses, and educational settings, among other locations.

Curiously, while clinical psychology has come such a long way, its progress has sometimes occurred, not because of, but in spite of, the APA. Several times, the clinical psychologists resigned from the APA to form their own independent group. Each time they later decided to rejoin the APA. The differences of opinion between the applied clinical professionals and the majority academic and scientific members of APA have been a fact of life since the APA was founded. The tension between the science and practice of psychology will likely continue.

Today, contemporary clinical psychology seeks to address and incorporate the important issues of diversity, scientific advances, and changes in professional training and economic factors affecting health care in this country. Ultimately, the science and practice of clinical psychology have contributed broadly to our understanding and treatment of human difficulties. The science and application of clinical psychology have proved effective in enhancing the quality of life for numerous people throughout the world. It certainly is an exciting time in the clinical psychology field. This excitement is likely to continue for future clinical psychologists.

Key Points

1. Following World War II, over 40,000 veterans were hospitalized in VA hospitals for psychiatric reasons. The overwhelming need for clinical services for these men resulted in a huge increase in clinical psychologists providing a full range of comprehensive psychological services, including psychological testing, psychotherapy, consultation, and research. In 1946, the VA requested about 4,700 clinical psychologists to be employed in the VA system.

2. The APA Committee on Training in Clinical Psychology met in 1947 and sought to develop training standards and guidelines for graduate and internship training in clinical psychology. Ultimately, the committee's guidelines became the gold standard for clinical training. The report included the notion that clinical psychologists should be trained rigorously in a four-year doctoral program as well as with a one-year clinical internship and be trained as both scientists and clinicians. The committee recommended that training be comprehensive in research, treatment, and assessment. In 1949, a committee met in Boulder, Colorado, and developed the Boulder model (also known as the scientist-practitioner model) of clinical training.

3. During the 1950s, 1960s, and 1970s, many new treatment and intervention approaches and perspectives were offered as an alternative to the traditional psychodynamic approach. Psychologists were becoming well established in their psychotherapy skills in addition to their testing services. The family systems, behavioral, cognitive-behavioral, and humanistic approaches to intervention emerged as compelling and popular alternatives to the more traditional theories and interventions. Furthermore, the rise of the community mental health movement in the 1960s as well as the advent of psychotropic medication to treat mental illness exerted powerful influences on clinical psychology.

4. A turning point in the philosophy of clinical psychology training occurred during the 1973 Vail Conference. The most significant outcome of the Conference was the acceptance of a new training model for clinical psychology. In addition to the Boulder, or scientist-practitioner, model, the Vail, or the scholar-practitioner, model was endorsed. This model suggested that clinical training could emphasize the delivery of professional psychological services while minimizing research training. Furthermore, the conference endorsed the notion that graduate training did not need to occur only in academic psychology departments at major universities but could also occur in freestanding professional schools of psychology. Finally, the Conference endorsed the PsyD degree as an alternative to the PhD degree.

5. In 1977, George Engel offered the biopsychosocial approach as the best possible model of understanding and treating physical and mental illness. The approach suggests that all physical and psychological illnesses and problems are likely to have a biological, psychological, or social element, which should be understood in order to provide the most effective intervention strategies. The biopsychosocial model has been widely accepted in both medicine and psychology with strong research support to demonstrate its effectiveness. The biopsychosocial perspective has quickly become an influential model in clinical psychology.

6. In recent years, clinical psychology has moved to treatment models that highlight empirically supported and evidence-based practices that more often than not use cognitive-behavioral approaches to intervention. The Task Force on Promotion and Dissemination of Psychological Procedures (1995) of the APA Division

of Clinical Psychology (Division 12) has developed guidelines for psychotherapy treatments based on solid research findings. Empirically supported treatments are well-established treatment approaches that have received significant research support demonstrating their efficacy.

Key Terms

Academy of Psychological Clinical Science
Behavioral
Biopsychosocial
Boulder model
Clinical practice guidelines
Clinical scientist model
Cognitive-behavioral
Community mental health movement
Empirically supported treatments
Evidence-based practice
Family systems
Humanistic
Integrative
Psychotropic medication
Scholar-practitioner model
Scientist-practitioner model
Vail model
Veterans' Administration

For Reflection

1. Why was the VA hospital system so supportive of clinical psychology?
2. Why did the government feel compelled to financially support the training of clinical psychologists?
3. What was the major outcome of the Boulder Conference?
4. What was the major outcome of the Vail Conference?
5. What do the changes in health care have to do with clinical psychology?
6. What theoretical orientations became popular between 1950 and 1980?

7. Compare and contrast the behavioral, cognitive-behavioral, humanistic, and family systems approaches.
8. How did psychotropic medication revolutionize the field of clinical psychology during the 1950s?
9. What does the biopsychosocial approach have to do with clinical psychology?
10. What are empirically supported treatments?

Real Students, Real Questions

1. Is family therapy still popular today? Does insurance pay for it?
2. How has technology impacted the likely direction of psychology?
3. Why is there so much tension between different branches of clinical psychology?
4. How does a school become accredited and why would it lose accreditation?
5. If a school loses accreditation, what are the implications for current students?
6. If the Salt Lake City conference wanted programs associated with a university, why are there so many professional schools not associated with universities still in existence?

Web Resources

http://www.apa.org/archives/apa-history.html

www.cop.es/English/docs/brief.htm
Learn more about the history of clinical psychology

http://www.apa.org/divisions/div12/aboutcp.html
Learn more about the Society of Clinical Psychology, Division 12 of APA

Research: Design and Outcome

Chapter Objective

To outline the most critical issues in understanding research in clinical psychology.

Chapter Outline

4

Chapter

Most people think of psychologists as practitioners who conduct psychotherapy rather than investigators who conduct research. Yet research forms the very foundation of clinical psychology. Basic and applied research provides many of the clues to important questions about diagnosis, treatment, and general human behavior, thus allowing practitioners to implement their techniques and theories with confidence. In fact, psychology is the only mental health discipline that has its roots in academic research rather than in practice. Psychiatry, social work, and marriage and family counseling, for example, all have their roots in practice rather than in research. Even the academic degree awarded in psychology reflects its unique role and foundation in research: The PhD (Doctor of Philosophy) is historically a research degree awarded from an academic department at a university. In contrast, the MD (Doctor of Medicine), JD (Doctor of Law), and MSW (Master of Social Work) degrees are generally awarded from professional schools at universities and emphasize practice rather than research. The scientist-practitioner, or Boulder, model, the scholar-practitioner, or Vail, model, and the new clinical scientist model of training in particular in clinical psychology emphasize the value placed on conducting research and remaining an informed consumer of research. In many ways, the Vail model in psychology, usually associated with the PsyD degree, is similar to the professional school degrees awarded in medicine, law, and social work in that emphasis is generally placed on practice and consuming research rather than conducting research. However, research is fundamental to both the science and the practice of clinical psychology regardless of the training model used in graduate school.

Clinical psychologists conduct research in hospitals and clinics, in schools and universities, in the military, and in business settings. Some researchers use questionnaires, whereas others perform laboratory experiments with people or animals. The research may be archival, using data from existing charts or records, or it may involve the study of a single subject over time. Research skills and knowledge are important even for clinical psychologists who do not actively conduct research studies. Those who maintain professional independent practices, for example, must be able to ascertain what new findings and discoveries are worthy of incorporation into their clinical work.

Research is needed not only to better understand human behavior but also to develop psychological assessment techniques and treatment strategies that are reliable, valid, and effective. Nevertheless, as discussed in Chapter 3, tensions have existed between the research and applied interests of psychology since clinical psychology began in 1896. For example, clinicians often feel that researchers conduct studies that are too obscure or irrelevant to be of help with actual patients, while researchers often feel that clinicians provide services that feel right rather than selecting those that are supported by empirical research. Furthermore, researchers often do not provide clinical services in a practice setting, and clinicians often do not conduct empirical research. This situation tends to enlarge the distance between science and practice. This chapter examines the research foundation of clinical psychology and discusses the manner in which research is designed and conducted. Several important research challenges in clinical psychology are highlighted.

Research Methods and Designs

The general goal of research in clinical psychology is to acquire knowledge about human behavior and to use this knowledge to help improve the lives of individuals, families, and groups. Clinical psychologists use the scientific method in conducting research activities. The scientific method is a set of rules and procedures that describe, explain, and predict a particular phenomenon. This method includes the observation of a phenomenon, the development of hypotheses about the phenomenon, the empirical testing of the hypotheses, and the alteration of hypotheses to accommodate the new data collected and interpreted.

During the first stage of inquiry, the clinical psychologist must objectively describe a given phenomenon. One important research tool for this purpose is the *Diagnostic and Statistical Manual, fourth edition, text revision* (*DSM-IV-TR*), published by the American Psychiatric Association. The manual describes numerous clinical syndromes and lists highly specific diagnostic criteria for each psychiatric problem, thus enabling researchers to better ensure that the same criteria are used to describe each population studied. The diagnostic criteria describe the thinking, feeling, and behavior associated with a particular clinical syndrome. The *DSM-IV-TR* is discussed in more detail later. While other diagnostic manuals are used, such as the International Classification of Impairments, Activities and Participation (ICIDH) and others, the DSM system is most commonly used in the United States and Canada (American Psychiatric Association, 2000; Mjoseth, 1998). Once a careful description is constructed, a hypothesis must be developed and tested to adequately explain the behavior of interest. For example, researchers may be interested in learning more about the sexual response changes experienced by patients utilizing Prozac versus Elavil, two very different antidepressants. They may hypothesize that unlike the inhibited orgasms experienced by women taking Elavil, Prozac users do not experience this particular side effect to any noticeable degree. Researchers may be interested in examining the influence of poverty on urban elderly residents' cognitive functioning by measuring their memory and motor performances in comparison to those members of other elderly groups. Once a hypothesis is developed, it must be tested to determine its accuracy and usefulness and adapted to accommodate consistent and inconsistent research findings. A valid hypothesis can then be used both to explain and to predict behavior. Accurately predicting behavior based on hypotheses becomes an index demonstrating that those hypotheses are indeed valid. Many different types of research experiments and investigations are used to test hypotheses.

Experiments

Conducting an experiment is the fundamental way to utilize the scientific method in answering research questions. For example, suppose we were interested in designing a procedure for reducing student test-taking anxiety. We wish to find out if relaxation or aerobic exercise might be useful in helping to reduce test anxiety prior to a stressful exam.

First, a hypothesis is needed. In this case, we may believe that while both aerobic exercise and relaxation might help to lower test-taking anxiety relative to a control (comparison or baseline) condition, the relaxation technique might prove the superior method. Relaxation has been shown to be helpful with other types of fears and anxieties, and it helps to reduce the physiological arousal (e.g., elevated heart rate and blood pressure) associated with anxiety.

Identifying Independent and Dependent Variables: After a hypothesis is proposed, an experiment must be designed to evaluate the hypothesis. The researcher must select both independent and dependent variables. The *independent* variable is manipulated by the researcher and provides the structure for the study. Therefore, treatment condition (i.e., relaxation, aerobic exercise, or a control condition) would be the independent variable in the test-anxiety study. The *dependent* variable is the variable that is expected to change as a result of the influence of the independent variable. In other words, the dependent variable is what is measured by the researcher to determine whether the hypothesis can be supported. In this case, scores on a test-anxiety scale following treatment might be the dependent variable. Research studies evaluate the influence of the independent variable(s) on the dependent measure(s). The study must be constructed such that all other factors that might influence the dependent variable are controlled, with the exception of the independent variable.

Minimizing Experimental Error: A critical goal of all experiments is to minimize experimental error. Experimental error occurs when changes in the dependent variable are due to factors other than the influence of the independent variable. For example, if the experimenter is aware of the hypothesis that relaxation is superior to aerobic exercise in reducing test-taking anxiety, yet conducts both laboratory sessions with the research subjects, his or her biases may influence the results. The experimenter might behave differently toward the subjects in the relaxation condition, perhaps being more friendly to them than to subjects in the exercise or control conditions. This scenario is termed *experimenter expectancy effects.*

The experimenter must minimize potential error or bias by controlling potentially influencing variables (other than the independent variable manipulated by the experimenter). For example, the experimenter might avoid bias in conducting the laboratory sessions by using a research assistant who was unaware of (and uninvested in) the hypotheses of the study. The research assistant might also be instructed to read from a prepared script and wear the same lab coat so that all interactions with each subject are consistent.

Furthermore, the experimenter would minimize potential error or bias caused by unknown or uncontrollable influences by using a randomization procedure. The experimenter randomly varies a variable across experimental and control conditions such that the influence of the variable does not differentially affect one or more of the experimental or control conditions. For example, test-anxious students may differ in the intensity or degree of their anxiety, in their belief that test-anxiety intervention techniques might prove useful to them, in academic performance, and in a host of other variables. Because all of these potentially confounding (influencing) variables cannot be controlled or accounted for in the experiment, the researcher would randomly assign the pool of research subjects to experimental and control conditions. Therefore the potential influence of these variables would be (theoretically) evenly distributed across experimental and control conditions.

Experimenters must use both reliable and valid measures of assessment in research studies as well. *Reliability* refers to the stability or consistency of a measurement procedure. For example, a method for assessing test anxiety should result in similar scores whether the test is administered early in the day, late in the day, or by different research assistants. *Validity* refers to the notion that an instrument should measure what it was designed to measure. An instrument measuring test anxiety should indeed measure the construct we call "test anxiety" rather than other constructs such as depression, general anxiety, or low self-esteem. Any measures used in a research study must demonstrate that they have adequate reliability and validity.

Furthermore, experimenters can make errors in their choice of instruments and in data collection, scoring, and analysis. Objective and precise scoring methods that are both reliable and valid must be designed and implemented to minimize error. Checking and rechecking of coded data, data entry, and data analysis are necessary in order to spot mistakes and ensure that the data are completely free of error.

Maximizing Internal and External Validity: Research experiments must be designed not only to minimize experimental error and bias but also to maximize both internal and external validity. Internal validity refers to the condition in which only the influence of the independent variable in an experiment accounts for results obtained on the dependent variable. Any potential extraneous influences on the dependent variable (other than the influence of the independent variable) becomes a *threat to* the experiment's **internal validity.** Thus, the experimenter designs a well-constructed and methodologically sound research study to ensure internal validity.

Extraneous variables that may threaten the internal validity of any research study include the effects of history, maturation, testing, instrumentation, statistical regression, selection bias, and experimental mortality (Campbell & Stanley, 2002). **History** refers to events outside the experimental situation (e.g., earthquakes, death of a loved one, marriage) that could have a significant impact on the results of the study. **Maturation** refers to changes within subjects over the passage of time (e.g., aging; becoming fatigued, bored, or stronger) that may influence the experimental results. For example, students who report that they are test anxious at the beginning of an academic year may feel less anxious as the term proceeds owing to positive experiences with in-class exams. Others may feel more anxious because of negative experiences with in-class exams and stress associated with approaching finals. Someone participating in a lengthy study may become tired and bored and therefore answer research questions differently at the end of the study than at the beginning. **Testing** concerns the influence of the testing or evaluation process itself on research results such as in the use of repeated measures obtained on the same subjects over time. For example, one might answer a series of questions following treatment for test anxiety in a similar manner as prior to treatment due to practice or familiarity effects. **Instrumentation** refers to the influences of the tests and measurement devices used to measure constructs in the study. For example, the test-anxiety scale may not be validated for use with the intended population or it may not reliably assess test anxiety. Furthermore, subjects may respond differently on a scale at different periods of the experiment.

Statistical regression concerns the tendency of extreme scores on a measure to move toward the mean over time. For example, subjects who score very high in test-taking anxiety only to score lower at a later date may reflect regression toward the mean rather than a reduction in anxiety associated with treatment. **Selection bias** refers to a differential and problematic selection procedure for choosing research subjects. For example, bias would occur when students selected to participate in the experimental treatment groups on test-taking anxiety are selected from a campus student health clinic while control subjects are selected from an introductory psychology class. Bias occurs since the treatment and control subjects were selected from different populations of students. As discussed earlier, random assignment into experimental and control conditions is usually performed to minimize the chance of any selection bias. Finally, **experimental mortality** refers to attrition or subject dropout in an experiment. For example, experimental mortality would be a problem if 50% of the subjects in the control condition dropped out of the experiment on test-taking anxiety while only 10% of the subjects in the experimental condition did so. Experimenters must evaluate their research designs in order to minimize the influence of these seven threats to internal validity prior to conducting an experiment. If any threat is operating in a research study, results are likely to be uninterpretable and the experimenters will be unable to reach meaningful conclusions based on their data.

External validity refers to the generalizability of the research results. The more similar the research experiment is to a "real world" situation, the more generalizable the findings. However, the more careful an experimenter is about maximizing internal validity, the more likely he or she will minimize external validity. A high degree of control and precision is necessary to minimize experimental and random error and thus maximize internal validity. Therefore, carefully constructed laboratory-based research maximizing internal validity may jeopardize the generalizability (external validity) of the results. For example, in the experiment on test-taking anxiety, all subjects completed the same stressful "IQ" test administered in a laboratory rather than a "real" test such as a final examination in one of their college courses. Allowing subjects in this study to take a real examination would increase the generalizability of the results but compromise the internal validity of the study because course exams cannot be uniform. Some

exams are in chemistry, physics, psychology, or business. Exams can be multiple choice, essay, or oral. Furthermore, some exams are scheduled on a Monday, some on a Friday, some in the morning, and some in the afternoon. All these conditions might influence the results if they are not uniform or constant for all experimental and control subjects.

Researchers must carefully examine *threats to external validity* prior to conducting their experiments. These threats include testing, reactivity, multiple-treatment interference, and the interaction of selection biases (Campbell & Stanley, 2002). **Testing** refers to the use of a questionnaire or other assessment device that may sensitize and alter the subject's response and therefore influence the dependent measure. For example, completing questionnaires on anxiety may increase the research subject's experience of anxiety. **Reactivity** concerns the subject's potential response to participating in an experiment. The subject may behave differently in an experiment than in the natural environment. For example, a subject who knows that he or she is being observed during an experiment may behave in a more socially desirable manner. **Multiple-treatment interference** refers to exposing a subject to several treatment conditions or factors such that the experimenter cannot isolate any specific condition or factor. For example, a subject in the relaxation condition may receive a videotape that presents relaxing music, nature scenes, and instructions in guided imagery and progressive muscle relaxation. So many different treatment influences (e.g., gentle music, pretty images, progressive muscle relaxation instruction, distraction) could be in operation that the isolation of only one influencing factor becomes impossible. Finally, the **interaction of selection biases** concerns the notion that subjects in one group may have been differentially responsive to the experimental condition in some unique manner. For instance, subjects assigned to a relaxation group for test-taking anxiety may enjoy or respond differently than subjects assigned to another treatment condition (e.g., exercise). Responses may be a by-product of their enjoyment of the activity and not due to assumed therapeutic value of the activity itself. Thus, experimenters must carefully evaluate these threats to external validity as well as balance the dual goals of maximizing both internal and external validity prior to conducting an experiment and drawing conclusions based on obtained research data.

Another important threat to external validity includes the specific population sampled and how similar or different the group is relative to the overall population of interest to the researchers. For example, if all of the students in the test-taking anxiety example were middle-class Caucasian college students, then the results could not be generalized to include non-middle-class Caucasian students or to students in elementary or high school settings. Therefore, researchers must pay careful attention to the population sampled to ensure that the group adequately represents the larger population of interest.

Experimental Designs

There are many different means of carrying out a research experiment. Each approach offers unique advantages and disadvantages. No single approach is superior to another for answering every research question, and all can be rendered useless if not carefully designed and applied. The trick is to use the right **experimental design** with the right research question and to construct each experiment to maximize both internal and external validity.

True Experimental Designs: To demonstrate cause-and-effect relationships (e.g., specific treatment may cause improvement in functioning), **true experiments** that use randomization procedures with experimental and control conditions must be conducted, and all efforts made to minimize and control potential error and bias as well as to maximize both internal and external validity. *Randomization* is a procedure where research subjects are selected in such a way that they all have an equal chance of being placed in the different experimental and control groups. No bias can

occur in deciding which conditions subjects are placed into during the experiment. In conducting experiments using randomization procedures, the experimenter is best able to determine that outcome measures obtained on the dependent variable must be due to the influence of the experimenter-manipulated independent variable and unlikely due to error or other factors. However, several unique challenges are associated with such studies in clinical psychology:

- It is often impossible or unethical to randomly assign human beings to certain experimental or control conditions. For example, an experimenter interested in the effects of sexual abuse and maternal deprivation on depression could not randomly assign children to an experimental group in which the children would be either sexually abused or deprived of contact with their mothers.

- It is often impossible or unethical to assign patients to a control condition in which they do not receive treatment. For example, it would be unethical to assign suicidal patients to a control condition for several months without any form of treatment. Furthermore, many patients would refuse to wait for treatment or knowingly accept a placebo treatment.

- Certain disorders are fairly rare, making it difficult to obtain enough subjects for various experimental and control conditions. For example, an experimenter interested in different treatment approaches for children with trichotillomania (i.e., a disorder that involves compulsively pulling out one's hair) may be unable to find enough subjects for group-designed research conditions in a timely manner.

- Because many patients experiencing psychological distress have several diagnoses, comorbidity (two or more diagnoses) is likely to be the rule rather than the exception. Thus, it is often difficult to find people who experience only the specific disorder under investigation. For example, many children with attention deficit disorders also experience depression, oppositional defiant disorder, learning disabilities, low self-esteem, and other problems. An experimenter might think that he or she is treating the attention deficit disorder, whereas the personal contact between child and therapist might actually be treating the depression.

In addition to true experimental designs that include randomization, there are quasi-experimental designs; between-, within-, and mixed-group designs; analogue designs; case studies; correlational methods; epidemiological methods; and longitudinal and cross-sectional designs. Many of these designs are not mutually exclusive. For example, correlational designs can be either longitudinal or cross-sectional, or both. A study can include both between- and within-group designs. The experimental and quasi-experimental approaches can also use between-, within-, and mixed-group designs. A brief review of each of these alternative designs follows.

Quasi-Experimental Designs: When random assignment to experimental and control conditions is not possible because of ethical or other limitations, an experimenter may choose to use a **quasi-experimental** design. For example, a treatment-outcome study conducted at a child guidance clinic must use patients already being treated at the clinic (Plante, Couchman, & Diaz, 1995). Client satisfaction as well as assessment of problematic symptoms are conducted at the beginning, during, and at the end of treatment. Control subjects may include persons not being treated at the clinic or those on a waitlist for treatment. Because the experimenters cannot always decide who can receive treatment and who must remain waitlisted, randomization is impossible. Therefore, many important differences between treated children and children not being treated at the clinic may exist and cannot be adequately controlled. Such practical limitations require much more caution in the interpretation of research findings than is the case with true experimental techniques, and direct cause-and-effect relationships cannot be inferred.

Between-Group Designs: **Between-group** designs use two or more separate groups of subjects, each of which receives a different type of intervention or, in the case of a control condition, no intervention. Therefore, the independent variable is manipulated by the experimenter so that different groups of subjects receive different types of experiences. In the test-taking anxiety example, one group of subjects received relaxation, a second group received aerobic exercise, while a third group received a control condition (i.e., magazine reading). Ideally, subjects are randomly assigned to treatment and control conditions in a between-group design. The experimenter then assumes that all other factors that could potentially influence the study results (e.g., age, motivation, intelligence, severity of anxiety) will be evenly distributed between the groups. To ensure that potential factors that might influence the results do not differentially affect the experimental and control groups, the experimenter may wish to use a matching procedure. For example, to ensure that gender and age are similar in each experimental and control condition, the experimenter would match subjects such that males and females as well as different ages are evenly distributed across the groups. Or in the test-taking anxiety example, to ensure that the severity of test-taking anxiety is evenly distributed among the groups, the experimenter would match subjects in each group on the basis of the severity of anxiety.

There are several different types of between-group research designs. The *pretest-posttest control group design* includes two or more subject groups. While one group receives treatment, the other does not. Subjects are evaluated both before and after treatment on the dimension of interest. For example, a test-anxiety questionnaire might be used both before the treatment begins and after the completion of treatment. Control subjects (i.e., those not receiving treatment) would complete the test-anxiety questionnaire at the same time the experimental group completes the materials. One disadvantage of the pretest-posttest design is that the administration of a pretest might sensitize subjects or influence their response to treatment. A posttest-only control group could be added to control for pretest sensitivity.

Another between-group design, the *factorial design*, provides an opportunity to study two or more factors in a given study. Therefore two independent variables of interest (e.g., gender and ethnic background of therapist) can be examined at the same time. For example, treatment might be conducted with four groups: male African American therapist, female African American therapist, male Caucasian therapist, female Caucasian therapist. This would be considered a 2 × 2 factorial design. Adding two additional ethnic groups to the design (e.g., Asian American, Hispanic American) would create a 2 (gender) × 4 (ethnicity) factorial design. An advantage of conducting factorial-designed studies is that the experimenter can examine the role of interactions between factors.

Within-Group Designs: **Within-group** designs are used to examine the influence of the independent variable (such as treatment) on the same subjects over time. Subjects are not assigned to different experimental and control groups as they are in a between-group design but are all assigned to experience the same research procedure, treatment, or protocol. The same patient is examined at different points of time, such as during a baseline or pretreatment period, a treatment intervention period, and a follow-up or post-treatment period. Thus each subject serves as his or her own control. For example, subjects at risk for the development of hypertension were asked to participate in a study to examine their blood pressure and heart rates while they performed different intellectual and cognitive tasks (Plante, Lantis, & Checa, 1997). All subjects had their heart rates and blood pressures taken before, during, and after a series of laboratory experiences. Changes within the same subjects over time allowed the experimenters to study the association between stress and physiological reactivity among hypertensive high-risk persons.

There are several within-group designs to choose from in conducting clinical psychology research. Since experimenters using within-group designs must be especially careful with ordering or sequencing effects, most variations on the design methods attempt to control for these influences. *Ordering effects* refers to the influence of the order in which treatment or experimental conditions are presented to the subjects. The experimental or treatment condition in the *crossover design* switches or "crosses over" during the course of the experiment. Generally, two or more groups receive the same treatments; only the order of presentation is altered for each group. The crossover design counterbalances the treatments so that order of presentation is controlled. For example, the hypertension study just discussed (Plante et al., 1997) counterbalanced two laboratory stressors (i.e., a stressful IQ test and the Stroop Color Naming test) such that for half the subjects one stressor was presented before the other, while for the other half the second stressor was presented before the first.

Three or more treatments make crossover designs very complicated. These designs are called *multiple-treatment counterbalanced designs*. For example, if three treatments or experimental conditions are used, six counterbalanced presentations are needed. Suppose three different treatment strategies were being used to treat cannabis abuse. These could include behavioral contracting, group therapy, and interpersonal psychotherapy. All subjects would receive the same three treatments, but the order of presentation would be altered so that various subgroups of subjects would receive the treatments in different order. Controlling the order of presentation is necessary because treatment effects could be influenced by which treatment was experienced first, second, or third. If group therapy were provided to all subjects first, it would be difficult to determine if subjects benefitted from the behavioral contracting or interpersonal psychotherapy procedure because of carryover or residual effects of the group treatment experience. Table 4.1 outlines

Table 4.1   **Order of Presentation in a Three-Treatment Counterbalanced Design**

First	Second	Third
Treatment 1	Treatment 2	Treatment 3
Treatment 2	Treatment 3	Treatment 1
Treatment 3	Treatment 1	Treatment 2
Treatment 1	Treatment 3	Treatment 2
Treatment 2	Treatment 1	Treatment 3
Treatment 3	Treatment 2	Treatment 1
Example:	Treatment 1 (relaxation training)	
	Treatment 2 (aerobic exercise)	
	Treatment 3 (thought stopping)	

the different counterbalanced presentations needed in a three-treatment study.

Mixed-Group Designs: **Mixed-group** designs include elements of both between- and within-group designs. In mixed-group designs, experiments are constructed in such a way that different groups of subjects receive different treatment or experimental experiences (between group) while subject responses are assessed over time at different phases of the experiment (within group). For example, in the hypertension study mentioned earlier, control groups of subjects who were not at risk for the development of hypertension were also used. Thus, the presence or absence of hypertension risk acted as a between-group variable, while the experimental tasks were within-group variables. Mixed-group designs, which are more complex than between- or within-group designs alone, are very commonly used in clinical psychology.

Analogue Designs: **Analogue**-designed studies use procedures, subjects, and measures that approximate a real-life clinical situation and are usually conducted in a laboratory where experimental conditions can be controlled better than in the natural environment. For example, subjects may or may not be suffering from disorders that are of interest to

the experimenter. Procedures may or may not be identical to those used in the natural or clinical environment. Therapists may or may not be licensed mental health providers. The test-anxiety experiment previously mentioned was conducted in a laboratory using a testing condition that was somewhat removed from testing conditions experienced by test-anxious students (e.g., final examinations). The subjects were students who identified themselves as being test anxious and who scored high on a questionnaire measuring test anxiety rather than students who sought treatment for the condition at a campus counseling center. Furthermore, the treatment conditions of relaxation training and aerobic exercise were conducted in the laboratory rather than in a more natural setting (e.g., a dorm room or campus apartment, a health club, a clinic). Analogue studies may use trained research assistants to conduct "treatment conditions" and may involve subjects who do not meet specific diagnostic criteria for a particular disorder. The advantages of analogue designs are that they maximize internal validity more effectively than studies conducted in a more natural environment. However, disadvantages include threats to external validity, since generalizability of research findings may be compromised. For example, subjects may respond less genuinely and honestly in a laboratory environment than in a clinical environment, or, treatment provided by research assistants may differ in important ways from treatment provided by licensed clinicians in practice.

Case Studies

A **case study** is an in-depth investigation, observation, and description of a single person or situation. The case study method was the primary technique used by Sigmund Freud and his colleagues to describe cases of hysteria and other problems. Case studies are not experiments, because they lack dependent variables, experimenter manipulation of independent variables, and randomized assignment of subjects into treatment and control conditions. Rather, case studies provide an intensive observation of a person and phenomenon that allows for the development of hypotheses and theories. Case studies can be especially helpful for examining a new, rare, or unusual phenomenon or during the early descriptive stages of a research program. Theories developed through case study methods can be tested later with more intensive research designs. One of the most famous case studies in psychology is the case of Anna O. described by Joseph Breuer and Sigmund Freud (Breuer & Freud, 1895/1957). Anna O. experienced *hysteria*, or what the *DSM-IV-TR* would term a *conversion disorder* today. She was healthy and relatively problem free until she was 21 years old, and caring for her failing father. After several months of care giving, Anna O. developed unusual vision difficulties as well as motor problems with her right arm and legs that could not be explained medically. She also had trouble speaking and developed other symptoms (e.g., headaches, recurrent cough, fear of drinking). She sought treatment from Breuer, who conducted hypnosis and treated one symptom at a time. Breuer noticed that symptoms disappeared following the hypnosis. The development of both hypnosis as well as psychoanalytic theory (e.g., theories of repression) occurred partly through the case study of Anna O. Specific single-case research designs have been developed to further objectify the case study method. Empirical experimental procedures applied to single case studies will be briefly reviewed here.

Single-Subject Designs: Single case designs blend case study and experimental techniques. While these designs offer the scientific rigor of experimental methods, they also allow for practical clinical relevance because they are used with only one patient or case. Therefore, clinicians can use these methods to both study and treat individual patients in their practice. Another advantage of the single-subject design is its robustness in that it avoids the problems associated with variability among a large number of subjects.

Single-subject designs use time-series methodologies (Barlow, Hayes, & Nelson, 1984), which require a series of measures conducted on the same person over a period of time (i.e., a pretreatment phase, a treatment phase, and a post-treatment phase). Rather than using a separate control group or control subject, the individual patient acts as his or her own control during the baseline phase when data are collected on a phenomenon of interest without any active treatment or intervention. For example, binge-eating behavior might be assessed in a bulimic patient by using a questionnaire before, during, and after treatment and during follow-up. Changes in self-reported binge-eating behavior can then be compared with baseline measures in order to document change. Various baseline and intervention phases or conditions can be implemented to examine the short-term and long-term effectiveness of the intervention.

One of the most commonly used single-subject designs is the *ABAB design.* The ABAB refers to alternating between baseline (or no treatment) and treatment phases during a single-subject intervention for a particular clinical problem. The ABAB is both a single-subject design and a within-subject design. It is also referred to as an *intra-subject-replication* design. Thus an initial baseline period (A) occurs when the problem behavior is assessed without any intervention, followed by a treatment intervention (B), followed by a return to no treatment (A), followed by a second treatment intervention (B). Treatment/no-treatment phases can alternate numerous times depending on the needs of the research and/or treatment. For example, a child who has an attention deficit/hyperactivity disorder (ADHD) might frequently and impulsively leave his or her seat in a classroom setting. This behavior might be highly disruptive to other students and the teacher and prevent the child from completing classroom assignments. The teacher might use social reinforcement such as praise when the child is behaving appropriately while sitting in his or her chair. The teacher might record the number of times the child leaves the chair without any reinforcement (i.e., A), and then the number of times the problematic behavior occurs while offering the social praise reinforcement (i.e., B). The teacher then withholds reinforcement, continuing to count the frequency of the problem behavior (i.e., A), and then reinstates the social praise reinforcement condition (i.e., B). Collected data (e.g., number of times child left classroom seat without permission) can be tabulated for each baseline and intervention period for analysis of the success of the intervention.

One cautionary note expressed about ABAB designs concerns the ethics associated with withdrawing helpful treatment during the A phases of the design. For example, some children engage in problematic head-banging or other self-destructive and aggressive activities that could be highly dangerous if allowed to be untreated during baseline assessment and treatment withdrawal phases. A second concern regarding ABAB designs is the limitation of focusing on only one problematic behavior. Rarely do patients present with only one specific target behavior. For example, the child mentioned earlier may not only leave the classroom seat but also impulsively and poorly complete assignments, interrupt and disturb other children, and have temper tantrums. An adult who is depressed may also have obsessive-compulsive traits, an eating or sleeping disturbance, suicidal thoughts, relationship conflicts, and alcohol abuse problems. Multiple baseline designs are used when more than one target behavior is evaluated and treated. An additional problem with the ABAB design is that it is often impossible to withdraw treatment because a new skill has been learned in the A condition. Therefore, once a new skill has been learned it may be impossible to "unlearn" it during the B condition.

Multiple-Baseline Designs: With a multiple-baseline design, baseline data are collected for all the behaviors of interest. Then treatment is provided for one target behavior while baseline data are still collected on the other behaviors. Treatment intervention might then target a second behavior while continuing

or removing treatment for the first behavior. For example, the child with attention deficit disorder mentioned earlier might not complete homework assignments and might also get into frequent fights with other children during recess periods at school. Baseline data such as the daily frequency of these problematic behaviors are tabulated. Reinforcements such as earning points toward a special gift or privilege might be used to target improvement in getting homework assignments completed. Following several weeks of treatment, reinforcement for the homework assignments is supplemented with social praise for playing cooperatively with other children. Social praise is used to improve the child's social behavior for several weeks. Data concerning the frequency of the problematic behaviors are collected continuously throughout the various baseline and intervention periods. If target behaviors do not improve during the intervention periods, new intervention strategies can be developed and implemented later on. Figure 4.1 shows results of a multiple-baseline design used for several children with autism to improve both social interaction and reading skills through tutoring.

Although all single-subject designs can provide a great deal of information about treatment for one individual, generalizing and applying the findings to others is of serious concern. Treatment interventions, for example, may work well for one person but not for another. Replication of the interventions aimed at target behaviors would need to be conducted with many others to determine whether generalizability exists. Whereas most single-subject study designs such as ABAB are used by professionals with behavioral or cognitive-behavioral orientations, the principles can be extended to assess any range of interventions as well as integrated into biopsychosocial or multimodal approaches.

Multiple-baseline designs can be used to investigate two or more behaviors, settings, or individuals. Multiple-baseline designs are often used when a return to baseline without reinforcement might prove to be problematic or dangerous. For example, if a child with

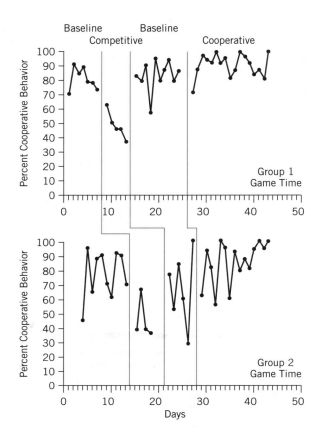

Figure 4.1

Example of multiple-baseline approach for several children with autism.
Source: From "Cooperative Games: A Way to Modify Aggressive and Cooperative Behavior in Young Children," by A. K. Bay-Hinitz, R. F. Peterson, and H. R. Quilitch, 1994, *Journal of Applied Behavioral Analysis, 27,* pp. 435– 446.

attentional and impulsivity problems engages in dangerous behaviors such as running into a busy street, it would likely be too dangerous to withdraw reinforcement and risk that the child could get injured or killed. A multiple baseline design might be used to first collect baseline data at school and home and then provide reinforcement (e.g., social praise, rewards) at the school setting first, followed by reinforcement at the home setting. Once the reinforcement begins, it is not withdrawn. If reinforcement works, it would be expected that improvements in behavior would be noted in the school environment first, followed by the home environment.

Multiple-baseline designs can mix individuals, settings, and behaviors and may withdraw interventions at some levels but not others. For instance, Bay-Hinitz, Peterson, and Quilitch (1994) conducted a study that used a multiple-baseline design to investigate the influence of competitive and cooperative games on aggression and cooperative behavior among preschool children. Children from four different preschool classes were used in the study. Results demonstrate that while cooperative games increased cooperative behavior and decreased aggressive behavior, competitive games increased aggressive behavior and decreased cooperative behavior. Figure 4.2 provides data from this study.

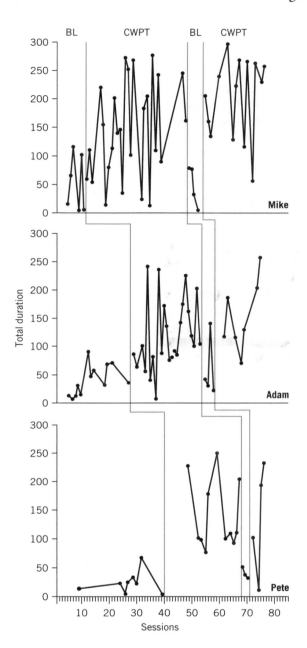

Figure 4.2

Multiple-baseline results for cooperative behavior among children in several preschool classes.
Source: From ''Classwide Peer Tutoring: An Integration Strategy to Improve Reading Skills and Promote Peer Interactions among Students with Autism and General Education Peers,'' by D. M. Kamps, P. M. Baretta, B. R. Leonard, and J. Delquadri, 1994, *Journal of Applied Behavior Analysis, 27,* pp. 49–61.

Correlational Methods

The *sine qua non* of experimental research, random-assignment experimental and control conditions, is often impossible to implement in clinical psychology research. Single case study designs are also not feasible in many clinical or research settings. Ethical, legal, and other limitations on experimentation with human beings must be taken into consideration before a research design can be selected. Many of the limitations that prevent experimental methods from being used can be alternatively addressed through the application of correlational methods. **Correlational** designs examine the degree of association between two or more variables. While correlational designs do not allow cause-and-effect conclusions (e.g., treatment cured a problem), they do provide researchers and clinicians useful information concerning the degree of association between constructs of interest. Thus, correlational methods inform the experimenter how closely two or more variables tend to correspond to each other.

Correlations can be either positive or negative. A positive correlation refers to two or more variables that move in the same direction. As one variable increases, so does the other. For example, the more depressed someone feels, the more hopeless he or she may feel. Thus depression and hopelessness tend to correlate and in the same direction (i.e., high degrees of depression are associated with high degrees of hopelessness, whereas low degrees of depression are associated with low degrees of hopelessness). The more marital arguments a couple experiences, the more dissatisfied they are with their marriage. The more alcohol one consumes, the more work or school days he or she is likely to miss.

A negative correlation refers to two or more variables that move in opposite directions. As one variable increases, the other decreases. For example, the more television a student watches, the less time he or she devotes to studying. Thus, television viewing and studying tend to go together in different directions

(i.e., a lot of time watching television is associated with little time studying, whereas little time watching television is associated with a lot of time studying). The more depressed someone feels, the less time he or she spends with friends. Therefore, negative correlations imply that two or more variables tend to go together in opposite directions.

None of these correlations or associations between variables is perfect. In other words, some variation is expected in all the examples presented. For instance, some couples who tend to have frequent arguments may report high marital satisfaction, while some students who watch a great deal of television may still be able to spend many hours studying. The degree of association between variables is expressed by a correlation coefficient. A *correlation coefficient* is a score ranging from −1.00 to +1.00. Scores close to −1.00 reflect a nearly perfect negative correlation, that is, while one variable is high, the other is low. For example, if hours of television watching and studying were assessed in a large class and it was determined that all of the students who watched a lot of television studied infrequently while all of the students who did not watch television studied frequently, a perfect −1.00 correlation coefficient would likely surface from the statistical equation that calculates the coefficient. Scores close to +1.00 reflect a nearly perfect positive correlation; as scores on one variable increase, so do the scores on the other. Furthermore, a positive correlation also occurs when scores on both variables of interest are low. For example, if scores on depression and scores on hopelessness are assessed in a large group of people, they are likely to be positively correlated. Thus, those who tend to score high on depression are also likely to score high on hopelessness, while those who score low on depression are also likely to score low on hopelessness. When there is no correlation between two variables (e.g., shoe size and intelligence), the correlation is close to .00.

It is important to emphasize that the association between two or more variables does not mean that one necessarily caused the other. Correlation does not imply causality. Thus, television viewing does not necessarily cause inadequate studying, and depression does not necessarily cause hopelessness. Additional variables not assessed in a given experiment or study may operate to influence the correlation coefficient. For example, perhaps unmotivated students watch a great deal of television and spend very little time studying. Perhaps these students would spend very little time studying no matter how much television they watched. Other factors (e.g., interest in the subject matter) may also play a role.

Epidemiological Methods

Clinical psychologists are often interested in the use and results of epidemiological research methods. *Epidemiology* refers to the examination of the incidence or distribution of a particular clinical problem or variable of interest.

Epidemiological research describes the prevalence and incidence of a particular issue of concern, seeking to answer questions such as "How many people have alcohol problems? How many college students are clinically depressed? How many people have schizophrenia? How many new cases of attention deficit/hyperactivity disorder were diagnosed last year? How many adolescent girls have unwanted pregnancies?" Epidemiological data may be collected from a variety of sources including government census, survey approaches, and hospital records. For example, epidemiological research has indicated that approximately 750,000 people die of heart disease each year (American Heart Association, 2009), and that about 11 million people in the United States are alcoholics (National Institute on Alcohol Abuse and Alcoholism, 2000). Epidemiological research has shown that approximately 1% of the United States population experiences schizophrenia, and between 0.5% and 1% of female adolescents or young adults experience anorexia nervosa (American Psychiatric Association, 2000). Not only does epidemiological research attempt to accurately estimate the number of people who experience certain problems, but it also tries to provide detailed information concerning other demographic characteristics of interest (e.g., ethnic, economic, age, or gender differences in those who have heart attacks before age 55). Data from epidemiological research are usually collected from government documents and records, hospital and clinic records, and national polls, and generalized from large-scale multisite research projects and other sources of information usually outside of the controlled laboratory experiments.

Cross-Sectional and Longitudinal Designs

Experimental, correlational, epidemiological, and even single-case designs can be constructed to be cross-sectional or longitudinal. Many studies can incorporate both cross-sectional and longitudinal methods into the same investigation and are called *cross-sequential* designs. **Cross-sectional** designs provide a "snapshot" view of behavior at a given moment in time. Most of the research in clinical psychology as well as most other areas of psychology applies cross-sectional methods because they are generally easier and less expensive to complete. The study on test-taking anxiety mentioned earlier is an example of a cross-sectional research design. Test-anxious subjects were provided laboratory "treatment" and then participated in a simulated "IQ test" during one brief laboratory session. The study provided a snapshot view of test-anxious students to determine whether a brief treatment might be useful in reducing anxiety during one isolated laboratory session. **Longitudinal** designs generally collect research data over a long period of time. Examining test-anxious subjects throughout the course of their high school and college education would be an example of a longitudinal design method. In this example, levels of test-taking anxiety would be assessed periodically during high school and college and thus would take approximately eight years to collect.

Suppose a clinical psychologist were interested in determining whether the development of hypertension (high blood pressure) was associated with a person's reaction to stress over time. Using a cross-sectional approach, the psychologist might take self-report and physiological (e.g., blood pressure) measures during a stressful laboratory procedure. He or she might be interested in determining whether hypertensive patients experience greater reactivity to the laboratory procedure than do non-hypertensive control subjects. On the other hand, a researcher who decided to use a longitudinal approach might assess a random group of people on their self-reported and physiological responses to laboratory stress periodically for many years. Then the researcher would determine which subjects developed hypertension and which subjects did not. The researcher would then determine whether earlier measurements could have predicted the later development of hypertension. While longitudinal designs can be extremely useful, their cost and other limitations often make this type of research difficult to conduct.

Highlight of a Contemporary Clinical Psychologist

Alan E. Kazdin, PhD, ABPP

Photo: Courtesy Alan E. Kazdin

Dr. Kazdin maintains a full-time academic career focusing on research methodology, conduct disorders, parenting, and child-rearing.

Birth Date: January 24, 1945

College: San Jose State University (BA, Psychology/Philosophy), 1967

Graduate Program: Northwestern University (MA, PhD, Clinical Psychology), 1970

Clinical Internship: North Shore Association, Evanston, IL

ABPP: Cognitive-Behavioral Psychology

Current Job: John M. Musser Professor of Psychology and Child Psychiatry; Director, Yale Parenting Center and Child Conduct Clinic

Pros and Cons of Being a Clinical Psychologist:

Pros: "A career in clinical psychology has an extraordinary number of options. I have worked at three universities (Pennsylvania State University, University of Pittsburgh School of Medicine, and Yale University). My current job is in the department of psychology, but in my career I have spent several years in departments of psychiatry at medical schools (in Pittsburgh and at the Yale University School of Medicine). Psychology and psychiatry jobs have different duties and responsibilities in relation to teaching, patient care, and administration, but convey options in settings and duties readily available to a clinical psychologist. There are scores of other career paths (e.g., in hospitals, industry, armed forces, government agencies) for clinical psychologists that I have not pursued. Over the years, there have been many opportunities to consult with state and federal government agencies and various hospitals and schools. In this work, one meets with scientists from many other fields (genetics, neuroscience, health policy, psychiatry, social work, mathematics, government and law, and others). I mention this because within the career, there many stimulating opportunities to learn and contribute according to one's intellectual and personal tastes.

"My current position as a faculty member in a department of psychology has built-in diversity. I teach undergraduate and graduate students, carry out and supervise research, direct a clinic where we see children and families, and work with other faculty on issues within the department or university (e.g., faculty recruitment). I see families in need of help each day and work with a remarkably committed and talented staff interested in helping these families in palpable ways and in generating questions research ought to answer to improve how we can understand and help such families.

"My area of interest is developmental psychopathology, which focuses on understanding adjustment, adaptation, and clinical dysfunction among children and adolescents. The area is particularly rich in career opportunities, including working on clinical problems (e.g., child depression, anxiety, trauma), their onset, path and course, and what can be done (e.g., prevention, treatment, social policy) to reduce or eliminate them. There are many opportunities to work and collaborate with colleagues from related disciplines (e.g., epidemiology, genetics, psychiatry, sociology) that are critical to understanding psychological processes and their emergence and course. My own energies permit consideration of only a few topics, including aggressive and antisocial behavior, child-rearing practices, and child and adolescent psychotherapy."

Cons: "I have not experienced cons of being a clinical psychologist, with one exception. At the few social events and parties I attend, once people learn I am a psychologist, they automatically refer to a 'friend' with a problem they want me to talk about. This is not what psychology is about! For a period of several years, once in these social situations I started telling people I taught history (instead of psychology). It worked. People nodded courteously and then went off to refresh their beverage, usually without even asking me 'what kind of history' (my standard reply was, 'the kind that is about

the past'). The exchange reveals a 'con' about psychology. As a field, we have not conveyed to the public that there is a huge scientific body of literature that relates to core areas of functioning (e.g., decision making, learning, brain development, language mastery, persuasion, social behavior, determinants of social action, attraction, interpersonal relationships—it is endless). (I stopped this practice after befriending a few colleagues who are historians.)

"I mentioned that the overriding advantage of a career in clinical psychology, at least for me, is the range of options in light of the many roles clinical psychology can play in health-care settings, industry, the legal system, the military, and all sorts of private and government institutes and agencies. Within university settings alone, there is a rather amazing set of choices within different levels of community colleges and small or large private or public colleges and universities, each with its own rewards and challenges. These options are important as they allow one to find one's niche and as needed to piece together different options (e.g., part-time teaching, part-time consulting) to accommodate that. The cons of any job or career are very much like those of an intimate relationship; it would be horrible to be in one place if your heart really lies in another. The cons for me would be if I were in another place doing something else."

Future of Clinical Psychology: "My concerns and interests are with psychology more broadly rather than clinical psychology in particular. I have no special insights about psychology in the future. I very much hope that psychological science is infused more broadly into areas that can help public life. For example, climate change and fostering behaviors that sustain the environment are world priorities and psychological science can contribute enormously to changing attitudes and behaviors in ways that make a difference. As another example, interpersonal violence, especially against women and children, is responsible for lifelong suffering in our country and certainly worldwide. Our research on prevention and treatment can help. We need more work but also to disseminate the work we have. A hope rather than a prediction is that we partner with other sciences to disseminate what we already know that can make a difference on critical issues as illustrated by these two examples.

"Within clinical psychology there are some natural tensions. The main one is between clinical practice and science. Among the issues is getting our best scientific findings in the hands of those who do clinical work. A related tension is in clinical practice of psychology with and versus other disciplines (e.g., social work, family therapy, psychiatry). Most individuals ($\sim$ 70%) in the United States in need of psychological services because of social, emotional, behavioral, and psychiatric problems do not receive treatment. The model of providing individual therapy for those who want to come to treatment sessions is not working well and simply cannot reach those in need. The future of psychology and health care more generally hopefully will address such issues in ways that make a difference.

"A career goal for me is to apply our very best science—all of psychology—to serve the public. That broad goal has been helpful to me because public needs and priorities shift (e.g., prevention of HIV/AIDS, treatment of child-hood obesity, climate change) in response to a changing world. Many topics remain constant (e.g., child-rearing, developing reading) and extending our science here is critically important. The path toward a better future can be guided by many questions. The two for me are: (1) What do we know from our scientific findings that can be used to address critical issues in public life (e.g., discrimination, healthy life-style, child-care, prevention of abuse, care for the elderly), and (2) what basic research needs to be done so we can address question #1 in a way that makes a genuine difference?

"The challenge is not to forecast the future but to work hard to shape it. There is little I might be able to do directly to have an impact, but I have the privilege of working with graduate and undergraduate students who have a commitment and longer timeframe.

As we influence each other, we also join in what we can do to have the impact needed to make a difference in public life."

Typical Schedule: "My day begins very early in the morning—too early to even mention. Very early in the morning is when I can do my writing and have myself as the only excuse for not being able to concentrate. A wonderful feature of the job is that writing requires reading to be sure that one is sufficiently current on a topic. Keeping up in a few areas of work is daunting. New research appears regularly and in multiple journals. Also, many areas that seem to be unrelated to one's interest can really shape thinking and so some of these areas should be perused as well. Clearly, the goal of keeping up can be only approximated. If I have a class that day, I also use this quiet time to review the lecture to see if there are last-minute additions to make in light of something pertinent I have read within the past few days.

"By mid-morning, I go to the university or my clinic for meetings or to do class-related work (e.g., preparation materials, grading papers). At some point, I am likely to have a class or two that consists of a formal lecture or seminar. One day each week I have a 'lab' class in which interested graduate students and I meet to discuss and plan research. A goal is to help students develop their areas of interest and expertise, to translate that interest into concrete studies, and then help the students begin their studies. Some of my supervision of graduate student master's degree research and doctoral dissertations are part of this class.

"By mid-afternoon, I may go or return to my clinic on campus (about three-quarters of a mile away from my office), an outpatient service where I meet with therapists, discuss cases, and watch ongoing treatment (via video cameras). The clinic serves children 2 to 14 who are referred for oppositional, aggressive, and antisocial behavior. In recent years, with gentle pressure from the community, we also see parents who want help with the normal challenges of parenting (e.g., toilet training, tantrums, and teen 'attitude') and whose children are not experiencing clinically significant problems or impairment. The clinical service is where I conduct research and work with and supervise graduate and undergraduate students who wish to learn the treatments we have developed.

"Each week I do an hour or two of media work, usually for magazines and radio or TV stations. The work is to provide background material on articles or shows related to children and families, parenting practices, and related research in the news. Also, each week, I review manuscripts for journals and books or book proposals of colleagues around the country. While I am doing this, others are doing the same with my work—all done anonymously.

"By very late afternoon or early evening, the day is ended and I return home. I am perplexed at how the day went so quickly, why I really did not get much done, and what might be in store tomorrow. I ponder whether it might be more honest and accurate if I renamed my 'To Do' list as the 'Still Not Done' list. These deep thoughts continue until I finally arrive home."

Further Information

www.yale.edu/psychology/FacInfo /Kazdin.html
www.yale.edu/childconductclinic
www.alankazdin.com

Treatment Outcome Research

Clinical psychologists conduct research to answer questions on the development of reliable and valid assessment instruments, on strategies to better understand and diagnose clinical syndromes, and on predicting problematic behavior such as aggression and suicide. But perhaps the most frequently asked and compelling research questions concern treatment outcome: Does psychotherapy work? Which type of therapy works best for which type of condition? Is longer term treatment better than shorter term treatment? Which therapist characteristics are associated with treatment

success? Which patient characteristics are associated with treatment success? A great deal of research in clinical psychology attempts to answer one or more of these questions. Treatment outcome research has become critical in recent years. Although treatment outcome research has been conducted for many years, the changes in the health-care delivery and reimbursement systems have demanded that treatment outcome research demonstrate that psychological and other forms of treatment do indeed work and therefore justify the expenditure of funds.

In recent years, much attention has focused on **randomized clinical trials** (RCTs) that focus on random assignment of clients into well-controlled and -assessed treatment and control conditions with particular agreed-upon standards for the implementation and reporting of this research (Hollon, 2006).

To conduct research on treatment outcome, different strategies are employed depending on the specific question of interest. Kazdin (1991) outlined seven **treatment outcome research strategies** for effectively evaluating treatment outcome research. These include treatment "package" strategy, dismantling treatment strategy, constructive treatment strategy, parametric treatment strategy, comparative treatment strategy, client and therapist variation strategy, and process research strategy (Table 4.2). Each method will be briefly described in the following section.

Treatment Package Strategy

The **treatment package** strategy approach attempts to answer the basic question, "Does treatment work?" This approach seeks to determine whether a specific treatment is effective for a specific clinical problem or disorder. In this approach, a treatment package is usually employed, while a control condition such as a no-treatment control or a waitlist control group is used for comparison. *Package* refers to the fact that most treatment approaches include a variety of potentially helpful components. For example, relaxation training

Table 4.2 **Treatment Outcome Research**

Treatment Outcome Research Strategy Approach	Research Questions Attempted to Answer
Treatment	Does treatment work?
Dismantling	What part of treatment works?
Constructive	What could be added to an effective treatment to make it even better?
Parametric	What element of treatment could be changed to make treatment work better?
Comparative	Which treatment approach is best?
Client and therapist variation	With which type of therapist or patient is treatment most likely to be effective?
Process	How does the process of treatment impact outcome?

Source: Kazdin (1991).

might include the learning of specific breathing techniques, muscle relaxation techniques, and visual imagery techniques, as well as problem-solving strategies to use the techniques on a daily basis. A package approach does not isolate one or several highly specific components that are believed responsible for the positive therapeutic effects. Because many nonspecific factors (e.g., attendance at sessions, belief that therapist is helpful and knowledgeable) could also be involved in patient improvement, researchers usually include a control condition that involves some form of *pseudotreatment.* A pseudotreatment might involve many aspects of real treatment (e.g., meeting with a mental health professional in a professional setting, discussion of problems, regular sessions) but would not involve what the researchers believe are the active ingredients of treatment (e.g., specific techniques or strategies). For example, suppose researchers conducting the test-anxiety study mentioned earlier wanted to know if relaxation training actually helped test-anxious students reduce anxiety. One group might receive relaxation therapy including instructions on specific techniques presented on videotape. Another group might watch a videotape that had pleasant pictures and music but no specific

instructions on how to use relaxation techniques. A third group might receive nothing. Additional groups could be used to determine if other strategies helped to reduce anxiety.

Dismantling Treatment Strategies

Dismantling treatment strategies attempt to answer the question, "Which aspect of treatment works?" The focus of dismantling treatment strategies is to identify the active ingredient of a particular treatment strategy after the treatment has been determined effective. To conduct a dismantling research study, different patients or groups of patients receive different aspects of a given treatment. Some may receive the entire treatment, while others receive the treatment without an important component. For example, interpersonal psychotherapy has been found to be helpful in treating patients with binge-eating disorder (Agras et al., 1995; Cooper & Fairburn, 2009; Wilfley et al., 1993). A dismantling strategy might include one group that receives standard interpersonal psychotherapy conducted by a licensed psychologist in a clinic setting. Another group might receive the same treatment, conducted by a fellow group member in a self-help format. A third group might receive the same treatment but use a workbook rather than an actual treatment provider. Therefore, the therapist role is examined using a dismantling strategy to determine whether experience, training, and face-to-face contact are necessary for interpersonal psychotherapy to work in the case of binge eating. The dismantling strategy thus seeks to determine the basis for change during treatment.

Constructive Treatment Strategies

Constructive treatment strategies attempt to answer the question, "What might be added to an effective treatment to make it even more effective?" The constructive treatment approach adds various components to the treatment to determine whether the additions will improve treatment outcome. For example, interpersonal treatment for binge eating might be enhanced if the treatment also included additional sessions with family members or a reading list for patient use. Furthermore, adding cognitive-behavioral treatment to the interpersonal therapy may be helpful (Agras et al., 1995; Cooper & Fairburn, 2009). One group of patients might receive the standard treatment, while others receive the standard treatment with different additional components. The constructive treatment approach allows the researcher to empirically construct a treatment package by adding new components piece by piece.

Parametric Treatment Strategy

The parametric treatment strategy seeks to answer the question, "What aspect of treatment can be altered to make treatment work better?" This approach changes a specific aspect of the treatment to determine whether the change can enhance treatment effectiveness. Often the parametric approach involves altering the treatment time or intensity. For example, interpersonal therapy for binge eating might be enhanced (i.e., fewer symptoms following treatment and client reported satisfaction with treatment) if the standard treatment were conducted for a longer period (e.g., 90-minute sessions instead of 60 minutes,

20 weeks of treatment instead of 12 weeks) or with scheduled follow-up sessions. Thus, a parametric treatment strategy might include one group of patients receiving standard treatment while another group receives longer and more intense treatment.

Comparative Treatment Strategy

The comparative treatment strategy attempts to answer the question, "Which treatment approach works better?" This approach generally compares different strategies for producing change in a clinical problem. For example, a comparative treatment approach to binge eating might include one group receiving cognitive-behavioral psychotherapy, a second group receiving interpersonal psychotherapy, and a third group receiving a combination of both cognitive-behavioral and interpersonal psychotherapy. Each group of patients would be evaluated to determine whether symptoms were reduced more in one group relative to the others.

Client–Therapist Variation Strategy

The client–therapist variation strategy seeks to answer the question, "With which type of therapist or for which type of patient is treatment most likely to be effective?" Thus, the client–therapist variation strategy alters the types of therapists or patients to determine which combinations optimize treatment outcome. For example, would treatment work better if the therapist were of the same gender, sex, or ethnicity as the patient? Might treatment outcome improve if the therapist has also experienced the disorder first-hand (e.g., sponsors in Alcoholics Anonymous)? Might treatment be more effective if the patient is highly motivated rather than only moderately motivated?

Process Research Strategy

Finally, the process research strategy attempts to answer the question, "How does the actual process of therapy impact treatment outcome?" This research approach seeks to determine which aspects of the psychotherapeutic process are associated with positive treatment outcome. The process approach might attempt to answer specific process questions such as, "What makes a satisfying and productive session between a therapist and patient?" For example, patient hostility, therapist friendliness, and level of patient disclosure might affect treatment process and outcome.

Questions and Challenges in Conducting Treatment Outcome Research

Conducting treatment outcome research is extremely challenging. Problems associated with the design, implementation, and interpretation of research results are common to this realm of research. Several common questions regarding treatment outcome research will be briefly reviewed here.

Is a Research Program's Treatment Similar to the Treatment in Actual Practice?

To conduct an effective research study, a great deal of control and precision are needed to determine whether changes in the dependent variable are due to the manipulation of the independent variable. Therefore, research strategies must be employed very carefully in any study. However, treatment designed for a research study may or may not be typical of the treatment provided in the professional community. For example, suppose a researcher wished to compare cognitive-behavioral therapy with psychodynamic therapy for a particular clinical population such as obsessive-compulsive disorder. To ensure that patients receive the same type of therapy, the researcher might use treatment manuals and instruct the therapists participating in the study never to deviate from the manual as they work with obsessive-compulsive research subjects and patients. To ensure that

the therapists do not deviate from the treatment manuals, sessions might be videotaped and evaluated by trained experts. To control the duration of treatment for the two groups, each therapist might be required to see the patients for 12 consecutive weeks (1 session per week) and terminate treatment on the twelfth session. These strict limitations generally do not occur in actual clinical practice. Patients may often be seen for longer or shorter lengths of time; integrative treatment approaches using, for example, both psychodynamic and cognitive-behavioral techniques are common in actual practice; videotaping of sessions rarely occurs in most practices; and participation in a research study in and of itself might alter the patient's perception of the treatment. Therefore, results from the study may not be generalizable. Researchers must design studies that approximate the real world as much as possible to maximize the external validity of their study, while monitoring experimental control to maximize its internal validity.

Are the Patients and Therapists Used in a Research Study Typical of Those in Actual Practice?

A patient who is willing to receive treatment provided in a research study may or may not be typical of someone who seeks treatment privately through the services of a mental health professional in the community. Often patients who agree to participate in a research study are able to get professional services at no cost or may even be paid to participate. These financial incentives may or may not result in securing a pool of research patients who are typical of the patient population at large. Furthermore, research studies often need to be very specific about the criteria used to select patients for the study. For example, if a researcher is interested in studying obsessive-compulsive disorder, he or she may wish to secure a patient subject pool that meets the *DSM-IV-TR* diagnostic criteria for obsessive-compulsive disorder without also having other coexisting psychiatric problems (e.g., depression, personality disorder, eating disorder). While selectivity in deciding who should participate in the research project enhances the internal validity of the study, the resulting subjects may or may not be representative of patients with obsessive-compulsive disorder in the general population.

Similar concerns exist regarding the selection of therapists. Therapists participating in the study may or may not be representative of therapists in the community providing treatment. For example, research experiments may use mental health professionals or trainees working in a hospital, clinic, or university setting or research assistants with no professional license to practice. Research studies often use clinicians who are primarily researchers rather than clinicians. Researchers may use therapists with highly specialized treatment approaches (e.g., hypnosis for pain control) that may not reflect the type of approaches the average clinician in the community might choose to use. Again, efforts to enhance internal validity may compromise external validity. Therapist characteristics such as age, gender, ethnicity, experience, warmth, orientation, and other factors must be taken into consideration as well.

What Are Some of the Ethical Problems with Treatment Outcome Research?

Although ethical issues in both research and practice are discussed in detail in Chapter 13, it is important to mention some of the challenging ethical issues and potential disadvantages associated with treatment outcome research here. While it is clear that it is important to have a scientific basis for clinical interventions and that treatment outcome research is an integral part of developing the scientific understanding about what works and doesn't work in clinical practice, a variety of challenging ethical issues are a byproduct of this effort to increase our knowledge and ultimately offer the best possible services to those who need them. First, patient needs must be balanced with the research protocol in such a way that patients are not put at significant risk. For example, if a suicidal patient is involved with a treatment outcome study that is evaluating a particular type of treatment on severe depression, it is possible that the patient might be at risk of hurting him- or herself and the treatment protocol or manual may not allow for additional interventions beyond the scope of the particular treatment being evaluated and offered. It might then be in the best interest of the patient to withdraw from the study so that professional services can be tailored to his or her individual needs. Patient withdrawal or dropout from the research study might then jeopardize the integrity of the study if too many people withdraw from the investigation or if they do so in significantly different numbers from one particular treatment group relative to another. Researchers may feel pressure to do everything they can to keep patients involved with the study in order to minimize the problems associated with too many withdrawals. Their need to complete their research might make them less able to clearly see what is in the best interest of the patients and their wellbeing.

The use of control and placebo groups presents challenging ethical problems in treatment outcome research as well. For example, in the hypothetical study on treatment for severe depression, it may be ethically questionable to ask a group of highly depressed patients to be in a non-treatment control or placebo group or in a waitlist control group and not receive much-needed services for several months or more. When people want to get help for emotional, behavioral, psychological, or relational problems no matter how severely or mildly distressed they are, they generally want the services to begin as soon as possible. Being placed in a control condition of any kind might not be suitable for those in great need of help such as suicidal patients. Yet, not using control, waitlist, or placebo groups compromises the quality of the research project.

These problems underscore the challenge in conducting high-quality research in the context of significant human problems and concerns. While these and other research problems are not insurmountable, they do need to be carefully and thoughtfully considered before undertaking the task of treatment outcome research.

How and When Is Treatment Outcome Measured?

The assessment of treatment outcome is much more complicated than, at the end of treatment, merely asking patients if they feel better or are no longer troubled by specific problems. Bias and demand characteristics may operate in affecting how a patient or therapist perceives the success of treatment. For example, both a therapist and a patient would likely be highly motivated to believe that treatment was useful after investing a significant amount of time and energy into the process. To overcome potential bias, outcome measures must be obtained in a variety of ways (e.g., direct observation, self-report, other report). Outcome measurements might include the viewpoint of the patient, of the therapist, and of significant others (e.g., spouse, boss, coworkers, parents), as well as that of impartial outside observers. Furthermore, reliable and valid instruments must be used in any attempt to measure outcome. Many instruments and programs have been developed to specifically measure treatment effectiveness as well as client satisfaction with treatment (e.g., Ellsworth, 1981; Murphy, Parnass, Mitchell, Hallett, Cayley, & Seagram, 2009; Nguyen, Attkisson, & Stegner, 1983; Overall & Pfefferbaum, 1962; Plante et al., 1995; Plante, Couchman, & Hoffman, 1998; Speer & Newman, 1996). The timing of the assessment is critical as well. Assessment of treatment effectiveness or outcome is needed not only at the termination of treatment but also during periodic follow-up sessions one to several years after treatment is completed (Craighead, Stunkard, & O'Brien, 1981; Jacobson, 1984; Speer & Newman, 1996). Treatment outcome measurements conducted at the end of treatment may reveal different results than

measurements conducted several weeks or months later.

Statistical versus Clinical Significance

To determine whether research hypotheses are supported, probability and statistical significance have been traditionally used in psychology as well as in most other scientific fields. Statistical significance refers to the very small probability of obtaining a particular finding by error or chance. The convention is that if there is less than a 5 in 100 times chance that the means of two groups come from the same population, then the null hypothesis (i.e., no difference) is rejected and the hypothesis of the study is supported. This is referred to as $p <$ .05; that is, the probability of error is less than 5%. A number of statistical techniques or tests can be used to derive this probability statement for a given study (e.g., t-test, analysis of variance, multiple analysis of variance). Statistical tests have also been developed to measure the size of a given effect beyond merely determining statistical significance. These tests measure what is referred to as *effect size*. Effect size reflects the strength or degree of impact a given result or effect has on the results of the study. The design and purpose of the study determine which statistical test is used.

Many researchers feel that demonstrating statistical significance in treatment outcome and other clinical psychology research is insufficient. They argue that researchers must be able to demonstrate clinical or practical significance in addition to statistical significance for a research finding to have meaning (Jacobson & Revenstorf, 1988; Kazdin, 1991; Kendall, Holmbeck, & Verduin, 2004; Kendall & Norton-Ford, 1982; Moleiro & Beutler, 2009). For example, a study was conducted to examine personality differences among 80 hospitalized clergy who sexually abused minors and 80 hospitalized clergy who did not sexually abuse minors (Plante, Manual, & Bryant, 1996). All the clergy were hospitalized in a psychiatric facility that specialized in the treatment of clergy. A number of psychological tests were administered to the patients, including both personality and cognitive tests. One of the findings of the study included a significant difference between the two clergy groups on a measure of over-controlled hostility from the Minnesota Multiphasic Personality Inventory-2 (MMPI-2). Over-controlled hostility refers to the tendency to try to suppress aggressive and hostile impulses. Using analysis of variance (ANOVA), the researchers found that the over-controlled hostility measure was significantly higher in the sexually abusive group ($p < .05$). Therefore, hospitalized clergy who sexually abused minors tended to experience more over-controlled hostility than those who did not sexually abuse minors. However, the actual mean score on over-controlled hostility for the sexual abusive group was 56, whereas for the non-abusing clergy it was 53. Although the difference between the two scores might be statistically significant if the study had used a large number of subjects, little practical or clinical significance can be obtained from these results. It would therefore be inappropriate for a clinician to use the over-controlled hostility measure as a screening instrument for sexual abuse based on this study. Another example might include measuring change in depression following a given treatment. Patients may have lower scores on measures of depression following treatment but still may feel depressed. While they may be less depressed than they were when they entered treatment and score significantly lower on a standard measure of depression (e.g., Beck Depression Inventory), they may still feel unhappy when they terminate treatment. It has been suggested that treatment outcome research use other criteria more relevant than statistical significance to determine treatment effectiveness (Kendall et al., 2004; Moleiro & Beutler, 2009). These criteria might include a return to pre-morbid or baseline level of functioning, change that results in improvement in social or occupational functioning, or the elimination of the presenting symptoms (Jacobson & Revenstorf, 1988; Kendall & Norton-Ford, 1982). Many investigators have

called for treatment outcome and other clinical psychology research to move away from the use of statistical significance as the only measure of success and to use more useful and practical measures such as evidence that the patient has moved from a dysfunctional to a more functional state (Kazdin, 1991; Moleiro & Beutler, 2009; Speer & Newman, 1996).

One method to mathematically define clinical significance is the use of the **reliable change index** (RCI; Jacobson & Truax, 1991). The RCI calculates the number of clients or patients who have moved from a dysfunctional to a more functional level of experience. The RCI measures the difference between post- and pretreatment scores and then divides by the standard error of measurement. The RCI thus examines the degree of change and the reliability of the measure to estimate the significance of the change in functioning. It is a valuable tool when used with good measurements (Kendall et al., 2004).

How Can Treatment Outcome Decisions Be Made When Studies Reach Different Conclusions?

Research investigations attempting to answer similar research questions often do not agree. Threats to both internal and external validity may play a role in what appear to be contradictory conclusions. Furthermore, research must be replicated in order to develop confidence in the conclusions obtained. One popular yet controversial method to examine all the research conducted on a given topic or question is the use of meta-analysis (Smith, Glass, & Miller, 1980). **Meta-analysis** is a statistical method for examining the results of a large number of research studies. Effect size, or result, is estimated by, for example, subtracting the average outcome score of a control group from the average outcome score of the treatment or experimental group and then dividing the difference by the standard deviation of the control group. The larger the effect size, the larger the treatment effect. For example, in a frequently quoted study of the use of meta-analysis for psychotherapy treatment outcome, Smith and Glass (1977) reported that the effect size for the studies they reviewed was 0.68 and concluded that the average patient would have a better outcome with psychotherapy than without psychotherapy about 75% of the time.

Many authorities have criticized the M. Smith and Glass (1977; Smith et al., 1980) studies for a wide range of procedural and statistical reasons (e.g., Landman & Dawes, 1982; G. Wilson & Rachman, 1983). Critics argue that only high-quality research studies should be used when conducting meta-analysis, and that using results from mediocre or flawed studies will result in erroneous conclusions—in other words, "garbage in, garbage out." In addition to statistical techniques such as meta-analysis, the development of a program of research examining research findings and designing additional studies to continue fine-tuning hypotheses is also used by researchers. A program of research allows one study to inform the development of a second study, which then informs the design and implementation of further studies in a step-by-step and organized manner.

What Is a Program of Research and How Is It Conducted?

One research study can never answer an important research question. Newspapers frequently report the results of a recently published study and make sweeping generalizations based on those results. For example, a study may report that oat bran lowers cholesterol or that drinking moderate amounts of red wine reduces the risk of heart attack. A single research study, however, rarely provides a full understanding of a particular phenomenon. Even the best designed and completed studies have limitations. Furthermore, replication is needed to ensure that the results are consistent and stable and not due to chance or unknown factors. Therefore, the understanding of various phenomena develops through a series of related research studies or programs of research rather than from a single study.

Agras and Berkowitz (1980) outlined a research program method to assist in gaining a better understanding of the treatment outcome of new intervention techniques. First, a new technique or procedure can be used in several case studies to determine whether it appears to be a reasonable intervention. Then short-term outcome studies can be designed to compare the new procedure to no treatment. If the short-term effectiveness of the procedure is supported, then studies can be designed to examine the most effective and efficient manner to utilize the procedure as well as to understand the basic ingredient that results in positive treatment outcome. The next step is to conduct field effectiveness research to determine whether the procedures developed and studied in a laboratory setting can be applied to various clinical settings (e.g., private practice, clinics). All the research designs and approaches discussed in this chapter (e.g., single case study designs, correlational designs, experimental designs) could be utilized in various stages to determine the usefulness of a new therapeutic technique or procedure. Usually these **research programs** start with

Table 4.3   **Different Levels of Research from Basic Research to Clinical Practice**

Level 1	Basic lab research on issues associated with behavior change.
Level 2	Analogue treatment research to examine elements of therapeutic approaches in controlled lab conditions.
Level 3	Controlled clinical research with actual patients.
Level 4	Clinical practice. Therapists assess outcome in case studies or clinical trials.

Source: Wilson (1981).

uncontrolled case studies and then lead from single case study designs to between-group designs with a small number of patients over a short period of time, followed by between-group designs with a large number of patients over a long period of time. Wilson (1981) also proposes a model of research that starts in the laboratory and ends in the consultation room of a clinician (Table 4.3).

Contemporary Issues in Clinical Psychology Treatment Outcome Research

Research conducted in clinical psychology has evolved to a high level of sophistication and complexity. Contemporary clinical psychology treatment outcome research involves much more than determining whether a particular treatment approach works relative to a control group conducted by a few therapists in one clinic location. While there are many fascinating current issues and trends in contemporary clinical psychology treatment outcome research, several selected compelling ones will be highlighted in this section. These include research regarding biopsychosocial approaches to psychopathology research, meta-analysis, empirically validated treatments, large comprehensive and collaborative multisite research projects, and large-scale community-wide interventions.

Biopsychosocial Approaches to Psychopathology Research

Research on psychopathology historically focused on specific and unidimensional influences on the development, maintenance, and treatment of psychopathology. Some researchers would focus on the biological influences while others would investigate psychological or social influences. Whereas many researchers continued their focus on the influence of a very specific variable on human behavior and psychopathology, researchers now recognize the complex influence of numerous interacting factors. As more and

more research has been conducted, complex and interactive biopsychosocial influences on psychopathology have been described, and research designs adapted to better study these complex interactions. Alcohol abuse is an excellent example of a complex biopsychosocial problem. Biological factors including genetic predisposition, physical dependency, and tolerance conspire with psychological vulnerabilities (e.g., depression, denial, stress) and social factors (e.g., friends gather at local pub, raised in family where drinking was excessive, media depictions of drinking as macho) to create the pervasive physical, interpersonal, intrapsychic, and work-related difficulties associated with alcoholism. Treatments are therefore largely multidimensional. In order to evaluate the efficacy of a treatment program that utilizes inpatient detoxification, group therapy, and antabuse follow-up (i.e., a medication that causes violent illness when combined with alcohol), a constructive treatment strategy research design may be applied. Thus, outcome measures would be taken at baseline, after the completion of inpatient treatment, then after the addition of group therapy, and finally, again after the addition of antabuse. Thus, the relative contributions of each component and their synergistic effects can be statistically analyzed and scientifically tested.

Depending on the specific research questions of interest to an experimenter, research investigating treatment outcome must take these biopsychosocial influences into consideration. For example, programs of research in these and other areas may use a variety of research design strategies to answer important questions. Although all of the designs discussed earlier may be used in a particular study, the comparative and constructive treatment strategies as well as longitudinal designs are often especially useful. These designs better reflect the types of complex questions asked of researchers in contemporary clinical psychology regarding the multiple influences on clinical problems.

Comprehensive biopsychosocial treatments often must intervene at multiple

Empirically Supported Treatments and the Tension between Research and Practice

Empirically supported treatments have taken the clinical psychology professional community by storm in recent years. Following the 1995 APA Division 12 (Clinical Psychology) task force report (APA, 1995d), numerous articles have been published about the pros and cons of empirically supported services. Nearly all researchers and clinicians would agree that clinical practice should be informed by the best available research evidence. However, great controversy exists regarding the ability of empirically supported and manualized treatments to adequately help actual clinical patients who can be highly unique in their biopsychosocial constellation of symptoms, life circumstances, motivation for change, support systems, and so forth. In general, many researchers insist that clinical practice should use only empirically supported treatments that closely follow treatment manuals. Practitioners generally resist manualized treatments, citing the highly unique needs of each client even if they share a similar diagnostic problem (Plante, Boccaccini, & Andersen, 1998). Recent writings and controversy about empirically supported treatments underscore the historical tensions between researchers (who rarely if ever treat real clinical patients in the real world) and clinicians (who rarely conduct or even read much of the empirical research literature).

Research that studies treatment for various clinical problems must use very clear procedures for the selection of patients and therapists, the administration of treatment, and the evaluation of treatment outcome and follow-up. Many have argued that the important experimental efforts to conduct high-quality research that maximizes the internal validity of the treatment protocol make it difficult if not impossible to generalize to the real world of clinical work. Therefore, efforts to increase internal validity often result in a decrease in external validity. For example, if we were interested in developing a quality empirically supported treatment for panic disorder, we would want to study those with this condition using a specific treatment protocol. David Barlow from Boston University has done exactly this and has published a variety of articles and treatment manuals about panic disorder (e.g., Barlow & Craske, 2000). If we used the standard protocol with Mary, the panic patient discussed throughout this text (see Chapter 5), we would find some difficulties in following the manualized treatment approach. For example, in addition to panic, Mary experiences a variety of other concerns and conflicts that need to be addressed when they emerge. She may experience a conflict with her husband or son that is not related to her panic symptoms and might wish to discuss them for a number of weeks rather than focusing on her panic symptoms. She may experience alcohol problems, marital difficulties, physical illness, and so forth that need attention. Since Mary, like most people who seek psychological services, experiences comorbidity and thus contends with several different diagnostic problems, it is often difficult to determine the use and effectiveness of various techniques when there are a number of target symptoms to work on at the same time. Mary may also not respond to all of the exposure and response prevention techniques offered in the panic disorder treatment manual. She may like or agree with some but not others. She may cooperate with some aspect of the treatment but not with all.

Variability in therapist skills, personality, and interests as well as variability in therapy conditions (e.g., managed care, private practice), and clients (e.g., comorbidity, ethnicity, race, gender, support systems) all interact in a way that may make the rigid use of empirically supported treatment manuals unrealistic and even undesirable in certain circumstances (La Roche & Christopher, 2008; M. Lambert, Bergin, & Garfield, 2004; Norcross, 2001, 2002; Norcross et al., 2006). Most critics and commentaries on empirically supported treatments tend to conclude that while the scientific emphasis on developing and investigating treatments that work are noble and worth pursuing, they must be tailored to the individual needs of clients and therapists in order to make them useful in the real and very complex world of clinical practice (APA, 2006; Beutler, Moleiro, & Talebi, 2002; Garfield, 1998; Ingram et al., 2000; Kazdin & Weisz, 2003; M. Lambert et al., 2004; Plante, Boccaccini, et al., 1998). Efforts are needed to bridge the gap between the scientists who develop and publish empirically supported treatments and the clinicians who need to treat complex clients with many different needs (DeLeon, 2003; La Roche & Christopher, 2008; Lilienfeld, 2007; Norcross, Beutler, & Levant, 2006; Sheldon, Joiner, Pettit, & Williams, 2003). The American Psychological Association (2006) has recently addressed this tension through the development of a Task Force and position statement regarding evidence-based practice that seeks to attend to quality clinical research findings yet also the clinical nuances faced by real people coping with real and often complex problems and treated by experienced professionals and not technicians.

---

levels and examine or account for multiple influencing factors. For example, treatment outcome research for schizophrenia must reflect realistic clinical practice and examine the role of medication, social support, individual, family, and group psychotherapy, vocational counseling, housing assistance, and other possible intervention strategies. Contemporary treatments rarely use one narrowly defined intervention strategy but rather attempt intervention at multiple biological, psychological, and social levels. Therefore, researchers now must follow suit and design research programs that take this complexity into account.

Meta-Analysis

As mentioned earlier, meta-analysis is a statistical technique that allows researchers to examine the results from numerous research studies. Ever since Smith and Glass (1977; Smith et al., 1980) conducted their landmark studies on the effectiveness of psychotherapy, meta-analytic approaches have been widely used in treatment outcome research. Because hundreds and perhaps thousands of research studies examining treatment outcome and other topics have been conducted over the years, this technique is especially useful in consolidating overall results across studies. Criteria are developed to determine which studies to include and which must be excluded. The measurement of effect size or the strength of a treatment effect relative to control conditions is determined for each study and evaluated with other studies. The use of well-designed and controlled research studies is fundamental to the meta-analysis technique (G. Wilson & Rachman, 1983). More and more research conducted in contemporary clinical psychology utilizes meta-analysis techniques (Kendall et al., 2004; Leichsenring & Rabung, 2008; Taylor & Harvey, 2009).

Comprehensive and Collaborative Multisite Clinical Trial Research Projects

Whereas clinical psychology treatment outcome research was conducted historically in isolated clinic, hospital, or practice settings by one primary investigator, contemporary research approaches use comprehensive and collaborative multiple sites in large-scale studies. Conducting collaborative research in many different sites across the country and using many different therapists enhances the external validity of treatment studies by representing more of a cross section of treatment situations. One of the best-known and most-often-cited comprehensive and **collaborative multisite research projects** in treatment outcome is the National Institute of Mental Health (NIMH) depression study (Elkin, 1994; Elkin, Parloff, Hadley, & Autry, 1985; Elkin et al., 1989). The NIMH study will be briefly discussed as an example of these research methods.

The goal of the 'NIMH depression study was to utilize a large-scale collaborative clinical trial study to evaluate the effectiveness of several brief treatments for depression. Large-scale collaborative clinical trials have been used frequently in medicine to investigate the effectiveness of medication and other medical interventions but had not been used in clinical psychology until this study. A collaborative

clinical trial is a well-controlled treatment outcome study in a wide variety of settings that provides support for the reliability, validity, and generalizability of results. The NIMH depression study compared cognitive-behavioral psychotherapy, interpersonal psychotherapy, and medication with case management for treating depression at three research sites (University of Pittsburgh, George Washington University, and University of Oklahoma) as well as at three training sites (Yale University, Clark University, and Rush Presbyterian–St. Luke's Medical Center). A medication with case management placebo control condition was also included. Two-hundred-fifty patients were randomly assigned to the four treatment conditions at the three research sites. Experienced clinicians were used as therapists in the study and were audiotaped to ensure that they followed treatment protocols. Results included assessment before, during, and after treatment. These results revealed that all treatments proved useful relative to the control condition. Medication resulted in a quicker treatment response but psychotherapy proved equally as effective as medication over time. Collaborative multisite treatment outcome studies have been conducted investigating other disorders such as panic and attention-deficit disorders (Sholomskas et al., 1990).

Photo: Courtesy Zach Plante.

Community-Wide Interventions

Contemporary clinical psychology research seeks to study and influence entire communities in addition to involving individuals

(Cohen, Stunkard, & Feliz, 1986). While there are many examples of research and intervention projects being conducted on a large-scale community level, the Stanford Heart Disease Prevention Program (Meyer, Maccoby, & Farquhar, 1980; Meyer, Nash, McAlister, Maccoby, & Farquhar, 1980) serves as an excellent example of this type of clinical research project. The purpose of the Stanford program was to alter health-damaging behavior in several California communities. Two towns were provided with an intense mass-media campaign to encourage residents to stop smoking and improve their diet and exercise in an effort to lower their risks of developing cardiovascular disease. Television, radio, mailings, and telephone contacts were all employed to attempt to help residents live a healthier lifestyle. A third town served as a control condition and thus was evaluated without any intervention.

In addition to mass-media appeals, specific behavioral instructions were provided to at-risk subjects. Results indicated that lower blood pressure and reductions in smoking occurred as a result of the community-wide intervention project (Meyer et al., 1980). Other **community-wide intervention** projects such as the Multiple Risk Factor Intervention Trial (MRFIT) following 320,000 men over 16 years and the North Karelia project in Finland have been used to alter high-risk behavior. Studies designed to minimize teen pregnancy, sexually transmitted diseases, and violence have been developed as well. In this way, clinical psychology has expanded its techniques to influence the behavior and health of entire communities.

Cross-Cultural Research

For too many years, research in clinical psychology (and psychology in general) used convenient samples of college students and then attempted to generalize findings to the wider community. For example, if a treatment or diagnostic procedure appeared to work well with a sample of Caucasian college students,

then it might be applied to clinical samples that are heterogeneous in terms of age, ethnicity, race, socioeconomic status, and so forth. In recent years, it has become clear that our increasingly multicultural community demands quality research that reflects the diversity of the general population (APA, 2003b; La Roche & Christopher, 2008; Rogler, 1999). Research studies must be designed that are sensitive to cultural, ethnic, racial, gender, and other differences. This has implications in terms of being sure not only that various groups are represented in the research studies but also that questionnaires and other assessment devices are in the appropriate language and that cultural traditions are respected. For example, having research associates or consultants from the culture being studied can often maximize the chances that quality multicultural research can be conducted successfully.

How and Where Is Research Conducted in Clinical Psychology and How Is It Funded?

Research in clinical psychology is conducted in numerous settings including colleges and universities, hospitals, outpatient clinics, independent research institutes, and even private practices. However, most clinical psychology research is conducted in academic settings such as colleges, universities, and university-affiliated medical settings or in institutions (e.g., clinics, hospitals).

Research is funded by various sources. Grants from government agencies such as the National Institute of Mental Health (NIMH), the National Institutes of Health (NIH), the Veterans Administration (VA), and the National Science Foundation (NSF) fund research in clinical psychology. In the United Kingdom, the Medical Research Council funds many projects. Private foundations such as the American Heart Association, the March of Dimes, the American Cancer Foundation, the John D. and Catherin T. McArthur Foundation, and the James T. Irvine Foundation also fund clinical psychology research projects. Many colleges, universities, hospitals, and corporations budget some money to provide small grants to researchers affiliated with their institutions. A researcher completes an application form and research proposal, hoping that his or her project will be selected for funding. Most national granting programs are highly competitive with only a small percentage being actually funded.

Often research can be conducted without grant money or other financial support. Many agencies allow some release time from clinical, teaching, or other professional responsibilities to allow time for research projects; they may also provide support such as secretarial time as well as photocopying, computer, and telephone services to assist in the completion of research projects. Finally, volunteers such as college and graduate students are often instrumental in helping to complete research projects.

How Are Research Results Communicated and Incorporated into Practice?

Completed research is usually communicated to the professional community through publication in scholarly professional journals and through presentation at international, national, and regional conferences. When a project is submitted to a professional journal, it is generally e-mailed to several experts in the field for peer review. Usually two to four professionals as well as the editor or associate editor of the professional journal carefully review the research paper to determine whether it is worthy of publication. To minimize potential bias, the reviews are sometimes conducted anonymously, with the authors' names and affiliations removed from the research paper while under review, and the names of the reviewers are withheld from the authors of the paper. The review process often takes three to eight months to complete before feedback is provided to the authors. The reviewers may accept the paper as written, or with revisions

requested, or they may reject the paper. If a paper is rejected, the authors usually incorporate the feedback of the reviewers to enhance the quality of the paper on subsequent investigation. Once a paper is accepted and the requested revisions are made, it can take several months to a year or more before the paper is published. Therefore, several years can elapse between the time a research project is submitted and when it is actually published. Authors are allowed to submit their research to only one professional journal at a time. Nor do they get paid for their article when it is accepted and published in a professional journal. In recent years, most professional journals have made great efforts to speed up the submission and review process. Many now allow electronic submission of articles and request faster electronic review of manuscripts by their consulting reviewers. Additionally, some professional journals have moved to an online format that also speeds up the publication process.

Whereas, this peer-review process has a number of disadvantages (e.g., the length of time for publication), advantages include careful review by experts in the field to maximize the chances that only high-quality and significant research is published. Although researchers are interested in learning more about their field of inquiry and sharing their findings with the professional community, regular publishing is generally expected and required for job retention (e.g., tenure) and promotion in academic, medical, and other settings. The well-known phrase "publish or perish" captures these publishing requirements and pressures. Of the numerous professional journals in clinical psychology, some are highly competitive, accepting few papers submitted to them by researchers; others are moderately competitive; and still others are fairly uncompetitive.

The peer-review process is also used for submissions to professional conferences. Most professional organizations at both the national and regional levels (e.g., American Psychological Association [APA], American Psychological Society, Western Psychological

Association, New England Psychological Association, Society of Behavioral Medicine) hold a yearly conference for their members and others interested in the field. Papers, posters, and symposiums are presented over several days in various cities across the country (for national organizations) or across the region (for smaller regional conferences). Research papers are submitted about six months prior to the conference and are reviewed by experts in the field.

Many have expressed concern that research findings tend to be communicated more to the research community than to the clinical community (e.g., APA, 2006; Addis, 2002; Beutler, Williams, Wakefield, & Entwistle, 1995; Fensterheim & Raw, 1996; Hayes, 2002; Nezu, 1996). For example, practitioners often do not read many of the professional scientific journals nor do they regularly attend national or regional conferences. Rather, they learn of new techniques and strategies by attending continuing-education workshops or hospital grand rounds presentations. Some argue that because research precision is so highly valued and many projects focus on such specialized areas of study, they are not useful to the average clinician practicing in the field. The dilemma is exacerbated by the fact that many researchers know few clinicians and many clinicians know few researchers. Hence, academic and clinical circles do not always overlap. This separation between research and practice has been an important issue in psychology since the field began in 1896 and continues to be a hotly debated topic (APA, 2006; Addis, 2002; Clement, 1996; Fensterheim & Raw, 1996; Hayes, 1996; Nezu, 1996; Rice, 1997).

Researchers often argue that some clinicians are misguided and uninformed in their efforts to help their patients and that quality research is needed to correct this problem (Davison & Lazarus, 1994; Garfield, 1994). Clinicians often feel that many research studies are oversimplified and that researchers are not in touch with the complicated challenges that clinicians face in trying to help their patients (Clement, 1996; Edelson, 1994;

Havens, 1994). However, some studies suggest that clinicians value research more than researchers generally believe they do, and that clinicians try to incorporate research findings into their practices, whereas researchers tend less often to incorporate the concerns of clinicians into their research (Addis, 2002; Beutler et al., 1995).

Several professional journals have been developed to specifically bridge the gap between research and practice (e.g., *Clinical Psychology: Science and Practice; In Session: Psychotherapy in Practice*). Talley, Strupp, and Butler (1994) proposed that research be made more relevant to clinicians by providing a therapeutic context for research results and interpretation, and that research funding be made more sensitive to the needs of clinicians. Stricker and Trierweiler (1995) and Clement (1996) suggested that clinicians bring the same rigorous scientific thinking and attitude to their practice as researchers bring to their experiments. Fensterheim and Raw (1996) suggested that clinical research and practice are such distinct areas that they should "deintegrate clinical research from clinical practice so that workers from each area can meet as peers, each accepting that the other has different modes of thinking, of researching, and respecting that difference" (p. 170).

The Big Picture

Research is fundamental to the goals and activities of clinical psychology. Research provides helpful answers to important questions about human nature and ways to improve the quality of life for many. For instance, quality research can be used to design studies investigating improved ways to assess and treat numerous clinical problems. Research can also help validate and fine-tune biopsychosocial models of psychopathology and treatment. Furthermore, research training helps to develop critical thinking skills that can be employed in both research and non-research activities and settings. Psychologists have developed a wide variety of sophisticated research design methods to use with various research and clinical questions. All of the different designs and research methods seek to study a particular issue of importance to clinical psychology while minimizing or eliminating potential research error and bias but maximizing internal and external validity. The scientific method is used in all areas of clinical psychology research and can be successfully employed in clinical practice as well as in research laboratories. Conducting high-quality, ethical, and useful research programs and incorporating these findings into the actual practice of psychologists is a challenging goal for contemporary psychology. Clinical psychologists who do not actually conduct research must be informed consumers of research in order to evaluate findings and incorporate the information into their clinical or other professional work. Future clinical psychologists will likely use more sophisticated research methods to answer more complex questions about the workings of the mind and behavior. These strategies will likely integrate methods and knowledge from other disciplines such as medicine, sociology, and epidemiology.

Key Points

1. Research is at the very foundation of clinical psychology. Basic and applied research provides many of the answers to important questions about diagnosis, treatment, and general human behavior, thus allowing both researchers and practitioners to use their techniques and theories with confidence. Research is fundamental to both the science and practice of clinical psychology.

2. The general goal of research in clinical psychology is to acquire knowledge about human behavior and use this knowledge to help improve the lives of others. Clinical psychologists use the scientific method in conducting their research activities. The scientific method is a set of rules and procedures that describe, explain, and predict a particular phenomenon.

3. Conducting an experiment is the typical and basic way to utilize the scientific method in answering research questions. Experiments must identify the independent and dependent variables, minimize experimenter error and bias, and maximize internal and external validity.

4. There are several types of extraneous variables that threaten internal and external validity, which must be considered and addressed in any research study. Threats to internal validity include the effects of history, maturation, testing, instrumentation, statistical regression, selection bias, and experimental mortality. Threats to external validity include testing, reactivity, multiple-treatment interference, and the interaction of selection biases.

5. There are many different approaches to constructing and carrying out a research experiment. Many of the different experimental designs offer unique advantages and disadvantages. These include experimental designs, quasi-experimental designs, between-group designs, within-group designs, mixed-group designs, analogue designs, case studies, correlational designs, epidemiological designs, cross-sectional designs, and longitudinal designs.

6. The cornerstone of true experiments that allow cause-and-effect statements is randomization. Randomization of subjects into experimental and control conditions is the hallmark of true experiments. However, randomization is often impossible in many clinical psychology research studies due to legal, ethical, and practical limitations.

7. Between-group designs use two or more separate groups of subjects, each of which receives a different type of intervention or no intervention in the case of a control condition. Therefore, the independent variable is manipulated by the experimenter in such a way that different groups of subjects receive different types of experiences that are being investigated.

8. Within-group designs examine the influence of the independent variable (such as treatment) with the same subjects over time. Therefore, subjects are not assigned to different experimental and control groups as they are in a between-group design but are all likely to experience the same research protocol. In within-group designs, comparisons are made with the same patient at different points of time, such as during a baseline or pretreatment period, during a treatment intervention period, and during a follow-up or post-treatment period.

9. Case studies provide an intensive observation of a person and phenomenon, which allows for hypotheses and theories to be developed. Case studies can be especially helpful when researchers and clinicians are interested in examining a new, rare, or unusual phenomenon, or during the early descriptive stages of a research program.

10. Analogue designs use procedures, subjects, and measures that approximate a real-life clinical situation and are usually conducted in a laboratory where experimental conditions can be controlled better than in the natural environment.

11. Correlational designs examine the degree of association between two or more variables. While correlational designs do not allow cause-and-effect conclusions to be made (e.g., treatment cured a problem), they do provide researchers and clinicians alike useful information concerning the degree of association between constructs of interest.

12. Cross-sectional studies provide a "snapshot" view of behavior at a given moment of time while longitudinal designs generally collect research data over a long period of time.

13. While clinical psychology research is conducted to investigate numerous research questions, the evaluation of treatment outcome is one of the most common areas of study. There are many different ways to conduct research on treatment outcome. Different strategies are employed depending on the specific research questions of interest. Kazdin (1991) has outlined seven specific research strategies for effectively evaluating treatment outcome research. These include the treatment strategy approach, the dismantling treatment strategy approach, the constructive treatment strategy approach, the parametric treatment strategy approach, the comparative treatment strategy approach, the client and therapist variation strategy approach, and the process research strategy approach.

14. Research in clinical psychology is conducted in numerous settings including colleges and universities, hospitals, outpatient clinics, independent research institutes, and even private practices. However, most research in clinical psychology is conducted in academic settings such as colleges, universities, and university-affiliated medical settings or in institutions (e.g., clinics or hospitals) that are affiliated with academic facilities.

15. One research study rarely results in a full understanding of a particular phenomenon being studied. Even the best-designed and -completed studies have limitations. Furthermore, replication is needed to ensure that the results of a particular study are consistent and stable and not due to chance or some unknown factor or factors. Therefore, understanding various phenomena occurs through a series of related research studies or a program of research rather than from a single study.

16. Contemporary clinical psychology treatment outcome research involves much more than determining whether a particular treatment approach works relative to a control group conducted by a few therapists in one clinic location. Current issues include biopsychosocial approaches to psychopathology research, meta-analysis, empirically supported treatments, large

comprehensive and collaborative multisite research projects, and large-scale community-wide interventions.

Key Terms

Analogue
Between group
Case study
Client–therapist variation
Collaborative multisite research projects
Community-wide intervention
Comparative
Constructive
Correlational
Cross-sectional
Dismantling
Empirically supported treatments
Epidemiological
Experimental designs
Experimental mortality
History
Instrumentation
Interaction of selection biases
Longitudinal
Maturation
Meta-analysis
Mixed group
Multiple-treatment interference
Parametric
Process
Quasi-experimental
Randomized clinical trials
Reactivity
Reliable change index
Research program
Selection bias
Statistical regression
Testing
Threats to external validity
Threats to internal validity
Treatment
Treatment outcome research strategy
Treatment package
True experiments
Within group

For Reflection

1. Why is research needed in clinical psychology?
2. What are the considerations that are needed to design a quality research experiment?
3. What are the different design methods used in clinical psychology and what are the advantages and disadvantages to each?
4. What are the different methods to conduct treatment outcome research and what are some of the advantages and disadvantages of each?
5. How are research ideas communicated?
6. How do research findings get incorporated into practical clinical activities such as professional practice?
7. How is research funded?
8. What are some advantages and disadvantages of the peer-review process for publishing research findings?
9. How can the need to maximize internal validity and external validity be balanced?
10. How are error and bias minimized in research studies?
11. Design a research study to investigate three treatments for depression.
12. Why is a program of research important and beneficial when compared with the results of one research study?
13. Why is meta-analysis used in research?
14. Why are biopsychosocial approaches needed in treatment outcome research?
15. What are some advantages of large-scale collaborative multisite research projects?
16. Why should research studies consider multicultural issues?

Real Students, Real Questions

1. How do professors and researchers choose what they want to research? Is it personal interest? Do they get suggestions by the

school or by the department of what topics to study?

2. When companies such as drug or tobacco producers offer research claiming their products are good, do they have valid tests and researchers to back them up? How do they get the results they want?

3. What is the process for getting a research grant?

4. How can the gap between researcher and clinician be bridged?

5. What is the influence of drug companies on research?

6. What's the average amount of time between starting a research study and seeing it in print?

7. Can you obtain a good sample of subjects by using ads in a local newspaper?

Web Resources

www.abct.org
Learn more about cognitive and behavioral approaches to treatment.

www.apsa.org
Learn more about psychodynamic approaches.

www.psychologicalscience.org
Learn more about the scientific side of clinical psychology from the American Psychological Society.

The Major Theoretical Models: Psychodynamic, Cognitive-Behavioral, Humanistic, and Family Systems

5

Chapter

Chapter Objective

To detail the four primary theoretical models used in clinical psychology and to apply these models to a clinical case.

Chapter Outline

The Four Major Theoretical Models in Clinical Psychology
Highlight of a Contemporary Clinical Psychologist: Marcia Johnston Wood, PhD
Understanding Mary from Different Theoretical Orientations

The field of clinical psychology in the contemporary era has been founded on four predominant theoretical models or orientations to the understanding and treatment of human difficulties. Theoretical models can be understood as worldviews or philosophies about human behavior that provide a conceptual framework for research, assessment, and treatment of psychological problems. These four psychological orientations include the psychodynamic, cognitive-behavioral, humanistic, and family systems models and each have received substantial research and clinical support. Whereas Chapter 3 introduced these theories and persons responsible for their development from a historical perspective, these fundamental psychological perspectives are reviewed in greater depth in this chapter in terms of how they are applied to actual clinical issues. Although each approach can be used to understand behavior in a wide range of settings, the use of each method in treatment of psychological and behavioral problems is highlighted here. Discussing how each approach is used in the treatment of behavioral problems helps illustrate the differences between them and how they can be applied to actual clinical problem areas. Keep in mind, however, that in contemporary science and practice, it has become increasingly difficult to adhere to one single **theoretical orientation** in considering all problems and questions regarding human behavior. Although some professionals still closely align themselves with one of these orientations, most psychologists today use a combination of these perspectives to fully understand and assist others. A sound knowledge of each of the four major theoretical models is essential to a thorough grounding in the building blocks of contemporary clinical psychology.

The theoretical models are used throughout the chapter to understand the panic and other problematic symptoms experienced by Mary, a middle-aged Caucasian woman presented in the case study.

The Four Major Theoretical Models in Clinical Psychology

The Psychodynamic Approach

The **psychodynamic** approach began with the work of Sigmund Freud. Often people assume that those who utilize the psychodynamic approach are Freudian and that they most likely look and act like Freud. People frequently picture a psychodynamic psychologist as a middle-aged or elderly man with a beard, sporting a tweed jacket replete with a pipe. They often envision someone who will analyze everything and require that their patients lie on a couch, talk about their relationship with their mother, and disclose all of their sexual fantasies. Various films and other media influences have perpetuated this stereotype of the psychodynamic therapist. This narrow stereotype of psychodynamically oriented professionals is obviously outdated and inaccurate. Psychologists of all ages, ethnicities, and both genders identify themselves as being psychodynamically oriented. While Freud is usually credited with being the founding father of the psychodynamic perspective, many neo-Freudians and other revisionists have greatly adapted, broadened, and challenged Freud's basic approach over the past 100 years. Freud, if alive today, might even be surprised (or appalled) to behold the array of current theories and intervention strategies utilized by modern psychodynamic psychologists.

The psychodynamic perspective maintains certain assumptions about human behavior and psychological problems (Table 5.1). First, the psychodynamic perspective holds that human behavior is influenced by *intrapsychic* (within the mind) drives, motives, conflicts, and impulses, which are primarily unconscious. Second, various adaptive and maladaptive ego defense mechanisms are used to deal with unresolved conflicts, needs, wishes, and fantasies that contribute to both normal and abnormal behavior. Third, early experiences and relationships, such as the relationship between children and their parents, play a

critical and enduring role in psychological development and adult behavior. Fourth, insight into these mostly unconscious influences combined with working through them (discussing and integrating them into everyday life) help to improve psychological functioning and behavior. Finally, the analysis of the *transferential* relationship that develops between the patient and therapist also helps to resolve conflicts and improve psychological functioning and behavior. **Transference** involves the projection of early relationship dynamics onto the therapist, who represents an authority figure similar to the patient's parents, for example. **Countertransference** involves projection by the therapist onto the patient in response to the patient's transference behavior.

The psychodynamic approach can be generally classified into several categories, including the traditional Freudian perspective, the revisionist perspective, and the modern object relations perspective. While there are numerous further divisions of psychodynamic theory, these three major views will be presented here.

Freud's Psychoanalytic Perspective: Freud's psychoanalytic perspective is often called *classical analysis* or *classical Freudian analysis*. Freud developed an understanding of human behavior based on three mental structures that are usually in conflict. The **id**, developed at birth, operates on the pleasure principle and represents all of our primitive wishes, needs, and desires. The **ego,** developed at about age one, operates on the reality principle and represents the rational and reasonable aspects of our personality helping us to adapt to a challenging world. Finally, the **superego,** developed at about age 5 following the successful resolution of the Oedipus complex, represents the internalization of familial, cultural, and societal norms and mores. The superego includes the *ego ideal* (the perfect image or representation of who we are and who we can become) and our *conscience* (the rules of good and bad feelings, thinking, and behavior). The conscience involves what we perceive to be "right" and "wrong."

Table 5.1   **Examples of Psychodynamic Techniques and Concepts**

Free association	Stating whatever is on the patient's mind without filtering. For example, Mary is encouraged to say whatever is on her mind, no matter how silly or embarrassing it may be to her.
Transference	Projecting the issues and dynamics between the patient and significant figures in his or her life (e.g., mother, father) onto the therapist. For example, Mary's feelings of love and longing for her father are projected onto her male therapist.
Insight	Better understanding unconscious influences and impulses. Making the unconscious conscious. For example, Mary learns that she really hates her mother and her panic is partially a guilt reaction to her wish that her mother died when she experienced episodes of panic.
Working through	Assimilating and incorporating new insights into daily life. For example, Mary learns to accept and cope with her new insight concerning the hate she experienced regarding her mother.
Dream analysis	Understanding the unconscious influence of dreams in everyday life. For example, Mary reports that she had a dream that she came to a therapy session and her therapist was not there to see her. In discussing her dream, she reports fears of being abandoned by her therapist as well as other important figures in her life.
Countertransference	Therapist responding to the transference of the patient through projecting their needs, wishes, and dynamics onto the patient. For example, Mary's therapist experiences Mary as being similar to his mother and behaves toward her as he would behave toward his mother.

Case Study: Mary

Mary is a 60-year-old Irish Catholic Caucasian woman who experiences panic, weight, and marital problems and lives with her husband. She is the mother of three adult children and has never worked outside of the home. She is significantly overweight. Following the death of her father from a cardiac arrest when she was 5, she was raised by a single mother who also suffered from panic attacks and was the eldest of two children, having a brother two years her junior.

Presenting Problem: Mary experiences frequent and severe panic attacks involving symptoms of rapid breathing, trembling, faintness, and intense fear. During these episodes, which occur only outside her home, she fears that she will die of a heart attack. Her symptoms have confined her to her home and several other "safe" locations such as her church and her daughter's house. She is also expressing some marital conflict centering around her perceived inability to work despite a recent financial setback in the home.

Inevitable conflict between the id, ego, and superego lead to anxiety and discomfort and the need to utilize ego defense mechanisms. **Defense mechanisms** are strategies developed by the ego to protect the person from these internal and mostly unconscious conflicts (Table 5.2). Thus, they help us cope, either adaptively or maladaptively, with the inevitable anxiety and discomfort associated with being human. There are a variety of

Table 5.2   **Examples of Ego Defense Mechanisms Using the Case Study of Mary**

Repression	Mary's hate of her mother is so anxiety and guilt provoking she does not allow these feelings to become conscious—keeping them repressed into her unconscious.
Denial	Mary denies having hateful feelings toward her mother.
Reaction formation	Mary's hateful feelings toward her mother are so powerful and frightening that she feels and behaves in a very loving manner toward her mother. She expresses a great deal of affection for her and has difficulty not being in close contact with her.
Projection	Mary's dislike of her mother is projected onto her female therapist, who she feels is cold, aloof, and uncaring.
Sublimination	Mary's hate of her mother has led her to channel these feelings into nonprofit organizations that work to prevent child abuse. She has become an active volunteer in efforts to help children who are abused by their parents.
Displacement	Mary's hate toward her mother cannot be channeled toward her for fear of retaliation along with the experience of extreme anxiety and guilt. However, Mary becomes very irritable and critical of her husband for no apparent reason.

ego defense mechanisms individuals can draw upon. Examples include **repression** (keeping unpleasant thoughts, feelings, wishes, and conflicts out of consciousness), **denial** (denying that problematic feelings, thoughts, or behaviors exist), *reaction formation* (consciously thinking or feeling the opposite of the unconscious impulse), *projection* (one's own unconscious conflicts, feelings, and drives are perceived in someone else), *sublimation* (channeling unacceptable impulses and desires into socially acceptable activities), and *displacement* (channeling unacceptable impulses toward less threatening sources). The maladaptive use of these defense mechanisms to cope with anxiety and conflict often leads to psychopathology.

Freud also outlined several **psychosexual stages** of development that he regarded as universal. These include the oral, anal, phallic, latency, and genital phases. Libidinal or life energies are channeled toward different areas of the body that demand gratification during each of these phases. Potential conflicts and problems can develop as a byproduct of fixations at any one of these stages. For example, one might become fixated at one stage of development (e.g., oral) due to

too much or too little stimulation during that stage. This fixation may then result in problems in adulthood such as smoking, eating, or drinking too much. Freud especially focused on the **Oedipus complex** (named after a character in the Greek tragedy, *Oedipus Rex*) that occurs during the phallic stage of development. Although one of Freud's most well-known theories, this complex notion was not a central feature of many of his writings. During the oedipal phase, a boy develops incestuous and murderous desires, wishing to be unified with his mother while necessarily eliminating his father. The resulting fears of retaliation and castration result in repression of these impulses and the use of reaction formation to identify with the father instead. Freud felt that a similar situation occurs for girls involving the desire for unification with the father and elimination of the mother. This female variation of the Oedipus complex is referred to as the *Electra complex* although Freud himself did not like or use this term.

The goal of Freud's approach was **insight** (understanding the unconscious factors that lead to problematic feelings, thinking, and behavior) and **working through** of the insights to improve daily functioning. The working-through process involves a careful and in-depth examination of the role of unconscious wishes, drives, impulses, and conflicts in everyday life. Techniques such as **free association** (saying whatever is on one's mind without censoring), dream analysis and interpretation, and the analysis of transference as well as everyday thoughts, feelings, and behavior were used to help understand and treat various problems. Furthermore, understanding and analyzing inevitable defensiveness and resistance to treatment is also a goal of psychodynamic therapy.

The Revisionist or Neo-Freudian Perspective:
The psychodynamic perspective proposed by Freud has been expanded and adapted in various ways by numerous theorists since the days of Freud. These revisions actually began during Freud's lifetime. Carl Jung (1875–1965) was one of the first members of Freud's inner circle to disagree with fundamental aspects of Freud's theory and develop a revision of the psychodynamic perspective. In fact, Freud had hoped that Jung would be his protégé and heir, carrying on his work after his death. Freud's disappointment with Jung's iconoclasm led to a great deal of bitterness and many angry letters between the two men.

Most adaptations of Freud's original theories focus on the role of development beyond childhood, the role of societal and cultural influences, and the role of interpersonal relationships, and involve a de-emphasis on unconscious and id-driven impulses and behaviors such as sexuality. Erik Erikson (1909–1993), for example, developed a lifespan perspective stating that psychosocial development continues far beyond the five psychosexual stages of childhood outlined by Freud. Alfred Adler (1870–1937) felt that Freud's emphasis on the id and sexuality as well as his underemphasis of the ego were critical flaws in his approach. Furthermore, unlike Freud, Adler felt that compensation for feelings of inferiority was very important in the formation of personality and psychological functioning. Carl Jung also rejected Freud's emphasis on sexuality. Furthermore, Jung emphasized spiritual influences as well as the role of the collective unconscious (symbols and innate ideas that are shared with our ancestors). Harry Stack Sullivan (1892–1949) focused on the role of interpersonal relationships in personality and psychological development. Karen Horney (1885–1952) took issue with Freud's theories of penis envy and the role of women.

The contributions of these neo-Freudians, or **revisionists,** significantly diverged from Freud's original theories. Fundamentally, Freud's emphasis on the id was deemphasized among the revisionists, who developed theories that focused more on the functioning of the ego. Thus, the theories of many of the revisionists have become known as forming the basis of ego psychology. Furthermore, most of the revisionists agreed that the role of interpersonal relationships was fundamental in the development of personality and psychological functioning. Finally, the revisionists generally agreed that psychological development continues beyond the early years addressed by Freud. These aspects of the revisionists' theories set the stage for current object relations theory.

The Object Relations Perspective:
Even though Freud's psychoanalytic theory focused heavily on early childhood experiences, he never once treated a child in psychoanalysis. Freud made inferences about childhood development and experiences through his analysis of adult patients who reflected on their childhoods. Critics of Freud often state that because his theories were based on his experience of treating a small number of upper-class and primarily adult female patients in Vienna during the Victorian period rather than on more broad and scientifically based research and experience, his theories are suspect. One of the first psychoanalytic writers who focused on the direct treatment of children was Melanie Klein (1952). Klein felt that the internal emotional world of children focuses on interpersonal relationships rather than on the control of impulses and drives. Klein and several colleagues including W. R. D. Fairbairn (1954)

and Margaret Mahler (1952) became known as the British School of object relations theory, whereas the American contributions of Otto Kernberg (1975, 1976, 1984), James Masterson (1981), and Heinz Kohut (1971, 1977, 1984) further developed **object relations** theory in the United States. Object relations theorists have been especially influential in further developing and fine-tuning current psychodynamic theory, research, and practice.

The object relations theorists view infants as being relationship or *object* seeking rather than pleasure seeking. The early relationship with the mother provides the framework for the development of the sense of self. Thus, attachment to the mother provides the structure and approach for the development of psychological functioning and future relationships. Through interactions with the mother during breast feeding and other activities, the child internalizes, or *introjects* various qualities of the person or object with whom he or she is interacting. The child then separates, or *splits* these internalized aspects of the mother into various positive (the good rewarding mother, or the "good breast") and negative (the bad or punishing mother, or the "bad breast") aspects. Attachment to the mother may be either secure or insecure. These divisions provide a template for future interactions with the world in general. Therefore, if the mother–child relationship is primarily negative and filled with unsatisfying and frustrating experiences, the child is likely to have a difficult time developing an adequate and positive sense of self or achieving satisfying and trusting intimate adult relationships. Therefore, object relations theorists tend to view behavior as a manifestation of early childhood experiences with the mother and other important figures in the child's life. Object relation theorists, however, generally neglected the influence of the father–child relationship. The early relationship foundation develops the sense of self as well as a framework for negotiating all future interpersonal relationships.

Psychodynamic professionals today are likely to focus on early childhood experiences and relationships, the enduring personality structure of a person, and the influences of unconscious fantasies, wishes, and impulses. The analysis of dreams, transference, and resistance with the goal of increased insight into the unconscious are still important goals of current psychodynamic approaches. Psychodynamic psychotherapy historically would take years to conduct and involve four or five sessions each week. More recent psychodynamic theorists have developed short-term treatments (Goldfried, Greenberg, & Marmar, 1990; Horowitz, Marmar, Krupnick, Wilner, Kaltreider, & Wallerstein, 1984; Laor, 2001; Rappoport, 2002; Strupp & Binder, 1984), which focus on the application of psychodynamic principles in treatment over the course of several weeks or a few months. Research has found that these brief psychodynamic treatments are effective (E. Anderson & Lambert, 1995). In fact, brief psychodynamic psychotherapy is considered to be an empirically supportive treatment by the American Psychological Association (APA) when applied to opiate dependence and depression (Chambless et al., 1996).

The Behavioral and Cognitive-Behavioral Approaches

The behavioral psychologist is often thought to control and manipulate behavior by giving reinforcements (such as M&M candies) to people when they behave in a desired manner and punishments (such as electric shocks) when they behave in an undesirable manner. Sometimes people assume that psychologists who are behavioral in orientation are not warm and caring and that they have little interest or tolerance for non-observable behavior such as feelings and fantasies. Popular films also help to perpetuate the image of a cold, aloof, mechanistic behaviorist concerned with specific behaviors rather than individuals. Similar to the stereotype of the psychodynamic professional, the stereotype of the behaviorist is also outdated and inaccurate.

Both behavioral and cognitive (thoughts and beliefs) focuses make up the broad behavioral/cognitive-behavioral perspective. Although some would argue that the behavioral and cognitive-behavioral viewpoints are separate, in this review, I combine these perspectives because they are generally more similar than divergent in their assumptions about human nature and behavioral change. Furthermore, the cognitive-behavioral approach generally draws on behaviorism rather than cognitive neuroscience or cognitive psychology. However, many contemporary cognitive theorists use cognitive science and information processing methods to enhance their theories and applications. I refer to the cognitive-behavioral perspective as including both the strictly traditional behavioral perspective (the theories of B. F. Skinner) as well as the newer cognitive perspective. Like the psychodynamic approach, the cognitive-behavioral approach subsumes a wealth of subperspectives associated with specific leading authors who develop and advocate certain theories and techniques. These leaders in cognitive-behavioral psychology include Albert Ellis, Aaron Beck, Arnold Lazarus, Leonard Krasner, Joseph Wolpe, B. F. Skinner, Donald Meichenbaum, Marsha Linehan, among others.

The cognitive-behavioral approach is historically based on the principles of learning and has its roots in the academic experimental psychology and conditioning research conducted by B. F. Skinner, John Watson, Clarke Hull, Edward Thorndike, William James, Ivan Pavlov, and others. The cognitive-behavioral approach focuses on overt (i.e., observable behavior) and covert (non-observable behavior such as thinking) behaviors acquired through learning and conditioning in the social environment (Table 5.3). Basic assumptions that provide the foundation of the cognitive-behavioral approach include a focus on current rather than past experiences, the emphasis on measurable and observable behavior, the importance of environmental influences on the development of both normal and problematic behavior, and an emphasis on empirical research methods to develop assessment and treatment strategies and

interventions. Cognitive-behavioral perspectives include principles of operant conditioning, classical conditioning, social learning, and attribution theories to help assess and treat a wide variety of difficulties (Table 5.3). For example, operant conditioning may be used to help a child improve his or her behavior and performance in a classroom setting. A child might obtain reinforcements such as stickers or social praise from the teacher for improved classroom behavior that is defined, for example, as being more attentive, talking less with peers during classroom instruction, and improving test scores. **Contingency management** (changing behavior by altering the consequences that follow behavior) and **behavioral rehearsal** (practicing appropriate behavior) may also be used. Classical conditioning techniques might be used to help someone overcome various fears and anxieties. Someone who is fearful of dogs, for example, might learn to overcome this fear through the use of systematic desensitization (a technique developed by Wolpe, 1958), **counterconditioning** (developing a more adaptive response to dogs), or by **exposure,** such as a gradual approach to being with dogs. Social learning might be used to help a child undergoing a painful medical procedure (such as a bone marrow transplant) to cope with the anxiety and pain associated with the procedure. For example, the child might watch an educational video of other children who cope well with the medical procedure. Furthermore, longstanding and maladaptive beliefs may contribute to many psychological problems such as depression and anxiety. Maladaptive irrational and automatic thoughts such as, "I'm a failure," "No one will love me," and "I can't do anything right," might be examined, challenged, and altered using cognitive-behavioral techniques such as **thought stopping** and rehearsal of positive self-statements. There are numerous cognitive-behavioral techniques that may be employed to help assess and alter behavior. Each of these general frameworks (classical, operant, social learning, and cognitive) is reviewed next.

Table 5.3   **Examples of Cognitive–Behavioral Techniques and Concepts**

Contingency management	Changing behavior by altering the consequences that follow behavior. For example, Mary takes the bus after the friendly bus driver and her children offer social praise.
Counterconditioning	Developing a more adaptive response to environmental stimuli. For example, Mary does aerobic exercise when feeling anxious rather than taking anti-anxiety medication.
Exposure	Gradual or all-at-once approach to the feared situation or stimuli. For example, Mary is encouraged to gradually take longer and longer bus rides.
Behavioral contract	An agreement between therapist and patient that outlines specific consequences of behavior. For example, Mary agrees to decrease coffee consumption by two cups per week until she no longer drinks caffeinated coffee.
Participant modeling	Demonstrating the desired behavior for the patient. For example, Mary watches others confidently learn to drive a car without fear before she tries to do the same.
Behavioral rehearsal	Practicing how one might handle a given problem situation. For example, Mary frequently practices diaphragmatic breathing techniques so that they become automatic.
Thought stopping	Stopping irrational or defeating thoughts by interrupting the negative or problematic pattern of thinking (e.g., yelling ''stop'' to oneself, snapping an elastic band around the wrist) and inserting more positive and adaptive thoughts (e.g., ''I can handle it, I'm as worthy of love as anyone else''). For example, Mary stops her thoughts that she cannot handle walking into the bank by yelling ''stop'' to herself when she finds herself engaged in maladaptive and negative thinking, and inserts more positive thoughts in their place, such as ''I enjoy my new-found independence by going to the bank anxiety free.''

The Classical Conditioning Perspective: The **classical conditioning** perspective originated with the work of Ivan Pavlov as well as the work of Joseph Wolpe and Hans Eysenck. This viewpoint maintains learning occurs, and subsequently behavior, through the association of conditioned and unconditioned stimuli. Thus, two or more random events (stimuli) that are paired together become associated over time. For example, a psychologist using the classical conditioning perspective with Mary might examine the pairing of Mary's panic and fear with going to church, the grocery store, and the bank. When Mary had her first panic attack at church, she associated the church with the uncomfortable and frightening feelings that accompany panic, thereby causing her to avoid the church in the future. Panic attacks in other places such as the grocery

store, on the bus, and in the bank all become associated through classical conditioning, resulting in more and more avoidance of various places. Furthermore, generalization occurs; for example, although Mary may have had a panic attack at one specific branch office of a bank, she feels fearful of entering any bank. A therapist using a classical conditioning approach may choose to treat Mary's anxiety with *systematic desensitization* (SD; Wolpe, 1958). The therapist would ask Mary to create a hierarchy of anxiety-provoking situations from less-anxiety-provoking situations such as walking on the sidewalk outside of her home to extremely anxiety-provoking situations such as flying in an airplane. The therapist would train Mary in a relaxation procedure and then pair relaxation with each of the anxiety-provoking situations that she would imagine. Thus, each step of the hierarchy would be paired with re-laxation using classical conditioning strategies.

The Operant Perspective: The **operant perspective** of the behavioral approach originated with the work of B. F. Skinner. This viewpoint maintains that all behavior can be understood through a functional analysis of antecedents (the conditions present just before a target behavior occurs) and consequences (what occurs following the target behavior) of behavior. This is often referred to as *functional behavioral analysis* or the *A-B-Cs* of behaviorism: *antecedents, behavior, consequences.* Thus, behavior is learned and developed through interaction with the environment. If behavior is reinforced in some way, it will continue, while behavior that is punished or not reinforced will be diminished. The gradual shaping of desired behavior is achieved by reinforcing small increments toward the target behavior. Problematic behavior, such as aggressiveness in children, fears and phobias, and overeating can be altered by changing the reinforcements associated with the target behavior (Plaud & Gaither, 1996). For example, a psychologist using the operant perspective might be concerned that Mary, the patient with panic disorder, might receive reinforcement for her panic behavior (e.g., not having to work, attention from her husband and other family members). Intervention might include an analysis of the antecedents (the conditions present just before her panic symptoms) and consequences of her panic behavior followed by reinforcement of desired behavior (e.g., praise when Mary has no panic symptoms while taking a bus). The reinforcement would likely include shaping the successive approximations of targeted behavior toward the goal of engaging in specific activities outside of the home such as food shopping and other errands.

The Social Learning Perspective: The social learning perspective originated with the work of Albert Bandura. This viewpoint maintains that learning occurs through observational or vicarious methods. Thus, behaviors can be learned and developed by watching others perform various behaviors rather than

by practicing a behavior or being personally reinforced for a given behavior. For example, someone might learn to avoid walking through a surprisingly deep puddle by watching someone else get uncomfortably wet when they walk through it. The psychologist working with Mary might use the **social learning** perspective in understanding how Mary learned panic behaviors from her mother, who also had panic attacks. Mary's mother might have been reinforced for her panic behavior through attention, distracting family members from other problems or conflicts, and avoiding work or household chores. Thus, by observing her mother, Mary may have learned that panic behaviors result in a variety of secondary gains such as avoiding things you do not want to do.

The social learning perspective also incorporates the role of expectations in behavior development. For example, Julian Rotter (1954) proposed that behavior develops as a byproduct of what someone expects to happen after they make a given response. The importance of the desired outcome also impacts the likelihood of that behavior. For example, someone will pay a large sum of money and dedicate several years of his life to obtain a college degree because he expects that a college degree will result in a satisfying career and life. Thus, Mary avoids the grocery store, the bank, and her church because she expects that she will experience a panic attack at these locations. The fear of having a panic attack is so great that she makes a great effort to avoid these places.

An important variation concerning the role that expectations play in behavior involves the concept of **self-efficacy** (Bandura, 1986). Self-efficacy refers to the belief that one can successfully perform a particular behavior. For example, someone is more likely to kick a field goal in football or make a free throw in basketball if the person believes that he or she can accomplish these athletic tasks. Thus, confidence in one's ability to successfully accomplish a task results in greater likelihood of success in the given task. Mary is more likely to take the bus to the grocery store if she believes that she will be able to adequately cope with her anxiety by practicing positive self-statements such as "I can handle this," employing breathing techniques, and feeling confident that she can shop with minimal stress.

The Cognitive Perspective: Beliefs, Appraisals, and Attributions: The cognitive perspective originated with the work and writings of several professionals, notably including Aaron Beck and Albert Ellis. The cognitive perspective suggests that our beliefs, appraisals, and attributions play a significant role in behavior and behavioral problems. Appraisals include the manner in which we examine or evaluate our behavior. For example, if a soccer player thinks her athletic abilities are mediocre, she will evaluate all of her successes and failures in this light. If the soccer player has an exceptionally great game, she may attribute her good fortune to luck or poor performance on the part of the opposing team. If Mary feels that her attempts to develop more independence are hampered by marginal skills and motivation, she will more likely fail.

Attributions refer to theories regarding the causes of behavior. We generally make attributions about behavior based on several factors. These factors include the concepts of the internal versus external locus of control as well as situational versus dispositional characteristics. Internal locus of control refers to feeling that we have control and influence over much of our life experiences while external locus of control refers to feeling that we have very little control or influence over what happens to us. For example, success in life due to hard work and being smart reflects an internal locus of control, whereas luck or fate reflects an external locus of control.

Situational factors refer to external influences impacting behavior, and *dispositional* factors refer to enduring characteristics of the person impacting behavior. For example, driving through a red light without stopping due to distraction from a heated conversation with a passenger would reflect a situational attribution, whereas driving through the red light because the person is a careless and reckless driver would reflect a dispositional attribution. Thus, a professional football player might attribute missing an easy field goal to distraction from a loud audience or from the sun in his eyes (external locus of control), low self-esteem or anxiety during the game (internal locus of control), having a bad day (situational), or being a bad player in general (dispositional). Depression and learned helplessness can develop, for example, in people who make frequent dispositional and internal locus of control attributions about their perceived problematic feelings and behavior (Rosenhan & Seligman, 1989; Seligman, Peterson, Kaslow, Tanenbaum, Alloy, & Abramson, 1984). For example, Mary feels depressed and hopeless believing that she will never get over her panic attacks because she experiences her fears as being due to her long-term "character flaws" and "weaknesses."

Albert Ellis (1962, 1977, 1980) and other professionals have focused on irrational beliefs and self-talk that lead to problematic feelings and behavior. For example, common beliefs such as "everyone should agree with me," "everyone should appreciate me and my talents," "no one could love someone as unattractive as me," and "I should always be patient with my children and spouse" result in inevitable failure and disappointment. Ellis and others use techniques such as rational-emotive therapy (RET) to help individuals think and process beliefs in a more rational manner. These techniques involve using logic and reason to challenge irrational and maladaptive thoughts and beliefs (e.g., "So do you really think that everyone you meet must like you in order to be a worthy human being?"). This approach relies on persuasion and reason to alter beliefs about self and others. For example, Ellis's focus on irrational beliefs is related to Mary's beliefs about her panic. Mary feels that if she experiences even a little anxiety while taking a bus or sitting in church, she is a failure and a weak person. The therapist helps Mary to see that her beliefs are irrational and unrealistic and encourages her to develop more adaptive self-talk regarding her anxiety (e.g., "Even if I'm anxious, I can still overcome my fear and take the bus. I don't need to have my anxiety control me; I can control it").

Aaron Beck (1963, 1976) developed *cognitive therapy* (CT) to treat depression and other disorders. Beck posits that as people develop, they formulate rules about how the world works that tend to be simplistic, rigid, and often based on erroneous assumptions. A schema or template develops to the extent that all new incoming data is filtered through these rules and distortions. Thus, overgeneralization (e.g., "everyone at work hates me"), all-or-none thinking (e.g., "If I don't get this job my career will be ruined"), or exaggeration or downplaying the meaning or significance of events (e.g., "my divorce was no big deal and didn't affect me or my children at all") are typical ways of interpreting our world and experiences. Problematic behavior and attitudes are associated with these unrealistic and erroneous rules and interpretation of events. Like Ellis, Beck evaluates and challenges these beliefs and assumptions and trains people to monitor and alter their automatic thoughts. However, Beck focuses on the treatment of beliefs as hypotheses that must be tested and evaluated to best determine whether the beliefs are useful and realistic.

A variety of variations on cognitive-behavioral psychotherapy has emerged over the years. For example, Marsha Linehan developed *dialectical behavior therapy* (DBT) to treat people experiencing borderline personality disorders (Linehan, 1993). DBT uses cognitive-behavioral strategies along with psychodynamic, client-centered, family systems, and crisis intervention perspectives. DBT focuses on acceptance of self and experiences along with efforts toward behavioral change. These changes are sought through a three-stage process that includes a pretreatment commitment phase, an exposure and emotional processing phase of past events, and a synthesis phase integrating progress from the first two stages to achieve treatment

goals. A related, fairly new approach is *acceptance and commitment training* (ACT) developed by Steven Hayes (Hayes, 2008; Hayes & Smith, 2005). ACT blends elements of cognitive behavioral therapy with mindfulness and relational frame theory. It seeks to increase psychological flexibility and improve behavior by integrating cognitive defusion skills, acceptance, mindfulness, and behavior change. An additional example includes David Barlow's *panic control treatments* (PCT) developed to help those experiencing panic attacks (Barlow & Craske, 2000). In PCT, patients are exposed to the sensations that remind them of their panic attacks. For example, patients would participate in exercise to elevate their heart rates or shake their heads to create dizziness. Attitudes and fears about these induced panic-like symptoms are explored and demonstrated as harmless to the patient's health. Furthermore, patients are taught breathing and relaxation exercises to help reduce anxiety.

The Humanistic Approach

The stereotype of the **humanistic** practitioner typically conjures a warm and supportive individual who does not provide any direct advice or suggestions to his patients. The stereotype of the humanistic psychologist involves an individual who, although friendly, says little more than "*hmmm . . .*" and benign comments such as "I hear you" or "I feel your pain." Images of encounter groups or T-groups from the 1960s might emerge. Again, like the behavioral and psychodynamic orientations, stereotypes about the humanistic approach are also outdated and inaccurate.

The humanistic approach has its roots in European philosophy as well as in the psychotherapeutic work of Victor Frankl, Carl Rogers, Abraham Maslow, Rollo May, Fritz Perls, and other mental health professionals. In rejecting the basic assumptions of the psychodynamic and behavioral theories, the humanistic theorists assume a *phenomenological* approach that emphasizes each individual's perception and experience of his or her

Table 5.4   **Examples of Humanistic Concepts and Techniques**

Active listening	Intense listening to the patient using paraphrasing, summaries, reflection, and other techniques.
Empathy	Conveying a sense of being heard and understood.
Unconditional positive regard	Fully accepting the feelings and thoughts of the patient.
Congruence	Being genuine in behavior.
Self-actualization	Innate movement toward growth and fulfilling one's potential.
Peak experiences	Moments when self-actualization is reached.

world (Table 5.4). The humanistic perspective tends to view people as being active, thinking, creative, and growth oriented. Helping others is partially accomplished through understanding concerns, feelings, and behavior through the eyes of the patient. Humanistic professionals tend to assume that people are basically well-intentioned and that they naturally strive toward growth, love, creativity, and self-actualization. Self-actualization helps to produce the forward movement in life toward greater growth, peace, and acceptance of self and others. Rather than focusing on the influences of the past, humanistic theorists focus on the "here and now" or present. The client-centered approach of Carl Rogers, the humanistic approach of Abraham Maslow, and the Gestalt approach of Fritz Perls will be briefly reviewed next. Of course, there are many additional perspectives and variations of these approaches. However, the contributions of Rogers, Maslow, and Perls have been the most influential within the humanistic perspective.

The Client-Centered Perspective: The **client-centered** perspective of Carl Rogers stands out as the most classic example of the humanistic approach. Rogers used nondirective techniques such as **active listening, empathy,** congruence, and unconditional positive regard to understand and help others. Rogers felt that sincere empathy was needed in order for people to feel accepted and understood, and ultimately to enable growth to occur. **Unconditional positive regard** refers to the belief that no one should be negatively

judged or evaluated in the therapy experience or elsewhere. Rather, respect and acceptance should prevail. Unconditional positive regard can be a challenge for professionals working with individuals who have attitudes or behaviors that one finds offensive (e.g., sexual abuse of children, stealing, racist comments). Unconditional positive regard does not mean that these behaviors or attitudes are accepted as being okay. Rather, it is the person who is fully accepted. Therefore, respect and a nonjudgmental attitude are advocated. **Congruence,** or genuineness, refers to harmony between one's feelings and actions. Thus, the professional should strive toward emotional honesty in his or her relationship with others. Genuineness also implies that the professional will not try to hide his or her feelings from others, yet still presents a professional attitude and demeanor. Rogers was also instrumental in developing ways to assess treatment process and outcome. This included an individualized assessment technique such as the Q-sort (sorting a variety of cards with descriptive feelings into several categories) to assess functioning and outcome. The client-centered approach maintains that people have an innate drive toward growth. Because the development of the self and attempts at growth are often met with various social consequences (such as praise or punishment), individuals may develop patterns of behavior that are inconsistent with growth. For example, a parent may wish that his child will eventually take over the family accounting business. However, the child may be very creative and prefer to pursue interests in music and dance. The parents may exert pressure on the child through conditioned love to pursue education and skills in accounting and business rather than the creative arts. The child, wishing to please his parents may do so, but at a high price in terms of incongruence with his self-actualizing motive and potential. Mary, for example, may feel "boxed into" her role as housewife and mother. She actually had harbored a strong interest in joining religious life as a nun. However, her parents more highly valued family life and encouraged her to get married and have children, thus discouraging her call to religious life. This conflict with her family resulted in incongruence, causing her to feel trapped, out of control in her life, and possibly, more prone to anxiety.

Maslow's Humanistic Perspective: Abraham Maslow (Maslow, 1954, 1971) originated a further variation of the humanistic approach. He emphasized the importance of **self-actualization,** which refers to the impulse and desire to fully develop one's potential. His focus on self-actualization highlighted the role of unmet needs. He felt that humans have a hierarchy of needs beginning with basic biological requirements for food, water, and warmth. Once these needs are met, one is free to focus on higher level needs such as safety and security. Again, as these higher level needs are met, one can then focus on needs for love, belonging, and acceptance. Finally, at the top of the hierarchy is self-actualization. Maslow believed that people who experienced self-actualization were characterized by an acceptance of themselves and others, efficient perceptions of reality, social interests, creativeness, mystical or **"peak" experiences,** as well as other qualities (Maslow, 1971). Although Maslow believed that everyone has the potential to achieve self-actualization, few were thought to succeed because of unmet needs at lower levels. Maslow felt that less than 1% of the population ever reach self-actualization. Therefore, problems in feelings, thoughts, behavior, and relationships emerge because many people are deficiency-motivated in that they are trying to fulfill unmet needs. Maslow referred to those moments

when self-actualization is actually reached as peak experiences. Although Maslow's theories have received a great deal of attention and acceptance, he offered little in terms of specific techniques to use in psychological assessment or treatment.

The Gestalt Perspective: The **gestalt** perspective within the humanistic approach originated with the work of Fritz Perls (Perls, 1947, 1969). Assumptions of the gestalt approach include the notion that problems occur due to our inability to be truly aware of our current feelings, thoughts, and behavior and to our inordinate focus on the past and future rather than the present. The gestalt approach focuses on being keenly aware of one's here-and-now or present experience. The gestalt approach seeks to help people live in the immediate moment by frequently requesting that people work toward an awareness of current thoughts and feelings. Taking personal responsibility for one's feelings, thoughts, behavior, and choices is also of paramount importance for those using the gestalt perspective. Techniques include making believe that an important someone such as a spouse, boss, or mother is in the room with you sitting in an empty chair. Talking to the person as if they were there helps someone become better in touch with feelings and behavior. For example, Mary might be asked to pretend that her mother is in the room with her. The gestalt therapist might encourage Mary to talk with her mother as if she was sitting in an empty chair in the office. Mary would be asked about her immediate feelings and thoughts as she spoke with her mother in the room.

An example of a more contemporary approach to humanistic models includes self-determination theory (Deci & Ryan, 2002; Sheldon et al., 2003). The approach focuses on three fundamental psychological needs of humans: competence, autonomy, and relatedness. Nurturing these three needs tends to result in more psychological wellbeing, moving a person toward self-actualization (Sheldon et al., 2003). The theory is used to provide autonomy support with clients. This suggests that the therapist fully respects the selfhood of the client, taking his or her perspective and allowing for maximum freedom. The therapist is encouraged to see the world through the eyes or worldview of clients and ensure that their autonomy and choices are respected so that the therapist is not telling them what to do and how to do it. Although it is not a directive approach, it encourages therapists to give clients a variety of informed and reasonable options to choose from with respect to their desires to move in directions that support their freedom to choose.

The Family Systems Approach

The **family systems** approach emerged to overcome the limitations of other perspectives seeking to work only with the identified individual patient. The family systems approach emerged from research and treatments geared to address problems associated with interpersonal communication among schizophrenic patients and between family members. As mentioned in Chapter 3, the family systems approach began with the Bateson group in Palo Alto, California, during the 1950s.

The goals of the family systems approach commonly include improved communication among family members and a de-emphasis on the problems of any one member in favor of attention to the family system as a whole. Family systems professionals meet with all family members rather than with just the person who has the identified problem(s). Family systems professionals might also involve extended members of the family or other significant figures in the life of the family such as neighbors, friends, and teachers in their therapeutic work. Family systems perspectives maintain a systemic view of problems and relationships. That is, they suggest that any change in the behavior or functioning of any one member of the family system is likely to influence other members of the system. Therefore, even if improved psychological functioning and behavior is achieved in individual members, others must adjust to

and contribute to these new changes in family functioning. Paradoxically, improvements among some family members may lead to problems among other family members. For example, if Mary becomes less fearful and more independent, she may no longer need her husband to drive her around town for errands. Her husband would then lose an important and powerful role in his relationship with his wife, perhaps feeling somewhat uncomfortable and even threatened by her new-found independence. This change might result in marital discord that may encourage Mary to relapse into her panic behaviors.

Like the previously reviewed approaches, there are many variations of the family systems approach identified with individual professionals (Table 5.5). These include, for example, the communication approach of Virginia Satir, the structural approach of Salvador Minuchin, the strategic perspectives of Jay Haley and Milton Erickson, and the narrative approach of Michael White. While there are many other perspectives within family systems, five main orientations are briefly presented.

The Communication Approach: The communication approach was developed by Virginia Satir (1967) and colleagues at the Mental Research Institute (MRI) in Palo Alto, California.

The approach suggests that problems in effective communication contribute to family problems and dysfunction. Unspoken and unreasonable expectations, rules, and assumptions about how family members should relate to one another and live their lives result in conflict and problems in family functioning. Satir outlined several communication styles in families, which include placating, blaming, superreasonable, irrelevant, and congruent. In problem families, the father may be *superreasonable,* maintaining a rational style and keeping his feelings to himself. The mother may placate the father by agreeing with him and not expressing her feelings. One of the children may use a *blaming* style, attributing all of his or her problems in school and at

Table 5.5   **Examples of Family Systems Concepts and Techniques**

Reframing	Altering the way one understands and interprets a given behavior. For example, Mary's panic might be reframed as an attempt to engage her husband in her life and assist him in feeling more manly.
Paradoxical intention	Prescribing the problematic symptom in order to combat resistance to treatment. For example, ask Mary to schedule a number of panic attacks each day.
Joining	Therapist attempts to connect with the family and become part of the family unit rather than act in a detached observer manner in the sessions.
Enmeshment	Over- and maladaptive involvement in the lives of family members. For example, Mary's overinvolvement in her son's life results in her being highly critical of all work and relationship decisions that he makes that are not consistent with her interests.
Disengagement	Over-detachment of one family member from others. For example, Mary's daughter has little interest in activities and functioning of the family and prefers to stay out of any emotional involvement with the family.

home to someone else. *Irrelevant communication* might involve annoying habits on the part of a sibling. Satir encourages family members to embrace *congruent communication,* which focuses on expressing genuine feelings.

A communications approach may encourage Mary to express her true feelings more directly about needing to be taken care of by her husband. Her panic behavior might be viewed as a way to communicate a need for attention and care by her husband and others. Her husband may be encouraged to express his feelings about his need to feel important and useful in the relationship. Taking care of Mary during panic episodes may be a way to feel powerful and important in the relationship.

The Structural Approach: The structural approach was developed by Salvador Minuchin (1974) and focuses on altering and restructuring the pattern of relationships between family members. The structural perspective focuses on appropriate and adaptive levels of **differentiation, enmeshment,** and **disengagement** among family members (Minuchin, 1974; Minuchin & Fishman, 1981). For example, a mother and daughter may be overly enmeshed with each other, resulting in distance and disengagement in the father. Furthermore, the daughter's overinvolvement

in her mother's life and troubles may make it difficult for her to develop satisfying peer relationships and levels of independence. The mother's overinvolvement with her daughter may result in less interest and energy for her relationship with her husband. Due to dysfunctional family patterns, conflicts and problems emerge within the family unit as a whole. The **structural** perspective emphasizes more functional, balanced, and hierarchical family relationships. The therapist may actually rearrange seating in the therapy session in order to join the family and to alter the structure of family dyads and interactions. For example, Mary may be overly involved with her son, resulting in resentment from her daughter and husband. Furthermore, her son may feel that her overinvolvement makes it difficult for him to develop more independence and greater connection with his father. The therapist might try to assist Mary in disengaging from her son (starting by having her sit away from her son during the session) and engaging more with her daughter and husband.

The Milan Approach: In the **Milan approach,** the professional is viewed as an integral part of the family system or unit (Boscolo, Cecchin, Hoffman, & Penn, 1987).

Positive Psychology

Clinical and other specialties in psychology have focused on *positive psychology* in recent years (Keys & Haidt, 2003; Seligman, Ernst, Gillham, Reivich, & Linkins, 2009; Snyder & Lopez, 2009). Positive psychology is the "scientific study of ordinary strengths and virtues" (Sheldon & King, 2001, p. 216). During Dr. Martin Seligman's year as the president of the American Psychological Association in 1998, he developed a variety of initiatives to focus on positive psychology (Seligman & Csikszentmihalyi, 2000). He and others felt that psychology too often focused on problems such as child abuse, violence, major psychopathology, and other significant problems in society without enough efforts to understand what is good and right about humans and human relationships. Positive psychology focuses on topics such as hope, love, ethics, optimism, resilience, happiness, spirituality, forgiveness, and other noble aspects of human behavior. While historically clinical psychologists have focused much of their professional activities and energy on the diagnosis and treatment of psychopathology and significant problems experienced by individuals, couples, families, and groups, recent efforts in positive psychology have tried to better train clinical psychologists and others to appreciate what we know about these more positive human qualities and ways that we can maximize human experience. For example, the benefits of spirituality and religious faith for mental and physical health have received a great deal of professional and popular attention that can be applied to all sorts of concerns and issues (Plante, 2009; Plante & Sherman, 2001; Plante & Thoresen, 2007). Much of the research examining happiness can be applied to help others maximize the chances that they can be happy regardless of the stressors they face (Myers, 2000). For example, resilient people are not necessarily those who experience the least amount of stress but are those who have coping strategies and personality styles that tend to help them deal better with the stressors that come their way relative to less resilient people (Masten, 2001; Seligman et al., 2009). The new emphasis on positive psychology will hopefully help clinical psychologists better help those who come to them for counseling and consultation and help the public learn more about what is right about the human condition (Snyder & Lopez, 2009). Positive psychology has become so popular that a new journal (*Journal of Positive Psychology*) was developed in 2006 and expanded in 2009.

The Milan approach highly values neutrality as well as acceptance and respect for the family system. The Milan approach uses hypothesizing as well as positive, logical connotation (Selvini Palazzoli, Boscolo, Cecchin, & Prata, 1980) to assist in better understanding family dynamics. Hypothesizing helps to better understand the function and dynamics of the family, whereas positive, logical connotation reframes the behavior of the family in more positive and accepting terms.

The Milan school also encourages the use of a team approach. For example, family systems professionals using the Milan approach might request that Mary bring her entire family to the treatment sessions. While a therapist meets with Mary's family, several colleagues observe the session using a one-way mirror. Efforts at hypothesizing and positive, logical connotation would be aimed at a better understanding of family interactions and a more acceptable, positive reframing of family issues. The treatment team discusses the session as it occurs and offers suggestions to the therapist working with the family via a telephone in the treatment room. Following the session, the family might be invited to observe the treatment team as they discuss the session with the treating therapist. The Milan school also uses "rituals," asking the family to behave in certain prescribed ways between sessions.

The Strategic Approach: The **strategic** approach was developed by Jay Haley (1973, 1987) and others such as Milton Erikson (1980) to help professionals deal more effectively with resistance in their work. The approach utilizes very active and direct involvement by the clinician. The strategic perspective maintains that any attempt to change a member or set of members within a family system will be met with resistance and sabotage (conscious or unconscious). Therefore, the professional must find ways to combat this resistance by directing and altering the behavior of the family. One of the most common and well-known examples of a strategic intervention involves the use of paradoxical techniques. Paradoxical approaches are often referred to by the general public as "reverse psychology."

Paradoxical techniques involve prescribing the symptom of concern in an exaggerated form and so it appears to contradict the goals of intervention. For example, a child who terrorizes the family with frequent and intense temper tantrums might be encouraged by the professional to yell and scream louder: "Yell louder—I don't think you are trying hard enough and I'm sure people in the next room cannot hear you." Strategic theorists believe that since people resist direct interventions to

change the family system, the clinician can assist others in reaching intervention goals by asking the client to do the opposite of those goals. For example, a strategic therapist might encourage Mary to schedule her panic attacks throughout the day and to never leave her house. Since resistance can be expected, Mary would likely have difficulty scheduling frequent panic attacks and have trouble staying in her home. Therefore, the ultimate goals of therapy (decreased panic and increased independence) are likely to be met. Using these paradoxical techniques is both controversial and risky (e.g., asking an anorexia nervosa patient to further decrease food consumption could be ill-advised and tantamount to malpractice).

Strategic techniques assume that people will be resistant to the suggestions. They also assist the client in being more aware of the undesirability of the problematic behaviors as well as provide the client with a greater sense of control. For example, Mary may find it dull to stay home all day beyond her usual at-home schedule and she may wish to do something other than have a panic attack at the therapist's prescribed time of day.

Another technique utilized by strategic clinicians is reframing. Reframing involves reinterpretation of a behavior or issue in a new and different light. Therefore, behaviors considered negative by the family may be reinterpreted as being positive. For example, a child who steals might be viewed as trying to alert the family to her emotional deprivation and neediness. Mary's panic behavior might be reframed as being an attempt to stay close to her husband and to help him feel more powerful and masculine. An adolescent who has run away from home and made poor choices could be viewed as "doing the wrong things for the right reasons" (i.e., increased independence).

The Narrative Approach: The **narrative** approach (White, 1986; White & Epston, 1990) holds that family members conceptualize their problems and concerns through a series of stories about their lives and various members of the family system. Using techniques such as externalizing and relative influence questioning, professionals assist family members in relating their stories in a more objective manner, allowing them to take a less negative and blaming approach to family problems. The narrative approach highlights the restraining influence that certain ideas and stories place on people. For example, an abusive male may feel that women are property and that they should have less power and influence than men. He may feel that he protects his weak, unstable, and inferior wife and that she would be in a great deal of trouble trying to survive without him. He may describe their relationship as one where he constantly protects her while she resists his efforts. These myths and worldviews influence his behavior toward women. Mary and her family might be asked, for example, to relate their story of Mary's mother's panic attacks and the role Mary's mother had in the development of family relationships and activities. They may be asked to discuss family stories about Mary's mother and examine what beliefs and myths play a role in current family functioning.

Highlight of a Contemporary Clinical Psychologist

Marcia J. Wood, PhD

Photo: Courtesy
Marcia J. Wood

Dr. Wood works in a part-time private practice, is President of the Oregon Psychological Association, and is the mother of two children.

Birth Date: 1956

College: Williams College, 1979 (English)

Graduate Program: Long Island University, Clinical Psychology, 1987

Clinical Internship: Yale University School of Medicine

Postdoctoral Fellowship: New York Hospital–Cornell Medical Center

Current Job: Private Practice, Portland, OR

Pros and Cons of Being a Clinical Psychologist:
Pros: "(1) Emotional and intellectual stimulation; (2) satisfaction and interest in helping people understand and change their lives; and (3) flexible schedule and autonomy."

Cons: "(1) At times emotionally draining and anxiety provoking (e.g., suicidal clients); (2) always "on call" (unless away on vacation and arrange coverage with colleagues); and (3) people's resistance to change."

Future of Clinical Psychology: "The need for psychotherapeutic help is not going to disappear and I hope that health-care reform includes improved access for mental health needs and is included in primary care as well as specialized settings. As more outcome and therapy research is done, therapies are becoming more tailored to effectively address particular diagnostic groups and problems so they can be targeted more specifically to match a client's needs."

Nature of Practice: "I see older adolescents, adults, and couples in psychotherapy. Rarely, family members may attend a session if it is helpful to the client. I see many clients who are depressed, suicidal, have relationship problems, grief, parenting, or other life problems/issues to solve, as well as clients with personality disorders, bipolar disorder, schizoaffective, and so on. Frequently my clients (most often for mood disorders or anxiety) are also on psychiatric medication so I coordinate treatment with a psychiatrist, LPN, or other primary-care doctor. Occasionally, I have to help arrange hospitalization for a severely depressed or suicidal client.''

Which theoretical models do you generally find most helpful in your work? ''I was trained psychodynamically. While that still forms the basis of my work, the longer I have been in practice, the more I incorporate and use theoretical as well as practical elements of other models; objection relations, interpersonal, and cognitive theories and therapies are the primary other influences on my work.''

Can you give an example of how your theoretical model impacted what you did with a patient? ''I had begun to treat a young woman in her late twenties who had been chronically depressed most of her life. She spent the first several sessions mostly 'complaining,' and telling me all the reasons that everything I suggested wouldn't work, or that she had already 'tried those suggestions with many previous therapists and they didn't work.' I became slightly confrontive about her resistance and tried to clarify what she wanted out of therapy. Her response was that she just wanted 'someone to complain to,' someone who would listen to her long list of complaints and not try to 'push or change her.' My next response was even more confrontive until I began to reflect on it over the next couple of sessions. At this point I began to wonder about secondary gain for her maintaining a depressed stance, but I also began to speculate that her stated complaint wasn't being addressed in the right way or at the right developmental level. This led me to substantively change my stance to be much more supportive and empathic, without the expectation that she look more rigorously at changing anything or doing anything different, yet. My reflection had led me to consider more strongly

the role and impact of early disrupted object relationships for her, in other words, that the pathological relationships with her family members had never provided a safe and secure holding environment. This led me to consider the reparative work that might need to precede a more confrontive approach, which was focused on later trauma and dynamics. This change in approach proved very helpful and under the guise of 'listening to her complain' and not challenging or pushing this client too far or too fast, we worked on early relationship issues through the therapy relationship, laying the groundwork for continued later progress. Without my shift to emphasize the perspective of both object relations and interpersonal therapy, I think this client would have dropped out of therapy after the first couple of months and would have added mine to the long list of unsuccessful therapies she had experienced.''

Typical Schedule: ''Three days a week I work during the school day and one day a week I work from mid-afternoon through mid-evening, to accommodate clients who cannot take time out during the day. One Friday every two months is a full-day Oregon Psychological Association Board meeting. Every other week there is an hour lunchtime conference call with OPA's Legislative Committee. The one morning and one full day a week I do not work I make sure to get in workouts for myself and often have lunch with friends or colleagues.''

8:45	Psychotherapy patient: 20-year-old Caucasian woman experiencing depression with suicidal thinking.
9:30	Psychotherapy patient: 30-year-old Caucasian woman experiencing post-partum depression and parenting issues.
10:15	Psychotherapy patient: 43-year-old Latino woman experiencing relationship and work conflicts associated with a personality disorder.
11:15	Psychotherapy patient: 29-year-old Caucasian man experiencing anxiety, depression, and spiritual issues.

1:00   Psychotherapy patient: 41-year-old Caucasian man with bipolar disorder coming to grips with the aftermath of first major bipolar break.

1:45   Couple in their fifties working on commitment issues in the aftermath of one partner's extramarital affair.

3:00   Pick up children from school and do "mom time" and other after-school activities almost every day.

5:00   Spend a couple of hours on work-related e-mail. At least 90% of this is related to my role as President of the Oregon Psychological Association, and less than 10% with clients.

Understanding Mary from Different Theoretical Orientations

One of the major theoretical models frequently is applied to clinical cases encountered by practicing psychologists. Mary's case study will be presented and separate psychodynamic, cognitive-behavioral, humanistic, and family systems formulations applied to illustrate the use of these models in actual practice. It is important to note the unidimensional nature of the formulations presented, as they further illustrate the usefulness of integration and multidimensional intervention subsequently emphasized in Chapter 6.

Psychodynamic Formulation and Plan

Mary's panic attacks and agoraphobia (fear of leaving home and other safe places) date back to the intense anxiety and guilt associated with the loss of her father during the heightened attachment of the oedipal period of development. Mary has not worked through this loss, so this interrupted attachment has led to tentative object relations, a view of the world as unpredictable and dangerous, and intense insecurity and lack of ego strength, which manifests in overt panic away from home, church, and other secure attachments. Mary's

own mother's depression and anxiety after her husband's death may have rendered her emotionally unavailable to Mary, thus heightening Mary's oral dependency needs and weight problem. Psychoanalytically oriented treatment would focus on working through the loss of her mother. Transference themes involving ambivalent attachment to the therapist (i.e., conflicting feelings of neediness and fear of loss), anger at anticipated loss and rejection, and the desire to be emotionally nurtured likely will be areas of focus leading ultimately to greater trust in relationships, a strengthened ego, and the ultimate resolution of her symptoms.

Cognitive-Behavioral Formulation and Plan

Mary's panic and agoraphobia are the result of learned behavior modeled by her own mother's struggle with these behaviors. Mary learned a set of beliefs through her mother's example: The world was not safe, sudden death was imminent, and she had little resources with which to cope independent of the help of others. Mary and her mother also attained significant reinforcement for their symptoms, as their confinement to home, inability to work, and dependent behaviors successfully solicited assistance, nurturance, and protection from others. Treatment would best incorporate cognitive-behavioral techniques involving exposure, response prevention, shaping, and reinforcement. Thus, Mary would be encouraged to recreate her symptoms of panic in the therapist's office, and develop strategies to interrupt and overcome these symptoms. She would be encouraged to gradually expose herself to feared situations, such as taking a bus or going alone to the store, and learning that each situation does not result in panic. Her therapist will teach her relaxation techniques such as diaphragmatic breathing to afford her tools for alleviating her own symptoms if and when they occur. Reinforcers, such as her family's admiration and praise and greater freedom to leave home, will encourage healthy behavior. A behavioral program could also be implemented to assist Mary with weight loss. Thus, a set of cognitive-behavioral interventions will be useful in reducing Mary's symptoms of panic, agoraphobia, inability to work, and obesity.

Humanistic Formulation and Plan

Mary's panic mirrors her existential anxiety and phenomenological experience of the world as lonely and risky. Mary has been deprived of support, empathy, and validation for her internal experience, and by feeling disempowered, has not assumed responsibility for herself and her life. Humanistic therapy would involve a highly supportive and empathetic approach wherein the therapist listens with respect and positive regard for Mary without judging or pathologizing her experience. The therapist would encourage Mary to express all of her feelings, fears, and beliefs while supportively affirming her experience and gently helping her move toward assuming greater levels of acceptance and responsibility for herself.

Family Systems Formulation and Plan

Mary, the identified patient, is manifesting symptoms of a larger dysfunctional system. Mary's family of origin encouraged dependent behavior in the service of keeping family members closely tied to one another. In Mary's present family, Mary's dependent role is supported by her husband and children in several ways. First, generational boundaries have been altered such that Mary's children assumed a parentified role in taking care of her, affording them a closer alliance with their father and a relief from their mother's threatened anxiety attacks. Mary's husband had been empowered in his role as Mary's driver, escort, and sole breadwinner, until recent financial circumstances threatened the

family system. Treatment would involve family sessions with the entire family initially and later with Mary and her husband. A strategic intervention might involve having Mary's family members insist on escorting her everywhere and helping her with everything, exaggerating her symptoms to the point where these interactions become unbearably smothering, resulting in her insistence on independence. Her symptoms could be reframed as forms of communication. Instead of expressing panic, Mary could be encouraged by family members to explicitly state the intended communication, for example, ''I need to know that I am cared about.'' Generational boundaries would be restructured such that Mary and her husband unite in the parental role and enable the children to assume less responsibility for Mary's needs in the future.

Conclusion

The case example of Mary explicates how each of the four major theoretical models might be applied toward understanding and treating problematic behavior. Each school of thought has strengths and weaknesses and makes some contribution to both understanding Mary's concerns and offering intervention strategies. However, the reality of contemporary psychology involves integrative ideas and efforts. For example, it may be useful to provide cognitive-behavioral interventions to Mary in the context of a supportive therapeutic relationship that assists her in resolving the death of her father and developing a heightened sense of self-efficacy. Involving her husband in the treatment may also have numerous benefits. Collaboration with medical professionals, her priest and church community, and other resources may provide a comprehensive and perhaps optimal treatment approach. All of these efforts must be evidence based as well. Chapter 6 fully expands this theme of integration in contemporary clinical psychology and explores the advances and applications of integrative perspectives to emotional and behavioral problems that are evidence based.

The Big Picture

Theoretical approaches provide a comprehensive framework for understanding behavior and planning intervention. Whether a psychologist is conducting research, teaching, or providing clinical services, using a theoretical approach helps to provide competent and theory-driven strategies. Without these perspectives, a professional would "wing it" each time he or she engaged in professional activities, deprived of useful guidelines for direction in his or her work. Some professionals mistakenly maintain rigid adherence to a particular approach, hoping that it can be universally applied to each and every situation and person. Strict adherence to a theoretical approach can result in limited, rigid views of human behavior and behavioral change and cult-like zealousness. Whereas each approach has its advantages for understanding behavior and offers ideas for intervention, this limited view might lead a psychologist to overlook important alternatives to understand, explain, and treat patients and thus fail to provide effective assessment and treatment.

Some perspectives lend themselves to research better than other approaches. For example, research has been extensively conducted on assessment and treatment using the behavioral approach while much less research has been conducted using the humanistic/existential approach. The vast majority of empirically validated treatments favor the behavioral approach. However, it would be incorrect to suggest that the behavioral approach is the superior approach. Each of the four major psychological perspectives offers a helpful way to view human behavior and useful strategies for assessment and intervention. Furthermore, all four approaches have been enormously influential in contemporary clinical psychology and have been integrated into current theory and practice.

The evolution of clinical psychology has witnessed increasing integration of various theoretical perspectives. While some argue that integrating approaches is a mistake and akin to mixing apples and oranges, more and more psychologists are integrating various theoretical perspectives and techniques with success. Biological, psychological, and sociological factors clearly influence emotional, behavioral, and interpersonal functioning. Furthermore, as more research and clinical experience help to uncover the mysteries of human behavior, approaches need to be adapted and shaped in order to best accommodate these new discoveries and knowledge. The future will likely further expand the biopsychosocial perspective by better understanding the interplay between biological, psychological, and social influences on behavior and targeting interventions that better suit these influences.

Key Points

1. Theoretical approaches are worldviews or philosophies about human behavior. They provide a psychologist with a conceptual understanding of why humans behave as they do, and a coherent structure for conducting research, assessment, treatment, and consultation concerning emotional, behavioral, or interpersonal problems. As clinical psychology has evolved over the past several decades, more integrative perspectives have emerged.

2. The psychodynamic perspective suggests that human behavior is influenced by intrapsychic drives, motives, conflicts, impulses, and other largely unconscious forces. Various adaptive and maladaptive defense mechanisms are used by the ego to deal with conflicts, needs, wishes, and anxieties. Early experiences and relationships are viewed as playing a critical and enduring role in development and adult behavior. Insight into these mostly unconscious influences, as well as the working-through process, help to improve psychological functioning and behavior. The psychodynamic method subsumes Freud's psychoanalytic approach, the revisionist approaches, and object relations theories.

3. Basic assumptions that comprise the foundation of the cognitive-behavioral

approach include: emphasis on current rather than past experiences and measurable and observable behavior, the importance of environmental influences on the development of both normal and problematic behavior, and empirical research methods to validate assessment and treatment strategies. Operant conditioning, classical conditioning, social-learning, and cognitive perspectives represent variations within the cognitive-behavioral perspective.

4. The humanistic perspective assumes a phenomenological approach that emphasizes the person's perception and experience of his or her world. The humanistic perspective tends to view people as being active, thinking, creative, and growth oriented. Helping others is partially accomplished through understanding concerns, feelings, and behavior as viewed by the patient. Humanistic therapists tend to assume that people are basically well intentioned and that they naturally strive toward growth, love, creativity, and self-actualization. The humanistic perspective includes the client-centered approach, Maslow's hierarchy of needs, and the gestalt approach.

5. The family systems approach focuses on improved communication among family members and a de-emphasis on the problems of any one member of the family. The family systems approach emphasizes systems theory, that is, any change or problem in one aspect of the system impacts and alters other aspects of the family system. Structural, strategic, Milan, and narrative methods represent some of the variations within family systems theory and practice.

Counterconditioning
Countertransference
Defense mechanisms
Denial
Differentiation
Disengagement
Ego
Empathy
Enmeshment
Exposure
Family systems
Free association
Gestalt
Humanistic
Id
Insight
Joining
Milan approach
Narrative
Object relations
Oedipus complex
Operant
Paradoxical technique
Peak experience
Psychodynamic
Psychosexual stages
Reframing
Repression
Revisionists
Self-actualization
Self-efficacy
Social learning
Strategic
Structural Superego
Theoretical orientation
Thought stopping
Transference
Unconditional positive regard
Working through

Key Terms

Active listening
Behavioral rehearsal
Classical conditioning
Client-centered
Cognitive-behavioral
Congruence
Contingency management

For Reflection

1. What are theoretical approaches in clinical psychology and how are they used?
2. What are the advantages and disadvantages of using theoretical approaches?
3. What are the advantages and disadvantages of integrating theoretical approaches?

4. Compare and contrast the psychodynamic, cognitive-behavioral, humanistic, and family systems approaches. What are the strengths and weaknesses of each approach?
5. How does the Freudian approach differ from the revisionist and object relations approaches?
6. How does the operant approach differ from the classical conditioning and social-learning approach?
7. How does the cognitive approach differ from the strict behavioral approach?
8. How does the client-centered approach differ from the gestalt approach?
9. How does the structural approach differ from the strategic approach?
10. Who are the founders of the psychodynamic, cognitive-behavioral, humanistic, and family systems approaches?
11. What unique contribution is provided in understanding behavior and offering assessment and intervention strategies for each of the major theoretical approaches?

Real Students, Real Questions

1. Integration of approaches seems much harder than just using one approach with everyone. Is it?
2. What kind of tensions exist between different professions regarding integrating approaches?

3. How does the integrative biopsychosocial approach mesh with the emphasis on empirically supported treatment approaches?
4. How can you use the humanistic approach if the patient is a sociopath or someone who has done terrible things like murder or child abuse?

Web Resources

www.americanheart.org
Learn more about heart disease from the American Heart Association.

www.cancer.org
Learn more about cancer from the American Cancer Society.

www.adaa.org
Learn more about anxiety disorders.

www.ocfoundation.org
Learn more about obsessive-compulsive disorder.

www.abct.org
Learn more about cognitive and behavioral approaches to treatment.

www.apsa.org
Learn more about psychodynamic approaches.

http://www.ppc.sas.upenn.edu/
Learn more about positive psychology.

Integrative and Biopsychosocial Approaches in Contemporary Clinical Psychology

Chapter Objective

To highlight and outline how contemporary clinical psychology integrates the major theoretical models using a biopsychosocial approach.

Chapter Outline

6

Chapter

Having now reviewed the four major theoretical and historical models in psychology in Chapter 5, this chapter illustrates how integration is achieved in the actual science and practice of clinical psychology. In addition to psychological perspectives per se, a full integration of human functioning demands a synthesis of psychological factors with both biological and social elements. This combination of biological, psychological, and social factors comprises an example of contemporary integration in the form of the biopsychosocial perspective. This chapter describes the evolution of individual psychological perspectives into a more comprehensive biopsychosocial synthesis, perhaps first touched upon 2,500 years ago by the Greeks.

The Call to Integration

While there are over 400 different types of approaches to psychotherapy and other professional services offered by clinical psychologists (Karasu, 1986), the major schools of thought reviewed and illustrated in Chapter 5 have emerged during the past century as the primary perspectives in clinical psychology. As mentioned, these include the psychodynamic, cognitive-behavioral, humanistic, and family systems approaches. Prior to the 1980s, most psychologists tended to adhere to one of these theoretical approaches in their research, psychotherapy, assessment, and consultation. Numerous institutes, centers, and professional journals were (and still are) devoted to the advancement, research, and practice of individual perspectives (e.g., *Behavior Therapy* and *International Journal of Psychoanalysis*). Professionals typically affiliate themselves with one perspective and the professional journals and organizations represented by that perspective (e.g., Association for Behavioral and Cognitive Therapies), and have little interaction or experience with the other perspectives or organizations. Opinions are often dogmatic and other perspectives and organizations viewed with skepticism or even disdain. Surprisingly, psychologists with research and science training sometimes choose not to use their objective and critical thinking skills when discussing the merits and limitations of theoretical frameworks different from their own. Choice of theoretical orientation is typically a by-product of graduate and postgraduate training, the personality of the professional, and the general worldview held of human nature. Even geographical regions of the country have been historically associated with theoretical orientations among psychologists and other mental health professionals. For example, the psychoanalytic approach has been especially popular in the northeastern part of the United States, and the behavioral approach has been especially popular in the midwestern and southern parts of the United States.

However, unidimensional approaches have been found to be lacking and of limited use in their approach to the full spectrum of psychological problems. Research has generally failed to demonstrate that one treatment perspective is consistently more effective than another for all patients (Beckham, 1990; Lambert, Shapiro, & Bergin, 1986; Luborsky et al., 2002; Messer & Wampold, 2002; Norcross & Goldfried, 2005; Smith et al., 1980). About 45% of the improvements in psychotherapy, for example, may be attributable to common factors found in all major theories and approaches (Lambert, 1986). Furthermore, some research has suggested that less than 15% of treatment outcome variance can be accounted for by specific techniques (Beutler, Mohr, Grawe, Engle, & MacDonald, 1991; Lambert, 1986; Luborsky et al., 2002). Studies have suggested that a combination of perspectives and techniques may even have powerful synergistic effects (Lazarus, 1989; Messer & Wampold, 2002; Norcross & Goldfried, 2005). Therefore, both research and practice suggest that religious adherence to only one perspective may be counterproductive and naive for most clinical problems.

In reviewing the major theoretical approaches in clinical psychology, it may seem clear that each perspective offers unique contributions toward a better understanding of human behavior and assisting those who seek professional psychological services (Beutler & Groth-Marnat, 2003; Norcross & Goldfried, 2005; O'Brien & Houston, 2000). Adherence to only one school of thought, however, can be rigid and ultimately limiting. In the words of Arnold Lazarus (1995), "Given the complexity of the subject matter, it seems unlikely that any single approach can possess all the answers. So why wear blinders? Why not borrow, purchase, pilfer, import, and otherwise draw upon conceptions and methods from diverse systems so as to harness their combined powers" (p. 399). While no one theory has a lock on the truth or the keys to behavior change, perhaps each has something very important to offer in the greater puzzle of "truth." Furthermore, debate about which school of thought reigns supreme seems to become moot in the ensuing context of integration (Arnkoff & Glass, 1992; Norcross et al., 2006). As expressed by Sol Garfield and Allen Bergin (1986), "a decisive shift in opinion has quietly occurred . . . the new view is that the long-term dominance of the major theories is over and that an eclectic position has taken precedence" (p. 7).

Finally, recent surveys have found that integrative approaches continue to be what most practicing psychologists report doing in their clinical work (Norcross, Karpiak, & Santoro, 2005).

Commonalities among Approaches

With so much emphasis on differences, it is often overlooked that there is some degree of overlap among many of these perspectives. For example, some of the major concepts articulated in one perspective are also expressed in other perspectives, using different terms and language. Those immediate and unfiltered thoughts and feelings that come to mind are referred to as *free associations* for those from a psychodynamic perspective and *automatic thoughts* in the cognitive-behavioral lexicon. Both approaches highly value and integrate free association/self-talk into their understanding and treatment of human behavior. Attempts to translate the language of one perspective into another have occurred since 1950, beginning with the work of Dollard and Miller. Since research tends to support the notion that one theoretical framework is not superior to another in treating all types of problems, the examination of common denominators among the different theoretical perspectives has attempted to isolate common factors (Goldfried, 1991). This research has suggested that providing the patient with new experiences within and outside of the therapy session is common in all types of psychotherapies (Brady et al., 1980). Goldfried (1991) stated that all psychotherapies encourage the patient to engage in corrective experiences and that they all provide some form of feedback to the patient. Additional similarities discussed by Frank (1982) and others include a professional office associated with healing and being helped; a trained mental health professional who is supportive, thoughtful, professional, and perceived as an expert in human behavior; enhanced hope that thoughts, feelings, and behaviors can change for the better; fees associated with service; and the avoidance of dual relationships (e.g., avoidance of sexual relationships or friendships with patients). James Prochaska (1984, 1995, 2000, 2008) discussed commonalities among theoretical orientations by examining the process of change across different types of problems and different methods of treatment. In his analysis of different orientations to behavior change, he isolated a variety of universal stages, levels, and processes of change. His theory includes five stages of change (i.e., pre-contemplation, contemplation, preparation, action, and maintenance), five levels of change (i.e., symptoms, maladaptive cognition, current interpersonal conflicts, family/systems conflicts, past interpersonal conflicts), and ten change processes (i.e., consciousness raising, catharsis/dramatic relief, self-evaluation, environmental reevaluation, self-liberation, social liberation, counterconditioning, stimulus control, contingency management, and helping relationship). It is

beyond the scope of this chapter to outline the specifics of Prochaska's model; for a more detailed account see Prochaska (1984, 1995, 2000, 2008) and Prochaska and Norcross (2002). Although Prochaska's perspective has a cognitive-behavioral flavor to it, his theory of change is atheoretical in that it is not based on any one theoretical perspective and can be applied to all perspectives.

Efforts toward Integration

The integration of theoretical and treatment perspectives is challenging and complex. Each perspective has its own language, leaders, and practices. Furthermore, research is challenging to conduct because what happens in a laboratory or research clinic may be very different from what happens in a clinician's office. For example, a treatment manual that clearly specifies a behavioral intervention for panic disorder used in research is likely not used in clinical practice. Efforts at **integration** tend to occur in one of three ways: (1) integrating the theories associated with each perspective, (2) developing an understanding of the common factors associated with each perspective, and (3) using eclecticism in a practical way to provide a range of available intervention strategies (Arkowitz, 1989, 1992; Norcross & Goldfried, 2005). Most attempts to integrate perspectives have involved the integration of psychodynamic and behavioral approaches. Perhaps this is due to the fact that during most of the twentieth century, the majority of clinical psychologists have identified themselves (with the exception of eclecticism) as being either psychodynamically or cognitive-behaviorally oriented.

Paul Wachtel (1977, 1982, 1987, 2002, 2008) has been a significant contributor to the evolving framework of integration between the psychodynamic and behavioral points of view. Wachtel was one of the first professionals to integrate psychodynamic and behavioral approaches. For example, Wachtel uses the psychodynamic perspective in focusing on early childhood experiences as well as the notion that unconscious conflicts result in problematic feelings and behaviors. He uses the behavioral principle of reinforcement in the present environment to understand various ongoing emotional, psychological, and behavioral problems. Wachtel further notes that behavioral interventions can improve insight while insight can lead to behavioral change (Wachtel, 1982).

Many authors (e.g., Castonguay, Reid, Halperin, & Goldfried, 2003; Gill, 1984; Messer 2001, 2008; Norcross & Goldfried, 2005; Nuttall, 2002; Ryle, 2005; Stern 2003; Wachtel, 2008) report that psychodynamic and cognitive-behavioral theories have clearly been integrated with much success. Psychodynamic therapies have increasingly incorporated cognitive-behavioral theories and practices into their perspectives. For example, many psychodynamic thinkers have become interested in the cognitive influences of maladaptive beliefs about self and others in interpersonal relationships (Horowitz, 1988; Messer 2001, 2008; Ryle, 2005; Strupp & Binder, 1984). Furthermore, interest in providing briefer treatments has resulted in the incorporation of cognitive-behavioral problem-solving strategies in dynamic therapy (Strupp & Binder, 1984). Some psychodynamic approaches have also endorsed the behavioral and humanistic principles of focusing on the present or *here and now* (Weiner, 1975). Contemporary cognitive-behavioral orientations have incorporated the psychodynamic view that attention must be paid to the nature of the therapeutic relationship between the therapist and patient as well as the need for insight to secure behavioral change (Dobson & Block, 1988; Mahoney, 1988; Ryle 2005). Other efforts toward theoretical integration have occurred using family systems theory (D. A. Kirschner & S. Kirschner, 1986; Lebow, 1984), humanistic approaches (Wandersman, Poppen, & Ricks, 1976), and interpersonal theory (Andrews, 1991). For example, the humanistic orientations have endorsed the scientific approach of the cognitive-behavioral orientation (Bugental, 1987) as well as the role of cognition in promoting growth (Bohart, 1982; Ellis, 1980). The behavioral approaches

have incorporated family systems theory into their efforts at developing behavioral family therapy (Jacobson, 1985; Jacobson & Margolin, 1979). Using a broader framework, some authors have looked toward an integration of biological, cognitive, affective, behavioral, and interpersonal elements of human behavior (Andrews, 1991; Beckham, 1990; Schwartz, 1984, 1991; Messer 2001, 2008; Norcross & Goldfried, 2005). Rather than looking at the major theoretical perspectives as being mutually exclusive, these authors experience them as all having some corner of the truth, which needs to be examined and pieced together in order to understand behavior and offer useful intervention strategies (Beutler & Groth-Marnat, 2003; Norcross & Goldfried, 2005; O'Brien & Houston, 2000). For example, Stanley Messer's assimilative integration approach includes psychodynamic, cognitive-behavioral, family systems, and even Yogic/Buddhist approaches (Messer 2001, 2008).

Eclecticism

Professionals maintaining an eclectic or integrative approach to their work tend to use whatever theories and techniques appear to work best for a given patient or problem. Of course, these approaches should be evidence based. Thus, once the psychologist has an adequate understanding of the patient's problems or symptoms, he or she uses strategies from various perspectives to design a treatment plan best suited to the unique needs of each patient. Lazarus (1971, 2005) argued that professionals can use techniques from various theoretical orientations without necessarily accepting the theory behind them. For example, a psychodynamically oriented psychologist might help a patient learn relaxation techniques such as diaphragmatic breathing or muscle relaxation in order to help control feelings of anxiety and panic. The therapy would continue to pursue the underlying basis for these symptoms while affording the patient some immediate relief. A cognitive-behaviorally oriented psychologist might ask a patient who is troubled by insomnia associated with frequent nightmares to describe his or her disturbing dreams and inquire about the patient's insights into these dreams. A humanistic psychologist might invite a patient to examine irrational beliefs. Irving Weiner stated that, "effective psychotherapy is defined not by its brand name, but by how well it meets the needs of the patient" (Weiner, 1975, p. 44). This has become the "battle cry" of many clinical psychologists. In many ways, someone seeking the professional services of a clinical psychologist is much more interested in obtaining help for his or her particular problem(s) than embracing the particular theoretical orientation of the psychologist. Also, they generally want immediate help with what ails them, not an intellectual discussion or understanding about the philosophy of human behavior. They usually want an approach that is consistent with their personality and their own perspective to problems. However, Eysenck (1970) and others have warned that eclecticism can be a "mish-mash of theories, a hugger-mugger of procedures, a gallimaufry of therapies" (p. 145). Concerns about eclecticism suggest that it can result in a passing familiarity with many approaches but competence in none, as well as muddled and unfocused thinking. Nonetheless, numerous surveys have revealed that eclectic approaches have become more and more common and popular among clinical psychologists (e.g., Norcross, Hedges et al., 2002; Norcross et al., 2005). In fact, integrative approaches have been the most commonly endorsed theoretical approaches by clinical psychologists during the past several decades (Norcross et al., 2005).

An excellent and influential example of an eclectic approach is the *multimodal* approach of Arnold Lazarus (1971, 1985, 1986, 1996, 2005). In the multimodal approach, treatment reflects the patient's needs based on seven aspects of behavior. These include behavior, affect, sensation, imagery, cognition, interpersonal relationships, and drugs (referred to as BASIC ID). Interventions include cognitive-behavioral techniques such as imagery, biological interventions such as medication, and humanistic strategies such as empty chair exercises and reflection. Although the work of Lazarus has a cognitive-behavioral slant, many non-cognitive-behavioral techniques and approaches are used in the multimodal approach.

Beyond Psychological Models

As clinical psychology has evolved, more complex theories of human behavior and behavior change have developed utilizing and integrating the major theoretical psychological perspectives in conjunction with biological and social factors. Furthermore, multidimensional and integrative approaches to intervention that reflect a biopsychosocial synthesis have become the trend in contemporary clinical psychology (Lam, 1991; Norcross et al., 2002; Norcross & Goldfried, 2005). Formal education in the biological, psychological, and social influences of behavior have become a requirement for licensure in most states. No longer can a psychologist master only one theoretical perspective while remaining oblivious to other perspectives and hope to obtain a license to practice in his or her state. For example, if a patient requests treatment by a clinical psychologist for tension headaches associated with stress, the psychologist must be able to appreciate the biological, psychological, and social influences on the patient's symptoms. While not all psychologists can treat all problems, it is incumbent on practitioners to at least know when to make appropriate referrals. The headaches might be associated with stress but they could also be associated with medical problems such as a migraine, brain tumor, or other serious neurological condition. The competent psychologist would request that the patient be evaluated by a physician in order to rule out these other important medical possibilities prior to treating the headaches with biofeedback, relaxation training, psychotherapy, or other psychosocial interventions and strategies in conjunction with any appropriate medical treatment. If a member of a particular religious or ethnic group seeks treatment for an emotional problem, it is important to have adequate awareness and understanding regarding the influences of culture on the behavior or problem in question (American Psychological Association [APA], 2003b; Sue & Sue, 2003, 2008; Sue, 1983, 1988). Ignorance regarding the role of ethnicity, culture, religion, and gender in behavior is no longer tolerated in most professional circles. Examining the biological, psychological, and social influences on behavior has become fundamental in clinical psychology and defines the biopsychosocial framework.

For example, a disabled Latino child, recently immigrating from El Salvador, experiences depression and posttraumatic stress disorder following an experience of sexual abuse perpetrated by a family member. The school teacher notices an increase in sexualized and inattentive behaviors and refers the child to a psychologist who consults with the school. The child tells the psychologist about the sexual abuse and the psychologist, as required by law, must break confidentiality and report the abuse to the state child protection agency. The bilingual psychologist might treat the child and members of the family with a variety of intervention strategies. The range of interventions might include (a) psychodynamic approaches to increase insight and access unconscious anger and resentment, (b) cognitive-behavioral strategies to manage anxiety symptoms and inattentive behavior at school, (c) referral to a psychiatrist for evaluation of the possible use of medication to address the depression, (d) referral to a pediatrician to evaluate potential medical problems associated with the abuse, (e) social and community support and interventions to address cultural issues associated with being an El Salvadoran immigrant as well as legal issues associated with the victimization, (f) family systems approaches to help the entire family cope with the current crisis and avoid future abuse, and (g) humanistic approaches to help support and accept the feelings and behavior of the child and family. This example demonstrates the need to intervene broadly with a wide arsenal of tools given the complexity of issues within the individual and larger family and social systems.

Biopsychosocial Integration

Whereas psychologists have increasingly utilized combined and multimodal psychological models and interventions, contemporary psychology has looked beyond even its own field into biological and sociological realms to enhance its scope and usefulness. The combined effects of biological, psychological, and social factors on behavior have led to the term *biopsychosocial,* and represents an increasingly appreciated comprehensive approach in clinical psychology. While biological, psychological, and social factors are all viewed as relevant in this perspective, they may not each be equal in their contribution to every problem or disorder. Thus, in the case of a primarily biological disorder such as childhood leukemia, for example, psychological and social factors provide important contributions to the course and treatment of the disease but are not given equal etiological or treatment consideration. Similarly, while a grief reaction following the loss of a loved one may at first glance appear purely psychological, social factors such as family and community support as well as biological factors such as sleeping and eating patterns can complicate or alleviate the severity of symptoms. Thus, an intelligent blending and weighing of these three factors comprise the challenge of biopsychosocial integration. Melchert (2007, p. 34) states the need for biopsychosocial integration when he says, "replacing the traditional reliance on an array of theoretical orientations with a science-based biopsychosocial framework would resolve many of the contradictions and conflicts that characterized (earlier) era(s) in (professional psychology)." Having described the major psychological approaches in detail in Chapter 5, the nature of biological and social factors in behavior will be described in this section, leading to clinical examples of biopsychosocial integration in contemporary practice.

Drugs and Obesity

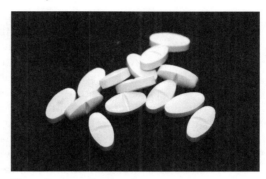

Photo: Courtesy Stockvault.net

Obesity has increased significantly in recent years in the United States and elsewhere. Efforts to help overweight people lose weight are the frequent topic of newsmagazines, television shows, blogs, and scientific research. The biopsychosocial model is needed in the evaluation and treatment of eating disorders such as obesity. Psychological and behavioral interventions that focus on food intake, selection, and the role of emotions such as anxiety, depression, and low self-esteem must be considered as well as social and cultural factors (e.g., access to high-fat foods, ability and motivation to exercise). Furthermore, interventions such as medication can be used effectively in the treatment of eating disorders such as obesity. Although there is no magic pill that will allow people to eat whatever they want and never gain weight, a number of medications have been approved by the Food and Drug Administration (FDA) to help treat obesity. For example, Orlistat (also known by the trade names Xenical and Alli), which is a medication that inhibits pancreatic lipase, reduces dietary fat by approximately 30%. Research suggests that those on the medication are more likely to lose weight and regain less weight than control groups after treatment (Aronne, 2001; Bray, 2008; Rivas-Vazquez, Rice, & Kalman, 2003). Side effects include gastrointestinal upset, fecal urgency, oily or soft stool, diarrhea, and flatus with discharge (Bray, 2008; Rivas-Vazquez et al., 2003).

Sibutramine (also known by the trade names Meridia and Reductil) is another approved medication to treat obesity that inhibits the reuptake of several neurotransmitters such as serotonin and norepinephrine. Like Orlistat, those who take Sibutramine tend to be more likely to lose weight and regain less weight than others following treatment (Aronne, 2001; Bray, 2008; Rivas-Vazquez et al., 2003). Side effects include increases in heart rate and blood pressure, upset stomach, and dry mouth.

Research continues to find other biological interventions for obesity. For example, ciliary neurotrophic factor (CNTF) is a promising protein that activates the intracellular signaling pathways in the hypothalamus,

(continued)

which regulates both body weight and food consumption (Bray, 2008; Rivas-Vazquez et al., 2003). Thus, it activates the satiety center in the brain to signal that the person is no longer hungry. Research suggests that it is effective in helping control weight.

These medications, when used in combination with other biopsychosocial interventions, may be useful to the millions of Americans who are obese. However, too often the public gets overly invested and excited about a promising "easy" way to control weight. Numerous medications, fad diets, and gadgets have been sold to the public only to be found to be ineffective or even dangerous. A good example is the excitement regarding the obesity medication, phentermine resin-fenfluramine or "phen-fen," which was very popular in the early and mid-1990s. The FDA banned the drug in 1997 when it became clear that patients on the medication were at higher risk for heart valve problems. One must proceed cautiously with weight-loss products such as medications, allowing research to adequately determine the effectiveness and safety of the product.

Biological Factors

Since Hippocrates, the close association between biology and behavior has been acknowledged, but not always fully integrated into treatment. Recent advances in medicine and the biological sciences have furthered our awareness of the intimate connection between our physical and psychological selves (Institute of Medicine, 2001; Lambert & Kinsley, 2005). A full understanding of any emotional or behavioral problem must therefore take into consideration potential biological factors.

Some authors have attempted to explain human behavior in terms of biological, genetic, and evolutionary influences (Barkow, 2006; Pinker, 2003; Thase & Denko, 2008). For example, it is well known that there is a strong genetic influence on physical characteristics such as height, weight, hair color, and eye color. Furthermore, it is well known that a variety of physical illnesses such as Huntington's chorea, phenylketonuria (PKU), Tay-Sachs, Down Syndrome, heart disease, cancer, mental retardation, and psychiatric illnesses such as schizophrenia, bipolar disorder, and alcoholism have strong biological or genetic influences (e.g., Dykens & Hodapp, 1997; Gottesman, 1991; Lambert & Kinsley, 2005). This does not mean that a psychiatric condition such as schizophrenia is completely attributable to genetic influences. In fact, an identical twin has about a 50% chance of *not* developing schizophrenia if his or her twin has the disorder (Gottesman, 1991; Gottesman & Erlenmeyer-Kimling, 2001). Biological and genetic influences have a significant but incomplete contribution to the development and course of many illnesses (Lambert & Kinsley, 2005; Pinker, 2003).

Genetically based chromosomal dysfunction can lead to a number of conditions that involve behavior and learning problems of interest to clinical psychologists. For example, Fragile X, Williams, and Prader-Willi syndromes all involve deletion or dysfunction of chromosomes due to genetic influences, resulting in a variety of cognitive, intellectual, learning, and behavioral problems (Bouras & Holt, 2007; Dykens & Hodapp, 1997; Hodapp & Dykens, 2007). Behavioral and learning problems associated with these disorders have intervention implications that involve both biological and psychosocial strategies.

Even personality traits such as shyness have been shown to have a genetic component (e.g., Kagan, Reznick, & Snidman, 1988; Pinker, 2003; Plomin, 1990; Posner & Rothbart, 2007). Research studying identical twins reared apart from birth have revealed many striking findings that support the notion of a strong biological influence associated with human health, illness, and behavior. Of course, genetic and **biological vulnerabilities** and predispositions do not necessarily result in the expression of a particular illness or trait. For example, while someone may inherit the vulnerability to develop PKU, environmental factors such as diet determine if the trait is expressed. Therefore, biological predispositions must be examined in the context of the environment (Hodapp & Dykens, 2007; Pinker, 2003; Posner & Rothbart, 2007).

Furthermore, additional biological influences on behavior, such as the role of brain chemicals called neurotransmitters, have demonstrated that brain functioning plays a significant role in human behavior. For example, serotonin (5-hydroxytryptamine or 5-HT) is a neurotransmitter associated with a variety of instinctual behaviors such as eating, sexuality, and moodiness. Low levels of serotonin at the synapse have been associated with impulsive behavior and depression (Institute of Medicine, 2001; Risch, Herrell, Lehner, Liang, Eaves, et al., 2009; Spoont, 1992; Thase, 2009). Another neurotransmitter, dopamine, has been linked to schizophrenia. Therefore, many psychologists and others maintain that biological influences such as inherited characteristics and brain neurochemistry (such as the role of neurotransmitters) greatly influence both normal and abnormal behavior (B. J. Sadock, V. A. Sadock, & Ruiz, 2009; Thase, 2009). The goal of the biological approach is to understand these biological and chemical influences and use interventions such as medication to help those with certain emotional, behavioral, and/or interpersonal problems.

Professionals with strong biological training, such as many psychiatrists, generally favor biological interventions in treating patients. Various types of psychotropic medications such as antipsychotic, antianxiety, and antidepressant medications are frequently used to treat a wide variety of emotional, psychological, and behavioral problems (Barondes, 2005; Glasser, 2003; Risch et al., 2009;

Sadock et al., 2009; Sharif, Bradford, Stroup, & Lieberman, 2007). For example, lithium is typically used to treat bipolar disorder (commonly referred to by the general population as manic-depression), while neuroleptics such as Haldol, Thorazine, Risperdal, and Zyprexa are often used to treat psychotic disorders such as schizophrenia. The benzodiazepines such as Valium and Xanax are frequently used to treat anxiety-based disorders such as panic and phobia. Finally, tricyclics such as Elavil, the monoamine oxidase (MAO) inhibitors, and a class of medications called the selective serotonin reuptake inhibitors (SSRIs), which include Prozac, are used to treat depressive disorders. Newer classes of drugs similar to the SSRIs yet different enough to be considered in their own category, including nefazodone (Serzone) and venlafaxine (Effexor), impact the norepinephrine as well as serotonin neurotransmitters while Bupropion (Wellbutrin and Zyban) also impacts the dopamine system (Nemeroff & Schatzberg, 2007; Sadock et al., 2009; Stahl, 1998). Tricyclics such as imipramine are also used to treat panic and phobic disorders. Electroconvulsive therapy (ECT) is frequently used to treat severe and resistant depression. The technique involves applying a small amount of electrical current (usually 20 to 30 milliamps) to the patient's temples for about one minute while the patient is sedated. The treatment results in a seizure or convulsion, which is subsequently associated with a reduction in symptoms in about 60% of the cases (Fink, 2003; Sadock et al., 2009).

These biological interventions are not without side effects. For example, the benzodiazepines can cause drowsiness, tolerance, and both physical and psychological dependence or addiction (American Psychiatric Association, 2000; Baldessarini & Cole, 1988; Hayward, Wardle, & Higgitt, 1989; Spiegal, 1998). Antidepressants such as Prozac can cause insomnia, nervousness, and inhibited orgasms (Sadock et al., 2009). Antipsychotic medication can produce muscle rigidity, weight gain, dry mouth, constipation, a shuffling walk, and an irreversible condition called *tardive dyskinesia* characterized by involuntary facial and limb movements (Breggin, 1991; Spaulding, Johnson, & Coursey, 2001; Sadock et al., 2009). Tardive dyskinesia can render patients socially impaired if the symptoms cannot be managed by other medications. Although research has failed to find that ECT causes structural damage to the brain (Devanand, Dwork, Hutchinson, Blowig, & Sackheim, 1994; Devanand & Sackheim, 1995; Scott, 1995), relapse rates and memory deficits, usually associated with events occurring around the time of ECT administration, are a common problem (Fink, 2003) and thus this technique remains controversial for these and other reasons (Reisner, 2003). Biological interventions may be used effectively with certain patients but also have important side effects. A perfect pill or "magic bullet" that completely fixes a problem without any side effects or negative factors does not exist.

While medication can greatly help to minimize or eliminate problematic symptoms, additional problems associated with a mental illness may continue to exist. For example, antipsychotic medication or neuroleptics such as Thorazine, Risperdal, or Zyprexa may reduce or eliminate the hallucinations and delusional thinking associated with schizophrenia. Therefore, the patient is bothered no longer by hearing voices or beliefs that have no basis in reality. However, problems with social skills, self-esteem, fears, and comfort with others may not be altered by the use of these powerful medications and must be dealt with using other means (e.g., social skills training, psychotherapy, job skill training).

In addition to medications and other biological treatments such as ECT, technological advances such as the development of computer neuroimaging techniques (CT and PET Scans, and functional MRIs) have improved our understanding of brain–behavior relationships (Mazziotta, 1996; Sadock et al., 2009). Computerized axial tomography (CT) scans were developed in the early 1970s to better view the structures of the brain. CT scans provide computer-enhanced multiple-X-ray-like pictures of the brain from multiple angles. CT scan research has, for example, discovered

that schizophrenics have enlarged ventricles or spaces in the brain and experience cortical atrophy over time. Positron emission tomography (PET) scans use radioactive isotopes injected into the bloodstream of a patient to create gamma rays in the body. PET scans not only provide a view of brain structure but also provide information on brain function. Research using PET scan technology has revealed changes in brain blood flow during different intellectual tasks and during different emotional states such as anxiety (Fischbach, 1992). PET scan research has determined that panic is associated with brain cells located in the locus ceruleus in the brainstem, which are also sensitive to the benzodiazepines (Barlow, 2002; Barlow & Craske, 2002; Reiman, Fusselman, Fox, & Raichle, 1989; Sadock et al., 2009). Finally, magnetic resonance imaging (MRI) was developed in the early 1980s and provides a detailed visual reconstruction of the brain's anatomy (Andreasen & Black, 1995; Sadock et al., 2009). The MRI analyzes the nuclear magnetic movements of hydrogen in the water and fat of the body. MRI research has helped to uncover the role of possible frontal lobe damage among schizophrenic patients (Andreasen, 1989) as well as potential tissue loss in bipolar patients (Andreasen & Black, 1995).

Clinical psychologists are unable to prescribe ECT, medication (in most states), or any other biological interventions (e.g., CT or PET scans, MRI). Therefore, psychologists interested in the use of these interventions must work collaboratively with physicians (such as psychiatrists). However, recent efforts have been underway by the U.S. military, the APA, and other organizations to work toward allowing psychologists, with the appropriate training, supervision, and experience, to legally prescribe medications. Psychologists now can prescribe medication in some states (e.g., New Mexico, Louisiana, Guam). This allows psychologists to more fully integrate biological interventions with the psychosocial interventions that they already provide. Prescribing medications by psychologists will be discussed in more detail in Chapter 14.

Some authors also view evolutionary influences as powerful contributors to human behavior (Wilson, 1978, 1983, 1991, 2003; D. S. Wilson & E. O. Wilson, 2007). Although speculative and not based on controlled scientific experimentation, evolutionary explanations for a variety of behaviors and behavioral problems have become popular in recent years. For example, some researchers report that many experiences and difficulties with intimate relationships can be traced to evolutionary influences (Buss, 2003, 2005; Fisher, 1995, 2004). Fisher (1995, 2004) explained that divorces occur often and usually fairly early in a relationship (after about four years) for evolutionary reasons, because about four years were needed to conceive and raise a child to a minimal level of independence. Once a child is about 3 years old, members of a clan could adequately continue with child rearing. Fisher, Buss, and others explain infidelity as evolutionarily helpful because by distributing our genes by mating with a number of partners, we will most likely keep our genes from dying out. Because life was tenuous for our ancestors—death was a realistic daily possibility—having some reproductive options with several people increased the possibility of mating as well as having help taking care of young infants. Maximizing reproductive success and perpetuating the species is enhanced if people mate often and with a variety of partners. Whereas these researchers provide compelling explanations for human intimate relationships from studying the behavior of animals as well as the behavior of our ancient ancestors, people are often very quick to proclaim that human behavior is driven by strong biological forces and, therefore, we cannot help being who we are and behaving as we do. Thus, someone engaged in an extramarital affair who blames the behavior on his or her genetic makeup is likely (and rightfully) to be viewed with skepticism.

Biologically oriented factors emphasize the influence of the brain, neurochemistry, and genetic influences on behavior. They typically lead to biologically oriented approaches to study, assess, and treat a wide range of emotional, psychological, medical, and behavioral problems. Evolutionarily oriented professionals focus on understanding human behavior in the context of our sociobiological roots. The biological and evolutionary perspectives on behavior have become increasingly influential. New discoveries in genetics such as genetic markers for depression, panic, anxiety, obesity, and schizophrenia as well as new discoveries in brain structure and function associated with schizophrenia, homosexuality, and violence have contributed to the ascendancy of the biological perspective. Finally, psychiatry's emphasis on biological theories of mental illness and medication interventions has also fueled the current focus on biological factors in understanding, diagnosing, and treating mental illness (Fleck, 1995; Glasser, 2003; Kramer, 1993; Michels, 1995; Nemeroff & Schatzberg, 2007; Sadock et al., 2009; Thase, 2009; Valenstein, 2002).

Social Factors

Many clinical psychologists have begun to focus more on both cultural and social influences on behavior. Sociologists, anthropologists, and social workers have been investigating these influences for many years. While most practicing clinical psychologists primarily work with individuals, couples, and families rather than with large organizations or groups, issues such as culture, socioeconomic factors, ethnicity, sexual orientation, religious background, social support, and community resources have received a great deal of attention concerning their important influences on human behavior (APA, 1993b, 2002, 2003; Brown, 1990; Caracci, 2006; Greene, 1993; Jones, 1994; Lopez et al., 1989; National Mental Health Association, 1986; Plante, 2009; Sue & Sue, 2003, 2008; Sue, 1983, 1988; Tharp, 1991; U.S. Department of Health and Human Services, 1990, 2001).

Professionals maintain that individual behavior is often influenced by the cultural environment as well as by larger social and even political factors. Homelessness, poverty,

Case Study: Mary—Integrating Biological Factors

Given the significant research into biological aspects of panic disorder, several key insights are germane to Mary's case. First, panic and other anxiety disorders have a strong familial contribution, in that individuals whose family members have these disorders are at increased risk of also developing the disorders. Second, neurotransmitters associated with the GABA-benzodiazepine and serotonergic systems have been implicated in the development of panic disorder (American Psychiatric Association, 2000; Bell & Nutt, 1998; Charney et al., 2000; Deakin &

Graeff, 1991; Gray, 1982, 1991; Roy-Byrne & Crowley, 2007; Sadock et al., 2009). Therefore, medications prescribed by a physician such as benzodiazepines (e.g., Valium and Xanax) and antidepressants (e.g., Zoloft and Lexapro) may be helpful in altering the biological neurochemistry associated with Mary's panic symptoms (e.g., Asnis et al., 2001; Roy-Byrne & Crowley, 2007). However, potential side effects including addiction potential would need to be fully discussed and Mary clearly informed as to her biological and other treatment options.

---

racism, ethnicity, underemployment, abuse, and even the weather can influence behavior (APA, 1993b, 2003; Caracci, 2006; Cardemil, & Battle, 2003; Economic Report of the President, 1998; Lewis, 1969; Lex, 1985; Roysircar, Sandhu, & Bibbins, 2003; Tharp, 1991). Thus, individual human behavior cannot be viewed apart from the larger social context. For example, compelling research has demonstrated that developing schizophrenia is 38% more likely for those living in urban environments relative to rural environments (Caracci, 2006; Lewis, David, Andreasson, & Allsbeck, 1992; van Os, Hanssen, Bijl, & Vollebergh, 2001). While no one would suggest that city living alone would cause someone to become schizophrenic, perhaps vulnerable persons who are at risk for the development of schizophrenia are more likely to develop symptoms in an urban rather than a suburban or rural environment. Depression and drug abuse are also more prevalent in urban environments while alcoholism is more common in rural places (Caracci, 2006; Eaton et al., 1984; Regier et al., 1984). Although disorders such as schizophrenia, depression, and substance abuse can be found in all cultures and countries, social factors such as culture, social expectations, racism, and economic factors often determine how symptoms are presented.

For example, while auditory hallucinations are most common in developed countries such as the United States, visual hallucinations are most common in less-developed countries such as those in many parts of Africa and Central America (Ndetei & Singh, 1983).

Social relationships appear influential in protecting individuals from a variety of physical and psychological problems, including depression, hypertension, and alcoholism (Brown, Nesse, Vinokur, & Smith, 2003; Ellison & Gray, 2009; House, Landis, & Umberson, 1988). In fact, research studies in several countries have found that a large network of social contacts increases the chance of living a long life (Brown et al., 2003; Berkman & Syme, 1979; Ellison & Gray, 2009; House, Robbins, & Metzner, 1982). The relationship between social support and longevity exists even after accounting for other important risk factors such as hypertension, smoking, and alcoholism. Social support also helps people cope more effectively and recover more quickly from both physical and psychological problems (Ellison & Gray, 2009; Mahoney & Restak, 1998; McLeod, Kessler, & Landis, 1992; T. Seeman, 2001).

Social factors can be damaging as well. Social influences can be so powerful that they can even lead to death. For example, disease

Poverty and Mental Health

Photo: Courtesy Zach Plante.

Tragically, 37 million Americans live below the poverty line with about 13% of all Americans living in poverty (U.S. Census Bureau, 2008). Twenty-five percent of African American and Latina women live below the poverty line and a third of women who head households live in poverty. The United States has the highest poverty rate among wealthy nations (Belle & Doucet, 2003). The richest 1% of the population in America owns more wealth than the bottom 95% (Wolff, 1998) with an average CEO earning 475 times as much as his employees (Giecek, 2000).

What does poverty have to do with mental health? Most researchers and clinicians say plenty (Wan, 2008). For example, depression is very common among the poor and most especially among poor women and children (Eamon & Zuehl, 2001; Wan, 2008). Those who are poor rarely get mental health or health-care services (Coiro, 2001; Conger & Donnellan, 2007; Wan, 2008). Sadly, 83% of low-income mothers have been physically or sexually abused and usually both while one-third experience posttraumatic stress disorder (Belle & Doucet, 2003). According to the Institute of Medicine (2001), the poor are more likely to be exposed to health-damaging toxins, have fewer social support systems and networks, and are much more likely to face discrimination.

Therefore, fighting poverty likely increases the chances for better mental and physical health among the poor (Conger & Donnellan, 2007; Nelson, Lord, & Ochocka, 2001; Wan, 2008). Clinical psychologists who work with the poor are well aware of the challenges facing these populations. Community resources have steadily decreased in recent years to help the poor in the United States, Canada, the United Kingdom, and elsewhere (Conger & Donnellan, 2007; Nelson et al., 2001; Wan, 2008).

and death frequently closely follow separation from a spouse through death or divorce. This relationship is especially common among elderly men (Arling, 1976; Bowling, 2009).

Professionals with a great deal of training and experience in the social influences on behavior, such as social workers, generally favor social interventions in helping patients. Interventions such as improved housing and employment opportunities, community interventions such as Project Head-Start, providing low-cost and high-quality preschool experiences for low-income and high-risk families, and legal strategies such as laws to protect battered women and abused children are often the focus of many of these professionals.

The powerful influences of cultural and ethnic background as well as social issues such as poverty, homelessness, racism, violence, and crime have been associated with psychological functioning and human behavior, lending support to the importance of more global social and systems thinking (APA, 1993b, 2003; Bowling, 2009; Cardemil & Battle, 2003; Ellison & Gray, 2009; Lopez et al., 1989; Schwartz, 1982, 1984, 1991; Sue & Sue, 2003, 2008; Tharp, 1991). No contemporary clinical psychologist can overlook social context when seeking to understand and treat psychological problems. The APA provides guidelines to psychologists that include that they "recognize ethnicity and culture as significant parameters in understanding psychological processes" (APA, 1993b, p. 46; see APA, 2003a). These issues are further discussed in Chapter 14.

Synthesizing Biological, Psychological, and Social Factors in Contemporary Integration

Several theories have influenced the development of this integrative and contemporary biopsychosocial perspective and a brief review of them is warranted. This group includes the diathesis-stress perspective, the reciprocal-gene-environment perspective, and the psychosocial influence on biology perspective.

The Diathesis-Stress Perspective

The **diathesis-stress** perspective is a causal perspective for illness or problems. It suggests that a biological or other type of vulnerability in combination with psychosocial or environmental stress (e.g., divorce, financial troubles, unemployment) creates the necessary conditions for illness to occur (Bremner, 2002; Eisenberg, 1968; Meehl, 1962; Segal & Ingram, 1994; Taylor & Stanton, 2007; Zubin & Spring, 1977). The diathesis-stress perspective states that people have a biological, genetic, cognitive, or other tendency toward certain behaviors and problems. A susceptibility emerges such that certain individuals are more prone to developing potential traits, tendencies, or problems. For example, if someone has one biological parent with hypertension (i.e., high blood pressure), she has a 45% chance of developing high blood pressure herself even if she maintains normal weight, minimizes her fat and salt intake, and obtains adequate physical exercise. If both biological parents have hypertension, the odds soar to 90% (S. Taylor, 2009). Another example includes schizophrenia, since in fact much of the research supporting the diathesis-stress perspective focuses on this serious mental illness (Eisenberg, 1968; Walker & Tessner, 2008 Zubin & Spring, 1977). Schizophrenia occurs in about 1% of the population. However, if a person has an identical twin with schizophrenia, there is a 48% chance of developing the disorder. If a person has a fraternal twin with schizophrenia, there is a 17% chance of developing the disorder (Gottesman, 1991; Gottesman & Erlenmeyer-Kimler, 2001; Walker & Tessner, 2008). Therefore, diathesis means that someone is susceptible to developing a particular problem due to some inherent vulnerability. When certain stressors emerge or the conditions are right, the problem then becomes manifest.

A disorder will occur when the biological or other vulnerability and environmental stressors interact in a sufficient manner to unleash the problem (Figure 6.1). For example, people with significant family histories of

Genetics and Psychology

New and exciting research in genetics highlighted by the international efforts of the human genome project and the successful cloning of several animals has resulted in an explosion of information about genetics that has enormous implications for understanding disease and behavior (International Human Genome Sequencing Consortium, 2001; Kaiser, 2008; Miller & Martin, 2008). The resulting research will undoubtedly alter our methods of predicting, understanding, preventing, and treating a host of gene-related problems such as cancer, heart disease, Alzheimer's disease, learning disabilities, and numerous other problems (Miller & Martin, 2008). As scientists have been able to fully map the human genome and use genetic information to clone animals, many questions and issues emerge that clinical psychologists can be very helpful with managing. For example, if genetic testing results in the knowledge that a patient has a high risk of passing on a potentially fatal genetically based illness (e.g., breast cancer, colorectal cancer, cystic fibrosis) to their potential offspring, they may wonder if they should have children. If genetic testing suggests that a young woman is very likely to develop a potentially fatal disease such as breast cancer, should she consider having a prophylactic mastectomy? If prenatal genetic testing suggests that your child is highly likely to suffer from a genetically based illness that is troublesome but not life threatening (e.g., Tourette's syndrome, Asperger's syndrome), should you consider an abortion? If a couple is biologically unable to have children, should they consider cloning if the technology and service is available to them? Should stem cells be harvested from a fetus in order to use the cells to treat another person with a potentially fatal disease? How do you manage the stress of knowing from genetic testing that you will definitely develop a fatal disease in the foreseeable future? The science associated with genetics is highly relevant to clinical psychologists who may conduct research on genetically based illnesses or who clinically treat patients who either suffer from these illnesses or must make important life decisions based on their risk profiles.

schizophrenia may experience their first psychotic episode during the stress of moving to a new city or starting college. Or individuals with a family history of alcoholism might develop the problem during college when many opportunities to drink are available and reinforced by peers. For example, Mary (the case example) may have a biological predisposition to panic and anxiety disorders due to her genetic and biological makeup. The stress of her father's death and her failure to develop necessary levels of self-confidence may have resulted in this predisposition becoming expressed in the form of a panic disorder.

The Reciprocal-Gene-Environment Perspective

Some argue that genetic influences might actually increase the likelihood that an individual will experience certain life events (Rende & Plomin, 1992). Thus, certain individuals

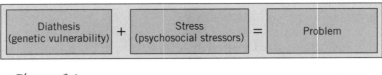

Figure 6.1
The diathesis-stress model.

may have the genetic tendency to experience or seek out certain stressful situations. For example, someone with a genetic tendency toward alcoholism may develop a drinking problem that results in work, relationship, and financial strains. These stressors may result in further drinking, thus worsening both the alcohol problem and life stressors. Someone with a genetic predisposition toward attention deficit hyperactivity disorder (ADHD) is likely to be impulsive. This impulsivity might result in making poor decisions concerning potential marital partners, leading to divorce and other relationship problems. Stressful relationships and divorce may then exacerbate their attention problems. The reciprocal-gene-environment perspective suggests that there is a close relationship between biological or genetic vulnerability and life events such that each continuously influences the other. Some research suggests that the reciprocal-gene-environment perspective may also help to explain depression (Kalat, 2008; McGuffin, Katz, & Bebbington, 1988) and even divorce (McGue & Lykken, 1992).

Psychosocial Influences on Biology

In addition to the notion that biology influences psychosocial issues, an alternative theory suggests that psychosocial factors actually alter biology (e.g., Bremner, 2002; Chida & Steptoe, 2009; Kalat, 2008). For example, research has found that monkeys reared with a high degree of control over their choice of food and activities were not anxious but were aggressive when injected with an anxiety-inducing medication (i.e., a benzodiazepine inverse agonist) that generally causes anxiety compared with a group of monkeys raised with no control over their food and activity choices (Insel, Champoux, Scanlan, & Soumi, 1986). Early rearing experiences greatly influenced how monkeys responded to the effects of medication influencing neurotransmitter activity. Other research has demonstrated that psychosocial influences can alter neurotransmitter and hormonal circuits (Anisman, 1984; Institute of Medicine, 2001; Kalat, 2008). Animals raised with a great deal of exercise and stimulation have been found to have

Case Study: Mary—Integrating Social Factors

A number of social factors further contribute to an understanding of Mary. First, Mary's Irish Catholic upbringing was marked by repression of feelings and a tendency to experience intense guilt. Her current social environment is exceedingly narrow, limited by her agoraphobia and avoidance of new situations. It may therefore be useful to first engage her priest and church community in working through deeply held religious beliefs that contribute to her sense of guilt and emotional restriction as well as toward broadening her contact with others. Connection to social support through her church community could lead to some volunteer responsibilities and eventually greater contact and involvement in the larger community. Thus, sociocultural and religious factors contribute largely to Mary's experience and can be used in a positive manner to assist her.

more neural connections in various parts of the brain than animals without an active background (Greenough, Withers, & Wallace, 1990). Social status has also impacted hormone production such as cortisol, which impacts stress (Institute of Medicine, 2001; Kalat, 2008). Other psychosocial factors appear to impact biological functioning as well. For example, social isolation, interpersonal and environmental stress, pessimism, depression, and anger have all been found to be closely associated with the development of various illnesses and even death (Bremner, 2002; Chida & Steptoe, 2009; Kalat, 2008). These illnesses include cardiovascular disease such as hypertension and heart attacks as well as cancer (see Chida & Steptoe, 2009; Goleman, 1995; Kalat, 2008; Kiecolt-Glaser, McGuire, Robles, & Glaser, 2002; and Shorter, 1994 for reviews). Hostility, for example, has been found to be an independent risk factor for coronary heart disease. It is believed that the heightened physiological arousal associated with chronic feelings of anger may promote problematic atherogenic changes in the cardiovascular system (Chida & Steptoe, 2009; Miller, Smith, Turner, Guijarro, & Hallet, 1996).

Development of the Biopsychosocial Perspective

In 1977, George Engel published a paper in the journal *Science* championing the **biopsychosocial** perspective in understanding and treating physical and mental illness. This perspective suggests that all physical and psychological illnesses and problems have biological, psychological, and social elements that require attention in any effective intervention. The biopsychosocial perspective further suggests that the biological, psychological, and social aspects of health and illness influence each other. The biopsychosocial perspective has been accepted in both medicine and psychology with research support demonstrating its validity (Carmody & Matarazzo, 1991; Fava & Sonino, 2008; Johnson, 2003; Miller, 1987).

The biopsychosocial perspective became the foundation for the field of health psychology in the early 1980s (Schwartz, 1982), and has quickly become an influential perspective in clinical psychology and other fields (Fava & Sonino, 2008; Johnson, 2003; Lam, 1991; Levy, 1984; McDaniel, 1995; Melchert, 2007; Sweet et al., 1991; Taylor, 2009). In fact, Melchert (2007, p. 37) states that "it has been incorporated into the curricula in nearly all medical schools in the United States and Europe ... and officially endorsed by the APA ... and 22 other health care and social service organizations." Melchert further states that "Although other comprehensive, integrative perspectives on human development and functioning have been developed, none enjoys the widespread recognition and acceptance the (biopsychosocial) approach does" (p. 37). It is important to mention that the biopsychosocial approach is not another term for the medical model. Nor is it another term for a biological approach to psychology and clinical problems.

The biopsychosocial approach is contextual and states that the interaction of biological, psychological, and social influences on behavior should be addressed in order to improve the complex lives and functioning of people who seek professional health and mental health services (Engel, 1977, 1980; Lam, 1991; McDaniel, 1995; Schwartz, 1982, 1984). The biopsychosocial framework applies a systems theory perspective to emotional, psychological, physical, and behavioral functioning (Lam, 1991; Levy, 1984; McDaniel, 1995; Schwartz, 1982, 1984). The "approach assumes that all human problems are biopsychosocial systems problems; each biological problem has psychosocial consequences, and each psychosocial problem has biological correlates" (McDaniel, 1995, p. 117). Miller (1978), for example, discussed seven levels of systems, each interdependent on the other. These include functioning at the cellular, organ, organism, group, organization, society, and supernatural levels. Furthermore, Miller outlined 19 additional sublevels present at each of the major 7 levels of functioning. Dysfunction at any level of functioning leads to dysregulation, which in turn results in dysfunction at other levels. Thus, changes in one area of functioning (such as the biological area) will likely impact functioning in other areas (e.g., psychological area). Chemical imbalances might occur at the cellular level in the brain, which leads to mood dysfunction in the form of depression. The depressive feelings may then lead to interpersonal difficulties that further impact job performance and self-esteem. Stress associated with these problems at work and home may then lead to further brain chemical imbalances and further depression. Similarly, in an adolescent, Japanese-American female with anorexia nervosa, the intimate interactions between (a) psychological needs for control and mastery, (b) cultural expectations of thinness in women and achievement in Japanese-American culture, combined with (c) pubertal hormonal changes, all conspire to create a dysregulated system with biological, psychological, and social factors each compounding and contributing to the dysfunction the others. Thus, the systems perspective of the biopsychosocial perspective highlights the mutual interdependence of all systems. The biopsychosocial perspective is holistic in that it considers the whole person and specifically the holistic interaction of biological, psychological, and social influences (Fava & Sonino, 2008).

Highlight of a Contemporary Clinical Psychologist

Stephanie Pinder-Amaker, PhD

Photo: Courtesy Stephanie Pinder-Amaker

Birth Date: June 19, 1960

College: Duke University, BS, May 1982

Graduate Program: Vanderbilt University, PhD, 1988

Clinical Internship: Yale University School of Medicine, New Haven, CT, July 1986–June 1987

Current Job(s): Director, College Mental Health Initiative, McLean Hospital and Instructor in Psychology, Harvard Medical School

Pros and Cons of Being a Clinical Psychologist:

Pros: "So many exciting career opportunities are available throughout academic, clinical, research and administrative realms."

Cons: "The compassion that we have as clinicians can sometimes interfere with the judgment needed to become a good administrator. There are excellent training courses that can assist with developing the latter."

Influence of Theoretical Models in Your Work: "I had the experience of attending Vanderbilt at a time when they encouraged graduate students to take courses in two theoretically and organizationally distinct programs. One was cognitive-behaviorally oriented and the other was psychodynamic. I learned both theoretical models from faculty who were very passionate and committed to their respective approaches. In the end, I was able to appreciate and integrate the best of both worlds and discovered that both approaches have a great deal more in common than I had expected. Both schools influenced my clinical work and made me a more flexible practitioner."

Future of Clinical Psychology: "Our training lends itself to being able to address many contemporary challenges. For example, higher education administration is leaning heavily upon clinical psychology to address the college mental health crisis. The economic crisis has all industries looking to us for guidance in navigating these difficult times. As the field continues to grow and technology expands the 'classroom,' we should remember the basics— that we also have the training and expertise to become outstanding educators. Because undergraduate students are naturally drawn to psychology, we have the unique opportunity to engage students in creative ways. An 'Intro to Psychology' course (where most students first encounter the field) can be so inspiring if we embrace the challenge of highlighting for students the significant impact they can have in the profession and the relevance that clinical psychology will always have for their lives."

Typical Schedule:

9:00	Review schedule and daily list of college students who have been admitted to the hospital; follow up accordingly.
10:00	Chair CMHI Student Advisory Committee.
11:00	Meet with postdoctoral fellow or program assistant for ongoing supervision.
12:00	Lunch (often with hospital staff or students).
1:00	Explore funding opportunities (e.g., grants, development) for program development.
2:00	Chair College Mental Health Initiative Work Group meeting.
3:00	Meet with regional counseling center directors or visit a local campus.
4:00	Manage e-mails, make phone calls, draft/edit proposals for new projects.
5:00	Review college database and follow up re: incomplete/missing entries.

Application of the Biopsychosocial Perspective to Contemporary Clinical Psychology Problems

The biopsychosocial perspective is generally viewed as a useful contemporary approach

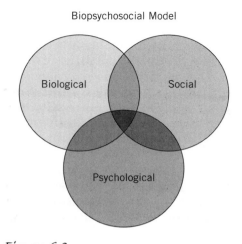

Biopsychosocial Model

Figure 6.2

The integrative biopsychosocial perspective.

to clinical psychology problems (Figure 6.2; Fava & Sonino, 2008 Johnson, 2003; Lam, 1991; McDaniel, 1995; Taylor, 2009). We next illustrate how this multidimensional, systemic, and holistic approach is employed with the complex problems faced by clinical psychology and related disciplines.

Obsessive-Compulsive Disorder

Obsessive-compulsive disorder (OCD) is an anxiety disorder involving obsessions (recurrent and persistent thoughts, images, impulses) and compulsions (repetitive behaviors such as hand washing, checking, ordering, or acts) (American Psychiatric Association, 2000). Frequent obsessions might include wishing to hurt oneself or others, or fear of contamination through contact with germs or others. Compulsions might include repeatedly checking to ensure that the stove is turned off or that the door is locked, constantly washing hands to avoid germs and contamination, or performing bizarre rituals. OCD occurs among approximately 3% of the population (American Psychiatric Association, 2000). However, milder forms of obsessions and compulsions that are not severe enough to be considered a disorder commonly occur among many people. OCD tends to be more common among males than females and symptoms generally first appear during adolescence or early adulthood (American Psychiatric Association, 2000).

Brain imaging techniques have found that OCD patients have hyperactivity in the orbital surface of the frontal lobe, the cingulate gyrus, and the caudate nucleus (Breiter, Rauch, Kwong, & Baker, 1996; Damsa, Kosel, & Moussally, 2009; Insel, 1992; Micallef & Blin, 2001). Furthermore, the neurotransmitter, serotonin, appears to be particularly active in these areas of the brain. OCD patients are believed to have less serotonin available than non-OCD controls (Kalat, 2008; Lambert & Kinsley, 2005). It is, however, unclear what causes these brain differences. Does the biology impact the behavior or does the behavior impact the biology? In other words, does the activity of neurotransmitters in certain sections of the brain cause people to develop OCD symptoms or do the symptoms themselves alter brain chemistry? Research evidence suggests that there may be an interaction (Baxter et al., 1992; Damsa et al., 2009; Insel, 1992; Kalat, 2008; Lambert & Kinsley, 2005). For example, a person can develop OCD following surgery to remove a brain tumor in the orbital frontal area of the brain (Insel, 1992). Thus, a specific trauma to the brain can result in OCD in individuals never troubled by obsessions or compulsions. Evidence has also shown that psychological interventions such as the cognitive-behavioral techniques of exposure and response prevention can alter brain circuitry (Baxter et al., 1992). Thus, an interaction between biological and psychological influences is likely to create or reduce OCD behavior. Additionally, social influences such as culture, religious faith, and social support influence the nature, course, and prognosis of OCD (Greist, 1990; Insel, 1984, 1992; Micallef & Blin, 2001; Plante, 2009; Riggs & Foa, 1993). Current treatments may involve a biopsychosocial approach that includes a drug such as Prozac that inhibits the reuptake of serotonin; neurosurgery (in extreme cases); cognitive-behavioral psychotherapy using exposure and response prevention techniques;

social support and education through psychoeducational groups; and psychotherapy, which may include marital and/or family counseling as well as supportive and insight-oriented approaches (Foa & Franklin, 2001; Franklin & Foa, 2008; Koran, Thienemann, & Davenport, 1996).

Panic Disorder and Anxiety

Anxiety-related panic disorder provides another useful application of the biopsychosocial perspective. While everyone has experienced anxiety at various times in their lives, some experience full-blown panic attacks. Panic attacks are characterized by an intense fear that arises quickly and contributes to a variety of symptoms including heart palpitations, sweating, chest pain, shortness of breath, dizziness, and depersonalization (American Psychiatric Association, 2000). While intense fear can be an adaptive mobilizing response in the face of real danger (e.g., preventing a car accident or running away from an assailant), people with panic attacks have a maladaptive response to an imagined threat that often prevents them from engaging in a variety of activities most people take for granted, such as grocery shopping, traveling over bridges, or leaving their home to run errands in a car. About 4% of the population experience panic disorder with onset typically occurring during adolescence or early adulthood (American Psychiatric Association, 2000). Although panic disorder is found throughout the world, symptoms manifest differently depending on the cultural context.

Biopsychosocial factors influence the development, maintenance, and prognosis of panic behavior (Barlow & Craske, 2000; Fava & Morton, 2009; Graeff & Del-Ben, 2008; Roth, 1996). First, evidence suggests that a combination of genetic factors make some people vulnerable to experiencing anxiety or panic attacks (Barlow, 2002; Charney et al., 2000; Fava & Morton, 2009; Graeff & Del-Ben, 2008). Furthermore, neurotransmitter activity, specifically the influence of gamma amino butyric acid (GABA), serotonin, and

Empirically Supported Treatment of Obsessive-Compulsive Disorder among Children

Approximately 1 in every 200 children under the age of 18 experiences obsessive-compulsive disorder that is severe enough to significantly disrupt school and social functioning (March & Mulle, 1998). Sadly, OCD in children is frequently not diagnosed. Treatment reflects biopsychosocial principles using a combination of medication (such as Prozac, Zoloft, or Anafranil when needed and when symptoms are especially difficult to manage and treat) and cognitive-behavioral psychotherapy that offers exposure and response prevention strategies.

John March and Karen Mulle offer an empirically supported treatment protocol for OCD in children (March, 2006; March & Mulle, 1998). It includes a manual for up to 21 sessions. Treatment begins with psychoeducational information presented to the parents and impacted child. Session 2 focuses on presenting the notion of an OCD toolkit of a variety of cognitive-behavioral techniques that can be used to fight off and cope with OCD. One technique includes "talking back" to OCD in an effort to not let OCD "boss you around." "OCD mapping" includes efforts to self-monitor or make regular assessments of OCD symptoms and triggers as well as the impact they have on the child's daily experience at home, school, and elsewhere. Subsequent sessions highlight the need to practice exposure and response prevention strategies to deal with OCD problems both small and large moving up a stimulus hierarchy. Family sessions are scheduled periodically as well during the course of treatment. Later sessions focus on relapse prevention strategies as well as periodic booster sessions. The treatment manual is informative for parents and clinicians alike and includes a variety of exercises, assessment tools, references, and practical tips. Treatment also takes into consideration co-morbid diagnoses, potential cultural issues, and other factors that make treatment appropriate for any given child and family. The March and Mulle approach to OCD in children represents one of many new emerging evidence-based treatment approaches specifically designed for children and adolescents (Barrett, Farrell, Pina, Peris, & Piacentini, 2008; Kazdin & Weisz, 2003).

norepinephrine, have been associated with people who experience panic (Charney et al., 2000; Deakin & Graeff, 1991; Fava & Morton, 2009; Graeff & Del-Ben, 2008; Gray, 1991). Neurotransmitter activity in the brain stem and midbrain have been implicated (Fava & Morton, 2009; Graeff & Del-Ben, 2008; Gray, 1991). Second, psychological contributions to the development of panic involve learning through modeling (Bandura, 1986) as well as emotionally feeling out of control of many important aspects of one's life (Barlow, 2002; Barlow & Craske, 2000; Li & Zinbarg, 2007). Cognitive explanations and situational cues also appear to contribute to panic (Clark, 1988; Roth, 1996; Teachman, Woody, & Magee, 2006). For example, heart rate increases due to exercise or excitement may result in fear that panic is imminent. Panic sufferers are thus more vigilant regarding their

Case Study: Hector Experiences Obsessive-Compulsive Disorder (Biopsychosocial)

Hector is an 18-year-old first-generation Mexican American living with his immigrant parents, two sisters, and maternal grandmother. Hector has recently completed high school, and has deferred his acceptance to a university due to the severity of his current symptoms. Hector's first language is Spanish, and he is also fluent in English.

Presenting Problem: Hector suffers from an obsessive-compulsive disorder that first emerged at age 14. His symptoms involve fears of contamination through contact with germs, blood, or other people. His fears compel him to wash his hands excessively throughout the day, disinfect his room at home, repeatedly cleanse any foods he consumes, wear gloves in public, and refuse to use public restrooms or restaurants. Hector's symptoms have greatly interfered with his social life, and he is largely isolated from peers or others outside of his immediate family. He is underweight due to his fear of many food items' safety and because of the extensive rituals he performs to cleanse anything he consumes. He also expresses some depressive symptoms in light of his feeling a prisoner to his obsessions and compulsions and due to their negative impact on his social and career goals.

Biological Factors: Hector's family history is positive for several paternal relatives having symptoms suggestive of obsessive-compulsive disorder, and research strongly supports a prominent biological/genetic role in the etiology of this disorder. Therefore, abnormalities in neurochemistry may be contributing greatly to his debilitating obsessions and compulsions.

Psychological Factors: Hector has always had a cautious personality, marked by a desire for order and predictability and a perfectionistic style. His ability to achieve success through highly ordered, careful, and perfectionistic behavior has ultimately served to reduce anxiety and enhance his self-esteem and family's pride in him. His high need for control extends into his grooming, exercising, eating, socializing, and academics.

Social Factors: Hector's family-centered upbringing has nurtured his increasing desire to stay within his home, to perform well, to aspire toward educational achievement and career success, and to feel a deep attachment to his family and Mexican heritage. Due to his parents' experience as primarily Spanish-speaking immigrants, he shares their suspicion of mental health professionals and other services that are perceived as having "official" or government ties.

Biopsychosocial Formulation and Plan: Hector's significant family history of obsessive-compulsive behavior speaks to a strong biological/genetic vulnerability to obsessive-compulsive disorder. While viewed by many as primarily a biological disorder, both psychological and social factors and interventions are essential to any successful treatment with Hector. Both his personality style and stressful school environment and social context that encourages achievement, home life, and suspicion of mental health professionals may subtly impact the course and treatment of Hector's obsessive-compulsive symptoms.

Treatment should involve a comprehensive approach sensitive to the experience of Mexican Americans and immigrants, and should involve a bilingual clinician to assist communication with Hector's parents and extended family members. Treatment

Case Study (Continued)

might incorporate medication to decrease obsessive-compulsive impulses and behavior as well as cognitive-behavioral techniques such as exposure, response prevention, thought stopping, relaxation, and problem solving to manage symptoms and to learn new adaptive skills. Psychoeducational group therapy may be used to help Hector learn more about the disorder as well as obtain group support from others experiencing similar problems. Psychotherapy might assist Hector to better understand and cope with his struggles; discuss feelings of anxiety, depression, and alienation; and obtain additional support. Family consultation might also assist in providing an optimal treatment approach by helping family members better understand Hector's condition.

---

bodily sensations. This awareness fuels further panic, resulting in a cycle of anxiety. Panic thus becomes a learned alarm (Barlow, 2002; Barlow & Craske, 2000; Landon & Barlow, 2004; Teachman et al., 2006). Finally, social factors such as family and work experiences, relationship conflicts, and cultural expectations may all contribute to the development and resolution of panic. Biological vulnerability coupled with psychological and social factors create the conditions for fear and panic to occur.

Treatment for panic also reflects the biopsychosocial nature of the disorder. Medications that impact the serotonin and norepinephrine neurotransmitter systems such as tricyclic antidepressants (e.g., imipramine) as well as benzodiazepines (e.g., Xanax) are often used (American Psychiatric Association, 2000; Asnis et al., 2001; Kalat, 2008; Klosko, Barlow, Tassinari, & Cerny, 1990; Roth, 1996; Roy-Byrne & Crowley, 2007) in conjunction with psychological treatments that involve gradual exposure to the feared situations, relaxation training, breathing exercises, cognitive therapy, and both insight-oriented and supportive psychotherapy (Barlow, 2002; Barlow & Craske, 2000; Klosko et al., 1990; Landon & Barlow, 2004; Teachman et al., 2006). Group treatment, contact with social support systems, and access to community resources also may provide a social component in treatment.

In addition to panic disorder, less severe forms of anxiety that are experienced by many can also be viewed from a biopsychosocial perspective. School phobia, separation anxiety, posttraumatic stress disorder, and other anxiety-based problems pose frequent clinical challenges. For example, many students experience test anxiety. Test anxiety not only results in feelings of intense discomfort prior to completing examinations but can also significantly impact performance. Some students are so anxious prior to an examination that they have difficulty sleeping and eating prior to the test. Some even routinely vomit. Biological vulnerability to anxiety as previously discussed is also a factor for many who experience test anxiety. They often tend to be more anxious in general and have family members who are anxious. This anxiety creates problems with bodily functioning such as eating and sleeping, which contributes to further anxiety about an exam in that they may feel more vulnerable to failure because they have been unable to sleep and eat. Psychological factors such as fear of failure, low self-esteem, and depression also contribute to test anxiety. Social factors such as expectations from parents, cultural norms, minority or language differences, and comparison to peers, siblings, and others may further increase anxiety.

Case Study: Nicole Experiences School Phobia (Biopsychosocial)

Nicole is a 9-year-old Caucasian female who lives with her mother. Nicole's father has never lived with the family and has not been in contact for many years. Nicole is a fourth-grade student at an urban elementary school and her mother works as an assistant at a veterinary hospital. Nicole and her mother moved to the city within the past year.

Presenting Problem: For the past several weeks, Nicole has increasingly refused to attend school. Initially, Nicole claimed illness in order to stay home, but lately has been tearfully refusing to go to school because she "wants to stay home" and is "scared to go back" to her classroom. Her mother has been forced to take time off from work, and occasionally enlists neighbors to stay with Nicole when she has to work. School officials are insisting that Nicole return to school immediately or begin a program of home tutoring.

Biological Factors: Nicole has always been an anxious child who had difficulty with separation and new experiences. While her mother is unaware of any family history of anxiety disorders, she claims that Nicole has seemed "edgy" and "fearful" from "day one." Nicole's diet is significant for her lack of appetite—excessive consumption of caffeine-rich cola beverages (approximately 6 cans per day)—and she also complains of sleep difficulties.

Psychological Factors: Nicole is deeply attached to her mother who works full time. Her mother finds it challenging to parent such a needy child. Nicole is beset by ongoing anxiety, particularly in response to separation experiences such as going to school and sleepovers at friends' homes. She has numerous strengths, such as her high intellect, loving nature, and artistic skill. She

has poor self-esteem, and is riddled with feelings of inadequacy.

Social Factors: Nicole lives and attends school in an urban environment. Having moved to the city only recently, Nicole and her mother feel relatively isolated and feel tentative in a big city with significant crime and hustle-bustle. Nicole's relatives all live in distant cities, and her mother's work demands have limited their ability to make social or community connections.

Biopsychosocial Formulation and Plan: Nicole, who may or may not have a biological tendency toward anxiety, is certainly not benefiting from the high levels of caffeine she is consuming. Caffeine may be contributing to some degree to her sleeplessness, low appetite, and possibly even her anxiety. Most prominent, however, appears to be Nicole's sense of isolation in a new and intimidating environment and her necessary dependence on her single, full-time working mother. By staying home from school, Nicole (perhaps unconsciously) succeeds in securing her mother's presence, or at least the attention of a neighbor. Nicole's school refusal may be inadvertently reinforced by the companionship and attention of her mother and neighbors, as well as by relief from the more challenging aspects of getting to school on public transportation and contending with school demands. The lack of a secure social support network appears to be enhancing her dependency on her mother and generating fearfulness and school refusal.

Treatment should progress in a number of ways. First, a behavioral program should be instituted whereby shaping is utilized to gradually reinforce Nicole's reentry to school. For example, Nicole's mother could spend the first hour of her school day during her first week back at school, then only

---

Case Study (Continued)

the first 30 minutes, then merely accompany her to school, and so forth. Nicole's successes could be reinforced by special time with her mother, enjoyable experiences with friends, or other desirable incentives. This behavioral plan should be augmented by some supportive psychotherapy to help Nicole express her fears and dependency needs, both verbally and through nonverbal means such as play

and drawing. Efforts should also be encouraged for the family to extend their social network, and consultation could be provided to determine available resources and strategies. Nicole's participation in activities (such as group art projects), which can enhance her sense of esteem and competence, would also be beneficial. Finally, all caffeine should be eliminated from Nicole's diet.

Cardiovascular Disease

Photo: Courtesy Zach Plante.

In addition to common mental health problems such as obsessive-compulsive disorder, anxiety and depressive disorders, and schizophrenia, the use of the biopsychosocial perspective in clinical psychology has been effectively extended to understand and treat major medical diseases. Thus, clinical psychologists are now involved in disorders that fall directly under the purview of medicine. Cardiovascular disease provides an excellent example of the biopsychosocial perspective's utility for clinical psychology in better understanding, preventing, and treating this problem. Cardiovascular disease (CVD) is the nation's number-one killer, resulting in 40% of all deaths and having been the leading cause of premature death in the United States since the 1930s (American Heart Association, 2009). As mentioned earlier, it has been estimated that 50% of the top ten causes of all deaths

are due to lifestyle factors such as smoking, drinking alcohol, high-fat diets, and sedentary lifestyles (Institute for the Future, 2000; S. Taylor, 2009; Schenck-Gustafsson, 2009; van Dam, Li, Spiegelman, Franco, & Hu, 2008). These lifestyle factors are especially closely associated with the development of CVD (American Heart Association, 2009; Dimsdale, 2009; Gump, Matthews, & Raikkonen, 1999; Krantz, Contrada, Hill, & Friedler, 1988; van Dam et al., 2008). In addition to lifestyle factors, personality, anger, anxiety, family medical history, and gender also contribute to CVD (Barlow, 2002; Contrada & Krantz, 1988; Institute of Medicine, 2001; Jorgensen, Johnson, Kolodziej, & Schreer, 1996; Schum, Jorgensen, Verhaeghen, Savro, & Thibodeau, 2003; S. Taylor, 2009; Thoresen & Powell, 1992). Even how one responds to stressful life events may contribute to CVD, as high stress responsivity has been reported to be an independent risk factor for the development of hypertension (Dimsdale, 2009; Jorgensen et al., 1996; Matthews, Woodall, & Allen, 1993). Anger expression has been found to be associated with the development of CVD in many studies (e.g., Institute of Medicine, 2001; Schum et al., 2003). Thus, *how* one responds to stress even when family history, gender, lifestyle, and personality factors are statistically accounted for and controlled is associated with the development of CVD. Furthermore, cultural, occupational, and socioeconomic factors also contribute to CVD. For example, Type A

Case Study: Taylor Experiences Cardiovascular Disease, Job and Family Stress, and Type A Personality (Biopsychosocial)

Taylor is a 60-year-old biracial male of African American and Korean heritage who works as a trial lawyer. Taylor has been divorced from his wife for the past three years following a highly contentious settlement and has one adult son who is married with two children.

Presenting Problem: Taylor recently experienced a cardiac arrest after a longstanding history of hypertension. He smokes a pack of cigarettes a day, exercises rarely, and works long hours in a high-stress job. His father died of a heart attack in his fifties, and cardiovascular disease is rampant throughout his paternal family history. Taylor's cardiologist has recommended that he make significant lifestyle and behavioral changes to maximize his opportunities for medical rehabilitation.

Biological Factors: Taylor's extensive family history of cardiovascular disease and his African American ethnicity clearly place him at increased risk for hypertension and heart attack. Taylor's cigarette smoking, lack of exercise, and stressful work likely exacerbate his medical condition.

Psychological Factors: Taylor manifests the classic Type A personality as a hard-driving, competitive, high-achieving, aggressive, time-urgent individual. The Type A personality is associated with cardiovascular disease, as are high-stress jobs and lifestyles. Thus, Taylor's personality, stressful work, and personal life may be contributing to his health problems. Finally, his smoking and lack of exercise further reflect his tension and poor health.

Social Factors: Taylor's recent divorce and lack of social life outside his work contribute to his high stress level and lack of support. Taylor's biracial ethnicity has prompted him to feel the need to perform exceptionally well in order to succeed as an ethnic minority in the field of law. Finally, Taylor has identified more strongly with his mother's Korean ancestry and traditions, which were actively integrated into the home, and yet has ultimately felt conflicted and alienated from both heritages given his dominantly African American appearance and love for his father as well.

Biopsychosocial Formulation and Plan: In addition to the regimen of medication and follow-up prescribed by his physician, Taylor would benefit from a number of other interventions as well. While his physician has told him to "stop smoking and start exercising," behavior and lifestyle are exceedingly difficult to change, and Taylor may well benefit from psychological consultation to develop a smoking cessation and exercise program. Cognitive-behavioral, group, and medical (e.g., nicotine patch, nicotine gum) interventions may be combined to assist with smoking cessation, while a behavioral program may be developed in conjunction with an exercise physiologist to develop a gradual build-up in exercise.

Psychological intervention would also be useful in contending with Taylor's Type A personality and response to the considerable work and personal stressors in his life, such as cognitive-behavioral, psychoeducational, and supportive techniques. Finally, Taylor may benefit from increased social support. Consultation regarding his family relationships, ethnic attitudes and identities, and leisure needs could be beneficial.

personalities in so-called white-collar positions are more likely to develop CVD than Type A personalities in blue-collar positions (Eaker, Pinsky, & Castelli, 1992; Haynes, Feinleib, & Kannel, 1980). Women with low levels of education are at higher risk for developing CVD than women from higher educational levels (American Heart Association, 2009; Institute of Medicine, 2001; Eaker et al., 1992; Schenck-Gustafsson, 2009; van Dam et al., 2008). African Americans are twice as likely to develop hypertension as other Americans (American Heart Association, 2009; Anderson & Jackson, 1987). Finally, poverty is closely associated with CVD in men, for example, being 2.5 times more likely to die from CVD if their annual income is below $10,000 compared to getting over $25,000 per year (Dimsdale, 2009; National Center for Health Studies, 2002).

Research suggests that those who have an immediate parental history of CVD are more likely to develop CVD as compared to those lacking this family history even when diet, weight, exercise, life stress, and other commonly known correlates of hypertension are statistically controlled (Fredrickson & Matthews, 1990; Jorgensen et al., 1996). For example, it has been estimated that 95% of those offspring whose biological parents both experience hypertension will develop hypertension, while 45% of offspring with one biological parent demonstrating hypertension will develop the condition (Smith et al., 1987).

Biopsychosocial factors play a significant role in the development of CVD. Furthermore, evidence suggests that these factors interact with and influence each other (Barlow, 2002; Carmody & Matarazzo, 1991; Haynes et al., 1980; Institute of Medicine, 2001; Schenck-Gustafsson, 2009; Sweet et al., 1991; Taylor, 2009). Treatments for CVD's symptoms including hypertension, cardiac arrhythmias, postmyocardial infarction, and other cardiac-related diseases reflect the biopsychosocial emphasis. These treatments may include an individualized approach involving surgery, medication, education, lifestyle management,

relaxation treatment, biofeedback, psychotherapy, and social support depending on the diagnosis and progression of the disease as well as the individual needs of the patient and the patient's family (Carmody & Matarazzo, 1991; Dimsdale, 2009; Institute of Medicine, 2001; Taylor, 2009).

Cancer

Cancer is another serious medical problem that is of interest to contemporary clinical psychologists. Principles of the biopsychosocial perspective offer assistance in understanding the disease as well as in developing intervention strategies for prevention and rehabilitation (Andersen, 1996, 2002; Skrzypulec, Tobor, Drosdzol, & Nowosielski, 2009). Cancer is the second leading cause of death in the United States, affecting approximately 25% of the population and killing about 570,000 people per year (American Cancer Society, 1997, 2000, 2009; Kort, Paneth, & Vande Woude, 2009; Ngo, 2009; S. Taylor, 2009). Deaths associated with cancer have increased steadily during the twentieth century, with large increases in lung cancer (especially among women) and both breast and prostate cancer (American Cancer Society, 1996, 2009). However, in most recent years, the death rate from cancer has actually decreased by about 2% due to improvements in cancer detection and treatment (J. Brody, 1996; Ngo, 2009; Skrzypulec et al., 2009; S. Taylor 2009). *Cancer* is a general term that subsumes more than 100 types of illnesses that have several similarities (S. Taylor, 2009). These primarily include problems associated with maladaptive cell growth and reproduction programmed by DNA at the cellular level. Some forms of cancer have a well-known etiology, such as exposure to cancer-causing toxins associated with poisons and pollutants. The poison DDT, the building material asbestos, as well as cigarette smoke and sun exposure are good examples. However, many forms of cancer develop without known causative factors. Some forms of cancer are easier to diagnose and treat than

Case Study: Marilyn —Biopsychosocial with Cancer

Marilyn is a 68-year-old Jewish female who lives with her husband. She has three adult children and five grandchildren. She has been retired from a long career as a high-level school administrator.

Presenting Problem: Marilyn has recently been diagnosed with invasive lobular breast carcinoma, a serious form of breast cancer discovered in a very early stage during a routine mammogram. Marilyn's mother died from bilateral lobular breast cancer diagnosed at age 69. Marilyn must decide on a course of treatment: mastectomy without radiation or lumpectomy with radiation and chemotherapy.

Biological Factors: Breast cancer is a disease that tends to run in families. Marilyn's mother's history of the disease places her at increased risk; however, unknown environmental and biological factors may also contribute to the development of breast cancer. Genetic concerns will cause her additional worry over her own daughter and three granddaughters.

Psychological Factors: In combating this fundamentally biological disease, emotional factors weigh heavily in treatment choice, outcome, and even ultimate mortality. First, Marilyn's surgical options are highly personal, and involve her sexuality, appearance, and feelings about both surgery and radiation. Second, adjusting to the long-term fears

and vulnerabilities associated with being a cancer victim poses a significant challenge. Psychoeducational needs also vary among individuals. In Marilyn's case, her desire to be well informed must be integrated into any treatment plan.

Social Factors: Social support has been shown to be a significant factor in outcome and longevity in breast cancer survivors. Both family and group support will be essential to Marilyn's decision making, adjustment, and long-term quality of life. Her husband's support will also be critical in Marilyn's adjustment to the bodily changes associated with surgery, as will the support of her many friendships developed over years of involvement in her temple and Hadassah.

Biopsychosocial Formulation and Plan: Marilyn's treatment would best integrate psychoeducational and social supportive interventions into her medical regimen of surgery, radiation, and chemotherapy. A "no-nonsense" type of person, Marilyn would likely benefit from informational access to physicians, libraries, and other breast cancer survivors in both group and individual contexts. Sensitive consultation on the part of medical and mental health professionals could assist Marilyn in making highly personal medical decisions and obtaining needed emotional support from community and family resources.

others, and cell growth associated with cancer can be rapid and life threatening or slow and easy to abate. Many forms of cancer are curable when caught and treated early in the development of the disease (American Cancer Society, 2000, 2009; Ngo, 2009; McCaul, Branstetter, Schroeder, & Glasgow, 1996).

Biopsychosocial factors interact and contribute to the development of many forms

of cancer. First, genetic factors influence the development of many types of cancer (Klausner, 1998; Kort et al., 2009; Skrzypulec et al., 2009). For example, colon and breast cancer have been found to be highly associated with genetic factors and tend to run in families. Specific inherited genes have been found to place some people at much higher risk for developing cancer than others.

Second, some cancers are related to lifestyle and ethnic factors (American Cancer Society, 1989, 1996, 2000, 2009; Andersen, 1996; Kort et al., 2009; Skrzypulec et al., 2009). For example, Caucasian men are more likely to develop skin and bladder cancer than non-Caucasians. Women from northern European backgrounds are at much higher risk for developing breast cancer than Asian women. African American men are at higher risk for prostate cancer, whereas Japanese Americans are at higher risk for stomach cancer (American Cancer Society, 2009). Third, cancer is related to lifestyle factors such as high-fat diets, sunbathing, smoking, alcohol consumption, and sedentary lifestyles (American Cancer Society, 1989, 1996, 2000, 2009; Fitzgibbon, Stolley, Avellone, Sugerman, & Chavez, 1996; Kort et al., 2009; Levy, 1983; Skrzypulec et al., 2009). Finally, psychosocial factors such as social support, stress, mood (e.g., depression and hopelessness), and even personality (e.g., repressiveness) have been associated with cancer in some studies (Andersen, 2002; Classen, Koopman, Angell, & Spiegel, 1996; B. Fox, 1988; G. Kaplan & Reynolds, 1988; Scherg, 1987; Sklar & Anisman, 1981). Although the relationships between all of these biopsychosocial factors and the development of cancer are unclear and even controversial, it appears that biological or genetic vulnerability interacts with life events and environmental factors (e.g., exposure to toxins, stress) to set the stage for the emergence and course of many forms of cancer.

Once cancer develops, the interaction of biopsychosocial factors contributes to the course of the illness. For example, negative emotions have been found to be associated with poorer prognosis among skin and breast cancer patients (Classen et al., 1996; Temoshok, 1987; Williamson, 2000). Depression among smokers leads to poorer outcome than among either nondepressed smokers or nonsmokers (Linkins & Comstock, 1988). In fact, these authors found an 18.5-fold increase in cancer risk among depressed smokers compared to nondepressed smokers. Stress has been hypothesized to interfere with

DNA repair, also resulting in poorer cancer prognosis (Levy, 1983; McGregor & Antoni, 2009). Furthermore, health-promoting behaviors such as healthy diets, exercise, stress reduction; compliance with medical evaluations and treatments; and the minimization of health-damaging behaviors such as alcohol and drug consumption, smoking, sunbathing, and exposure to environmental and occupational toxins are often necessary to improve recovery (American Cancer Society, 2000, 2009; Andersen, 1996; Fitzgibbon et al., 1996; Levy, 1983; McCaul et al., 1996; McGregor & Antoni, 2009; S. Taylor, 2009).

Treatment for cancer also reflects the biopsychosocial perspective. In addition to medical treatments such as chemotherapy, radiation, and surgery, social support and psychotherapy have been found to enhance rehabilitation and sometimes even longevity (Classen et al., 1996; Spiegal, Bloom, Kraemer, & Gottheil, 1989; McGregor & Antoni, 2009). Medical treatment for cancer often has problematic side effects such as nausea and vomiting associated with chemotherapy and a host of problems following surgery such as the loss of bodily function, pain, and fatigue. Cancer patients are understandably often depressed and anxious (Andersen, 2002; McGregor & Antoni, 2009; Williamson, 2000). They must learn to cope with both the physical and emotional ramifications of a truly frightening disease. Marital and family relationship and work-related problems also are common among cancer patients. Psychosocial treatments including hypnosis, visual imaging, relaxation training, psychotherapy, group therapy, and peer support have all been used with cancer patients (Andersen, 1992, 1996, 2002; Burish & Trope, 1992; Manne & Glassman, 2000; McGregor & Antoni, 2009; Turk & Fernandez, 1990; Williamson, 2000).

Many additional medical problems such as AIDS, arthritis, pain, headaches, and irritable bowel syndrome all involve biological, psychological, and social components in their development, maintenance, and outcome (Fava & Sonino, 2008; Gatchel & Blanchard, 1993;

Case Study: Mary—Biopsychosocial Synthesis

We now reexamine the case of Mary from an integrative biopsychosocial perspective.

Biological Factors: Mary may have a biological/genetic predisposition to panic disorder, agoraphobia, and anxiety-related conditions in light of her mother's history of these symptoms and research highlighting this association. She may be prone to experiencing anxiety through intense physiological reactions, especially under certain psychological and environmental conditions.

Psychological Factors: Mary presents a personality profile that places her at risk for anxiety. The sudden death of her father and subsequent loss of her mother due to her grief and anxiety resulted in tremendous emotional vulnerability to loss and separation. This underlying insecurity is further compounded in Mary by her failure to develop an internal sense of competence and developmentally appropriate independence to assist her in traversing life's challenges. Together, Mary experiences both her internal and external worlds as fragile and is vulnerable to genuine panic away from known safety zones.

Social Factors: Mary's Irish Catholic cultural and religious upbringing has provided both resources and liabilities. First, the traditions, rituals, and strong religious faith of her family and church community have contributed a sense of belonging, meaning, and safety in these contexts. However, her family's emphasis on the common good as opposed to individual development thwarted her separation from home; her cultural context that favored repression over expression of feelings and needs has stifled her expression and development; and her perceived view of the church's

teachings as encouraging self-sacrifice and denial of personal needs has perhaps contributed to Mary's inability to develop autonomous coping skills and values. Finally, Mary's role model of womanhood in our society, her mother, perhaps taught her the dependency and fearfulness she herself experiences.

Biopsychosocial Formulation and Plan: Mary's biological vulnerability to anxiety has been spurred into a full-blown panic disorder in the context of her personality and cultural development. A multidimensional treatment approach is clearly indicated and should include the following integrated components:

1. Individual psychotherapy that combines a supportive therapeutic relationship wherein Mary can safely explore her difficulties, work through her losses, and develop enhanced tools for autonomous and competent functioning.
2. Cognitive-behavioral strategies will be essential in assisting Mary with her immediate symptoms of panic, including the techniques of relaxation, exposure, and response prevention.
3. Adjunctive couples work may be useful in enlisting Mary's husband's support and encouragement for Mary to take on a more healthy and autonomous role without feeling her attachment to her husband (and others) threatened.
4. Utilization of church resources to assist Mary in greater mobility and in addressing some of her religious concerns.
5. Consultation with a psychiatrist may be useful in exploring the possible benefits and side effects associated with the use of psychoactive medication in treating Mary's symptoms of panic.

S. Taylor, 2009). These and other medical problems often involve biological vulnerability, environmental stress, personality, culture, and their ultimate interaction. Contemporary clinical psychology, along with traditional medical intervention, is useful in developing comprehensive prevention and intervention approaches for many of these problems.

Conclusion

The biopsychosocial perspective provides invaluable and comprehensive means of understanding and treating a wide variety of physical and emotional problems. Research evidence and clinical practice both tend to support the use of this perspective in treating many types of problems that are of interest to clinical psychologists and other professionals. Human difficulties are certainly complex with unidimensional theories proving less and less fruitful as more information becomes available concerning how people develop problems in their lives. The biopsychosocial perspective serves as an example of a current integrated orientation aimed at managing this complexity by approaching problems in a holistic, systemic, and multidimensional manner (Fava & Sonino, 2008; N. Johnson, 2003; Skrzypulec et al., 2009).

The Big Picture

It has become important for contemporary clinical psychologists to heed the call to integration in an increasingly complex field and society. The intelligent and sensitive synthesis of psychological approaches with relevant biological and social factors has led to an increasingly integrative field. While biological, psychological, and social factors may not always share equal weight in either cause or treatment, on a case-by-case basis, attention to the delicate interaction between these factors richly informs any study or intervention regarding clinical issues. Biopsychosocial integration in many ways is intimate with contemporary clinical psychology, expanding the range and usefulness of its efforts. As more research evidence emerges concerning the interplay of biological, psychological, and social influences on behavior, contemporary clinical psychologists will incorporate new knowledge to develop better applications in their efforts to help others.

Key Points

1. Today, the vast majority of clinical psychologists identify themselves as being integrative in orientation rather than adhering to one singular theoretical point of view. Clinical psychology has evolved in such a way that one theoretical approach no longer appears to adequately provide a satisfactory theory of human behavior and behavior change for most professionals. Integration of theoretical approaches and available techniques has become the norm rather than the exception.

2. The integration of approaches is a complex and challenging endeavor. Each approach has its own language, leaders, and practices. However, attempts at the integration of these major theoretical approaches tend to occur in one of three ways: (1) integrating the theory associated with each approach, (2) developing an understanding of the common factors associated with each approach, or (3) using eclecticism in a practical way to provide a range of available techniques to assist others.

3. The biopsychosocial approach is contextual and suggests that the interaction of biological, psychological, and social influences on behavior must be carefully addressed in order to understand the complexities of human behavior and help improve the lives of people who seek professional health and mental health services. The biopsychosocial approach applies a systems theory perspective to emotional, psychological, physical, and behavioral functioning in that each of these areas is intimately related and interdependent.

4. Professionals with a biological viewpoint generally favor biological interventions. As a result, they tend to treat problems suited to this approach. For example, electroconvulsive therapy (ECT) and medications are frequently used to treat depressions, mania associated with bipolar disorder, and schizophrenia.
5. Many clinical psychologists have begun to increasingly focus on the cultural and social influences on behavior that sociologists and anthropologists have been investigating for many years. While most practicing clinical psychologists still primarily work with individuals, couples, and families, rather than large organizations or groups, the influence of issues such as culture, socioeconomic factors, ethnicity, and community has received a great deal of attention concerning their relative contributions to human functioning and variation.

Key Terms

Biological vulnerability
Biopsychosocial
Diathesis-stress
Integration

For Reflection

1. Why is it harder to conduct research on some of the approaches than others?
2. Which approach has the most research support and why?
3. What are the disadvantages of adherence to one approach?
4. What theoretical approaches have generally been integrated?

5. What are some of the advantages of approach integration?
6. What is the biopsychosocial approach and how does it apply to clinical psychology?
7. What are the advantages and disadvantages of the biopsychosocial approach?
8. Use the biopsychosocial approach to discuss schizophrenia, depression, and cancer.

Real Students, Real Questions

1. How are the symptoms of panic disorder different in different cultures?
2. If integrative approaches are now the norm, why do people like Freud still get so much attention?
3. Are there any clinical problems where the biopsychosocial model is *not* useful?

Web Resources

www.psychologicalscience.org
Learn more about the scientific side of clinical psychology from the American Psychological Society.

www.americanheart.org
Learn more about heart disease from the American Heart Association.

www.cancer.org
Learn more about cancer from the American Cancer Society.

www.adaa.org
Learn more about anxiety disorders.

www.ocfoundation.org
Learn more about obsessive-compulsive disorder.

ROLES AND
RESPONSIBILITIES

Photo: Courtesy Zach Plante.

Contemporary Psychological Assessment I: Interviewing and Observing Behavior

7
Chapter

Chapter Objective

Discuss issues in conducting evaluations and focus on strategies for conducting interviews, behavioral observations, checklists, and physiological testing.

Chapter Outline

Goals, Purposes, and Types of Assessment
Reliability and Validity
Interviewing
Types of Interviews
Highlight of a Contemporary Clinical Psychologist:
Stanley Sue, PhD
Potential Threats to Effective Interviewing
Behavioral Observations
Checklists and Inventories
Physiological Testing

Assessing an individual's psychological makeup in the course of a few meetings is a formidable undertaking. This ability to access, identify, describe, and meaningfully integrate the quintessential workings of an individual's mind and emotional soul challenges both the human and intellectual resources of the psychologist.

Since the earliest days of professional psychology, assessment and testing have been important clinical activities. *Psychological assessment* is the process psychologists use to collect and evaluate information to make diagnoses, plan treatment, and predict behavior. Assessment may include interviewing the patient, reviewing past records (such as medical or school records), observing behavior, and administering psychological tests to measure various cognitive, behavioral, personality, family, and even biological factors. *Psychological testing* involves specific assessment techniques utilizing reliable and valid testing instruments that enable the psychologist to compare individual scores with the scores obtained from normative samples.

Assessment was the primary applied activity of clinical psychologists from the emergence of clinical psychology in 1896 to the end of World War II. As discussed in Chapter 3, the need to evaluate not only children who were struggling in school but also military recruits in the two world wars quickly propelled clinical psychology into the assessment and testing enterprise. Today, many clinical psychologists specialize in general psychological testing or the testing of specific populations (e.g., neuropsychological testing of elderly stroke patients, cognitive testing of preschoolers, personality testing of disturbed adolescents). In fact, psychological assessment and testing, with its numerous procedures and products, has become a multimillion-dollar industry.

In this chapter, psychological assessment through interviewing and behavioral observation is reviewed. In Chapter 8, the major undertakings of cognitive and neuropsychological assessment as well as personality assessment are discussed. Throughout, case examples are utilized to illustrate the actual use and application of assessment tools and measures.

Goals, Purposes, and Types of Assessment

People requesting the services of a clinical psychologist are typically motivated to seek help because of certain thoughts, feelings, or behaviors that cause them or others discomfort and concern. The symptoms they present may include anxiety, depression, anger, poor grades, interpersonal conflict, overeating, sleeplessness, loneliness, or irritability. They find such symptoms distressing and wish to obtain professional help in eliminating them. Routinely, important questions emerge during the sessions. The psychologist's job is to help answer fundamental questions such as the following:

Why is my son not behaving in school?

Why can't I get over the breakup with my girlfriend six months ago?

How can I overcome my intense fear and panic whenever I drive over a bridge?

What can I do to help my adult son cope with his bipolar illness?

How can my husband and I get along better?

Is my child mentally retarded?

Are my headaches caused by stress or by some serious medical problem like a brain tumor?

Why do I feel so depressed when things in life appear to be going fine?

How can I overcome the low self-esteem that prevents me from doing better at work?

Before the psychologist can help the patient, an initial assessment is necessary. The goal of assessment is usually to size up the situation by developing a fuller understanding of the factors that contribute to the presenting problem(s). Then the psychologist can make a diagnosis and outline a subsequent treatment or intervention plan. For example, someone may come to a psychologist for help in coping with frequent hallucinations and delusions. Various biological, psychological, and/or social factors might contribute to these symptoms. The person may have a medical problem, such as a tumor, or the hallucinations and delusions may be associated with amphetamine abuse or seizures. The symptoms may also be associated with posttraumatic stress disorder or schizophrenia, or with important social factors, for example, a financial crisis or violent trauma. Thus, the hallucinations and delusions could be associated with a variety of biological, psychological, and social factors. An assessment of the influence of these factors is critical in developing a satisfactory diagnostic and treatment plan. For example, treatment would be vastly different if the hallucinations and delusions were associated with amphetamine abuse, schizophrenia, bipolar illness, posttraumatic stress disorder or organic brain disease.

Sometimes the presenting problem or symptom is not the real problem. For instance, someone may seek help specifically for the treatment of tension headaches. Perhaps the patient is interested in using biofeedback or developing relaxation strategies to reduce the frequency, duration, and intensity of the headaches. However, after a session or two, the patient reports that her marriage is falling apart and she is fearful that her spouse is having an affair. The headaches may be associated with the stress of marital discord, but focusing on the headaches during the first few sessions might have felt less threatening than launching into the more compelling and painful topic of marital discord and infidelity. Thus, the headaches were a "ticket" into psychotherapy with marital issues comprising the core area of concern.

Depression is another example of a symptom that can be due to many causes. Again, an assessment of the biological, psychological, and social influences on each case of depression is necessary in order to develop an adequate diagnostic understanding and intervention strategy. For example, depression often runs in families and research suggests that there is frequently a genetic or biological vulnerability to depression among family members. Thus, if several biological relatives such as a parent, sibling, and/or grandparent have a history of a depressive disorder, the odds are higher that other family members will also develop depressive symptoms. Furthermore, depressive symptoms may be a side effect of various medications or may be associated with a number of physical ailments and conditions (e.g., heart disease, diabetes, cancer, chronic fatigue syndrome, chronic illness, sleep apnea). Psychological factors associated with depression may include stress at home or work, significant losses (e.g., death or separation from loved ones), relationship conflicts, personality disorders such as borderline personality, as well as numerous other psychological factors. Social factors including homelessness, cultural conflicts, racism, sexual harassment, financial problems, and other issues could also play a significant role in the manifestation of depressive symptoms. For many people, a constellation of biological, psychological, and social factors leads to depressive symptoms. Finally, other potential psychiatric problems are also associated with depression, such as attention deficit hyperactivity disorder, posttraumatic stress disorder, oppositional defiant disorder, eating disorders (e.g., obesity, anorexia nervosa, bulimia), and thought disorders (e.g., schizophrenia) among others. Therefore, comorbidity, defined as the coexistence of two or more clinical problems, needs to be adequately addressed in order to more fully understand the factors contributing to the depressive symptoms and the development of an appropriate diagnostic and treatment plan.

Assessment is fundamental to any professional psychological service and may take many different forms. For example, it could include clinical interviews with a patient or significant other (family member, friend, colleague); behavioral observations (classroom observation, role plays); the use of checklists, inventories, and psychological tests (IQ and personality tests); the review of previous records (medical charts, school records); and discussions with other professionals familiar with the person or situation in question (physician, school teacher, school counselor, clergy, probation officer, attorney). The choice of assessment tools depends on the nature of the presenting problem(s), the skills and perspective of the psychologist, the objectives and willingness of the patient, and practical matters such as cost and time.

Reliability and Validity

Regardless of the assessment approach used, the method must be both reliable and valid to be useful. *Reliability* is a term used to refer to the consistency of results. To develop conclusions and general principles from collected data, the data must be deemed reliable or consistent. Reliability might concern the ability of an examiner to obtain similar test scores on the same person on two different occasions. For example, scores obtained on an IQ test given to a child on Monday should not significantly differ if the test was administered by the same person to the same child on Wednesday. Reliability also may involve the ability to obtain the same scores on a test regardless of the identity of the examiner. For example, the child in the previous example should obtain the same IQ score whether Dr. A, B, or C is the test administrator. Reliability might also involve having several people or raters observe the same behavior of interest and provide independent ratings or scores for comparison. This refers to *interrater* or *interobserver* reliability. For example, while Dr. A is conducting an IQ test with a child, Dr. B and Dr. C observe the testing administration and score the test as well. There should be a high degree of agreement between the raters for the test to be reliable.

There are many different types of reliability that evaluate the consistency of an assessment procedure. These include test-retest reliability, alternate-form reliability, split-half reliability, Kuder-Richardson reliability and Cronbach's coefficient alpha, and scorer or interrater reliability (Anastasi & Urbina, 1997). *Test-retest* reliability refers to obtaining the same results when the test is given on two separate occasions. *Alternate-form* reliability refers to getting the same results even when two different but equal versions of the test are administered. *Split-half* reliability concerns getting the same results even when the test is evaluated in separate but equal parts (e.g., comparing scores from the odd-numbered items with the even-numbered items). *Kuder-Richardson* and *Cronbach's coefficient alpha* reliability refer to statistical procedures that measure the internal consistency of an assessment procedure. Finally, *scorer* reliability concerns how well two or more examiners conduct the evaluation and are consistent in their testing administration and scoring. Each of these types of reliabilities measures a different type of consistency. Reliability is rarely perfect and a small amount of error or imperfection can be expected from all tests. For example, a child may not obtain the exact same scores on two equivalent forms of an IQ test or two raters may not agree on every aspect of their evaluation of the same person. However, for a test to be reliable, the conclusions drawn from these scores must be the same.

In addition to reliability, assessment procedures must be valid. *Validity* refers to how well the assessment approach measures what it purports to measure. Does an IQ test really measure intelligence? Does a personality test really measure personality? Does the SAT really measure college aptitude? Like reliability, there are many different types of validity: Results from research must be deemed valid in order to draw conclusions and generalize findings. These include content, criterion (predictive and concurrent), construct validity, and discriminant (Anastasi & Urbina, 1997). *Content validity* refers to whether the assessment procedure covers a representative sample of the behaviors it is designed to measure. For example, an IQ test that includes only vocabulary items would not adequately represent all aspects of intelligence (e.g., problem-solving, abstract reasoning, visual-motor skills). *Criterion validity* refers to how well an assessment instrument predicts performance on another test or in a specific activity. For example, performance on an SAT should highly correlate with college performance. This is *predictive* criterion validity since SAT scores taken during high school are used to predict performance in college at a future date. *Concurrent validity* occurs when the two measures of interest are available at the same time. For example, SAT scores may be used to assess concurrent validity with the ACT examination, an alternative high school test used in place of the SAT in many high schools. Since the SAT and ACT can both be administered at about the same time, concurrent validity is assessed. *Construct validity* refers to how well the assessment device measures the theoretical construct it purports to measure. For example, does a test of anxiety truly measure the construct of anxiety? *Discriminant validity* refers to two or more measures that are appropriately unrelated. For example, SAT scores should be unrelated to shoe size, height, and social skills. Like reliability, the assessment of validity is rarely perfect. Some degree of error in measurement can be expected. For example, SAT scores do not perfectly predict college performance. Acceptable levels of validity may differ depending on the criteria of an investigator or the purpose of the validity assessment.

The assessment approaches discussed in this chapter and the next are used to diagnose, describe, explain, and predict behavior in a reliable and valid manner. Typically, assessment then leads to recommendations regarding treatment, selection (e.g., job or school program selection), or other intervention strategies. Since assessment is used to make important decisions affecting the lives of many, it is critical that reliable and valid procedures are used and used cautiously. Therefore, these measures must have appropriate clinical utility. *Clinical utility* refers to the notion that assessment devices must maximize the number of true positives and true negatives while minimizing false positives and false negatives. For example, if testing is used to determine who might be admitted to a psychiatric inpatient unit against their will (i.e., involuntary commitment), it is imperative the testing maximizes the odds of making a correct decision and minimizes any possibility that someone would be admitted against his or her will based on faulty, unreliable, and invalid test findings.

Interviewing

Most helping professionals use interviewing as a standard approach to assessing problems and formulating hypotheses and conclusions. Talking with appropriate, interested, and knowledgeable parties (the patient, family members, school teachers, physicians) is usually an important early step in conducting an assessment. Interviewing in clinical psychology entails much more than posing a series of questions to collect data about a case. Asking critical questions, carefully listening to answers, attending to missing or inconsistent information, observing nonverbal behavior, developing hypotheses, and ruling out alternative hypotheses are all part of the interviewing process.

The interview is a thoughtful, well-planned, and deliberate conversation designed to acquire important information (facts, attitudes, beliefs) that enables the psychologist to develop a working hypothesis of the problem(s) and its best solution. Whereas some interviews are highly structured with very specific questions and directions (e.g., those provided by the Diagnostic Interview Schedule [DIS] and the Structured Clinical Interview for *DSM-IV* [SCID]), others are unstructured and evolve as the conversation develops. While structured interviews are often used in research settings, unstructured interviews are generally used in practice settings. Structured interviews provide more precision but do not allow the flexibility to tailor the experience to the individual needs of the person being interviewed.

The use of structured or unstructured interviews is based on the goals of the interview. Effective interviewing is both an art and a science. Although a great deal of research has been conducted on interviewing skills, the psychologist does not read a manual on how to conduct an interview and then become an expert. Effective interviewing is developed over time with practice, supervision, experience, and natural skill.

While the actual information obtained might vary greatly depending on the specific purpose of the interview, generally a list of standard data is collected and discussed (Table 7.1). This includes demographic information such as name, address, telephone number, age, gender, or grade in school, occupation, ethnicity, marital status, and living arrangements. Information about current and past medical and psychiatric problems and treatments is also usually requested. The chief complaint or a list of symptoms experienced by the patient is discussed as well as the patient's hypotheses regarding the contributing factors

Table 7.1   Typical Information Requested during a Standard Clinical Interview
Identifying information (e.g., name, age, gender, address, date, marital status, education level)
Referral source (who referred the person and why)
Chief complaint or presenting problems (list of symptoms)
Family background
Health background
Educational background
Employment background
Developmental history (birth and early child development history)
Sexual history (sexual experiences, orientation, concerns)
Previous medical treatment
Previous psychiatric treatment
History of traumas (e.g., physical or sexual abuse, major losses, major accidents)
Current treatment goals

associated with the development and maintenance of the problem(s). The interviewer often wants to know how the person has tried to cope with the problem(s) and why he or she wishes to obtain professional services now.

Interviewing is used for a wide variety of purposes. For example, an interview is typically conducted whenever a psychologist begins psychotherapy with a new patient. Interviews are also conducted to determine whether someone is in a crisis and might be at risk for self-injury or injury to others. An interview might be conducted to determine the current mental status (e.g., is alert and oriented toward time, place, and person) of a patient at a given moment. An interview is generally conducted as part of any psychological evaluation. Although numerous different interviewing situations exist, certain techniques and skills are necessary for nearly all types of interviews. These include developing rapport, effective listening skills, effective communication, observation of behavior, and asking the right questions.

Rapport

When patients talk with a psychologist about problems they are experiencing, they are often uncomfortable sharing their intimate concerns with a complete stranger. They may have never discussed these concerns with anyone before, including their best friends, parents, or spouse. They may worry that the psychologist might make negative judgments about their problems. They may feel embarrassed, silly, worried, angry, or uncomfortable in a variety of ways. An individual from an ethnic, racial, or sexual minority may fear being misunderstood or maltreated. To develop a helpful, productive, and effective interview, the psychologist must develop rapport with the person he or she is interviewing. **Rapport** is a term used to describe the comfortable working relationship that develops between the professional and the interviewee. The psychologist seeks to develop an atmosphere and relationship that is positive, trusting, accepting, respectful, and helpful.

Although there is no specific formula for developing rapport, several principles are generally followed. First, the professional must be attentive. He or she must focus complete attention on the patient without interruption from distractions such as telephone calls or personal concerns. Second, the professional must maintain a rapport-building posture—for example, by maintaining eye contact and facing the patient with an open posture without a physical barrier such as a large desk impeding communication. Third, the psychologist actively and carefully listens to the patient, allowing him or her to answer questions without constant interruption. Fourth, the psychologist is nonjudgmental and noncritical when interacting with the patient, especially in regard to personal disclosures. The professional also strives toward genuine respect, empathy, sincerity, and acceptance, without acting as a friend or a know-it-all. He or she tries to create a supportive, professional, and respectful environment that will help the patient feel as comfortable and as well understood as possible during the interview.

Effective Listening Skills

In addition to the development of rapport, an effective interviewer must be a good listener. While this may appear obvious, good listening skills are important to develop and generally do not come naturally for most people. People often find it challenging to fully listen to another without being distracted by their thoughts and concerns. Many are too focused on what they are thinking or want to say rather than on listening to someone else. Furthermore, careful listening must occur at many different levels. This includes the *content* of what is being said as well as the *feelings* behind what is being said. Listening also involves paying attention to not only what is being said but how it is presented. For example, someone may deny feeling anger and yet have his or her arms crossed and teeth clenched, thus suggesting otherwise. Listening also includes paying attention to what is not being said. Thus, listening involves a great deal of attention and skill, including the ability to read between the lines.

Effective interviewers must learn to use and develop active listening skills, which include paraphrasing, reflection, summarization, and clarification techniques (Cormier, Nurius, & Osborn, 2008). Paraphrasing involves rephrasing the content of what is being said. It means careful listening to another's story and then attempting to put the content of the story into a brief summary. The purpose of paraphrasing is to help the person focus and attend to the content of his or her message. In contrast, reflection involves rephrasing the feelings of what is being said in order to encourage the person to express and understand his or her feelings better. Summarization involves both paraphrasing and reflection in attempting to pull together several points into a coherent brief review of the message. Summarization is used to highlight a common overall theme of the message. Finally, clarification includes asking questions to ensure that the message is being fully understood. Clarification is needed to ensure that the interviewer understands the message as well as to help the person elaborate on his or her message.

Examples of these techniques are provided in the following example of a couple trying to decide if they should get married. Eduardo is a 36-year-old Latino man who has been dating Janice, a 33-year-old Caucasian woman, for several years. He feels that he cannot commit to marriage because he feels unsure if Janice is the "right one" for him. Janice wants to marry Eduardo and reports feeling frustrated that he has so many doubts. Eduardo further reports that he is unsure if he could stay faithful to one person for the rest of his life.

EDUARDO: "I'm not much of a believer in the institution of marriage. It seems to me that it made sense when the average life span was only 30 years or so. How can someone make a decision like this during their 20s or

30s and have it be a good decision for 50 years or more? My parents are still married after 50 years but they hate each other. I don't know why they stay together. Janice is really nice and I like being with her but who knows what the future will hold for us. She has a lot of great qualities but some characteristics drive me nuts. For example, I really don't like some of her friends. They are boring. She's really a practical person, which I like, but sometimes there isn't a lot of excitement in our relationship."

Examples of active listening techniques offered by the therapist follow:

PARAPHRASE: "So you seem to be unsure if marriage to Janice or anyone for that matter is right for you."

REFLECTION: "To some degree you feel bored in your relationship."

SUMMARIZATION: "You are unsure if marriage is right for you and you are concerned that Janice may not be the right person for you regardless of your views on marriage."

CLARIFICATION: "When you say that your relationship lacks excitement are you also referring to your sexual relationship?"

Effective Communication

To conduct a successful interview, effective communication is a requirement. The professional must use language appropriate to the patient, whether a young child, an adolescent, or a highly educated adult. The interviewer generally avoids the use of professional jargon, or psychobabble, and speaks in terms that are easily understood. The interviewer tries to fully understand what the patient is trying to communicate and asks for clarification when he or she is unsure.

Observation of Behavior

The interviewer pays attention not only to what is being said during a clinical interview, but also to how it is being said. Observation of

Multicultural Issues and Communication in Conducting Interviews

Communication styles can be very different based on cultural background. In our increasingly multicultural society, it is important for interviewers to be attentive to the influence of culture on communication and interviewing styles. D. Sue and Sue (2008) outline a number of important subtle differences in communication style associated with various ethnic groups. For example, their review of the literature suggests that Caucasians tend to speak loud and fast using head nods, eye contact, and quick responses, in objective and task-oriented communication. However, African Americans tend to speak with affect, use eye contact more when speaking than when listening, and use more affective and interpersonal communication styles. Asian Americans and Latino/a populations tend to speak more softly, avoid eye contact when listening as well as speaking to a high-status person, and use low-key and indirect communication styles. They suggest that psychologists must be sensitive to different communication styles and learn more about how race, culture, and gender impact these styles.

---

nonverbal communication (e.g., body posture or body language, eye contact, voice tone, attire) provides potentially useful information. For example, a patient may describe severe depressive symptoms and suicidal thoughts, yet smile a great deal and appear energized and in good spirits during the interview. Another patient might state that he or she feels completely comfortable, yet sits with arms and legs tightly crossed while avoiding eye contact. Inappropriate dress (e.g., T-shirt and shorts on a very cold winter day or for a job interview) or a disheveled appearance may provide further insight into the nature of the patient's difficulties.

Asking the Right Questions

A good interviewer must ask the right questions.

All too often, inexperienced interviewers forget to ask a critical question only to remember it after the patient has left. Experience with interviewing and a solid understanding of psychopathology and human behavior are needed in order to ask the right questions. Typical questions deal with issues such as the frequency, duration, severity, and patient's perception of the etiology of the presenting problem. A careful understanding of the symptoms as well as the patient's efforts to cope with the problem is usually important. A comprehensive examination of biological, psychological, and social factors associated with the problem is useful, as are questions pertaining to suicide risk and other dangerous behaviors where indicated.

In the following case study, the interviewer's questions lead to a better understanding of the factors that may be associated with Joe's depression. Joe's long work hours as well as his conflictual relationships with both his boss and his father appear to play important roles in his self-esteem and depression. On the basis of the information given, the depression does not appear severe enough to require hospitalization or other dramatic interventions (e.g., electroconvulsive therapy, medication). Continued individual therapy appears warranted, however.

Types of Interviews

There are many different types of interviews conducted by psychologists. Some interviews are conducted prior to admission to a clinic or hospital, some are conducted to determine if a patient is in danger of injuring herself or someone else, some are conducted to determine a diagnosis. Whereas some interviews are highly structured with specific questions asked of all patients, others are unstructured and spontaneous. While not an exhaustive list, this section briefly reviews examples of the major types of interviews conducted by clinical psychologists.

Initial Intake or Admissions Interview

The purpose of the initial intake or admissions interview is to develop a better understanding of the patient's symptoms or concerns in order to recommend the most appropriate treatment or intervention plan. Whether the interview is conducted for admission to a hospital, an outpatient clinic, a private practice, or some other setting, the initial interview attempts to evaluate the patient's situation as efficiently as possible (Figure 7.1). In addition to learning more about the patient's problems and needs, the psychologist also seeks to determine whether the services provided by the hospital, the clinic, or the practitioner can adequately meet the patient's needs. For example, someone might request services for treating depression, yet during the course of the initial interview, the patient reveals that he has a significant alcohol and cocaine problem. If the psychologist feels that substance abuse treatment is warranted, he or she might refer the patient to a colleague or clinic that specializes in substance abuse problems rather than undertaking treatment of a problem outside his or her area of expertise. Another goal of the initial interview is to orient the patient to the hospital, clinic, or practice. The psychologist typically discusses treatment and payment options, informs the patient about

Photo: Zigy Kaluzny, Tony Stone Images, New York, Inc.

Figure 7.1

A psychologist conducts a clinical interview.

the policies and procedures of the treatment facility or practice, and answers the patient's questions about the services offered. Finally, the initial interview often attempts to instill trust, rapport, and hope that the treatment professional(s) and/or facility will professionally and competently deal with the patient's concerns.

Mental Status Interview

Often a mental status interview is conducted to screen the patient's level of psychological functioning and the presence or absence of abnormal mental phenomena such as delusions, delirium, or dementia. Mental status exams include a brief evaluation and observation of the patient's appearance and manner, speech characteristics, mood,

Case Study: Joe Experiences Depression

Joe is a 35-year-old Caucasian middle manager of a large construction company. He has been married for five years and has no children.

Presenting Problem: Joe is concerned about his feelings of depression. He experiences sadness, hopelessness, feelings of worthlessness, and general lassitude. He reports that these feelings occur about 10 or so days each month and are usually associated with a conflict or problem at work. The following is a transcript from a segment of the initial interview conducted by a clinical psychologist.

Interviewer: How long have you had these feelings of depression? (duration of problem)

Patient: Oh, probably about 20 years.

Interviewer: Do you remember what happened 20 years ago that started these feelings? (etiology of problem)

Patient: No.

Interviewer: Have you ever sought professional help for these problems during the past 20 years? (previous history of treatment)

Patient: No. I have never seen a psychologist or anyone else about them before. In fact, other than my wife, I don't think anyone knows about them.

Interviewer: What made you decide to do something about them now? (antecedents for current help seeking)

Patient: Well, my wife encouraged me to see someone—I think because she recently saw a psychologist for feelings of panic and anxiety whenever she drives over a major bridge. Since she found it helpful, she thought I might talk this over with someone. Also, my new insurance plan at work allows me up to 12 free sessions, and so I thought I might as well take advantage of it.

Interviewer: Do you feel comfortable doing this? (assess feelings associated with help seeking)

Patient: Yes. I feel good about finally doing something about my depression.

Interviewer: What exactly happens when you feel depressed? (assess patient symptoms)

Patient: Well, I just feel worthless, like my self-esteem takes a hit.

Interviewer: So you generally feel bad about yourself?

Patient: Yes, definitely.

Interviewer: Any troubles or changes with sleeping or eating? (assess vegetative signs)

Patient: Not really. I sleep okay and eat fine. In fact, I probably could lose a few pounds. I have a weak spot for chocolate, especially dark chocolate cremes.

Interviewer: How do you try to cope with these feelings when they occur?

Patient: I generally talk it over with my wife, who is very supportive. I also usually try to do some exercise like taking a hard run or bike ride. I think the distraction of exercise helps me a great deal. Sometimes, when I feel especially bad, I cry a little and the release makes me feel better.

Interviewer: So you either distract yourself with physical activity or cry when things are really bad.

Patient: Right.

Interviewer: Do other members of your family have trouble with depression or other mood problems?

Patient: Not really. My mother had bouts of depression now and then but nothing serious. My brothers and sisters, my father, my grandparents all seem to have no significant trouble with depression or mood problems.

Interviewer: Do you (or any family members) ever experience the opposite of depression? Do you or do they ever feel very

Case Study (Continued)

euphoric, maybe get little sleep, spend a lot of money, feel on top of the world?

Patient: No, if you mean do I ever feel manic, I don't. No one in my family does either, that I know of.

Interviewer: Do you ever feel so low that you think of hurting yourself?

Patient: Not really, I might have a fleeting thought that I wish I were dead, but I never feel what I would call suicidal and I would never hurt myself.

Interviewer: Have you ever tried to hurt yourself?

Patient: No, never.

Interviewer: What do you think contributes to your feelings of depression?

Patient: Well, I work really hard. Usually I start work at 7 A.M. and finish at 7 to 8 P.M. Sometimes my boss drives me crazy. He is so controlling. You always feel like he stands over your shoulder and tells you how you could be doing your job better. Generally, I like my job. It pays

very well and I like the type of work I do, but I don't like the hours or my boss.

Interviewer: So the job has some major pros, like money, yet major cons like long hours and a challenging boss.

Patient: Right.

Interviewer: Does your boss remind you of anyone else in your life?

Patient: Well, to tell you the truth, he does remind me of my dad a bit. My dad, bless his heart, is a loving guy, and I have a good relationship with him, but his one major flaw is that he is controlling and always has an opinion on how you could do something better. He means well, but he sure can be annoying.

Interviewer: Do you think the similarity between your boss and your father might have anything to do with your depressive feelings?

Patient: I'm not sure. I never really thought about it or made a connection between the two.

---

thought processes, insight, judgment, attention, concentration, memory, and orientation. Results from the mental status examination provide preliminary information about the likely psychiatric diagnoses experienced by the patient as well as offering some direction for further assessment and intervention (e.g., referral to a specialist, admission to psychiatric unit, evaluation for medical problems that impact psychological functioning). For instance, mental status interviews typically include questions and tasks to determine orientation to time (e.g., "What day is it? What month is it? What year is it?"), place ("What city are you in? Where are you now? Which hospital are you in?"), and person ("Who am I? Who are you? Who is the president of the United States?"). Also, the mental status interview assesses short-term memory (e.g., "I am going to name three objects I'd like you to try

and remember: dog, pencil, and vase") and attention-concentration (e.g., "Count down by 7s starting at 100. For example, 100, 93, and so forth").

Baker and Trzepacz (2005) offer a useful outline or checklist for mental status examinations. This includes the assessment of (1) appearance, attitude, and activity (e.g., level of consciousness, attire, appropriate eye contact, degree of cooperativeness and resistance, appropriate voluntary, involuntary, and automatic movements), (2) mood and affect (e.g., appropriate type, intensity, range, and reactivity of emotion), (3) speech and language (e.g., fluency, comprehension, quality of speech), (4) thought process, thought content, and perception (e.g., possible delusions, hallucinations, ruminations, obsessions, suicidal or homicidal ideation, peculiar thoughts), (5) cognition (e.g., attention, concentration, short- and long-term memory, orientation to time, place, and person), and (6) insight and judgment (e.g., awareness of internal and external realities, appropriate use of defense mechanisms).

While there are some mental status examinations that are structured, resulting in scores that can be compared to national norms, most are unstructured and do not offer a scoring or norming option. During the examination, the interviewer notes any unusual behavior or answers to questions that might be indicative of psychiatric disturbance. For example, being unaware of the month, year, or the name of the current president of the United States usually indicates mental problems. This can result in bias based on the interviewer's clinical judgment during an evaluation unless objective scoring can be conducted (Herbert, Nelson, & Herbert, 1988).

Crisis Interview

A crisis interview occurs when a patient is in the middle of a significant and often traumatic or life-threatening crisis. The psychologist or other mental health professional or paraprofessional (e.g., a trained volunteer) might encounter such a situation while working at a suicide or poison control hotline, an emergency room, a community mental health clinic, a student health service on campus, or in many other settings. Although many of the interviewing principles discussed earlier still apply (e.g., asking the right questions, attentive listening), the nature of the emergency dictates a rapid, "get to the point" style of interview as well as quick decision making in the context of a calming style. For example, it may be critical to determine whether the person is at significant risk of hurting him- or herself or others. Or it may be important to determine whether the alcohol, drugs, and/or medication the person ingested is a lethal dose. The interviewer must maintain a calm and clearheaded manner while asking critical questions in order to deal with the situation effectively. The interviewer may need to be more directive

(e.g., encouraging the person to phone the police or to unload a gun, providing instructions to induce vomiting, or to step away from a tall building or bridge); break confidentiality if the person (or someone else, such as a child) is in serious and immediate danger; or enlist the help of others (e.g., police department, ambulance).

Diagnostic Interview

The purpose of a diagnostic interview is to obtain a clear understanding of the patient's particular diagnosis. Thus patient-reported symptoms and problems are examined in order to classify the concerns into a diagnosis. Typically, the *Diagnostic and Statistical Manual-IV-TR* (*DSM IV-TR;* American Psychiatric Association, 2000) is used to develop a diagnosis based on five categories, or axes (Table 7.2). The *DSM-IV-TR* is used by hospitals, clinics, insurance companies, and the vast majority of mental health professionals to classify and diagnose psychiatric problems. While this is the most widely used diagnostic classification of psychiatric disorders in the United States, other classification systems exist and have both advantages and disadvantages (Beutler & Malik, 2002; Mjoseth, 1998). The five axes for each diagnosis provide information concerning the clinical syndromes, influence of potential personality disorders, medical problems, psychosocial stressors, and level of functioning. Specifically, Axis I includes the presence of clinical syndromes (e.g., depression, panic disorder, schizophrenia). Axis II includes potential personality disorders (e.g., paranoid, antisocial, borderline). Axis III includes physical and medical problems (e.g., heart disease, diabetes, cancer). Axis IV includes psychosocial stressors currently experienced by the patient (e.g., fired from job, marital discord, financial hardship). Axis V (Global Assessment of Functioning or GAF) includes a clinician rating of how well the patient is coping with his or her problems (1 = poor coping, 100 = excellent coping). The interview is conducted to rule out inapplicable diagnoses and rule in

Table 7.2   **Diagnostic Categories in the *DSM-IV-TR* and Examples**

Disorders Usually First Diagnosed in Infancy, Childhood, or Adolescence (e.g., Mild Mental Retardation Autistic Disorder, Attention Deficit Hyperactivity Disorder, Conduct Disorder)
Delirium, Dementia, and Amnesia and Other Cognitive Disorders (e.g., Dementia of the Alzheimer's Type, Vascular Dementia, Dementia Due to Parkinson's Disease)
Mental Disorders Due to a General Medical Condition (e.g., Personality Change Due to Head Injury)
Substance-Related Disorders (e.g., Alcohol Abuse, Caffeine Intoxication, Cannabis-Induced Anxiety Disorder, Inhalant Abuse)
Schizophrenia and Other Psychotic Disorders (e.g., Schizophrenia, Paranoid Type, Schizoaffective Disorder, Shared Psychotic Disorder)
Mood Disorders (e.g., Major Depressive Disorder, Bipolar I Disorder, Dysthymic Disorder, Cyclothymic Disorder)
Anxiety Disorders (e.g., Panic Disorder with Agoraphobia, Social Phobia, Posttraumatic Stress Disorder, Obsessive-Compulsive Disorder)
Somatoform Disorders (e.g., Hypochondriasis, Conversion Disorder, Body Dysmorphic Disorder)
Factitious Disorders (e.g., Factitious Disorder with Predominantly Physical Signs and Symptoms)
Dissociative Disorders (e.g., Dissociative Amnesia, Depersonalization Disorder)
Sexual and Gender Identity Disorders (e.g., Sexual Aversion Disorder, Male Erectile Disorder, Exhibitionism, Pedophilia)
Eating Disorders (e.g., Anorexia Nervosa, Bulimia Nervosa)
Sleep Disorders (e.g., Primary Insomnia, Sleepwalking Disorder, Nightmare Disorder)
Impulse-Control Disorders Not Elsewhere Classified (e.g., Kleptomania, Pathological Gambling, Trichotillomania)
Adjustment Disorders (e.g., Adjustment Disorder with Depressed Mood, Adjustment Disorder with Disturbance of Conduct)
Personality Disorders (e.g., Paranoid Personality Disorder, Borderline Personality Disorder, Histrionic Personality Disorder)
Other Conditions That May Be a Focus of Clinical Attention (e.g., Psychological Factors Affecting Physical Condition, Relational Problems, Malingering, Religious or Spiritual Problem)

applicable ones. Thus, the goal of the interview is to determine whether the patient meets the diagnostic criteria of a particular disorder.

Diagnostic interviewing can be challenging. It is frequently difficult to ascertain the precise diagnosis through interview alone. Also, comorbidity may complicate the clinical picture. For instance, a patient who has been losing a lot of weight might be interviewed to determine whether he or she has anorexia nervosa, a disorder that results in self-starvation. Anorexia nervosa is especially prevalent in adolescent girls. Significant weight loss may also be associated with a number of medical problems (e.g., brain tumor)

or other psychiatric problems (e.g., depression). To determine whether the weight loss symptoms might be associated with anorexia nervosa, the clinician may wish to conduct a diagnostic interview to see if the patient meets the *DSM-IV-TR* diagnostic criteria for anorexia nervosa. Furthermore, additional possible diagnoses may need to be considered as well (e.g., depression, phobia, borderline personality). While some clinicians might choose to use a structured clinical interview (see next section for description of structured interview approaches), most would conduct their own clinical interview. Table 7.3 provides several examples of diagnoses among children.

Table 7.3   **Examples of *DSM-IV-TR* Diagnoses for Three Children**

Jim:	
Axis I:	Separation Anxiety Disorder (309.21)
	Learning Disorder NOS (315.90)
Axis II:	No Diagnosis on Axis II (V71.09)
Axis III:	Type I Diabetes
Axis IV:	Psychosocial Stressors: is picked on in school, mother has cancer
Axis V:	GAF: Current (61), Past Year (65)
Peter:	
Axis I:	Attention Deficit/Hyperactivity Disorder, Predominantly Inattentive Type (314.01), Mild Disruptive Behavior Disorder, Not Otherwise Specified (312.9), Mild Depressive Disorder, Not Otherwise Specified (311.00)
Axis II:	No Diagnosis on Axis II (V71.09)
Axis III:	None reported
Axis IV:	Psychosocial and Environmental Problems: father lost job, shares room with two other siblings in very small apartment
Axis V:	GAF: Current (55), Past Year (65)
Beth:	
Axis I:	Oppositional Defiant Disorder (313.81)
	Academic Problem (V62.30)
Axis II:	Mild Mental Retardation (317.00)
Axis III:	Allergies
Axis IV:	Psychosocial Stressors: parents divorce, moved to new school
Axis V:	GAF: Current (55), Past Year (65)

SPOTLIGHT

The Diagnostic and Statistical Manual of Mental Disorders (DSM)

For more than 50 years, the *DSM* has been the "psychiatric bible" for the diagnosis of mental disorders. It was originally published by the American Psychiatric Association in 1952 and has been revised several times (in 1968, 1980, 1987, 1994, and most recently in 2000). The *DSM* is the standard for defining a wide range of mental health diagnoses and is used for diagnosis, treatment planning, and insurance reimbursement. Over the years, the number of diagnoses have grown from 106 in the first edition to 365 in the current version (Beutler & Malik, 2002).

The current manual (*DSM-IV-TR*) provides diagnoses on a multiaxial system using five axes. Axis I includes major clinical disorders such as schizophrenia, bipolar, mood disorders, and such. Axis II includes personality disorders and mental retardation. Axis III includes any medical problems such as heart disease, cancer, diabetes, and so forth. Axis IV lists psychosocial problems while Axis V is a 1-to-100 global assessment of functioning where 100 is excellent functioning and 1 is great dysfunction.

Despite the universal use of the manual, there are a number of problems with it. First, competent clinicians agree on diagnoses using the *DSM* only 70% of the time (Kirk & Kutchins, 1992). This is especially true for personality disorders (Lowe & Widiger, 2009). Second, there is a great amount of overlap or comorbid diagnostic criteria so that it can be difficult to determine how one disorder is truly different from another (Lowe & Widiger, 2009; Widiger & Clark, 2000). Furthermore, many have reported that the *DSM* system is not attentive enough to multicultural issues and women's issues (Beutler & Malik, 2002; Kirmayer, 2001). Finally, many have concerns about the political nature of the *DSM* development process. Leading psychiatrists meet to discuss the diagnostic criteria in several task forces and then ultimately vote on what should or should not be included. Some have called for a more research and empirical basis for the development of a diagnostic system (Beutler & Malik, 2002; Lowe & Widiger, 2009; Widiger & Clark, 2000). The political issues extend to financial matters in that a *DSM* diagnosis is generally always needed in order to receive health insurance benefits. Therefore, clinicians may use a diagnosis that does not truly reflect what a patient experiences in order to maximize the odds that an insurance claim will be paid. Although many have suggested that the *DSM* system should be changed, there is little likelihood that the *DSM* system will be abandoned anytime soon. The next edition, DSM V, is scheduled to be released during 2013.

Structured Interviews

In an effort to increase the reliability and validity of clinical interviews, a number of structured interviews have been developed (e.g., The Anxiety Disorders Interview Schedule for Children, Silverman & Nelles, 1988; Diagnostic Interview Schedule [DIS], Robins, Helzer, Croughan, & Ratcliff, 1994; Structured Clinical Interview for *DSM-IV* [SCID-I and SCID-II], First, Spitzer, Gibbon, & Williams, 1997, 2002; Structured Interview for the Five-Factor Model of Personality [SIFFM], Trull & Widiger, 1997). Although the SCID interview is the most common one used, each has both advantages and disadvantages depending on the goals of the interview and the patient involved (First, Spitzer, et al., 1997, 2002). Structured interviews include very specific questions (e.g., "Have you ever had a spell or attack when all of a sudden you felt frightened, anxious, or very uneasy in situations when most people would not be afraid?" Robins et al., 1994) asked in a detailed flowchart format. The goal is to obtain necessary information to make an appropriate diagnosis, to determine whether a patient is appropriate for a specific treatment or research program, and to secure critical data that are needed for patient care. The questions are generally organized and developed in a decision-tree format. If a patient answers yes to a particular question (such as in the example about panic), a list of additional questions might be asked to obtain details and clarification (e.g., "During this spell did your heart pound? Did you have tightness or pain in your chest? Did you sweat? Did you tremble or shake?" Robins et al., 1994). If the patient answers no to a particular question, the follow-up questions are skipped. Clinical judgment and spontaneity are minimized or eliminated in structured interviews. The interview proceeds

Table 7.4   **Example of Part of a Structured Interview from the SCID-I**

SPECIFIC PHOBIA	SPECIFIC PHOBIA CRITERIA	SCREEN Q #7	
		YES	NO
If Screening Question #7 Answered "No," Skip to Obsessive-Compulsive Disorder		IF NO: GO TO OBSESSIVE-COMPULSIVE DISOR-DER	
IF QUESTION #7 ANSWERED "YES": You've said that there are other things that you've been especially afraid of, like flying, seeing blood, getting a shot, heights, closed places, or certain kinds of animals or insects . . .			
IF SCREENER NOT USED: Are there any other things that you have been especially afraid of, like flying, seeing blood, getting a shot, heights, closed places, or certain kinds of animals of insects? Tell me about that. What were you afraid would happen when (CONFRONTED WITH PHOBIC STIMULUS)?	A. Marked and persistent fear that is excessive or unreasonable, cued by the presence of anticipation of a specific object or situation (e.g., flying, heights, animals, receiving an injection, seeing blood).	? 1 2 3 ↓ GO TO OBSESSIVE-COMPULSIVE DISORDER	F67
Did you always feel frightened when you (CONFRONTED PHOBIC STIMULUS)?	B. Exposure to the phobic stimulus almost invariably provokes an immediate anxiety response, which may take the form of a situationally bound or situationally predisposed panic attack. Note: in children, the anxiety may be expressed by crying, tantrums, freezing, or clinging.	? 1 2 3 ↓ GO TO OBSESSIVE-COMPULSIVE DISORDER	F68
Did you think that you were more afraid of (PHOBIC STIMULUS) than you should have been (or than made sense)?	C. The person recognizes that the fear is excessive or unreasonable. Note: in children, this feature may be absent.	? 1 2 3 ↓ GO TO OBSESSIVE-COMPULSIVE DISORDER	F69

? = inadequate information   1 = absent or false   2 = subthreshold   3 = threshold or true

Source: Specific Phobia section of the Structured Clinical Interview for *DSM-IV* Axis I Disorders, or SCID-I. From *Structured Clinical Interview for* DSM-IV *Axis I Disorder,* by M. B. First, R. L. Spitzer, and J. B. W. Williams, pp. F16–F19. Copyright © 1996 Biometrics Research. Reprinted by permission.

in the same precise manner no matter who conducts it. Thus, the interview resembles an oral questionnaire more than a conversation. Structured interviews have become a popular means of objectifying the interviewing process (Edelbrock & Costello, 1984; First, Spitzer, et al., 1997; First, Gibbon, Spitzer, Williams 1997, 2002; Robins et al., 1994; Silverman & Nelles, 1988; Trull & Widiger, 1997; Wiens, 1989). Semi-structured interviews offer some degree of flexibility in the questions asked by the interviewer. Structured and semi-structured interviews tend to be used in research environments more than in clinical environments such as private practice or clinics. Paraprofessionals, nonprofessionals, and clinical or research assistants are often trained to conduct structured interviews to reduce the costs and enhance the uniformity associated with the interview process. An example of part of a structured interview examining phobia is provided in Table 7.4.

Computer-Assisted Interviews

A next step in the evolution of structured interviews involves computer interviewing. As computers become more sophisticated and less expensive, programs can be developed to administer highly complex, efficient, and effective interviews. Computers can be used to ask patients questions and record their responses in a very objective manner. Numerous decision trees can be employed for appropriate follow-up questions to patients' answers. Furthermore, some patients feel more comfortable answering sensitive and potentially embarrassing questions via computer rather than talking face-to-face with a human interviewer (DiNitto, Busch-Armendariz, Bender, Woo, Tackett-Gibson et al., 2008; Farrell, Complair, & McCullough, 1987). However, some people are uncomfortable with using computers in this way and prefer to talk with a professional person about problems.

Computer-assisted interviews have been used in clinic settings where patients can answer a variety of questions about their concerns while in a waiting area prior to their face-to-face meeting with a counselor.

Results from the computer interview can be provided to the counselor to help in the treatment process. Confidentiality concerns must be addressed when sensitive material is being requested in a public area (e.g., waiting room) and when access to computer files is not closely controlled.

Exit or Termination Interview

After treatment is completed, an exit or termination interview may be used to help evaluate the effectiveness of treatment or to smooth the patient's transition to the next psychotherapeutic step (e.g., discharge from a hospital to a group home or to an outpatient facility). The interview might focus on how the patient experienced the treatment, what the patient found useful or not useful, and how he or she might best deal with problems in the future. Another goal of the exit interview may be to determine what residual problems still need to be addressed or to give the patient a sense of closure regarding the therapeutic experience. The interview may or may not be conducted by the treating professional. Especially in large treatment facilities such as hospitals and clinics, someone other than the treating professional might conduct a termination interview in order to minimize bias. For example, it may be difficult for a patient to tell his or her therapist directly that the treatment was unhelpful or to criticize the clinician's techniques. However, in smaller treatment facilities, such as a solo independent practice, the treating professional usually conducts the termination interview.

1. Be prepared for the interview.
2. Know the purpose of the interview.
3. Be sure the purpose and parameters of the interview are clear to the interviewee.
4. Ensure that the interview is understood as a collaborative experience between the client and the interviewer.
5. Listen very closely to the interviewee.
6. Consider the use of structured interviews.
7. Encourage the interviewees to describe their symptoms and concerns in behaviorally and operationally defined terms.

8. Use other assessment tools (such as checklists, inventories, psychological testing) with the interview data to supplement the findings.

9. Identify the antecedents and consequences of problem behaviors and symptoms.

10. Avoid unreasonable expectations and biases.

11. Don't jump to conclusions too soon but allow the interview to be finished before making diagnostic, treatment, or other conclusions.

Highlight of a Contemporary Clinical Psychologist

Stanley Sue, PhD

Photo: Courtesy
Stanley Sue

Dr. Sue maintains a full-time academic career focusing on Asian American and ethnic minority mental health issues.

Birth Date: February 13, 1944

College: University of Oregon (BS, Psychology), 1966

Graduate Program: University of California at Los Angeles (PhD, Clinical Psychology), 1971

Clinical Internship: Student Health Psychiatric Clinic, University of California at Los Angeles

Current Job: Professor of Psychology and Asian American Studies, University of California at Davis

Pros and Cons of Being a Clinical Psychologist:
Pros: "Interesting and important work with people. Variety of possible roles in teaching, research, clinical practice, consulting, and administration."

Cons: "Can experience burnout in clinical practice. Must be able to manage work and time or serious overcommitment can occur."

Future of Clinical Psychology: "The future looks bright. Employment possibilities are relatively strong despite managed care. In the future, better integration of research findings with clinical practice."

What should clinicians keep in mind when conducting interviews and behavioral observations with people from various cultures? "Because clinicians may be unfamiliar with the cultural backgrounds of clients and the precise meaning of client behaviors, they should avoid quick judgments and learn to form and test hypotheses concerning the meaning of client behavior."

How can rapport be nurtured when working with people from various cultural groups? "Show respect, listen and learn from the client, and try to provide some gifts to the client such as support, cognitive structure, reduction of anxiety and depression, so that the clinician can achieve some credibility with the client. Understand the culture of the client."

Typical Schedule:

8:00	Handle e-mail.
9:00 to 10:00	Prepare for lecture and courses.
11:00	Meet with students concerning research about the importance of culture in mental health assessment issues.
12:00	Handle e-mail.
1:00 to 2:00	Research and writing. Working on paper for publication and grant application concerning training culturally competent mental health professionals.
3:00	Teach Clinical Psychology class.
4:00	Office hours.

Potential Threats to Effective Interviewing

Bias

Interviewers may be biased. Their personality, theoretical orientation, interests, values, previous experiences, cultural background, and other factors may influence how they conduct an interview, what they attend to, and what they conclude. Interviewers may consciously or unconsciously distort information collected during an interview based on their own slant on the patient or the patient's problems. For example, a psychologist is an expert on child sexual abuse. She treats patients who have been sexually abused as children and publishes professional articles and books on the topic. She is often asked to give lectures around the country on the subject. When a patient describes symptoms often associated with child sexual abuse such as depression, anxiety, low self-esteem, relationship conflicts, and sexuality concerns, the psychologist assumes that the symptoms are associated with sexual abuse. When a patient denies any experience of sexual abuse, the psychologist assumes that the patient has repressed or forgotten the traumatic memory. She then works to help patients uncover the repressed memory in order to realize that they have been abused. Clearly,

this example illustrates how **bias** can lead to distorted or even destructive approaches.

Reliability and Validity

Reliability and validity may also be threatened. For example, if two or more interviewers conduct independent interviews with a patient, they may or may not end up with the same diagnosis, hypotheses, conclusions, or treatment plans. Furthermore, patients may not report the same information when questioned by several different interviewers (Cormier et al., 2008; Hubert, Wachs, Peters-Martin, & Gandour, 1982). Interviewer gender, race, age, religion, and skill level are some of the factors that may affect patient response during an interview (Cormier et al., 2008; Grantham, 1973; Plante, 2009). Emotional level may also have an impact on reporting of information (Kolko, Kazdin, & Meyer, 1985). For example, personal questions regarding sexual behavior, alcohol use, child abuse, or other sensitive issues may elicit varying responses from patients under different circumstances. Reliability and validity may be enhanced by using structured interviews, asking similar questions in different ways, using multiple interviewers, and supplementing interview information from other sources (e.g., medical records, observers, questionnaires).

Behavioral Observations

Seeing is believing. Behavioral observations are an attempt by the psychologist or other trained observer to watch the problems and behaviors in question unfold naturally in the real world. While a clinical interview can provide a psychologist with a great deal of helpful information, this approach to assessment has a number of limitations. Perhaps most importantly, the clinical interview relies on self-report information that may or may not be accurate. Interview information is filtered through the perception, experience, and impression management orientation of the person being interviewed. Therefore, information

Autism and Related Disorders

Autism is a childhood disorder that occurs before the age of three and includes a wide range of problems in social relationships and interactions, communication, as well as activities and interests (American Psychiatric Association, 2000). Problems in social interactions include a lack of nonverbal social connection such as eye contact and facial responses such as smiling as well as the inability to develop mutual social contact, reciprocity, and relatedness. Communication problems might include delayed or minimal spoken language development or unusual communication styles. Activity and interest deficits might include a preoccupation with very particular objects, engaging in highly repetitive movements such as head banging or rocking, and a compulsive adherence to certain rituals or routines.

Asperger's syndrome reflects problems in social relatedness, activities, and interests, but there tends to be no significant language or cognitive ability deficits. Therefore, children with Asperger's syndrome tend to do fine in school from an academic standpoint with fairly minimal problems in educational activities, but tend to do poorly from a social and peer standpoint.

Autism and related disorders such as Asperger's syndrome have received a great deal of attention recently. Part of this renewed interest in these disorders is due to well-known celebrities who have children with these disorders (e.g., football quarterback Doug Flutie, musician Neil Young, actress Jenny McCarthy), popular movies that feature these disorders (e.g., *Forrest Gump*, 1994), and many reports that these disorders are increasing in frequency. Some news reports have suggested that autism might be associated with the administration of childhood vaccines routinely given to young children (although quality research has failed to support this hypothesis as of this date). Other reports suggest that the criteria for diagnosis is lower than what it used to be and therefore more children are being identified as autistic. Additional reports suggest that autism is found among more highly educated populations and that perhaps exposure to some toxin that is not yet identified may contribute to the dramatic increases in this diagnosis. Finally, other reports suggest that training and public awareness have improved such that children who have these problems are more likely to be identified by school personnel, mental health professionals, pediatricians, and concerned parents than in the past. Since more and more efforts have been made to have autistic children in regular classrooms rather than segregated to special education classrooms, more and more children and families are likely to have contact with autistic children.

Clinical psychologists are involved with the diagnosis and treatment of autism as well as working with families and schoolteachers who are trying to cope with living with or teaching autistic children. Clinical psychologists conduct research on autism and are often involved in policy and advocacy work as well.

obtained through an interview may be biased. For example, patients may minimize the degree of distress they experience. People with an alcohol problem may underreport the daily amount of alcohol they consume because of embarrassment and/or denial that they have a problem. Children who are reportedly disruptive and inattentive in class may appear attentive and well-behaved during an interview session when talking one-on-one with a psychologist. Information provided in an interview session may be intentionally or unintentionally distorted. Behavioral observations, whether naturalistic, self-monitoring, or controlled, provide an opportunity for the psychologist to see for himself or herself the concerns in question.

An important concept in behavioral observations includes functional analysis (Skinner, 1953). **Functional analysis** refers to a behavioral analysis of the antecedents, or what led up to the behavior in question, as well as the consequences of the behavior. For example, if a child is disruptive in class, the behavior in question might involve speaking to his peers, leaving his seat, and refusing to complete assignments. A functional analysis of the behavior may reveal that being ignored by a teacher may precede the display of the problematic disruptive behavior and the consequences might include a great deal of attention (although negative attention) from the teacher and perhaps other school personnel (e.g., teacher's aide, principal) following the behavior. Functional analysis assumes that behaviors are learned and that antecedents result in the opportunity for the behavior to manifest itself while consequences maintain or reinforce the behavior.

Another important concept regarding behavioral observations includes selection of target behaviors. *Target behaviors* are specific behaviors that are examined, evaluated, and hopefully altered by interventions (Hawkins, 1987). It is often very difficult to isolate target behaviors. Many people seeking the consultation of a psychologist have vague complaints that may be difficult to observe and understand. For example, the teacher in the example

might complain that a child is "unmotivated" in school and not "working to potential." The man mentioned on p. 175 who is unsure if he should marry might complain of a lack of passion in the relationship and feelings of boredom. Behavioral observations must identify clear target behaviors to observe. Developing operational definitions (i.e., specifically defined behaviors or concepts using reliable and valid measures for assessment) to clearly define target behaviors is needed for effective behavioral observations. For example, the term *unmotivated* might involve target behaviors such as not attending class, sloppy and incomplete homework, and looking out the window during classroom instruction. Lack of passion might be defined as infrequent sexual contact and/or highly unsatisfying sexual experiences.

Naturalistic Observation

Photo: Courtesy Zach Plante

Observing patients in their natural environments often helps psychologists develop a more comprehensive and realistic understanding of the problems that need to be addressed. For example, a child may be highly disruptive in class, get into frequent fights on the playground, and have numerous conflicts at home over homework or household chores. Teachers or parents may suspect an attention deficit disorder and refer the child to a psychologist for evaluation. In addition to conducting an interview with the child, family, and teachers, the psychologist might wish to observe the child at home and/or at school. In doing so, the psychologist can obtain firsthand information about the child's problematic behavior as well as examining the environmental and social influences (e.g., teacher, peer, and/or parental response to disruptive behavior, classroom seating arrangements) that may reinforce or encourage the child's disruptive behavior. Therefore **naturalistic observation** involves entering into the world of the patient to observe the person interacting with the environment in which problems occur.

Although there are many obvious advantages to observation in a natural environment, several important disadvantages should be addressed. First, naturalistic observations can be time consuming and expensive. The psychologist must travel to the home, school, ball field, or work environment as well as conduct the observation and then travel back to the office. The psychologist can therefore spend many hours out of a day involved with just one case. Second, confidentiality can be compromised when teachers, coworkers, peers, colleagues, teammates, and others know that a psychologist is coming to observe so-and-so. Third, most people behave differently when they know they are being watched. This is referred to as *reactivity*, reflecting the notion that people often behave differently in private than in public while being watched by certain others (e.g., researchers or parents). For example, a disruptive child may be on his or her best behavior knowing that a psychologist is observing in the classroom or on the playground. Fourth, the problematic behavior may or may not occur when the psychologist is conducting his or her observation. The observation is a small snapshot of behavior that may not represent typical behavior. Finally, the observation may be biased. The psychologist may expect to see certain behavior (e.g., inattentiveness, impulsivity, and disruptive behavior) based on the information collected during the interview session. Furthermore, interested parties may try to influence the psychologist's judgment because they have a hidden agenda in the outcome of the evaluation. For example,

a teacher may wish to have a perceived problem student taken out of the class. Thus, the psychologist may focus on expected behaviors and ignore unexpected behaviors. These disadvantages often prohibit most psychologists from conducting on-site observations. Those who do conduct naturalistic observations often work on-site where direct observation is convenient and inexpensive. For example, school psychologists who work in an elementary or secondary school can easily observe a classroom or playground that may be located on the same premises as their office.

Many efforts have been made to increase the convenience, reliability, and validity of naturalistic observations. For example, Patterson (1977) developed the Behavioral Coding System (BCS), which provides a structured and research-based observational coding system for trained observers to record and classify disruptive behavior at home. Others have developed structured observational coding methods for specific populations (e.g., children, mentally challenged adults, hospitalized psychiatric patients) and problems (e.g., depression, anxiety, work behaviors; Jones, Ulicny, Czyzewski, & Plante, 1987; Lewinsohn & Shaffer, 1971; Mariotto & Paul, 1974; O'Leary & Becker, 1967). Many of these scales can be used by trained paraprofessionals to reduce the costs associated with conducting naturalistic observations. However, most of these techniques and scales are still employed primarily for research purposes and only infrequently for clinical purposes.

Self-Monitoring

Whereas naturalistic observations are conducted by a trained clinician, researcher, paraprofessional, or appropriate person other than the patient, **self-monitoring** is conducted by the identified patient. The patient is instructed in how to observe and record his or her own behavior in an objective manner. Self-monitoring has become a very commonly used tool not only for assessing problems but also as an intervention.

Patients are instructed to maintain a diary or log where they can record the problematic behaviors as well as other important information such as feelings and thoughts associated with each behavioral occurrence. For example, someone who is trying to lose weight might be asked to write down everything he or she eats for several weeks. The food item, quantity, and time might be recorded for each eating episode. The person might be asked to also record feelings and thoughts at the time as well as what happened before and after each eating episode. In this way, both patient and psychologist develop a better understanding of the target behavior, or problem, as well as the factors that may encourage or reinforce it. These self-monitoring diaries can then be analyzed in various ways. For instance, total calorie consumption, percentage of fat in the diet, and stress-related eating episodes can be more closely assessed using this method than with a traditional interview. Although many people might find self-monitoring boring and a chore, computer technology (e.g., self-monitoring computer software and small datebook-size hand-held computers or an iTouch) as well as other methods have made self-monitoring easier and more pleasant (e.g.,Taylor, Agras, Losch, Plante, & Burnett, 1991). Self-monitoring has been successfully employed with a large number of problem behaviors other than eating problems, including smoking (O. F. Pomerleau & C. S. Pomerleau, 1977), sleeping problems (Miller & DiPilato, 1983), anxiety symptoms (Cooper & Clum, 1989), criminal behavior (Shapiro, 1984), and sedentary behavior (Strath et al., 2003). Much research and press has attended to helping people become more physically active by using low-cost pedometers such as the Digiwalker. The small and inexpensive device reliably counts steps and people are encouraged to accumulate 10,000 steps (or five miles) of walking each day (Figure 7.2).

There are also several important disadvantages to self-monitoring. First, patients often have some reaction to the process of recording their behavior, which changes the very

Photograph: Courtesy New Lifestyles, Inc. (Kansas City, Missouri)

Figure 7.2

The digi-walker is a contemporary and popular self-monitoring device that measures physical activity.

behavior that is being assessed. Paradoxically, this disadvantage in getting an accurate assessment can become a treatment advantage. For example, if patients know that they must write down everything they eat, they may think twice before impulsively eating a high-fat, high-calorie treat such as candy or cookies (Table 7.5). Thus self-monitoring is often used as both an intervention and an assessment technique. A second disadvantage is that few people are willing to self-monitor for a long period of time. Thus, compliance to the self-monitoring task can be a challenge for many. Finally, embarrassment and denial may prevent people from honestly completing the self-monitoring assignment. For example, someone who has to report in to a professional might shy away from recording a binge-eating episode for fear of reproach.

Controlled Observations

In a controlled observation, the psychologist attempts to observe behavior in a prescribed manner. Rather than waiting (and hoping) for target behaviors to unfold in the natural environment or for the patient to report on the behavior using a self-monitoring technique,

Table 7.5   Self-Monitoring Example Form for Weight Loss

Name _____

Current Weight _____

Goal Weight _____

Date _____

Time	Food Item	Quantity	Calories	Thoughts/Feelings	Behavior

controlled observations force the behavior of interest to occur in a simulated manner. For example, a person who is interested in reducing public-speaking anxiety may be asked to present a speech in front of the psychologist and other patients who also have public-speaking anxiety. In this way the psychologist can observe firsthand the patient's behavior in a controlled, confidential, and unthreatening environment. Stress interviews are another kind of controlled observation. To determine how someone copes with stress, the person may be asked to participate in a stressful interview situation or be required to complete a stressful task while being observed. These techniques were especially popular in the military following World War II (OSS Assessment Staff, 1948; Vernon, 1950). One example employed by a graduate school admissions committee involved asking a candidate to open a window in a room with several members of the committee present. The window, unbeknownst to the applicant, had been nailed shut. The committee observed how the applicant handled the impossible task of trying to open the window. Another technique entails the use of leaderless groups (Ansbacher,

1951). Small groups of people without a designated leader are required to solve a problem or participate in a discussion, with observers watching behind a one-way mirror. The observers see who develops as a leader in the group and who takes a passive role.

Perhaps the most commonly used type of controlled observation is the role play. Role plays require people to act as if they were in a particular situation that causes them concern. For example, patients who have trouble making new friends might be asked to role play with the psychologist (or a research or clinical assistant) how they might try to meet a new neighbor. People who have trouble being assertive with family members might be asked to role play telling their mothers they are not coming home for Thanksgiving dinner. Thus, in conducting a role play, the patient and other participants are requested to act as if they were in a brief play. They are asked to stay in role as if they were indeed in the prescribed situation. Role plays might be videotaped to review later for teaching purposes. Role plays can be used both for the assessment of a particular problem and for treatment interventions. For example, they are frequently used to help people become more assertive or socially skilled (Plante, Pinder, & Howe, 1988).

Checklists and Inventories

Interviews and behavioral observations can provide a great deal of helpful information in a psychological assessment. However, a major disadvantage of both methods is that they generally take a lot of time to complete and therefore tend to be expensive. It is not uncommon for several hundred and even thousands of dollars to be billed for interview and observational assessments. Additionally, if many assessments are needed (e.g., screening military recruits, factory workers, hospital employees), it is often impractical to conduct intensive interviews and behavioral observations for each person. Concerns regarding reliability and validity also emerge when using these techniques. As mentioned earlier, the expectations, interests, perspectives, and prejudices of the interviewer and observer may uniquely influence each assessment.

To avoid these disadvantages, many psychologists utilize checklists and inventories to assess behavior. These are brief pencil-and-paper questionnaires that assess one or more traits or problem areas. They can be administered to a large number of people at one time, are inexpensive, and can be quickly scored and analyzed. Clinical information obtained from checklists and inventories tends to be more reliable and valid than information collected through most interview and observational methods. This is because extensive research is conducted on most of these measures before they become available for purchase and use. Numerous checklists and inventories have been developed to assess and diagnose a wide variety of problems such as anxiety, depression, eating disorders, and attention deficit disorders. These instruments generally are very brief, easy to complete, and need little instruction or supervision from a professional. They may focus on feelings, thoughts, and/or behavior and are typically either hand or computer scored. While seemingly straightforward, checklists and inventories also need to be sensitively interpreted in the context of other measures as well as biological, psychological, and social factors. This section highlights three of the most commonly used instruments in clinical psychology: the Beck Inventories, the Child Behavior Checklist, and the Symptom Checklist 90—Revised.

Beck Inventories

Aaron Beck, a founding father of cognitive-behavioral psychotherapy, has developed a series of inventories to assess depression, anxiety, hopelessness, and suicidal ideation (thoughts of hurting oneself). All of the **Beck Scales** are brief (all include 21 items, except the 20-item hopelessness inventory) and are used with persons who range in age from 17 to 80 years. Each scale takes only 5 to 10 minutes to complete and employs a simple scoring system so that hand scoring is both easy and quick. The Beck Depression Inventory (BDI; Beck, 1987, 1993; Beck, Steer, & Brown, 1996) has become the most widely used checklist instrument to assess the severity of depressive symptoms. The BDI has been revised and updated several times with the most recent version (BDI-II) published in 1996. The Beck Anxiety Scale (BAS; Beck, 1990, 1993) is a popular instrument for assessing the intensity of anxiety symptoms. The Beck Hopelessness Scale (BHS; Beck, 1988, 1993) assesses hopelessness about the future and examines feelings regarding the loss of motivation and expectations. The Beck Scale for Suicide Ideation (BSS; Beck, 1991) assesses suicidal thinking. Newer scales include those that measure obsessive-compulsive symptoms, youth troubles, and medical issues (e.g., Beck, Beck, & Jolly, 2005). Research demonstrates that the Beck Scales are both reliable and valid. These inventories often are used during an initial assessment evaluation as well as during the course of psychotherapy to assess progress and treatment outcome.

Assessing Suicidal Risk

Conducting an assessment for suicidal behavior is one of the most important and difficult assessments for psychologists and other mental health professionals. The stakes are very high if a psychologist makes an error in judgment that might result in someone hurting or even killing him- or herself. Although it is very difficult and sometimes impossible to predict with great confidence who will and who will not attempt to take his or her own life, years of research and clinical practice in this area have provided guidelines that can help clinical psychologists and others make reasonable judgments about risk factors for suicide. Pope and Vasquez (2005) offer a useful list of risk factors, including:

1. The best predictor of future behavior is past behavior. If someone has made serious attempts at suicide in the past, they are more likely to make them again in the future.
2. Admitting to suicidal behavior or ideation. Clients willing to honestly state their suicidal intentions should be taken seriously.
3. Specific plan. A person might have a specific plan or method in mind such as overdosing on prescription medications, jumping off a particular bridge, using a gun that they have at home.
4. Depression. Not surprisingly, experiencing depression is a risk factor for suicidal behavior.
5. Substance abuse. Abusing substances such as alcohol or other drugs is a risk factor for suicide as well.
6. Gender differences. Women tend to be more than three times as likely to make suicide attempts and gestures than men but men tend to make more lethal attempts.
7. Age. Risk of suicide increases with age and the elderly population tend to make more lethal attempts than younger persons.
8. Religion. Protestants tend to have higher suicide rates than Catholics and Jews.
9. Isolation. Suicide rates tend to be higher among those living alone.
10. Stressful life events. Suicide rates are higher among those who have experienced the death of a close friend or relative, been the victim of trauma, incest, unemployment, divorce, chronic or life-threatening illness (e.g., AIDS).
11. Impulsivity. Those with poor impulse control in general are at higher risk for self-destructive behavior.
12. Release from hospitalization. Suicidal risk curiously is high following release from hospitalization for depression or suicidal thoughts and gestures.

The Achenbach System of Empirically Based Assessment (ASEBA)

The ASEBA (Achenbach, 2009; Bérubé & Achenbach, 2007) is a group of symptom checklist assessment questionnaires used with children and adults of all ages to closely and empirically evaluate behavioral and psychiatric symptoms. Perhaps among the most well known and most often used of these checklists is the **Child Behavior Checklist** (**CBCL**; Achenbach, 1997, 2009; Achenbach & Rescorla, 2001; Bérubé & Achenbach, 2007), which is a checklist of over 100 problem behaviors or symptoms (e.g., disobedient at school, cries a lot) experienced by children ages 6 through 18. Parents are asked to evaluate their child using a 3-point scale on each of the symptoms. The CBCL also includes a series of questions concerning the child's activities, chores, friends, and grades. A teacher's version of the checklist is available (i.e., Teacher's Report Form [TRF]) as well as a self-report form for children ages 11 through 18 to complete (i.e., Youth Self-Report [YSR]). Preschool and adult (including elderly) versions are also available. Furthermore, a semi-structured clinical interview (i.e., the Semi-structured Clinical Interview for Children and Adolescents [SCICA]) and a direct observation form (i.e., DOF) are also available.

Each of the measures is hand or computer scored and compared with national norms. Separate scores are obtained on a number of both internalizing symptoms (e.g., anxious/depressed, social problems, attention problems) and externalizing symptoms (e.g., delinquent behavior, aggressive behavior). The CBCL and related instruments have satisfactory psychometric properties in terms of reliability and validity (Achenbach, 2009; Bérubé & Achenbach, 2007). Like the Beck Scales, the ASEBA scales are frequently incorporated into an initial evaluation and periodically both during and following treatment to evaluate progress and outcome.

The Symptom Checklist 90—Revised (SCL-90-R)

The **SCL-90-R** (Derogatis, 1994) is a brief and multidimensional self-report measure to screen persons for major psychiatric symptoms. The SCL-90-R consists of 90 items, scored on a 5-point scale, that reflect nine validated symptom dimensions (e.g., anxiety, depression, interpersonal sensitivity, obsessions, psychoticism). The checklist can be administered to people ages 13 through adulthood and generally takes 10 to 15 minutes to complete. A brief form of the SCL-90-R (i.e., the Brief Symptom Inventory [BSI]; Derogatis, 1994) that includes only 53 items is also available. In addition to scores on each of the nine dimensions, a Global Severity Index is calculated to assess the depth of the disorder, and a Positive Symptom Distress Index is designed to assess the intensity of the symptoms. Reliability and validity research indicates that the SCL-90-R has satisfactory psychometric properties. It is also used throughout evaluation, treatment, and follow-up periods to evaluate progress and outcome.

Other Checklists and Inventories

In addition to the checklists and inventories already outlined, many other instruments have been developed for specific populations or clinical problems. These include, among others, the Conner's Rating Scales—Revised (Conners, 2000), which focus on the assessment of hyperactivity and other child behavioral problems; the Children's Depression Inventory (CDI; M. Kovacs, 1985); and the Goldfarb Fear of Fat Scale (GAFFS; Goldfarb, Dykens, & Gerrard, 1985), used with eating-disordered patients. The Asperger Syndrome Diagnostic Scale (ASDS; Myles, Bock, & Simpson, 2001) is used to evaluate Asperger syndrome among children ages 5 through 18. It consists of 50 yes/no test items and takes about 15 minutes to complete and provides an Asperger syndrome or AS Quotient. It evaluates

Case Study: José and the BDI, CBCL, and SCL-90-R

José is a 17-year-old Hispanic high school junior. He lives with his parents and three siblings. José identifies himself as homosexual.

Referral Question: José's parents have noticed an abrupt shift from José's typically cheerful and energetic demeanor to a pattern of tearfulness, lethargy, anxiety, irritability, and inability to eat or sleep adequately. José has told his parents that he has been feeling depressed and anxious about his college applications, stating "I don't know what I want to do with my life." He was referred by his parents for a psychological evaluation to determine the nature of his current symptoms and obtain appropriate recommendations. There is significant family history of depression and anxiety.

Tests Administered: Interview, BDI, CBCL, and SCL-90-R

Brief Summary and Interpretation of Results: José's score on the Beck Depression Inventory (23) places him in the "severely depressed" range of this measure. On the Child Behavior Checklist (Parent Report Form), significant elevations were obtained on the Anxious/Depressed, Attention Problems, Somatic Complaints, and Withdrawn scales. On the SCL-90-R, significant elevations were revealed on the Interpersonal Sensitivity, Depression, Anxiety, Paranoia, and Positive Symptom Distress Index scales. Taken together, these checklist measures clearly corroborate significant levels of depression and anxiety in José's profile. However, the cause, nature, and content of these symptoms still remain unanswered by these measures alone.

Results from the clinical interview revealed that José had become deeply depressed following the discovery that his former boyfriend tested positive for HIV, the virus associated with Acquired Immune Deficiency Syndrome (AIDS). This revelation has plummeted José into a state of fear, guilt, hopelessness, and ultimately, major depression. While he has shared his sexual orientation with his parents, he has been afraid of telling them about his former boyfriend's HIV, and even more frightened to obtain an HIV test himself. His family history of depression and anxiety may make him biologically vulnerable to depression in the context of significant psychosocial stress.

The clinical psychologist assessing José made the following recommendations. First, José requires ongoing therapy with a supportive clinician who can assist him in traversing this difficult crisis. A clinician especially sensitive to homosexuality, terminal illness, and Hispanic culture would be indicated. Second, adjunctive work with José's parents, given his consent, will be useful in assisting them in supporting their beloved son. Third, a psychiatric consultation may be useful to determine whether antidepressant medications are indicated to assist in treating José's depression. Fourth, assisting José in developing contacts with community resources, such as a group for young gay men and AIDS information hotline, would be beneficial. Fifth and finally, processing with José the emotional and medical implications of obtaining an HIV test while remaining alert to his fears will be necessary to assist him in making a responsible choice with adequate preparation.

people on five areas of behavior, including cognitive, maladaptive, language, social, and sensorimotor skills. Table 7.6 provides a list of checklists and inventories used in clinical practice and research.

Like all assessment procedures, checklists and inventories have some disadvantages as well as advantages. Because these instruments rely on self-report information, people may distort their answers or try to present

Table 7.6   **Examples of Checklists and Inventories**

Adolescent Anger Rating Scale
Adolescent Drinking Index
Career Assessment Inventory
Childhood Autism Rating Scale
Children's Depression Inventory
Checklist for Child Abuse Evaluation
Coping Response Inventory
Dementia Rating Scale-2
Eating Disorder Inventory-2
Emotional Problems Scale
Goldfarb Fear of Fat Scale
Guilford-Zimmerman Temperament Survey
Hamilton Depression Inventory
Hare Psychopathy Checklist—Revised
Health Status Questionnaire
Occupational Stress Inventory—Revised
Parenting Stress Index
Personality Assessment Inventory
Quality of Life Inventory
Santa Clara Strength of Religious Faith Questionnaire
State-Trait Anxiety Inventory
State-Trait Anger Expression Inventory-2
Suicidal Ideation Questionnaire
Trauma Symptom Inventory
West Haven–Yale Multidimensional Pain Inventory

themselves in a favorable or unfavorable light. Furthermore, checklists and inventories do not provide the depth and complexity of information obtainable through interview, observation, and other assessment measures. Thus, they are typically used as a screening tool rather than for an in-depth analysis of a particular person or problem. Screening is a useful means of determining the need for further assessment in specific areas. Cognitive and personality testing seeks to obtain more detailed, complex, and comprehensive data than available from checklists and inventories.

Physiological Testing

Physiological tests have increasingly been integrated into contemporary clinical psychology. Psychological states such as anxiety and stress can be assessed through noninvasive techniques that measure physiological activity (e.g., blood pressure, heart rate, and sweating, respiration, and muscle tension; Blascovich & Katkin, 1993; Gatchel & Blanchard, 1993). Physicians may order and interpret **neuroimaging** techniques such as magnetic resonance imaging (MRI, fMRI) (Figure 7.3), computerized axial tomography (CT), and positron emission tomography (PET) scans to examine physiological activities associated with mood and other psychological states. Some clinical psychologists use polygraph or biofeedback equipment to assess physiological activities such as blood pressure, heart rate, respiration, and muscle tension, which indicate levels of arousal, stress, and anxiety. **Polygraphs,** or lie detector tests, measure physiological reactions but have been highly criticized for being unreliable and invalid (Iacono, 2008; Lykken, 1991). Whereas polygraphs measure physiological activity in a reliable and valid way, most professionals feel that to attribute certain physiological states to the act of lying is a stretch that is not supported by research data.

Biofeedback equipment is similar to polygraphs in that it measures physiological activity. Unlike polygraphs, biofeedback provides information to patients or subjects about their level of physiological arousal through visual or auditory feedback (e.g., high-pitched tone sounds when heart rate is fast and low-pitched tone sounds when heart rate is slow). Technological advances have resulted in the development of small and inexpensive devices that measure these physiological states. Thus, the devices can be used in professional offices or at home by patients. They are also used to assess and treat people with disorders

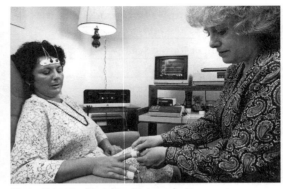

Photo: S. Grant, Monkmeyer, Grantpix   Photo:Grant Le Duc, Monkmeyer, LeDuc

Figure 7.3

(*left*) A medical technician operates a Magnetic Resonance Imaging (MRI) installation with brain image on screen and patient module in background; (*right*) a patient receives biofeedback treatment.

associated with overactivity of the sympathetic nervous system (e.g., Raynaud's disease, irritable bowel syndrome, Type A behavior pattern, headaches, and anxiety disorders).

Biofeedback provides this information to patients who then try to lower their physiological arousal through the use of relaxation or other techniques. For example, thermal biofeedback, which provides patients with information regarding their hand temperature, is the treatment of choice for Raynaud's disease, a condition of restricted blood flow that causes cold and often pain in the hands and feet (Freedman, 1993; Malenfant, Catton, & Pope, 2009). The use of these technological advancements is likely to be helpful in the assessment of a wide variety of mental and physical health problems of interest to clinical psychologists and others in the future.

The Big Picture

Clinical psychologists provide a unique and extremely challenging and useful skill in the form of psychological testing. Interviews, behavioral observations, checklists and inventories, and physiological measures provide important information that can be used in conjunction with other tests to make diagnostic conclusions and intervention decisions. Always, these tests need to be contextualized given the unique constellation of biopsychosocial factors affecting individuals and their test results. Future clinical psychologists will likely fine-tune these instruments, making them more reliable, valid, and useful among diverse populations. In Chapter 8, the assessment of cognitive functioning and personality is described, as these tools assist the clinical psychologist in delving deeper and deeper into the intellectual, emotional, and interpersonal worlds of patients.

Key Points

1. Since the earliest days of clinical psychology, assessment and testing have been important professional activities. Psychological assessment and testing are the major professional activities of many clinical psychologists.

2. Psychological assessment is the process psychologists use to collect and evaluate information in order to make diagnoses, plan treatment, and predict behavior. Assessment may include interviewing the patient, reviewing past records (such as medical or school records), observing behavior, and administering psychological tests to measure various cognitive, behavioral, personality, family, and even biological variables. Psychological testing is a specific assessment

technique utilizing reliable and valid testing instruments. Tests usually compare individual scores with the scores obtained from normative samples.

3. The goal of assessment is usually to size up the situation by developing a fuller understanding of the factors that contribute to the presenting problem(s). An assessment is necessary to make a diagnosis and outline a subsequent treatment or intervention plan.

4. The clinical interview is a thoughtful and deliberate conversation designed to acquire important information (facts, attitudes, beliefs) that allows the psychologist to develop a working hypothesis of what the problem(s) is/are about. Although there are numerous examples of interviewing situations (initial intake or admissions interview, mental status interview, crisis interview, structured interview, computer-assisted interview, exit, or termination interview), several techniques and skills are necessary for all types of interviews. These include developing rapport, active listening, effective communication, observation of behavior, and asking the right questions.

5. Potential threats to effective interviewing include bias as well as inadequate reliability and validity. The patient's background and other factors may bias or influence the manner in which an interview is conducted as well as what might be attended to and concluded. Interviewers may consciously or unconsciously distort information collected during an interview based on their own slant on the patient or the patient's problems. Reliability and validity may also be threatened. Two or more professionals interviewing the same person may come to very different conclusions.

6. Behavioral observations are an attempt by the psychologist or other trained observers to watch the problems and behaviors in question unfold naturally in the real world. There are several different types of behavioral observations including naturalistic, self-monitoring, and controlled. Naturalistic observations involve entering into the world of the patient in order to observe the person interacting with the environment in which problems occur. Self-monitoring is conducted by the identified patient who is instructed in how to observe and record his or her own behavior in an objective manner. Controlled observations force the behavior of interest to occur in a simulated manner, such as during a role play.

7. Checklists and inventories are brief pencil-and-paper questionnaires that assess one or more traits or problem areas. They provide a quick, inexpensive, reliable, and valid way to obtain useful clinical information. Examples are shown in Table 7.6.

8. Psychological states such as anxiety and stress can be assessed through noninvasive techniques that measure physiological activity (e.g., blood pressure, heart rate, and sweating, respiration, and muscle tension). Clinical psychologists often use polygraph or biofeedback equipment to assess physiological activity such as blood pressure and heart rate, which indicate levels of arousal, stress, and anxiety.

Key Terms

Achenbach System of Empirically Based Assessment (ASEBA)
Active listening
Beck scales
Bias
Biofeedback
Child Behavior Checklist (CBCL)
Clarification
Controlled observation
Functional analysis
Mental status interview
Naturalistic observation
Neuroimaging
Objective testing
Paraphrasing
Polygraph
Projective testing
Rapport
Reflection
Self-monitoring
Structured interview

Summarization
Symptom Checklist 90—Revised (SCL-90-R)

For Reflection

1. Why is assessment needed in clinical psychology?
2. How are psychological assessment and psychological testing the same or different?
3. What are the factors that contribute to effective interviewing?
4. What are the different types of clinical interviews?
5. What are major threats to effective interviewing?
6. What are the major methods to directly observe behavior in an assessment?
7. What are some of the advantages of checklists and inventories?
8. What types of constructs are checklists and inventories likely to assess?
9. What are examples of assessment procedures that measure physiological activity?
10. Why might a psychologist be interested in assessing physiological activity?

Real Students, Real Questions

1. About how many sessions does it take to build rapport?
2. How do you keep yourself calm and level headed during a crisis interview?
3. What do you do if the patient refuses to participate in the interview or is uncooperative in other ways?
4. What happens if you misdiagnose?

Web Resources

www.psychologynet.org
Learn about the *DSM* criteria for all mental disorders.

www.unl.edu/buros
Learn more about various psychological inventories and assessment devices.

Contemporary Psychological Assessment II: Cognitive and Personality Assessment

Chapter Objective

To discuss cognitive and personality evaluations and issues in making clinical judgments and communicating testing results to others.

Chapter Outline

Cognitive Testing

Highlight of a Contemporary Clinical Psychologist: Lori Goldfarb Plante, PhD

Personality Testing

Clinical Inference and Judgment

Communicating Assessment Results

This chapter expands the discussion of assessment in clinical psychology. Cognitive assessment measures a host of intellectual capacities and encompasses the subspecialty of neuropsychological assessment that examines brain–behavior relationships. Personality testing accesses both underlying intrapsychic issues as well as overt behavioral manifestations of each individual's unique psyche. Once all the assessment data are collected and examined by the psychologist, decisions can be made regarding diagnosis, treatment plans, and predictions about future behavior. How does the psychologist integrate and draw conclusions from all the data? How does he or she communicate results to the patient and other interested parties (e.g., family members, school teachers, physicians, attorneys)? This fascinating and unique clinical psychology endeavor is explored in depth.

Cognitive Testing

Cognitive testing is a general term referring to the assessment of a wide range of information-processing or thinking skills and behaviors.

These comprise general neuropsychological functions involving brain–behavior relationships, general intellectual functions (such as reasoning and problem solving) as well as more specific cognitive skills (such as visual and auditory memory), language skills, pattern recognition, finger dexterity, visual-perceptual skills, academic skills, and motor functions. Cognitive testing may include aptitude testing (which assesses cognitive potential such as general intelligence) and achievement testing (which assesses proficiency in specific skills such as reading or mathematics). Cognitive testing uses well-known tests such as the Scholastic Aptitude Test (SAT) and intelligence quotient (IQ) tests of all kinds. Thus, cognitive testing is an umbrella term that refers to many different types of tests measuring many different types of thinking and learning skills. While it is beyond the scope of this book to consider all the specific tests available, intelligence testing is discussed in detail.

Intelligence Testing

Measuring intellectual ability has long been a major activity and interest of clinical psychologists. As noted in Chapter 3, the goals of **intellectual testing** during the earliest years of the field were to evaluate children in order to help them maximize their educational experience and to assist teachers in developing curricula for children with special needs. Intelligence testing was also used to screen military recruits. Today, it is still used for these purposes. However, it is also employed for vocational planning, assessing learning disabilities, determining eligibility for gifted and special education programs, and examining brain–behavior relationships following head injuries, strokes, or other medical conditions. Intellectual testing is used not only to obtain an IQ score, but to learn more about an individual's overall cognitive strengths and weaknesses. Thus, it is used not only to measure intelligence but to assess cognitive functioning in general.

Many myths and misconceptions about intelligence testing persist. Alfred Binet (1857–1911), creator of the first IQ test, expressed concern about the misinterpretation, overgeneralization, and misuse of his test almost immediately after it was developed. Unfortunately, IQ testing has been frequently misused by some professionals as well as the public. Often people erroneously assume that IQ tests are perfect measures of an innate and stable ability we call "intelligence" and that these scores perfectly predict success in life and self-worth. Controversy continues over the reliability, validity, meaning, and usefulness of IQ scores and testing. Questions concerning IQ testing and racial bias, for example, have been the topic of bestselling books, feature articles in national magazines, and even legislative initiatives (Herrnstein & Murray, 1994). Some people have used the IQ as a way to perpetuate racist beliefs that certain ethnic groups are innately less intelligent than other groups. Before discussing the major intelligence tests, a brief discussion of the definition of intelligence is warranted.

What Is Intelligence? Unfortunately, there is no definition or theory of intelligence that all experts agree upon. Controversy exists among the numerous professionals who specialize in intelligence research and testing concerning how best to define and understand intelligence (Sternberg, 1997, 2008; Zhang & Sternberg, 2009). In fact, there are so many definitions that Sternberg and Kaye (1982) suggested that there were more definitions than experts! Even as early as 1923, Boring (1923) cynically defined intelligence as what intelligence tests measure. The most influential and often-cited definitions and theories of intelligence include those offered by Spearman (1927), Thurstone (1931, 1938), Cattell (1963, 1971, 1979), Guilford (1967, 1979, 1985), Piaget (1952, 1970, 1972), and, more recently, Sternberg (1996, 1997, 2008), Gardner (1983, 1986, 1994, 2006), and Goleman (1995, 2006, 2007). While it is beyond the scope of this book to present detailed descriptions of all of these definitions and theories, a brief overview will help put in context the types of tests currently available to measure intellectual, or cognitive, functioning.

Spearman (1927), well known and respected for his development of statistical techniques, offered a two-factor theory of intelligence that suggested that any intellectual task or challenge required the input of two factors: *general* abilities of intelligence (which Spearman referred to as *g*) and *specific* abilities of intelligence (referred to as *s*). Overall, Spearman emphasized through factor analysis research that intelligence was primarily a broad-based and general ability. Factor analysis is a complex statistical technique that helps to identify specific factors from sets of variables. Spearman's notion of intelligence as a comprehensive overall general ability has greatly influenced not only the conception of intelligence but also the development of intelligence tests for many years.

Also using factor analysis, Thurstone (1931, 1938) disagreed with Spearman and suggested that intelligence included nine unique and independent skills or *primary mental abilities:* verbal relations, words, perceptual ability, spatial ability, induction, deduction, numerical ability, arithmetic reasoning, and memory. Thurstone thus focused on distinct and separate abilities that together comprise intelligence.

Cattell (1963, 1971, 1979) expanded Spearman's two-factor theory regarding the notion of a broad-based general intelligence (*g*) factor and suggested that it consisted of two components that included both fluid and crystallized abilities. Cattell defined *fluid abilities* as the person's genetic or inborn intellectual abilities, whereas *crystallized abilities* are what a person learns through experience, culture, and various opportunities arising from interaction with the world. Fluid abilities resemble Spearman's *g* and refer to general problem-solving abilities, abstract reasoning, and ability to integrate and synthesize information quickly and efficiently. Crystallized abilities resemble Spearman's *s* and refer to specific skills developed and nurtured through training and experience. Cattell and colleagues also included the role of motivation, personality, and culture in their investigation and understanding of intelligence.

Guilford (1967, 1979, 1985) provided a comprehensive classification system of 150 specific intellectual abilities in his attempt to define intelligence. In contrast to the statistical and factor analytic approach and theories of Spearman, Thurstone, and Cattell, Guilford reasoned that intelligence consisted of three categories: operations (i.e., mental activity needed to solve a particular intellectual problem), contents (i.e., the specific issue or problem needing to be addressed), and products (i.e., the end result, or bottom line, of the mental activity). Guilford outlined five types of operations (i.e., memory, cognition, evaluation, divergent production, convergent production); five categories of content (i.e., visual, auditory, semantic, symbolic, and behavioral); and six products (i.e., class, relation, system, unit, transformation, implication). Each intellectual task required, according to Guilford, at least one element from each of the three categories for a possible combination of 150 factors of intelligence.

Unlike the theories of intelligence mentioned, Piaget (1952, 1970, 1972) added a developmental perspective to intellectual theory.

Piaget sought to develop a theory of how humans understand their world through actively adapting and interpreting their life experiences. He suggested that humans have four major stages of cognitive development (i.e., sensorimotor, preoperational, concrete operational, and formal operations), each having a variety of substages. Piaget used the terms *assimilation* to refer to gathering information and *accommodation* to refer to changing existing cognitive structures (or schemes) to allow for the newly incorporated and assimilated information. Rather than using laboratory or statistical analyses, Piaget conducted cognitive tasks and experiments with his own children to develop his theories of intellectual and cognitive development.

These traditional theories of intelligence tend to focus on the discovery and understanding of the structure or components of intelligence. Tests were used and developed based on these theories in an attempt to measure a variety of skills such as reasoning, analytical thinking, and language skills. These theories and tests were designed to measure what we know or what we are able to accomplish with a new problem. More recent theories of intelligence use an information-processing model to better understand the process or manner in which we attempt to solve problems (Gardner, 2006; Hersen, 2003; Sternberg, 2008). The speed, level, and type of processing someone experiences when trying to solve problems are of interest to many experts in the field of intelligence research and testing today. Furthermore, contemporary views of intelligence include practical, creative, social, and emotional aspects in addition to more traditional abstract reasoning and academic abilities (Gardner, 1994; Goleman, 1995, 2006, 2007; Sternberg, 1996, 2008). Particularly influential developments in theories of intelligence include the work of Robert Sternberg (1996, 1997, 2008) and Howard Gardner (1983, 1986, 1994, 2006), and reflect a more biopsychosocial perspective in the description of intelligence.

Sternberg offered a triarchic theory of intelligence that identifies three categories of intelligence: componential, experiential, and contextual. This theory is consistent with the holistic biopsychosocial perspective. The *componential* aspect of intelligence includes analytical thinking, and the *experiential* factor includes creative abilities. The *contextual* factor refers to good "street smarts" and the ability to adapt to and manipulate the environment. Thus, Sternberg views intelligence as involving practical and creative elements, with biological, psychological, and social underpinnings, traditionally ignored in both research and assessment of intellectual functioning.

Gardner (1983, 1986, 1994, 2006) developed a theory of multiple intelligences comprising six different types of intelligence: linguistic, logical-mathematical, musical, bodily-kinesthetic, spatial, and personal. Gardner's view thus includes music and body awareness, which have been ignored in earlier views of intelligence. Both Sternberg and Gardner have attempted to develop theories of intelligence that emphasize the practical aspects of human existence, accounting for a wider variety of skills and tasks and cultural contexts utilized to survive and thrive in the world. Emphasis on emotional and social intelligence (Goleman, 2006, 2007) further highlights the more holistic approach to understanding intellectual functioning and suggests that social skills and emotional functioning play an important role in "intelligence" as well as the ability to achieve goals and be successful. Knowing and managing one's emotions and recognizing emotions in others are part of emotional intelligence, and have tremendous biopsychosocial implications. For example, social experiences may enhance or squelch the appreciation of and opportunities for the development of social skills and managing emotions to maximize social relationships. Psychological stress and trauma may also contribute to the inability to manage emotions and understand the emotions of others. At this time, however, these views of intelligence offered by Sternberg, Gardner, and others have not resulted in the development of new tests that are commonly used in clinical psychology. Therefore, the traditional IQ tests will be presented here, and

their interpretation highlighted with a more biopsychosocially informed appreciation.

How Do Clinical Psychologists Measure Intelligence? There are hundreds of tests that propose to measure intelligence or cognitive ability. Different tests have been developed for use with various populations such as children, adults, ethnic minority group members, the gifted, and the disabled (e.g., visually, hearing, or motorically impaired individuals). Some tests are administered individually, while others are administered in groups. Some tests have used extensive research to examine reliability and validity, whereas others have very little research support. Some are easy to administer and score, while others are very difficult to use. Although there are many intelligence tests to choose from, only a small handful of tests tend to be used consistently and widely by most psychologists. Clearly, the most popular and frequently administered tests include the **Wechsler Scales** (i.e., the Wechsler Adult Intelligence Scale—Fourth Edition [WAIS-IV], the Wechsler Intelligence Scale of Children—Fourth Edition [WISC-IV], the Wechsler Primary and Preschool Scale—Third Edition [WPPSI-III]). The second most frequently used intelligence test is the Stanford-Binet (Fifth Edition). Other popular choices include the Kaufman Assessment Battery for Children (Second Edition) (K-ABC-II) and the Woodcock-Johnson III Cognitive Abilities Assessment.

Wechsler Scales

WECHSLER SCALES FOR ADULTS: The Wechsler-Bellevue Intelligence Scale was developed and published by David Wechsler (1896–1981) in 1939. The test was revised in 1955, 1981 (WAIS-R), 1997 (WAIS-III), and most recently in 2008 as the fourth edition (WAIS-IV; Wechsler, 2008); thus the WAIS-IV is the current version of the test in use today (Table 8.1). The WAIS-IV consists of four separate verbal comprehension subtests (Information, Similarities, Vocabulary, and Comprehension), five perceptual reasoning subtests (Picture

Table 8.1   **Descriptions of the WAIS-IV Subtests**

Subtest	Description
Picture Completion	A set of color pictures of common objects and settings, each of which is missing an important part that the examinee must identify
Vocabulary	A series of orally and visually presented words that the examinee orally defines
Coding	A series of numbers, each of which is paired with its own corresponding hieroglyphic-like symbol. Using a key, the examinee writes the symbol corresponding to its number
Similarities	A series of orally presented pairs of words for which the examinee explains the similarity of the common objects or concepts they represent
Block Design	A set of modeled or printed two-dimensional geometric patterns that the examinee replicates using two-color cubes
Arithmetic	A series of arithmetic problems that the examinee solves mentally and responds to orally
Matrix Reasoning	A series of incomplete gridded patterns that the examinee completes by pointing to or saying the number of the correct response from five possible choices
Digit Span	A series of orally presented number sequences that the examinee repeats verbatim for Digits Forward and in reverse for Digits Backward
Information	A series of orally presented questions that tap the examinee's knowledge of common events, objects, places, and people
Comprehension	A series of orally presented questions that require the examinee to understand and articulate social rules and concepts or solutions to everyday problems
Symbol Search	A series of paired groups, each pair consisting of a target group and a search group. The examinees indicates, by marking the appropriate box, whether either target symbol appears in the search group
Letter-Number Sequencing	A series of orally presented sequences of letters and numbers that the examinee simultaneously tracks and orally repeats, with the number in ascending order and the letters in alphabetical order
Visual Puzzles	A series of abstract visual puzzles that ask the respondent to select the components of each target puzzle to assess nonverbal reasoning
Figure Weights	A series of objects on scales that ask the respondent to determine which objects will balance the scales to assess quantitative and analogical reasoning
Cancellation	A sequence of colored abstract objects with particular ones to be crossed out or cancelled by the respondent. The subtest measures visual perceptual speed

Source: From *Wechsler Adult Intelligence Scale*, Fourth Edition, by D. Wechsler, 2008, Minneapolis, MN: Pearson Assessments.

Completion, Block Design, Matrix Reasoning, Visual Puzzles, and Figure Weights), three working memory scale subtests (Arithmetic, Digit Span, and Letter-Numbering Sequencing), and three processing speed subtests (Symbol Search, Coding, and Cancellation). Each subtest includes a variety of items that assess a particular intellectual skill of interest (e.g., the vocabulary subtest includes a list of words that the respondent must define). The WAIS-IV generally takes about one to one-and-a-half hours to individually administer to someone between the ages of 16 and 90. Four IQ index scores are determined using the WAIS-IV: a Verbal Comprehension Index Score, a Perceptual Reasoning Index Score, a Working Memory Index Score, and a Processing Speed Index Score. A Full Scale IQ Score (combining the index scores) is also provided. The mean IQ score for each of these three categories is 100 with a standard deviation of 15. Scores between 90 and 110 are considered within the average range of intellectual functioning. Scores below 70 are considered to be in the mentally deficient range, while scores above 130 are considered to be in the very superior range. The individual subtests (e.g., Vocabulary, Block Design) have a mean of 10 and a standard deviation of 3. These subtests form the basis for subtle observations about the relative strengths and weaknesses possessed by each individual.

The Wechsler Scales have been shown to have acceptable reliability, validity, and stability (Anastasi and Urbina, 1997; Hersen, 2003; Parker, Hanson, & Hunsley, 1988; Wechsler, 1981, 1997a, 2003, 2008).

Edith Kaplan and associates have developed an expanded version of the Wechsler Scales called the WAIS-R as a Neuropsychological Instrument (WAIS-R NI; Kaplan, Fein, Morris, & Delis, 1991). The WAIS-R NI contains additional subtests (e.g., Sentence Arrangement, Spatial Span, Symbol Copy) as well as modifications for administration and scoring (e.g., using pencil and paper for the Arithmetic subtest and multiple choice for the Vocabulary, Information, and Similarities subtests) in order to be more useful for individuals who may

have brain dysfunction. Kaplan and associates developed a similar test for children called the WISC-III as a process instrument (WISC-III PI; Kaplan, Fein, Kramer, Delis, & Morris, 1999). These are just a few of an arsenal of neuropsychological tests utilized in psychology, an area of testing covered more fully later in this chapter.

In addition to overall IQ scores, most psychologists make inferences about cognitive strengths and weaknesses by examining the pattern of scores obtained on each WAIS-IV subtest. For example, high scores on the vocabulary subtest relative to very low scores on the block design subject might suggest that the person has good use of language in solving problems and a poorer ability to solve problems using certain perceptual and motor integration skills. Additionally, the Wechsler Scales can be helpful in learning about neuropsychological problems such as brain damage (Kaplan et al., 1991; Kaplan et al., 1999), as well as psychological and personality functioning (Allison, Blatt, & Zimet, 1968).

Finally, IQ tests should always be interpreted in the context of other assessment measures. As subsequent examples will illustrate, even a seemingly straightforward IQ test needs to be integrated with other test results as well as the panoply of biopsychosocial factors impacting the individual and his or her performance. Otherwise, the scores in isolation can be rendered meaningless or even misleading.

THE WECHSLER SCALES FOR CHILDREN: The Wechsler Intelligence Scale for Children (WISC) was first published in 1949 and was revised in 1974 (WISC-R) and revised again in 1991 (WISC-III) and again in 2003 (now named the Wechsler Intelligence Scale for Children—Fourth Edition; WISC-IV). The WISC-IV is the version currently used today. The WISC-IV has both verbal and nonverbal subscales similar to those used in the WAIS-III. However, WISC-IV questions are generally simpler because they were developed for children aged 6 to 16 rather than for adults. Furthermore, they are clustered in

Case Study: Paul—WAIS-IV (Intellectual Assessment)

(Case provided by clinical psychologist John Brentar, PhD)

Age: 20 years
Education: College Junior

Wechsler Adult Intelligence Scale, Fourth Edition (WAIS-IV) The Wechsler Adult Intelligence Scale, Fourth Edition (WAIS-IV) is a standardized measure of intelligence designed to assess verbal comprehension, perceptual organization, working memory, and processing speed. Scaled scores between 8 and 12 and standard scores between 90 and 109 (25th to 75th percentiles) reflect age-appropriate functioning.

Verbal Comprehension	Scaled Score	Perceptual Reasoning	Scaled Score
Similarities	11	Block Design	13
Vocabulary	12	Matrix Reasoning	9
Information	11	*Visual Puzzles	13 (19)

Working Memory	Scaled Score	Processing Speed	Scaled Score
Digit Span	7	Symbol Search	7
Arithmetic	7	Coding	7

Index Scores	Standard Score	Percentile
Verbal Comprehension	107	68
*Perceptual Organization	109 (121)	73 (92)
Working Memory	83	13
Processing Speed	84	14
*FULL SCALE IQ	98	45

*Scores in parentheses indicated performance when time limits tested.

Paul's overall score on the WAIS-IV indicated that his cognitive skills are in the mid-average range of functioning. However, there were significant discrepancies among domain scores, as well as between his performance under standard timed conditions and when given credit for correct responses after the time limits. Specifically, Paul displayed verbal and nonverbal reasoning abilities in the high end of the average range under standardized conditions compared to significant weaknesses in his auditory working memory and speed of processing skills, both below average. However, his overall performance on tests of nonverbal reasoning improved from the average to superior range when time limits were tested due to his exceptional performance on the Visual Puzzles subtest without time constraints.

Within the Verbal Comprehension domain, Paul displayed average verbal reasoning and knowledge. Specifically, his performance indicated age-appropriate word knowledge (Vocabulary = 75th percentile) and abstract reasoning (Similarities = 63rd percentile). His fund of knowledge (Information) was also average, at the 63rd percentile. Of note, Paul required time to consider the questions and often struggled to formulate his responses, causing him visible frustration.

Paul's overall performance on tests of his nonverbal reasoning skills was impacted by his deliberate pace when faced with complex problems, and he displayed average skills when standard, timed conditions were used. However, when limits were tested and he was given credit for correct responses after the time limit, his overall performance improved to the superior range. This was due to the significant impact of time on his performance on the Visual Puzzles subtest, which measured his ability to analyze and synthesize abstract visual stimuli. Indeed, his performance under timed conditions was at the 84th percentile and improved

(continued)

Case Study (Continued)

to the 99.9th percentile when given credit for the items he answered correctly after the 30-second time limit. In fact, Paul answered all of the problems correctly, 6 after the time limit, and spent as much as 2 minutes on some problems. The impact of time was not as apparent during the Block Design subtest, which measured visual-motor and spatial organization, although Paul did not receive some of the bonus points for working quickly despite answering all items correctly. During this subtest, he talked his way through the problems and exhibited a systematic approach to constructing the designs. Paul had the most difficulty on the Matrix Reasoning subtest, which measured his reasoning skills for abstract visual information, at the 37th percentile. He appeared flustered during this subtest, commenting "Why am I not putting this together?" and also seemed to rush to provide answers. His anxiety appeared to worsen as the test progressed, which likely impacted his overall performance.

Paul's auditory working memory, or his ability to hold information in memory in order to complete a task, was in the low average range of functioning, at the 13th percentile, indicating a significant weakness.

During the Digit Span subtest, he appeared confused about the task requirements, and especially struggled when asked to recall digits backward. Additionally, Paul's performance on the Arithmetic subtest was impacted by his need for more time, and he answered 5 questions correctly after the time limit. He used helpful strategies during this subtest, including "writing" on the desk when solving the problems, and requested that the examiner repeat many of the problems. This approach improved his accuracy but slowed his performance. Overall, Paul appeared to benefit from the context provided by the items of the Arithmetic subtest compared to the less meaningful number lists, but he required time to fully consider the more complex problems.

Paul's overall performance on tests of processing speed indicated a significant weakness, at the 14th percentile. Specifically, he demonstrated weak performance when completing the Coding subtest, which assesses speeded graphomotor coordination, at the 16th percentile. Similarly, his visual scanning skills as assessed by the Symbol Search subtest were below average, also at the 16th percentile.

four categories that represent different areas of intellectual functioning. These include Verbal Comprehension, Perceptual Reasoning, Working Memory, and Processing Speed. Each of these four areas of intellectual functioning include both "core" or mandatory subtests that must be administered to derive an index or IQ score as well as at least one "supplementary" or optional subtest that is not included in the index or IQ score. The Verbal Comprehension category consists of three core subtests including Similarities, Vocabulary, and Comprehension as well as two supplementary subtests that include Information and Word Reasoning. The Perceptual Reasoning category

also consists of three core subtests, including Block Design, Picture Concepts, and Matrix Reasoning, as well as one supplementary subtest called Picture Completion. The Working Memory category consists of two core subtests including Digit Span and Letter-Number Sequencing as well as one supplementary subtest entitled Arithmetic. Finally, the Processing Speed category consists of two core subtests, Coding and Symbol Search, as well as one supplementary subtest entitled Cancellation.

The WISC-IV provides four index score IQs as well as an overall or full-scale IQ based on the scores from all of the four index scores. These IQ scores all are set with a mean of 100 and a standard deviation of 15. The four factor scores (i.e., Verbal Comprehension, Perceptual Reasoning, Working Memory, and Processing Speed) were developed using factor analytic techniques and numerous research studies to reflect human intellectual functioning. Each of the subtests use a mean of 10 and standard deviation of 3. The WISC-IV has been shown to have excellent reliability, validity, and stability (Wechsler, 2003).

The Wechsler Preschool and Primary Scale of Intelligence (WPPSI) was developed and published in 1967 for use with children aged 4 to 6. The test was revised in 1989 (WPPSI-R) and revised again in 2002 as the WPPSI-III. The WPPSI-III is the current version of the test being used today. The WPPSI-III is used for children ranging in age from 2 to 7. Like the other Wechsler scales (WAIS-IV, WAIS-R NI, WISC-IV), the WPPSI-III has both Verbal and Performance scales resulting in four IQ scores: Verbal IQ, Performance IQ, Processing Speed IQ, and Full Scale IQ. Similar to the other Wechsler scales, IQ scores have a mean of 100 and a standard deviation of 15, while the subtest scores have a mean of 10 and a standard deviation of 3. The Verbal IQ score consists of the Information, Vocabulary, and Word Reasoning subtest while the Comprehension and Similarities subtests are not included in the calculation of the Verbal IQ score. The Performance IQ consists of the Block Design, Matrix Reasoning, and Picture Concept subtests while the Picture Completion and Object Assembly are not included in the calculation of the Performance IQ score. The Processing Speed IQ score consists of the Symbol Search and Coding Subtest. The WPPSI-III has been shown to have satisfaction, reliability, validity, and stability (Wechsler, 2002).

Stanford-Binet Scales: The Stanford-Binet is a revised version of the first standardized intelligence test, developed by Alfred Binet in 1905. The test has been revised many times—in 1916, 1937, 1960, 1986, and most recently, in 2003. The current version of the test is called the Stanford-Binet—Fifth Edition (Roid, 2003) The Stanford-Binet can be used with individuals from 2 years of age through adulthood.

The Stanford-Binet Scales consist of Nonverbal (NV) and Verbal (V) domains. Together, they produce a full-scale IQ score. Furthermore, factor scores or indexes are provided in five areas: Fluid Reasoning (FR), Knowledge (KN), Visual-Spatial Processing (VS), Working Memory (WM), and Quantitative Reasoning (QR).

Fluid Reasoning subtests include Object Series/Matrices, Early Reasoning, Verbal Absurdities, and Verbal Analogies. Knowledge subtests include Vocabulary, Procedural Knowledge, and Picture Absurdities. Visual-Spatial processing subtests include Form Board, Form Patterns, and Position and Direction. The Working Memory subtests include Block Span, Memory for Sentences, and Last Word. Finally, Quantitative Reasoning subtests include one subtest called Quantitative Reasoning. Unlike the Wechsler Scales, only certain Stanford-Binet subtests are used with certain subjects. The age of the subject determines which subtests are used in any given evaluation. Scores from all subtest categories are used to derive IQ scores based on a mean of 100 and a standard deviation of 15. Research suggests that the Stanford-Binet has satisfactory reliability, validity, and stability (Anastasi & Urbina, 1997; Roid, 2003; Thorndike, Hagen, & Sattler, 1986).

Other Tests of Intellectual Ability: Numerous tests other than the Wechsler and Stanford-Binet are available for use with specific populations. For example, alternative tests may be used with special populations such as gifted children, nonverbal or hearing-impaired individuals, or minority group members. They may also be used as a second opinion following a Wechsler test or Stanford-Binet or to obtain additional cognitive information not available through the administration of the Wechsler or Stanford-Binet scales (e.g., reading achievement). While it is beyond the scope of this book to discuss all the available tests in detail, some of the more popular are discussed next. You may wish to consult other resources for

Multicultural Issues and Testing

Although we use the term *objective* to describe many psychological tests and inventories, many of these tests must be used with great caution in our increasingly diverse multicultural world. Testing instrument developers such as the Pearson Assessments work diligently to ensure that minority groups are represented and reflect America's diverse cultural landscape when developing and producing norms for tests. However, many instruments still may be inappropriate to use with many minority group members. For example, most of the tests reviewed in this book assume that the testee has an excellent command of the English language. For example, the MMPI-2 or the WAIS-IV would be very difficult to complete if the client was not well versed in English. Lack of adequate English skills could result in lower IQ scores, which might be wrongfully attributed to lower intelligence and cognitive functioning rather than English-language skills. Additionally, level of acculturation and assimilation of minority group members into society must be taken into consideration when using any psychological tests as well. Although individuals' English skills might be acceptable, their cultural background may impact their testing performance.

In a remarkable 1986 landmark decision in California (*Larry P. v. California*), a judge ruled in favor of the Association of Black Psychologists' claim that standard individually administered intelligence tests such as the WISC and Stanford-Binet could not be used with African American students in public schools. It was decided that the improper use of these instruments can lead to discriminatory educational decisions such as placing students in lower-performing class environments. The court felt that these tests do more harm than good for African American children and thus should no longer be used. This decision underscored the notion that cultural factors must be carefully considered in the use of any psychological test and that efforts to assess skills and functioning must always take culture into consideration.

One important issue in assessment of ethnic minority persons includes the issue of acculturation. It would be unreasonable to expect that all members of a particular minority group would have the same cultural issues operating if they recently moved to the United States or Canada from other countries compared to moving decades or even centuries ago. Gonzalez (1998) states that acculturation depends on the level of assimilation and integration into the majority culture. Therefore, in addition to cultural or ethnic group membership, it is important to assess a client's level of acculturation into the majority culture as well. This can be done by interview or actual tests used specifically to assess acculturation. These include the Acculturation Rating Scale for Mexican Americans (ARSMA-II; Cuellar, Arnold, & Maldonado, 1995), the Bicultural Involvement Scale (Szapocznik, Kurtines, & Fernandez, 1980) and the Suinn-Lew Asian Self-Identity Acculturation Scale (Suinn, Ahuna, & Khoo, 1992), to name a few.

Case Study: Donald—WISC-IV (Intellectual Assessment)

Donald L. is a 9-year-old boy who comes from a mixed racial family where his father is Caucasian and his mother is of Asian descent. He was referred for an evaluation by his parents to obtain a comprehensive assessment of his cognitive and academic strengths and weaknesses. He has been diagnosed with an auditory processing disorder. A speech and language evaluation revealed a weakness in language reasoning skills. His parents requested this evaluation to determine the best ways to support Donald's performance in school. Currently, Donald is a fourth grader.

Mrs. L. reported that Donald is struggling with the significant increase in his workload this year. He has difficulty organizing himself; for example, he has not turned in work even if it was complete. Donald's teacher reported that he has difficulty knowing where to start when she asks him to clean his desk area; Mrs. L. has noticed a similar difficulty at home. Mrs. L. reported that it is difficult to get his attention at times. Once you are able to secure his attention, Donald generally attends well. At other times (e.g., while reading), he is prone to hyperfocus. Donald also has difficulty processing multistep directions and needs directions stated in a concrete and explicit manner.

Mrs. L. reported that Donald is a good speller and reader. She is concerned, however, that his comprehension skills may weaken as he faces more abstract concepts in the future. Donald struggles with his higher-order thinking skills and with writing. His lowest scores on standardized tests tend to be in written language. Donald's math skills are good.

Donald works with a speech and language therapist in school for two 30-minute sessions per week to address his pragmatic language skills. Mrs. L. reported that he is prone to talk loudly and struggles with maintaining reciprocal conversations. Donald is also working with a psychotherapist to address symptoms of anxiety. Donald has been seen by physical and occupational therapists in the past due to weakness in gross motor functioning as a result of mild cerebral palsy. Despite his motor difficulties, he has played soccer and baseball; however, Donald learned to ride his bike only after three years of training. He has also worked on his penmanship and struggles with alignment and spacing of letters.

Test Results:

	Scaled Score	Percentile
Verbal Comprehension		
Similarities	12	75
Vocabulary	18	99.7
Comprehension	09	37
Perceptual Reasoning		
Block Design	08	25
Picture Concepts	15	95
Matrix Reasoning	10	50
Picture Completion	10	50
Working Memory		
Digit Span	10	50
Letter-Number Sequencing	13	84
Arithmetic	15	95
Processing Speed		
Coding	06	09
Symbol Search	06	09
Cancellation	10	50

Composite Scores	Standard Score	Percentile
Verbal Comprehension	116	86
Perceptual Reasoning	106	66
Working Memory	107	68
Processing Speed	78	07
FULL-SCALE IQ	105	63

Brief Summary of IQ Results: The results of intelligence testing indicate that Donald's cognitive capabilities are in the average range overall. His Composite Scores provide a good picture of areas of strengths and weaknesses. Donald's verbal comprehension

(continued)

Case Study (Continued)

skills are an area of strength, with skills in the above-average range. He performed at age-level in the areas of perceptual reasoning and working memory. In contrast, Donald scored significantly lower on the Processing Speed Composite, indicating that this is an area of relative weakness among his cognitive skills.

Among subtests comprising the Verbal Comprehension Composite, Donald's scores are variable. He displayed gifted skills in word knowledge (Vocabulary), scoring at the 99.7 percentile. Donald performed in the higher end of the average range on Similarities, a measure of abstract reasoning. He scored relatively lower on Comprehension, a test of social reasoning and problem solving, although his score was still in the average range. His language reasoning weaknesses likely contributed to his relatively lower score on this test.

Donald's scores were also variable on the Perceptual Reasoning subtests. He exhibited a clear strength on Picture Concepts, which allowed Donald to access his language skills to solve this visual reasoning task. Donald performed at age-level on another visual reasoning task (Matrix Reasoning) that did not lend itself to a language-based strategy. He scored at a comparable level on Picture Completion, a test of attention to detail. Donald's lowest score was on Block Design, a visual problem-solving test involving colored blocks. He scored in the lower end of the average range, reflecting a relative weakness in visual-perceptual functioning.

In the area of working memory, Donald performed in the superior range on a test of mental arithmetic (Arithmetic). His strength in math and his ability to use contextual verbal information undoubtedly enhanced his performance on this test. Donald scored in the above-average range on Letter-Number Sequencing. In this test, he was presented with random series of numbers and letters. Donald was asked to sequence the numbers in numeric order and the letters in alphabetical order. He reported that he tried "really hard" on this test because he knew that it would be challenging for him. Donald scored in the average range on Digit Span, a test of rote memory for numbers. He was equally proficient in recalling numbers in the forward and reverse directions.

Processing speed appears to be an area of relative weakness among Donald's cognitive skills. He scored in the average range on Cancellation, a timed test that measured his ability to quickly locate pictures of animals among a random array of pictures. He was equally proficient in locating animals when the pictures were placed randomly across two pages and when the pictures were arranged in rows and columns. Donald did not appear to use a clear organizational strategy to manage this task. He scored in the below-average range on the remaining two processing speed tests, Coding and Symbol Search. Donald's higher score on Cancellation may reflect his increased level of engagement on the brightly colored Cancellation tasks. His self-talk strategy may have also enhanced his performance.

Brief Interpretation Summary of WISC-IV Results: The results of intelligence testing indicate that Donald's overall intellectual functioning is in the average range. He displays a relative strength in verbal comprehension (scoring in the above-average range). Donald performed at age level on tests of perceptual reasoning and working memory. He scored relatively lower in the area of processing speed, reflecting an area of weakness among his cognitive skills.

more information concerning these tests (e.g., Anastasi & Urbina, 1997). Examples of these alternative tests include the Kaufman Tests (Kaufman Assessment Battery for Children [K-ABC-II]; Kaufman & Kaufman, 2004), which offer, for example, African American norms, the Kaufman Brief Intelligence Test (K-BIT-II; Kaufman & Kaufman, 2004), the Kaufman Adolescent and Adult Intelligence Test (KAIT; Kaufman & Kaufman, 1993), the Peabody Picture Vocabulary Test—Fourth Edition (PPVT-IV; Dunn & Dunn, 2007), the Woodcock-Johnson Psycho-Educational Battery (WJ III; Woodcock, McGrew, & Mather, 2001), Raven's Progressive Matrices (Raven, 1993; Raven, Raven, & Court, 2003), the General Ability Measure for Adults (GAMA; Naglieri & Bardos, 1997), and the System of Multicultural Pluralistic Assessment (SOMPA; Lewis & Mercer, 1978; Mercer & Lewis, 1979). The K-ABC-II and SOMPA will be briefly outlined next.

The K-ABC-II is administered to children between the ages of 3 and 13 and has five global scales including Sequential Processing, Simultaneous Processing, Learning Ability, Planning Ability, and Crystallized Ability. Scores are then combined to create a Mental Processing Index (MPI) and a nonverbal index. The development of the K-ABC reflects a different theoretical approach to intellectual assessment relative to the Wechsler Scales. Sequential processing refers to problem-solving skills that use a step-by-step approach while simultaneous processing uses information from several sources to arrive at an answer all at once. Means are set at 100 with standard deviations of 15. The K-ABC-II was developed from research and theory in neuropsychology and, unlike both the Wechsler and Stanford-Binet scales, has achievement scores to measure skills such as reading ability. Many clinicians feel that the K-ABC-II is more enjoyable and engaging for children than the Wechsler Scales and Stanford-Binet, as well as a less verbally dependent test. Furthermore, the K-ABC-II generally takes less time to administer than the Wechsler and Stanford-Binet.

The SOMPA is a comprehensive assessment of intellectual functioning for children aged 5 to 11 and is especially designed for children from minority groups such as African-American and Latino populations. SOMPA provides nine different measurements of cognitive functioning and includes a structured parent interview as part of the evaluation process. Many professionals feel that the SOMPA is much more useful with minority groups than the Wechsler and Stanford-Binet measures. Issues regarding testing bias among minority groups will be addressed later in this chapter.

Other Tests of Cognitive Ability: Some tests are not merely intelligence tests per se, but also measure cognitive abilities. For example, the Bayley Scales of Infant Development, Second Edition (BSID-II; Bayley, 1993), measures mental, motor, and developmental abilities among very young children aged 1 month to 42 months. The Cognitive Assessment System (CAS; Das & Naglieri, 1997) evaluates cognitive processing such as planning, attention, and simultaneous and successive cognitive functioning for children ages 5 through 17. The Vineland Adaptive Behavior Scales, Second Edition (Sparrow, Balla, & Cicchetti, 2005), and the Adaptive Behavior Scales, Second Edition (N. Lambert, 1993), examine adaptive behavior (e.g., dressing and eating independently) among children by focusing on socialization and the development of social competence. These scales are critical, for example, in documenting mental retardation in conjunction with IQ scores. Thus, IQ scores below 70 (reflecting 2 standard deviations below the mean) in conjunction with adaptive behaviors significantly below expectation for a given age are used to diagnose mental retardation. The Wide Range Achievement Test-4 (WRAT-4; Wilkinson & Robertson, 2006) measures reading, writing, and mathematical skills for individuals aged 5 to 75. The Woodcock-Johnson test includes an achievement as well as aptitude component, measuring skills such as reading, writing, and mathematics.

Learning Disabilities Assessment by Clinical Psychologist John Brentar, PhD

In 1968, the federal government developed a definition of *learning disabilities* that was operationalized in the *Federal Register* in 1977 as a severe discrepancy between intellectual ability, based on IQ test scores, and achievement in academic areas such as reading, writing, or math. This model helped to promote the development of the field of learning disabilities because it acknowledged that a child was not mentally deficient because he or she struggled to learn. It also provided a standardized way to assess learning disabilities. More recently, however, researchers in the learning disability field have argued that IQ tests contribute little reliable information for developing, implementing, and evaluating instructional interventions and that the use of the discrepancy model should be discontinued. Their arguments are:

- The discrepancy model has become associated with underachievement, which makes it very difficult to identify children early enough for preventive interventions (i.e., it can take a long time for achievement scores to drop low enough to be discrepant with IQ scores). Therefore, intervention programs often occur after a child has already failed or are too late to significantly impact the child's skills, usually by the second grade or later.
- There is a bidirectional influence between IQ and achievement: not only does IQ set limits on achievement, limited achievement impacts performance on IQ tests.
- Time-consuming assessments involving traditional IQ tests provide teachers with little information that can be used to develop immediate intervention services.
- Children's processing problems can affect their performance on specific IQ subtests, thereby reducing the chance for a significant discrepancy between IQ and academic achievement test scores.
- It is often difficult to document a discrepancy in bilingual children, ethnic minority children, and children with very high or low-average/below-average IQ scores.

Alternative models have been proposed that focus on assessment of processing skills that are presumed to underlie academic performance problems. The benefits of this type of model include:

- It would not require children to fail in school prior to diagnosis.
- It could help target all children who have learning problems and not merely those who satisfy the discrepancy criterion.
- It could help focus instruction in areas of greatest need. Specifically, children at risk could be identified as early as preschool and kindergarten,

allowing for early intervention. The child's response to the interventions could then be assessed and a designation of "learning disability" could be made based on the child's lack of progress to the intervention.

The educational system's ability to quickly adopt this processing skills model is compromised by several significant problems:

- Researchers do not have a complete understanding of the processing skills that are needed to learn efficiently across all academic areas. For example, while critical processing skills have been identified for reading, they have not been clearly identified for math.
- Researchers do not necessarily know whether performance problems on tests designed to assess processing skills purely measure the processing skill or are impacted by other factors, such as acquired knowledge or previous experience with similar tasks.
- Most school psychologists and educational specialists are not trained in these assessment measures, nor do they have easy access to them.
- Most teachers have not received specialized training in how to develop effective intervention strategies based on children's processing strengths and weaknesses. Therefore, the processing skills model might not be easily implemented unless teachers and assessors (such as school psychologists) are better educated to understand processing skills and their relationship to academic achievement.

This dilemma suggests that IQ tests will remain an important assessment instrument in the diagnosis of learning disabilities in the near future for the following reasons:

- IQ tests provide a context by which to interpret a child's performance on other tests based on his or her ability level in verbal and nonverbal (visual-perceptual) domains.
- Most psychologists who perform learning disability assessments use the IQ test as a way to generate initial hypotheses about a child's processing skills and select subsequent assessment measures to test those hypotheses.

When handled sensitively and interpreted by a competent psychologist, IQ tests used in combination with other information, such as scores from processing and academic tests, history, clinical observations, and parent/school reports, can be an important tool in the assessment of a child's learning skills. With this approach, learning disabilities can still be diagnosed even if an ability-achievement discrepancy is not present.

Neuropsychological Testing: Other tests focus on brain–behavior relationships and thus measure neuropsychological functioning. Brain impairment due to head injury, substance abuse, stroke, or other illnesses and injuries often impacts the cognitive ability to use language, think and make appropriate judgments, adequately perceive and respond to stimuli, and remember old or new information. **Neuropsychological testing** assesses brain–behavior skills such as intellectual, abstract reasoning, memory, visual-perceptual, attention, concentration, gross and fine motor, and language functioning. Since neuropsychological topics are highlighted in Chapter 11, this testing approach will be only briefly addressed here.

Neuropsychological tests include test batteries as well as individual tests. The Halstead-Reitan Battery (Boll, 1981; Halstead, 1947; Reitan & Davison, 1974) and the Luria-Nebraska Battery (Golden, Hammeke, & Purisch, 1980) are the most commonly used with adults. The Halstead-Reitan Battery can be administered to persons aged 15 through adulthood and consists of 12 separate tests along with the administration of the MMPI-2 and the WAIS-IV. The battery takes approximately 6 to 8 hours to administer and provides an overall impairment index as well as separate scores on each subtest assessing skills such as memory, sensory-perceptual skills, and the ability to solve new learning problems (Table 8.2). Other versions of the test are available for children between ages 5 and 14. The Luria-Nebraska Battery consists of 11 subtests for a total of 269 separate testing tasks. The subtests assess reading, writing, receptive and expressive speech, memory, arithmetic, and other skills. The Luria-Nebraska battery takes about 2.5 hours to administer.

Another neuropsychological testing approach is represented by the **Boston Process Approach** (Delis, Kaplan, & Kramer, 2001; Goodglass, 1986; Kaplan et al., 1991, 1999; Milberg, Hebben, & Kaplan, 1986). The Boston Process Approach uses a variety of different tests depending on the nature of the referral question (Table 8.3). Rather than using a standard test battery, the Boston Process Approach uses a subset of a wide variety of tests in order to answer specific

Table 8.2 **Halstead-Reitan Neuropsychological Test Battery**

Category Test	Current learning, abstract concept formation
Tactual Performance Test	Motor speed, psychomotor coordination
Rhythm Test	Attention, concentration, auditory perception
Speech Sounds Perception Test	Attention, concentration, coordination of language processing
Finger Oscillation Test	Finger tapping skill
Trail Making Test	Psychomotor speed, sequencing, maintain and shift sets
Strength of Grip Test	Gross motor strength
Sensory-Perceptual Examination	Ability to perceive stimuli to both body sides
Tactile Perception	Tactile finger localization
Modified Halstead-Wepman Aphasia Screening Test	Screening of language skill
Wechsler Adult Intelligence Scale-III (WAIS-III)	Intellectual functioning
Minnesota Multiphasic Personality Inventory-2 (MMPI-2)	Personality and psychological functioning

Table 8.3   **Sample of Tests Used in the Boston Process Approach to Neuropsychological Assessment**

Intellectual and Conceptual Skills

Wechsler Adult Intelligence Scale-IV (WAIS-IV)
Standard Progressive Matrices
Shipley Institute of Living Scale
Wisconsin Card Sorting Test
Proverbs Test

Memory Skills

Wechsler Memory Scale—Third Edition
Rey Auditory Verbal Learning Test
Rey-Osterrieth Complex Figure
Benton Visual Recognition Test
Consonant Trigrams Test
Cowboy Story Reading Memory Test
Corsi Blocks

Language Skills

Narrative Writing Sample
Tests of Verbal Fluency (Word List Generation)

Visual-Perceptual Skills

Cow and Circle Experimental Test
Automobile Puzzle
Parietal Lobe Battery
Hooper Visual Organization Test

Academic Skills

Wide Range Achievement Test

Motor and Impulse Control Skills

Porteus Maze Test
Stroop Color-Word Interference Test
Luria Three-Step Motor Program
Finger Tapping

---

neuropsychological questions. Performance on one test determines which tests or subtests, if any, will be used next. The testing process could be short or long, involving few or many tests and subtests depending on what is needed to adequately evaluate strengths and weaknesses in functioning. For example, if a neuropsychological evaluation of a head-injured patient was to focus on memory skills

following a car accident, several tests would be considered for use. These might include the Benton Visual Retention Test, the Wechsler Memory Scale-III, and the Wisconsin Card Sorting Test. Each of these tests measures a different facet of memory functioning. Results provide a clearer picture of short- and long-term memory as well as visual, auditory, and sensory memory. If, during testing, language problems were detected, the receptive and expressive language sections of the Luria-Nebraska might be added to the battery to assess language skills. The language assessment might help to better understand the relationship between memory and language skills in this patient.

Some of the commonly used individual neuropsychological tests include the Wechsler Memory Scale-III (Wechsler, 1997b), the Benton Visual Retention Test, Fifth Edition (Benton, 1991), and the WAIS-R as a Neuropsychological Instrument (Kaplan et al., 1991), the WISC-III as a Process Instrument (Kaplan et al., 1999), the Kaufman Short Neuropsychological Assessment Procedure (K-SNAP; Kaufman & Kaufman, 1994), the California Verbal Learning Test (Delis, Kramer, Kaplan, & Ober, 1987, 2000) and the California Verbal Learning Test—Children's Version (Delis, Kramer, Kaplan, & Ober, 1994), and the Wisconsin Card Sorting Test (Grant & Berg, 1993). The Delis-Kaplan Executive Function System (D-KEFS; Delis, Kaplan, & Kramer, 2001) provides a comprehensive evaluation of executive functioning or high-level thinking and processing as well as cognitive flexibility. It can be administered to both children and adults from ages 8 through 89. It assesses the integrity of the frontal lobe area of the brain, and examines potential deficits in abstract and creative thinking. The D-KEFS consists of 9 subtests, including the Sorting, Trail Making, Verbal Fluency, Design Fluency, Color-Word Interference, Tower, 20-Questions, Word Context, and the Proverb tests. These tests measure various aspects of cognitive functioning that reflect strengths and weaknesses associated with brain–behavior relationships. Results from these tests are compared with national norms to develop a clearer understanding of the interaction between brain functioning and behavior, emotions, and thoughts as well as to help locate the site of brain impairment.

The Spanish and English Neuropsychological Assessment Scales (SENAS: Mungas, Reed, Crane, Haan, & Gonzalez, 2004) include a variety of cognitive tests that are used with older adults from diverse ethnic groups. These include 12 tests assessing a variety of cognitive skills. The SENAS is an excellent example of the efforts needed to develop testing procedures that can be used in diverse settings with those who may not speak English.

Some authors have suggested that physiological tests such as evoked potentials, electroencephalography (EEG), and reaction time measures may be useful in the assessment of intelligence and cognitive abilities (Matarazzo, 1992; Reed & Jensen, 1991; Sternberg, 2008). Evoked potentials assess the brain's ability to process the perception of a stimulus, and EEG measures electrical activity of the brain. Although psychologists are currently not licensed to administer or interpret neuroimaging techniques such as computerized axial tomography (CT), magnetic resonance imaging (MRI and fMRI), and positron emission tomography (PET), these techniques allow examination of brain structure and function, which is useful in assessing brain–behavior relationships such as cognitive abilities. For example, cortical atrophy, shrinkage, or actual loss of brain tissue has been associated with schizophrenia, Alzheimer's disease, anorexia nervosa, alcoholism, and mood disorders (e.g., Andreasen, 1989, Andreasen & Black, 1995; Fischbach, 1992; Storandt, 2008).

Contemporary neuropsychological testing integrates specialized tests along with additional sources of information. The tests are often used in conjunction with data obtained from clinical interviews, behavioral observations, and other cognitive, personality, and physiological assessment tools. Thus, neuropsychological testing is not isolated from other evaluation techniques used by contemporary clinical psychologists. While neuropsychological assessment is a subspecialty of clinical psychology, it overlaps with many of the skills and techniques of general clinical psychologists. In addition to specialized testing, neuropsychologists must have a high level of understanding of brain structure and functioning.

Questions and Controversies Concerning IQ and Cognitive Testing: ARE WE BORN WITH A CERTAIN IQ? Often people assume that we are born with an innately determined level of intellectual ability that is not influenced by social, emotional, and environmental factors (Herrnstein & Murray, 1994). Some suggest that **IQ** differences found among different racial groups might be due to inborn differences in intelligence. A great deal of controversy has raged in this debate for many years. The publication of the book *The Bell Curve* (Herrnstein & Murray, 1994) reignited this controversy by suggesting that African Americans were innately less intelligent than Caucasians while Caucasians were less intelligent than Asians. Research examining genetic influences on intelligence generally studies the heritability (i.e., the estimate of genetic contribution to a given trait) of IQ using twin studies. Identical (monozygotic) and fraternal (dizygotic) twins reared together and reared apart present a unique research opportunity for examining the influence of both genetic and environmental contributions to a wide variety of traits. It has been estimated that the heritability of intelligence is between .40 and .80. Thus between 16% and 64% of the variance in intellectual ability is due to genetic influence (Hale, 1991; Sattler, 1988, 1992, 2008). Research generally supports the notion of at least some significant genetic influence in intellectual ability (Deary, Spinath, & Bates, 2006; Neisser et al., 1996). However, biological (e.g., prenatal care, genetics, nutrition), psychological (e.g., anxiety, motivation, self-esteem), and social (e.g., culture, socioeconomic status) influences all appear to be associated with intelligence or at least with IQ scores on standardized tests (Hale, 1991; Neisser et al., 1996; Sattler, 2008; Sternberg, 2008).

ARE IQ SCORES STABLE OVER TIME? Measures of attention, memory, and other cognitive abilities assessed during the first year of life generally are moderately associated (i.e., $r = .36$) with intelligence test scores assessed later in childhood (McCall & Garriger, 1993). Often people assume that an IQ score obtained in childhood is stable over time. Thus, many people erroneously believe that someone who obtained an IQ of 120 in the first grade will also have an IQ of 120 in adulthood. Intelligence tests, however, provide an index of current functioning, and scores may change significantly over time. Many factors influence the stability of IQ scores. First, scores obtained when a child is very young (e.g., age 3) are likely to be less stable than scores obtained when a child is older (e.g., age 16). This is partially because early childhood tests focus on perceptual and motor skills, whereas tests for older children and adults focus more on verbal skills (Anastasi & Urbina, 1997; Brody, 1997; Hale, 1991; Sattler, 1988, 1992, 2008). Second, the longer the time between testing administrations, the more unstable the IQ score will appear. Thus, the difference between scores obtained at ages 3 and 30 is likely to be greater than the difference between scores obtained at ages 16 and 19. Furthermore, environmental factors such as stress, nutrition, educational opportunities, exposure to toxins such as lead, and illness, among other influences, all play a role in the determination of IQ scores (Anastasi & Urbina, 1997; Hale, 1991; Hersen, 2003; Sattler, 1988, 1992, 2008).

ARE IQ SCORES BIASED? Many people are concerned about potential bias in intelligence testing (Cole, 1981; Greenfield, 1997; Helms,

---

Case Study: Robert Experiences a Head Injury and Resulting Antisocial Behaviors (Neuropsychological)

Robert is a 17-year-old Caucasian male who is a senior in high school. He lives with his father and younger sister. Robert was shot in the head when he was 11 years old during a robbery at a neighborhood store. His mother was shot and killed during the robbery. Robert has received surgery to obtain a cranial plate and a glass eye. He experiences seizures and is being administered 100 milligrams of Dilantin per day.

Referral Question: Robert has been evidencing antisocial behavior over the past three years, including lying, stealing, truancy, and angry and aggressive outbursts. Neuropsychological testing was requested to determine the basis for his behavior in light of his brain damage.

Tests Administered: The Halstead-Reitan Neuropsychological Battery

Brief Summary and Interpretation of Test Results: Robert achieved an average full-scale IQ, above-average Verbal IQ, and average Performance IQ. Test results indicated some difficulties in sensory-perceptual functioning such that he experiences mild to moderate right upper extremity sensory-perceptual dysfunction consistent with left posterior frontal (i.e., sensory strip) and parietal compromise. Thus, he has difficulty moving and feeling with his right arm and shoulder. The nature of Robert's mild neuropsychological compromise is chronic, nonprogressive, and residual from his head trauma. Therefore, only a portion of his current behavioral problems can be attributed to neuropsychological compromise. Personality testing is recommended to evaluate the psychosocial basis for his antisocial behavior in the context of his traumatic brain injury.

1992; Neisser et al., 1996; Sandoval, 1989; Schiele, 1991; Sattler, 2008; Sue & Sue, 2008). For example, many feel that IQ testing may be biased in that children from high-socioeconomic-level homes tend to perform better on standardized tests than those from lower-socioeconomic-level homes. Furthermore, some argue that currently available intelligence tests may not be appropriate for use with individuals from many ethnic minority groups (Sandoval, 1989; Sattler, 1988, 1992, 2008; Schiele, 1991; Sue & Sue, 2003, 2008; Suzuki & Valencia, 1997). In fact, California passed legislation that prohibited intelligence testing from being used for school placement of African-American children (*Larry P. v. Wilson Riles*). The ruling suggested that intelligence testing was biased against African Americans and that they were disproportionately represented in educable mental retardation (EMR) classrooms. Bias is determined by examining the test's validity across different groups. A test is biased if the validity of the test varies from group to group. Research suggests that most standardized IQ tests such as the Wechsler and Stanford-Binet scales are not biased (Hale, 1991; Reynolds, 1982; Wechsler, 2008). However, tests can be misused by both unqualified and well-meaning people (Sattler, 2008; Sue & Sue, 2003, 2008; Suzuki & Valencia, 1997).

Curiously, IQ scores have increased dramatically over generations, which has become known as the *Flynn effect* (Flynn, 1984, 1987, 2007). This is likely due to a confluence of influences such as better education, improved nutrition, smaller family sizes, better education, and technological advances. Flynn (2007) reports that the modernization of our environment and culture that includes intellectual demands and stimulation as well as improved nutrition and health care may all interact to produce higher IQ scores today than in previous years.

SHOULD THE TERMS *INTELLIGENCE QUOTIENT* OR *IQ* CONTINUE TO BE USED? A number of misconceptions and myths about IQ exist. These include the notion that the IQ measures an innate or genetically determined intelligence level, that IQ scores are fixed and never change, and that IQ scores generated from different tests mean the same thing (Hale, 1991; Sattler, 1988, 1992, 2008). These concerns have led some experts to suggest that general IQ scores be eliminated (Turnbull, 1979) in favor of standard scores that more accurately describe specific skills. In fact, many recent tests of intellectual and cognitive ability have not used the terms *intelligence quotient* or *IQ* at all. These include the Woodcock-Johnson Psychoeducational Battery, the Kaufman Assessment Battery for Children, and the newest version of the Stanford-Binet.

Conclusion: Tests of cognitive ability are used to answer a wide variety of important clinical questions. In addition to identifying overall intellectual skills and cognitive strengths and weaknesses, these tests are frequently employed to assess the presence of learning disabilities, predict academic success in school, examine brain dysfunction, and assess personality. Any competent psychologist must be cautious in the use of intellectual, neuropsychological, achievement, and all other forms of cognitive testing (Sattler, 2008; Sternberg, 2008; Turner, DeMars, Fox, & Reed, 2001). Professionals must be aware of the limitations of the testing situation and the limitations of the particular test they have chosen. They must be careful to use tests for the purpose for which the test was developed and researched, and in conjunction with other appropriate tests. They must also be able to understand the results in terms of the context of the individual's testing response style and the biopsychosocial influences that might affect particular scores. For instance, scores may not accurately reflect potential if a child is distracted due to severe stress or family conflict or chronic illness; compromised by poor nutrition; or disadvantaged due to poverty or frequent school disruption. In fact, some research has indicated that stress level and coping abilities are significantly associated with performance on intelligence and other tests of cognitive abilities (Hersen, 2003; Plante,

Highlight of a Contemporary Clinical Psychologist

Lori Goldfarb Plante, PhD

Photo: Courtesy Lori Goldfarb Plante

Dr. Plante maintains a private practice and serves on the Clinical Faculty at Stanford University Medical School in training psychology interns.

Birth Date: January 22, 1959

College: Pitzer College (BA, Psychology), 1982

Graduate Program: University of Kansas (MA, PhD in Clinical Psychology), 1987

Clinical Internship: Yale University School of Medicine (1986–1987)

Postdoctoral Fellowship: Cornell University Medical College, New York Hospital (1987–1988)

Current Job: Private Practice, Menlo Park, CA; Adjunct Clinical Assistant Professor, Stanford University School of Medicine

Pros and Cons of Being a Clinical Psychologist:

Pros: "Clinical psychology affords a tremendously engaging and rewarding role in alleviating suffering and improving the lives of others. It also enables fascinating insight into human psyches and systems. Opportunities to teach and train students also enliven and inform clinical practice. Finally, I greatly appreciate the flexibility and versatility it affords in roles, settings, populations, and work/home balance."

Cons: "By definition, the nature of clinical work requires solidarity with deeply distressed people and therefore entails a certain burden of responsibility and stress. Private practice can be isolating in the absence of ongoing engagement with students, organizations, or other clinicians. Finally, it is becoming increasingly difficult for individuals and families to afford needed psychological services."

Future of Clinical Psychology: "First, prescription privileges will become increasingly important for psychologists to secure as psychopharmacology continues to influence treatment. Funding sources may continue to decline and necessary services will become inaccessible to more people. There will sadly be a virtual extinction of projective tests used in assessment, and an increasing reliance on strict self-report and behavioral data. Psychotherapy, especially long-term approaches, will become less affordable and less popular."

Typical Daily Schedule:

8:00–12:00	Patient hours (psychotherapy and consultation)
1:00–2:00	Supervision of psychology intern
2:00–3:00	Calls, reports, paperwork
3:00	Home to meet son after school
5:00	Patient hour

Goldfarb, & Wadley, 1993; Plante & Sykora, 1994; Sattler, 2008).

Personality Testing

Personality testing in a sense accesses the heart and soul of an individual's psyche. Personality testing strives to observe and describe the structure and content of personality, which can be defined as the characteristic ways in which an individual thinks, feels, and behaves. Personality testing is particularly useful in clarifying diagnosis, problematic patterns and symptoms, intrapsychic and interpersonal dynamics, and treatment implications. Personality testing involves a wide variety of both objective and projective measures, both of which will be discussed in detail after the following explanations of the concepts *personality* and *psychological functioning*.

What Are Personality and Psychological Functioning?

Each human being has a unique manner of interacting with the world. Some people tend to be shy and withdrawn, while others are generally outgoing and gregarious. Some tend to be anxious worriers, while others are generally calm and relaxed. Some are highly organized and pay attention to detail, while others are disorganized and impressionistic. *Personality* refers to the enduring styles of thinking and behaving when interacting with the world (Hogan, Hogan, & Roberts, 1996; MacKinnon, 1944; McCrae & Costa, 2003). Thus, it includes characteristic patterns that make each person unique. These characteristics can be assessed and compared with those of others. Personality is influenced by biological, psychological, and social factors. For example, research has shown that between 20% and 60% of the variance in personality traits (e.g., extroversion, sociability) are influenced by genetic factors (Loehlin, 1992; Plomin, 1990; Plomin, Defries,

McClearn, & McGuffin, 2008), with the remainder influenced by psychosocial factors (e.g., relationships that develop with parents, siblings, and friends, as well as life events; Bouchard & McGue, 1990; Maccoby, 2000). While the nature versus nurture debate rages on well beyond statistical models, personality development clearly reflects biological, psychological, and social factors.

Personality theories provide a way to understand how people develop, change, and experience generally stable and enduring behavior and thinking patterns. These theories also help us to understand the differences among people that make each person unique. Ultimately, personality theory is used to understand and predict behavior. This understanding is then used to develop intervention strategies to help people change problematic patterns.

Psychological functioning is a more general term referring to the individual's cognitive, personality, and emotional worlds. Thus, psychological functioning includes personality as well as other aspects of emotional, behavioral, cognitive, and interpersonal functioning. In this section, psychological functioning refers to particularly non-cognitive areas of functioning such as mood and interpersonal relationships. For example, while anxiety, depression, and anger may all be enduring personality traits, they can also be temporary mood states. Someone facing stressful life events, such as the death of a loved one or criminal victimization, may experience severe anxiety, depression, or anger. However, these mood states may not be associated with enduring personality characteristics. Thus, the individual may feel and behave in an anxious or depressed manner as a reaction to the stressful event(s) but does not tend to be anxious or depressed most of the time. Therefore, psychological functioning can be viewed as encompassing the gamut of component psychological processes as they impact one's ability to cope with life's pleasures and demands and uniquely combine to define personality.

Test User Qualifications

Who is competent enough to administer psychological, intelligence, educational, and other tests? Many people other than psychologists now administer these types of tests. Learning specialists, social workers, doctors, marriage and family therapists, speech and language therapists, and others may potentially use psychological tests. Furthermore, psychologists do not necessarily have the training and experience to administer and interpret all of the numerous tests that are available on the market. There are thousands of psychological tests available for use that measure a wide range of intellectual, education, personality, and psychological constructs. It is unrealistic to expect that psychologists will be competent in all of these tests. Furthermore, since so many tests are regularly updated, it is unrealistic to expect that psychologists can keep on top of all of the latest developments in test revisions. For example, someone who specializes in the evaluation and treatment of adults may be untrained and thus unqualified to administer tests to children. Since testing has become a multibillion-dollar-per-year industry and since there are so many tests available, a current challenging issue for clinical psychology is how can we determine who is qualified to use these tests?

The American Psychological Association Task Force on Test User Qualifications (TFTUQ) was established in October 1996 to help develop important guidelines so that both the general public and professionals could have a better understanding of the responsible use of psychological tests by competent professionals. These guidelines outline specific recommendations for the use of tests and can be found in the TFTUQ (Turner, DeMars, Fox, & Reed, 2001). The guidelines state that testers should have coursework and competence that adequately cover classical test theory, descriptive statistics, reliability and measurement error, validity and the meaning of test scores, normative interpretation of test scores, selection for appropriate tests, test administration procedures, and issues pertaining to ethnic, racial, cultural, gender, age, linguistic, and disability variables. They should also have adequate supervision and experience.

However, these aspirational guidelines and goals must be applied to day-to-day decisions about individual persons giving tests to individuals with unique issues and concerns. Hopefully, ethically minded clinical psychologists are careful to ensure that they are adequately trained and competent enough to administer and interpret the tests that they use, and they continuously update their skills and information to stay on top of the newest developments and versions of tests that come on the market. For example, tests such as the Wechsler Scales that assess intelligence are updated every few years. It is important that psychologists who administer these tests are retrained each time a new edition is made available so that they can competently administer and interpret these new versions of the tests. Busy professionals may find it challenging to keep up with all of these

(continued)

developments as they unfold yet must work hard to ensure that they do everything necessary (e.g., attend training workshops, receive appropriate consultation or supervision) in order to be sure that they are adequately trained to use these instruments. The guidelines for competent test use are useful but they are indeed only guidelines. Individual psychologists must make individual decisions about their level of expertise and know when they should refer testing requests to other competent professionals.

Is Personality Really Enduring?

The famous psychologist William James (1890) stated that by the age of 30 personality was "set in plaster." While a tremendous amount of research has been conducted on personality, controversy still exists concerning its definition and characteristics (Beutler & Groth-Marnat, 2003; Kenrick & Funder, 1988; Plomin et al., 2008; West & Graziano, 1989). Some people question the very notion of personality, suggesting that enduring behavioral characteristics do not exist. While many believe that behavior is consistent across situations (e.g., a shy person is likely to behave in a shy manner wherever he or she goes), many argue that behavior is generally situation specific. Thus, someone may behave in a shy manner in a social situation with people he or she does not know very well while he or she might behave in a very outgoing manner at work or with close friends. Most professionals in the area of personality theory, research, and practice support an interactional approach (Kenrick & Funder, 1988). This approach suggests that behavior is predictable but is not rigidly consistent in an absolute sense. Therefore, people have personality styles that are generally consistent but interact with situational factors (McCrae & Costa, 2003); personality and behavior differs somewhat from situation to situation.

How Do Clinical Psychologists Measure Personality and Psychological Functioning?

In addition to using interviews, observations, checklists, inventories, and even biological assessments (e.g., neuroimaging techniques such as fMRI scans), clinical psychologists generally use a range of tests to assess personality and psychological functioning. Most of these tests can be classified as either objective or projective. **Objective testing** presents very specific questions (e.g., Do you feel sad more days than not?) or statements (e.g., I feel rested) to which the person responds by using specific answers (e.g., yes/no, true/false, multiple choice) or a rating scale (e.g., 1 = strongly disagree, 10 = strongly agree). Scores are tabulated and then compared with those of reference groups, using national norms. Thus, scores that reflect specific constructs (e.g., anxiety, depression, psychotic thinking, stress) may be compared to determine exactly how anxious, depressed, psychotic, or stressed someone might be relative to the norm. The checklists described in the previous chapter are examples of objective tests. **Projective testing** uses ambiguous or unstructured testing stimuli such as inkblots, incomplete sentences, or pictures of people engaged in various activities. Rather than answering specific questions using specific structured responses (e.g., yes/no, true/false, agree/disagree), subjects are asked to respond freely to the testing stimuli. For example, they are asked to tell stories about pictures, or describe what they see in an inkblot, or say the first thing that comes to their mind when hearing a word or sentence fragment. The theory behind projective testing is that unconscious or conscious needs, interests, dynamics, and motivations are projected onto the ambiguous testing stimuli, thereby revealing the internal dynamics or personality. Projective responses are generally much more challenging to score and interpret than objective responses.

Objective Testing: There are hundreds of objective tests of personality and psychological functioning. The reader may wish to consult other resources for detailed information about these instruments (e.g., Anastasi & Urbina, 1997; Corr & Matthews, 2009). Clinical psychologists usually employ a small set of objective tests to evaluate personality and psychological functioning. By far the most commonly used test is the Minnesota Multiphasic Personality Inventory (MMPI), now in its second edition (MMPI-2). The MMPI also includes an adolescent version called the Minnesota Multiphasic Personality Inventory—Adolescents (MMPI-A). Other objective tests such as the Millon Clinical Multiaxial Inventory-III (MCMI-III), the 16 Personality Factors Questionnaire, Fifth Edition (16PF), and the NEO-Personality Inventory—Revised (NEO-PI-R) will also be briefly discussed below.

THE MINNESOTA MULTIPHASIC PERSONALITY INVENTORY (MMPI, MMPI-2, MMPI-A, MMPI-2-RF):

The original MMPI was developed during the late 1930s and published in 1943 by psychologist Starke Hathaway and psychiatrist J. C. McKinley. The MMPI was revised and became available as the MMPI-2 in 1989. The MMPI was also revised again in 2008 as the MMPI-2-RF, where RF refers to "Restructured Form." The MMPI-2-RF provides a briefer version of the MMPI-2 and focuses on the diagnosis of psychopathology. The original MMPI consisted of 550 true/false items. The items were selected from a series of other personality tests and from the developers' clinical experience in an effort to provide psychiatric diagnoses for mental patients. The original pool of about 1,000 test items were considered and about 500 items were administered to psychiatric patients and visitors at the University of Minnesota hospitals. The **MMPI** was designed to be used with individuals ages 16 through adulthood. However, the test has been frequently used with adolescents younger than 16. The MMPI

takes about one to one-and-a-half hours to complete.

Scoring the MMPI results in a large number of validity measures and clinical measures. The primary validity scales include the L (Lie), F (Infrequency), and K (Correction) scales. Admitting to many problems or "faking bad" is reflected in an inverted V configuration with low scores on the L and K scales and a high score on the F scale. Presenting oneself in a favorable light or "faking good" is reflected in a V configuration with high scores on the L and K scales and a low score on the F scale. The primary clinical scales include Hypochondriasis (Hs), Depression (D), Hysteria (Hy), Psychopathic deviate (Pd), Masculinity-femininity (Mf), Paranoia (Pa), Psychasthenia (Pt), Schizophrenia (Sc), Hypomania (Ma), and Social Introversion (Si). Scores are normed using standardized *T*-scores, meaning that each scale has a mean of 50 and a standard deviation of 10. Scores above 65 (representing one-and-one-half standard deviations above the mean) are considered elevated, and in the clinical range. While 65 is the cutoff score on the MMPI-2, MMPI-2-RF, and MMPI-A, 70 is used with the original MMPI. Table 8.4 provides a description of each of the primary MMPI scales.

Since the MMPI was originally published, a large number of additional subscales have been developed, including measures such as Repression, Anxiety, Ego Strength, Overcontrolled Hostility, and Dominance. It has been estimated that there are now hundreds of subtests of the MMPI (Graham, 2006). The MMPI has been used in well over 10,000 studies that examine a wide range of clinical issues and problems (Graham, 2006). Although the original MMPI was the most widely used psychological test, a revision was needed. For example, the MMPI did not use a representative sample when it was constructed. The original sample included Caucasians living in the Minneapolis, Minnesota, area who were either patients or visitors at the University of Minnesota hospitals. Also, many of the more sophisticated methods of test construction and analysis used today were not available

Table 8.4   **MMPI-2 Primary Scales and Personality Dimension Measured**

Scale Name Personality	Dimension Measured
Primary Validity Scales	
? (Cannot Say)	Number of items unanswered
L (Lie)	Overly positive self-report
F (Infrequency)	Admitting to many problems
K (Correction)	Defensiveness
S (Superlative Self-Presentation)	Presenting oneself in a highly favorable light
Major Clinical Scales	
1 Hypochondriasis (Hs)	Concern regarding bodily functioning
2 Depression (D)	Hopelessness, pessimism
3 Conversion Hysteria (Hy)	Psychological conflict and distress manifested as somatic problems
4 Psychopathic Deviate (Pd)	Oppositional, disregard for social convention
5 Masculinity-Femininity (Mf)	Traditional masculine or feminine interests
6 Paranoia (Pa)	Mistrust, suspiciousness
7 Psychasthenia (Pt)	Fears, guilt, anxiety
8 Schizophrenia (Sc)	Idiosyncratic thinking, unusual thoughts and behavior
9 Hypomania (Ma)	Overactivity, emotional excitement
0 Social Introversion (Si)	Shy, insecurity

in the late 1930s when the test was developed. Therefore, during the late 1980s, the test was restandardized and many of the test items were rewritten. Furthermore, many new test items were added, and outdated items were eliminated. The resulting MMPI-2 (Butcher, Dahlstrom, Graham, Tellegen, & Kraemmer, 1989) consists of 567 items and can be used with individuals aged 18 through adulthood. The MMPI-2 uses the same validity and clinical scale names as the MMPI. Importantly, many have noted that the names reflecting each of the MMPI (or MMPI-2) scales are misleading. For example, a high score on the Schizophrenia (Sc) scale does not necessarily mean that the person who completed the test is schizophrenic. Therefore, many clinicians and researchers prefer to ignore the scale names and use numbers to reflect each scale instead. For example, the Schizophrenia (Sc) scale is referred to as Scale 8 (see Table 8.4). Like the original MMPI, the MMPI-2 has numerous subscales, including measures such as

Type A behavior, posttraumatic stress, obsessions, and fears.

The Minnesota Multiphasic Personality Inventory—Adolescent (MMPI-A) (Butcher et al., 1992) was developed for use with teens between the ages of 14 and 18. The MMPI-A has 478 true/false items and includes a number of validity measures in addition to those available in the MMPI and MMPI-2. The Minnesota Multiphasic Personality Inventory-2—Restructured Form (MMPI-2-RF) (Ben-Porath & Tellegen, 2008) includes 338 Items and is used with adults 18 years and older. The shortened test takes about 45 minutes to complete and offers restructured clinical scales such as antisocial behavior (RC4), cynicism (RC3), and dysfunctional negative emotions (RC7). The MMPI, MMPI-2, MMPI-A, and MMPI-2-RF can be scored by hand using templates for each scale or they can be computer scored. Most commercially available computer-scoring programs offer in-depth interpretive reports that fully describe the testing results and offer suggestions for treatment or other interventions. Scores are typically interpreted by reviewing the entire resulting profile rather than individual scale scores. Profile analysis is highlighted by examining pairs of high-scores combinations. For example, high scores on the first three scales of the MMPI are referred to as the *neurotic triad* reflecting anxiety, depression, and somatic complaints. Research indicates that the MMPI, MMPI-2, MMPI-A, and MMPI-2-RF have acceptable reliability, stability, and validity (Ben-Porath & Tellegen, 2008; Butcher et al., 1989; Butcher et al., 1992; Graham, 2006; Parker et al., 1988). However, controversy exists concerning many aspects of the test. For example, the MacAndrew Scale was designed as a supplementary scale to classify those people with alcohol-related problems. The validity of the scale has been criticized and some authors have suggested that the scale no longer be used to examine alcohol problems (Gottesman & Prescott, 1989). Figure 8.1 provides an example of an MMPI-2 profile of a 60-year-old male high school teacher convicted of sexually abusing adolescent boys. The evaluation, which included a comprehensive psychological battery, revealed him to be actively alcoholic, depressed, and suffering from a personality disorder.

THE MILLON CLINICAL MULTIAXIAL INVENTORIES: The **Millon Clinical Multiaxial Inventories (MCMI)** include several tests that assess personality functioning using the *DSM-IV-TR* classification system and the Theodore Millon theory of personality (Millon, 1981). Unlike the MMPI-2, the Millon was specifically designed to assess personality disorders outlined in the DSM such as histrionic, borderline, paranoid, and obsessive-compulsive personalities. The first Millon test was published in 1982; additional tests and revisions quickly developed during the 1980s and 1990s. The current tests include the Millon Clinical Multiaxial Inventory-III (MCMI-III; Millon, Millon, Davis, & Grossman, 2008), the Millon Adolescent Clinical Inventory (MACI; Millon, Millon,

Davis, & Grossman, 1993), the Millon Pre-Adolescent Clinical Inventory (M-PAC; Millon, Millon, Davis, & Grossman, 2001), and the Millon Behavioral Medicine Diagnostic (MBMD; Millon, Antoni, Millon, Minor, & Grossman, 2001), among several others. The MBMD, however, is a health behavior inventory and not a measure of personality or psychological functioning per se. The MCMI-III will be highlighted here. The MCMI-III is a 175-true/false-item questionnaire designed for persons ages 18 through adulthood and takes approximately 30 minutes to complete. It was designed to assess personality disorders and syndromes based on the *DSM-IV-TR* system of classification. The MCMI-III includes 24 scales, including 14 personality pattern scales and 10 clinical syndrome scales. Furthermore, the MCMI-III also includes several validity measures. Table 8.5 provides a list of the measured characteristics.

THE SIXTEEN PERSONALITY FACTORS (16PF): The **16PF** was developed by Raymond Cattell and colleagues and is currently in its fifth edition (Cattell, Cattell, & Cattell, 2002). It is a 185-item multiple-choice questionnaire that takes approximately 45 minutes to complete. The 16PF is administered to individuals ages 16 years through adulthood. Scoring the 16PF results in 16 primary personality traits (e.g., apprehension prone) and five global factors that assess second-order personality characteristics (e.g., anxiety). Standardized scores from 1 to 10 or sten scores are used with means set at 5 and a standard deviation of 2. Table 8.6 lists the 16PF scales. The 16PF has been found to have acceptable stability, reliability, and validity (Anastasi & Urbina, 1997; Cattell et al., 2002).

THE NEO-PERSONALITY INVENTORY—REVISED (NEO-PI-R): The NEO-PI-R (Costa & McCrae, 1985, 1989, 1992, in press) is a 240-item questionnaire that uses a 5-point rating system. A brief 60-item version of the NEO-PI-R called the NEO-Five Factor Inventory (NEO-FF) is also available as well as an observer

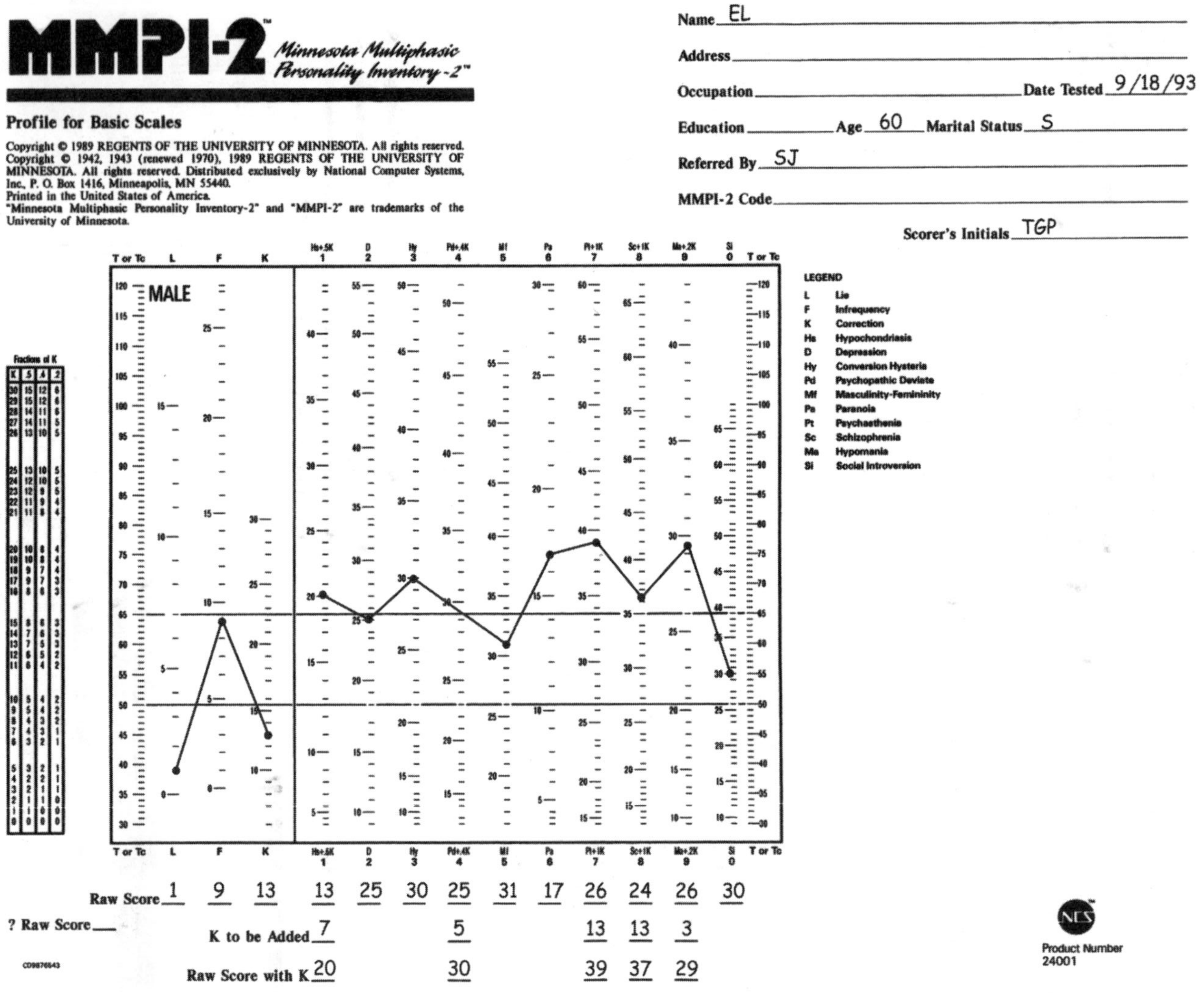

Figure 8.1

Minnesota Multiphasic Personality Inventory-2, profile of EL, a 60-year-old high school teacher convicted of sexual abuse of minors. Reprinted from MMPI-2™ (Minnesota Multiphasic Personality Inventory-2)™ *Manual for Administration, Scoring, and Interpretation, Revised Edition.* Copyright © 2001 by the Regents of the University of Minnesota. Used by permission of the University of Minnesota Press. All rights reserved. "MMPI-2"

Table 8.5   **MCMI-III Scales**

Clinical Personality Patterns Scales

Scale 1	Schizoid
Scale 2A	Avoidant
Scale 2B	Depressive
Scale 3	Dependent
Scale 4	Histrionic
Scale 5	Narcissistic
Scale 6A	Antisocial
Scale 6B	Aggressive (Sadistic)
Scale 7	Compulsive
Scale 8A	Passive-Aggressive (Negativistic)
Scale 8B	Self-Defeating

Clinical Syndrome Scales

Scale A	Anxiety
Scale H	Somatoform
Scale N	Bipolar: Manic
Scale D	Dysthymia
Scale B	Alcohol Dependence
Scale T	Drug Dependence
Scale R	Posttraumatic Stress Disorder

Severe Syndrome Scales

Scale SS	Thought Disorder
Scale CC	Major Depression
Scale PP	Delusional Disorder

Severe Personality Pathology Scales

Scale S	Schizotypal
Scale C	Borderline
Scale P	Paranoid

Modifying Indices (Correction Scales)

Scale X	Disclosure
Scale Y	Desirability
Scale Z	Debasement

Table 8.6   **16PF (Fifth Edition) Measures**

Global Factors Scales

EX	Extroversion
AX	Anxiety
TM	Tough-Mindedness
IN	Independence
SC	Self-Control

16 Primary Personality Traits

A	Warmth
B	Reasoning
C	Emotional Stability
E	Dominance
F	Liveliness
G	Rule Consciousness
H	Social Boldness
I	Sensitivity
L	Vigilance
M	Abstractedness
N	Privateness
O	Apprehension
Q1	Openness to Change
Q2	Self-Reliance
Q3	Perfectionism
Q4	Tension

rating version (Form R). The NEO-PI-R measures the big five personality dimensions: neuroticism, extroversion, openness, agreeableness, and conscientiousness. The *big five* or the five-factor model has been found to be consistent in personality dimensions from factor analytic research conducted for over 40 years and across many cultures (Digman, 1990; McCrae & Costa, 2003, in press). The NEO-PI traits are referred to as the big five because in many research studies they have been found to account for a great deal of variability in personality test scores (McCrae & Costa, 2003; Wiggins & Pincus, 1989). The NEO-PI-R has been found to be both reliable and valid (Costa & McGrae, 1992, in press). Unlike the other objective tests mentioned, the NEO-PI-R does not include validity scales to assess subject response set.

OTHER OBJECTIVE TESTS: Additional objective personality tests include the Edwards Personal Preference Schedule (EPPS: Edwards, 1959), a 225-item paired-comparison test assessing 15 personality variables, and the Eysenck Personality Questionnaire (Eysenck & Eysenck, 1975), measuring three basic personality characteristics: psychoticism, introversion-extroversion, and emotionality-stability. Many other tests are available as well; however, they generally are not as commonly used as those previously discussed.

Projective Testing: Just as there are numerous objective personality and psychological functioning instruments, there are many projective instruments. Most psychologists use a small number of preferred projective tests—typically the Rorschach, the Thematic Apperception Test (TAT), Projective Drawings, and Incomplete Sentences.

THE RORSCHACH: The **Rorschach** is the famous inkblot test (Rorschach, 1921/1942, 1951, 1998). Many people are fascinated by the idea of using inkblots to investigate personality and psychological functioning. Of course, many people (including psychologists) are skeptical of projective techniques such as the Rorschach, questioning its validity as a measure of psychological functioning (Dawes, 1994; Wood, Lilienfeld, Garb, & Nezworski, 2000; Wood, Nezworski, Lilienfeld, Garb, 2003). The Rorschach is often mentioned in television shows or in films depicting psychological evaluations. Curiously, the idea of seeing objects in inkblots came from a common game in the 1800s called Blotto. Someone would put a drop of ink on a blank piece of paper and fold the paper in half, creating a unique inkblot. Others would then take turns identifying objects in the inkblots. Alfred Binet used this technique to examine imagination among children. Swiss psychiatrist Hermann Rorschach noticed that mental patients tended to respond very differently to this game relative to others. Thus, Blotto became the basis for the Rorschach test (Exner, 1976).

The Rorschach consists of 10 inkblots that are symmetrical; that is, the left side of each card is essentially a mirror image of the right side. The same 10 inkblots have been used (in the same order of presentation) since they were first developed by Herman Rorschach in 1921 (Rorschach, 1921/1942). Half of the cards are black, white, and gray, and half use color. While there are several different ways to administer the Rorschach and score, the vast majority of psychologists today use the method developed by John Exner (Exner, 1974, 1976, 1986, 1993, 2003; Exner & Weiner, 1995;

Weiner, 2003). Each card is handed to the patient with the question, "What might this be?" The psychologist writes down everything the patient says verbatim. During this free-association portion of the test, the psychologist does not question the patient. After all 10 cards are administered, the psychologist shows the patient each card a second time and asks questions that will help in scoring the test. For example, the psychologist might say, "Now I'd like to show you the cards once again and ask you several questions about each card so that I can be sure that I see it as you do." With each card, he or she asks a nonleading question such as, "What about the card made it look like a_____ to you?" The psychologist looks for answers that will help him or her score the test in several categories such as location (i.e., the area of the blot being used), content (i.e., the nature of the object being described, such as a person, animal, or element of nature), determinants (i.e., the parts of the blot that the patient used in the response, such as form, color, shading, and movement), and populars (i.e., the responses typically seen by others). This portion of the test is referred to as the *inquiry.* Once the test is completed, scoring involves a highly complex system and analysis. Each response is carefully scored based on the content, location, determinants, and quality of the response. An actual scoring sheet, once completed, resembles a highly specialized and foreign language. Because the scoring process can be very complicated and may take a long time to complete, many experienced psychologists do not score the test in fine detail but rely on their clinical inference, experience, and judgment to answer clinical questions such as, Is the patient psychotic or not? Is the patient repressive or not? Is the patient depressed? The case studies of Martha and Xavier illustrate the use of the Rorschach.

Various aspects of the Rorschach responses are associated with psychological functioning. For example, the frequent use of shading is generally considered to be reflective of anxiety and depression. The use of human movement and adequate number of popular

Case Study: Martha Experiences Severe Depression and Borderline Personality (Rorschach)

Martha is a 24-year-old biracial (Caucasian and Iranian) woman who was referred for psychological testing by her psychiatrist. She had several hospital admissions due to depression and suicide attempts. Martha was diagnosed with both major depression and a borderline personality disorder. She was resistant to testing and complied only because "my shrink and father are making me do this." The following represents the free-association portion of the first five cards of the Rorschach administration.

Card I:

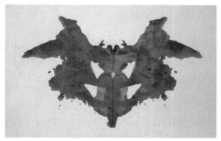

Psychologist: What might this be?
Martha: (long pause) You mean besides just a blot of ink?
Psychologist: Yes.
Martha: Well, some kind of big black animal looking into the water. An ugly animal.
Psychologist: Most people see more than one thing.
Martha: Well I don't. That's it.

Card II:

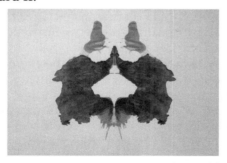

Psychologist: What might this be?
Martha: This looks like a head and hands touching and feet here (points). That's the only thing I see. They all look like mirror reflections so far. There's blood there (points).

Card III:

Psychologist: What might this be?
Martha: Two people spinning. I don't know what these red things are. Could be they got shot. Would you like me to move the cards around?
Psychologist: It's up to you.
Martha: That little figure looks like a person leaning back with their legs in front of them and that looks sort of like a fish. Looks like a human fish.

Card IV:

Psychologist: What might this be?
Martha: This seems stupid. I don't see how this will help me. I don't know, it looks like some sort of charred monster. I suppose you want to know how it looks like a monster.

(continued)

Case Study (Continued)

Psychologist: Sure.

Martha: This is the head and claws, big feet here, and a tail coming through the bottom (points).

Card V:

Photos: Courtesy Wikipedia

Psychologist: What might this be?

Martha: Looks like a moth or a bat or something. That looks like an alligator or crocodile head, at least part of it does.

---

responses are usually associated with adaptive and well-integrated psychological functioning. Numerous responses that attend to minor details of the blots often reflect obsessive-compulsive traits. Frequent use of the white space around the blot is generally associated with oppositionality and/or avoidance.

Many have argued that the Rorschach is not a reliable and valid instrument. In fact, Robyn Dawes calls the Rorschach a "shoddy (instrument that) . . . is not a valid test of anything" (Dawes, 1994, pp. 123 & 146). Many graduate training programs have stopped using it. Some attempts to improve the psychometric properties of the Rorschach, such as the development of the Holtzman Inkblot Technique (HIT; Holtzman, 1975; Holtzman, Thorpe, Swartz, & Herron, 1961), have not caught on with clinicians. However, the development of John Exner's Comprehensive System and his research on the Rorschach (Exner, 1974, 1976, 1986, 1993, 2003; Exner & Erdberg, 2005; Exner & Weiner, 1995; Weiner, 1996, 2003) have helped to improve the scientific basis of the test. Exner has developed a method with highly precise scoring criteria and has used this method to demonstrate reliability and validity of the approach. Many have criticized

Exner for not publishing his findings in peer-reviewed journals. Others question some of his assumptions regarding reliability and validity (Dawes, 1994; Wood et al., 2000, 2003). Others suggest that it is not appropriate to use with various ethnic minority groups (). Thus, many still remain skeptical of the Rorschach's use even with the available and much-improved scoring and interpretation techniques. However, a review of Rorschach research revealed reliability coefficients to be in the .80s and the average validity coefficient to be about .42 (Ornberg & Zalewski, 1994; Parker et al., 1988; Weiner, 1996, 2003), suggesting that the Rorschach does maintain acceptable levels of reliability and validity (Exner & Erdberg, 2005; Weiner, 1996, 2003). Ultimately, it may be reasonable to refer to the Rorschach and other projective instruments as *tools* as opposed to tests *per se.*

In recent years, copyright protection of the Rorschach has expired since the procedure was published many years ago in the 1920s. Therefore, the famous inkblots are in the public domain and can be seen at will online through Wikipedia and other sources.

THE THEMATIC APPERCEPTION TEST (TAT):

The **TAT** (Murray & Bellack, 1942; Tomkins,

Case Study: Xavier Experiences Bipolar Disorder (Rorschach)

Xavier is a 48-year-old Caucasian attorney hospitalized for mania associated with a bipolar disorder. He was spending a great deal of money, which he could not afford to do, and behaving in a hypersexual manner, not sleeping, and getting into fights. The following represents the free-association portion of the first five cards of the Rorschach administration. Compare Xavier's responses to those of Martha. Remember that they are both looking at the same five Rorschach cards and yet their responses differ greatly.

Card I:

Psychologist: What might this be?
Xavier: It's a butterfly. It could be a Halloween mask, too. Here, at the top, it looks like dogs. It also looks like something sinister going on inside, a horror mask. It looks like a vagina in the middle. Little children are looking out from the womb of the mother.

Card II:

Psychologist: What might this be?

Xavier: Two long-snouted animals kissing in the middle with their hearts in the middle. The top red part is a mask or something. Looks like little sheep, teddy bears, or dogs.

Card III:

Psychologist: What might this be?
Xavier: Looks like Africans dancing around pots. This looks like a bow tie or a hip bone. This looks like an inverted fish that swims.

Card IV:

Psychologist: What might this be?
Xavier: This looks sinister. Looks like I'm looking on top of this huge rug or rodent. Maybe a bat looking down from the top. This looks like antenna or antlers. Maybe an Indian rug.

Card V:

Psychologist: What might this be?
Xavier: It looks like a bat or butterfly. It also could be a rodent.

1947) was developed during the late 1930s by Henry Murray and Christiana Morgan at Harvard University. The TAT was originally designed to measure personality factors in research settings. Specifically, it was used to investigate goals, central conflicts, needs, press (i.e., factors that facilitate or impede progress toward reaching goals), and achievement strivings associated with Henry Murray's theory of *personology* (Murray, 1938). The TAT consists of 31 pictures (one of which is blank), almost all of which depict people rather than objects. Some of the pictures are designed to be administered to males, some to females, and others to both genders. Generally only a selected number of cards (e.g., 10) are administered to any one patient.

The psychologist introduces the test by telling the patient that he or she will be given a series of pictures and requested to tell a story about each. The patient is instructed to make up a story that reflects what the people in the picture are thinking, feeling, and doing and also to speculate on what led up to the events depicted in the picture and what will happen in the future. After each card is presented to the patient, the psychologist writes down everything that is said verbatim. Although a variety of complex scoring approaches have been developed (Murray, 1943; Shneidman, 1951), most clinicians use their clinical experience and judgment to analyze the themes that emerge from the patient's stories. Since clinicians generally do not officially score the TAT, conducting reliability and validity research is challenging. Many feel that the TAT and other projective tests are more like a clinical interview than a test, and that the experience, training, and clinical judgment of the clinician determines the usefulness and accuracy of these instruments.

Other tests similar to the TAT have been developed for special populations, such as the Roberts Apperception Test for Children-2 (Roberts 2; Roberts, 2005; McArthur & Roberts, 1982), for use with elementary school children. The 27 pictures depict children interacting with parents, teachers, and peers. The Children's Apperception Test (CAT; Bellak, 1992) was developed for very young children and depicts animals interacting in various ways.

PROJECTIVE DRAWINGS: Many clinicians ask both children and adults to draw pictures in order to assess their psychological functioning. Typically, people are asked to draw a house, a tree, a person, and their family doing something together. For the Draw-a-Person test (Machover, 1949), the House-Tree-Person Technique (Buck, 1948), and the Kinetic Family Drawing Technique, the patient is instructed to draw each picture in pencil on a separate blank piece of paper and to avoid the use of stick figures. Variations on the instructions have been used by many clinicians. For example, a popular variation on the Draw-a-Person test instructs the patient to draw persons of the same and opposite sex and a person in the rain. Attempts to develop scoring criteria as well as research on the reliability and validity of these drawing techniques have been only moderately successful. Some researchers have been involved with developing scientific scoring procedures that maximize both reliability and validity and can be used as screening measures for cognitive and emotional impairment (A. L. Sopchak, A. M. Sopchak, & Kohlbrenner, 1993; Trevisaw, 1996). Yet these attempts have not generally been embraced by practicing clinicians. Many clinicians feel that these techniques are quick and easy methods to establish rapport with children or with those who have great difficulty expressing their feelings verbally. Unfortunately, some clinicians overinterpret

projective drawings without adequate research support to justify their interpretations.

SENTENCE COMPLETION TECHNIQUES: Another projective technique involves the use of **sentence completion.** There are many different versions of this technique (e.g., Forer, 1957; P. A. Goldberg, 1965; Lanyon & Lanyon, 1980; Rotter, 1954; Rotter & Rafferty, 1950). The patient is presented (either orally by the examiner or in writing through a questionnaire) a series of sentence fragments. These might include items such as, "When he answered the phone he ..." or "Most mothers are ...." The patient is asked to give the first response that he or she thinks of and complete the sentence. Again, like projective drawings and the TAT, several scoring systems have been developed to assist in interpretation. However, these scoring approaches are generally used only in research settings; most clinicians prefer to use their own experience and clinical judgment to interpret the themes that emerge from the completed sentences.

Questions and Controversies Concerning Personality and Psychological Testing

ARE PERSONALITY RESULTS ASSESSED THROUGH TESTING STABLE? Traditionally, many psychologists have assumed that personality is a fairly stable phenomenon—that each individual's personality traits and style are consistent over time and in varying situations (e.g., home, work, school). Thus, someone who tends to be friendly is likely to be friendly most of the time and in most circumstances. Personality testing using the MMPI-2, MCMI-III, or 16PF, for example, might be considered useful in evaluating and measuring fairly stable personality characteristics. However, several researchers have demonstrated that personality is not as stable as many people assume but instead partially depends on specific environmental and situational circumstances (Mischel, 1968, 1973). For example, rather than thinking of someone as an anxious person, it is

---

Case Study: Debbie Experiences Alcoholism, Depression, and Phobic Anxiety (TAT)

Debbie is a 24-year-old physically disabled Caucasian female patient who has experienced alcoholism, depression, and intense feelings of death anxiety. She also reported feeling stressed from too many job and home responsibilities as well as alcoholism among several family members. She felt that she was the "glue that keeps the family together" and had been overly responsible for her family's functioning and happiness. The following is an example of Debbie's response to one of the TAT cards depicting three people (2 female and 1 male) in an outdoor farm scene.

Debbie: I've seen this one before, okay, she is her daughter and she just came home from school and is looking around at her father and her pregnant mother and wondering if school will get her out of this achorion (i.e., fungus-like) existence (laughs). She looks concerned that she'll end up like her mother. She's going to be in the same trap and never be out of this crummy situation.

Psychologist: How does the father feel?

Debbie: He's pretty tired and has his back towards her. He knows she's there. It's late in the day and he's still plowing and she doesn't identify with that or doesn't want to.

Psychologist: What will happen in the future?

Debbie: She looks despondent and looks like she'll be in the same situation as her mother or father.

Debbie's response to the TAT card likely reflects her concerns about the marital problems between her parents and her worries about what her future relationships might be like. Her response suggests that she feels that following in her mother's footsteps might be inevitable.

---

more useful to evaluate and understand the circumstances in which he or she is likely to show anxiety (e.g., testing situations, speaking engagements, asking someone for a date). Mischel and others (Bem & Funder, 1978; Epstein, 1979; Magnusson, 1981) have advanced the person–situation interaction theory of personality. While recognizing that somewhat stable individual differences can exist in cognitive styles, the psychologist must consider behavior across similar situations, and self-reported personality traits, emphasizing situational factors and influences, Personality testing results must then be evaluated in light of these situation-specific factors, which should, of course, be part of any integrative biopsychosocial evaluation.

ARE PROJECTIVE TECHNIQUES RELIABLE AND VALID? Over the years, numerous reviews have concluded that projective techniques have not demonstrated adequate reliability and validity to justify their use with patients (e.g., Cronbach, 1956; Dawes, 1994; Eysenck, 1958; Lilienfeld, Wood, & Garb, 2000; Rotter, 1954; Suinn & Oskamp, 1969; Wood et al., 2000, 2004) or in court cases for child custody, for example (Erickson, Lilienfeld, & Vitacco, 2007). Some proponents of projective testing have argued that it is inappropriate to use the same criteria for both objective tests and projective tests. They state that unlike objective tests, in which scores are determined and compared to national norms, projective tests are similar to structured interviews, whose purpose is to better know, understand, and describe a person (Blatt, 1975; Frank, 1948; Tomkins, 1947).

Most of the debate concerning the reliability and validity of projective testing has centered around the Rorschach. Many reviews of the literature on the Rorschach have found little

Case Study: Xavier (Sentence Completion)

Xavier is the attorney who was hospitalized during a manic episode of bipolar disorder. The following is a sample of his responses on a sentence completion test.

I used to feel I was being held back by *limited people.*

He often wished he could *fulfill his potential.*

Sometimes he wished he *could do it all.*

I was most annoyed when *big egos demand attention and don't work.*

I feel guilty about *overspending.*

More than anything else, he needed *love.*

Case Study: Elias Experiences Anxiety and Depression (Sentence Completion)

Elias is a 37-year-old African-American computer programmer who is seeking psychotherapy for symptoms of anxiety and depression. He has recently had several poor job performance ratings and has been told that he is not a "team player." The following is a sample of his responses on a sentence completion test.

Most fathers *don't spend enough time with their sons.*

I used to feel *that I was being held back by my lack of people skills.*

My father always *doesn't understand me.*

I was most annoyed when *my Dad pooh-poohed my ideas.*

At times he worried about *getting bad reviews at work.*

I felt most dissatisfied when *I did not get the recognition I thought I should.*

Sometimes I feel *that my boss doesn't care about my career interests.*

He felt inferior *when he got bad reviews at work relating to his people skills.*

support for the technique (Dawes, 1994; Lilienfeld et al., 2000; Sackett & Lievens, 2008; Schofield, 1952; Suinn & Oskamp, 1969; Windle, 1952; Wood et al., 2000, 2004; Ziskin & Faust, 1988; Zubin, 1954). However, others studies have been more favorable in their analysis of the psychometric properties of the Rorschach (Exner, 1974, 1986, 1993; Exner & Edberg, 2005; Exner & Weiner, 1995; Parker et al., 1988; Weiner, 1996, 2004). I. Weiner (1996) concluded his review of research on the validity of the Rorschach by stating that "properly used by informed clinicians … it functions with substantial validity and considerable utility in answering certain kinds of important questions related to personality processes" (p. 213). Now that

the Rorschach copyright has expired and it is readily available online, there are concerns about continued use of the instrument, and its validity is more severely questioned.

Research on the psychometric properties of the TAT and projective drawing techniques has generally failed to provide support for their reliability and validity (Harris, 1972; Lilienfeld et al., 2000; Swartz, 1978). Yet, these and other projective tests continue to be used by clinical psychologists (Lubin, Larsen, Matarazzo, & Seever, 1985; Piotrowski & Keller, 1989). Many clinicians report that these instruments provide useful information that helps them develop a better understanding of the patient, particularly when interpreted in concert with other measures. However, the percentage of clinical psychologists who report using projective testing had dramatically decreased in more recent years from about 72% in 1986 to 39% in 2003, for example (Norcross et al., 2005, 2008).

ARE PERSONALITY AND PSYCHOLOGICAL TESTS APPROPRIATE FOR USE WITH MINORITY GROUP MEMBERS? The early developers of most personality and psychological tests such as the MMPI, Rorschach, and TAT did not consider ethnic and other diversity issues during the test construction and validation process. For example, using the original MMPI with members of ethnic minority groups is questionable since the test was validated using only Caucasians. Furthermore, many tests (e.g., Stanford-Binet) were first developed among people from the middle or upper-middle socioeconomic classes; thus using these tests for low-socioeconomic groups may also compromise validity. Today, the professionals who update these tests and construct new ones are much more sensitive to issues of diversity. For example, the revisors of the MMPI (i.e., the MMPI-2) and the WISC (i.e., WISC-IV) were careful to use a standardization sample that reflected geographic, socioeconomic, and ethnic diversity. Additionally, many of these instruments are now available in multiple languages. Psychologists must be aware of the limitations of the tests that they use and be sensitive to diversity issues when making judgments based on psychological tests used with diverse populations (American Psychological Association [APA], 1992a, 1993b, 2002, 2003b).

SHOULD PERSONALITY AND PSYCHOLOGICAL TESTS BE USED FOR EMPLOYMENT DECISIONS? Many employers use personality and psychological tests to screen job applicants for psychiatric disorders or personality problems that may interfere with work performance. Others are interested in screening for personalities that match the requirements for a particular position. As mentioned earlier, a shy and withdrawn person may not succeed as a salesperson; someone who is not detail-oriented may not succeed as an accountant.

Some have argued that personality tests such as the MMPI-2, MCMI-III, Rorschach, and WAIS-IV were not specifically designed and validated for use in employment settings and therefore should not be used for employment decisions (Guion, 2008). Others claim that personality measures can be successfully and appropriately used in employment settings (Bentz, 1985; Hogan et al., 1996; Plante, 2004b). Still others have designed specialized tests that have been validated for personnel selection in specific industries (Clarke, 1956; Gough, 1984).

Clinical Inference and Judgment

Psychological assessment and testing involve much more than administering tests and computing scores. Once a psychologist completes an interview, conducts a behavioral observation, and administers intellectual and personality testing, he or she must pull all the information together and make some important decisions regarding diagnosis and treatment recommendations. All of the information gathered may or may not agree with other data collected. Integrating convergent and divergent information from many different sources requires a great deal of skill, training, and experience (Beutler & Groth-Marnat, 2003; Grove, Zald, Lebow, Snitz, & Nelson, 2000). Although clinicians make many efforts to objectify **clinical judgments** by using structured interviews, computer interviewing, objective testing, and input from other highly skilled and experienced professionals, the clinician ultimately uses his or her own judgment, impressions, and experience along with objective data to make decisions. These judgments are not only needed to make sense of all of the data gathered to answer specific clinical questions about psychological functioning, diagnosis, prognosis, and treatment but are also used to decide which instruments and assessment approaches should be administered in the first place. There are many available tests and assessment approaches that can be enlisted to evaluate a person. Choosing the right techniques can often be a complex task.

The quality of clinical judgment can be enhanced by the use of multiple assessment sources (e.g., interview, case history, tests, observations). For instance, if a patient reports feeling depressed, if many of the stories that the patient tells in response to the TAT include depressive themes, and if the patient's scores on the MMPI-2, the Beck Depression Inventory (BDI), the Symptom Checklist 90—Revised (SCL-90-R), and depression index on the Rorschach are all elevated, it is likely that the clinician will accurately conclude that the patient is indeed depressed. Unfortunately, clinical decisions are not always so clear. For example, a patient may report feeling depressed, but scores on psychological tests measuring depression are not elevated. Alternatively, a patient may deny feeling depressed during the clinical interview, while testing scores indicate that he or she is depressed. Furthermore, depression may be associated with numerous diagnoses. Patients with a variety of medical conditions (e.g., irritable bowel syndrome, cardiac problems, diabetes, chronic pain) may feel depressed. People who experience personality disorders (e.g., dependent, borderline) may also feel depressed. Depression is often associated with attention deficit disorders, learning disabilities, and other syndromes. Depression can be moderate in severity and chronic (i.e., dysthymia) or severe in intensity and of shorter duration (i.e., major depression). Someone may falsely report being depressed in order to get medical attention (e.g., Munchausen's syndrome) or to obtain some other type of secondary gain (e.g., obtaining sympathy and attention from loved ones, staying home from work). Furthermore, many people who are depressed express their feelings through somatic complaints and do not consciously recognize their depression. Numerous factors in the environment may also lead to depression (e.g., loss of job or a loved one). How can the psychologist sort out all the available data and make judgments regarding diagnosis and treatment planning? Psychologists must examine all of the pieces of the puzzle and then make sense of them.

Their theoretical framework, prior experience, clinical training, and intuitions all come into play. Clinicians do not put all of the data into a formula or computer program and get a fully objective answer to their questions. However, much research suggests that clinical judgments can be unreliable and invalid (Aegisdóttir et al. 2006; Dawes, 1994; Faust, 1986; Grove et al., 2000; Lilienfeld et al., 2000; Lilienfeld, 2007; Meehl, 1954, 1965; Mischel, 1986; Spengler et al., 2009; Wood et al., 2000, 2004)—not only in psychology but in medicine and other fields (Sanchez & Kahn, 1991). Others have criticized this research, stating that these studies are flawed and do not reflect the types of decisions typically made by practicing clinicians (Garb, 1988, 1989; Lambert & Wertheimer, 1988). Efforts are often made to increase the reliability and validity of clinical judgments. For example, many managed-care insurance companies require clinicians to use highly specific assessment tools and to objectify target symptoms in psychological evaluations and treatment. Assessment is also encouraged on a regular basis rather than in a single snapshot of a person at the beginning of treatment. Initial formulations and impressions are constantly being challenged based on the discovery of further information. Given the complex nature of psychological assessment, psychologists make case formulations and an initial plan for treatment, for example, that is continually reassessed and revised as the need arises.

Some have suggested that psychologists should employ actuarial (i.e., statistical) approaches in their decision making rather than relying solely on clinical judgment. Thus, test scores, presenting symptoms, and other information can be quantified and entered into statistical equations to help determine a diagnosis and develop a treatment plan (Dawes, 1979, 1994; Gough, 1962; Grove et al., 2000). Others argue that the complexity of human nature cannot be quantified so easily and that professional clinical judgment is always needed (Blatt, 1975; Garb, 1988, 1989;

Where Psychologists Get These Tests

Given all of the information about psychological tests provided in this chapter and the previous one, you might wonder where psychologists get these testing instruments. They are not available in bookstores or department stores. There are several companies that make and distribute these tests for those who they determine are qualified by training and experience to purchase them. Typically, you need to demonstrate that you are a licensed psychologist or have appropriate training to purchase psychological tests. Some of the major testing companies include:

Achenbach System of Empirically Based Assessment

ASEBA/Research Center for Children, Youth and Families
1 South Prospect Street
St. Joseph's Wing (3rd Floor, Room# 3207)
Burlington, VT 05401 (802-656-5130, www.aseba.org)

Consulting Psychologists Press (CPP)

1055 Joaquin Road, 2nd Floor
Mountain View, CA 94043 (800-624-1765, www.cpp.com)

Institute of Personality and Ability Testing (IPAT)

1801 Woodfield Drive
Savoy, IL 61874 (800-225-4728, www.ipat.com)

Pearson Assessments

Box 1416
Minneapolis, MN 55440 (888-1627-7271, www.pearsonassessments.com)

PRO-ED

8700 Shoal Creek Boulevard
Austin, TX 78757-6897 (800-897-3202, www.proedinc.com)

Psychological Assessment Resources (PAR)

16204 North Florida Avenue
Lutz, FL 33549 (800-331-8378, www.parinc.com)

Reitan Neuropsychological Laboratory

Box 66080
Tucson, AZ 85728 (520-577-2970, www.reitanlabs.com)

Riverside Publishing

3800 Golf Road, Suite 100
Rolling Meadows, IL 60008 (800-323-9540, www.riverpub.com)

(continued)

University of Minnesota Press

111 Third Avenue South, Suite 290
Minneapolis, MN 55401 (800-388-3863, www.upress.umn.edu)

Western Psychological Services

12031 Wilshire Boulevard
Los Angeles, CA 90025 (800-648-8857, www.wpspublish.com)

MacDonald, 1996). Whereas many clinicians find it distasteful to rely on actuarial techniques, others feel it is critical to use any approach that has proved reliable, valid, and useful (Aegisdóttir et al. 2006; Dawes, 1979, 1994; Grove et al., 2000). Most practicing clinicians rely more on clinical judgment than on actuarial approaches, whereas most researchers rely on actuarial approaches. The reality is that psychologists will likely always be required to make professional clinical judgments that are based on training, experience, and intuition as well as those that are evidence based. Efforts to increase their skills and achieve reliable, valid, and useful conclusions is certainly a worthy and welcomed endeavor (Beutler & Groth-Marnat, 2003; Grove et al., 2000; Lilienfeld, 2007; MacDonald, 1996; Sackett & Lievens, 2008).

Communicating Assessment Results

After testing is completed, analyzed, and interpreted, the results are usually first communicated orally to patients and other interested parties. Results are communicated to others only with the explicit permission of the person unless extraordinary conditions are involved (e.g., the patient is gravely disabled). After a psychological evaluation, the psychologist will often schedule a feedback session to show the patient the results, explain the findings in understandable language, and answer all questions. Often psychologists must also explain their assessment results to other interested parties such as parents, teachers, attorneys, and physicians.

In addition to oral feedback, the psychologist typically prepares a written report to communicate test findings. Table 8.7 provides

---

Table 8.7   **Outline of Typical Psychological Report**

1. Identifying information (name, sex, age, ethnicity, date of evaluation, referring clinician)

2. Referral question (when is the person being evaluated now and what questions need to be answered)

3. Background Information (relevant history of psychiatric, medical, legal, family, and so forth)

4. Assessment procedures and tests administered

    a. Cognitive Functioning (current cognitive functioning including intellectual, memory, and perception)

    b. Affective and mood (current affective functioning such as depression and anxiety as well as general mood)

    c. Relational functioning (relationships with family, work, peers)

5. Diagnostic impressions (including DSM-IV-TR categories and codes)

6. Summary of impressions and findings

7. Recommendations (assessment of risk factors, need for medication, treatment, and possible further evaluation)

Case Study: Thomas Experiences Aggressive Behavior Associated with Asperger's Syndrome (Psychological Assessment Report)

Patient: Thomas X
Date of Birth: January 12, 2004
Age: 6 years
Parents: Mr. and Mrs. X
Dates of Testing: January 22, 23, 2010
Clinician: Dr. Z

Thomas is a 6-year-old adopted Caucasian boy who has recently completed kindergarten. His adoptive mother is Japanese American and his adoptive father is Caucasian. Little is known about Thomas's biological parents, who apparently were teenagers who felt ill-prepared to care for a child. Thomas's parents chose to adopt due to infertility. Thomas was born at 27 weeks' gestation, three months premature.

Thomas's parents are seeking an evaluation of Thomas in order to assist them with a number of school-related decisions. First, it is unclear whether Thomas is ready for first grade, primarily in light of "explosive aggression" at school. His mother reports that while shy and introverted during preschool, Thomas has been highly aggressive in kindergarten, hitting, pushing, and punching other children. He is described as very active, bossy with other children, but bright and academically on track. Psychological testing was requested in order to shed light on Thomas's social difficulties and determine an optimal educational program.

Tests and Procedures Administered:

Wechsler Intelligence Scale for Children-IV (WISC-IV)

Child Behavior Checklist (completed by his mother)

Sentence Completion Test (Haak version)

Child Depression Inventory

Robert's Apperception Test—2nd edition

Rorschach

Projective Drawings

Clinical Interview with Thomas's mother

Conversation with kindergarten teacher

Conversation with educational consultant

Interview Data: Thomas's development is significant for behavioral rigidity and fixated interests. Thomas's mother describes him as having tremendous difficulty adapting to changes in plans, frequently prompting tantrums. Similarly, Thomas is described as controlling and bossy with his peers, insisting that they play what and how he wants. Beginning at age 2, Thomas has developed rigid food preferences and bedtime rituals; for example, Thomas must have his mother bring him a glass of water in bed. In terms of interests, he "becomes fixated for months at a time" on one particular preoccupation—currently sharks and previously dinosaurs.

He is an active child, but neither his teacher nor his mother feel that he is unusually overactive. He is also not described as unusually distractible or inattentive. He is, however, regarded by both his teacher and mother as impulsive, and easily frustrated. In the sensory realm, Thomas often licks objects and sniffs at foods before consuming them. In addition to the aggression with other children, he is unable to read social cues, appears to misperceive other children's communication, and is not attuned to others' emotions. He also compulsively labels other individuals according to their racial status, for example, stating: "Joey is Mexican. His Mommy is Mexican, too." There is no known history of significant trauma

(continued)

Case Study (Continued)

outside of Thomas's adoption experience. He is presently in excellent physical health.

Behavioral Observations: Because the evaluation was conducted during the summer, an in-class observation was not possible. In the office, Thomas engaged enthusiastically, cheerfully, and cooperatively in the testing. He demonstrated good attention and concentration despite being physically restless and squirmy during verbal portions of the assessment. He was easily redirected at each of these points. Thomas was tangential and preservative in his speech, frequently telling long stories unrelated to the task. Many of his verbalizations were difficult to follow, and he spoke with a singsong prosody in an overly loud voice.

Intellectual Functioning: Thomas is currently functioning within the above-average range of general mental abilities, achieving a full-scale IQ score of 118. There were no significant differences between index scores.

Results of Personality and Psychological Functioning Tests: Emotionally, Thomas's test results revealed feelings of mild depression, anxiety, and aggressive content. On the Child Behavior Checklist (CBCL) completed by his mother, Thomas's profile shows significant levels of Anxiety/Depression, Aggression, and Social Problems. On the Child Depression Inventory administered directly (and orally) to Thomas, he scored in the mildly depressed range (i.e., score of 11). These findings are consistent with a child who is aware to some degree of his present difficulties and is responding with understandable sadness and frustration.

On projective tests, Thomas first drew a series of person drawings significant for their tiny size, often associated with low self-esteem in children. These drawings are further suggestive of some tension due to the extremely heavy pencil pressure and darkly shaded areas. Obsessive detail was also noted. His Sentence Completion

Test responses were notable for the degree of difficulty meeting his social and emotional needs, for example, stating: I feel sorry when I have . . . "no friends around to play with." Thomas's story responses to the Robert's cards were significant for aggression, sadness, tangentiality, and perseverativeness. Thomas's Rorschach responses focused on nonhuman, strange, or extraterrestrial figures, for example, perceiving a "flying robot," "a really strange guy," and "a sea monster." Aggressive images were also pervasive. These responses may reflect Thomas's feelings of social alienation and the use of aggression to assert himself. On all of the protective measures, Thomas repeatedly referred to the racial status of himself and others, mentioning race no fewer than 22 recorded times during the evaluation, indicative of both his perseverative style and extreme focus on this issue.

Integration and Formulation: Thomas presents a complex profile of significant strengths and difficulties, and given his rapid development as a robust 6-year-old, caution must be taken in applying diagnostic labels. Thomas's history and current test results are suggestive of a diagnosis of Asperger's Disorder, often viewed as "social dyslexia" or the highest-functioning end of the Pervasive Developmental Disorders continuum. Consistent with this potential understanding is Thomas's pattern of behavioral rigidity, fixated interests, sensory abnormalities, social difficulties and inability to perceive social cues, tangential speech and lack of relatedness in conversation, and associated feelings of frustration, anger, sadness, and anxiety.

Thomas's clinical picture is further complicated by his premature birth, adoptive status, and confusion regarding his racial identity in an interracial family. Thus, medical, cognitive, family, sociocultural, and emotional factors all deserve further attention in order to best assist Thomas in meeting the challenges ahead.

Case Study (Continued)

Recommendations:

1. Social skills training (in a group context) is indicated to assist Thomas in acquiring improved tools for contending with peers and more effectively meeting his social needs and decreasing his aggressive behavior. The use of cognitive-behavioral techniques in a highly structured group format is indicated.

2. Parent consultation is recommended to support Thomas's parents, assist the family in processing adoption and racial issues, and in developing a behavioral program that breaks down social behavior into small steps and rewards desirable social behavior both at home and in school.

3. A speech and language evaluation is recommended in order to rule out a language learning disorder that may be contributing to Thomas's expressive and social difficulties.

4. Thomas is cognitively and academically prepared to move on to a first-grade classroom that can collaborate with Thomas's parents and clinicians in assisting with and providing support for his social and behavioral difficulties.

---

an outline of a typical assessment report. Most testing reports include the reason for the referral and the identification of the referring party, the list of assessment instruments used, actual test scores (such as percentile ranks), the psychologist's interpretation of the scores and findings, a diagnostic impression, and recommendations. It is important to ascertain the audience for whom the report is being written. A report directed to another mental health professional may be very different from one to a school teacher or a parent. Most psychologists avoid professional jargon so that their reports will be understandable to non-psychologists. Psychologists also must handle reports confidentially and send them only to appropriate persons.

Integrated Psychological Assessment Report

Having described various components of psychological assessment, the case study for Thomas will be used to demonstrate the actual integration of a complete psychological assessment battery. Note the diversity of measures, theoretical perspectives and biopsychosocial elements synthesized in the course of this evaluation.

This complex, integrative, and contemporary example of a psychological assessment case serves to illustrate several critical issues. First, a combination of psychological tests was utilized to fully assess this child through observational, interviewing, intellectual, objective personality, and projective personality measures. Second, an integrated theoretical approach was utilized, taking into consideration intrapsychic psychodynamic issues (e.g., loneliness, low self-esteem), cognitive-behavioral factors (e.g., need for behavioral reinforcement program and social skills training), humanistic concerns (e.g., need for support and understanding in both Thomas and his parents), and family issues (e.g., adoption). Third, the intimate connection between biological (e.g., Asperger's is a neurological condition), psychological (e.g., social impairments, aggression), and social (e.g., interracial issues, classroom milieu) factors must be integrated into a meaningful formulation and set of recommendations. Finally, what on the surface may have appeared to be simply a boy having problems with aggression in the classroom was revealed through psychological assessment to be far more complex and elusive.

The Big Picture

Psychological testing is truly a unique and invaluable skill offered by clinical psychologists. In addition to the interviewing and observational tools described in Chapter 7, the major areas of cognitive, neuropsychological, and personality assessment provide tremendous insights into the human mind and psyche. Formal psychological assessment, when carefully integrated with selected measures and biopsychosocial contexts, richly informs both diagnosis and treatment. Future clinical psychologists will improve these measures in order to make them more useful to diverse clinical populations. Information obtained from research and practice will be used to develop improved measures that increase reliability, validity, and utility. Future instruments will also likely attempt to assess psychological and other relevant constructs in a more efficient manner.

Key Points

1. Cognitive testing is a general term referring to the assessment of a wide range of information-processing or thinking skills and behaviors. These include general neuropsychological functioning involving brain–behavior relationships, general intellectual functioning (such as reasoning and problem-solving), as well as more specific cognitive skills such as visual and auditory memory, language skills, pattern recognition, finger dexterity, visual-perceptual skills, academic skills, and motor functioning.

2. Experts disagree on the definition of intelligence. Theories proposed by Spearman, Thurstone, Cattell, Guilford, Piaget, Sternberg, Gardner, and others have been considered. The Wechsler Scales are the most commonly used tests of intelligence assessing preschool children (WPPSI-III), elementary and secondary school children (WISC-IV), and adults (WAIS-IV). The Stanford-Binet, Kaufman Scales, and other intelligence tests are also frequently used. In addition to overall intellectual skills and cognitive strengths and weaknesses, these tests are frequently used to assess the presence of learning disabilities, predict academic success in school, examine brain dysfunction, and assess personality.

3. Other cognitive tests include neuropsychological tests (e.g., the Halstead-Reitan, the Boston Process Approach, the Luria-Nebraska) and other nonintellectual tests of cognitive, social, and motor development.

4. Controversy exists concerning cognitive testing. Some have argued that many tests are biased and misused with minority group members. Others assume that cognitive skills such as intelligence are stable throughout the life span and are innately determined.

5. Many tests exist to measure personality and psychological functioning such as mood. Most of these tests can be classified as either objective or projective instruments.

6. Objective instruments present very specific questions or statements to which the person responds using specific answers. Scores are tabulated and then compared with those of reference groups, using national norms. The most commonly used objective personality tests include the Minnesota Multiphasic Personality Inventory (MMPI-2, MMPI-2-RF, MMPI-A), the Millon Clinical Inventories (MCMI-III, MACI, M-PACI, MAPI, MBMD), and the 16 Personality Factors Questionnaire (16PF).

7. Projective tests use ambiguous or unstructured testing stimuli. Subjects are asked to respond freely to the testing stimuli, such as telling stories about pictures, describing what they see in an inkblot, or saying the first thing that comes to their mind when hearing a word or sentence fragment. The most common projective tests used include the Rorschach, the TAT, Incomplete Sentences, and Drawings.

8. Traditionally, many psychologists have assumed that personality is a fairly stable phenomenon—that each person's personality traits and style are consistent over time and in varying situations (e.g., home, work, school). However, several researchers have demonstrated that personality is not as stable as many people assume but instead partially depends on specific environmental and situational circumstances.

9. Many authors have questioned the reliability and validity of projective tests. Over the years, numerous reviews have concluded that projective techniques have not demonstrated adequate reliability and validity to justify their use with patients. Most of the debate concerning the reliability and validity of projective testing has centered around the Rorschach. Many conclude that research failing to support the reliability and validity of these tests does not deter them from using the instruments if they believe that helpful clinical information can be obtained. Now that the Rorschach copyright has run out, it is readily available online and elsewhere.

10. The developers of most personality and psychological tests such as the MMPI, Rorschach, and TAT did not consider ethnic and other diversity issues during the test construction and validation process. The professionals who update these tests and construct new ones are much more sensitive to issues of diversity. Psychologists must be aware of the limitations of the tests that they use and be sensitive to diversity issues when making judgments based on tests administered with special populations.

11. Many employers use personality and psychological tests to screen job applicants for psychiatric disorders or personality problems that may interfere with work performance. Others are interested in screening for personalities that match the requirements for a particular position.

12. Psychologists must examine all of the available assessment data and make sense out of it. Their theoretical framework, prior experience, clinical training, and intuition play a role in decision making. However, research suggests that clinical judgments are sometimes unreliable. Some have suggested that psychologists employ actuarial approaches in their decision making rather than relying solely on clinical judgment. Most practicing clinicians rely more on clinical judgment than actuarial approaches while most researchers rely on actuarial approaches.

13. Assessment results are often communicated verbally to interested parties. After a psychological evaluation, a psychologist will often schedule a feedback session to show the person who was tested the results and explain the findings in language that is understandable to a non-psychologist. In addition to oral feedback, the psychologist typically prepares a written report to communicate test findings. Most psychologists avoid professional jargon so that their reports will be understandable to non-psychologists.

Key Terms

Boston Process Approach
Clinical judgments
Flynn effect
Intellectual testing
Intelligence quotient (IQ)
Millon Clinical Multiaxial Inventories (MCMI)
Minnesota Multiphasic Personality Inventory (MMPI)
Neuropsychological testing
Objective testing
Personality testing
Projective drawings
Projective testing
Rorschach
Sentence completion
Sixteen Personality Factors Questionnaire (16PF)
Stanford-Binet Scales
Thematic Apperception Test (TAT)
Wechsler Scales

For Reflection

1. What is cognitive testing?
2. What are the main approaches to assess intelligence?
3. What is neuropsychological assessment?
4. Will an IQ score obtained at age 5 be the same as an IQ score obtained at age 40 for the same person? Why or why not?
5. What are some of the different tests used to measure IQ and how are they similar and different?
6. What are the differences between objective and projective psychological testing?
7. List the major objective and projective tests used in clinical psychology.
8. What are the main types of personality tests used?
9. Are projective tests valid?
10. Should psychological tests be used to hire employees? Why or why not?
11. Are psychological tests appropriate to use with people from ethnically diverse backgrounds?
12. How do psychologists make decisions based on testing data?
13. How are testing results communicated to others?
14. What are the advantages of and disadvantages of using an actuarial approach rather than a clinical approach in making clinical judgments?
15. Why are multiple approaches to assessment often advantageous?

Real Students, Real Questions

1. Does the variation in IQ scores over time suggest that an individual's level of intelligence continues to change over the course of his or her life?
2. Is it possible to give effective therapy without administering any cognitive or personality tests? How do you know when these tests are necessary?
3. Who is qualified to give intelligence tests? Can only psychologists give them?
4. What do you do when different tests produce conflicting results?
5. What do you do when test results don't seem to mesh with the clinical interview or the diagnosis?

Web Resources

Learn more about psychological testing and products offered from psychology's largest testing companies. These web sites give you a good deal of additional information about psychological testing:

Consulting Psychologist Press
(www.cpp.com)

Institute of Personality and Ability Testing
(IPAT; www.ipat.com)

Pearson Assessments
(www.pearsonassessments.com)

PRO-ED (www.proedinc.com)

Psychological Assessment Resources
(PAR; www.parinc.com)

Reitan Neuropsychological Laboratory
(www.reitanlabs.com)

Riverside Publishing
(www.riverpub.com)

University of Minnesota Press
(www.upress.umn.edu)

Western Psychological Services
(www.wpspublish.com)

General issues about psychological testing
(www.guidetopsychology.com/testing.htm)

Psychotherapeutic Interventions

9
chapter

Psychotherapy, to many, is the *sine qua non* of clinical psychology. The cumulative power of psychology's many efforts in research and assessment is perhaps best seen in the ultimate helpfulness it achieves in relieving suffering and effecting positive change. Psychotherapy is the general umbrella term for an enormous range of interventions, modalities, and integrative strategies employed in the service of improving quality of life and health. Contemporary psychotherapy combines the synergistic power of a wealth of biological, psychological, and social resources to create a multidimensional, integrative, and evidence-based treatment requiring a great deal of creativity, competence, and collaboration on the part of the clinician. In this chapter, psychotherapy is defined, its goals, common denominators, stages, and modes delineated, and finally, its contemporary incarnation

in the form of integrative and evidence-based approaches is illustrated through case studies.

The word **psychotherapy** means caring for another person's soul or being, as derived from the Greek word *psyche* meaning "soul" or "being" and *therapeutikos* meaning "caring for another" (Kleinke, 1994). A useful definition, developed by Norcross (1990), follows: Psychotherapy is "the informed and intentional application of clinical methods and interpersonal stances derived from established psychological principles for the purpose of assisting people to modify their behaviors, cognitions, emotions, and/or other personal characteristics in directions that the participants deem desirable" (p. 218). While psychotherapy implies being treated by someone to cure or care for problems, *counseling* refers to providing advice and suggestions.

Psychotherapy is a unilateral professional relationship that is circumscribed by limits on time, frequency of contact, content of discussions, and level of intimacy in which a person may talk over problems with a specialist in human behavior. Confidentiality is assured in a professional relationship, so that a client or patient can express whatever is on his or her mind without concern that the information will be disclosed to others. As will be discussed in Chapter 13, there are, however, ethical and legal limits to confidentiality, including serious and immediate danger to self and others and evidence of child abuse. A professional relationship also must not be compromised by the development or maintenance of unethical exploitative dual relationships. A psychologist will not be effective if also trying to be a friend, a colleague, a business partner, or a lover. One of the differences between talking to a friend and talking to a psychologist is that the professional relationship is a primarily unilateral, or "one-way," relationship in which the problems or concerns of the patient or client are discussed, not the needs or concerns of the psychologist. Thus, psychotherapy involves consulting with a mental health professional to obtain assistance in changing feelings, thoughts, or behaviors that one experiences as problematic and distressing. Psychotherapy utilizes theories of human behavior as well as a carefully integrative plan to improve the psychological and behavioral functioning of a person or group.

An extensive review of all the research studies concludes that those who choose to receive psychotherapy from a mental health professional tend to benefit from the experience (Barlow, 1996; Hollon, 1996; VandenBos, 1996). Generally 70% to 80% of those treated in psychotherapy are improved (Smith et al., 1980). Most people who participate in a psychotherapy experience are satisfied with their treatment (*Consumer Reports*, 1998; Seligman, 1995). Some psychologists are critical of psychotherapy, feeling that much more effort should be directed toward prevention rather than treatment of psychological problems (Albee & Gullotta, 1997; Albee & Perry, 1996).

Contemporary Integration in Psychotherapy Using Evidence-Based Approaches

Contemporary approaches to treating emotional distress and behavioral troubles in psychotherapy are multidimensional, comprehensive, integrative, and evidence based (American Psychological Association, 2006; Beutler & Groth-Marnat, 2003; O'Brien & Houston, 2000). An integrative biopsychosocial perspective maintains that biological, psychological, and social influences on behavior interact and must be taken into consideration in both psychological and medical treatment. Although psychotherapy conducted by psychologists is primarily a psychological and behavioral (rather than biological or social) intervention, the biological and social influences on behavior are assessed, discussed, and taken into consideration during psychotherapy. Often, social or medical interventions are sought through other professionals or resources. Leading experts expect that psychotherapy will become more integrative, psychoeducational, problem-focused, brief, and evidence based in the future (APA, 2006; Norcross et al., 2002; Sue & Sue, 2008; Weisz & Gray, 2008).

For example, suppose a patient seeks psychotherapy for depression. The patient may have a *biological* or genetic predisposition to depression and other affective or mood disorders. The patient's mother, father, siblings, grandparents, and/or other relatives may also have depressive disorders. Research has demonstrated that emotional problems such as depression tend to be two to three times more likely to occur if someone has a relative with depression (American Psychiatric Association, 2000; Gershon, 1990; Levinson, 2006). Relatives usually share both genetic and environmental similarities. Twin studies have revealed further support for the genetic influence in the development of depression. For example, Bertelsen, Harvald, and Hauge (1977), Nurnberger and Gershon (1992), and others (e.g., Sullivan, Neale, & Kendler, 2000) report that an identical twin is about three times more likely to develop a mood disorder when their twin has a mood disorder compared with nonidentical (fraternal) twins. Depressed patients also appear to have lower levels of neurotransmitters such as serotonin, norepinephrine, and dopamine (Levinson, 2006; Spoont, 1992; Thase, 2009; Thase & Denko, 2008). Furthermore, endocrine involvement is associated with depression in that depressed patients experience elevated levels of the stress hormone cortisol relative to nondepressed persons (Thase & Denko, 2008; E. B. Weller & R. A. Weller, 1988). Thus, people may be biologically vulnerable to developing certain types of psychological disorders such as depression, attention deficit hyperactivity disorder, schizophrenia, bipolar disorder, or panic disorder. The psychologist may discuss this biological aspect with the patient to help him or her better understand and cope with this aspect of the illness. The psychologist may, for instance, refer the patient to a psychiatrist for biological treatments such as the use of antidepressant medication or electroconvulsive therapy (ECT).

The patient also inevitably experiences *psychological* concerns related to the depression. Low self-esteem, hopelessness, loss of pleasure in activities and relationships, and perceived inability to achieve one's goals may all be distressing for the depressed patient. Attitudes and the interpretation of stressful life events may also contribute to feelings of depression. Beck and colleagues (Beck, 1963, 1976; Beck & Alford, 2009) have suggested that depressed persons maintain a "negative schema," which is a stable negative cognitive belief about their life. Thus, depressed people maintain automatic negative interpretations of life events, perhaps seeing the glass as half empty rather than half full. Seligman (1975, 1994, 2006; Seligman et al., 2009) suggested that depressed persons develop a pessimistic style of understanding their world and maintain a "learned helplessness" feeling that they have no control over their life. Object relations theorists (e.g., Kernberg, 1976; Klein, 1952; Kohut, 1971) suggest that impaired early attachments make

one vulnerable to depression. Psychological interventions generally focus on such concerns by examining the thoughts and feelings associated with depression.

Finally, *social* influences on depression might include the depressed patient's interaction with family members, work associates, friends, and the larger cultural context. Stressful life events such as divorce are highly associated with the onset of depression, especially among men. While divorced women are three times more likely to develop severe depression relative to women who remain married, men are nine times more likely to develop depression following a divorce (Bruce & Kim, 1992). Cultural influences may also play an important role in depression. For instance, in various cultural groups, many members tend to express depressive symptoms through somatic complaints such as headaches and gastric discomfort (APA, 2003b; Shorter, 1994; D. Sue & D. M. Sue, 2008; Tsai & Chentsova-Dutton, 2002). How emotional distress is expressed is partially determined by the social and cultural context in which the distress is experienced. Some cultural groups are more apt than others to encourage the expression of feelings and support the concept of psychotherapy. Therefore, these influences must be examined in order to better understand and treat the patient. Involving family members in the psychotherapy or using culture-specific interventions or consultations may prove useful for the depressed patient.

In short, in even the seemingly straightforward "psychological" example of depression, biopsychosocial factors interact uniquely and importantly to inform and direct treatment. Additionally, assessment and treatment of depression and other troubles must be evidence based in that research findings must be well integrated into psychotherapeutic work (American Psychological Association, 2006). In the following discussion of psychotherapy, this complexity and richness will best be illustrated in the integrative case examples provided for each therapeutic modality described.

Goals of Psychotherapy

The list of possible goals of psychotherapy is endless. Goals may include behavioral change, enhanced interpersonal relationships, insight, support, or concrete outcomes such as finding a job or a partner, staying out of the hospital, or staying alive. The goals may also be different for the patient, for the significant others in the patient's life (e.g., spouse, parents, coworkers, teacher), and for the psychologist. Whereas the patient may have one goal (e.g., reduction of anxiety), the psychologist may have another (e.g., increased insight), and the patient's spouse may have yet a different goal (e.g., getting a job).

Kleinke (1994) described six fundamental therapeutic goals common to almost all psychotherapies: (1) overcoming demoralization and gaining hope, (2) enhancing mastery and self-efficacy, (3) overcoming avoidance, (4) becoming aware of one's misconceptions, (5) accepting life's realities, and (6) achieving insight. Common concerns that bring many to psychotherapy (e.g., anxiety, depression, loneliness, low self-esteem, problematic symptoms and/or relationships) often lead to the patient's feeling hopeless and demoralized. Psychotherapy usually seeks to return or develop a sense of hope or optimism. Increasing one's sense of mastery, efficacy, and control can also heighten one's sense of hope. Avoidance of issues can lead to more serious problems. Denying, avoiding, and minimizing problems prevent a person from dealing directly with them. Psychotherapy often seeks ways to help patients confront problems and concerns in order to deal more effectively with them. Insight into the intrapsychic, interpersonal, biological, and social factors that lead to symptoms and problems is likely to assist a person in coping more effectively with his or her concerns.

The goal of psychotherapy may include changing very specific problem behaviors. For example, the goal might be to reduce or minimize temper tantrums, fear while speaking in public, nail biting, binge eating, or smoking. Other goals might include improving certain target behaviors such as attention in class, performance on examinations, polite behavior, exercise, and healthy food consumption; enhancing awareness of and insight into anxieties, attitudes, beliefs, and feelings; or increasing self-efficacy and mastery over problems. Goals of treatment might also involve careful management of a crisis (e.g., trauma, suicidal or homicidal threats). The objectives of psychotherapy may change several times during the course of the therapy experience. Accordingly, psychotherapy hopes to address many different types of goals, depending on the specific needs, interests, and concerns of all interested parties. Sometimes the goals are difficult to define and articulate until the psychologist evaluates or gets to know the patient. Overall, the ultimate objective is to improve quality of life through self-understanding, behavioral and lifestyle change, improved coping and adaptation, and/or enhanced relationships. Psychotherapy attempts to utilize what is known about the biopsychosocial influences on human behavior and apply that knowledge to help individuals and groups contending with a wide range of difficulties.

Similarities or Common Denominators in Psychotherapy

Common denominators in all psychotherapy include a professional person or "expert," professional behavior or manner on the part of the expert, a professional setting where services meant to help the client are rendered, fees, and a schedule of sessions. All psychotherapy also includes (or should include) ethical conduct. Many professionals report that factors such as the development of a therapeutic relationship, a sense of mastery and control, and corrective emotional experiences are helpful to patients and can be found in all psychotherapies (Kleinke, 1994; Lambert, 2005; Norcross, 2002; O'Brien & Houston, 2000; Prochaska & Norcross, 2007; Sprenkle, David, & Lebow, 2009). Grencavage and Norcross (1990) report

89 commonalities in psychotherapy, which generally fall into one of two categories: positive expectations and a helpful therapeutic relationship. These common factors are discussed in detail in the next chapter. Professional person, manner, setting, fees, and schedule issues are briefly discussed here.

Professional Person

Almost all psychotherapies involve working with a licensed mental health professional (e.g., psychologist, psychiatrist, social worker, psychiatric nurse, marriage and family counselor) or a formally supervised trainee in a mental health discipline. These professionals learn evidence-based principles of human behavior and apply them to the individual needs and concerns expressed by those who seek their services. Most professional organizations suggest that the practice of psychotherapy is a challenging art and science. Most encourage or require their members to obtain many years of intensive training, experience, and supervision prior to licensing. Psychologists, psychiatrists, social workers, nurses, marriage and family counselors, and others have specific requirements for certification and continuing education. Curiously, the terms *counselor, advisor, coach,* or *therapist* are not regulated by states. Therefore, anyone can use these terms without any specific training or certification. A wide variety of psychotherapy approaches and techniques are offered by untrained or marginally trained persons. Although some of these counselors can provide excellent services, many do not (Norcross, 2002; Singer & Lalich, 1996). All the professional mental health disciplines demand that anyone who wishes to provide psychotherapeutic services be fully trained and supervised to protect both the public and the profession from potential harm.

Professional Manner

Almost all psychologists maintain a professional manner. This entails observing appropriate professional boundaries (e.g., not discussing one's own problems) as well as behaving in an attentive, caring, and helpful manner. Professional manner also requires being physically and psychologically available to the patient during sessions. Psychologists should not, for example, take telephone calls, fall asleep, eat, be late for appointments, act impulsively, dress provocatively, or allow themselves to be distracted from their patients during the session.

Professional Setting

Most psychotherapy occurs in the professional office of the service provider (Figure 9.1). The office is usually equipped with comfortable seating and space and also allows for private conversation (e.g., so that others cannot see or hear the conversation). Although some professionals may meet with patients outside the office setting (e.g., at school), the vast majority of psychotherapy takes place in the office of the mental health professional. Whenever psychotherapy is conducted outside the professional office setting, clinicians should have a compelling reason to do so. Home visits and meetings at school or in public places may be appropriate under certain circumstances. For example, a psychologist treating someone with an airplane phobia may appropriately conduct a session at an airport, and someone who is severely disabled and cannot leave home may be treated by the psychologist at home. However, psychotherapy sessions over lunch at a restaurant are considered unprofessional and inappropriate. Maintaining confidentiality and professional boundaries must be considered carefully when meeting outside the office setting.

Fees

Almost all psychotherapy involves fees. Patients and/or their insurance companies are required to pay for the psychotherapy sessions. Fees range from about $30 per hour in low-fee training or community clinics to

Photo: Zigy Kaluzny, Tony Stone Images, New York

Figure 9.1

Psychologist conducting a psychotherapy session.

$200 or more per hour. Generally, mental health disciplines that require more years of training (e.g., psychiatry and psychology) charge more than disciplines requiring fewer years of training (e.g., social work, marriage and family counseling). Geographic location can also impact professional fees. Fees tend to be higher for professionals with more years of experience who live in expensive areas (e.g., New York City, San Francisco, Toronto). Some professionals use a sliding fee schedule to accommodate those who cannot afford the expense or whose health insurance does not cover mental health services. Some psychologists offer services to a certain number of people for free, or *pro bono,* in order to help those who need services but cannot pay for them. Psychologists must manage their fees in an appropriately professional manner.

Duration of Sessions

Psychotherapy usually involves about an hour of service per session (e.g., 50 minutes). Longer sessions (e.g., 80 minutes) are often scheduled for family or group psychotherapy. Although there is nothing magical about meeting for 50 minutes, most psychologists do not deviate significantly from the 50-minute session format. Fifty minutes (rather than a full hour) allows the psychologist to take notes following the session as well as make quick telephone calls and conduct other administrative tasks relevant to patients. Most psychologists have a clock that is easily seen by the therapist and the patient so that both can monitor their time and use it wisely.

Frequency of Sessions

Most outpatient psychotherapy is conducted on a once-per-week basis, whereas inpatient or hospital-based psychotherapy is usually conducted daily. However, there may be compelling reasons to alter the once-per-week format. For example, some outpatient psychotherapy is conducted twice, three times, or, in the case of psychoanalysis, four or five times per week. Frequency of sessions may change during the course of psychotherapy. Some people prefer once every other week, once per month, or on an as-needed basis, and each of these arrangements affords pros and cons. Insurance companies generally have guidelines concerning the frequency or number of sessions that they will reimburse. During a crisis, someone may schedule psychotherapy sessions several times a week and switch to a weekly, bimonthly, or an as-needed basis following the resolution of the crisis. After most of the goals of psychotherapy are reached, periodic follow-up or booster sessions are scheduled as needed to monitor progress and deal with potential relapse.

Stages of Psychotherapy

Most psychotherapy is carried out in several stages: an initial consultation, assessment of the problem and situation, development of treatment goals, implementation of treatment, evaluation of treatment, termination of treatment, and follow-up.

Initial Consultation

An initial consultation generally involves a discussion of why the patient has decided to seek help and what the patient hopes to gain from the psychotherapy experience. The consultation provides an opportunity to determine whether there is a good fit between the needs, goals, and interests of the patient and the skills of the psychologist. Furthermore, the psychologist usually outlines the terms of professional services such as limits of confidentiality, fees, available appointment times, therapeutic approach, and so forth. The initial consultation helps both the patient and the psychologist answer the question, "Am I likely to be able to work with this person successfully?"

Following the initial consultation, several decisions are made regarding whether to schedule a second session. The patient may evaluate how adequately his or her needs can be met by working with the psychologist, and whether the practical terms of the therapy are acceptable (e.g., session availability, fees, office location, psychologist approach). The patient may also consider whether the psychologist has an appealing personality or professional manner. Additionally, given the information presented during the consultation session, the psychologist may determine whether he or she has the expertise to work effectively with the patient. Thus, both patient and psychologist mutually decide whether additional sessions are advisable.

The initial consultation may result in the decision not to continue services. The patient may decide that his or her goals and needs cannot be adequately met by the psychologist

for a variety of reasons. For instance, the psychologist may seem too direct, quiet, aloof, old, young, expensive, or inexperienced. Or the patient's goals may no longer seem as reasonable as initially thought. For example, the patient may have requested global personality change during the course of limited sessions or may wish to reduce a longstanding problem that is not amenable to psychotherapy. Then, too, the patient may feel better and have some sense of direction after the initial consultation and thus feel less compelled to continue sessions. The psychologist may also refuse to provide continued services for several reasons. For example, the patient may reveal an alcohol problem, and the psychologist might wish to refer him or her to a specialist in the assessment and treatment of substance abuse problems. The psychologist may decide not to proceed if the goals outlined by the patient are unrealistic or inappropriate. Research discussed later in this chapter suggests that a sizable number of initial consultation sessions do not result in a second session.

Assessment

The psychologist must perform an assessment of the patient. This may involve formal psychological testing or extended interviews. Essentially, the psychologist must size up the patient and situation to develop a reasonable level of understanding concerning the diagnosis and direction for designing a treatment program. The psychologist must gain some insight into the factors that led to the development of the problem(s), the maintenance of the problem(s), and appropriate strategies for helping the patient obtain relief from the problem(s).

Some psychologists perform formal assessments for each new patient in their practice. Many clinics, hospitals, prisons, and other facilities use a standard battery of tests for all persons undergoing psychotherapy. For example, each adult patient might be asked to complete the Minnesota Multiphasic Personality Inventory (MMPI-2 or MMPI-2-RF) and

Multicultural Counseling

Photo: Courtesy Zach Plante.

Given the increasingly diverse multicultural environment, clinical psychologists as well as other mental health and health-care professionals must work to be more aware and skilled at providing services in a multicultural society (APA, 2003b). Sue and Sue (2003, 2008) offer several useful suggestions regarding ways to increase cultural competence for clinical psychologists. These experts define *cultural competence* as "the ability to engage in actions or create conditions that maximize the optimal development of client and client systems. Multicultural counseling competence is defined as the counselor's acquisition of awareness, knowledge, and skills needed to function effectively in a pluralistic democratic society (ability to communicate, interact, negotiate, and intervene on behalf of clients from diverse backgrounds) . . ." (p. 21).

Sue and Sue suggest that psychologists first become more aware of their own culturally-based assumptions, values, and biases. Although it is often challenging and uncomfortable confronting one's own biases associated with "racism, sexism, heterosexism, able-body-ism, and ageism" (p. 18), one must strive to work toward the realization that well-meaning psychologists may enter a multicultural world with problematic views that negatively impact their work with people of color.

Psychologists must learn to understand and appreciate the worldview of culturally diverse clients. Although a psychologist cannot expect to fully know exactly what it feels like to live as a minority group member who may not be similar to their own cultural experience, they can still develop some degree of understanding and empathy for others.

Finally, psychologists need to develop appropriate culturally informed intervention strategies and techniques. For example, research suggests that many minority group members prefer more active and directive approaches to treatment rather than inactive and nondirective approaches.

Furthermore, Sue and Sue caution that the traditional "one-to-one, in-the-office, objective form of treatment aimed at remediation of existing problems may be at odds with the sociopolitical and cultural experiences of their clients" (p. 23).

Sue and Sue offer several specific tips for psychologists, including adopting a more active style, working outside of the office, helping change environmental conditions rather than changing the client, viewing the client as experiencing problems rather than having a problem, focusing on prevention, and accepting more responsibility for the course and outcome of their consultation work.

Symptom Checklist-90—Revised (SCL-90-R) no matter what the presenting problem(s) might be. All parents might be asked to complete a Child Behavior Checklist (CBCL) or a Conner's Rating Scale prior to treatment services for their child. Other treatment facilities and individual practitioners may make assessment decisions on a case-by-case basis after the initial interview. Furthermore, many professionals weave assessment and treatment together, evaluating treatment goals, symptoms, and satisfaction with services on a regular basis throughout treatment as well as after its termination.

Development of Treatment Goals

Once a reasonable level of understanding about the nature of the problem(s) is established, treatment goals and objectives can be developed. Whereas many psychologists explicitly detail treatment goals with their patients and use formal instruments to complete this process, others are less formal about the development of written treatment goals. It is important, however, for both patient and psychologist to have some understanding of the goals that each has in mind so that both parties can work toward the same ends. Once treatment goals are developed, a treatment plan should be outlined to reach them.

Implementation of Treatment

The actual treatment is provided with the hope of reaching the treatment goals. The treatment

plan may include individual, couple, family, or group psychotherapy in weekly, biweekly, or daily sessions. Inpatient, outpatient, and partial hospitalization all may be utilized in the implementation of treatment. Different theoretical approaches might be used as well, and biological, psychological, and social interventions carried out. The treatment might include homework, self-help readings, or consultation with other professionals (e.g., physicians, clergy, vocational counselors, school teachers). The various combinations and permutations of the treatment plan can be as unique as each person seeking psychotherapy.

Evaluation of Treatment

During the course of treatment, an evaluation of the treatment should be regularly conducted to determine whether the treatment plan is working effectively or needs to be altered to be more useful to the patient. Although some psychologists, treatment facilities, and even health insurance companies conduct periodic and formal treatment evaluations using questionnaires, checklists, and other instruments, most choose to discuss the progress of the treatment informally with their patients during periodic sessions. Treatment may be altered or even terminated based on the evaluation.

Termination

Once psychotherapy has successfully reached the treatment goals, psychotherapy is usually terminated. Sometimes treatment is terminated prematurely due to a variety of factors such as the patient's financial or time constraints or resistance to change; a job change or move on the part of the patient or psychologist; changes or limitation in insurance coverage; and so forth. A discussion concerning relapse strategies and a review of psychotherapy progress usually occur during termination. Psychotherapy termination can be difficult for both patients and psychologists who have spent much time working closely together.

Follow-Up

Often, follow-up sessions are scheduled or at least offered to the patient to ensure that the changes achieved during the course of therapy are maintained after treatment is terminated. Periodical booster sessions might be scheduled to review progress and to work on problems that emerge later. Follow-up can provide a sense of continuity for patients, and alleviate the abruptness of termination after therapy.

Modes of Psychotherapy

Meeting individually with a psychologist is not the only way psychotherapy can occur. Psychotherapy can be provided in individual, couple, group, or family modes, and people may participate in several different modes at the same time. Each mode has advantages and disadvantages as well as different potential goals and objectives.

It is difficult to understand what psychotherapy might be like without using actual case examples. Confidentiality concerns prevent most students and other interested parties from witnessing psychotherapy sessions in person or on videotape. Several examples of actual psychotherapy cases are provided in this chapter in a manner that protects patient confidentiality. Each of these cases provides a description of psychotherapy with either groups, couples, or individuals regarding specific difficulties.

Individual Psychotherapy

Individual psychotherapy is the most commonly practiced and researched mode of psychotherapy (Bergin & Garfield, 1994; Norcross, Hedges, et al., 2002; Norcross, Karpiak, & Santoro, 2005). Goals, techniques, and perspectives on how to conduct individual psychotherapy vary widely. Perhaps the only common configuration is that the patient meets alone with a psychologist. Individual psychotherapy involves conversations between a psychologist and patient who work as a team to help the patient overcome problems, improve insight and/or behavior, and enhance his or her quality of life. These conversations may focus on many different topics, depending on the problems and symptoms experienced by the patient as well as the skills and orientation of the psychologist. The discussion can focus on the development of techniques to cope with symptoms (e.g., thought stopping, relaxation), on feelings associated with symptoms (e.g., alienation, fear), or on the actual relationship between the psychologist and patient (e.g., the transference and countertransference).

Whereas individual psychotherapy for adults involves discussions with a psychologist, for young children it often incorporates play activities. Play therapy includes activities that are observed and interpreted by a psychologist. It is assumed that children work though emotional conflicts in their play, and that themes that develop and become reenacted during play sessions assist in the healing process. Play is also used with children to aid communication and as a distraction to assist children in feeling less self-conscious when talking about sensitive topics.

Group Psychotherapy

Group psychotherapy comes in many shapes and sizes with various goals, techniques, and objectives. Some groups are conducted in hospital settings and meet daily or several times per week. Outpatient groups generally meet once per week or every other week.

Case Study: Shawna Experiences Enuresis (Individual Child Therapy)

Shawna is an 11-year-old Caucasian girl who lives with her parents, older sister (15), and two cats. She is presently in the sixth grade in a public school where she is performing very well academically. Shawna's family lives in a wealthy suburban area where achievement and success are strong community values. There are no significant current stressors in the home or past traumas identified.

Presenting Problem: Shawna has been troubled by almost nightly enuresis, or bedwetting, ever since she was "out of diapers." Both Shawna and her parents are deeply embarrassed by this problem, which has remained a deep family secret and prevented Shawna from the normal range of overnights and sleep-away activities with her peers. Assessment of the enuresis does not reveal any consistent stressors or emotional antecedents to the almost nightly occurrences. However, the consequences of the wetting involve Shawna's mother or older sister changing her bedclothes and informing her father: "Another wet night."

Key Biopsychosocial Factors:

Biological: The clinician needs to rule out a medical basis for enuresis (e.g., bladder disease or abnormality). Some children sleep so deeply as to not heed the physiological sensation of a full bladder.

Psychological: The clinician needs to rule out an emotional basis for enuresis (e.g., anxiety, trauma, stress). For example, shame and isolation as well as a lack of developmentally appropriate independence and autonomy may play a role.

Social: Community values on success intimidate this family from sharing problems with friends and extended family and increase sense of shame and isolation.

Treatment Goals and Plans: Treatment will focus on resolving the enuresis, working through the shame and secrecy, and increasing Shawna's sense of competence and social access.

The treatment plan involves the following components.

1. A medical examination is required to rule out any physical basis for the enuresis.
2. In the absence of a medical problem, a behavioral program using a special device that buzzes at the first drop of moisture in bed will be employed. This technique requires that Shawna take responsibility for attaching the device to her bed each night, and as soon as the alarm is activated, she is to get out of bed and go to the bathroom to urinate. (Eventually, children become conditioned to the association between a full bladder and the buzzer, and learn to awaken on their own.) Shawna is to record each morning whether the buzzer woke her, whether she woke herself, and other relevant details. She is also to handle her own linens, with family members involved only at her direct request.
3. Individual sessions will discuss the progress of this behavioral program while exploring her feelings of shame, success, isolation, and so on.
4. Intermittent family sessions will ensure that the family is allowing Shawna more autonomy and afford an opportunity to discuss embarrassment and the pressure to "always look good" in their community. As Shawna's enuresis resolves, her newfound pride and independence can be integrated through discussion and ventures into overnights, and therapy sessions eventually tapered.

This example illustrates the use of individual and family modalities in a combined behavioral and humanistic approach to understand, support, and increase self-efficacy around a specific problem. Medical consultation in addition to an understanding of the meaning of the problem in the larger sociocultural context further adds to the treatment efficacy.

Some groups are homogeneous, specializing in the treatment of people who share a common clinical problem (e.g., bulimia, social phobia, alcoholism), whereas other groups are heterogeneous, with patients experiencing a wide range of concerns and diagnoses. All of the major theoretical orientations and their integration can be used to structure a psychotherapy group and formulate its goals. About 20% of clinical psychologists conduct group therapy (Norcross et al., 2005).

Groups that are psychoeducational in orientation provide both useful information for patients experiencing similar problems and an opportunity for group support (e.g., sharing and expressing feelings and concerns and obtaining feedback from group members). Much like classroom instruction, information is provided, followed by group discussion and support (Figure 9.2). Many psychoeducational groups also include guest speakers on relevant topics. Most hospitals offer psychoeducational support groups for patients with diabetes, cancer, multiple sclerosis, heart disease, bipolar disorder, smoking, alcohol, obsessive-compulsive disorder, or other problems. Patients who share the same diagnosis meet together to learn how to manage their illness; they also share stories and give and receive support from each other. Group support not only is helpful for psychological health but has been associated with physical health and wellbeing among cancer patients and others (Forsyth & Corazzini, 2000; Spiegal, 1990, 1992; Hansen, Enright, Baskin, & Klatt, 2009). Recently, much attention has been given to forgiveness groups (Luskin, 2002; Hansen et al., 2009; Wade & Meyer, 2009). These groups include people who may experience both mental and physical health problems associated with chronic feelings of anger and bitterness associated with the inability to forgive themselves or others.

Other forms of group psychotherapy may focus on interpersonal skill development rather than psychoeducation. These groups generally provide a forum for support and peer feedback as well as for the development of interpersonal skills. Patients can gain new insights and practice new ways of interacting with others during group sessions. Group cohesion and a sense of hope often

Photo: Robert E. Daemmrich, Tony Stone Images, New York, Inc.

Figure 9.2

School-based discussion group among adolescents.

Case Study: James Experiences Bipolar Disorder (Individual Psychotherapy)

James is a 55-year-old biracial (Hawaiian and Caucasian) executive who lives alone following the death of his wife seven years ago. He has one adult daughter who has a family of her own.

Presenting Problem: James presents in a manic stage of bipolar disorder, having had a number of previous episodes. James's maternal uncle and grandfather also had bipolar illness. This episode involved James discontinuing his lithium use, traveling to Los Angeles in the hopes of becoming an actor, spending thousands of dollars on extravagant merchandise, and finally being arrested for drunk and disorderly conduct at a nightclub. James was hospitalized in an inpatient unit briefly and is now seeking outpatient treatment.

Key Biopsychosocial Factors:

Biological: There is a family (genetic) history of bipolar disorder as well as research supporting a biological basis of bipolar disorder. Medication is an essential treatment component.

Psychological: James's lack of compliance with his lithium regimen, denial regarding chronicity of his bipolar disorder, enjoyment of the manic high, need for control and independence, emotional losses pertaining to wife's death, and a severe chronic psychiatric condition all play a role in his illness.

Social: Family and cultural traditions that (in James's family) distrust Western medicine and cultural and general social isolation also are likely to impact his illness.

Treatment Goals and Plan: James requires medication management in addition to individual therapy in order to achieve several immediate and long-term goals. After an initial consultation and assessment period with James, the following treatment goals were determined. First, James will seek to work through the various impediments to his reliable use of lithium medication. These involve not only his need to be in control and not dependent on drugs (or others), but his family of origin's negative feelings about Western medicine. Second, James finds that when he becomes depressed, he longs for the "high" associated with mania. Therefore, the causes of his depression will be determined as well as improved coping skills. Third, James is lonely, misses his wife, and feels isolated from the Hawaiian heritage he cherishes. Thus, treatment will also address his interpersonal, social, and cultural needs.

The treatment plan involves the following components:

1. Collaboration with James's physician regarding his lithium regimen.
2. Behavioral contracting, which involves James's commitment to maintain his lithium regimen for at least the first six weeks of psychotherapy.
3. Exploratory work to understand James's disdain for dependence and impediments to developing a more satisfying interpersonal life.
4. Psychoeducational materials regarding bipolar illness, lithium, and traditional Hawaiian healing techniques and rituals to aid James in understanding the similarities, differences, and potential virtues and liabilities of both traditions.
5. Problem solving regarding increasing social contacts and cultural identification.
6. Developing improved awareness and skills for combating depression and curtailing future manic episodes.
7. Examination of the transference relationship between James and his psychologist to better understand James's interpersonal issues as well as his need for control and independence.

Case Study (Continued)

This case example illustrates how personality and culture impact compliance with medical regimens such as medication, and the need to work through a variety of intrapsychic and social issues in managing a major psychiatric problem such as bipolar illness. The treatment by necessity is multidimensional and mindful of the biopsychosocial influences on human functioning.

---

emerges through these sessions. Patients frequently feel better knowing that they are not alone and that others, like them, struggle with similar issues and concerns. Advice, suggestions, and general feedback from peer group members can often be more powerful than those provided by the group leader(s). Table 9.1 provides a list of **curative factors** associated with group psychotherapy.

Children's groups can be helpful for children having difficulty with socialization. Those who experience problems such as attention deficit hyperactivity disorder, perva-

sive developmental disorders, social phobia, and anxiety can often benefit from regular group psychotherapy. Children experiencing parental divorce, sexual abuse, or chronic illness also benefit from being with other children who share similar concerns and experiences. Groups for young children tend to have fewer verbal activities such as talking and usually include play, art, and other activities. Peer interactions, support, and feedback can be useful in all of these group activities to improve self-esteem, social skills, and general interpersonal functioning.

Table 9.1   **Curative Factors in Group Psychotherapy (Yalom, 1985)**

Imparting information:	Advice and suggestions offered by group members and leaders.
Instilling hope:	Others learning and dealing with concerns enhances hope.
Universality:	Others share same problems and concerns.
Altruism:	Helping others enhances self-esteem and confidence.
Interpersonal learning:	Learning from others in open and honest manner.
Corrective recapitulation of the Group often takes on a family-like quality. New ways of primary family:	interacting with others helps to improve ways of dealing with others.
Catharsis:	Expressing emotions in a safe and trusting manner.
Group cohesion:	Feeling connected and close to the group.
Development of socializing techniques:	Group provides chance to develop and improve social skills.
Imitative behavior:	Group members learning by observing and modeling other group members as well as the group leader.
Existential factors:	Group members learn about meaning in life, that life is not always as you plan, and that feelings of loneliness are common.

Couples Psychotherapy

Couples psychotherapy is often useful for those experiencing marital or couples discord. Rather than meeting with one person to discuss problems in the relationship, both parties meet with the psychologist to work on *in vivo* issues pertaining specifically to the relationship (e.g., communication problems, sexual concerns, commitment issues; see Figure 9.3). Couples therapy includes unmarried as well as married partners and heterosexual as well as homosexual partners. There are as many approaches to couples psychotherapy as there are to individual psychotherapy; however, the focus is usually on improved communication and problem-solving strategies. About 55% of clinical psychologists do couples or marital psychotherapy (Norcross et al., 2005).

Family Therapy

Family psychotherapy involves the entire family—parents and children, and sometimes also grandparents, aunts and uncles, or various subsets of the family (e.g., mother-and-child dyad or pair). There are numerous approaches and perspectives to family psychotherapy. Like couples psychotherapy, the goals of family psychotherapy often include improving both communication between family members and problem-solving strategies. There is often an "identified patient" (e.g., an adolescent who is acting out), yet treatment focuses on how each family member is contributing to the maintenance of disharmony within the entire family system. About 39% of clinical psychologists are involved with family therapy (Norcross et al., 2005).

Photo: Judy S. Gelles, Stock, Boston

Figure 9.3

A marriage therapy session.

Highlight of a Contemporary Clinical Psychologist

John C. Norcross, PhD

Photo: Courtesy John
C. Norcross

Dr. Norcross combines a full-time academic career with a part-time private practice. He is also president of the APA Division of Clinical Psychology and edits the *Journal of Clinical Psychology: In Session* (Wiley/Blackwell).

Birth Date: August 13, 1957

College: Rutgers University (BA, Psychology), 1980

Graduate Program: University of Rhode Island (MA, PhD, Clinical Psychology), 1984

Clinical Internship: Brown University School of Medicine

Current Job: Distinguished University Fellow and Professor of Psychology, University of Scranton; private practice (part-time); journal editor (part-time)

Pros and Cons of Being a Clinical Psychologist:

Pros: "(1) Diversity of professional activities (e.g., teaching, psychotherapy, research, supervision); (2) enhancing the life functioning and satisfaction of fellow humans (i.e., making a difference); and (3) combining the best of science and humanism ('thinking with the mind of a scientist and feeling with the heart of the humanist,' as I like to say)."

Cons: "The only serious con that comes to mind is that it can be quite exhausting at times."

Future of Clinical Psychology: "Innovation and expansion will define our future. Innovation in designing and researching new, evidence-based treatments, tests, and preventions; expansion into new areas and populations, such as health psychology, prescription privileges, and primary care. Psychotherapy will come of age by customizing the treatment methods and relationship stances to the unique needs of the individual client. Psychotherapy integration will become the predominant model."

What do you think will be the major changes in psychotherapy practice during the next decade? "Most attempts to predict the future fail either because they are the author's magical wish fulfillments or because they are based on one individual's limited perspective. For these reasons, my colleagues and I conducted a Delphi poll of 62 psychotherapy experts to predict psychotherapy trends in the next decade. The future will appear more cognitive-behavioral, culture-sensitive, and eclectic/integrative in terms of theories. Directive, self-change, and technological interventions will be in the ascendancy. Master's-level psychotherapists along with Web-based therapy services will flourish. Forecast scenarios with the highest likelihood center on the expansion of evidence-based therapy, practice guidelines, behavioral medicine, and pharmacotherapy."

How do you think integrative approaches will evolve in the foreseeable future?
"Integrative therapies will evolve in at least three directions. First, integration/eclecticism-psychotherapy will continue to be the most popular orientation among practitioners. Practically all psychotherapists now recognize the limitations of using any single theoretical orientation for all clients and appreciate the superior effectiveness of different treatments for some clients and particular disorders. Second, psychotherapy integration will be increasingly taught in graduate school. In place of learning different theories and then pledging allegiance to one of them, students will learn evidence-based principles of change that cut across theories. For example, what are the best change principles and therapy relationships for a client wanting to reduce trauma symptoms or a client with impulse-control problems or someone who is undecided about his or her religious convictions? Different strokes for different folks—prescriptive treatments—will be standard fare. And third, the definition of integration will expand—no longer only a blending of different theories, but now a synthesis of behavior change methods: psychotherapy, self-help, medication, exercise, technology, meditation, religion, and so on. Integrative approaches will increase the bandwidth of how people change and grow."

Typical Schedule:

8:00	Conference call with Board of Directors of the APA Division of Clinical Psychology
9:00	Office hour at university.
10:00–12:00	Teach class—Clinical Psychology (lecture on psychotherapy integration).
12:00	Meet with research assistants concerning a large survey of APA-approved doctoral programs.
1:00	Clinical supervision with intern.
2:00	Play tennis or racquetball.
3:00	Travel to my private practice; paperwork.
4:00	Individual psychotherapy with 50-year-old Latino social worker with couple difficulties and occupational stress.
5:00	Individual psychotherapy with 32-year-old Italian American woman coping with the death of her only young child.
6:00	Individual and family therapy with 18-year-old man suffering from ADHD.
7:00	Couple therapy session with Caucasian couple in their fifties regarding marital problems associated with an extramarital affair.

Nonpsychotherapy Approaches to Treatment: Biological and Social Interventions

Although clinical psychologists primarily rely on psychotherapy utilizing models (see Chapter 4) to treat difficulties, nonpsychotherapy interventions are also frequently used. Nonpsychotherapy interventions may include biological interventions such as the use of psychotropic medication, electroconvulsive therapy (ECT), and biofeedback or social interventions such as large-scale community education programs, structured residential communities (e.g., halfway houses), and various types of prevention programs. Nonpsychotherapy treatment and prevention interventions may be used in addition to psychotherapy or without psychotherapy. For example, a patient may routinely take an antidepressant medication such as Prozac or an antianxiety agent such as Xanax with or without participating in psychotherapy. The medications might be provided by a trained mental health professional such as a psychiatrist or by someone with minimal mental health training such as an internal medicine or family practice physician. A clinician might use biofeedback with or without psychotherapy to treat a range of problems such as anxiety, phobia, headaches, or irritable

SPOTLIGHT

Women and Depression

It is estimated that about seven million women in the United States experience clinical depression, which is about twice the rate found among men (Nolen-Hoeksema, 2002; Nolen-Hoeksema & Hilt, 2008; Nolen-Hoeksema & Puryear Keita, 2003; Schwartzman & Glaus, 2000). This pattern of more frequent depression among women relative to men has been found across different countries, most ethnic groups, and various age groups starting during the teen years (Nolen-Hoeksema, 2002; Nolen-Hoeksema & Hilt, 2008). This difference is found even when controlling for a number of variables such as willingness to admit to problems and concerns, hormonal activity, socioeconomic status, and so forth (Coiro, 2001; Eamon & Zuehl, 2001; Nolen-Hoeksema & Hilt, 2008). Some researchers have suggested that part of the problem with female teen onset of depression is related to society expectations for beauty and success with more conflictual and mixed society expectations for girls relative to boys (C. Hayward, Gotlib, Schraedley, & Litt, 1999). Females are more likely to be pressured to look model-like, be feminine, yet be achievement oriented and successful. Some of the risk factors associated with depression among women include low socioeconomic status, gender discrimination, posttraumatic stress, sexual and physical abuse, and conflicts about role and society expectations, among other factors (Eamon & Zuehl, 2001; Nolen-Hoeksema & Hilt, 2008; D. Sue & Sue, 2003, 2008). Treatment is challenging because most women who experience depression will likely not seek treatment and they are much more likely to both consider and attempt suicide than men (Welch, 2001).

bowel syndrome. Finally, a patient may enroll in a halfway house for substance abuse with or without individual, family, or group psychotherapy.

Biological Interventions

Currently psychologists in most states are unable to provide invasive biological or medical interventions such as prescribing psychotropic medications or using ECT. However, psychologists have limited prescription privileges in several locations (i.e., New Mexico, Louisiana, Guam, the military), thereby allowing them to provide medications for their patients without physician supervision (Beutler, 2002; Read, Larsen, & Robinson, 2009). (This issue will be discussed in more detail in Chapter 14.)

Although most psychologists at present cannot prescribe medication and thus must work with physician colleagues in treating patients using these medications, clinical psychologists need at least a basic understanding of commonly used psychotropic medications to best serve their clients. They must be familiar with medications and their side effects and know when to refer a patient to a physician for a medication evaluation or treatment.

The most common classes of medications used in psychiatric treatment include antidepressant, antianxiety, and antipsychotic agents (American Psychiatric Association, 2000; Julien, 2007; Valenstein, 2002). However, psychostimulants and lithium are two other types of medication used for specific clinical problems. Antidepressant medication

Case Study: Inpatient Group Psychotherapy

Patients hospitalized on an inpatient medical/psychiatric unit participate in daily group psychotherapy. The participants experience both medical and psychiatric problems such as eating disorders, chronic pain disorders, alcohol abuse and dependence, colitis, and Alzheimer's disease. Many of the patients have experienced depression, anxiety, and/or personality disorder as well. In addition to comprehensive individual medical and psychiatric treatment, patients attend psychoeducational groups (e.g., "How to Manage Your Illness"), as well as the psychotherapy group sessions conducted by a psychologist and a nurse. Patients are generally hospitalized for several days or weeks, and individuals are admitted to and discharged from the unit several times each day. Therefore, the composition of the psychotherapy group changes almost daily.

The purpose of the group is to encourage patients to discuss feelings and concerns in a safe and trusting environment. The group is highly structured, provides support, and emphasizes a "here-and-now" perspective. Structure, such as starting and ending the session on time, providing an introduction to the group so that all group members understand what can be expected from the group experience, introducing all members, and trying to elicit feelings and reflections from all members during the course of the session is provided to ensure that the group runs smoothly and that all patients have a positive group experience. Support is necessary to create a comfortable, accepting, and nonjudgmental environment. The "here and now" helps each group member stay focused on the present rather than revealing long stories about the past or worries about the future.

The following patients attended one of these actual inpatient group sessions:

- Anna is a 58-year-old Latino woman who is hospitalized with obesity, sleep apnea, and depression. Her internal medicine physician is concerned that her obesity is making her sleep apnea (episodes of breathing cessation while asleep) much worse and that since she is depressed, she is unwilling to attempt to lose weight to minimize her health risks. In fact, Anna reports that she is very unhappy about family stress and conflicts and would prefer to die in her sleep. She hopes that her sleep apnea will kill her without pain.
- Beth is a 19-year-old Caucasian college student with severe anorexia nervosa. She currently weighs 83 pounds and is 5' 7" tall. She is also obsessive-compulsive and depressed. She refuses to gain weight and had to withdraw from her classes due to her recent hospitalization.
- Carl is a 34-year-old African American with severe colitis. He is highly anxious and experiences several phobias. He has recently had surgery for colon cancer as well. His doctors do not think that he will live for more than a few years.
- Diane is a 43-year-old Caucasian woman who is dependent on alcohol, Valium, and several pain medications. She has been hospitalized many times during suicidal episodes as well as for detoxification. She is also diagnosed with borderline personality disorder and major depression. She was severely sexually abused as a child by her father and is currently married to a man who physically abuses her.
- Esther is an 84-year-old African American who is depressed, has Alzheimer's disease, and recently had hip-replacement surgery. She is concerned that she must leave her own home and enter a nursing home when she is discharged from the hospital. She would like to stay hospitalized as long as possible to delay her inevitable move to the nursing home.

(continued)

Case Study (Continued)

- Fran is a 34-year-old Asian American married woman who has a somatization disorder. While she has no known medical problems, she has numerous medical symptoms and complaints. She left her work on disability several years ago, and her husband and two children take turns caring for her. She complains that she can't walk well, move her arms, or see very well. She is also diagnosed with a histrionic personality disorder. She is especially angry because she feels that all the doctors and nurses think her problems are "all in her head." She has had over 20 hospitalizations for these symptoms.

An excerpt from a group session follows:

Psychologist: Welcome to the group. We meet every day at 11:00 A.M. for one hour. The purpose of the group is to talk about feelings and issues in the moment. Anger, sadness, anxiety, interpersonal conflicts are, for example, typical topics that we discuss. We try to avoid talking about things in the past or future problems and concerns because we don't feel that we can be very helpful on these topics within our limited amount of time and given the number of people that participate in the group. Let's quickly go around the room and introduce ourselves and then let us go around a second time and state what topic or agenda you would like to talk about in our group today. My name is Dr. Gerard and I am a psychologist on the unit.

(Group members introduce themselves and then each states what his or her topic or agenda is for the day.)

Anna: I really have nothing to say today.

Psychologist: Anna, you seemed angry when you said that. Are you feeling angry today?

Anna: Yes, I guess I am. I want to just go home. I'm sick of being locked up here. My doctor tells me that he thinks I should stay for at least another 4 days, but I don't think it is doing me any good.

Psychologist: Perhaps discussing your feelings of anger and frustration would be useful in the group today.

Anna: Okay, I guess so. I suppose it can't hurt since I'm here anyway.

Psychologist: Okay, Anna, we'll get back to that issue. Beth, how about you?

Beth: I'm feeling very anxious and guilty today. I can't believe I had to drop out of school this term. I'll never graduate with my class and maybe never graduate at all. I feel like a total failure.

Psychologist: Thanks Beth, we'll come back to you. Carl?

Carl: I feel down, too. I feel crummy. Angry, too. I'm sick of being sick all the time. It stinks. I wish I didn't have to deal with this.

Diane: I'm okay today. I feel pretty good, actually. I'm leaving the hospital later today and feel that I've made some good progress this time. I'll miss Beth, we've had some good talks since I've been here. I hope you'll stay in touch. I'm a bit anxious about how I'll do outside of the hospital, but I'm pretty excited about leaving. I've been here long enough.

Psychologist: We'll be sure to say our goodbyes and best wishes to you, Diane, before the group ends today.

Esther: I'm okay. I don't have anything to say.

Psychologist: How are you feeling right now, in the moment?

Esther: Okay, nothing really.

Psychologist: Okay, let us know, however, if something comes up for you and we'll check in with you as well.

Fran: I think this is all B.S. I'm sick of all this talk, talk, talk. I need answers to my medical problems and everyone around here wants me to talk about my feelings. I can't believe I even agreed to be admitted here. What a mistake. There is no way I'd do this again.

Psychologist: You sound pretty angry, Fran. Perhaps we could talk about that in the group today.

Fran: See what I mean? Talk, talk, talk. I don't know. I'm angry for sure but I don't think talking will help much.

Case Study (Continued)

Psychologist: I hope that you'll try, Fran. While talking may not cure any of the medical problems that you experience, perhaps it will help you to feel better. Now that we've heard from everyone, let's try to work through the issues that were brought up in the group today. Anna and Fran are feeling pretty angry today, while Carl says that he's feeling down and Beth is feeling angry and guilty. Esther is doing okay and doesn't have an agenda in the moment. Let's do the best we can to talk about each agenda. Let's start with Anna and Fran's anger.

This brief excerpt from an inpatient group psychotherapy session illustrates several key themes. First, this particular psychotherapy is one part of a complex, multidimensional treatment program that utilizes biological, psychological, and social interventions and various modalities during this inpatient phase of treatment. Second, it is clear from even these brief summaries of each patient's problems that clinical cases are usually highly complex and involved. Finally, the psychologist in this group provides structure, support, and clarification in an effort to assist patients in dealing with their immediate emotional states.

---

is usually classified in one of three categories. The first category includes the selective serotonin reuptake inhibitors (SSRIs) such as Prozac, Zoloft, and Paxil. Additionally, a new subclass of medications called the serotonin and norepinephrine reuptake inhibitors (SNRIs), such as Effexor, Cymbalta, and Pristiq, have become available and popular in recent years (Julien, 2007; Stahl, 2002). The second class includes the tricyclics, such as Elavil, Tofranil, and Anafranil. The third class includes the monoamine oxidase inhibitors (MAOIs), such as Parnate and Nardil. Antianxiety medications usually include the benzodiazepines, such as Xanax, Valium, and Ativan. Antipsychotic medications (often called neuroleptics) include older or first-generation medications such as Haldol, Mellaril, and Thorazine and second-generation or atypical medications such as Risperdal, Zyprexa, and Seroquel. Psychostimulants such as Ritalin and Dexedrine are used to increase attention and concentration among children with attention-deficit and/or hyperactivity problems (Castle, Aubert, Verbrugge, Khalid, & Epstein, 2007; Klein, 1995). Finally, lithium (lithium chloride) as well as anticonvulsant medications (e.g., Depakote, Neurontin, Tegretol) are used

to treat bipolar disorder (commonly known as manic-depression; Julien, 2007).

Each medication has advantages and disadvantages (Castle et al., 2007; Julien, 2007; Klein, 1995; Kramer, 1993; Nemeroff & Schatzberg, 2007; Valenstein, 2002). Some medications work well for some people but not for others, even if they share the same diagnosis. Some people have negative reactions to some medications while others do not. Although helping to relieve symptoms such as anxiety, depression, and psychotic thinking, many medications have undesirable side effects (e.g., dry mouth, weight gain, constipation, diarrhea, physical and/or psychological addiction). Some medications (e.g., MAO inhibitors) cannot be taken with certain foods (e.g., beer, wine, chocolate). Some are often extremely dangerous if used in suicide attempts (e.g., Valium). Some can be abused as well. Research and development by pharmaceutical companies and other researchers work toward improved medications that are safe and effective and have minimal negative side effects. Much attention has been given to the selective serotonin reuptake inhibitors such as Prozac in recent years (Julien, 2007). Many claim that Prozac is more effective than the other classes of antidepressant medications

Case Study: Hans and Marta Experience Severe Marital Discord (Couples Therapy)

Hans and Marta, a Caucasian couple of Austrian descent, have been married for two years, and each have two children from their previous marriages currently living in the home. They also have an infant daughter of their own. Thus, this blended family combines five children and the challenges of relating to involved ex-spouses. Hans is employed as a contractor and Marta does not work outside of her considerable duties within the home.

Presenting Problem: Hans and Marta report frequent fighting and very low marital satisfaction. Hans is reportedly physically abusive of Marta, and a number of times has struck one of the children. Marta is therefore afraid to confront Hans about her unhappiness and has been withdrawn and disinterested in sex. Hans reports that Marta ignores him, is focused only on the children, and sometimes he just "loses it." Hans and Marta are asking for help with the fighting, the physical abuse, and the extremely low level of positive marital interaction.

Key Biopsychosocial Factors:

Biological: Hans's father was physically abusive, which may represent a biological or an environmental predisposition to violence. Marta gave birth only six months ago and is still resuming her normal hormonal and physical functioning. The extent of the physical abuse needs to be assessed in terms of the health of Marta and the children, and all family members protected from further violence.

Psychological: Marta is a battered woman and lives in constant fear for her own and her children's safety. She is attached to Hans and is unable to separate from him or assert her needs in the face of his violence. Hans is a classic batterer in the sense that he denies responsibility for the abuse, blames Marta for his behavior, and states that if she were only more loving and available he would not need to resort to such anger.

Social: The larger sociocultural context for violence is well established in that we live in a violent society that does not adequately protect victims or treat perpetrators. Hans's own abuse at the hands of his father may have imparted this tendency through social learning or identification with the aggressor.

Marta may feel dependent upon Hans and afraid to separate due to her fear that she may be unable to adequately house, clothe, and feed her children, and perhaps even lose custody.

Treatment Goals and Plan: The prevailing goal of treatment must be the physical safety of Marta and her children. Given that physical abuse of the children is being reported, the psychologist is legally and ethically mandated to make a report to Child Protective Services. If the couple are willing to remain in treatment in spite of this report, several goals will include (1) cessation of all physical violence within the home, (2) development of alternative means of expressing and working through anger and frustration, (3) insight into the origins and triggers of violence, and (4) improved capacity for communication and intimacy.

The treatment plan will include:

1. Individual therapy for Hans to learn to control his temper and violence and for Marta to develop increased autonomy, assertiveness, and a plan of action in the face of future violence.
2. Develop alternative behavioral strategies for dealing with anger and create a contract between Hans and Marta for taking alternative steps to violence.

Case Study (Continued)

3. Family-of-origin work to understand the roots of violence for Hans and factors contributing to Marta's relationship to an abusive man.

4. Develop opportunities for the couple to engage in some mutually positive and pleasurable activities.

5. Locate social services and shelters for battered women.

6. Group therapy for Hans with other men who are abusive.

7. Collaboration with the individual psychologists, group therapist, family physician, child therapists, and social services worker monitoring abuse within the home.

This couple's therapy case illustrates the high stakes and complex layers of relational problems. The outcome of this case, like most others, will depend largely on the cooperation and motivation of Hans and Marta to acknowledge their serious difficulties and take the necessary steps toward improvement. Various modalities, techniques, and social and medical elements also come into play in this complex yet all-too-common situation.

SPOTLIGHT

Evidence-Based Practice

As in many areas of health care and education, more emphasis has been placed in recent years on demonstrating that interventions actually work. In the past, psychologists and other mental health professionals could follow their own views about what worked and didn't work in psychotherapy generally rooted in their theoretical orientation or treatment philosophy (e.g., psychodynamic, behavioral, humanistic). However, the movement to use empirically validated or supported treatments with treatment manuals that were found to be effective based on clinical research trials became popular in the late 1990s and early 2000s. Yet, controversy existed between researchers and clinicians such that researchers generally were highly supportive of manualized treatments while clinicians were skeptical. This topic will be discussed in further detail in Chapter 14. The American Psychological Association (2006) put together a Task Force to deal with these issues and published a policy statement in 2006 that highlighted the importance of evidence-based practice. Evidence-based practice takes into consideration research findings to inform clinical practice but also recognizes the wisdom of clinical experience and the complexity of applying research findings to actual clinical patients.

(i.e., tricyclics and MAO Inhibitors) without so many adverse side effects (Julien, 2007). Importantly, medication is generally prescribed in the context of a therapeutic relationship, and research supports the combined efficacy.

The positive effects of medication on disorders such as depression, anxiety, and schizophrenia do not imply that these disorders are strictly a biological problem (Beck & Alford, 2009; Castle et al., 2007; Cuipers

Case Study: The Kaplans Experience a Family Death and a Suicide Attempt in the Family (Family Therapy)

The Kaplan family consists of Mr. Kaplan and his 16-year-old son David and 13-year-old daughter Barbara. Mrs. Kaplan died one year ago after a long battle with lung cancer. The Kaplans live in an urban setting in a large city.

Presenting Problems: The Kaplans were referred for family therapy by David's individual psychologist, who is treating David following a serious suicide attempt. This psychologist feels that family therapy is indicated in order to address issues of unresolved grief, anger, parenting, and communication.

As a family, the Kaplans report that since Mrs. Kaplan's death, the family has been in extreme turmoil. Mrs. Kaplan had always assumed the primary parenting and housekeeping duties, while Mr. Kaplan worked long hours as a city planner. David has been performing poorly in school, experimenting with drugs, and withdrawing from his home. Barbara has been depressed, anxious, and both clingy and demanding with her father. Mr. Kaplan is depressed, overwhelmed, and frequently irritable with the children. All agreed that the family is in crisis, or as David put it: "Everything sucks."

Key Biopsychosocial Factors:

Biological: There is no known family history of psychiatric problems such as depression. Family members have not regulated well in the wake of their loss, and are eating and sleeping poorly.

Psychological: The Kaplans experience an ongoing grief reaction; depression in the wake of loss, associated anger and irritability, acting out of emotional distress; and reworking of attachments, roles, and structure within the family.

Social: The Kaplan children have experienced the loss of their mother as the keeper of family and religious traditions and rituals as well as changes in their social network, which was maintained by their mother.

Treatment Goals and Plan: The Kaplans agree to the following treatment goals in the context of family therapy: (1) Discuss each member's feelings regarding the loss of Mrs. Kaplan, (2) learn how these feelings impact current relationships within the family, and (3) figure out how to reorganize the household to reduce the present chaos and reclaim a sense of cohesion, stability, and organization.

The treatment plan involves the following components:

1. During each session, each member will discuss their feelings of grief, sadness, anger, confusion, and so forth regarding the untimely loss of Mrs. Kaplan and refer to one interaction with another family member where these feelings interfered (e.g., lashed out at another due to anger at loss, was afraid to be alone because of fear of feeling overwhelmingly sad).
2. Problem solving will be utilized to develop plans for carrying out household tasks, resuming important rituals and traditions, redefining roles, and, in a sense, creating a new household structure.
3. Consultation with David's psychologist with David and his father's signed consent in order to keep abreast of important developments in both therapies.

This case illustrates the use of family therapy to alter systemic factors potentially responsible for generating symptoms and problems. Collaboration between the two treating psychologists will be important as will monitoring of family members' biological, psychological, and social functioning through the course of treatment.

et al., 2007; Glasser, 2003; Horgan, 1996). Again a biopsychosocial view is needed to understand and treat these and other disorders. Many people respond positively to medication due to a placebo effect, since many believe that the medication will help them and expectation therefore ensures that it does. Many people also do not respond well to psychotropic medications. It has been estimated that about two-thirds of people using antidepressant medications experience no improvement or responded equally well to a placebo drug (Padesky & Greenberger, 1995). Although medications such as Prozac are enormously popular with more than 30 million people taking the drug (Valenstein, 2002), research has not demonstrated that Prozac is more effective than psychotherapy in treating depression (*Consumer Reports,* 1995; Glasser, 2003; Horgan, 1996; Seligman, 1995). Biofeedback (N. Miller, 1969; Schwartz & Beatty, 1977) is another example of a nonpsychotherapy biological approach to treatment.

Biofeedback provides patients with information concerning their physiological arousal as measured by heart rate, blood pressure, muscle tension, respiration, sweating, and body temperature. Some or all of these physiological states are measured during office or home sessions. Patients are asked to lower their level of arousal through the use of relaxation, imagery, prayer, or any other technique that works for them. Feedback is provided by visual or auditory means such as tones or computer graphics. Unlike psychotropic medication, biofeedback is noninvasive, and psychologists can legally and ethically use it with their patients as long as they have adequate training and experience with the technique.

Social Interventions

Social and community interventions and programs often seek to improve psychological, interpersonal, social, and occupational functioning. Clinical psychologists frequently are involved with the design, implementation, and evaluation of these programs. They usually employ a psychoeducational approach, providing education, skill-building training, and support for those at risk for or already struggling with a significant psychiatric, medical, or other problem(s).

Community programs generally attempt to help at-risk persons to prevent the development of serious problems or to minimize the impact of an already present problem. The programs are usually categorized as primary, secondary, or tertiary. Primary prevention programs seek to prevent problems from developing through the use of education. For example, Head Start is a program developed to give young children from disadvantaged homes an opportunity to attend preschool without charge. The goal was to give these children a head start in school and allow their parents the opportunity to work or obtain further education to improve their socioeconomic status and quality of life. Primary prevention programs have been developed to help teen mothers learn child care and other skills (Abma & Mott, 1991). Other programs have been designed to teach school children how to minimize unsafe and high-risk sexual behavior (Howard & McCabe, 1990).

Secondary prevention programs attempt to intervene early during the course of problems to minimize the development of more serious problems. For example, people arrested for driving under the influence of alcohol (DUIs) are often offered the opportunity to attend a training program about substance abuse in order to avoid the loss of their driver's license. The goal of the program is to educate first-time offenders about the dangers of driving under the influence of drugs, thereby helping to prevent future incidents of drunk driving. Similar programs have been developed for adolescents arrested for various offenses and for people who seek the services of prostitutes. Secondary prevention might also involve outreach to homebound elderly individuals to mitigate loneliness and provide social and intellectual stimulation.

Tertiary prevention programs endeavor to minimize the impact of serious psychiatric or other problem(s). They are basically the same as other treatments but usually refer to

Social Interventions: International Clinical Psychology in South Africa

Apartheid in South Africa ended in 1994, yet the implications of many years of racial tensions, violence, and prejudice live on. Clinical psychologists in the United States and South Africa have teamed up to help former soldiers and other combatants to develop job skills and receive psychosocial support as they adjust to the remarkable transformations in South Africa. These ex-combatants have a 66% unemployment rate, which is about twice the national average. They generally are about 40 years old and joined liberation forces aiming to create more democracy in South Africa while they were teenagers (Buhlungu, Daniel, Southall, & Lutchman, 2007). Now that South Africa has become more democratic, their skills and jobs are no longer needed. The Tswelopele project (meaning, "we will go forward together") helps these ex-combatants develop job skills and better job communication and attitudes as well as better behavioral and social skills. They are encouraged to discuss their past traumas in group settings as well. The project uses clinical psychology and other disciplines to best help these men and women transition to a more productive and satisfying life in the new South Africa (Buhlungu et al., 2007).

community-based interventions. For example, halfway houses are designed to help patients recently released from hospitals, drug treatment programs, or prisons. They allow patients to live and work in the community and still receive professional supervision and skill-building training. They help transition patients from the highly structured hospital, drug treatment, or prison setting back to the community. Halfway houses typically specialize in certain populations such as adolescents or former convicts, or in certain problems such as alcohol and drug dependence, schizophrenia, or physical disabilities. Other tertiary prevention programs offer education and support for those with serious illnesses. The American Cancer Society, along with other organizations, offers group support programs to help those coping with terminal or other forms of cancer. Alcoholics Anonymous (AA) is a well-known example of a tertiary prevention program. AA started in 1935 and provides over 100,000 support groups in about 100 countries around the globe for over 2 million

AA members (Alcoholics Anonymous, 2009). AA uses a 12-step treatment approach that involves confidential group support for alcoholics. AA members report a very high degree of satisfaction with the program (*Consumer Reports*, 1998, and some research suggests that participation in AA is generally effective (e.g., Finney & Moos, 1991; Humphreys & Moos, 2007; Kaskutas, 2009), although the research is not completely conclusive (Kaskutas, 2009).

Contemporary Case, Contemporary Treatment

Increasingly, psychologists are confronted with extremely "involved" cases, referring to the multidimensional complexities encountered in a typical caseload. Individuals are rarely "simple," and neither can treatment be simple or unidimensional. The following case illustrates this complexity and the siren call to integration in contemporary clinical psychology.

Media Violence

Much has been published in the popular press and elsewhere about the relationship between media violence and aggression in children and adolescents (Huesmann, Moise-Titus, Podolski, & Eron, 2003; Murray, 2008). Almost all homes in the United States have media access via television, DVD players, video game equipment, and personal computers (Federal Trade Commission, 2000). The average American child spends over 40 hours per week engaged with television, video-games, computers, or other media (Murray, 2008).

Sadly, the majority of television programming contains violent episodes with more and more violence portrayed in movies and accessible through computers (Huesmann et al., 2003; Murray, 2008). Research over the years has clearly demonstrated in a variety of cross-sectional and longitudinal studies that exposure to violence in the media is correlated with acting violent in the real world (Bushman & Anderson, 2001; Murray, 2008). In fact, the research evidence is so strong that six major professional organizations, including the American Psychological Association (APA), the American Psychiatric Association, and the American Academy of Pediatrics, among others, issued a joint statement in July 2000 warning of the hazards of allowing children to be exposed to media violence, stating that there is strong evidence of a causal link between exposure to media violence and aggressive behavior among children (Johnson, 2003). The effect size of this relationship is reported to be about 0.30, which represents a larger effect than the relationship between condom use and HIV infection, lead exposure and IQ scores, the use of the nicotine patch and smoking cessation, doing homework and academic achievement, and a variety of other well-known correlational relationships (Bushman & Anderson, 2001). Tragically, as more and more children are exposed to violence in the media, current research tells us that we can expect increasing amounts of aggression and violence among young people.

Clinical psychologists are involved in the media violence and aggression issue from a number of different perspectives. These include conducting research in this area, helping parents and children maintain activities that minimize violence exposure, lobbying Congress and other state and federal policymakers to take this research and relationship seriously and enact legislation and policies that minimize exposure to media violence among at-risk youth, and working with children who experience aggressive problems associated with media violence exposure.

Case Study: Mako Experiences Anorexia Nervosa—Integration of Theories, Techniques, Modalities, and Biopsychosocial Factors (Contemporary Psychotherapy)

Mako is a 14-year-old Japanese female who has lived in the United States since age 7. She lives with her parents and younger brother. Mako's father is a businessman who commutes between Japan and the United States, utilizing a work visa for himself and his family. Mako is in the eighth grade in public school, and attends a Japanese school three afternoons each week to maintain her Japanese language skills. Mako and her brother are fluently bilingual; her parents have some difficulty conversing in English.

Presenting Problem: Mako has been diagnosed with anorexia nervosa, a disorder that commonly afflicts adolescent females with a relentless drive toward thinness. Mako is severely emaciated due to self-starvation and excessive exercise, and also evidences amenorrhea (cessation of menstrual periods), intense fear of gaining weight, extreme fatigue, social withdrawal, and depression. She has received both a medical and a neurological evaluation to rule out a primary medical basis for her weight loss, and was determined to be suffering from anorexia nervosa.

Key Biopsychosocial Factors:

Biological: Mako experiences life-threatening malnutrition and emaciation, low heart rate and blood pressure, as well as hormonal and electrolyte imbalances. Mako's malnutrition also contributes to impaired reasoning and severe fatigue.

Psychological: Mako is presently genuinely terrified of losing control over her eating and becoming overweight. Her perfectionism and desire to achieve correspond to a strong need for control, yet also to underlying fears of inadequacy in confronting the psychosocial and developmental challenges of adolescence. Depression, feelings of stigmatization, and loss of esteem are also relevant.

Social: Mako's family and cultural values emphasize cooperation, achievement, conformity, and minimal expression of emotion and opinion. Mako is also experiencing cultural conflict in seeking to maintain her dual Japanese and American identities. The generally American premium on expressiveness and individuality is in direct conflict with her Japanese family's value on calm acceptance and conformity to parents and social norms. Finally, media and culture in both the United States and Japan glorify standards of thinness and beauty for females.

Treatment Goals: (1) Assist Mako in resuming a healthy weight and healthy eating behavior, (2) address the underlying psychological, developmental, and familial basis for her anorexia nervosa, (3) assist the family in contending with this serious illness in the family, (4) assist Mako in resuming school and social activities.

Course of Treatment: Mako was initially hospitalized on an adolescent eating disorders unit in order to stabilize her medical condition and lay the foundation for outpatient treatment. During hospitalization, Mako was initially confined to bed, during which time she was medically monitored, given intravenous fluids and electrolytes, and given the option of tube-feeding or eating substantially on her own. She opted to eat on her own (anorexics are typically ravenously hungry), and made good progress with gradual reintroduction of food.

Once stabilized, Mako was integrated into the ward milieu, participating in group psychotherapy where she learned that she was not alone with anorexia and was able to hear the experiences of others at varying stages of recovery. Mako began individual psychotherapy with a psychologist on the unit,

Case Study (Continued)

and learned information about anorexia nervosa, the general course of treatment, and for the first time entertained the idea that her dieting was not only about fearing fat but perhaps had other deeper causes as well. Family sessions were also begun while on the unit, and the stress of her illness, her father's frequent absences, and the challenges of straddling two cultures discussed. A behavioral contract guided her way toward some moderate weight gain, and contingencies were spelled out for continuing this progress outside the hospital lest she need to be rehospitalized. Her inpatient psychologist assisted Mako in discharge planning by locating a Japanese American therapist with bilingual abilities, conferring with her physician, and arranging for her reintegration into both of her schools.

After discharge, Mako began individual therapy with occasional family sessions integrated into the treatment. While her physician monitored her weight and medical status and communicated this to her psychologist, Mako focused on the psychological, cultural, and family aspects of her life. The psychologist explored Mako's sense of anxiety and dependency regarding ensuing adolescence, and her trepidation regarding the pressure she felt from American peers to separate from family members and prematurely explore sexual behavior. Her desire to integrate with her friends at school and adopt their more outgoing, expressive, even bold manner was in conflict with her family's style of quiet acceptance, good manners, and respect for authority. Mako discussed her perfectionism and obsessiveness regarding both schoolwork and eating behavior and developed cognitive-behavioral strategies with her psychologist to assist with

decision making, thought stopping, and re-examining her attitudes and expectations. Finally, when Mako's depression did not remit with adequate weight gain, she was referred to a psychiatrist for a medication consult and responded positively to Prozac.

Mako's family was integral to the treatment. In family sessions, her concerns were discussed and she found her parents remarkably respectful and attentive to her feelings. Her parents were encouraged to support her autonomous decisions when they did not contradict their values, and allow her to take steps toward independence while learning that her parents would neither condemn nor abandon her. The family was able to openly discuss the challenges of dual American and Japanese identities as well as the stress of Mako's father's frequent absences.

Mako's treatment proceeded extremely smoothly relative to the often difficult courses in many cases of anorexia nervosa. Nevertheless, her individual therapy and medication treatment continued for three full years, as she gradually overcame her anorexia and developed significantly enhanced psychological, social, and family resources.

This case illustration exemplifies the necessity and utility of integrative strategies in treating complex problems. In a case such as anorexia nervosa, where the biological, psychological, and social features are so compelling, neglect of any one factor can seriously limit or even compromise the treatment. This case demonstrates the trend in contemporary psychotherapy to integrate theories, techniques, modalities, and biopsychosocial factors to best meet the comprehensive needs of the patient.

The Big Picture

Psychotherapy is one of the most common activities conducted by clinical psychologists and one that brings relief and tremendous assistance to many individuals and groups. Each patient, each psychologist, and each psychotherapy experience is unique. Psychotherapy has evolved over the years from several distinct theoretical perspectives to an integrative, evidence-based, and biopsychosocial endeavor. No longer can a psychologist maintain an isolated practice while conducting routine, rigid, and narrowly conceived treatment. Today, integration of theory, technique, modality, and biopsychosocial factors is the state-of-the-art and evidence-based standard to which psychologists aspire. The future of psychotherapy will attempt to use research and practice evidence-based supported intervention strategies that can be administered in a brief, cost-effective manner to maximize treatment effectiveness while minimizing costs and time.

Key Points

1. Of all the professional activities conducted by clinical psychologists, psychotherapy is probably the most well known. Psychotherapy involves consulting with a mental health professional in order to obtain assistance in changing feelings, thoughts, or behaviors that the patient or client experiences as problematic and distressing. Psychotherapy includes theories of human behavior as well as specific treatment techniques to impact the psychological and behavioral functioning of a person or persons.

2. There are many different types of goals that psychotherapy hopes to reach depending on the specific needs, interest, and concerns of all of the interested parties. Overall, psychotherapy ultimately hopes to improve the quality of life through self-understanding, behavior and lifestyle change, coping with problems, and/or enhancing relationships. Psychotherapy attempts to utilize what is known about

human behavior and apply that knowledge to help a particular person better deal with the issues that cause distress in an evidence-based manner.

3. There are numerous types of psychotherapy. Psychotherapy may include individual, couple, family, group, or combinations of different types of treatment.

4. All psychotherapy tends to include several common denominators or certain similarities. They all include a professional person or "expert" of varying degree, professional behavior, or manner, on the part of the psychologist, a professional setting where services are rendered, fees, and a schedule of sessions.

5. No matter what type or approach to psychotherapy a psychologist uses, most psychotherapy occurs in several stages. Generally, these include an initial consultation, assessment of the problem and situation, the development of treatment goals, the implementation of the treatment, an evaluation of the treatment, termination of treatment, and, perhaps, follow-up.

6. A biopsychosocial perspective suggests that psychotherapy consider biological, psychological, and social influences on behavior and behavior change. Although psychotherapy conducted by psychologists is usually a psychological and behavioral (rather than biological or social) intervention, the biological and social influences on behavior are generally assessed and discussed during psychotherapy.

Key Terms

Curative factors
Psychotherapy

For Reflection

1. How does psychotherapy differ from talking problems over with a friend or someone else you know?
2. What is psychotherapy?

3. What do most psychotherapies have in common?
4. Describe the stages of psychotherapy.
5. What are some of the biological approaches used to treat psychological disorders?
6. What are some of the social interventions used to treat psychological disorders?
7. How does psychotherapy differ from what is depicted in television and in films?

Real Students, Real Questions

1. I often wonder how much we take an "American" view toward the treatment of people with behavioral or emotional problems. How do other countries like France, China, South Africa, and so forth differ in their treatment approaches?
2. Is group therapy useful for most people? What are some instances when it would be counterproductive?
3. How do you know when you have completed psychotherapy? Does the therapist or patient end the relationship usually?
4. What kind of places offer therapy for those who can't afford it or don't have insurance that will pay for it?

5. How available are therapists to their patients via e-mail, cell phone, and so on?
6. Would a therapist "friend" a patient on Facebook?

Web Resources

http://www.surgeongeneral.gov/library/mentalhealth/home.html
See the Surgeon General's report on mental health issues.

www.ndmda.org
Learn more about depression and bipolar disorder by contacting the National Depressive and Manic Depressive Association.

www.bpdcentral.com
Learn more about borderline personality disorder.

www.cmhc.com/disorder
Learn more about psychological disorders.

Psychotherapeutic Issues

10
Chapter

While psychotherapy has been in existence for over 100 years and today enjoys society's acceptance and popularity, this common professional activity of clinical psychologists still remains shrouded in a certain degree of mystery. Many fundamental questions regarding psychotherapy are on the minds of its many consumers and students, and deserve direct attention. This chapter addresses 10 critical issues commonly heard about psychotherapy, beginning with the very basic ''Does psychotherapy work?''

Does Psychotherapy Work?

Patients, insurance carriers, psychologists, and other interested parties (i.e., significant others of patients, school personnel, courts, clergy) frequently ask important questions about the usefulness of psychotherapy. For example: Are the time, expense, and effort of psychotherapy warranted by its results? Are people likely to be better off after psychotherapy than before? What are the expected benefits of psychotherapy? Unfortunately, such questions are difficult to answer and may vary from individual to individual and treatment to treatment. Psychotherapy is a highly personalized experience that is impacted by the skills, interest, training, motivation, and personality of the psychotherapist and by the specific symptoms (e.g., etiology, duration, severity), motivation, personality, and resources of the patient. Furthermore, the unique therapist–patient interaction that emerges during psychotherapy as well as a wide range of nonspecific factors such as beliefs, attitudes, and expectations all play a role

279

in treatment outcome. Positive treatment outcome may be associated not only with the psychotherapy experience but also with the passage of time (i.e., "time heals all wounds"), among many other factors. Thus, no two psychotherapy experiences can be exactly alike. Two patients with very similar symptoms seeing the same psychotherapist may experience two very different psychotherapies. Psychotherapy may be helpful to one but not to the other. Although many efforts have been made to make psychotherapy a precise scientific enterprise through the emphasis on empirically supported treatments and the use of evidence-based practices, psychotherapy involves a human relationship between therapist and patient: No human relationship can be reduced to a completely precise science.

How can we investigate whether psychotherapy works? Merely asking patients whether they believe that the services were useful provides important but not sufficient data to answer this important question. Demand characteristics are likely to influence a patient's report that psychotherapy was or was not useful. The situation creates an environment where a certain often positive response is expected. For example, it may be important for the patient to believe that psychotherapy was useful to justify spending a great deal of time, money, and effort in the psychotherapy process. Also, after spending so many sessions working with a psychotherapist, the patient may not want to tell him or her that the experience was not helpful. Therefore, determining whether psychotherapy is useful is a challenging research and clinical task.

Early psychotherapists used clinical case studies rather than controlled research investigations to evaluate treatment outcome. In fact, Freud felt that controlled research using statistical analysis was not a reasonable method for determining the effects of treatment (Freud, 1917/1963, 1933/1964). Freud and others felt that because psychotherapy was such a highly individualized experience, group findings based on averages and statistics were useless. Only since the 1950s have psychologists endorsed the notion that systematically

studying psychotherapy outcome is a worthy endeavor. After controlled investigations of psychotherapy outcome were conducted, thousands of studies followed. **Psychotherapy treatment outcome** has become one of the most common topics of investigation in all psychology research.

In a classic and frequently cited research project, Hans Eysenck (1952) examined 24 research studies concerning both psychodynamic and eclectic techniques used for nonpsychotic patients. The results of his study failed to demonstrate that psychotherapy was effective. Furthermore, Eysenck suggested that spontaneous recovery (i.e., recovery from symptoms without any treatment intervention) from neurotic types of problems (e.g., anxiety and depression) could be expected about 72% of the time. Therefore, he estimated that 72% of those experiencing psychological distress would improve without treatment. However, many critics of Eysenck's research methods have seriously questioned his conclusions (e.g., Bergin, 1971; Sanford, 1953; Strupp, 1963). For example, Bergin (1971) reexamined Eysenck's data and estimated that the rate of spontaneous recovery was about 30% rather than 72% and that the recovery rate from psychotherapy was much higher than that estimated by Eysenck.

In a much more rigorous and ambitious research project, Smith and Glass (1977) examined 375 research studies on psychotherapy treatment outcome by using meta-analysis and effect-size techniques. Results from the study revealed that patients receiving psychotherapy tended to be more improved than those who did not seek psychotherapy about 75% of the time. Furthermore, Smith and Glass examined the treatment outcomes of different types of psychotherapy (e.g., behavioral and psychodynamic) and failed to find superiority of one treatment approach over another. This comprehensive and extensive investigation contradicted the Eysenck study and provided compelling support for the effectiveness of psychotherapy. The Smith and Glass (1977) study, like the one by Eysenck

(1952), became one of the most frequently cited research studies in clinical psychology.

The Smith and Glass (1977) study received a great deal of attention and a large response from the professional community. Many strongly criticized both the method and the conclusions of the investigation (Eysenck, 1978, 1983; Kazdin & Wilson, 1978; Rachman & Wilson, 1980: Searles, 1985). For example, some questioned the wisdom of using a wide variety of studies that focused on so many different types of treatments and patient problems. Others felt that the authors paid too little attention to the quality of the studies evaluated. Still others questioned the interpretation of the meta-analysis results. Smith, Glass, and Miller (1980) later extended the analysis to include 475 studies and improved upon several of the procedures from the earlier study. The 1980 study confirmed the earlier results and found that those receiving psychotherapy tended to be more improved than 80% of untreated persons and that behavioral therapies were more effective than verbal therapies. Perhaps one of the most positive outcomes of the Eysenck (1952) and Smith & Glass, (1977) and Smith et al. (1980) investigations has been the subsequent stimulation of numerous research studies to assist in answering basic questions about the effectiveness of psychotherapy.

A large number of meta-analysis studies examining psychotherapy treatment outcome have been conducted since the Smith and Glass studies (e.g., Andrews & Harvey, 1981; Kazdin & Bass, 1989; Lambert et al., 2003; Landman & Dawes, 1982; Lipsey & Wilson, 1993; Matt, 1989; Searles, 1985; Shadish, Navarro, Matt, & Phillips, 2000; D. L Shapiro & D. Shapiro, 1982). The vast majority of these and other studies conclude that psychotherapy is generally effective. For example, Andrews and Harvey (1981) evaluated 475 controlled psychotherapy outcome studies and concluded that a patient receiving psychotherapy was better off than 77% of untreated control subjects and that relapse rates were very small. Smith (1982) examined over 500 controlled psychotherapy outcome studies and concluded that psychotherapy was effective in improving psychological wellbeing and that duration, mode, and therapist training and experience were unrelated to outcome. Furthermore, Smith (1982) concluded that behavioral therapies were more effective than verbal therapies and that the use of medication without therapy was not more effective than psychotherapy alone. The positive effectiveness of psychotherapy has also been found among studies focusing on special populations such as children. Casey and Berman (1985), for example, found that treatment of children was equally effective whether the treatment was provided individually or in groups.

The popular magazine, *Consumer Reports* (November 1998; Seligman, 1995), conducted an extensive survey of psychotherapy outcome and found that people who participated in psychotherapy found the experience effective and that long-term treatment was superior to short-term treatment. Furthermore, the survey concluded that psychotherapy with medication was not superior to psychotherapy alone and that psychologists, psychiatrists, and social workers were equally effective and were, as a group, superior to marriage counselors. The survey also concluded that no particular psychotherapy orientation (e.g., psychodynamic, behavioral) was superior to other orientations regardless of the clinical problem of interest. People who used community interventions such as Alcoholics Anonymous (AA) were found to be especially satisfied with these experiences. The *Consumer Reports* survey concluded that while psychotherapy does appear to work and people are generally highly satisfied with their psychotherapy experience, low- or no-cost self-help community interventions are equally helpful.

An extensive review of all the research studies generally concludes that psychotherapy does indeed work (American Psychological Association, 2006; Arkowitz & Lilienfeld, 2007; Barlow, 1996; Duncan, Miller, Wampold, & Hubble, 2009; Hollon, 1996; In-Albon & Schneider, 2007; Ingram et al., 2000; Lambert et al., 2003; Messer & Wampold, 2002; Nathan & Gorman, 2007; Shadish et al., 2000; VandenBos, 1996). Numerous research and clinical examples provide convincing evidence that psychotherapy is effective (Beutler, Bongar, & Shurkin, 1998; Nathan & Gorman, 2002, 2007) and even when compared to psychotropic medication use (Arkowitz & Lilienfeld, 2007). However, both researchers and clinicians have been trying to answer many additional follow-up questions that go well beyond whether psychotherapy works, such as: How does psychotherapy work and what types of treatment and therapists are effective for what types of problems and patients? Recent efforts by the American Psychological Association (APA) have attempted to identify specific treatment approaches for specific problem areas (Addis, 2002; American Psychological Association, 2006; Duncan et al., 2009; Chambless et al., 1996; Chambless & Ollendick, 2001; Task Force on Promotion and Dissemination of Psychological Procedures, 1995). These empirically supported treatments and evidence-based practices have received a great deal of recent attention and support but remain controversial. While many feel that specific treatments can be targeted for specific problems, others feel that psychotherapy is too unique and complicated to routinely fit human beings into standardized treatment protocols (Garfield, 1996; Havik & VandenBos, 1996; Norcross, 2002).

Seligman (1994) suggests that certain types of problems are more amenable to change than others. He states that the depth of a problem often predicts whether the problem can be altered significantly through psychotherapy. For example, problems that are primarily biologically oriented and pervade all aspects of life are less appropriate for psychotherapy than problems that are learned and are less pervasive. Thus, he suggests that problems such as panic and phobia are much more responsive to therapy than obesity and alcoholism.

Barry Duncan, Scott Miller, and colleagues (Duncan et al., 2009) offer several quality books and a number of articles that have well-articulated treatments that work in a variety of areas, expanding upon empirically supported treatments and evidence-based practices.

Long-Term Therapy versus Short-Term Treatment

Psychotherapy can last for one session or for hundreds of sessions over the course of many years. The duration of psychotherapy depends on the symptoms, interest, motivation, and financial resources of the patient as well as on the orientation and skills of the therapist. Some types of psychotherapy tend to be very short while others tend to be remarkably long. For example, the average length of treatment using psychoanalysis is about 1,000 sessions (Kernberg, 1973).

More and more emphasis is being placed on *brief psychotherapy*. Brief approaches to therapy are of interest to both patients and insurance companies. Patients who seek psychotherapy generally do so during an emotional crisis and wish to obtain relief as fast as possible. They generally expect to see quick results within just a few sessions, and complete recovery from presenting problems within 12 sessions (Garfield, 1986). Insurance companies and others are interested in briefer forms of treatment to reduce health-care costs.

Most psychotherapy experiences do tend to be fairly brief. The majority of patients in psychotherapy terminate treatment before 10 sessions, with the median number of sessions being about 6 (Garfield, 1986; Kleinke, 1994; Taube, Burns, & Kessler, 1984). In fact, about one-third of all persons who consult with a mental health professional for psychotherapy attend only one session (Bloom, 1981; Clarkin & Hull, 1991). Research has found that between 25% and 50% of people who consult with a mental health professional fail to attend a second session (Betz & Shullman, 1979; Phillips & Fagan, 1982; Sue, McKinney, & Allen, 1976). Research on more than 2,400 psychotherapy patients spanning over 30 years suggests that 50% of psychotherapy patients were significantly improved by 8 sessions and 75% were improved by 26 sessions (Howard, Kopta, Krause, & Orlinsky, 1986). More recent research using the 4,100 people who sought mental health services and

Empirically Supported Treatment Manuals: Overcoming Eating Disorders

Photo: Courtesy Stockvault.net

By definition, empirically supported treatments offer both therapists and clients the opportunity to use a step-by-step treatment manual as an integral part of the treatment process. One example of an empirically supported treatment manual is the one authored by Robin F. Apple and W. Stewart Agras from Stanford University School of Medicine entitled, *Overcoming Eating Disorders: A Cognitive-Behavioral Treatment for Bulimia Nervosa and Binge-Eating Disorder* (1997).

The manual is typical of other empirically supported treatment manuals in that it provides an easy to read and understand step-by-step program to change a problematic behavior. The manual begins with an assessment of the reader's eating problems and tries to help the client decide whether altering his or her eating behavior is the right thing to do at this time in the person's life. The manual examines some of the typical problems associated with behavior change such as motivation and willingness to change, emotional issues that get in the way of effective behavior change, and so on. The manual then provides an overview of the treatment process and separates the program into several key phases. These include a behavior-change phase, an identifying-binge-trigger phase, and a relapse-prevention phase. The manual encourages the client to self-monitor by

(continued)

using daily food records (i.e., writing down all of the food items as well as associated feelings and activities) each time food or drink is consumed.

Subsequent chapters examine understanding more about eating patterns, binge-eating cycles, and ways to think more productively about weight, body shape, and form. Additional chapters focus on feared or special problematic foods, understanding binge triggers, interpersonal and emotional triggers for eating, and ways to maintain changes after treatment is completed. Throughout the manual, there are many exercises, charts, workbook questions and answers, homework exercises, tips from the experts, and so forth. The therapist and client work through the workbook step-by-step in a structured format. Often, additional resources are available, such as record forms and videotapes.

who participated in the *Consumer Reports* Study (1998) found that most people experienced significant improvement in symptoms within the first 10 to 20 sessions (Howard, Moras, Brill, & Martinovich, 1996). Surprisingly, research has found that even a single session of psychotherapy or consultation is associated with positive therapeutic outcomes, such as a decrease in medical office visits (Goldberg, Krantz, & Locke, 1970) and in general medical utilization (Cummings, 1977). However, some meta-analysis research of treatment outcome has demonstrated that treatment duration is not necessarily associated with treatment outcome. For example, brief treatment results in about the same positive outcome as moderate or long-term treatment, according to Andrews and Harvey (1981). Others have found little support for treatment outcome successes for either short- or longer-term treatment (Strupp & Anderson, 1997). Yet a survey conducted by *Consumer Reports* magazine as well as several other studies including very recent ones have found that longer-term treatments tend to be more helpful than shorter-term treatments (Barlow, 1996; *Consumer Reports,* November 1998; Leichsenring & Rabung, 2008). Thus, whereas psychotherapy tends to be fairly brief in duration, it is difficult to make generalizations regarding the superiority of short- versus long-term treatment. Lambert and Ogles (2004) conclude that a majority of patients improve after 10 sessions and 75% will improve after 50 sessions.

Psychotherapy Dropouts

About a third of psychotherapy patients do not attend a second session. What factors might predict psychotherapy dropout? Several studies have found that socioeconomic status (Berrigan & Garfield, 1981; Dodd, 1970; Fiester & Rudestam, 1975; Kahn & Heiman, 1978; Pilkonis, Imber, Lewis, & Rubinsky, 1984) and educational level (Rabin, Kaslow, & Rehm, 1985) appear to be associated with psychotherapy dropout. Those from lower-socioeconomic spheres and those who have less education tend to be more likely to quit psychotherapy. Research focusing on the influence of age, sex, race, psychological test results, and other patient variables of interest has proved inconclusive (Garfield, 1993). Thus, social and cultural factors deserve further investigation to understand their impact on therapy duration and outcome.

If the socioeconomic status and educational level of the patient predict psychotherapy dropout, what characteristics of the therapist might also predict it? The skill of the therapist is positively associated with continuation of psychotherapy (Baekeland & Lundwall, 1975; Dodd, 1970; McNeill, May, & Lee, 1987; Sloane, Staples, Cristol, Yorkston, & Whipple, 1975). However, a therapist's sex and professional affiliation (e.g., psychologist, psychiatrist, social worker) appear unrelated to psychotherapy continuation or dropout (Carpenter & Range, 1982; Mogul, 1982), although many additional factors may play a role. Patients may feel that the crisis that led them to psychotherapy has passed, and thus motivation for continuing has significantly decreased. Often patients feel better after just one session and do not wish or need to continue (Goldberg et al., 1970). The therapist and patient might not "click" during the first session as well. Patients who do not like their therapist or who feel that their needs are not being adequately met are less likely to schedule or attend additional sessions.

Is One Type of Therapy Better Than Another?

Is psychodynamic psychotherapy better than cognitive-behavioral psychotherapy? Is individual psychotherapy better than family systems approaches to psychotherapy? Is any one type of psychotherapy superior to another? As discussed in earlier chapters, clinical psychology has had a long history of professionals claiming that their approach to psychotherapy is superior to other alternatives. However, as detailed in Chapter 4, more and more integrative approaches to psychotherapy have been developed and practiced during the past several decades as the field has grown and matured. Additionally, recent emphasis on providing evidence-based practices tends to focus on what treatments work best with less interest in particular theoretical orientations (American Psychological Association, 2006). Still, numerous research investigations have been and continue to be conducted to determine whether one type of psychotherapy is superior to others. The vast majority of these studies compare verbal or insight-oriented psychotherapies (e.g., psychodynamic, humanistic) to action-oriented psychotherapies (e.g., behavioral, cognitive). Additionally, research also tends to examine

how psychotherapy and psychosocial interventions compare to medication use (Arkowitz & Lilienfeld, 2007).

To ensure that these studies use pure forms of therapy and do not mix and match techniques and orientations, most of these research investigations incorporate treatment manuals and ask clinicians to follow these treatment manual protocols. These protocols provide specific guidelines in the administration of the treatment approach (e.g., Crits-Christoph & Mintz, 1991; Lebow, 2008; Luborsky & DeRubeis, 1984; Rounsaville, O'Malley, Foley, & Weissman, 1988). Of course, clinicians tend not to use treatment manuals in actual practice and rarely focus their treatment with the use of techniques and approaches from only one theoretical perspective (American Psychological Association, 2006; Barlow, 1996; Goldfried & Wolfe, 1996; Lebow, 2008; Norcross et al., 2006; Prochaska, 2008; Seligman, 1996). Most of the research studies have ultimately failed to find that one type of psychotherapy is consistently superior to another. In fact, since the mid-1970s, Luborsky, Singer, and Luborsky (1975) and many others (e.g., Luborsky et al., 2002; Stiles, Shapiro, & Elliott, 1986) have referred to the equality of different types of psychotherapy as the "dodo bird verdict." This term comes from *Alice in Wonderland,* where the dodo bird states that "everyone has won and all must have prizes." However, a number of authors believe that the dodo bird verdict is a myth (Chambless, 2002; London, 1988; Nathan & Gorman, 2007; Norcross, 1995; Norcross et al., 2006). They suggest that different types of psychotherapy often result in different specific effects, and that these effects are not exclusive to only one type of therapy (Chambless, 2002; Lebow, 2008; Norcross, 1995). When these studies find differences between therapies, they generally support the notion that cognitive and behavioral treatments tend to result in more positive outcomes (usually measured by symptom reduction and behavior change) than psychodynamic or other more verbal treatment orientations (Andrews & Harvey, 1981; Chambless, 2002; Kazdin & Weisz, 1998; Lebow, 2008; Searles, 1985;

Diversity: Do Clients Prefer Therapists from Their Own Cultural Group?

Zane and colleagues (2004) state that one of the most commonly asked questions about culturally sensitive therapy is whether minority group members prefer a therapist from their own cultural group. Many studies find that people do prefer working with therapists from their own cultural group and that this preference is especially true for African Americans. Research suggests that patient–therapist racial matching may result in more treatment sessions but may not result in better treatment outcome than mixed racial or ethnic pairings between patients and therapists among African Americans and Latino groups (e.g., Zane et al., 2004). However, treatment outcome seems to be enhanced when Asian Americans are paired with Asian American therapists and when Mexican Americans are paired with Mexican American therapists with similar language skills (Sue, Fujino, Ho, Takeuchi, & Zane, 1991). These associations are modest at best and thus it is unreasonable to expect that ethnic matching is a guarantee that a more positive treatment outcome will always occur (D. Sue & D. M. Sue, 2008; Zane et al., 2004). Furthermore, researchers have noted that client–therapist matching on race, ethnicity, gender, and sexual orientation may not necessarily be a match in other important variables like culture, language, socioeconomic status, acculturation, and so forth (D. Sue & D. M. Sue, 2008; Zane et al., 2004). Efforts to provide cultural sensitivity training for therapists and pre-therapy orientation for clients are likely to improve treatment effectiveness for culturally diverse patients (D. Sue & D. M. Sue, 2008). A variety of high-profile and engaged organizations, such as AFFIRM, which focuses on gay, lesbian, bisexual, and transgender, offer therapists and the public helpful information including bibliographies, resources, and therapist matching assistance.

D. L. Shapiro & D. Shapiro, 1982; Svartberg & Stiles, 1991). Thus, cognitive and behavioral approaches have come to dominate more empirically supported treatment manuals and evidence-based practice approaches (American Psychological Association, 2006).

Studies have also attempted to determine whether psychotherapy is as effective as medication in treating anxiety, depression, and other symptoms (see Arkowitz & Lilienfeld, 2007; Blackburn & Moore, 1997; Clay, 2000; Fava et al., 1998; Hollon, 1996; and Horgan, 1996 for review). An often-quoted and large-scale National Institute of Mental Health (NIMH) Collaborative Depression study compared cognitive-behavioral psychotherapy, interpersonal psychotherapy (i.e., a combination of psychodynamic and humanistic psychotherapy), medication (i.e., imipramine), and a drug placebo condition. The medication and drug placebo groups also received clinical case management. Two hundred fifty patients were treated in one of three major cities by either a psychiatrist or a psychologist. Results indicated that all the treatments, including the placebo condition, resulted in patient improvement and that differences in outcome between patients receiving the cognitive-behavioral and the interpersonal psychotherapy were minimal.

Thus, medication has not proved superior to psychotherapies in treating many common psychological problems such as anxiety and depression. Although isolated studies do sometimes support one type of therapy over another, the overall picture is that most professionally administered and legitimate psychotherapy approaches are equally effective for most people and that medication is not superior to psychotherapy (Horgan, 1996).

Although research does not support the notion that one type of legitimate psychotherapy is superior to another for treating all types of clinical problems, research that examines treatment approaches for very specific disorders does provide some support for the superiority of certain techniques. So, although no one type of therapy is superior to another for general issues of concern, several specific disorders tend to be treated more successfully using certain approaches. The Task Force on Promotion and Dissemination of Psychological Procedures (1995) of the APA Division of Clinical Psychology (Division 12) as well as the APA Task Force on evidence-based practices have developed guidelines for psychotherapy treatments based on these solid research findings of specific disorders (American Psychological Association, 2006; Chambless et al., 1996; Chambless & Ollendick, 2001). Empirically supported treatments and evidence-based practices have been developed for the treatment of a variety of problem areas such as chemical abuse and dependence, and anxiety, depressive, sexual, eating, and health problems. Examples of these treatments include exposure treatment for phobias and posttraumatic stress disorder, cognitive-behavior therapy for headache, depression, irritable bowel syndrome, and bulimia, and insight-oriented dynamic therapy for depression and marital discord (American Psychological Association, 2006; Lamberg, 2008; Lambert, 2005; Nathan & Gorman, 2007).

Enduring Psychotherapy Effects

What happens when someone stops psychotherapy? Do people generally relapse into maladaptive patterns of thinking, feeling, and behaving? Do the gains obtained through psychotherapy last? It may be unrealistic to expect that psychotherapy will "cure" a problem or eliminate symptoms without any relapse. If someone is treated with psychotherapy for depression at age 20, one cannot expect that the person will never again feel depressed. Numerous studies have investigated the long-term effects of psychotherapy to determine whether symptoms reemerge following termination. Most of the data collected on psychotherapy follow-up range from several months to several years after treatment.

Research generally supports the contention that gains obtained in psychotherapy do last (Andrews & Harvey, 1981; Barlow, 1996; Jorm, 1989; Lambert & Ogles, 2004; Landman & Dawes, 1982; Nicholson & Berman, 1983; Nietzel, Russell, Hemmings, & Gretter, 1987; Nathan & Gorman, 2007; Snyder & Ingram, 2000). For example, Jorm (1989) examined the results of studies treating anxiety and found that anxiety reduction was maintained one year after treatment when compared with control subjects. Feske and Chambless (1995) examined 21 research studies using cognitive-behavioral treatments for social anxiety and found improvements lasting up to a year after treatment relative to control conditions. Bakker et al. (1998) found similar results for panic patients up to eight years following treatment. Nietzel et al. (1987) investigated research that focused on the treatment of depression and found that treatment gains were maintained four months (on average) after termination of active treatment. Gallagher-Thompson, Hanley-Peterson, and Thompson (1990) also examined depression treatment outcome studies and found that therapy gains were generally maintained even two years after treatment. Similar findings have been reported when examining alcohol (Bellack & Herson, 1990), posttraumatic stress disorder (Foa et al., 1999), and headache treatments (Blanchard, 1987). However, relapse is a common and worrisome problem for many. Researchers have developed programs and strategies to maximize maintenance of psychotherapy gains (e.g., Annis, 1990; Brownell & Jeffery, 1987; Cummings, Gordon, & Marlatt, 1980; Kane, 2008; Marlatt & Donovan, 2008). Research tends to support the notion that the effects of psychotherapy last even after psychotherapy has terminated (Lambert & Ogles, 2004). However, some research suggests otherwise. Some authors believe that change related to psychotherapy may be due to a confirmatory bias, optimism, positive expectations, or cognitive dissonance (Myers, 2000)

Highlight of a Contemporary Clinical Psychologist

John Pina, PhD

Photo: Courtesy John Pina

Birth Date: August 2, 1963

College: University of Minnesota (BA, Psychology), 1995

Graduate Program: University of Minnesota (PhD, Clinical Psychology), 2000

Clinical Internship: Lucille Packard Children's Hospital & Children's Health Council, Stanford University, Palo Alto, CA

Current Job: Adolescent & Family Therapist—Private Practice, Los Gatos, CA

Pros and Cons of Being a Clinical Psychologist:

Pros: "I really like to help teens and families see their dysfunctional patterns of behavior and thinking. I love having the opportunity to firsthand observe and appreciate the differences in how people think."

Cons: "When clients erroneously believe that I am the one who can facilitate change, rather than they. When clients' expectations are a function of their problems, I can be put in a no-win situation."

Your Specialty and How You Chose It: "My specialty is dealing with serious behavioral issues in young teen males and females. Lots of these kids have oppositional behavior, as well as depression, anxiety, attention-deficit disorder (ADHD), and significant substance abuse histories. I also work with their parents, and my specialty there is to try to help the parents empower themselves, sometimes in situations where they feel they've lost all control with their kids. I don't know if I chose these specialties, or whether they seemed to be pervasive in our culture these days, but I felt I was good at communicating with both kids and parents at their respective levels."

Future of Clinical Psychology: "The future of my work basically depends on economic factors—economy, insurance, and so on. When times are good, people can use therapy for what it is intended—to help them figure out their maladaptive behavioral and thought patterns. When times are tough, clients can use therapy as basic crisis intervention, and therapy may unfortunately become less of a priority."

Typical Schedule: "I basically see clients Monday through Friday, from 11 A.M. until 5 P.M. I also do parent teaching seminars, usually monthly."

Common Factors Associated with Positive Psychotherapy Outcome

Overall, research suggests that psychotherapy is effective in treating numerous concerns compared with receiving no treatment, and that, in general, no one type of psychotherapy is superior to another (Lebow, 2008; Lambert & Bergin, 1994; Luborsky et al., 2002; Messer & Wampold, 2002; Norcross, 2002; Norcross & Goldfried, 2005; Norcross et al., 2006; Prochaska & Norcross, 2007; Wampold, 2001). However, in recent years, many cognitive-behavioral approaches have come to dominate the list of empirically supported treatments and evidence-based practice approaches. If most of the research over many years on psychotherapy outcome supports the notion that different types of legitimate treatment are about equally effective, then specific theories and techniques associated with different types of psychotherapy (e.g., psychodynamic, behavioral, and family systems) may not significantly account for the curative effects of the therapy experience. If specific theories and techniques may not account for treatment outcome, then what does? One potential answer is that there are certain commonalities among all types of psychotherapies and that these commonalities are associated with treatment effectiveness. One might speculate that merely having someone with whom to talk over problems or having the attention of a caring and nurturing professional might be a powerful curative factor in all types of psychotherapy. Furthermore, making an appointment to see a therapist forces clients to regularly attend to and think about ways to improve their situation and problems that brought them to psychotherapy in the first place. The search for common denominators or **common factors** in psychotherapy is important to understanding how psychotherapy might work (Duncan et al., 2009; Norcross, 2002; Norcross & Goldfried, 2005; Prochaska & Norcross, 2007; Roth & Fonagy, 2005).

Goldfried and colleagues (Goldfried, 1991; Goldfried et al., 1990) proposed that all psychotherapies encourage the patient to engage in corrective emotional experiences and that they all provide some form of corrective feedback to the patient. Karasu (1986) suggested that all useful psychotherapies include three common patient factors—affective experiencing, cognitive mastery, and behavioral regulation—and that all major schools of psychotherapy use these three ingredients to effect change. *Affect experiencing* refers to expressing feelings. *Cognitive mastery* refers to thinking about problems in a manner that enables the patient to experience control over attitudes, perceptions, and beliefs about his or her problems. *Behavioral regulation* refers to developing strategies for controlling impulses and problematic behaviors. Additional commonalities outlined by Frank (1982, 1993) and others include a professional office associated with being helped; a trained mental health professional who is supportive; enhanced hope that thoughts, feelings, and behaviors can change for the better; fees associated with service; and the avoidance of exploitive dual relationships.

In reviewing the literature, Weinberger (1995) outlined five common factors associated with positive psychotherapy outcome. These include the therapeutic relationship, expectations of success, confronting a problem, providing the experience of mastery or control over the problem, and an attribution of success or failure. Each of these factors will be briefly reviewed. All major approaches to psychotherapy emphasize that the working relationship between the therapist and patient should be positive and that therapists should generally be empathetic, genuine, warm, and professional (Duncan et al., 2009; Lafferty, Beutler, & Crago, 1991; Lambert, 1986; Lambert & Okishi, 1997; Norcross & Goldfried, 2005; Prochaska & Norcross, 2007; Roth & Fonagy, 2005; Teyber & McClure, 2000). This working alliance between therapist and patient is thought to be a critical ingredient for effective psychotherapy (Horvath & Symonds, 1991; Lambert, 1992; Lambert & Bergin, 1994; Norcross, 1995; Norcross & Goldfried, 2005;

Prochaska & Norcross, 2007; Salvio, Beutler, Wood, & Engle, 1992; Strupp, 1995; Teyber & McClure, 2000; Yalom, 1980). Strupp (1995), for example, states that "the quality of the interpersonal context is the *sine qua non* in all forms of psychotherapy" (p. 70) and that good therapists provide a patient with a corrective emotional experience and deal effectively with transference dynamics. Thus, Strupp concluded that therapists must have "the ability to manage therapeutically a complex human relationship and . . . avoid enmeshments in the patient's unconscious self-defeating scenarios" (p. 71). Connecting to a therapist whom the patient perceives as helpful and accepting is a powerful common factor in almost all types of psychotherapy (Lambert, 1992; Norcross, 1995; Norcross & Goldfried, 2005; Prochaska & Norcross, 2007; Teyber & McClure, 2000).

Expectancy is also a strong predictor of positive therapeutic outcome. Numerous studies have demonstrated and suggested that treatment is more effective when patients believe that the treatment is helpful (Bandura, 1989; Barker, Funk, & Houston, 1988; Frank, 1982, 1993; Kirsch, 1990; Lambert & Ogles, 2004; Rosenthal, 1987). Belief that psychotherapy can work is another important common factor in psychotherapy. In fact, because many improvements in psychotherapy may be attributed to placebos (Brody, 1983; Horvath, 1988; Myers, 2000), placebo control conditions must be utilized in treatment outcome research to ensure that outcome results are due to factors other than expectancy effects (Horvath, 1988; Kirsch, 1990; Weinberger, 1995).

Facing problems rather than avoiding, escaping, or denying them has been thought to be a critical variable in treatment outcome and is a common factor in all therapies (Kleinke, 1994; Lambert & Ogles, 2004; Norcross & Goldfried, 2005; Orlinsky & Howard, 1986; Prochaska & Norcross, 2007; Weinberger, 1995). All involve some degree of attention and plan of attack to confront problems and develop strategies to cope more effectively with various symptoms. Research

has even supported the healing aspects of confronting problems outside a psychotherapeutic context. For example, Liberman (1978) and Pennebaker (1990) found that merely writing or talking about a problem in isolation without a therapist present results in improvement of symptoms. Therefore, working on problems and focusing on ways to overcome them are powerful common factors in all types of psychotherapy and are effective even outside the formal psychotherapy experience.

Mastery, or a sense of control, over a problem is a powerful predictor of therapy outcome and is hypothesized to be a very important common factor in all therapies (Kleinke, 1994; Liberman, 1978; Rappoport, 2002; Roth & Fonagy, 2005; Weinberger, 1995). Belief that you have a reasonable plan to overcome a problem enhances your sense of self-efficacy (Bandura, 1989).

Finally, patient attributions concerning the factors that they believe contribute to change appear to be a powerful predictor of therapy success or failure. Success in treatment is generally associated with internal attributions (e.g., the patient's own efforts, improved coping skills, positive personality changes; Bandura, 1989; Roth & Fonagy, 2005; Weinberger, 1995).

Murphy, Cramer, and Lillie (1984) asked patients to describe what they thought were the most important factors associated with positive psychotherapy outcome. The majority reported that getting advice and talking with someone who understands and is interested in their problems, and gives encouragement and hope, were **curative factors**. Lazarus (1971) found that the personal qualities of the therapist (e.g., gentle, honest) were more important to patients than the actual psychotherapy techniques used. Thus, the therapeutic relationship, beliefs about psychotherapy, working on problems, and developing control and mastery all seem to be common curative factors in psychotherapy (Duncan et al., 2009; Lambert & Ogles, 2004; Roth & Fonagy, 2005; Wampold, 2001).

Change Is Challenging

Behavioral change, with or without the assistance of psychotherapy, is not easy to accomplish. Humans tend to be creatures of habit, and even behavior or thinking patterns that are destructive (e.g., temper tantrums, low self-esteem, smoking, eating high-fat foods, drinking too much alcohol) tend to be remarkably difficult to change. Furthermore, even positive change is not always welcomed. Often patients are ambivalent about change and may not be pleased with some of the consequences of change. For example, a patient who loses a lot of weight may find some of the attention he or she receives unpleasant. A patient who successfully overcomes panic attacks and other fears may be expected to develop more responsibility at home or at work. A child who no longer gets negative attention for temper tantrums in school may feel ignored. Resistance to change is very common among psychotherapy patients as well as, perhaps, the general public.

James Prochaska (1984, 2000, 2008) and colleagues have researched commonalities of behavioral change among theoretical orientations by examining the process of change across different types of problems and different methods of treatment. In his analysis of different orientations to behavioral change, Prochaska isolated a variety of universal stages, levels, and processes of change. His theory includes five stages of change (i.e., precontemplation, contemplation, preparation, action, and maintenance), five levels of change (i.e., symptoms, maladaptive cognition, current interpersonal conflicts, family/systems conflicts, interpersonal conflicts), and 10 change processes (i.e., consciousness raising, catharsis/dramatic relief, self-evaluation, environmental reevaluation, self-liberation, social liberation, counterconditioning, stimulus control, contingency management, and helping relationship). Although Prochaska's model has a cognitive-behavioral "flavor" to it, his theory of change is atheoretical since it is not based on any one model or perspective (Prochaska

& Norcross, 2002, 2007). Up to 40% of change can be attributed to expectation or placebo (Lambert, 1992), and because consciousness raising is considered a critical ingredient in behavioral change for most psychotherapies (Prochaska & Norcross, 2002), the desire to change is likely to be a very important factor in explaining behavioral change (Prochaska, 2000).

Change is not easy to accomplish. Although patients generally enter a psychotherapy experience seeking to change their behavior (or the behavior of others), paradoxically many people are highly resistant to change. Resistance to change in psychotherapy has been recognized and highlighted by psychotherapists since the days of Freud. Kleinke (1994) outlined several important factors explaining why change is difficult to achieve and why resistance is so common in psychotherapy. First, change is threatening. Familiar ways of thinking, feeling, and behaving offer some degree of comfort even if they are maladaptive. For example, people who suffer from agoraphobia may be frustrated by their inability to feel comfortable traveling on airplanes, going to the grocery store, or conducting other errands. They often feel most comfortable when they are close to home and can avoid the situations that provoke anxiety. Confronting these fears and working to increase independence is threatening and scary. Secondary gains (i.e., advantages to maintaining problems) associated with problematic symptoms may also be difficult to give up. For instance, the patient with agoraphobia may not work or be expected to run errands (e.g., picking up friends and family at the airport, grocery shopping). Family members and friends may be willing to do a lot for the agoraphobic person, affording the opportunity to avoid many difficult tasks. A third factor associated with resistance as outlined by Kleinke (1994) includes potential interference from others. Although a patient may wish to change behavior through psychotherapy, important others in the life of the patient may be motivated to maintain the status quo. For example, the spouse of the patient with agoraphobia may feel important

What Leading Experts Think about Psychotherapy Research Findings

A survey conducted by Rhode Island researchers Charles Boisvert and David Faust (2003) asked leading international experts on psychotherapy research to provide their opinions on what psychotherapy research outcome tells us about certain key issues. These 25 leading experts were the most highly cited authors among other experts in psychotherapy research.

The findings suggested very strong consensus that research supported the following results:

1. Psychotherapy is useful for most clients.
2. Most people obtain improvements fairly quickly in psychotherapy.
3. Clients are more likely to change due to common rather than specific factors associated with the various forms of psychotherapy.
4. Generally, different therapies obtain fairly similar treatment outcome results.
5. The best predictor of treatment success is the relationship that forms between the therapist and client.
6. Most therapists learn about effective approaches from experience rather than from research findings.
7. About 10% of clients get worse rather than better after their participation in psychotherapy.
8. Therapy is better than a placebo or waitlist control groups.
9. Therapist experience and training is not a strong predictor of treatment success.
10. Long-term treatment is not more effective than brief forms of treatment for most clients.

and needed by the patient. Increased independence may be experienced by the spouse as a threat to his or her power and role in the relationship. If a patient is interested in minimizing alcohol consumption, family and friends who frequently drink with the person may feel displaced, guilty, and uncomfortable if he or she stops drinking and they no longer have this activity in common. A person trying to lose weight may find it difficult to maintain friendships with others who enjoy dining out together. Finally, many people resist change when they feel that their freedom is threatened (Brehm & Brehm, 1981). If a therapist is perceived as moving too quickly or having high expectations for change, the patient will likely repel and resist the change even if it is in the desirable direction.

Level of Training for Psychotherapists

Does someone really need to have a PhD or other advanced degree (e.g., PsyD, MSW, MD) to be an effective psychotherapist? Does someone really need four to seven years of postgraduate training to get a license to practice as a mental health professional? Aren't many caring and empathetic persons excellent "therapists" or "counselors" even if they have no formal training? Aren't a lot of friends, colleagues, and grandparents excellent "therapists"? If common factors such as warmth, empathy, honesty, and interest on the part of the psychotherapist are important and even vital to treatment outcome, couldn't any "nice" person with minimal training be an effective psychotherapist? If placebo conditions are associated with positive treatment outcome, might not good placebos administered by almost anyone be appropriate therapy? These challenging questions all center on the notion that someone might not need to be a professional to be a therapist. Compared with performing surgery, constructing an office building, or programming a computer, discussing problems with people is a natural human activity. Most people have had the experience of talking over problems and concerns with their friends, relatives, colleagues, or even strangers. Not every potential patient will feel that a particular psychotherapist is good. The fit between the therapist and patient is not only important but highly individual. Research indicates that the therapist's psychological health and skill as well as a sincere interest in helping others are necessary qualities for being an effective psychotherapist (Davidson & Scott, 2009; Kleinke, 1994).

Several studies have failed to find a difference in psychotherapy outcome between therapies provided by professionals versus paraprofessionals (Berman & Norton, 1985; Stein & Lambert, 1984). Surprisingly, some studies have found that the use of paraprofessionals results in superior outcomes relative to professionals (Hattie, Sharpley, & Rogers, 1984; Lambert et al., 2003). The Hattie et al. study, however, has been severely criticized (e.g., Berman & Norton, 1985) for using poor quality research in their analysis and for considering social workers as paraprofessionals. Lambert and colleagues (2003) found that psychology trainees (e.g., interns) under staff supervision have better treatment outcomes than

professional staff therapists. However, other research has demonstrated that the experience and training of the therapist is important for positive therapeutic outcomes (Bergin & Lambert, 1978; *Consumer Reports*, 1998; Davidson & Scott, 2009; Dush, Hirt, & Schroeder, 1989; Lyons & Woods, 1991; Seligman, 1995; Teyber & McClure, 2000; Weisz, Weiss, Alicke, & Klotz, 1987). These studies have found that professionals with solid experience, training, and credentials were more helpful to patients than were those with minimal experience, training, and credentials. For example, the aforementioned survey by *Consumer Reports* magazine (November 1998; Seligman, 1995) found that patients were more satisfied and had better outcomes when treated by psychologists and psychiatrists than when treated by less-trained marriage counselors.

Although both well–trained and poorly trained therapists can potentially provide poor professional service and in fact do harm, minimally trained therapists are more likely to provide a very narrow range of treatment options that often are not based on solid research support (Singer & Lalich, 1996). For example, many attend a weekend workshop in a particular technique such as hypnosis, biofeedback, or EMDR and then attempt to apply these skills and techniques with all of their clients. Highly trained professionals are more likely to have a wide range of treatment options available to them and use rigorous integrative thinking and judgment based on scientific support.

Overall, the professional literature has failed to demonstrate convincingly that trained professionals are superior to less-trained professionals in positive therapeutic outcome. Effective therapists may not necessarily be those with the most training, experience, and credentials. However, it is generally advisable to trust the professional judgments of highly trained professionals rather than minimally trained persons (Davidson & Scott, 2009; Lambert et al., 2003; Lambert & Ogles, 2004; Singer & Lalich, 1996).

Health-Care Costs and Psychotherapy

Because a contemporary biopsychosocial perspective suggests that the mind, body, and social context are important in the development and maintenance of both physical and emotional health, one would expect that a more healthy emotional life might result in a healthier physical life as well. For example, an estimated 50% of all deaths are due to behavioral and lifestyle factors such as eating high-fat foods, being sedentary, and misusing alcohol (Taylor, 2009). Changing health-care behavior and attitudes through psychotherapy may lead to healthier living and fewer illnesses. Additionally, an important question for government agencies, insurance companies, and health-care facilities concerns the association between psychotherapy and health-care costs. Is a person experiencing psychotherapy less likely to need or seek out medical attention? Research suggests that the answer is yes (Blount et al., 2007). Psychotherapy does appear to reduce medical costs.

It has been estimated that 50% to 70% of patients who seek medical treatment have no medical problems and that their symptoms are primarily due to psychological factors such as anxiety, stress, and depression (Blount et al., 2007; VandenBos & DeLeon, 1988). Emotional problems (most notably anxiety and depression) are associated with many medical problems such as heart disease, diabetes, and cancer as well as psychophysiological diseases such as dermatitis, irritable bowel syndrome, chronic headaches, Raynaud's disease, and asthma (Gatchel & Blanchard, 1993; S. Taylor, 2009). Psychological interventions have also been found to be the treatment of choice for a number of medical problems such as tension headaches and irritable bowel syndrome (Chambless & Ollendick, 2001; Chambless et al., 1996). Treatment of emotional and psychological factors through psychotherapy assists in the treatment of many of these medical problems and symptoms.

Those who experience a mental illness tend to use medical services a great deal. It has been estimated that mental health patients use medical services more than twice as often as those who do not experience a mental health diagnosis (Brous & Olendzki, 1985). For example, about one-third of depressed patients experience somatic complaints as a by-product of their depression (Shorter, 1994). Patients who receive psychotherapy tend to seek much less medical care than those who do not receive psychotherapy (Brous & Olendzki, 1985). This is true for self-help groups as well (Humphreys & Moos, 2007). Medical patients with chronic illnesses such as hypertension and diabetes lower medical costs by 18% to 31% when they receive psychological interventions (Lechnyr, 1992). Therefore, psychotherapy not only enhances psychological functioning and wellbeing but also improves medical symptoms, which in turn reduces overall health-care costs (Blount et al., 2007).

Psychotherapy Harm

Psychotherapy is generally helpful for the majority of people who participate in it. Even psychotherapy critics and skeptics feel that the experience is benign and that people are usually not hurt as a result of it. Therapy, unlike a medical procedure such as surgery, does not seem to have life-and-death consequences if it goes poorly. The worst thing that could happen in psychotherapy is that someone might waste time and money and receive little if any benefit, right? Wrong! Actually, psychotherapy may not be appropriate or useful for everyone who wants it. Some people may actually deteriorate in functioning during or after psychotherapy (Berk & Parker, 2009; Lambert & Ogles, 2004; Lilienfeld, 2007; Mays & Frank, 1980, 1985; Mohr, 1995; Nicholson, Foote, & Grigerick, 2009; Singer & Lalich, 1996). In fact, Freud's most famous case example of Anna O. was a treatment failure: Anna O. had more severe symptoms after she began treatment with Freud. Research has found that a sizable number of psychotherapy patients are worse off after psychotherapy than before

Prevention

Photo: Courtesy Stockvault.net

Historically, both medicine and clinical psychology have been involved with treating problems that have already emerged. In more recent years, efforts have been more aggressively pursued to prevent problems before they occur. One excellent example of the interest in preventing problems from occurring includes school-based violence. There have been a number of school shootings perpetrated by minors in recent years. These shootings have occurred mostly in the United States but have also occurred in Germany, England, and elsewhere. Perhaps the incident that received the most publicity in the United States was the one that occurred at Columbine High School in Colorado during April 1999. Two students used a large number of sophisticated semiautomatic weapons as well as bombs to create terror at their high school. When their rampage was completed and before they committed suicide at the school, they had killed a number of students and teachers and injured many more.

Some wanted to blame the media for the events. The boys apparently stated that they were hoping that a movie would be made about their killing spree and they even had suggestions about which Hollywood actors would play their roles. Others wanted to blame the video game industry that provides children with numerous games of violence. Still others blamed the parents for not adequately supervising their children or being aware that their children were planning such a serious

(continued)

crime. They wondered how parents could be totally unaware that their children had a stockpile of weapons and ammunition hidden in their homes. Still others wanted to blame the gun industry, the National Rifle Association (NRA), and conservative lawmakers who have allowed our culture to have so many weapons available to citizens. Others wanted to blame the victims and the other students of Columbine High School for not treating these boys with care and compassion. It was reported that these boys were teased about being odd and not part of the popular crowd. Since the boys had had psychotherapy and actually completed an anger management course, many wanted to blame the mental health community for failing to prevent the tragedy. Fingers have been pointed toward many different people and institutions.

Everyone appears to agree that there is a need to improve our ability to prevent problems such as school-based violence from occurring. Research has found that 20% or more of children and teens experience symptoms of mental illness during the course of a year but about 80% of these children do not get appropriate professional services (U.S. Department of Health and Human Services, 2001). As the years go by, these alarming numbers appear to be getting worse and not better. Furthermore, about 30% of teens participate in multiple high-risk behaviors while an additional 35% are at moderate risk, engaging in one or several problematic behaviors (Taylor, 2009). Too many young people abuse alcohol and other mind-altering substances, experience physical, sexual, and/or emotional abuse and neglect, engage in premature or unsafe sexual practices, and are exposed to violence in their homes, neighborhoods, or through television, movies, and the Internet (Weissberg, Kumpfer, & Seligman, 2003). There are a number of model programs and research studies conducted to better identify high-risk youth and strategies to prevent at-risk children and teens from developing more significant problems and behaviors (Weissberg et al., 2003). However, knowledge obtained from well-conducted research projects and prevention programs ultimately needs to be disseminated to parents, school systems, law enforcement, and community agencies. Furthermore, lawmakers and policy developers need to be able to implement and adequately fund innovative preventive programs (Biglan, Mrazek, Carnine, & Flay, 2003).

Prevention programs may target a wide variety of problems in addition to school violence. These include substance abuse, smoking, adolescent pregnancy, bullying, immunizations, and arson prevention. For example, the Prevention of Alcohol and Trauma: A Community Trial project was conducted in communities in both California and South Carolina and involved community education, training bar employees to be more responsible in alcohol beverage service, and law enforcement education. The five-year project resulted in a 10% reduction in alcohol-related traffic accidents (Holder et al., 1997).

In examining prevention strategies that work well, Nation et al. (2003) have carefully reviewed the literature on prevention and have outlined several principles that tend to predict successful prevention programs. These include comprehensive programming (i.e., providing a variety of interventions to "address the salient precursors or mediators of the target problem," p. 451) in multiple settings, the use of varied teaching methods, providing a sufficient dosage or program intensity (e.g., quality and quantity of contact hours), and theory-driven programming that is scientifically justifiable and that involves positive relationships. The programming must also be appropriately timed and socioculturally relevant and should engage in outcome assessment and use a high-quality and well-trained staff (Nation et al., 2003). Appropriate financial and other resources must be made available if we are to increase the odds of having an effective prevention program.

Clinical psychologists offer prevention research and programming and a variety of talents and skills that range from conducting research and outcome assessment to offering individual, family, group, and organizational consultation, teaching, and therapy services. Furthermore, clinical psychologists are involved in policy and advocacy activities to promote these services to the community.

(e.g., Berk & Parker, 2009; Colson, Lewis, & Horowitz, 1985; Lilienfeld, 2007; Nicholson et al., 2009; D. Shapiro & Shapiro, 1982; Stone, 1985). Some research has shown that patients in waitlist or other control conditions may show less deterioration in functioning than some psychotherapy patients. For example, D. Shapiro and Shapiro (1982) found that about 11% of psychotherapies resulted in a negative outcome, and Colson et al. (1985) found that about 17% of patients were worse at psychotherapy termination than before psychotherapy began. Other studies generally report similar findings (e.g., Lilienfeld, 2007; Stone, 1985). Ogles, Lambert, and Sawyer (1995) found that 8% of clients in treatment for depression deteriorated whereas those in the control group did not. M. Lambert and Ogles (2004) conclude that 5% to 10% of patients in treatment can expect to get worse rather than better. Of course, a wide variety of factors associated with treatment failure may or may not be directly associated with the psychotherapy experience. These might, for example, include stressful life events that occur during the course of psychotherapy (e.g., divorce, loss of job, development of physical illness, death of a loved one). Furthermore, a number of both patient and therapist variables (e.g., patient diagnosis, therapist personality and technique) have been found to be associated with negative treatment outcome. Finally, minimally trained therapists have been found to be damaging when they offer inappropriate and even "crazy therapies" (Singer & Lalich, 1996).

How can psychotherapy result in deterioration in functioning, and what are the variables that predict negative outcome? Research has shown that a large number of variables are associated with poor treatment outcome such as characteristics of the patient and the therapist, and the interaction or lack of fit between patient and therapist. For example, patient diagnosis, severity of symptoms, and psychotherapy that includes experiential, insight-oriented, or confrontational approaches are all associated with poor treatment outcome among certain patients. Patients who experience psychotic disorders such as schizophrenia (Feighner, Brown, & Oliver, 1973; Stone, 1985) or are diagnosed with borderline personality disorder (Horowitz, 1974; Kernberg, 1973; McGlashan, 1986; Mohr, 1995; Stone, 1985, 1990) often deteriorate in these types of expressive therapies. Furthermore, a number of researchers have also found a high incidence

SPOTLIGHT

Repressed Memories

One remarkable controversy in clinical psychology that has made national headlines concerns the issue of repressed memories. Some reports have stated that physical or sexual abuse that occurred many years ago may be repressed or not recalled until many years later following psychotherapy or hypnosis. Several notable cases have involved women in their 30s or 40s recalling abuse and or reporting that they even witnessed murders decades earlier. The recent sexual abuse scandals in the Roman Catholic Church have also involved repressed memory cases. Reports of sexual victimization by priests were recalled by some victims decades after the events following the numerous news reports during 2002 and 2003.

Some clinicians and researchers claim that someone who experiences a significant trauma such as sexual abuse may repress or deny the memory for many years only for it to resurface many years later. Others suggest that repressed memories are most likely to be false memories implanted by therapists or others who make confident and constant suggestions that these events indeed happened. Both points of view have at least some research evidence to support their claims. A number of studies have documented that repressed memories can exist. For example, Williams (1995) examined 129 women who reported that they were sexually abused during the mid-1970s when they were prepubescent children. They were interviewed 17 years later and about a third of these now-adult women had no recollection of the abuse reported when they were children. However, Elizabeth Loftus and colleagues have conducted a variety of research studies that have convincingly demonstrated that false memories can be instilled through experimental procedures (Loftus & Pickrell, 1995). Other researchers have shown that repeatedly asking adults about childhood events that did not actually occur has resulted in up to 40% of the subjects claiming that they actually remember these false and implanted memories (Schacter, 1999). Some researchers such as Richard McNally and colleagues (e.g., McNally, 2001) have suggested that some women experience a cognitive style such that they are prone to believe that they experienced specific traumatic events such as sexual abuse when they actually experienced other types of childhood stress such as neglect or emotional abuse but not sexual abuse. Certain personality styles such as borderline personality have been found to be more likely to be reporters of repressed childhood traumatic events. This controversy has resulted in numerous media reports as well as litigation against mental health professionals who work with these patients. In fact, clinicians working with repressed memory cases increase the chances that a mental health professional will likely be sued at a later date.

Eye Movement Desensitization Reprocessing (EMDR)

Photo: Courtesy Zach Plante.

EMDR has been a fairly new treatment approach for helping those who experience posttraumatic stress and other anxiety disorders and symptoms (Shapiro, 1989, 2001, 2002). It involves eye movement training to help cope with the stress of painful memories and feelings associated with traumatic life events (e.g., war experiences, rape, child victimization, phobias). Once it was introduced to the public and professional community, many clinicians signed up for specialized training and were offering EMDR services to the public before adequate research was conducted to demonstrate its effectiveness. It has been somewhat controversial over the years (Singer & Lalich, 1996).

EMDR began in 1987 when Francine Shapiro (a then–graduate student in psychology) noticed that her rapid eye movements when walking in a park appeared to minimize her negative feelings about particular personal memories. She thought that her eye movements had a desensitizing or calming effect. She tested her theory about eye movements and negative emotions associated with traumatic memories in a case study and then several controlled studies. Her initial studies were published in 1989. Other studies soon followed, conducted by both her and her colleagues as well as other independent researchers who were not invested in the treatment outcome.

This research ultimately led to the recommendation by the APA Division of Clinical Psychology Task Force Empirically Supported Treatments to list EMDR as a supported treatment for the treatment of PTSD in combat veterans (Chambless et al., 1996). Something about the procedure seems to help patients who experience traumatic memories and feelings (Lilienfeld & Arkowitz, 2006; Rodenburg, Benjamin, de Roos, Meijer, & Stams, 2009).

According to Dr. Shapiro and other EMDR experts (Shapiro, 2001, 2002), EMDR is an eight-phase information processing therapy where the patient attends to current and previous anxiety-producing experiences or memories in brief sequential periods while focusing on an external

(continued)

stimulus. The patients focus on a problematic image, thought, or feeling while simultaneously moving their eyes back and forth in a rapid manner following the therapist's fingers as they move across the field of vision for about 30 seconds or so. Dr. Shapiro suggests that EMDR helps patients by processing the various parts of their upsetting memories in a more productive manner. She offers several neurobiological theories about how EMDR might work in the brain, but at this point the theories are speculative (Lilienfeld & Arkowitz, 2006).

---

of deterioration among obsessive-compulsive patients as well (Foa & Steketee, 1977; Vaugh & Beech, 1985). Expressive psychotherapies, which may prove useful for many people under certain conditions, may not be the best choice for therapists working with patients who have many psychotic, borderline, or obsessive-compulsive disorders.

Patients who have little motivation for change, have low tolerance for anxiety, and a history of inability to maintain satisfying interpersonal relationships also tend to do poorly in psychotherapy (Kernberg, 1973; Mohr, 1995; Strupp, 1980). Thus the old adage, "You can lead a horse to water but you cannot make him drink" may be an appropriate way to think about highly unmotivated patients or those who have tremendous difficulty maintaining a relationship and/or tolerating anxiety. Patients who are highly suspicious, mistrustful, and hostile also generally do poorly in psychotherapy (Mohr et al., 1990; Strupp, 1980). Not all persons who present themselves to a therapist for psychotherapy are good candidates for it.

In addition to patient and patient–therapy fit variables, therapist characteristics have also been closely associated with poor treatment outcome. For example, therapists who lack empathy and are impatient and authoritarian tend to be associated with poor psychotherapy outcome (Lafferty, Beutler, & Crago, 1991; Yalom & Lieberman, 1971). Furthermore, therapists who fail to focus the therapy session, fail to deal with negative feelings of the patient toward the therapist or treatment, and inappropriately use various techniques

are also associated with poor treatment outcomes (Sachs, 1983). Unethical and incompetent therapists can certainly do a great deal of harm to their patients. For instance, sexual relationships between therapist and patient can be highly damaging (Apfel & Simon, 1985; Gabbard, 1994). Patients seeing poorly trained therapists or therapists who offer only one type of intervention applied to all types of problems are associated with poor outcomes (Singer & Lalich, 1996). Patient, therapist, and patient–therapist fit must be taken into consideration prior to beginning psychotherapy in order to minimize potential harm to patients. Psychotherapy can be harmful if these factors are not examined and if both therapists and patients alike assume that a psychotherapy experience can do no harm (Berk & Parker, 2009; Nicholson et al., 2009). In recent years, lists of potentially harmful treatments (PHTs) have been developed and published; it would behoove therapists and clients alike to review these before treatment services are offered (Lilienfeld, 2007).

The Big Picture

Psychotherapy is one of the most common activities conducted by clinical psychologists. Each patient, each psychologist, and each psychotherapy experience are unique. What works well with one person may not work well with another. Conducting useful research on psychotherapy is important yet challenging due to the uniqueness of each psychotherapeutic experience. Psychotherapy has evolved over the years from several distinct theoretical perspectives to an integrative and biopsychosocial contemporary evidence-based practice. The good news is that research suggests that therapy does in fact work. Yet, the intricate process of change in therapy is dependent on a range of specific and nonspecific factors, and the benefits, length, and patient–therapist variables involved in each treatment are best assessed on a case-by-case basis.

Contemporary clinical psychologists must continue to work toward understanding what works well in psychotherapy and to provide this service in a cost-effective, efficient, and evidence-based manner. The future of psychotherapy is likely to include efforts for more specific research-supported clinical guidelines to maximize treatment effectiveness. However, psychotherapy will always be a unique experience shared between a therapist and patient(s).

Key Points

1. An extensive review of all of the research studies conducted to determine if psychotherapy works generally concludes that psychotherapy is effective.
2. Research suggests that most psychotherapies tend to be very brief in duration, with an average of six sessions per psychotherapy experience. While most research suggests brief treatment is as effective as longer treatment, some data suggest that longer treatments are more beneficial.
3. Those from lower-socioeconomic classes and those who have less education are more likely to drop out of psychotherapy.
4. No one type of psychotherapy has been determined to be generally better or more effective than any other overall. Many authors suggest that different types of psychotherapy often result in different specific effects and, yet, these effects are not exclusive to only one type of therapy. In recent years, cognitive-behavioral approaches have come to dominate the list of empirically supported and evidence-based treatments.

5. Several common factors found in most psychotherapies have been associated with positive psychotherapy outcomes. These include the therapeutic relationship, expectations of success, confronting a problem, providing the experience of mastery or control over the problem, and an attribution of success or failure. The therapeutic relationship, beliefs about psychotherapy, and working on problems developing control and mastery all seem to be common curative factors in psychotherapy.
6. Behavioral change, with or without the assistance of psychotherapy, is generally not easy to accomplish. Humans tend to be creatures of habit, and even behavior or thinking patterns that are destructive tend to be remarkably difficult to change.
7. The professional literature has failed to demonstrate convincingly that trained professionals are superior to less trained professionals in positive therapeutic outcome. Therefore, effective therapists may not necessarily be those with the most training, experience, and credentials. However, research and practice suggests that highly trained professionals are more likely to have a wide range of treatment options and skills available to them relative to minimally trained persons.
8. Those who experience a mental illness tend to use medical services a great deal. It has been estimated that mental health patients use medical services more than twice as much as those who do not experience a mental health diagnosis. After patients receive psychotherapy, they tend to seek much less medical care than those who need but do not receive psychotherapy. Medical patients with chronic illnesses such as hypertension and diabetes lower their future medical costs by 18% to 31% when they receive psychological interventions. Thus, psychotherapy not only improves psychological functioning and wellbeing but also improves many medical symptoms and conditions as well as reducing overall health-care costs.

9. Research has shown that there are a large number of variables associated with poor treatment outcome. These variables include characteristics of the patient, the therapist, and the interaction or lack of fit between patient and therapist. Patients who have little motivation for change, little tolerance for anxiety, and a history of an inability to maintain satisfying interpersonal relationships also tend to do poorly in psychotherapy. Unethical and incompetent therapists can certainly do a great deal of harm as well.

Key Terms

Common factors
Curative factors
Psychotherapy treatment outcome

For Reflection

1. Does psychotherapy work?
2. How might psychotherapy work?
3. Is long-term psychotherapy superior to short-term psychotherapy?
4. Which type of psychotherapy seems to work best?
5. Name curative factors associated with psychotherapy.
6. Under what circumstances might psychotherapy be harmful?
7. Is a volunteer paraprofessional likely to be as good a psychotherapist as a psychologist or psychiatrist? Why or why not?

Real Students, Real Questions

1. Is it expensive to have your own practice? Is it difficult to get clients?
2. Do you think that people would benefit from psychotherapy provided over the Internet?
3. How does a sliding fee scale work?
4. What would you do if a patient says something that is really offensive?
5. What do you do if you think therapy has been completed but the patient still wants to be seen regularly?
6. Have you ever had a patient who changed your life or impacted you in a big way?

Web Resources

http://www.nmha.org
Learn more about the National Mental Health Association.

http://www.divisionofpsychotherapy.org
Learn more about the Psychotherapy division of the American Psychological Association.

http://www.apahelpcenter.org
Learn more about psychological services from the American Psychological Association Health Center.

Areas of Specialization

Chapter Objective
To highlight four of the most common and popular
  subspecializations in clinical psychology.

Chapter Outline

11

Chapter

The principles and practices of clinical
psychology can be applied to many areas
of research and clinical service. The skills developed by a clinical psychologist can be used
to better understand and treat both children
and adults as well as a wide variety of special
populations such as substance abusers and neglected children. These principles and skills can
also be used in a wide range of settings including hospitals, clinics, businesses, government
agencies, and even courts. Most clinical psychologists cannot develop and maintain the
skills necessary to perform competently with
all of these populations and settings. Although
many psychologists maintain a general clinical practice, more and more are focusing their
skills in an area of specialization. Like many
evolving and maturing fields, clinical psychology has developed a number of specialty and
subspecialty areas.

Many years ago, physicians were trained in
general medicine and were often asked to treat
all potential medical problems that emerged in
the community where they practiced. The era
in which almost every physician was a general

practitioner is now long gone. As medicine
has become increasingly sophisticated, many
physicians have focused their training into
specialties such as pediatrics, oncology, psychiatry, radiology, internal medicine, neurology, and cardiology. In fact, medical schools
have trouble recruiting people to be general
practitioners in needy areas. These specialties have further evolved into subspecialties,
such as pediatric oncology and geropsychiatry. Residency and fellowship programs were
developed to train physicians in these specialty areas and board certification processes
were instigated to certify physicians as competent in these specific areas of clinical practice.
While many physicians still maintain an essentially general practice (e.g., family physicians
and internists), a large number have chosen
to specialize.

Clinical psychology has undergone a very
similar developmental process. Psychologists
have been historically trained in a general
manner and subsequently have applied their
skills to all patients and problems they could
competently evaluate and treat. As the field

303

has become more sophisticated regarding specific problems of interest to clinical psychology, specialties have emerged. Graduate training programs, internships, and postdoctoral fellowship programs have responded to the era of specialization by training psychologists in these specialty areas. Finally, similar to medical board certification, psychology now offers board certification of psychologists seeking to claim special expertise in one of a number of specialty areas.

Some of the more prominent specialty areas in clinical psychology are health psychology, child psychology, neuropsychology, and forensic psychology. Subspecialty areas have also emerged, such as pediatric neuropsychology and forensic health psychology. Within each specialty area many psychologists focus their research and/or practice on a particular population or problem area. For example, some professionals who specialize in clinical health psychology primarily work in the area of eating disorders, smoking cessation, or alcohol abuse. Some who specialize in neuropsychology focus their attention on elderly stroke victims, patients with epilepsy, or individuals with head and spinal cord injuries. Psychologists who specialize in working with children might focus on children with emotional disorders, traumatic histories, or learning disabilities. Furthermore, many professionals maintain expertise in a technique rather than a problem or patient population. For example, some psychologists have special expertise in biofeedback, exposure therapies, or group therapy approaches. The list of potential specialty and subspecialty areas is remarkably long.

Some of the specialty areas overlap and thus are not mutually exclusive. For example, a pediatric neuropsychologist might specialize in head injuries suffered by children and consequently be called on to undertake a great deal of forensic work. Thus, such a psychologist may be said to specialize in forensic pediatric neuropsychology. Another professional may specialize in geriatric health psychology working with Alzheimer's patients. Another

psychologist might focus her professional work in the area of chronic pain and workman's compensation litigation and thus specialize in forensic health psychology. In short, not only are there numerous specialty and subspecialty areas but there are many different ways that these areas blend and merge together.

How do we make sense of all these specialty areas? What makes them distinct? Why do so many overlap? Although there are no simple answers to these questions, several principles help to provide some of the answers. First, as clinical psychology evolves, grows, and matures, more and more information has become available through research and practice that can be applied to specific problems and populations. In fact, clinical psychology is no longer limited to issues involving mental illness, and many clinical psychologists do not work with mental illness issues at all. Medical problems such as cancer, head injury, heart disease, and AIDS as well as legal problems such as child custody decisions, competency to stand trial, and product liability are now within the domain of clinical psychology. Thus, as clinical psychology has broadened in scope and focus, specialization has become increasingly necessary. As the field continues to grow and change, new specialties emerge and others diminish. Second, contemporary clinical psychology, as previously discussed, uses an interactive and evidence-based perspective rather than rigid adherence to one particular and limiting orientation. An integrated and evidence-based biopsychosocial model can be used with many problem areas and populations, allowing for both growth and overlap of specializations. Third, specific postgraduate training programs as well as board and proficiency certification have become available in a number of specialty areas. The establishment of specific training programs and certification procedures contributes to the official recognition and monitoring of these specialty areas.

This chapter cannot hope to do justice to all of the specialty and subspecialty areas in clinical psychology, but it discusses the four major contemporary areas of specialization: clinical health psychology, clinical child psychology, neuropsychology, and forensic psychology. The types of clinical and research problems addressed with each of these specialties will be highlighted, along with examples of specific assessment and intervention strategies. Typical subspecialties within each of the specialties is also described.

Clinical Health Psychology

Clinical health psychology is currently one of the most popular and fastest growing specialties in clinical psychology. The specialty of clinical health psychology formally began around 1980 and has been defined as: "... the aggregate of the specific educational, scientific, and professional contributions of the discipline of psychology to the promotion and maintenance of health, the prevention and treatment of illness, the identification of etiologic and diagnostic correlates of health, illness, and related dysfunction, and to the analysis and improvement of the health care system and health policy formation" (Matarazzo, 1982, p. 4). Health psychology is closely related to the field of behavioral medicine, which is defined as: "The interdisciplinary field concerned with the development and integration of behavioral and biomedical science, knowledge, and techniques relevant to health and illness and the application of this knowledge and these techniques to prevention, diagnosis, treatment, and rehabilitation" (Schwartz & Weiss, 1978a, p. 250).

Thus, whereas behavioral medicine is an interdisciplinary field in which MDs, PhDs, RNs and other professionals practice, **health psychology** involves the contribution of one field (psychology) to problems associated with health and illness. Health psychologists work in numerous diverse settings including hospitals, clinics, universities, businesses, government agencies, and private practices. They use the principles of psychology and behavior change to study and help people cope

better with medical illnesses as well as prevent potential illnesses from developing or worsening. They conduct research on the relationships between behavior and health and consult with organizations to maximize health-promoting behavior and policies while minimizing health-damaging behavior and policies. More than a trillion dollars are spent each year on health care in the United States, and a national effort has been promoted to reduce these costs through improved health behaviors (Carmody & Matarazzo, 1991; National Center for Health Statistics, 2001; S. Taylor, 2009). Health psychology offers effective strategies to deal with numerous health-related problems and has been at the forefront of improving health in America. The brief clinical health psychology case descriptions that appear within this section demonstrate that many of the intervention strategies used in health psychology as well as the problems themselves are complex and multidimensional.

Influenza, measles, tuberculosis, and other infectious diseases were the cause of most deaths in the United States during the first part of the twentieth century and in earlier times. During the past 100 years, medical advances have conquered many of these problems. Today, lifestyle factors that reflect health-damaging behavior patterns account for most deaths in all developed countries. Smoking, high-fat diets, sedentary lifestyles, unsafe sexual practices, accidents, and other "behavioral pathogens" (Matarazzo, 1984) are the culprits in at least 50% of the top-ten leading causes of death (Centers for Disease Control, 2008, 2009; Institute for the Future, 2000; Murphy, 2000; National Center for Health Statistics, 1993, 2001, 2002; S. Taylor, 2009). Heart disease, cancer, stroke, and other common killers are also closely associated with lifestyle factors. As a nation, we eat and drink too much, exercise too little, and develop habits that compromise our health. Therefore, most health problems of today are intimately tied to problems in behavior. In fact, research demonstrated that the primary causes of illness are due to emotions, cognitions, social relations, and behavior (Johnson, 2003). Health psychology hinges on the understanding that by changing unhealthy behavior, a range of significant health problems can be eliminated or minimized (Institute for the Future, 2000).

The principles of clinical psychology have been used to help people live more healthy lifestyles in order to avoid developing illnesses. These principles have also been used to help cope with illnesses once they have developed. Diabetes, cancer, heart disease, arthritis, asthma, AIDS, autoimmune diseases such as lupus and multiple sclerosis, chronic pain control, and other serious health problems have all been of interest to health psychologists. Individual and group psychotherapy, education, biofeedback, relaxation training, coping skills training interventions, and other strategies have been effectively used to assist many of these problems. In fact, psychological interventions such as biofeedback and relaxation training have become an important adjunct treatment for a number of health problems such as irritable bowel syndrome and Raynaud's disease. Health psychology presents an excellent example of the contemporary and integrative and evidence-based biopsychosocial approach to both medical and mental health problems. Interventions integrate medical treatment along with education, psychotherapy, social support, social engineering, and other approaches to maximize health and minimize illness. While there are numerous health behaviors and illnesses that are of interest to contemporary clinical health psychologists, several stand out as especially compelling current problems that have received tremendous attention from health psychology in recent years. These include smoking, obesity, alcohol consumption, stress management, AIDS, and chronic pain. These issues are briefly highlighted here. Table 11.1 is a list of many of the topics of interest to health psychologists.

Table 11.1   **Health Psychology Areas of Focus**

Alcohol	Smoking
Irritable bowel syndrome	Eating disorders
Panic disorders	Hypertension
Raynaud's disease	Asthma
Cardiovascular disease	Ulcers
Pain	Headache
Diabetes	Cancer
Spinal injuries	Epilepsy
Sleep disorders	Cystic fibrosis
AIDS	Stress
Sexual disorders	Substance abuse

Smoking

Photo: Courtesy Stockvault.net

Smoking cigarettes is considered to be the largest preventable cause of premature death in the nation (American Heart Association, 2009; McGinnis, Richmond, Brandt, Windom, & Mason, 1992; U.S. Department of Health and Human Services, 1983, 2007; S. Taylor, 2009). The Centers for Disease Control and Prevention reports that 20% of deaths in the United States are attributed to smoking (Centers for Disease Control and Prevention, 2008, 2009). Smoking has been associated with many illnesses, including cancer and heart disease (Centers for Disease Control and

Prevention, 2008, 2009; McGinnis et al., 1992; McKim, 1991; S. Taylor, 2009). Furthermore, smokers are more likely than nonsmokers to engage in other health-damaging behaviors such as eating high-fat foods and leading sedentary lifestyles (French, Hennrikus, & Jeffery, 1996). Health psychology has been involved in all aspects of smoking cessation as well as psychoeducational programs to prevent people from beginning the smoking habit. Although almost everyone knows that smoking is damaging to health, approximately 25% of the American adult and teenage population smokes (National Center for Health Statistics, 2006). Fortunately, the number of adults who smoke has decreased in recent years (McGinnis et al., 1992; National Center for Health Statistics, 2006). Intervention programs and public policies of various sorts have been useful in decreasing the number of adult smokers. However, the percentage of teenagers who smoke has tragically increased steadily in recent years. In fact, today about 26% of male teens and 22% of female teens smoke (National Center for Health Statistics, 2006).

People generally begin the smoking habit during their teenage years due to peer pressure, cultural norms, modeling of family, friends, and celebrities, as an act of rebellion, as an assertion of independence, and for a host of other reasons (Centers for Disease Control, 2008b; Chassin, Presson, Rose, & Sherman, 1996; Redmond, 1999; S. Taylor, 2009; U.S. Surgeon General, 1994). As opposed to many other unhealthy habits such as the consumption of high-fat foods, people generally report that smoking is an acquired taste. In other words, the pleasurable effects of smoking tend to occur after a number of initial attempts at smoking and not during the first few smoking episodes. In fact, smoking may initially result in coughing, headache, nausea, or other aversive symptoms. Once accustomed to smoking, however, the addictive qualities of nicotine as well as the psychological dependence associated with smoking result in a very difficult

habit for most people to break. Furthermore, anxiety, depression, irritability, and anger are associated with nicotine withdrawal (S. M. Hall, Munoz, Reus, & Sees, 1993; S. Taylor, 2009). Therefore, smoking often is used to avoid the negative consequences of nicotine withdrawal.

The majority of people who attempt to quit smoking are unsuccessful (Cepeda-Benito, 1993; Ockene et al., 2000). While some people are able to quit smoking on their own, many need professional assistance in stopping the habit (American Cancer Society, 2009). Treatments include biological interventions such as the nicotine patch and gum, which supply a constant dose of nicotine without the detrimental effects on lungs or other organs induced by smoking. These treatments provide the drug effect without the psychological and social reinforcement that maintains the psychological dependence on smoking. Other treatment approaches include psychological interventions such as problem-solving and coping skills training, hypnotherapy, biofeedback, and behavior modification approaches. Educational and social interventions such as group support are also used (Ockene et al., 2000; O. F. Pomerleau & C. S. Pomerleau, 1988; Schwartz, 1987; Zhu, Stretch, Balabanis, & Rosbrook, et al., 1996). Finally, social engineering and public policy approaches such as smoking bans in public places and large taxes to increase the price of smoking also discourage smokers from maintaining their habit. Research indicates that multimodal and integrative biopsychosocial approaches tend to work best in treating smokers (Hall et al., 1993; Hatsukami, Jensen, Allen, & Grillo, 1996; Hughes, 1993; Ockene, 1986; Prochaska, Velicer, DiClemente, & Fava, 1988; S. Taylor, 2009). Thus, fading dependence on nicotine by using a nicotine patch along with cognitive-behavioral coping strategies in the context of a support group may work best. Community-wide interventions such as the Stanford Heart Disease Prevention Project

Prevention in Health-Care Settings

Sadly, the major causes of death (especially for children and adolescents) are related to preventable health and lifestyle behaviors (Centers for Disease Control and Prevention, 2009; S. Taylor, 2009; U.S. Department of Health and Human Services, 2001, 2007). *Healthy People 2000, 2010, and 2020* are reports by the U.S. Department of Health and Human Services that have clearly articulated the health objectives for the United States that mostly involve changing health behaviors. For example, the leading cause of death among children and teens is accidents, and most of these are motor vehicle accidents. Furthermore, at least half of these accidents are alcohol related (S. Taylor, 2009; U.S. Department of Health and Human Services, 2007). Among adults, it is estimated by the same government reports that half of all deaths are related to behavioral factors such as smoking, drinking alcohol to excess, poor diet, sedentary lifestyles, unsafe sexual practices, homicides, and suicides. Health-care settings such as local hospitals and health clinics as well as other community settings that people frequent (e.g., schools, sporting events, churches) offer a potentially useful opportunity to help educate people as well as screen and intervene in problem areas such as those noted. There are a number of examples of quality prevention programs used in health-care settings that have improved the behavior of target populations as well as being cost effective (see Bennett-Johnson & Millstein, 2003 for a review). These include weight control, prenatal care, lead poisoning, and sexually transmitted diseases such as HIV/AIDS among other problems. Clinical psychologists help to design and implement these programs as well as offer consultation and educational resources and services to various at-risk target populations. For example, many African Americans are at risk for the development of heart disease such as hypertension (S. Taylor, 2009). Offering blood pressure and cholesterol screenings on church property after church services has been used in a wide variety of communities in order to assist in finding and potentially preventing heart disease from developing among an at-risk population.

(Meyer, Nash, et al., 1980) among others (Zhu et al., 1996) have also had some success at decreasing smoking behavior in entire communities.

Preventing people from starting to smoke through educational campaigns has also met with some limited success. Peer modeling approaches, role-playing ways to cope with social pressure, self-monitoring of smoking attitudes and behavior, multimedia presentations, and other methods have been used. Although not always effective, research indicates that these programs do prevent many at-risk children and adolescents from beginning to smoke (Carter, Bendell, & Matarazzo, 1985; McGinnis et al., 1992; Ockene et al., 2000; S. Taylor, 2009).

Obesity

Overweight, often defined as weighing 20% more than ideal, affects approximately 60% of the adult American population while **obesity** affects 30% of Americans (Kopelman, 2000; Koretz, 2001; National Center for Health Statistics, 2006). As smoking is decreasing in the United States, obesity is on the rise. Especially disturbing is the fact that up to 40% of children are overweight, with 80% of them becoming obese adults (Nash, 2003; National Center for Health Statistics, 2006; S. Taylor, 2009). Tragically, for the first time in several centuries, it has been estimated that current children have a shorter life span than the previous generation of children due to rising rates of obesity and related health problems such as diabetes and cardiovascular disease (Belluck, 2005; S. Taylor, 2009). Obesity has been associated with coronary heart disease, several forms of cancer, gall bladder disease, skeletal-joint problems, diabetes, infections, and so many other illnesses (Brownell & Wadden, 1992; Hsu, Chou, Hwang, & Lin, 2008; Kopelman, 2000; Stoll, 1996; S. Taylor, 2009; Von Itallie, 1985). Morbid obesity (i.e., weighing 100% above ideal weight) is associated with premature death due to a wide spectrum of illnesses. Obesity, like smoking, has become a serious national health problem.

Biopsychosocial factors have been found to contribute to the development of obesity. Research has shown that genetic factors and family history account for up to 60% of the variance in body fat (Bouchard & Perusse, 1996; Cohen, 2009; Price, 1987). Lifestyle factors such as sedentary behavior, high-fat food consumption, and television viewing have also been associated with obesity. Psychological and social factors such as stress, depression, access to a variety of highly attractive and high-calorie foods, and cultural influences also play roles in the development of obesity (Shell, 2002; S. Taylor, 2009). The complex interaction between biological vulnerability in combination with psychological and social factors clearly demands an integrative and evidence-based biopsychosocial approach to prevention and treatment (Brownell & Wadden, 1992; Hsu et al., 2008; Institute of Medicine, 2001; Shell, 2002).

Like smoking, the majority of those trying to lose weight are not successful (Agras, Berkowitz, Arnow, & Telch, 1996; Fairburn & Brownell, 2002; National Institutes of Health, 1992). While most people try to diet on their own to lose weight, many choose to join community weight-loss programs such as Diet Ease, Jenny Craig, Weight Watchers, Overeaters Anonymous, and Take Off Pounds Sensibly (TOPS). These programs also generally use an integrative approach combining medical intervention with social support, education, and counseling (Wang, Wadden, Womble, & Noras, 2003). In fact, over 500,000 people attend these community programs each year (S. Taylor, 2009). Others use medically supervised programs offered by medical centers and clinics throughout the country (e.g., Agras et al., 1996). The weight-loss industry is a multibillion-dollar industry. Sadly, the vast majority of those who attempt to lose weight either on their own or in an organized and professionally run program do not maintain their weight loss (Wang et al., 2003). About 95% of those who lose weight tend to regain all weight lost within five years (Brownell, 1993; Wadden et al., 1989).

Treatments for obesity reflect the biopsychosocial model. Treatments include surgery, medication, and very-low-calorie liquid diets for those who are morbidly obese. Behavioral modification, problem-solving and coping strategies, hypnotherapy, psychotherapy, group support, nutritional information programs, and exercise programs are also used to treat obesity. Multimodal approaches thus integrate medical intervention along with various forms of education and counseling. In addition to individual treatment, public health and informational approaches have also been used (Jeffery, 1988; Meyer, Maccoby, & Farquhar, 1980; Wang et al., 2003). Multimodal treatments integrating biopsychosocial factors tend to be most successful (Agras et al., 1996; Brownell, 1993; Fairburn & Brownell, 2002; S. Taylor, 2009).

Alcohol Abuse

Photo: Courtesy Stockvault.net

Alcohol abuse remains a major threat to the health and wellbeing of many (Casswell & Thamarangsi, 2009; Center for the Advancement of Health, 2001). Alcohol abuse is estimated to cost the nation $184 billion per year, with 10% of all Americans considered as alcoholic or problem drinker (Dorgan & Editue, 1995; National Institute on Alcohol Abuse and Alcoholism, 2004). Alcohol is the third leading cause of death in the United States (Center for the Advancement of Health, 2001). Almost half of all college-age people admit to an alcohol binge of five or more drinks in recent weeks (Presley & Meilman, 1992; Wechsler, Seibring , Liu, & Ahl, 2004). College students ages 18 through 24 have the highest percentage of problem drinkers of any age group (Ham & Hope, 2003), with rates of binge drinking among female students increasing dramatically in recent years (Wechsler et al., 2004). Alcohol consumption begins remarkably early in life, with over 50% of Americans reporting some alcohol use by age 13 (Pandina, 1986). In addition to the numerous physical, psychological, and social problems caused by alcohol-related abuse and

dependence, it has been estimated that about 50% of all traffic accidents are alcohol related as well as most murders, suicides, rapes, and violent crimes (National Institute on Alcohol Abuse and Alcoholism, 2004; S. Taylor, 2009; Weinhardt, Carey, Carey, Maisto, & Gordon, 2001). Approximately 100,000 deaths in the United States each year are due to alcohol consumption (Institute of Medicine, 2001). Alcohol appears to disinhibit people's control over their behavior and makes them less concerned about the consequences of their actions.

Like smoking and obesity, biopsychosocial factors are associated with both the development of alcohol-related problems and their treatment. Alcohol problems are associated with genetic and biological vulnerability (Finney & Moos, 1991; Goodman, 2008; Goodwin, 1986), and many individuals thus seem to be inherently predisposed to developing an alcohol-related problem. Some people are fortunately unlikely to develop alcohol problems due to inherited inability to drink alcohol. For example, about 25% of Asian individuals have a negative physiological reaction to alcohol, which results in little alcohol abuse in that population. While the United States has an alcohol problem prevalence rate of 10%, Taipei has one that is less than 1% (Yamamoto, Silva, Sasao, Wang, & Nguyen, 1993). Curiously, the Korean alcoholism rate is 22%, which is a rate more than twice that of the United States. Cultural expectations regarding heavy drinking appear to override the physiological tendency toward moderate alcohol consumption in the Korean population (Lee, 1992).

Psychological factors such as anxiety and depression as well as social factors such as peer influence, low income, and stress also play an important role in the development of alcohol problems (Brennan & Moos, 1990; Zucker & Gomberg, 1986). Research suggests that alcohol is often used as a way to buffer stress and thus becomes a maladaptive coping strategy (M. Seeman, A. Z. Seeman, & Budros, 1988; Stewart, 1996). Those who experience many negative life events as well as little social support are at risk for developing alcohol problems (Brennan & Moos, 1990; Stewart, 1996). Furthermore, those who feel a sense of powerlessness are at risk (M. Seeman et al., 1988). Drinking alcohol is temporarily rewarding since it can help people to feel less stressed and distract them from problems in living.

Treatment and prevention programs for alcohol abuse also reflect an evidence-based biopsychosocial perspective (Casswell & Thamarangsi, 2009). Alcohol treatment might include the use of Antabuse (a medication that prevents the metabolism of acetaldehyde), which results in severe nausea and vomiting when alcohol is consumed (Nathan, 1993) and medical detoxification in an inpatient hospital facility with individual, family, group, and educational components. Psychotherapy as well as group support through professionally run programs such as Alcoholics Anonymous (AA) are also beneficial (Kelly, 2003; National Institute on Alcohol Abuse and Alcoholism, 2000, 2004). Relapse prevention approaches that focus on specific problem-solving strategies for alcohol abuse have also been used successfully with alcoholics (Marlatt & Gordon, 1985). Once again, multimodal approaches seem to work best (Casswell & Thamarangsi, 2009; Center for the Advancement of Health, 2001; Kelly, 2003). However, relapse is extremely high. For example, only about 50% of those treated for alcohol problems remain sober one year following treatment (Nathan, 1996), and 75% of those who join AA drop out within a year (Alcoholics Anonymous, 1990; National Institute on Alcohol Abuse and Alcoholism, 2000, 2004).

Stress Management

Stress has been associated with the development and maintenance of numerous physical and mental health problems. Ultimately, the human cost of excess stress is unquantifiable. Psychological and social stress adversely impact many systems of the body, including the immune (Ader & Cohen, 1984;

Bremner, 2002; Cohen, Tyrrell, & Smith, 1993) and endocrine systems (Krishman, Doraiswamy, Venkataraman, Reed, & Richie, 1991). Chronic psychosocial stress has been found to damage the brain through hypercortisol activity in the hippocampus and elsewhere (Bremner, 2002; Sapolsky, 1990; Sapolsky & Meaney, 1986). Thus, chronic stress can actually cause brain damage. People who lack a sense of control and self-efficacy in their lives appear especially vulnerable to stress-related problems (Bandura, 1986, 1989; Kobasa, 1982). Finally, environmental stressors such as poverty, violence, and other social ills contribute to poor physical and mental health and similarly need to be addressed at policy, preventative, and intervention levels (S. Taylor, 2009).

Stress management has been found to help people experiencing many physical and mental health problems, including cancer, heart disease, diabetes, AIDS, and chronic pain. Social support has also been found to help in the treatment of stress-related problems (Cohen, 1988; S. Taylor, 2009) as well as numerous medical problems. For example, social support and stress management strategies provided in group therapy have been found to assist in helping cancer patients cope better and even live longer (Spiegal, 1992). Stress management techniques such as relaxation training, meditation, biofeedback, diaphragmatic breathing, stress inoculation training, psychotherapy, visual imagery, and other approaches have been found useful in reducing stress (Scheufele, 2000; S. Taylor, 2009).

Acquired Immune Deficiency Syndrome (AIDS)

Tragically, about 1.1 million Americans are infected with the HIV virus, and about 500,000 deaths have occurred from **acquired immune deficiency syndrome (AIDS)** in the United States since 1981 (Centers for Disease Control, 2007; S. Taylor, 2009). It is estimated that about 40 million people are infected worldwide with two-thirds living in Africa

Women and AIDS

According to the Centers for Disease Control (CDC), HIV/AIDS rates among adolescent girls and women have increased significantly in recent years. This is especially true among ethnic minority females such as African American and Latina women. For example, the percentage of AIDS cases among women and girls in the United States increased from 7% in 1985 to 25% by 1999, and although minority women represent less than 25% of all women in the United States, they represent about 75% of all AIDS cases among American women (Center for Disease Control, 2007). The CDC suggests that psychologists and other health-care professionals aggressively develop prevention programs that target these at-risk women.

Clinical psychologists often work with at-risk women in both clinical and research settings. Many at-risk women may need help to better control their sexual health by avoiding high-risk sexual behavior such as failing to engage in protected sex. For example, a number of psychologists have developed prevention programs that assist women in developing better skills to encourage their male sexual partners to use condoms. Many of these women may have experienced physical or sexual abuse in the past or among their current sexual partners, and thus helping them to cope more effectively with their abuse is one way to help them more productively avoid unsafe sexual activity.

The National Institute of Mental Health is currently conducting a multisite longitudinal study aimed at minimizing HIV/AIDS among pregnant teens and young women. The study is a randomized controlled trial of 1,120 participants in both Atlanta and New Haven, Connecticut, where HIV/AIDS rates among young women are especially high. The project utilizes a structured approach to prenatal care development to hopefully use the window of opportunity of pregnancy to help these women adopt more safe sex and other techniques to minimize the odds of getting HIV/AIDS (World Health Organization, 2006).

(World Health Organization, 2006). AIDS is the fourth leading cause of death worldwide and is the second leading cause of death among young Americans ages 25 through 44 (Institute of Medicine, 2001). Changing problematic high-risk behavior is the best way to prevent AIDS from spreading since no vaccine is currently available. Engaging in safer sex as well as avoidance of shared needles among IV drug users are requisites to minimizing the spread of the infection. Multimodal psychoeducational programs that involve informational, motivational, skill-building, sexuality training, and public policy approaches have proved successful in reducing high-risk behaviors in a variety of populations (Ekstrand & Coates, 1990; Kelly & Kalichman, 1995; S. Taylor, 2009). For example, this type of program reduced unprotected sex in the San Francisco male gay community from 37% to 2% in one study (Ekstrand & Coates, 1990). Self-management training and social support have also proved useful in behavioral change among high-risk groups (Kelly, St. Lawrence, Hood, & Brasfield, 1989; S. Taylor, 2009). Finally, enhancing self-efficacy and perceived control

Case Study: Celeste Experiences Type A Personality and Irritable Bowel Syndrome

Celeste is a 40-year-old Korean American manager with a Type A personality (e.g., competitive, hard-driving, hostile, time urgent) and irritable bowel syndrome. She has frequent stomach aches and alternating patterns of constipation and diarrhea. Her father and grandfather both had colon cancer and one of her sisters also struggles with irritable bowel syndrome. She notices that her symptoms are worse when she is under stress. She tends to live life on the edge, always taking on more things than she can comfortably handle and waiting until the last minute to complete work assignments. She always feels that she is in a rush and reports that she frequently eats and even makes phone calls in her car while driving on the highway to work each morning. Certain foods seem to make her symptoms worse as well. Pizza and other high-fat fast foods seem to increase her stomach complaints.

After consulting with her physician, she was referred to a clinical health psychologist for assistance with her symptoms. Reflecting a biopsychosocial intervention approach, in addition to her medical treatment, she participated in efforts to change her lifestyle and increase her social support network. After a careful evaluation, Celeste and the psychologist agreed to work on many of the lifestyle factors that contributed to her symptoms. She agreed to work on developing a comprehensive relaxation program that included regular aerobic exercise, diaphragmatic breathing exercises, relaxation imagery, and cognitive restructuring concerning her need to be in a rush so much of the time. She also worked on changing her eating patterns to avoid problematic fast foods. She worked on getting up earlier to avoid the constant morning rush. She also worked on increasing her social support network of friends and took efforts to develop a satisfying intimate relationship. While it was very difficult for Celeste to alter these patterns, she did achieve reduction in symptoms after several months of consultation.

over sexual behavior has been found to predict safe-sex practices (Gerrard, Gibbons, & Bushman, 1996; O'Leary, 1992). The battle against AIDS provides another classic example of a devastating illness that is completely preventable through behavioral change (Institute of Medicine, 2001; S. Taylor, 2009).

Chronic Pain Control

It has been estimated that over 9 million Americans suffer from **chronic pain** with over $100 billion having been spent each year on medications to decrease various types of pain (Bonica, 1992; Farrugia & Fetter, 2009; S. Taylor, 2009). The severity of pain seems only remotely related to individual reactions to pain. Some people cope remarkably well with severe pain while others do not: Some people are incapacitated from somewhat milder forms of pain while others are not. Pain perception is thus largely a subjective experience, with biopsychosocial factors interacting to determine the unique pain experience for each person (Banks & Kerns, 1996; Farrugia & Fetter, 2009; Hoffman, Papas, Chatkoff, & Kerns, 2007; Keefe, Dunsmore, & Burnett, 1992). Psychological states such as anxiety and depression as well as pessimism, low self-efficacy, and little sense of control appear closely related to pain experience (Banks & Kerns, 1996; Hoffman et al., 2007; Keefe et al., 1992). Furthermore, those with little social support generally cope less well with pain (Farrugia & Fetter, 2009; Fordyce, 1988; Jamison & Virts, 1990). Relaxation techniques, coping skills training, psychotherapy, biofeedback, group therapy, hypnosis, and cognitive restructuring have all been found to be useful in conjunction with medical interventions in the treatment of chronic pain (Barlow & Rapee, 1991; Farrugia & Fetter, 2009; Hoffman et al., 2007; Keefe et al., 1992; Mercado, Carroll, Cassidy, & Cote, 2000; S. Taylor, 2009).

Conclusion

Health psychologists use the principles and procedures of clinical psychology and apply them to the field of medicine and health. Health psychologists are useful in helping people with a wide variety of health concerns and illnesses. Many health problems are associated with health-damaging behaviors and therefore health psychologists seek to help people develop lifestyles that are health promoting rather than health damaging. Eating healthy low-fat foods, minimizing alcohol consumption, eliminating smoking and unsafe sexual practices, wearing seatbelts, and better managing stress minimize the risk of premature death as well as the risk of developing a long list of health problems. Once health problems occur, health psychologists are involved with helping people cope better with their illnesses and minimize exacerbation or worsening of symptoms. Obtaining social support, learning information about the illness, finding strategies to cope with pain, adhering to the medical treatment regimens, and better understanding underlying causes of noncompliance to medical treatments are all of interest to health psychology.

Child Clinical Psychology

Child clinical psychologists specialize in working with children and their families. Specializing in child and family work is enormously popular among clinical psychologists (Brown, 2003; Kim-Cohen, 2007; Mash & Barkley, 1989; Roberts & Steele, 2009). In fact, as discussed in Chapter 2, most of the earliest clinical psychologists at the turn of the twentieth century specialized in working with children. Today, these psychologists obtain training in developmental psychology and both child assessment and treatment. They commonly work in community mental health clinics, child guidance clinics, schools, children's hospitals, and private practices. Some of the common problem areas that are the focus of work for child clinical psychologists include physical and/or sexual abuse, attention deficit hyperactivity disorder, conduct disorders, learning disabilities, autism, enuresis (bed wetting), depression, other mood and behavior disorders, and school phobia. These psychologists may provide consultation to schoolteachers, school counselors, pediatricians, day-care workers, parents, and others. They may assist teachers in classroom behavior management or assist parents in developing better parenting skills. Table 11.2 presents a list of topics of interest to child clinical psychologists.

Pediatric psychology is a blend of **child clinical psychology** and health psychology, and is often called child health psychology. Pediatric psychologists are child clinical psychologists who generally work with children and families in hospital settings where significant medical disorders are prominent in the clinical picture. These medical problems might include cancer, epilepsy, diabetes, asthma, eating disorders, or cystic fibrosis (Powers, Shapiro, & DuPaul, 2003; Rudolph, Dennig, & Weisz, 1995; Roberts & Steele, 2009; S. Taylor, 2009). The pediatric psychologist might offer pain management strategies to children or help the family cope more effectively with understanding and assisting a child undergoing significant medical problems. They may help the child and family cope with invasive medical procedures, anxiety and depression, or noncompliance with medical treatment. They may act as a consultant to various medical units and departments to assist physicians, nurses, and other professionals in responding to the emotional and behavioral sequelae of severe medical illnesses in children (Brown, 2003; Roberts & Steele, 2009;

Table 11.2 **Examples of Diagnostic Problem Areas of Focus among Child Clinical Psychologists**

Attention deficit hyperactivity disorder	Conduct disorders
Learning disabilities	Autism
Asperger's disorder	Pervasive developmental disorders
Tourette's disorder	Tics
Encopresis	Enuresis
Separation anxiety	School phobia
Selective mutism	Social anxiety and phobia
Child abuse and neglect	

In Hospital Settings

Cancer	Asthma
Seizures	Diabetes
Headaches	Cystic fibrosis
Medical problems resulting from child abuse and neglect	
Coping with painful medical procedures	

Case Study: Weight-Loss Treatment Program

People who are morbidly obese or 100% above ideal weight are offered a group treatment program through a university hospital. The program combines a very-low-calorie diet along with nutritional information, group support, medical monitoring, and a variety of psychological and social interventions. Patients are interviewed to ensure that they are appropriate for the group. Applicants with severe personality or other mental disorders or medical disorders that contraindicate rapid weight loss are not included in the program. Patients participate in weekly group meetings for six months while they use a very-low-calorie liquid food product. The weekly group meetings include social support discussion of issues important to individual group members as well as information about diet, exercise, food preparation, and contending with social situations involving food. Patients have a weekly medical appointment to ensure that their medical status is stable and that their weight loss is carefully monitored. Following six months of liquid diet, food is gradually reintroduced beginning with packaged frozen foods and, eventually, self-prepared foods. Packaged foods are used to minimize decision making regarding preparation and portion control. After about a year of the weekly program and a significant reduction in weight loss, group members are invited to participate in a twice-per-month maintenance group where support and information are available to assist in the challenging task of weight-loss maintenance.

Rodrigue, 1994; Rudolph et al., 1995). Pediatric psychologists also may assess neuropsychological functioning, level of cognitive functioning, and psychosis, and offer individual, group, and family therapy.

Attention Deficit Hyperactivity Disorder

Attention deficit hyperactivity disorder (ADHD) has received a great deal of national

Case Study: Joe Experiences Alcoholism

Joe is a 32-year-old Caucasian man with a severe alcohol problem. He reports that he drinks two bottles of wine per evening as well as a fifth of Scotch over the course of the week. His wife and children are very worried about his alcohol consumption and have insisted that he seek help from a psychologist specializing in alcohol abuse treatment.

Joe admits that he has an alcohol problem and feels that his stressful job contributes to the problem. He works in sales and has trouble reaching his sales quotas each month. Furthermore, he feels that his boss dislikes him a great deal and wants to find a way to fire him. Joe considers himself a wine connoisseur and enjoys collecting, tasting, and reading about fine wines. He says he has a special fondness for French wines from the St. Emilion region of Southern France.

After several sessions, Joe agrees to participate in an AA program near his home. He also agrees to see his physician to talk about the medical ramifications of his drinking. Psychotherapy focused on his stress at work and his extremely high expectations for himself and for others. Exercise and other more health-promoting behaviors were encouraged. Joe also had several treatment sessions with his wife in attendance to work on marital conflicts both involving and underlying his alcohol consumption. After a drinking binge, Joe was arrested for driving under the influence of alcohol and only then agreed to urine alcohol screening.

attention in recent years, being featured in the cover stories of major news magazines such as *Time* and *Newsweek* and as the topic of several best-selling books. Child clinical psychologists are frequently asked to conduct evaluations to diagnose ADHD; provide individual, family, and group treatment for ADHD children; and consult with teachers, pediatricians, and parents about social, behavioral, emotional, medical, and educational interventions with ADHD children. Many psychologists are at the forefront of research and public policy campaigns concerning ADHD (e.g., Barkley, 1993, 1996, 2000, 2009; Pelham, 1993). It is currently one of the most frequently encountered clinical issues faced by many child clinical psychologists.

ADHD affects approximately 3% to 5% of children, but is primarily found in boys (American Psychiatric Association, 2000; Barkley, 1993, 2000, 2009; Kelly, 2009). Symptoms include an inability to sustain attention and concentration as well as problems with impulsivity, overactivity, irritability, and moodiness. Children with ADHD often have trouble getting along with peers and are usually disruptive at home and in the classroom.

ADHD children tend to be very active and oppositional, and often get in trouble at both home and school (Barkley, 1989, 1993, 2000, 2009; Bradley & Golden, 2001; Kelly, 2009; Waschbusch, 2002). Restlessness and impulsivity are generally not well tolerated by parents, peers, and teachers. Attention and organizational problems among ADHD children are usually lifelong problems (Barkley, 1989, 2000, 2009). Adults who experienced ADHD as children often report that they have similar trouble with attention, impulsivity, and interpersonal relationships as adults (Barkley, 2009). Furthermore, they are also much more likely to develop antisocial and criminal behavior, underachievement, and both emotional and relational problems as adults (Barkley, 2009; Young, Toone, & Tyson, 2003).

Biopsychosocial factors play a role in the etiology, manifestation, and treatment of ADHD (Bradley & Golden, 2001; Barkley, 2009; Diller, Tanner, & Weil, 1996; Edwards, Schultz, & Long, 1995; Goos, Ezzatian, & Schachar, 2007; Kelly, 2009). Brain functioning in certain regions of the cortex and heredity are believed to play significant roles

Disabilities and the Americans with Disabilities Act (ADA)

Photo: Courtesy Stockvault.net

There are about 55 million Americans (or 20% of the population) who experience a physical or mental disability covered by the Americans with Disabilities Act (National Organization on Disability, 2009; Thomas & Gostin, 2009; Wellner, 2001).

According to the American Medical Association (2001), the most common forms of disabilities include arthritis, back and spine problems, and cardiovascular disease. Sadly, only 29% of those who experience disabilities work while 72% want to work (National Organization on Disability, 1998). Of those who work, those with disabilities earn only 66% of the income those without disabilities earn with the earning power of minority persons with disabilities even less (Atkinson & Hackett, 1998).

The Americans with Disabilities Act (ADA) was signed into law during 1990 and was recently amended in 2008, which took effect in 2009. It seeks to assist those with disabilities with potential discrimination. In addition to medical disabilities, the act also includes psychiatric disabilities as well as depression, bipolar, schizophrenia, personality disorders, obsessive-compulsive disorder, and panic. Substance abuse, impulse-control disorders such as gambling, and sexual impulse disorders are not covered under the ADA.

The ADA sought to protect disabled persons from experiencing discrimination and help them to obtain reasonable accommodations in their work, school, and other environments. These accommodations might include wheelchair access to buildings and offices, restrooms, and elevators, as well as sign-language interpreters, large-print materials, access for guide animals, and so forth.

Clinical psychologists must be attentive to their own feelings and reactions to people with disabilities as they would regarding anyone from a different culture or experience than their own. Psychologists

(continued)

need to help those with disabilities cope with the challenges that they face such as dealing with misunderstandings, prejudice, employment discrimination, and so forth. Psychologists must be abreast of both the ethical and legal guidelines applicable to those with disabilities as well as the limitations of their services (especially testing services) for these populations. Psychologists can better help their clients with disabilities if they are also aware of community resources and services that are available to them.

---

in the development of ADHD (Barkley, 1996, 2002, 2009; Beiderman et al., 1992; Frick, Strauss, Lahey, & Christ, 1993; Wilens, Beiderman, & Spencer, 2002). People with ADHD tend to have less brain activity in the frontal cortex and basal ganglia area than controls when tested (Bradley & Golden, 2001; Goos et al., 2007; Zametkin et al., 1990). ADHD also appears to be more common in family members with at least one other ADHD member (Barkley, 1993, 1996, 2000, 2009; Goos et al., 2007). Psychological and social factors such as child abuse have also been associated with the development of ADHD symptoms (Diller et al., 1996; Kelly, 2009). Children with ADHD usually receive a great deal of negative attention from parents, siblings, teachers, and peers, which results in few friendships, frequent teasing, and other social problems. These children often develop depression and low self-esteem as a result of these social interactions (Barkley, 1989, 1993, 1996, 2000, 2009). They also often experience learning disabilities, and develop conduct and substance abuse disorders later in life (American Psychiatric Association, 2000; Barkley, 2009; Levine, 2003a, 2003b).

ADHD is not easy to diagnose. Many biopsychosocial factors might contribute to impulsivity, inattention, and disruptive behavior without constituting ADHD per se. Marital discord, physical and/or sexual abuse, depression, posttraumatic stress disorder, poor child-rearing practices, learning disabilities, conduct disorders, and other problems may all result in ADHD-like symptoms (Barkley, 1996, 2000, 2009; Edwards et al., 1995; Kelly, 2009). Parents, teachers, and pediatricians may also quickly diagnose ADHD without a

careful evaluation. Many parents are invested in obtaining an ADHD diagnosis rather than confronting the possibility that their child-rearing practices are faulty or that there exist other emotional factors to account for the problematic symptoms. A careful diagnosis usually involves a thorough history, a close review of the child's behavior at home and at school, as well as psychological, cognitive, and educational testing.

Treatment of ADHD also reflects the biopsychosocial interplay of factors involved in the development and maintenance of ADHD symptoms. Stimulant medication such as Ritalin is often used and improves ADHD symptoms in approximately 75% of all cases (Barkley, 2000, 2009; Hazell, 2007; Pelham, 1993; Swanson et al., 1993; Wilens et al., 2002). However, stimulant medication has been found to improve attention and concentration even among many non-ADHD children. Cognitive problem-solving strategies to help children learn to think before acting have proved successful with ADHD children (Hinshaw, 2003; Kendall & Braswell, 1985; Whalen, Henker, & Hinshaw, 1985). Relaxation training and biofeedback have also shown some promise (Hinshaw, 2003; Raymer & Poppen, 1985). Parent and teacher consultation is also an important adjunct in successful treatment (Barkley, 1993, 1996, 2000, 2009; Fiore, Becker, & Nero 1993; Swanson et al., 1993). Group social skills training is also often used to help ADHD children learn to get along better with other children. A multimodal approach addressing biopsychosocial factors appears to be most comprehensive and effective (Barkley, 1993, 1996, 2000, 2009; Diller et al.,

1996; Kelly, 2009; Hazell, 2007; Hinshaw, 2003; Waschbusch, 2002; Wilens et al., 2002).

Learning Disabilities

Learning disabilities (LD) are another common clinical problem faced by child clinical psychologists. A learning disability is diagnosed when a child experiences a cognitive processing impairment (e.g., visual-motor, auditory) that impedes academic achievement in relation to aptitude measured by intellectual functioning (i.e., IQ). Many children experience problems in reading, writing, mathematics, and other academic areas as a result of one or more learning disabilities. While many children perform poorly in various school subjects due to lack of motivation and interest, poor study skills, or psychological, family, or social problems that interfere with school performance, many children have a learning disability that hinders their performance (Levine, 2003a, 2003b; Smith-Spark & Fisk, 2007). It is estimated that about 20% of school children have a diagnosable learning disability, with boys being much more vulnerable to this problem than girls (American Psychiatric Association, 2000; Heaton, 1988). Learning disabilities are a risk factor for dropping out of school (American Psychiatric Association, 2000; Levine, 2003a, 2003b; Wagner, 1990), adult unemployment (Morris & Turnbull, 2007; Shapiro & Lentz, 1991), and other psychological and social problems (Levine, 2003a, 2003b; Russell, 1997; Spreen, 1988). Children with learning disabilities often have negative school experiences and are more likely to experience low self-esteem, depression, anxiety, and disruptive behaviors. Learning disabilities often evade detection by parents and teachers who may alternately attribute difficulties in school to laziness, low intellectual ability, oppositionality, or other social or emotional problems (Levine, 2003a, 2003b).

Like ADHD, learning disabilities have received a great deal of clinical, research, and media attention in recent years. Fairly recently, many colleges have begun to offer special admission consideration to learning-disabled applicants. Untimed tests are also available at many schools and during national examinations such as the Scholastic Aptitude Test (SAT). Fortunately, learning disabilities have received enough attention to alert many parents, teachers, school administrators, and others of this potential basis of children's difficulties in school. However, learning disabilities has also become a popular diagnosis, which non–learning disability children and their parents seek in order to obtain the advantage of untimed SATs and school exams as well as special consideration for college admission.

Like ADHD, learning disabilities are not always easy to diagnose (Levine, 2003a, 2003b; Russell, 1997; Smith-Spark & Fisk, 2007). Many different problems can be associated with poor school performance. Psychological and social problems, marital discord, poor motivation, low aptitude, poor nutrition, large class sizes, stress, illness, poor teaching, and a host of other factors may contribute to poor school performance by any given child. Additionally, many children with serious psychiatric or medical problems also appear to have learning disabilities (real or supposed). Children with ADHD, *pervasive developmental disabilities*, Asperger's syndrome, depression, posttraumatic stress disorder, cultural or language differences, and other problems often have trouble with school performance.

The diagnosis of learning disabilities is usually made by child clinical psychologists in consultation with educational specialists. Intellectual, educational, and psychological testing along with interviews of teachers, parents, and the child are used to evaluate a potentially learning-disabled child. Generally, a learning disability is defined as a statistically significant difference between aptitude and achievement as well as a diagnosable processing problem, which might include visual or auditory difficulties. However, each state selects a specific criterion for the diagnosis and this criterion varies a great deal from state to state. For example, a 22.5-point difference (one and one-half standard deviation units) between aptitude assessed by a standard IQ test and achievement must be documented to meet the California state criterion for a learning disability.

A classic example of a learning disability is **dyslexia,** a reading disability that involves letter reversals such as confusing a *b* with a *d*. Dyslexia makes reading and learning difficult and can involve both visual and/or auditory discrimination problems. Aptitude testing is conducted using the standard IQ tests described in Chapter 8. Achievement testing involves educational testing as also described in Chapter 8. While psychologists frequently conduct both types of testing, they often work in conjunction with educational specialists who provide the achievement testing while the psychologist conducts the aptitude and psychological testing.

In addition to learning disabilities that involve reading, writing, math, and other academic skills, learning disabilities that primarily involve social relationships also impact children. Asperger's syndrome and *nonverbal learning disability* are two examples in which academic performance may be acceptable but social skills significantly impaired. These children are often unable to adequately interact with peers and teachers and have difficulty interpreting and responding to the subtleties of social interaction.

Prevailing theories concerning the etiology of learning disabilities involve genetic and neurological factors. Several studies have suggested that learning disabilities are heritable (Cardon et al., 1994; Myers & Hammil, 1990; Pennington & Smith, 1988). Other researchers suggest that early childhood or prenatal brain damage might cause learning disabilities (Hynd & Semrud-Clikeman, 1989; Russell, 1997). These biological influences interact with psychological, social, and educational issues to result in the manifestation of learning disabilities. Relationships with parents and teachers as well as the child's personality, ability to compensate for deficits, cultural expectations, and other factors are all integral to the expression and repercussions of learning disabilities. Optimal treatment therefore reflects this biopsychosocial

perspective. Special tutoring and computer-assisted techniques that help in compensating for learning challenges have proven useful. Furthermore, psychotherapy, parent education, and teacher consultation are also ideally incorporated into intervention programs. Children often need family and school support as well as psychotherapy to come to terms with a learning disability diagnosis. Feeling different from others, damaged, and contending with the self-esteem, depressive, and anxiety symptoms potentially associated with learning disabilities requires individual, family, and/or group psychotherapy (Levine, 2003a, 2003b; Smith-Spark & Fisk, 2007).

Child Abuse and Neglect

Photo: Courtesy Stockvault.net

Many clinical child psychologists and pediatric psychologists are involved in evaluation, treatment, research, and policy development concerning **child abuse and neglect** (Emery & Laumann-Billings, 1998; Shipman & Taussig, 2009). Sadly, many children are physically, sexually, and/or emotionally abused by parents, stepparents, other family members, family friends, and even strangers, with 76% of murdered children being under the age of 5 and harmed by one of their parents (U.S. Department of Health and Human Services, 2008). Some rare but high-profile cases involving abduction and murder receive a great deal of national and sometimes international attention and highlight the hideous problem of violence toward children. However, parents, rather than strangers, are responsible for the vast majority of children being abused, neglected, and even murdered. In fact, it is estimated that about 97% of all child abuse cases involve one or both parents as the perpetrator of the abuse (American Humane Association, 1984; Stith, Liu, Davies, Boykin, Alder, Harris, et al., 2009; References and further reading may be available for this article. To view references and further reading you must purchase this article. U.S. Department of Health and Human Services, 2008). Both boys and girls appear to be mistreated at about the same rate. According to the U.S. Department of Health and Human Services (2008), there were 794,000 cases of documented child abuse reported in 2007, with 60% being neglect cases, 11% being physical abuse cases, and 8% being sexual abuse cases. A third of the cases involve children younger than age 4. Sexual abuse cases tend to be more common among female victims than male victims.

A number of risk factors are associated with people who are more likely to abuse their children (Faust, Runyon, & Kenny, 1995; Stith et al., 2009; U.S. Department of Health and Human Services, 2008). The most prominent of these includes a personal history of abuse. Thus, parents who abuse their children generally were abused by their parents when they were children (Chafel & Hadley, 2001; Faust et al., 1995; Garbarino & Stocking, 1980; Stith et al., 2009). Alcohol and drug abuse, socioeconomic stress, occupational and marital stress, poor coping skills, and impulse-control problems all contribute to potential abuse (Faust et al., 1995; Stith et al., 2009). While child abuse and neglect is found in all segments of society, it generally comes to the attention of child protection services and law enforcement among the poor and disadvantaged (Chafel & Hadley, 2001).

All psychologists in every state are mandated to report suspected child abuse and neglect to child protective services and/or the police (Deisz, Doueck, & George, 1996; McDevitt, 1996). Therefore all psychologists must be trained in the signs and symptoms of child abuse. Child clinical psychologists are frequently involved in the assessment of possible abuse, in child custody evaluations, and in the treatment of both abused children and their families. Child clinical psychologists also often offer psychoeducational classes to help abusive parents learn better ways of interacting with their children. Child clinical psychologists might also work with legal professionals to determine appropriate home placements for abused children.

Children who are abused often suffer from anxiety, depression, oppositional and conduct disorders, and other problems (Barkley, Mash, Heffernan, & Fletcher, 2003; Shipman & Taussig, 2009; Willis, 1995). Troubles with trust, chronic fear, bodily vulnerability, self-esteem, and shame are also common. Abused children are also more likely to develop eating disorders as well (Goldfarb, 1987). Perpetrators of abuse often suffer from alcohol abuse and other problems associated with having been themselves victimized as children (Stith et al., 2009). Treatment of both victims and perpetrators of abuse can be very difficult (Kendziora & O'Leary, 1993; Shipman & Taussig, 2009). Funding of child abuse treatment programs frequently is reduced and eliminated during government budget-cutting periods. The embarrassment and humiliation of being abused often prevents children, especially adolescents and boys, from acknowledging victimization and willingly participating in treatment. The same is true of perpetrators, who also may face criminal prosecution. Many abused children find themselves living in various foster homes or with relatives, rendering consistent treatment a challenge. In addition to the victimization of the abuse, usually the child, rather than the victimizing parent, is taken from the home and placed in a new environment. Parents, foster parents, and other guardians are often wary and skeptical of mental health services that may be perceived as being closely connected with law enforcement. Treatment dropout among perpetrators of child abuse is remarkably high and estimated to be about 90% in the absence of court involvement and about 40% when it is specifically mandated by the courts (Shipman & Taussig, 2009; Wolfe, Aragona, Kaufman, & Sandler, 1980). Efforts by the courts and policymakers to preserve families by trying to keep abused children with abusive parents can dangerously backfire with repeated abusive episodes occurring even during treatment.

A unique form of child abuse seen among pediatric psychologists working in hospital settings includes *factitious disorder* or *Munchausen's by proxy disorder* (Eastwood & Bisson, 2008; Sanders, 1995). A factitious disorder involves the "intentional production or feigning of physical or psychological signs or symptoms" (American Psychiatric Association, 2000). In Munchausen's by proxy disorder, a parent (usually the mother) obtains gratification from the attention and support she receives from medical personnel when her child is ill. She therefore intentionally induces illnesses in her child through poisoning or other methods in order to seek treatment in the hospital setting. Frequent and mysterious illnesses among children might suggest that a parent is affected by Munchausen's by proxy disorder (Eastwood & Bisson, 2008; Sanders, 1995). Pediatric psychologists might evaluate the mother and child and contact child protective services to investigate allegations of potential abuse.

Anorexia Nervosa

Anorexia nervosa affects about 1% of the adolescent female population. Age of onset is generally around 17, though it can occur throughout adolescence and even into adulthood (American Psychiatric Association, 2000; Herzog, 1988). Only about 5% of anorexics are males. Anorexia is defined by body weight falling to less than 85% of ideal in conjunction with an intense fear of becoming fat and amenorrhea (American Psychiatric Association, 2000). While all anorexics restrict their food intake, some also engage in episodes of binge eating and purging. Purging might include self-induced vomiting or laxative use. Because anorexia can result in a threat to health and life, inpatient hospitalization is

needed in severe cases. Pediatric psychologists working in hospital settings are often involved in the diagnosis, treatment, and research of anorexia nervosa.

The etiology, symptoms, and treatment of anorexia reflect the biopsychosocial nature of the disorder and clinical psychology's response to it. Anorexia and other eating disorders may have a genetic component, with a 4 to 5 times higher incidence in first-degree relatives (Kaye, Fudge, & Paulus, 2009; Striegal-Moore, 2000; Strober & Humphrey, 1987). Anorexia *per se* might not be inherited, yet factors such as personality, impulsivity, body shape, impulse control, anxiety, and other characteristics that might place someone at greater risk for developing an eating disorder may be heritable factors (Fairburn & Brownell, 2002; Kaye et al., 2009). Once an eating disorder begins, neurochemical factors may perpetuate the problem. Some have suggested that the functioning of the hypothalamus via neurotransmitters such as dopamine, serotonin, and norepinephrine might be involved in anorexia nervosa (Hsu, 1990; Kaye et al., 2009; Polivy & Herman, 2002). Starvation itself also leads to irrational and rigid thinking, which further perpetuates the problem. Psychological factors including a lack of perceived control in life, poor self-esteem, stress, anxiety, and depression also play a role in the development and course of the illness (Fairburn & Brownell, 2002; Nicholls & Viner, 2009; Striegal-Moore, Silberstein, & Rodin, 1993). Social factors such as cultural ideals of thinness and beauty play a role in motivating the anorexic's relentless pursuit of thinness (Brownell, 1991a, 1991b; Nicholls & Viner, 2009; Pike & Rodin, 1991; Striegal-Moore, Silberstein, & Rodin, 1986). Intervention approaches include tube and/or intravenous feeding in medical emergencies, high-calorie liquid diets, and medication to assist with anxiety, depression, and compulsive symptoms. Individual, family, and group psychotherapy are usually provided in some combination during and following the hospital stay, or in lieu of inpatient treatment where weight loss is less extreme (Fairburn & Brownell, 2002).

Childhood Bipolar Disorder

Photo: Courtesy Stockvault.net

Following the publication of the book, *The Bipolar Child* in 1999 by Demitri Papolos, MD, and Janice Papolos (1999, 2002, 2006), the diagnosis of bipolar disorder among children has become very popular during the past decade in the United States. It increased almost 300% between 1994 and 2001 alone (Pavuluri, Birmaher, & Naylor, 2005). Although the diagnosis for children is not discussed in the DSM-IV-TR it has become what some refer to as the diagnosis of the decade (Fields & Fristad, 2009; Young & Fristad, 2007). Many have stated that the diagnosis is overused and that the diagnosis may reflect a relabeling of problematic child behavior that might have been called something else in the past, such as attention deficit/hyperactivity disorder (Blader & Carlson, 2007). Thus, many argue that one must proceed with caution while diagnosing and treating (usually with medications) bipolar disorder in youth (Blader & Carlson, 2007; Fields & Fristad, 2009; Papolos & Papolos, 2006; Young & Fristad, 2007). Thoughtful researchers have stated that the condition is rare and that co-morbidity is very common (Fields & Fristad, 2009).

Conclusions

Child clinical psychologists and pediatric psychologists work with the unique problems affecting children and adolescents and their families. They also work closely with a wide variety of other professionals involved in the lives of children such as school teachers, pediatricians, and legal authorities. Child clinical psychologists work with unique problems that face children and families such as attention deficit hyperactivity disorder, child abuse and neglect, depression, learning disabilities, school phobia, autism, and medical problems,

Highlight of a Contemporary Clinical Psychologist

Susan Steibe-Pasalich, PhD

Photo: Courtesy Susan
Steibe-Pasalich

Dr. Steibe-Pasalich is a clinical psychologist who directs the counseling services at the University of Notre Dame in South Bend, Indiana.

Birthdate: April 3, 1950

College: BA in psychology, the Catholic University of America, 1973

Graduate Program: PhD in Clinical Psychology, the University of Ottawa, Ontario, Canada

Clinical Internship: Psychological Services Centre, Ottawa, Ontario, 1978–1979

Current Job: Director, University of Notre Dame Counseling Center

Pros and Cons of being a Clinical Psychologist:
Pros: "Having the knowledge and skills to facilitate positive behavior change in individuals, groups, and organizations."

Cons: "Recognizing that change can be a slow process."

Future of Clinical Psychology: "There are several challenging issues facing the future of clinical psychology and clinical psychologists at counseling centers housed in university settings in the United States. First is balancing the mission of counseling centers on campuses of higher education with respect to treating and managing more seriously disturbed students while providing preventative outreach and service to those students experiencing typical developmental challenges. Second is the issue of student privacy versus the critical role of consultation with parents and/or other university administrators. Another emerging challenge is the role and place of clinical psychologists on threat assessment teams, groups designed to manage and assess risk as it pertains to high-profile or acting-out students on college campuses. And last but not least is the salient issue of the need for education still to be done on campuses in reducing or eliminating the stigma and misunderstanding associated with emotional illness."

In what kinds of consultation, administration, training, and practice activities are you involved? "I oversee the University Counseling Center, one of 12 departments in the Division of Student Affairs of a private, religiously affiliated university. The Center provides individual and group counseling, outreach, consultation, and crisis intervention services to a population of approximately 11,500 students, in addition to consulting with faculty, staff, parents, and concerned third parties about student concerns. I engage in providing intake and emergency services to the student population, and conduct individual counseling. I provide oversight to practicum and APA accredited internship training programs, as well as provide individual supervision to unlicensed practitioners. I provide creative leadership for the Center, and develop and implement policies governing programs, service delivery, and general Center operations. I administer a budget, recruit, supervise, and

8032787

evaluate staff, and function as chief psychologist for the Center. I monitor and maintain professional standards and ethics, and promote the professional development of the Counseling Center staff. I am responsible to establish and maintain cooperative relationships with other Student Affairs units, academic departments, and the campus community."

What are some of the challenges that you face in your work? "A major challenge is managing a talented staff of mental health providers in a way that is respectful of each person's career development and that strikes the appropriate chord between self-care and workload. It is also important to be the kind of leader that inspires and motivates people to do their best work, and work that is in line with the University's mission. Another big challenge is staying on top of the nitty-gritty of administration, and learning to delegate tasks appropriately."

Typical Schedule:

8:30–9:30	Respond to work-related e-mails, prepare meeting agendas, attend interdepartmental meetings, review policies and procedures.
9:30–10:00	Meet with Counseling Center staff to discuss emerging work or clinical issues.
10:00–11:30	Administrative tasks (budget preparation, staff recruitment, individual staff consultation).
11:00–12:00	Emergency coverage for students walking into the Center.
12:00–1:00	Lunch.
1:00–2:00	Clinical supervision with psychology intern/practicum counselor.
2:00–3:00	Participation in interdepartmental committee meetings (Sexual Assault Prevention, Wellness, Drug Testing, Student Welfare, etc.).
3:00–4:30	Administrative consultations with Center clinical, training, or outreach coordinators.
4:30–5:00	Clinical consultations with parent or faculty concerned about a student.

Some evening work to facilitate student focus groups/outreach presentations, or to complete rotation for 24/7 urgent crisis consultation.

to name a few (Barkley, 1996, 2000, 2008; Mash & Barkley, 1989; Shipman & Taussig, 2009; Smith-Spark & Fisk, 2007; Stith et al., 2009).

Clinical Neuropsychology

The subspecialty of clinical **neuropsychology** focuses on **brain–behavior relationships,** that is, how brain functioning impacts behavior and behavior problems (Davidson, 2000b; Jones & Butters, 1991; Kolb & Whishaw, 2008; Lezak, 1995; Lezak, Howieson, & Loring, 2004). Clinical neuropsychologists assess brain and behavior functioning and offer strategies for patients suffering from brain impairment due to problems that result in cognitive and neurological dysfunction. Table 11.3 lists some of the topics of interest to clinical neuropsychologists. Neuropsychologists must be well versed in neuroanatomy and neuropathology as well as clinical psychology (Kolb & Whishaw, 2008; Lezak et al., 2004). They assess a range of cognitive abilities including executive or higher-order cognitive functions, sensory and motor functioning, memory skills, and abstract reasoning. Many psychologists who specialize in neuropsychology are trained as clinical psychologists or they may have

Table 11.3 **Typical Problems Addressed by Neuropsychologists**

Seizures	Tumors
Head traumas	Alzheimer's disease
Stroke	Alcohol
Malingering	Language problems
Dementia	Impairment due to injury
Epilepsy	Impairment due to chemotherapy
AIDS	Disease

Case Study: Sam Experiences Autism

Sam is a 6-year-old biracial (East Indian and Filipino) boy who experiences difficulties in social relationships at school. His teacher and parents report that he engages in excessive self-stimulation behavior (e.g., rocks, hums) and is rigidly attached to certain objects and routines. They expressed concern that Sam gets upset over little things (e.g., being pushed at school, altered schedules, loud classroom), and shows very little interest in peers or adults.

Sam's parents have a high-conflict relationship and are planning to divorce. They both work many hours each week and frequently travel on business. Sam has a full-time nanny who takes care of him when his parents are working and traveling. Sam's father has an obsessive-compulsive disorder and takes medication to control his behavior. He also participates in an obsessive-compulsive disorder support and information group.

Cognitive testing using the WISC-IV revealed that Sam functions in the below-average range on overall intellectual functioning, with a lower verbal than performance IQ. Sam's performance on the Rey-Osterrieth Complex Figure Test as well as his performance on the Projective Drawing tasks suggest problems in fine motor skills as well as perceptual-motor integration abilities. His language abilities are significantly limited, despite English being his and his parents' only language.

Sam's problems in social, behavioral, and intellectual functioning were attributed to childhood autism, which is a severe, pervasive developmental disorder. Autism is a neurologically based syndrome that involves problems in social interactions (e.g., lack of spontaneous social behavior and problems in developing appropriate peer relationships and skills), combined with restricted patterns of behavior (e.g., inflexible adherence to specific routines or rituals), and impaired language and communication. The onset of symptoms generally occurs prior to the age of 3. The child clinical psychologist recommended a different classroom setting for Sam and a host of behavioral, supportive, and social interventions to assist Sam and his family in addressing his complex needs.

received training in cognitive science or neuroscience. Most neuropsychologists work in hospital, rehabilitation, or clinic settings. Some specialize in working with children, a field referred to as *child*, or *developmental*, *neuropsychology*. Many also work in private or group practice environments.

Assessment is the primary activity of the neuropsychologist who relies on testing results to provide recommendations for diagnosis, treatment, and rehabilitation. As discussed in Chapter 8, neuropsychologists administer and interpret a wide variety of specialty test batteries such as the Halstead-Reitan Neuropsychological Battery and the Luria-Nebraska Battery as well as individual tests such as the Rey-Osterrieth Complex Figure, the Benton Visual Recognition Test, the Wisconsin Card Sorting Test, and the California Verbal Learning Test, which evaluate language, motor, attention, concentration, and higher-order cognitive functioning such as problem solving. Furthermore, more commonly known tests such as the Wechsler Adult Intelligence Test-IV (WAIS-IV) and the Minnesota Multiphasic Personality Inventory-2 (MMPI-2) are often part of a comprehensive neuropsychological evaluation. These tests provide information concerning the cognitive and psychological functioning of people experiencing a wide range of potential problems that impact brain–behavior relationships. Neuropsychologists also provide consultation and rehabilitation services such as psychoeducational support groups, psychotherapy, coping and skill-building strategies, and family support

---

Case Study: Zoe Experiences Acting-Out Behaviors

Zoe is a 13-year-old Caucasian girl who attends the eighth grade. She lives with her adoptive parents and younger adoptive brother and sister. She was adopted when she was 4 months old after Child Protective Services removed her from her home due to physical abuse and neglect. Little is known about the medical, psychological, and social background of Zoe's biological parents.

Zoe is highly disorganized, forgetful, and distracted. Her parents also describe her as "hyper." She can't sit still and is always talking and moving around. She recently was suspended at school when she left a school dance with a few girlfriends to meet up with some older high school boys in a nearby baseball field. The girls drank a large amount of beer and returned to the dance intoxicated. Zoe's parents were especially upset because she was unconcerned about the consequences of her behavior and initially lied about her participation. They also report that when Zoe was 10 she left home late at night and was picked up by the police approximately two miles away at

12:30 A.M. They report that she left a note about being abducted. Again, the family was concerned about her impulsive behavior, her lying, and her inability to understand the consequences of her behavior and to exercise better judgment.

A complete psychological evaluation failed to confirm true attentional and other deficits consistent with an ADHD diagnosis. Psychological testing did, however, reveal below-average cognitive abilities and poorly modulated feelings of anger and sadness that contributed to Zoe's poor judgment, vulnerability to peer pressure, and impulsive acting out. The psychologist conducting the evaluation suggested that Zoe would benefit from tutorial assistance at school, individual therapy to assist her in contending with painful emotions related to her early history and adolescent autonomy strivings, and family therapy to negotiate rules and limits while addressing adoption issues long buried in the family. Zoe was diagnosed with an adjustment disorder with mixed disturbance of emotions and conduct.

---

for those experiencing head injuries and diseases impacting brain–behavior relationships. Finally, neuropsychologists conduct research into understanding, assessing, and treating these problems. While neuropsychologists are involved in assessment, treatment, consultation, and research in many problem areas that affect brain functioning, this section will highlight the problems of epilepsy, degenerative diseases, and head injuries.

Epilepsy

Epilepsy is a seizure disorder defined as excessive discharging of brain cells in a sudden, transient, and recurrent manner (Engel & Pedley, 2007; Goldensohn, Glaser, & Goldberg, 1984; McConnell & Snyder, 1997; Shuster, 1996). **Seizures** result in intense muscle spasms, a

complete or partial loss of consciousness, and sometimes unconscious purposeful behavior. Neurons in the brain become excited due to a variety of reasons that differ from person to person. For example, infections, metabolic abnormalities, and biochemical factors may all contribute to the development of a seizure. In addition to these physiological causes, psychological stress has been found to elicit seizures among those vulnerable to this disorder (Joëls, 2009; Williams, 1982).

Epilepsy affects about 1% of the population. Children are more likely to experience epilepsy than adults; children under the age of 5 and at puberty are the most vulnerable (Hauser, Annegers, & Anderson, 1983; McConnell & Snyder, 1997; Otero, 2009). Curiously, epilepsy is also more likely to occur among lower-socioeconomic groups (Hauser

Case Study: Sally Experiences Anorexia Nervosa

Sally is a 15-year-old Caucasian girl who was recently hospitalized with anorexia nervosa. She is currently 5'6" tall and weighs only 85 pounds. Her symptoms began when she was 14 years old following a diet in response to critical comments about her weight made by some girls at school. She first tried to lose weight by exercising and eliminating desserts, enjoying the positive comments about her weight loss made by friends and family members. After she lost several pounds she felt that she was still "too fat" and continued to diet and exercise even more rigorously. She began using laxatives to speed up the weight-loss process and relieve feelings of fullness, guilt, and anxiety after eating even small amounts. She became more withdrawn and depressed.

Her school performance decreased and she became more and more obsessed with food and dieting.

Sally's parents brought her to a pediatrician who encouraged her to seek professional help at the Eating Disorders Clinic at a local hospital. Sally denied that she had a problem and refused to get help. After Sally fainted following a run, her mother brought her to the hospital for treatment. She was admitted to the eating disorders unit of the children's hospital. Following an intake interview with Sally and her mother, Sally was provided with intravenous fluids and a regimen to increase weight. Individual, family, and group psychotherapy were provided in conjunction with medical care. Sally was diagnosed with anorexia nervosa.

---

et al., 1983; McCagh, Fisk, & Baker, 2009). Biopsychosocial factors contribute to the development of epilepsy with genetics, infections, socioeconomics, stress, nutrition, prenatal care, and other factors contributing to the development and maintenance of the disorder (Hanesian, Paez, & Williams, 1988; McCagh et al., 2009; Stears & Spitz, 1996).

The severity, duration, and age of onset of epilepsy is related to the level of potential impairment in cognitive functioning. Attention-concentration, memory, problem-solving, motor, and intellectual abilities all can be significantly impaired due to problems associated with repeated seizures (Ellenberg, Hirtz, & Nelson, 1986; Hanesian et al., 1988; McCagh et al., 2009). However, anticonvulsant medication causes side effects that adversely impact these skills; thus deficits in cognitive function may be related to medication rather than to the seizures per se (Corbet, Trimble, & Nicol, 1985; Engel & Pedley, 2007; McConnell & Snyder, 1997). In addition to neurological functioning, personality and mood are also altered by seizures. Complex partial seizures that are localized in the temporal lobe region of the brain have been associated with changes in mood, sexual activity, and aggressiveness (Engel & Pedley, 2007; Trimble, 1985). People with epilepsy are also at higher risk for the development of psychiatric problems such as anxiety, depression, psychosis, and antisocial behavior (Engel & Pedley, 2007; Hanesian et al., 1988).

Neuropsychologists are often requested to carefully evaluate the cognitive and personality functioning of patients with epilepsy. Medication and other treatment decisions are often determined partly on the basis of these test results. Neuropsychologists are also frequently asked to differentiate seizures from **pseudoseizure** disorders and **malingering.** Curiously, some people present with seizures that are psychologically based (e.g., hysterical seizures) or intentionally feigned (Bergen, 2008; Williams & Mostofsky, 1982). Sometimes patients with somatoform disorders, factitious disorders, or motivation to malinger consciously or even unconsciously fake having a seizure disorder for medical attention, financial incentives, or other reasons.

Treatment of epilepsy reflects contemporary, integrative, and biopsychosocial perspectives (Engel & Pedley, 2007; McCagh et al., 2009; Shuster, 1996). Anticonvulsant medication such as carbamazepine has proven to be effective in decreasing the frequency and intensity of seizures. Psychotropic medications such as benzodiazepines, antidepressants, and neuroleptics have all been successfully used to minimize the frequency, intensity, or duration (Hanesian et al., 1988; Perucca, Gilliam, & Schmitz, 2009; Trimble, 1985; Williams & Mostofsky, 1982). When medications prove ineffective and seizures are localized to the temporal lobe, for example, surgery to perform a temporal lobectomy may be performed to prevent onset. Psychotherapy, group therapy, social support, and psychoeducational opportunities are valuable adjuncts to medical treatment (Hanesian et al., 1988; McConnell & Snyder, 1997; Perucca et al., 2009). These approaches assist patients with the emotional, social, and behavioral challenges of coping with this chronic illness, thereby minimizing any limitations associated with seizures.

Brain Injuries

Brain injuries present another area of focus for neuropsychologists. Accidents causing brain injuries impact over 10 million people each year (including about 1 million children) and may occur from vehicular accidents, falls, war wounds, sport injuries, gunshot wounds, violent assaults, and other tragic events. Concussions (jarring the brain) and contusions (shifting of the position of the brain) that occur during accidents can impact brain functions such as memory, attention-concentration, and orientation (Anderson, Bigler, & Blatter, 1995; Langlois, Rutland-Brown, & Thomas, 2006; Newcombe, 1996). Strokes can also impair language, motor skills, personality functioning, and other neurocognitive abilities. Environmental toxins such as poisons, gas fumes, and metals such as mercury and lead can also result in brain injuries. It has been estimated that about 4% of American children have damaging levels of lead in their blood and brains, which can result in impaired intellectual abilities, problems in attention-concentration, confusion, and ADHD-like symptoms (Committee on Environmental Health, 2005; U.S. Department of Health and Human Services, 1985b). Neuropsychologists are asked to evaluate cognitive and psychological functioning as well as develop rehabilitation programs for brain-injured patients. Psychotherapy, group support, education, and medical treatment may all be involved, depending on the nature of the problem and the special needs of the patient and family.

Brain injury, also called *traumatic brain injury (TBI)*, has been a factor in many of the injuries among military soldiers during the recent wars in Iraq and Afghanistan over the past decade (Hildreth, 2009). It has been estimated that about 15% of injured soldiers experience brain injury (Martin, Lu, Helmick, French, & Warden, 2008). Psychologists who specialize in neuropsychology are needed to evaluate and treat returning veterans to determine how best to proceed with rehabilitation.

Brain injuries have also been found to be common among young athletes who participate in high-impact sports such as football and boxing. Head injuries among famous sports personalities such as Ben Roethlisberger, the 2009 Super Bowl champion quarterback, draw attention to the importance of head safety in sports.

Degenerative Diseases

Degenerative diseases represent an additional spectrum of impairment faced by neuropsychologists. These include Alzheimer's disease, dementia, Parkinson's disease, Huntington's chorea, and infectious diseases such as syphilis and other disorders. Gradual degeneration of neurological functioning results in problems in memory, attention, speech, judgment, movement, and other areas of functioning, depending on the specific disease process in each individual (Jucker, Beyreuther, Haass, Nitsch, & Christen, 2006; Lambert & Kinsley, 2005; Tuokko, Kristjansson, & Miller, 1995). Often patients with degenerative diseases develop depression, anxiety, irritability, personality changes, and loss of social support (American Psychiatric Association, 2000; Dunkin & Anderson-Hanley, 1998; Lambert & Kinsley, 2005; Sultzer, Levin, Mahler, High, & Cummings, 1993). Thus, these individuals also deserve sensitive, comprehensive care.

Dementia associated with Alzheimer's disease is perhaps the most well-known and prevalent degenerative disease. Alzheimer's disease involves memory loss, failure to recognize well-known people and objects, difficulty in organizing and planning, suspiciousness, and language problems (American Psychiatric Association, 2000; Bogerts, 1993; Edwards, 1994; Jucker et al., 2006; Katzman, 2008). It is estimated that Alzheimer's disease occurs among more than four million people in the United States (American Psychiatric Association, 2000; Edwards, 1994; Max, 1993; Katzman, 2008) and is likely to increase significantly in future years with an increasing aging population (Jucker et al., 2006; Katzman, 2008). It is more common among people with lower educational levels as well (Korczyn, Kahana, & Galper, 1991).

Alzheimer's disease may be due to genetically and environmentally induced brain atrophy and plaque formation and low levels of the brain neurotransmitters acetylcholine, serotonin, and noradrenalin (Jucker et al., 2006; La Rue, 1992). Defective genes located on chromosomes 1, 14, 19, and 21, with gene mutations involving the APP (amyloid precursor protein), PS1 (presenilin 1), PS2 (presenilin 2), and APOE (Apolipoprotein) genes, have been implicated in a number of Alzheimer cases (Jucker et al., 2006; Katzman, 2008; Petegnief, Saura, De Gregorio-Rocasolano, & Paul, 2001). Head trauma, malnutrition, drug and toxin exposure, viral infection, personality, and cultural factors all may play a role in the development, progression, and manifestation of Alzheimer's disease (American Psychiatric Association, 2000; Ikels, 1991; Jucker et al., 2006; Katzman, 2008; Korczyn et al., 1991).

Neuropsychologists are often requested to evaluate the cognitive and psychological functioning of these patients and assist in making a definitive diagnosis. However, often the diagnosis of Alzheimer's disease is made when no other apparent cause for symptoms can be identified. Often an evaluation helps to rule out other potential explanations for symptoms as well as assisting in the rehabilitation efforts. Psychologists also offer services including psychotherapy, group support, psychoeducational instructions, milieu therapy, behavior management, and consultation with physicians, nurses, family, and other caregivers. Treatment approaches also include careful work with family members who are usually highly stressed by caring for and facing the eventual decline and loss of a loved one. Treatments also include medication such as Cognex, Aricept, and Namenda, which alter the production of glutamate or acetylcholine (Jucker et al., 2006; Katzman, 2008).

Vascular dementia is sometimes confused with Alzheimer's disease. Although symptoms may appear similar in terms of memory and other dysfunctions, it is an illness that is different in its cause. It is due to cerebral infarcts or problems with blood supply to the brain and is often due to mini-strokes. Loss of brain cells and functioning that is associated with loss of blood supply to key regions in the brain tend to create symptoms that are very similar to Alzheimer's disease. Vascular dementia tends to impact the elderly and usually occurs after age 50.

Neuropsychology's Unique Contribution to Psychopathology

In addition to focus on assessment of brain–behavior relations and contributions to the understanding and treatment of specialized clinical problems, including seizure disorders such as epilepsy, brain injuries, and degenerative diseases such as dementia and

---

Case Study: Joseph Experiences Dementia and Depression

Joseph is a 71-year-old married Caucasian man who has a doctorate degree and has worked as a highly successful engineer for many years. He was hospitalized on a combined medical/psychiatric unit for depression and a variety of medical problems. He started several companies and had become independently wealthy as a result of his business success. His difficulties involved a number of cognitive and personality changes. He frequently became lost when traveling to familiar places in town and had difficulty remembering people and places. At times he was overtly hostile to friends and family. His impulsivity resulted in several poor financial decisions that were very costly for his family. The staff of the hospital unit evaluated whether Joseph had a neuropsychological problem associated with dementia. They were unsure if his problems in behavior might be associated with other potential medical or psychiatric problems. An abbreviated version of the Halstead-Reitan Battery was administered. The patient was uncooperative during much of the testing process. He expressed anger and resentment toward the hospital, staff, and examiner. Results indicated that Joseph did in fact experience dementia as well as a concurrent depressive disorder. Results suggested that his level of cognitive functioning (especially abstract reasoning, memory, and new learning) were significantly impaired.

Alzheimer's disease, the neuropsychology subfield of clinical psychology offers much in our understanding and treatment of general psychological troubles. For example, depression often is associated with neuropsychological dysfunction. Research has shown that about half of patients who experience a head injury to their left side of their brain will experience depression (Starkstein & Robinson, 1988). Curiously, the closer to the frontal portion of the left brain hemisphere, the more likely the depressive symptoms will occur and be severe. Other research has found that additional brain injuries to particular brain locations are more likely to result in depression (Mukherjee, Levin, & Heller, 2006) and that assessing depression following brain injury is an important component of treating these disorders. Another example includes the diagnosis and treatment of schizophrenia. Research has found that schizophrenics have both structural and functional abnormalities in their prefrontal cortex (Sapara, Cooke, Fannon, Francis, Buchanan, Anilkumar et al., 2007). Research has found that dysfunction most especially in the left brain hemisphere is commonly found among schizophrenic patients (Antonova, Sharma, Morris, & Kumari, 2004).

Thus, neuropsychology offers unique diagnostic tools and perspectives to help better understand important issues related to common psychological diagnoses such as depression, schizophrenia, and other problems often confronted by clinical psychologists. As newer diagnostic tools such as functional MRIs become more commonplace, we can likely expect that the influence and skills of neuropsychologists will only increase in coming years. Additionally, as the issues of head injuries continue to be highlighted in the news due to returning war veterans and sports injuries, efforts to increase both diagnosis and treatment of neuropsychological troubles will likely unfold in coming years.

Conclusions

Neuropsychology is a popular and rapidly developing subspecialty of clinical psychology. It blends psychology and medicine in understanding how problems with the brain impact behavior and psychological functioning.

Neuropsychology also highlights the contemporary biopsychosocial model. Brain injuries due to head trauma and disease cause illnesses impacting cognitive and psychological functioning. These disorders impact not only the patient but the patient's family. Genetic vulnerability as well as social and emotional factors interact in many of these problems to result in the development, manifestation, and progression of certain diseases. Neuropsychologists can be enormously helpful in assessment, treatment, rehabilitation, and research regarding disorders as diverse as Alzheimer's disease, epilepsy, AIDS, stroke, alcoholism, and gunshot wounds. Neuropsychology also overlaps to some degree with other subspecialty areas in clinical psychology, including health psychology, pediatric psychology, and forensic psychology.

Geropsychology

The number of elderly people living in the United States has increased from 3.1 million to 35 million during the past 100 years. Those over the age of 65 now represent one in every eight Americans. Furthermore, it is estimated that the growth of the elderly population will increase by 74% by the year 2030 (U.S. Census Bureau, 2008b). As more and more Americans live into their elder years, the need for research, consultation, and quality professional services from clinical psychologists specializing in issues salient to the elder population is greatly needed (Rosowsky, Casciani, & Arnold, 2009). Geropsychology or clinical geropsychology is an important and fast-growing specialty area of clinical psychology. Although about 70% of all psychologists evaluate or treat older adults in their clinical work, only 3% report that working with elders is their area of specialization (Dittmann, 2003; Rosowsky et al., 2009). Furthermore, the National Institute on Aging reports that 5,000 full-time geropsychologists will be needed by the year 2020 to accommodate the need for these services to the elderly (Dittmann, 2003). Currently, there are only about 700 geropsychologists.

The U.S. government has acknowledged this need by passing the Older Americans Act of 2000 (PL 89-73) to make grants available to train psychologists and other appropriate professionals to specialize in the behavioral health needs of older persons.

Sadly, the Department of Health and Human Services (2001) suggests that about two-thirds of all older adults who experience a mental disorder do not get the services they need and that only 3% see mental or behavioral health specialists. Many problems that elders experience could be helped by consultation with geropsychologists. For example, many patients experience urinary incontinence, insomnia, anxiety, depression, and bereavement challenges associated with a variety of illnesses that impact their cognitive functioning, such as degenerative diseases like Alzheimer's and stroke. Furthermore, there is often a dearth of social support services or experiences for elders.

Geropsychologists provide prevention, assessment, consultation, and intervention services to help elders (and their families) deal with the many problems and issues that can emerge in the later years of life. For example, they may provide treatment for depression and anxiety, help with assessing cognitive impairment, and help with coping with the loss of physical, mental, and family functioning. Several specific problems that geropsychologists focus on are discussed briefly.

Degenerative Diseases

Degenerative diseases such as dementia caused by Alzheimer's disease is a common area of research and clinical work for geropsychologists. This topic was reviewed earlier in the chapter in the section on neuropsychology. Other types of dementia and degenerative diseases are highlighted in this section.

Vascular dementia is the second most common type of dementia among the elderly. Technically, vascular dementia is a by-product of cerebrovascular disease that occurs when blood flow to the brain is interrupted, causing tissue damage to the brain. When this happens suddenly, it is called a stroke. Hypertension, an accumulation of fatty deposits in the arteries, and the interaction with other illnesses that damage the brain can create vascular dementia. Cognitive and psychological changes often accompany the physical brain changes that occur. The nature of these cognitive and psychological changes depends on both the nature of the patient's premorbid level of functioning and the specific areas of the brain that are affected (Desmond & Tatemichi, 1998; Rosowsky et al., 2009). Risk of stroke and other vascular dementia increases with age.

Parkinson's disease is a degenerative brain disorder that is due to the brain's inability to adequately produce the neurotransmitter *dopamine.* The disease includes symptoms such as involuntary tremors and muscle rigidity. About half of Parkinson's disease patients develop dementia during the advanced stages of the illness. Although Parkinson's disease has received a great deal of attention recently due to the illness of the well-known actor, Michael J. Fox, it is a disease more often seen among the elderly.

Geropsychologists may be involved with neuropsychological testing to help assess the degree of cognitive and psychological damage as well as assess the strengths remaining in those who experience dementia from vascular disease, Parkinson's disease, or other reasons. These professionals might also participate in individual, family, and group psychotherapy and psychoeducational activities to help both the patient and loved ones cope with the dementia in particular and the general illness. For example, behavior therapy is often used to help patients deal with emotional volatility (Dunkin & Anderson-Hanley, 1998; Rosowsky et al., 2009).

Cross-cultural research from a variety of different countries and cultures suggests that people with less education are more likely to be diagnosed with dementia than those with higher educational achievements (e.g., Katzman, 1993). This is supported by neuroimaging studies. It is possible that cognitive stimulation in general may act as a protective factor in forestalling the onset of dementia for those vulnerable to it.

Psychiatric Issues in Older Adults

Anxiety, depression, substance abuse, and bereavement issues are common among the elderly. Diagnosing and treating these problems can be especially challenging among the senior population since many of the psychological problems experienced by this population could be directly related to comorbid medical problems, medication side-effects, and potential bias due to preconceived notions about what is normal and not normal for elderly people to experience.

Anxiety: It is estimated that about 15% of people over the age of 65 experience a diagnosable anxiety disorder (Rosowsky et al., 2009; Scogin, Floyd, & Forde, 2000; Vink, Aartsen, & Schoevers, 2008). Whereas some of these patients have suffered from anxiety-related problems for much of their lives, many have not, such that problems with anxiety first emerge during the elder years. Frequently, the anxiety is related to health, safety, and concerns about the wellbeing of loved ones (Rosowsky et al., 2009; Scogin et al., 2000; Vink et al., 2008). Posttraumatic stress disorder (PTSD) is common among the elderly and is often associated with bereavement regarding the loss of a loved one such as a spouse or other close relatives or friends (Boananno & Kaltman, 1999; Bowling, 2009). Integrative biopsychosocial approaches using medication, cognitive-behavioral techniques, and humanistic supportive approaches have been demonstrated to be generally successful for elders dealing with significant anxiety (Bowling, 2009; Rosowsky et al., 2009; Stanley & Novy, 2000). Geropsychologists must work closely with physicians, family members, and others to tailor their services to the unique needs of elders experiencing anxiety.

Depression: It is estimated that about 15% of elders experience major depression while

Clergy Sexual Abuse in the Roman Catholic Church

Photo: Courtesy Zach Plante.

The sexual abuse scandals in the Roman Catholic Church publicized since January 6, 2002, with an investigative report published by the *Boston Globe* have resulted in an almost-hysterical response to the allegations, convictions, resignations, and coverups of priest sex offenders. All of the major newspapers, magazines, and television news programs throughout the United States and much of the world reported on the cases of Catholic priests who engaged minors in sexual activity. Remarkably, the clergy abuse crisis made front-page news in the *New York Times* for 41 days in a row during 2002. Catholics and non-Catholics alike have been furious with Church leaders for not better protecting unsuspecting children and families from sex-offending priests. Calls for reform have also been voiced about other challenging issues with the Roman Catholic Church such as the prohibitions against female, married, and homosexual priests. It is unlikely that the American Catholic Church has been in a more difficult crisis in decades (Plante, 2004b).

The best available data suggest that approximately 4% of Catholic priests in the United States have had a sexual encounter with a minor under the age of 18 and 81% of all priests who abuse minors abuse adolescent boys and not prepubescent children (John Jay College of Criminal Justice, 2004). So, the teen is more at risk than the altar boy or girls of any age. Therefore, most priest sex offenders aren't *pedophiles* but are **ephebophiles.** This could seem like a minor semantic difference but the implications for prevention and treatment are important.

The crisis in the Catholic Church has much to do with clinical psychology. First of all, 25% of the American population identify themselves as being Roman Catholic. Additionally, countless people (Catholics and many non-Catholics alike) have received elementary, secondary, and/or university education through Catholic schools and universities. Therefore, an enormous segment of the American population has had or continues to have direct contact with priests and the Catholic Church in at least some capacity. Second, the crisis in the Catholic Church is a crisis of behavior. This includes the behavior of priests and other male Catholic clergy (e.g., brothers) who have sexually engaged with minors in some capacity, and Church leaders for inadequate supervision and decisions regarding how to best manage Catholic clergy who behave in problematic ways. The morale among Catholics has been very low due to this problem. This crisis has shaken their trust in the Church as well as their faith. Therefore, the odds are quite high that the Catholic clergy sexual abuse crisis will impact the professional work of most clinical psychologists. Clinical psychologists evaluate and treat both victims and perpetrators of clergy abuse as well as consult with the Church about policies and procedures to both minimize the chances of clergy sexual abuse and help manage the problem once it emerges. These psychologists also work with Catholics who are distraught and depressed about what has happened to their Church. Finally, much of the research conducted on clergy abuse has been conducted by clinical psychologists (Plante, 1999, 2004a).

30% of elders in health-care institutions experience a severe form of depression (King & Markus, 2000; Vink et al., 2008). Depression can be especially deadly for elders as well. In fact, the suicide rate among elder Caucasian men is the highest of any group in the United States (Conwell, Pearson, & DeRenzo, 1996). Diagnosis and treatment can be especially challenging since elders are less likely to report depressive symptoms while being more likely to report somatic problems (King & Markus, 2000; Vink et al., 2009). Since depressive symptoms are more likely to be reported and experienced as somatic in origin and since physicians, family members, and others expect somatic complaints to increase with aging, frequently a depression diagnosis and possible treatment is not pursued by either the elder or those working and living with them. Depression among the elderly is often associated with bereavement, comorbid medical problems, and medication side effects (Bowling, 2009; King & Markus, 2000). Geropsychologists must be able to diagnosis and treat depression among elders as well as consult with physicians, other health-care professionals, and family members in order to help develop and implement a biopsychosocial strategy to best help the depressed elder.

Substance Abuse: We generally think of substance abuse as dealing with problems using alcohol or illegal drugs such as heroin, cocaine, ecstasy, marijuana, and other substances usually thought of as being more youth-oriented drugs. However, elderly persons often experience problems with older-adult-onset alcohol abuse and prescription drug abuse (Lisansky-Gomberg, 2000; Snow & Amalu, 2009). Older people are much more likely to use over-the-counter medications as well as prescription agents. The most common drugs used by the elderly include diuretics, cardiovascular medications, sedatives, analgesics, and laxatives (Lisansky-Gomberg, 2000). Alcohol problems can emerge since older persons metabolize alcohol more slowly, leading to higher blood concentrations, and the increased chance of elders living alone and being depressed and anxious relative to when they were younger. Potential bias among health-care professionals might also minimize the chances of noticing substance abuse problems in the elderly. For example, a professional might be more suspect of a young adult or adolescent abusing substances than an elderly person. Geropsychologists must be attentive to the potential of substance abuse among elders and be able to consult with other health-care professionals to alert them to possible abuse where it likely exists (Snow & Amalu, 2009).

Forensic Psychology

Forensic psychology is defined as the "application of psychology to legal issues" (Cooke, 1984, p. 29) and became a specialty area in psychology as a result of the legal case *Jenkins v. U.S.* in 1962 when a federal appellate court ruled that psychologists with appropriate training and competence could offer expert testimony regarding mental disorders (Otto & Heilbrun, 2002). The interested reader might wish to see Wrightsman (2001) and Weiner and Hess (2006) for a historical review of this field. Forensic psychologists specialize in utilizing principles of human behavior to inform the judicial and legal systems (Otto & Heilbrun, 2002; Weiner & Hess, 2006). They are often trained as clinical psychologists with a specialty in forensic work. Forensic psychologists may conduct psychological evaluations with defendants and present their findings as an expert witness in court. They may also provide evaluations for child custody arrangements, or be asked to predict dangerousness or determine if an individual is competent to stand trial. They may be asked to participate in worker's compensation claims, or serve as a consultant to attorneys who are selecting a jury. Forensic psychologists also assist in documenting mental anguish, pain and suffering, and brain injury in personal injury litigation. Injury may include physical accidents or psychological traumas associated with sexual harassment, rape, violence, discrimination, and other stressful experiences. In addition to being competent psychologists, they must thoroughly understand the law and legal system and be prepared to make court appearances. While forensic psychologists are involved in numerous aspects of the legal system, we highlight their work in legal cases involving involuntary commitment, the insanity defense, child custody, violence against women, and jury selection.

Involuntary Commitment

Each state has laws that allow someone to be committed to a psychiatric hospital if they are in serious and immediate danger of hurting themselves or others. While many people may have fleeting suicidal or homicidal thoughts, those who are in danger of acting on these thoughts must be protected from harming themselves or others. However, freedom is a fundamental human right and highly valued in our society. Therefore, depriving a citizen of this important right through forced, **involuntary commitment** to a psychiatric hospital is a serious matter. Throughout the course of history, commitment to a psychiatric facility or prison was exploited as a means of controlling people who maintained unpopular political, religious, or personal beliefs and activities. The ability to commit someone against their will has been clearly abused over the years and continues to occur in many countries. Even with the best intentions, it is often unclear if someone is indeed in serious danger of hurting themselves or others. Predicting dangerous behavior is very difficult and usually unreliable (Grisso & Appelbaum, 1992; Weiner & Hess, 2006). The legal system consults with psychologists to obtain guidance in determining whether someone should be involuntarily committed. In addition to danger to self and others, the criteria for involuntary commitment in most states include a diagnosable mental illness as well as the inability to adequately care for oneself due to being "gravely disabled."

Special efforts are needed to ensure that involuntary commitment laws are not abused. Famous cases such as the *O'Connor v. Donaldson* case, where a patient without any mental illness and who was not in danger of hurting anyone was hospitalized for many years against his will, highlight this issue. Forensic psychologists are asked to carefully evaluate a patient using assessment techniques such as clinical interviews, cognitive tests, and both objective and projective personality tests to determine whether someone is at high risk

Case Study: Austin Experiences Substance Abuse and a Severe Head Injury

Austin is a 16-year-old Caucasian male who was severely injured in a motorcycle accident associated with his use of the drug *crank* (i.e., methamphetamine). Austin experienced a severe head injury and was in a coma for one week prior to regaining consciousness. A neuropsychologist administered the Halstead-Reitan Battery and found that Austin evidences impaired judgment, abstract reasoning, and impulse control consistent with his frontal lobe concussion. In addition, Austin has visual deficits associated with his concussion from the impact on his occipital lobe. The neuropsychologist, in conjunction with Austin's physician, provided recommendations, information, and rehabilitation options to Austin and his family. In addition, a drug consultation was recommended for a future date.

Case Study: Margaret Experiences Problems Associated with a Stroke

Margaret is a 63-year-old African American woman who recently suffered a stroke. Since the stroke occurred, she has been unable to speak or write. She appears to recognize familiar friends and family members and is frequently upset and frustrated by her inability to communicate. Friends and family were initially very supportive and available to her but have recently appeared more distant. They feel uncomfortable being around her since they cannot communicate effectively. A neuropsychologist was asked to evaluate Margaret and offer treatment recommendations. The neuropsychologist found that Margaret has some ability to communicate via pictures and an adapted keyboard and helped to develop a communication system for Margaret in addition to offering strategies for rehabilitation to the medical team. The neuropsychologist also provided consultation to Margaret and her family to help them better understand and cope with Margaret's problems.

for harm to self or others as well as to determine whether a mental illness exists that renders them unable to provide adequate self-care. Since these criteria are very difficult to evaluate, psychologists make clinical judgments based on the totality of their experience, training, and the data that emerge from their evaluation. They often testify in court as well as consult with both attorneys and judges to make decisions that are in the best interest of both the patient and society.

Insanity Defense

Ever since the **M'Naghten Rule** of 1843, American and British law has struggled with the **insanity defense.** This rule was named after Daniel M'Naghten, who attempted to kill the prime minister of England because he felt that the government was persecuting him. Tragically, he mistakenly killed the prime minister's secretary. His symptoms were consistent with what *DSM-IV* would consider paranoid schizophrenia. The M'Naghten Rule suggests that someone is not responsible for his criminal actions if he suffers from a disorder that renders him unaware of what he is doing or that what he is doing is wrong. The M'Naghten Rule has been adapted several times over the years. For example, the **Durham Rule** of 1954 added a "medical disease or defect" to the criteria for insanity. However, since mental health professionals were unable to reliably demonstrate that a mental illness could cause someone to commit a crime, the Durham Rule was amended by the American Law Institute Rule of 1962, the Diminished Capacity Rule of 1979, and the **Insanity Defense Reform Act** of 1984.

Today's version, based on the Insanity Defense Reform Act, states that someone can be found innocent due to reasons of insanity if unable to understand that criminal behavior was wrong at the time of the crime due to a mental disease or mental retardation. Famous cases such as John Hinckley (who attempted to assassinate then-President Ronald Reagan), Charles Manson (who participated in multiple murders including the actress Sharon Tate), Jeffrey Dahmer (who committed multiple murders that involved cannibalism), Dan White (who murdered San Francisco mayor, George Moscone, and claimed that junk food made him unstable), and Andrea Yates (who murdered her five young children) have highlighted the use of the insanity defense. Most people think that the insanity defense is overused and that criminals too often get away with heinous crimes (Hans, 1986). This has led to efforts on the part of several states to abandon the insanity defense altogether (De Angelis, 1994) or develop a "guilty but mentally ill" verdict that would allow both treatment and punishment of criminals who meet this criterion (Callahan, McGreevy, Cirincione, & Stedman, 1992; Weiner & Hess, 2006). The insanity defense is rarely successful.

Forensic psychologists are asked to evaluate these accused offenders to determine whether they suffer from a mental illness that might meet the legal criteria of insanity and provide expert testimony to the court to assist in determining whether the accused should be held responsible for his or her crime. They complete clinical interviews and conduct psychological evaluations to inform their judgments.

Child Custody

About half of all marriages end in divorce. Many of these marriages involve children, leaving the question of the children's custody a critical and often hotly contested issue (Crosby-Currie, 1996; Weiner & Hess, 2006). Many years ago, children from divorced families were routinely given to the father. During the past 30 years, the mother has generally been awarded the children in custody disputes and the father has been allowed visitation rights and ordered to pay child support. In more recent years, these patterns have been challenged, and more and more joint custody arrangements are being worked out in court. **Joint custody** means that both parents retain custody of their children following divorce and that arrangements are made regarding living and financial matters to accommodate the needs and wishes of both parents. While joint custody can often be in the best interest of all of the parties involved, it is not without difficulties and can often be problematic for children. Since many divorces are highly conflictual, cooperation between parents regarding the care of their children is often difficult to establish in joint custody arrangements. Divorced parents must interact frequently in joint custody situations, and children are often placed in the middle of ongoing conflict. When divorced parents remarry and blended families enter the picture, the complexity and challenges often increase.

In addition to **child custody** arrangements due to divorce, custody matters are also decided when parental rights are severed due to child abuse, abandonment, and neglect. Adoption strategies as well as visitation rights are usually worked out through the family court systems. Efforts to keep the best interests of the child in mind while still trying to preserve the rights and freedoms of parents, combined with efforts to keep troubled families together, tend to dominate these decisions. Forensic psychologists are asked to evaluate parents, children, and other relevant parties (e.g., adoptive parents, foster parents, grandparents who may serve as legal guardians) to assist the court in determining who should have legal custody of children and what arrangements should be outlined for not only custody but visitation and other parental responsibilities. These psychologists may conduct psychotherapy with parents, children, other guardians, and families as well as provide expert testimony concerning their evaluative or intervention work with families.

Violence against Women

Tragically, about 15% of women in the United States have been raped and more than 20% have been physically assaulted by their partner (Renzetti, 2008; Tjaden & Thoennes, 2000). These statistics are even higher in many other parts of the world (Koss, 2000). Twenty percent of women report that they were sexually abused when they were children (Finkelhor, Hotaling, Lewis, & Smith, 1990). In addition to the physical threat, the emotional and psychological challenges are enormous, with the majority of these victims experiencing post-traumatic stress disorder (PTSD) and other problems (Koss, 1993, 2000; Renzetti, 2008; Weiner & Hess, 2006). Forensic psychologists might be asked to evaluate victims or perpetrators of abuse and testify in court proceedings. They may also conduct individual or group treatment with agencies to assist them in managing the potentially volatile situation between perpetrators and victims.

Jury Selection

Forensic psychologists often work as consultants to attorneys concerning **jury selection.** Famous cases such as the O. J. Simpson and Michael Jackson cases highlighted the efforts of attorneys to maximize their chances of selecting a jury that would likely be favorable to their client. Jury characteristics such as gender, race, socioeconomic status, occupation, interests, and a host of psychological factors may potentially contribute to the likelihood that a jury will be sympathetic to the defendant or plaintiff. Forensic psychologists also consult with attorneys regarding how best to interact with the selected jury to maximize the chances that the jury will accept their arguments. Presentation styles, attire, mannerisms, and methods of argument are adjusted to enhance the chances that the jury will be favorable to the attorney's point of view. These psychologists might conduct focus groups where research subjects act as juries and are interviewed during and after mock trials to determine which strategies work best.

Conclusions

Forensic psychology is another fast-growing subspecialty in clinical psychology. These psychologists act as consultants and expert witnesses in numerous types of civil and criminal cases. They use their assessment skills as well as their knowledge of the field of psychology to assist courts in determining many legal decisions. They may be hired by the court or by attorneys representing either side of a dispute. While their primary activity is evaluation and expert testimony, many forensic psychologists provide treatment and other services. Forensic psychology, like the other subspecialties reviewed in this chapter, overlap with other subspecialties. For example, forensic and child specialties overlap in child custody work, while neuropsychology and forensic psychology overlap in litigation regarding work-related accidents.

Other Subspecialties

In addition to health, child, neuropsychology, and forensics, there are a number of other subspecialties and areas of expertise in clinical psychology. Furthermore, there are specialties

Tests Used in Forensic Evaluations

Clinical psychologists who specialize in forensic psychology very frequently are asked to answer important questions in court environments. These often include trying to determine the mental status of a person at the time of an event (such as a crime), assessing the risk for violence (including sexual violence), competency to stand trial, and malingering. These psychologists generally are asked to conduct evaluations that include clinical interviews and the use of psychological tests. All of their procedures must be able to stand the test of cross-examination. Therefore, the psychologist must be sure that the procedures and tests used have adequate research and clinical support. A number of court rulings over the years have insisted that expert testimony by psychologists must be "scientifically valid and relevant" (Lally, 2003, p. 491). Whatever conclusions and results the psychologist offers will likely be challenged by attorneys.

Lally (2003) conducted a survey to determine which psychological tests were appropriate to use in forensic evaluations based on the legal questions that are being asked in court. He surveyed forensic specialists who are diplomats of the American Board of Forensic Psychology and found that certain tests were highly recommended in answering particular forensic questions. For example, the WAIS-III and MMPI-2 scales were recommended to be used in evaluations concerning the mental state of a person when an offense was committed, while the Psychopathy Checklist—Revised (PCL-R) was recommended for risk-for-violence evaluations. The survey also revealed tests that were considered unacceptable to use. Projective instruments such as drawings, sentence completion tests, and the Thematic Apperception Test (TAT) were found to be unacceptable to use for any of the forensic questions routinely asked of psychologists. In general, projective instruments were found to be more difficult to support in legal proceedings than more objective ones.

within subspecialties. For example, some clinical psychologists specialize in conducting neuropsychological evaluations among elderly persons who experience strokes. Others focus on treatment of children from specific minority populations. Still others specialize in psychopharmacology as it relates to certain illnesses among certain populations. New subspecialties regularly emerge, reflecting psychology's growing and changing evolution. While some specialties have specific professional organizations and standards for training and service, others are so new that these structures are not yet in place.

Case Study: The Lee Family Experiences Stress Associated with Divorce and Child Custody

The Lee family, an affluent Chinese American family, is in the midst of a child custody dispute. Mr. and Mrs. Lee were granted a divorce several years ago and were awarded joint custody of their 5-year-old son, Mark. Mr. Lee was promoted and transferred to another city about 400 miles away from Mrs. Lee. The Lees decided to have Mark live with Mrs. Lee for two weeks out of the month and live with Mr. Lee for two weeks of the month. Mark would fly between his two homes every other week. After several months of this arrangement, Mark began to show signs of significant stress. He began to develop a bed-wetting problem and was engaging in frequent temper tantrums. Mrs. Lee felt that the joint custody arrangement was unworkable and decided to seek sole legal custody of her son, allowing for generous visitation rights with Mark's father. Mr. Lee was outraged at Mrs. Lee's attempt to secure sole custody and fought her attempts. Since Mr. and Mrs. Lee had a bitter divorce and were still very angry with each other, they acted out their conflict regarding the custody arrangements and often did not keep their son's best interests in mind. The court referred the Lee family to a forensic psychologist to conduct a comprehensive family evaluation and make recommendations to the court regarding custody. The psychologist conducted the evaluation using clinical interviews and psychological evaluations of each family member. The psychologist then testified in court regarding these findings and offered recommendations regarding custody.

Case Study: Marie Experiences Suicidal Behaviors and Depression

Marie is a 32-year-old Latino woman who recently made a suicide attempt by cutting her wrists. Luckily, her roommate discovered her and called 911 shortly after Marie lost consciousness. After receiving medical treatment, she was admitted to a psychiatric unit for evaluation. Marie reported that she felt suicidal after the recent breakup with her boyfriend. She continued to feel suicidal during her hospital stay and admitted that she was angry at her roommate for interrupting her suicide attempt and demanded to be discharged immediately. The court asked for a psychological evaluation by a forensic psychologist to determine whether Marie was still in immediate and serious danger of hurting herself and whether she should be hospitalized for an additional 72 hours against her will for evaluation and observation. The psychologist interviewed Marie and asked her to complete a psychological battery including both objective and projective personality measures. The psychologist determined that Marie was still at risk for hurting herself and suggested that Marie continue to be hospitalized.

Case Study: Betty Experiences Job Stress

Betty is a 31-year-old Caucasian woman who was denied tenure at a major university. She was furious with the decision and felt that it was an unfair political decision because several members of the department and university tenure review committee did not agree with some of her views about faculty governance and other matters. She also perceived herself to be a victim of gender discrimination since there were no tenured female faculty in her English department. The university reported that her scholarship was not adequate for tenure and that she was only a mediocre teacher. Betty was also suing the university for lost revenue as well as for pain and suffering damages due to the stress she was under as a result of her dismissal. She reported that her stress-related health problems (i.e., lupus and migraine headaches) were primarily due to the university's decision. Her attorney sought to have a psychological evaluation conducted to demonstrate the level of stress she was under. The university also sought an evaluation from another psychologist to demonstrate that the university did not impose undue stress, and in fact that her health problems were a result of Betty's own preexisting emotional instability. The psychologists conducted independent evaluations and presented their results and conclusions to the court.

The Big Picture

Clinical psychology has grown and evolved to the point where subspecialties are necessary and commonplace. Subspecialty areas encompass work in many diverse settings dealing with many diverse problems. Psychology has proved to offer useful services to the legal, medical, psychiatric, and other communities. Paradoxically, the recent proliferation of managed health care has resulted in an emphasis on general and family medical practitioners (primary care providers) rather than specialists. Thus far, this has not been the case for clinical psychology, where specialization is the zeitgeist. What had once been viewed as the wave of the future is now very much realized in the current practice. Specialization has proven both viable and valuable, and will likely result in the growth of new specialties as our tools and knowledge base increase regarding specific populations, disorders, and systems. Advances in medical and computer technology as well as new problems may result in psychologists specializing in areas such as infertility, multicultural issues, computer assessment, and other areas yet to emerge in contemporary society. Although the future contemporary clinical psychologist will likely need highly specialized skills in one or several areas of focus, solid basic clinical skills will always be needed regardless of specialization.

Key Points

1. Some of the most popular specialty areas in clinical psychology include health psychology, child psychology, neuropsychology, geropsychology, and forensic psychology. Subspecialty areas have also emerged, such as pediatric neuropsychology. Within each specialty area many psychologists focus their research and/or practice on a particular population or problem area.

2. Health psychologists work in numerous and diverse settings including hospitals, clinics, universities, businesses, government agencies, and private practices. They use the principles of psychology and behavioral change to help people cope better with medical illnesses as well as prevent potential illnesses from developing or from getting worse. They conduct research

on the relationships between behavioral and health and consult with organizations to maximize health-promoting behavior and policies while minimizing health-damaging behavior and policies.

3. Common problems of interest to health psychologists include smoking, obesity, alcohol consumption, stress management, AIDS, and chronic pain.

4. Child clinical psychologists commonly work in community mental health clinics, child guidance clinics, schools, children's hospitals, universities, and in private practices. Some of the common problem areas of interest include physical and/or sexual abuse, attention deficit hyperactivity disorder, conduct disorders, autism, enuresis (bed wetting), encopresis (soiling), and school phobia.

5. Pediatric psychology is a blend of child clinical psychology and health psychology. Pediatric psychologists are child clinical psychologists who generally work with children and families in hospital settings where the child has a significant medical disorder. These medical problems might include cancer, epilepsy, diabetes, or cystic fibrosis. The pediatric psychologist might offer pain management strategies to children or help the family cope more effectively with understanding and assisting a child having significant medical problems. They may help the child and family cope with painful medical procedures or assist the family and hospital staff with noncompliance with medical treatment.

6. Clinical neuropsychology focuses on brain–behavior relationships. These are defined as how brain functioning impacts behavior and behavioral problems. Clinical neuropsychologists assess brain and behavior functioning and offer strategies for patients suffering from brain impairment due to problems such as dementia, head injuries, tumors, stroke, AIDS, Alzheimer's disease, epilepsy, and other diseases and traumas that result in cognitive and neurological dysfunction.

7. Geropsychology focuses on unique issues associated with the elderly. This might include physical and mental health issues commonly experienced among this population. Examples include dementia and bereavement.

8. Forensic psychology involves the application of psychology to legal issues. Forensic psychologists may conduct psychological evaluations with defendants and present their findings as expert witnesses in court. They may also provide evaluations for child custody arrangements, or be asked to predict dangerousness or determine whether an individual is competent to stand trial. They may be asked to participate in worker's compensation claims, or serve as a consultant to attorneys who are selecting a jury.

9. While forensic psychologists are involved in numerous aspects of the legal system, they may be best known for their work in legal cases involving involuntary commitment, the insanity defense, child custody, violence against women and others, and jury selection.

10. In addition to health, child, neuropsychology, geropsychology, and forensics, there are a number of other subspecialties in clinical psychology. New subspecialties regularly emerge, reflecting psychology's growing and changing evolution.

Key Terms

Acquired immune deficiency syndrome (AIDS)

Alcohol abuse

Alzheimer's disease

Anorexia nervosa

Attention deficit hyperactivity disorder (ADHD)

Brain–behavior relationships

Brain injuries

Child abuse and neglect

Child clinical psychology

Child custody

Chronic pain

Degenerative diseases
Dementia
Durham Rule
Dyslexia
Ephebophiles
Epilepsy
Geropsychology
Health psychology
Insanity defense
Insanity Defense Reform Act
Involuntary commitment
Joint custody
Jury selection
Learning disabilities
M'Naghten Rule
Malingering
Neuropsychology
Obesity
Pseudoseizures
Seizures
Smoking
Stress management

For Reflection

1. What are some advantages and disadvantages of having subspecialties in clinical psychology?
2. How might the subspecialties overlap?
3. What types of problems are of interest to those who specialize in clinical health psychology?
4. What types of problems are of interest to those who specialize in child clinical psychology?
5. What types of problems are of interest to those who specialize in neuropsychology?
6. What types of problems are of interest to those who specialize in forensic psychology?

7. What types of problems are of interest to those who specialize in geropsychology?
8. Speculate about possible future subspecialties in clinical psychology.

Real Students, Real Questions

1. What is the likelihood of recovery from anorexia nervosa, bulimia, and obesity?
2. Is it possible that an ADHD diagnosis is a way of controlling very active children?
3. What is the distinction between dementia and Alzheimer's?
4. What kind of medical training is required for neuropsychologists?
5. What are the long-term side effects of medications like Ritalin?
6. Does hypnosis really help with smoking cessation and weight reduction?
7. Do specialization areas overlap a lot?
8. How do you diagnose children if their parents think nothing is wrong with them?
9. Are schoolteachers mandated reporters for child abuse?

Web Resources

http://www.allpsychologyschools.com/faqs/psyspecialties
Learn more about specialties in psychology.

http://www.ptsd.va.gov
Learn more about PTSD.

www.cdc.gov
Learn more about the U.S. Centers for Disease Control and Prevention.

http://www.nia.nih.gov/Alzheimers/AlzheimersInformation/GeneralInfo/
Learn more about Alzheimer's disease.

Consultative, Teaching, and Administrative Roles

Chapter Objective

To introduce and highlight the roles of consultation, teaching, and administrative activities among clinical psychologists.

Chapter Outline

Consultation

Highlight of a Contemporary Clinical Psychologist: Julie B. (Sincoff) Jampel, PhD

Teaching

Administration

12

Chapter

Drs. A, B, and C are all clinical psychologists. Dr. A is a professor at a large university and teaches courses in abnormal psychology, psychological testing, and clinical psychology. Dr. B directs mental health services for a child guidance clinic, overseeing 30 mental health clinicians and managing a multimillion-dollar annual budget. Dr. C is a consultant to a law firm and provides advice about stress management, employee relations, ethics, and other matters involving human behavior. Drs. A, B, and C may or may not engage in the traditional clinical psychology activities discussed earlier such as research, psychological testing, or psychotherapy. They may not work with any patients at all. Yet their professional roles and activities are typical of what many clinical psychologists do for a living.

In addition to research, assessment, and psychotherapy, clinical psychologists often spend a significant amount of time involved in other professional activities. Consultation, teaching, and administration are three common professional services offered by clinical psychologists. In a survey of over 14,000 practitioner members of the American Psychological Association (APA), psychologists reported spending 11% of their time in teaching, 9% in administration, and 6% in consultation (Phelps, 1996). These activities are not necessarily separate or distinct. Psychologists may both teach and consult in addition to conducting psychotherapy, psychological testing, or research. Therefore, a high degree of overlap may exist among these professional activities. The purpose of this chapter is to discuss the consultation, teaching, and administration activities of clinical psychologists.

Consultation

Clinical psychologists are experts in human behavior. They study, research, and treat a wide range of problems and people who are distressed by problematic feelings, thoughts, and behaviors. Psychologists are knowledgeable about theories and principles of human behavior. This expertise can be used to help many individuals, families, groups, and institutions (Figure 12.1). Clinical psychologists are often asked to consult with others to assist in solving problems in diverse settings. Almost all clinical psychologists participate in some form of professional consultation. Five percent of clinical psychologists report that consultation

345

Photo: Rhoda Sidney, Stock, Boston

Figure 12.1

Informal consultation regarding a patient hospitalized in a psychiatric unit.

is their primary professional activity (Norcross et al., 1997a). Psychologists not only provide consultation but regularly receive consultation from others. Consultation is an integral part of their professional work. Consultation may be provided to other mental health professionals; to organizations, groups, and individuals; and to the general public. Examples of consultation questions in various settings are provided in Table 12.1.

Consultation Defined

Consultation in clinical psychology refers to the application of knowledge and theories of human behavior to specific questions and problems in various community settings such as hospitals, clinics, schools, businesses, and government agencies. Consultation involves offering professional advice to others concerning problems that exist in their setting. Consultation usually involves the participation of a *consultant* with specialized knowledge and skill and a *consultee* or client who benefits from the expertise of the consultant. Unlike one-to-one psychotherapy, a consultant has the opportunity to assist large groups of people and entire organizations through his or her work with

a consultee. Wallace and Hall (1996) defined consultation as "a broad helping approach in which qualified psychological consultants help consultees (1) resolve work-related issues pertaining to individuals, clients or programs that they are responsible for, (2) become active agents in achieving solutions to problems, or (3) strengthen consultees' work-related competencies to address similar issues in the future" (p. 10). Consultation might be thought of in terms of the popular phrase, "Two (or more) heads are better than one," especially where one possesses special expertise.

Consultation has become more widely practiced in recent years, with consultation skills more commonly taught to clinical psychology students and professionals (Brown, 1985; Clayton & Bongar, 1994; Conyne & O'Neal, 1992; Peltier, 2010; Wallace & Hall, 1996). In fact, a national survey of psychologists revealed that 72% agreed that regular consultation is a good or excellent way to obtain information and provide competent professional service (Pope, Tabachnick, & Keith-Spiegal, 1987). Furthermore, the Clayton and Bongar (1994) review of consultation literature

Table 12.1   **Examples of Consultation Questions by Setting**

Hospital

1. Physicians and nurses on a cardiology unit are wondering how to assist patients in losing weight and exercising after they leave the hospital.

2. Physicians and nurses on a pediatric unit request help in developing a program to minimize adolescents from being sexually involved with other patients on the unit.

3. Physicians and nurses are concerned about how to help dialysis patients cope with feelings of anxiety and depression.

School

1. Teachers in a sixth-grade class are concerned about how to best deal with conflicts between the boys and girls in class.

2. Teachers in a third-grade class are unsure how to handle the disruptive behavior of a child with an attention deficit disorder.

3. Teachers in a high school are anxious and angry about parents who seem too demanding and entitled. They wonder how best to deal with parents who want too much from them.

4. A school principal seeks guidance about how best to deal with a teacher who openly challenges her during faculty meetings.

Business

1. An employer is concerned about stress associated with numerous layoffs and wonders how he can help his employees deal with work stress.

2. A small company is unproductive and inefficient due to numerous personality conflicts in the office. The company president hopes that a psychologist can help to figure out ways to help his employees get along better.

3. A company is concerned about a company vice president who was recently hospitalized with a bipolar illness. The company is unsure how to understand and manage this person once he returns to work.

4. A company is interested in hiring employees, especially in selecting employees who are likely to be excellent workers.

Government

1. A police department is interested in helping officers deal with the stress of witnessing and sometimes being the victim of violent crime.

2. A fire department is interested in having a psychologist consult about screening job applicants.

3. A juvenile court system is interested in finding ways to prevent juvenile offenders from repeating their offenses once released.

4. A judge is interested in obtaining consultation regarding child custody evaluations.

reported that consultation activities by psychologists significantly improve quality of care, client satisfaction, and treatment outcome.

Consultation Roles

Consultants may assume many different roles during the course of consultation or between consultation assignments. G. Lippitt and R. Lippitt (1994) suggested that the role of consultant is based on a continuum between being directive and being nondirective. Consultants in a *directive* role are generally viewed as offering expert and technical consultation. They help consultees solve problems through their knowledge about issues of interest to the consultees. For example, a consultant may be highly knowledgeable about computer software that keeps track of patients' files. A clinic may hire the consultant to assist in purchasing the software and teaching employees to use it effectively. *Nondirective* consultants use their skills and expertise to facilitate the consultee's skills. For example, a consultant may be hired to help managers of a company do a better job at interacting with employees who will be "downsized." Managers with the difficult and often painful job of informing employees that their position will be eliminated often need assistance in learning how both to complete this task sensitively and to cope with the employees' distress. The nondirective consultant might conduct role plays and critique the performance to help managers practice this difficult task. Directive consultation generally is task-oriented (the consultants provide expert assistance in solving problems), whereas the nondirective approach is process oriented or facilitative (Matthews, 1983). The directive approach generally focuses more on results, while the nondirective approach usually focuses on process or growth (Champion, Kiel, & McLendon, 1990).

Dougherty (2004) defined the following six common consultation roles for clinical psychologists: expert, trainer/educator, advocate, collaborator, fact finder, and process specialist. The **expert** consultation role is the most common one (Gallessich, 1982). The

expert consultant is a technological advisor (Dougherty, 2004) who has the specialized skills, knowledge, or experience that the consultee needs to help solve a problem. For instance, an expert consultant may have special skills in conducting intelligence testing for children applying to a school system's gifted and talented program. The school hires the consultant to help them understand what the test scores mean and determine how best to screen applicants for the program.

Somewhat similar to the expert role, consultants are often asked to act as trainer/educators. Formal training may occur in workshops, seminars, and classes on a variety of topics. Informal training may occur in one-to-one training sessions with employees or clients. The **trainer/educator** role, like the expert role, assumes that the consultant has specialized information that is useful to the client and can be acquired through education. For example, a consultant may be asked to train employees of a company to manage stress better through the use of relaxation techniques. A trainer/educator consultant may teach day-care workers about child illnesses or patterns of physical abuse through several workshop sessions. A consultant who is knowledgeable about domestic violence may also train police officers to recognize the signs and symptoms of this problem.

The **advocate** consultant seeks to convince a consultee to do something that the consultant believes is desirable. Consultants can act as advocates in a wide variety of ways (Kurpius & Lewis, 1988; Peltier, 2010). For example, a consultant to a mental health clinic may advocate for the rights of severely disabled patients who have difficulty advocating for themselves. A consultant hired to participate in a school meeting to discuss an Individual Education Plan (IEP) might advocate for the provision of special education services for a learning-disabled child. An advocate consultant may help ensure that a physically disabled child or adult receives access to facilities and maintains optimal independence.

The **collaborator** consultant role suggests that the consultant is an equal partner working with a consultee to achieve a common goal. Both the consultant and consultee stand to benefit from their collaboration. For example, if a researcher is interested in learning more about the effect of exercise in the treatment of depression and knows a great deal about exercise but little about depression, he or she may decide to work with a collaborating consultant who is an expert on depression. As another example, an individual psychotherapist and a group psychotherapist treating the same patient might collaborate in order to coordinate their two psychotherapies and to learn more about the patient's progress in each treatment modality.

The **fact finder** consultation role involves seeking information and relaying the results to consultees who lack the expertise, time, energy, or psychological sensitivities to do the task themselves (Dougherty, 2004; Lippitt & Lippitt, 1994). For instance, a psychologist may be interested in buying special equipment for his research laboratory. He may hire a fact-finding consultant who is highly knowledgeable about the equipment to locate an appropriate product and service agreement at a reasonable price. Or a company concerned about poor morale might hire an outside fact-finding consultant to investigate the causes of the problem.

Finally, the role of the **process-specialist** consultant is to help the consultee better understand the process of events that might cause problems (Peltier, 2010; Schein, 1988). For example, a clinic manager dissatisfied with how staff meetings are run might hire a process-specialist consultant to observe the meetings and suggest ways to improve communication and staff participation. Consultants thus can assume many different roles or perform several roles during the same consultation experience.

Types of Consultation

Mental Health Consultation: Several types of consultation are typically conducted by clinical psychologists in mental health settings. These include (a) informal peer-group

consultation, (b) client-centered case consultation, (c) program-centered administrative consultation, (d) consultee-centered case consultation, and (e) consultee-centered administrative consultation.

Informal peer-group consultation is the most widely used and valued method of consultation in psychology (Allen, Nelson, & Sheckley, 1987; Cranston et al., 1988). It involves asking coworkers to consult on a challenging clinical case informally during lunch or other work breaks. For example, a psychologist may struggle with the treatment of a difficult patient where treatment seems stuck. The psychologist may believe that process has stopped and wonders how he or she might best alter the treatment plan to best assist the patient. The psychologist might ask a colleague to discuss the case with him or her in order to develop insight into better treatment strategies.

Client-centered case consultation involves consultation with a fellow professional such as another psychologist who is responsible for the treatment or care of a particular patient. The professional seeks the advice of the consultant in order to meet the specific needs of the patient more adequately. Both consultee and consultant have some responsibility for the care of the patient.

Program-centered administrative consultation focuses on a program or system rather than on an individual case. The consultation may involve an important aspect of the functioning of a clinic, practice, research program, or other more global issue. For example, a psychologist might seek consultation about the curriculum, structure, and advertising strategy of group psychotherapy programs for patients. Or the consultation might concern how best to conduct intake interviews and assign patients to therapists in a large community mental health clinic.

The focus of **consultee-centered case consultation** is on challenges experienced by the consultee rather than on problems concerning an individual case or client. Inexperience, lack of information, and mistakes made by the consultee are often the topic of discussion. For instance, a graduate student in psychology may seek consultation from an experienced supervisor about discomfort and anxiety experienced when conducting psychotherapy with patients who are older than the student.

Finally, **consultee-centered administrative consultation** generally involves working on administrative and personnel issues within an agency. For example, an outpatient clinic board of directors may wish to consult with a psychologist about problems in the leadership performance of their executive director.

Organizational Consultation: Clinical psychologists also frequently provide consultation to an enormous range of non–mental health agencies and organizations. Businesses, non-profit agencies, religious communities and groups, and government organizations all employ people who must work cooperatively to achieve a common purpose and keep the organization running effectively and smoothly (Hanna, 1988). As experts in human behavior, psychologists can offer useful advice on dealing with the interpersonal and organizational problems and conflicts that inevitably arise in organizational life.

Organizational consultation generally uses systems theory to understand and intervene in organizations (Hanna, 1988; Kurpius, 1985). As discussed earlier in this book, systems theory proposes that all aspects of a system (whether a family or a professional organization) interact and react to changes and behavior in each element of the system. Each element or subsystem within the large organizational structure is dependent on other elements or subsystems; therefore, changes that occur at one level will usually influence changes at other levels (Fuqua & Kurpius, 1993). For example, suppose that one division of a company is losing a great deal of money, has experienced several major failures, and has a leader perceived by most employees as incompetent. The division is unable to maintain employee loyalty and morale, and most of the employees are looking for work elsewhere. Systems theory would predict that the problems within this division are likely

to impact the entire company. Losses by the division may need to be compensated for by other more productive and successful divisions within the company. The successful divisions are likely to feel resentful for having to bail out a failing division. As a result, morale will probably decline in the successful divisions. Consultants to organizations must use systems theory to diagnose organizational problems and provide interventions. They know that tinkering with one aspect of an organization will probably have ripple effects on other parts of the organization, and must be mindful of the entire system when intervening.

Executive Coaching: In recent years, **executive coaching** has become extremely popular as a way to bring principles of psychology to business and industry executives (Auerbach, 2001; Hays & Brown, 2004; Kombarakaran, Yang, Baker, & Fernandes, 2008; Peltier, 2010; Williams & David, 2002). In fact, executive coaching is now a billion-dollar-per-year industry with thousands of coaches located worldwide (Peltier, 2010). Clinical psychologists, as well as other professionals from a variety of disciplines such as social work, marriage and family therapy, human resources, and so forth, have developed services for leading executives as executive coaches. They generally focus on ways to help executives become better leaders and managers as well as develop strategies to improve interpersonal relationships, productivity, and efficiency in companies. Executive coaches may consult with business leaders about stress management, goal setting, and a host of other topics and services related to human behavior and business.

Executive coaching has become a potentially new and lucrative area of work for many clinical psychologists looking to expand their range of professional activities and services (Hays & Brown, 2004; Kombarakaran et al., 2008; Peltier, 2010).

Stages of Consultation

Many of the stages that have been used to describe the psychotherapy process apply to consultation as well. These include (a) understanding the question, (b) assessment, (c) intervention, (d) termination, and (e) follow-up.

Understanding the Question: First the consultant must evaluate the situation in order to understand the nature of the referral question and the goals of the consultation. The consultant must determine whether he or she has the training, experience, and expertise to provide a competent and professional consultation. Frequently, the initial question posed by the person(s) seeking consultation changes during the course of the consultation. For example, a personnel director of a company may ask a psychologist to consult on stress management techniques for employees of her company. She tells the psychologist that downsizing and layoffs have resulted in a high degree of stress. She wants the psychologist to offer stress management workshops for small groups of employees as well as individual sessions for those interested in specialized one-on-one help. However, during the initial consultation it becomes clear to the psychologist (and the personnel director) that the management of the company has been ineffective and must be altered to reduce employee stress. Organizational management issues are much more salient than initially thought. The personnel director then decides that dealing with management issues should occur prior to offering the stress management workshops initially requested. Thus, psychologists who act as consultants must fully investigate the nature of the referral questions, knowing that the initial request may not be what is really needed. The consultant must also determine the fit between the needs of the consultee and his or her own expertise.

Sometimes before agreeing to be hired, a consultant must determine whether the organization requesting the consultation is actually ready for the experience. Paradoxically, an organization that initiates contact with a consultant and requests needed help may be resistant to change, to feedback, or to the results of the consultation. An organization's readiness for and openness to consultation are sometimes more important to the success of the consultation project than are the consultant's assessment and intervention (Beer & Spector, 1993).

Assessment: Once the appropriate questions are understood, psychologists hired as consultants need to assess the situation fully before offering intervention or advice. The assessment phase usually includes interviews and may also include formal psychological testing and/or review of records or other data. Ideally, the consultant should enter the organizational system "gaining acceptance and approval from consultees and other constituents" (Wallace & Hall, 1996, p. 29). However, the consultees may not trust the consultant if he or she appears to have personality traits, attitudes, or strategies that they view as negative. Even those who are in favor of obtaining help may be resistant and have an agenda concerning the consultant's findings. The consultant must assess the customs, beliefs, rules, and general climate of the organization as well as attempt to develop a trusting relationship with the consultees prior to offering advice (J. C. Conoley & C. W. Conoley, 1992).

Interviewing is the most common method of conducting a consultation assessment (Molyneaux & Lane, 1982). The consultant may choose to use either structured and standardized interviews or unstructured, conversational, and nonstandardized interviews. The consultant asks questions of relevant people involved with the organization. For example, a researcher may wish to consult with a psychologist on measures to assess depression for a particular study. The consultant interviews the researcher about the goals and design of the study. Once the consultant has a solid understanding of the needs of the researcher, he or she will be able to suggest relevant measures of depression. Or, as another example, suppose the recent reorganization of a small company has proved challenging and stressful for most employees. A psychologist consultant is asked to evaluate the reorganization process and to suggest how best to deal with the associated stress. The psychologist interviews first the company's management team and then each of the key employees. The series of comprehensive interviews enables the psychologist to assess the problem(s) before offering intervention strategies and advice. Surveys and questionnaires are a second common method of assessment in consultation.

Surveys allow large amounts of information to be collected efficiently and confidentially (Wallace & Hall, 1996). Direct observation is another approach to assessment in consultation (Dougherty, 1990, 2004). A consultant may informally observe an organization, sit in on meetings, and/or watch key people work and interact.

Once a comprehensive assessment is complete, the consultant develops a diagnostic impression of the problem(s) and outlines goals for intervention. The goals should be specific, realistic, measurable, and based on collaboration between consultant and consultees (Wallace & Hall, 1996).

Intervention: After the assessment phase, in which the consultant diagnoses a particular problem and sets consultation goals, the consultant can develop an intervention strategy or a response to the consultee's questions and problems. Intervention is the stage when the consultant provides the actual advice or suggestions for change. It is also the stage when implementation occurs. Intervention is what the person(s) seeking consultation hopes to get from the consultant. For instance, a physician may ask a psychologist to consult on a case that he or she is treating: Patient with sleep apnea and obesity is not being compliant with the doctor's treatment suggestions. The physician is frustrated and concerned because, without cooperation in her medical treatment, the patient is in jeopardy of dying. The consulting psychologist interviews the physician, the patient, and the patient's spouse and determines that she is highly depressed and wishes to die. The consultant suggests ways for the physician to treat the patient's depression, encourage psychotherapy, and manage the emotional factors affecting her illness.

Consultation intervention may include either individual intervention as in the previous example or group interventions such as training, conflict resolution, or team building (Wallace & Hall, 1996). Implementing the intervention (e.g., team building and training) is usually the responsibility of the consultee, with guidance from the consultant (Caplan, 1970; Dougherty, 1990, 2004).

Once an intervention is implemented, an evaluation is typically conducted to determine whether the intervention has been beneficial. Scriven (1967) classifies consultation evaluations as either formative or summative. Formative evaluations examine the process of consultation from start to finish. Each stage of the process is evaluated carefully. Summative evaluations highlight the consultation outcome. They assess whether the goals and objectives of the consultation were adequately reached.

Termination: After the goals of the consultation agreements have been met, or if the consultant determines that the goals cannot be achieved, then the termination phase of the consultation occurs (Kurpius, Fuqua, & Rozecki, 1993). Unfortunately, the consultation relationship may be terminated without thoughtful or appropriate consideration. Many authors suggest that careful attention be given to the termination phase to correct this problem (Dustin & Ehly, 1984; Hansen, Himes, & Meier, 1990; Kurpius et al., 1993). For example, Dustin and Ehly (1984) recommend conducting an exit interview at termination. The purpose of the exit interview is to enable the consultant and consultee(s) to discuss the consultation process, share feedback about the experience and intervention, resolve any residual issues, plan for follow-up if appropriate, and obtain closure for all participants.

Follow-Up: Interventions and advice provided by the consultant may or may not be used. The advice may not be what the consultee wanted to hear, the intervention plans may not be realistic, or they may be too difficult to implement. The consultee may have lost interest in the problems because of new crises that emerged after the initiation or termination of the consultation. Follow-up frequently maximizes the consultee's benefit from the consultation efforts. For example, the previously mentioned patient with sleep apnea may be treated for depression in addition to her sleep apnea and obesity in accordance with the recommendations of the consultant. However, family conflicts emerge that threaten the progress she has made. Follow-up consultation may prove useful in dealing with these new family concerns so that the therapeutic process can move forward. As another example, a consultant may offer stress management workshops for employees at a company that is undergoing layoffs and organizational restructuring. Although the workshops may be well received, old patterns of behavior may reemerge and good intentions may fade, causing the intervention to fail several weeks after completion of the workshops. Because behavior and habits are often difficult to change, periodic follow-up sessions or ongoing programs may be needed to maintain new patterns. The sessions may be scheduled during the intervention or termination phase or on an as-needed basis. Many consultants routinely provide follow-up in person, over the telephone, or by letter (Wallace & Hall, 1996).

To Whom Do Clinical Psychologists Offer Consultation?

Clinical psychologists frequently provide advice and consultation to their peers (Clayton & Bongar, 1994; Peltier, 2010). They may develop a high degree of expertise in a certain area less familiar to other professionals. For instance, a psychologist may be especially skilled in working with children who experience attention deficit hyperactivity disorder (ADHD). Because many different life events and situations may contribute to the impulsive and behavioral overactivity usually associated with ADHD (e.g., physical or sexual abuse, parental neglect, marital discord or divorce, learning disabilities), the diagnosis and treatment of ADHD is complex and should be conducted by specialists. A social worker, psychiatrist, marriage counselor, or fellow psychologist without a high level of expertise in this area may choose to ask another professional with these skills to consult on a given case. The consultant would determine what specific questions or issues need to be addressed (e.g., diagnosis, treatment recommendations) and perhaps meet with the family and child for an assessment. The consultant may offer advice about tests to use or may review testing and interview data to assist in making an appropriate diagnosis.

Psychologists may also consult with a colleague about a patient they treat in psychotherapy when they are unsure how best to handle a particular therapeutic situation. Discussing a case with an objective and unbiased colleague is often very useful. For example, a psychologist may feel frustrated in conducting psychotherapy with a patient who is angry and hostile. The patient experiences a borderline personality disorder, major depression, and chronic low-back pain. She frequently expresses anger, resentment, and even rage. During one of her therapy sessions the patient states that she has an urge to strangle the therapist. Furthermore, the patient has access to weapons, and the therapist is concerned that she may show up at a session with a gun. The psychologist tries to be understanding and helpful but feels angry, resentful, and fearful. The psychologist consults with a colleague to discuss the case and obtain advice on how to proceed in the best interest of the patient. The consultant listens carefully to the situation, asking questions of the therapist. They talk about strategies and options for treatment that the therapist can try to incorporate into the treatment sessions as well as discussing the therapist's feelings and reactions. They decide to meet several times to see how the therapy progresses, and the consultant offers follow-up advice.

Psychologists may also seek consultation when conducting psychological evaluations or testing. Some of the data obtained through an evaluation may be difficult to interpret or may conflict with data from other sources (e.g., interview, physician's report, teacher's report). The psychologist conducting the evaluation may seek a second opinion by asking a colleague to consult on the case and review the testing materials. For instance, a psychologist may be asked to conduct an evaluation of a child who does very poorly on school examinations. The child's teachers and parents all feel that the child is very bright and maintains good study skills. They wonder whether the child is overanxious about tests or perhaps has a learning disability that impairs testing performance. The psychologist interviews the parents, several teachers, and the child, and then administers intellectual, educational, and psychological tests to the child. However, the testing data seem somewhat contradictory, and it is unclear what the results actually mean. The psychologist decides to consult with an expert colleague who can review the data, offer an opinion about diagnosis, and suggest treatment plans. The consulting psychologist reviews the testing data and interviews the clinician. The consultant may also decide to interview the family and/or child as well. Psychologists conducting research also frequently consult with colleagues. A psychologist may seek the consultation of another to assist in interpreting research data, designing appropriate experiments, and determining which specialized equipment to use, or for help in other research questions. For example, a psychologist may be conducting experiments on the psychological benefits of exercise among anxious and depressed patients. She would like to have the patients exercise in a laboratory to determine how much exercise is needed to elevate mood. Unsure of what equipment to use and how intense the exercise sessions should be, she consults with several colleagues who are experts in this field for advice and guidance. The consultants also might provide useful journal articles or other reading materials or invite the psychologist to tour their laboratory to observe their testing and research protocols.

Consultation with Non–Mental Health Professionals: In addition to consultation with colleagues, many psychologists consult with professionals from other disciplines as well as with individual patients. Clinical psychologists frequently consult with school teachers and administrators, physicians and nurses, attorneys and judges, clergy, the military, and people working in business and industry. The number of potential areas and issues requiring consultation on human behavior is countless. Consultation is so popular that several companies specialize in providing psychological consultation to people in business and industry.

Psychologists also consult with medical personnel (e.g., physicians, nurses, physical therapists, nutritionists) concerning patient care (Gunn & Blount, 2009; McDaniel, 1995; Miller & Swartz, 1990; Pillay, 1990). Medical personnel often seek consultation from psychologists and other mental health professionals in order to assist patients experiencing a wide variety of medical problems. Many medical patients need assistance in coping with anxiety or depression associated with their own illness or illness in the family. Others may need assistance in changing their lifestyle to better accommodate their illness or cope more effectively with their medical problems. Still others need help complying with medical instructions to care more appropriately for their needs. In fact, many hospitals offer a consultation-liaison (C&L) service so that psychological consultation can be made available to every medical department at all times. For instance, patients recovering from a heart attack, obtaining dialysis for kidney failure, or receiving radiation/chemotherapy for cancer are often fearful and depressed. Consultation with a psychologist may assist these patients in coping more effectively with their treatment, diagnosis, feelings, and post-hospital adjustment. Many medical patients engage in health-damaging behavior such as eating too many high-fat foods, drinking too much alcohol, smoking cigarettes, and refusing to practice safe sex or wear seatbelts. Changing these and other destructive behaviors to

---

Case Studies: Consultation with Mental Health Colleagues

Dr. A is treating a young Caucasian woman with bulimia. During the course of several months of treatment, the woman inquires about the use of hypnosis as a possible adjunct to treatment. Since Dr. A is unfamiliar with the technique, he suggests that the patient consult with a colleague, Dr. B, who specializes in hypnotic techniques. After discussing the issue with Dr. A, the patient decides to consult with Dr. B. The patient signs a release to allow Dr. A and Dr. B to discuss her case and coordinate treatment. Dr. A continues to provide weekly individual psychotherapy sessions, while Dr. B schedules several hypnotherapy sessions.

Dr. C works in the consultation-liaison service of a large university teaching hospital. The attending psychiatrist on the geropsychiatric unit asks Dr. C for a consultation regarding a 72-year-old African American female patient who reports feeling severely depressed. The patient has had several trials of antidepressant medication and yet appears disoriented and reports no symptom relief. The psychiatrist on the unit is considering electroconvulsive therapy (ECT) as a last resort. Prior to administering the ECT treatment, the psychiatrist would like Dr. C to conduct an evaluation and consultation to determine what other personality or neuropsychological factors play a role in her reported symptoms. Dr. C meets with the patient and psychiatrist, conducts an interview, and administers a battery of neuropsychological tests. Dr. C concludes that the patient experiences senile dementia in addition to depression. Based on Dr. C's findings, the psychiatrist chooses not to administer ECT and further compromise her cognitive functioning.

Dr. D is interested in conducting a research project on the coping responses and strategies of Salvadoran immigrants to the United States. Dr. D decides to consult with his colleague, Dr. E, who is a native Salvadoran and psychologist. Dr. E helps Dr. D in securing access to the population of immigrants, translates questionnaires into Spanish, and helps Dr. D better understand the Salvadoran culture to improve his research study.

---

improve health and cope more effectively with illness is remarkably difficult. In fact, about 50% of all deaths are considered to be caused by lifestyle factors (Centers for Disease Control, 2009; S. Taylor, 2009).

Psychologists frequently consult with teachers and school personnel in day-care centers, preschools, elementary schools, secondary schools, and/or special-education schools. For instance, a psychologist may consult with a teacher about ways to manage the disruptive classroom behavior of a child. The psychologist might evaluate the child and family, observe the child in the classroom setting, and meet periodically with the teacher to help him or her interact more effectively with the child and class. A school principal may consult with a psychologist about how best to handle requests by parents and students for untimed tests for students with learning disabilities. Or a psychologist may be requested to consult with a day-care center to assist the staff in coping with children who have been victims of sexual abuse.

Many psychologists work regularly with the legal system and consult with attorneys and judges on various cases. For example, psychologists often act as expert witnesses and consultants in child custody cases. Parents who are going through divorce may each seek sole custody of a child or several children. When divorces are bitter and the couple experiences a high degree of conflict, their children may become the battleground for their conflict. The parents may be unable to agree on child placement, child-rearing strategies, or anything else pertaining to their children. The psychologist may be asked to evaluate each parent and the child and offer an expert opinion concerning child custody placement. Psychologists are often consultants in criminal cases as well. When a criminal defendant is attempting to use an insanity defense, the psychologist might be asked to conduct an evaluation and consultation, then provide expert opinion to the court about the diagnosis and mental status of the accused.

Psychologists often consult with the clergy as well (Pargament et al., 1991; Plante, 1999, 2004a, 2009). For example, a clergy member may wish to learn more about how to handle difficult parishioners or best help those suffering from mental illness when they ask for pastoral counseling or spiritual direction. Clergy may seek guidance and consultation on the selection process for clergy applicants or for better ways to conduct group sessions during retreats and other group activities.

Psychologists are frequently asked to consult with business personnel from many different industries regarding employee relations, selection, stress management, morale boosting, and so on (Tobias, 1990). For example, many police and fire departments are concerned about helping their employees deal more effectively with the stress associated with their jobs. Psychologists may be asked to consult on individual cases and on developing programs and procedures to help these individuals cope better. They may also be asked to consult on the selection and training of new police and fire recruits.

Effective Consultation

A number of skills are needed to be an effective consultant. Most researchers and practitioners of consultation highlight the primary importance of competent interpersonal and communication skills (J. C. Conoley & C. W. Conoley, 1992; Dougherty, 2004; G. Lippitt & R. Lippitt, 1994; Peltier, 2010). However, excellent group and problem-solving skills (Dougherty, 2004; Schindler-Rainman, 1985), the ability to work with organizations (Schein, 1988), and highly developed professional and ethical behavior (G. Corey, M. S. Corey, & Callanan, 1993) are also imperative. Dougherty (2004) offered consultants a detailed list of skills necessary for effective consultation. Briefly, these include empathy, genuineness, social skills, and ease in working with others. Consultants must be able to create a comfortable, trusting, collaborative environment with consultees. They must be effective listeners. They must be able to ask useful questions, provide feedback and criticism in a diplomatic manner, and both give and receive information as necessary. They must be able to define problems and be skilled at gathering, understanding, and interpreting information relevant to the consultation. Consultants must also be able to assess the working atmosphere or climate and culture of an organization. They must understand group dynamics and group process and be able to manage conflict in group settings. Finally, they must be professional and ethical, maintaining the highest level of competence and integrity.

Challenges in Consultation

Although consultants and consultees may readily agree on the need for and goals of a consultation relationship, several challenges often typically emerge. Resistance to the consultant and to his or her suggestions is very common. Many consultees have mixed feelings about having an outside expert enter their agency, organization, or work environment to tell them what they are doing wrong and how they should solve their problems. Airing dirty laundry before an outsider and admitting that problems cannot be solved without consultative help is often difficult and threatening. An internal consultant (someone who already works for the organization) may experience resistance as well. Other employees may resent that one of their own peers has been asked to investigate, diagnose, and offer suggestions regarding their problems. Although internal consultants are likely to know the organization and its social climate, culture, politics, power issues, and players much better than

Case Studies: Consultation with Non–Mental Health Professionals

Dr. F is called by an oncology (cancer specialist) physician treating a 36-year-old Caucasian woman for advanced breast cancer. The physician has been working with the woman for many years regarding her medical problems. Recently, she has refused chemotherapy and has failed to undergo scheduled diagnostic tests. Concerned that she might die prematurely, the physician asks Dr. F to consult on the case. Dr. F meets with the patient, her family, and the physician, and determines that the patient is highly depressed and suicidal. Apparently she hopes that she can hasten her death by terminating necessary medical treatment. Dr. F suggests both individual and family psychotherapy, a psychiatric consultation for antidepressant medication, as well as exploration between the patient and her physician of medical alternatives to aversive chemotherapy.

Dr. G is called by a private school headmaster to consult on a difficult situation. The parents of a 13-year-old Caucasian student attending the school insist on special treatment for their child and personalized attention from the teachers, and generally behave in a highly entitled manner. Furthermore, they are often late in paying for tuition and other bills and always have some excuse for the delay. Several teachers have expressed extreme frustration with the parents and have threatened not to include the student in their classes. The headmaster also feels at a loss as to how to deal with the parents' behavior. After interviewing the principal and several teachers, Dr. G helps them develop clear expectations, limits, and consequences for behavior and coaches them in dealing more firmly and effectively with the parents. A plan is developed prior to each interaction with the parents, and the psychologist reviews the plan and outcome following each interaction. The review helps to fine-tune future interactions and significantly decreases the tension between the parents and school personnel.

Dr. H is called by an executive director of a nonprofit organization specializing in the diagnosis and treatment of a racially diverse group of learning-disabled children. The executive director is trained in special education and business. She contacted Dr. H to obtain assistance in developing a treatment outcome and client-satisfaction program for her agency. Various sources of financial support (e.g., health insurance companies; state and county education contracts; federal, state, and private granting agencies) have requested information regarding treatment outcome and client satisfaction prior to considering funding the agency. Dr. H consults with the executive director and reviews the goals of the program, cultural sensitivity of staff, research design strategies, statistical methods, and specific assessment procedures to evaluate treatment outcome and client satisfaction. Dr. H also meets with several other agency administrators and clinical staff members. Together they develop a comprehensive evaluation program. The program is implemented and reviewed periodically by Dr. H to troubleshoot problems and suggest improvements.

outside consultants, they may not be taken seriously by their peers.

Another common problem in consultation is the concern that all the parties involved may not cooperate. Management executives of a company or agency may make the decision to hire a consultant while several employees may feel that consultation is not needed. Therefore, not everyone may agree or cooperate. While some may enthusiastically support the consultant's efforts, others may be resentful and even attempt to sabotage the work. Consultees may have hidden agendas as well. For example, a school principal may seek consultation from a psychologist about how to handle a very difficult student who does poorly in class and is a discipline problem. The consultant may suggest removing the student from the school. The principal may have wanted to remove the student all along, but sought validation from a professional consultant in order to convince the student's parents and teachers that the decision was justified. Consultants, being human, may also have their hidden agendas. Some may be more interested in promoting their services, seminars, books, training programs, and careers than in helping consultees with a particular problem.

Additionally, the consultee's expectations may be unreasonably high. By the time many consultees decide to hire a professional consultant, they may want the person to step into the organization and instantly fix the problems(s) (Conyne & O'Neil, 1992; Kombarakaran et al., 2008; Peltier, 2010). Developing expectations that are reasonable, realistic, and appropriate as well as intervention plans that are feasible represent challenging but essential tasks in all consultation relationships.

Finally, consultants themselves may contribute to problems. They may lack adequate knowledge, skill, experience, self-confidence, or professional objectivity and integrity to be effective (Dougherty, 1994).

Clinical psychology consultants are asked to deal with an endless variety of problems, populations, cultures, and questions. As more and more research and practical experience help to develop our understanding of human nature, consultants on human behavior come to be more in demand. A better understanding of behavior and ways to manage or change behavior in various settings is useful in almost all areas of work. Therefore, consultation activities provided by clinical psychologists are likely to increase in the future.

Highlight of a Contemporary Clinical Psychologist

Julie B. (Sincoff) Jampel, PhD

Photo: Courtesy Julie B. Jampel

Dr. Jampel uses her skills as a clinical psychologist to counsel students at a university counseling center.

Birth Date: December 1, 1961

College: Harvard University (BA, Psychology and Social Relations), 1984

Graduate Program: Yale University (PhD, Clinical and Developmental Psychology), 1990

Clinical Internship: Veterans Administration Medical Center, West Haven, CT, 1989–1990

Postdoctoral Fellowship: Harvard University Health Services, Mental Health Service, 1990–1991

Current Job: Director of Training, Counseling and Mental Health Service, Tufts University, Medford, MA

Pros and Cons of Being a Clinical Psychologist:

Pros: ''Being part of the larger field of psychology, which is ripe with interesting and important theories and research. Performing work that is challenging and stimulating and that affords an opportunity to get to know a broad range of people. Feeling that the work I do is relevant and useful.''

Cons: "At times the work can be time consuming and draining. It is also sedentary. Job opportunities and salaries in some settings may be poor."

Future of Clinical Psychology: "Clinical psychologists have identified many roles in which their training and expertise can help alleviate human suffering. While some of these roles remain constant, others change to accommodate the cultural forces and times in which we live. Clinical psychology is creative and resilient; the field will survive and adapt along with the human spirit."

What kind of consultative, administrative, and teaching activities are you engaged in? "I consult with university deans about students who have come to their attention for emotional or sometimes disciplinary reasons. I also consult with professors who are concerned about particular students as well as with the staff of various offices in the university charged with providing support services to students. Examples include the Academic Resource Center, International Student Center, Women's Center, and Residential Life. I supervise and lead a seminar for the postdoctoral psychology fellows who join our staff each year. The seminar covers a lot of ground, including late adolescent development and issues related to psychotherapy and consultation."

What are some of the challenges that you face in your work? "One of the more challenging aspects of working in college mental health is reaching those students who need services but who are reluctant to seek help, such as isolated students or international students who might feel that seeking counseling is a sign of weakness. Functioning in both the private role of a student's therapist and the public role of a member of the university community can also be challenging."

Typical Schedule:

9:00 Therapy session with a college student coping with a history of sexual abuse.

10:00 Therapy session with a graduate student from South America who feels isolated and overwhelmed.

11:00 Consultation with a residential hall advisor about a bulimic student on his floor.

12:00 Lunch and paperwork.

1:00 Therapy session with a college student struggling with a learning disability and social anxiety.

2:00 Team meeting to discuss clients' dispositions.

3:00 Supervision with a postdoctoral fellow who is worried about a suicidal client.

4:00 Therapy session with a graduate student suffering from bipolar disorder.

5:00 Private therapy session with a depressed adult who feels stuck in an unhappy marriage and meaningless job.

Teaching

As discussed in Chapter 3, psychology has its roots in academics, including both research and teaching activities. Teaching activities are a part of the professional duties of many psychologists. Although only 30% of clinical psychologists work primarily in academic environments such as colleges, universities, and medical schools (Norcross et al., 2005, 2008; Phelps, 1996), most psychologists participate in some teaching activity. However, teaching and supervision skills are often not a significant part of graduate school training in clinical psychology (Hoffman, 1990; Norcross et al., 2008; Russell & Petrie, 1994; Watkins, 1992).

Clinical psychologists frequently teach in a wide variety of settings and to a wide variety of audiences. Teaching may involve formal college classroom instruction, individual supervision of a psychologist-in-training, or lecturing on stress-management techniques to business firms or schools. Teaching may also be incorporated into psychotherapy and psychological testing activities. For instance, a psychologist may teach a patient how to use relaxation techniques to counter stress or teach a couple how to communicate better without blaming a partner in an angry and destructive manner.

Psychoeducational approaches involve teaching patients to cope with a wide range of medical and psychiatric problems. For example, support and psychoeducational groups helping patients with diabetes, cancer, irritable bowel syndrome, AIDS, and other illnesses use both teaching and psychotherapy methods. Part of the teaching function may be to review specific coping strategies, inform the participants about new treatment medications or procedures, and provide guest speakers on selected topics of interest.

Teaching in Academic Settings

Psychology Departments: Many clinical psychologists teach in psychology departments in colleges and universities across the country. They teach courses such as Abnormal Psychology, Clinical Psychology, Psychological Testing, Introduction to Psychology, Statistics, and Research Methods, among others. In addition to the ordinary duties of teaching such as classroom lectures and discussions; creating, administering, and scoring exams; and counseling students on academic and educational issues, academic psychologists conduct research and offer services to their department and university. They may teach undergraduates, graduates, and postgraduates.

In addition to offering courses in psychology, many clinical psychology professors provide individual and/or group supervision of clinical cases treated by advanced graduate or postgraduate students (Norcross et al., 2008, 2008; Russell & Petrie, 1994). They review the assessment, treatment, and consultation activities of students working with clinical patients and offer guidance, support, and advice, and ensure quality care regarding clinical methods and interventions. Further details regarding clinical supervision are presented in the section on medical schools and hospitals.

Full-time professors in college settings are usually classified as assistant, associate, or full professors. Although their teaching load and research activities may not differ based on academic rank or title, their status within the university as well as salary are determined, at least in part, by their academic rank. Newly hired faculty are generally given the *assistant professor* title. Assistant professors have a probationary status and are often given a yearly contract until the probationary period is completed. After approximately six years, they apply for promotion to associate professor and for tenure. Tenure provides job security by awarding a permanent job to the professor. After generally another six or more years in the rank of associate professor, the person may apply to become full professor. Full professor is a rank usually reserved for those who have made a significant impact on the profession through both research and teaching activities. Associate professors do not need to apply for full professor to maintain their job. Universities also hire part-time instructors who are not eligible for tenure or a more permanent full-time position. These part-time teachers are often called lecturers, instructors, or adjunct professors. These positions are non-tenure-track positions. Although tenure has been a part of academic life for many years, it is controversial in that many people feel that the guarantee of a permanent position might result in some professors spending less time and energy on their academic duties following the awarding of tenure.

Other Academic Departments: In colleges and universities, clinical psychologists teach in departments other than psychology, such as education, counseling, women's studies, business, law, and medicine. They may teach a wide variety of courses full time or part time in these departments.

Medical Schools and Hospitals: Clinical psychologists teach in medical schools and hospitals as well. They may teach seminars to various trainees and staff members, including medical students, residents, nurses, psychology interns, and postdoctoral psychology fellows, or they may be guest lecturers at courses, seminars, or department grand rounds. Each medical department generally offers weekly

Women Psychologists in Academe

Women now make up the majority of people earning doctorates in psychology and most especially in the applied areas of psychology such as clinical, counseling, and school psychology (American Psychological Association, 2000a, 2003a; Halpern, 2008; Snyder et al., 2000). Although women are now the majority of new psychologists, their salaries and status within the profession are not on par with those of men. For example, of the full-time employees in academic psychology, men are much more likely to hold the rank of full professor (45% of all male professors) relative to women (27% of all female professors) according to the American Psychological Association Task Force on Women in Academe (Kite et al., 2001). Furthermore, of these full-time academics, men are much more likely to have the status and job security of tenure (68% of male faculty) than women (44% of female faculty). These gender differences surface in salary as well. Women academic psychologists earn 84% of what men earn (National Center for Education Statistics, 1993; Settles, Cortina, Malley, & Stewart, 2006).

Given the fact that more and more women are entering the field of psychology, it is likely that these gaps will narrow in the future. However, Kite et al. (2001) warns that this alone will unlikely result in more equitable salary, status, and professional advancement for women. The American Psychological Association Task Force on Women in Academe offers a variety of recommendations for improving women's success in academia at all levels of academic decision making (e.g., university presidents, provosts, deans, department chairs) and can be found in the *American Psychologist* task force summary article by Kite et al. (2001). These include strategies to enhance women's service and leadership roles, enhancing the environment for women as both teachers and researchers, developing and disseminating important training materials, and special concerns for ethnic minorities, lesbians, and women with disabilities. The authors warn about complacency and that aggressive efforts by university decision makers must be made in order to close the gender gap in these areas. Hopefully, in the future, gender will be unrelated to salary, benefits, career satisfaction, promotion, and so forth not only for women psychologists in academic life but for women in all fields (Halpern, 2008; Settles et al., 2006).

or monthly grand rounds presentations where guest speakers provide a lecture on a topic of interest to members of a particular medical specialty such as psychiatry, pediatrics, oncology, cardiology, or neurology. Ongoing seminars (meeting weekly for several months or longer) may focus on numerous topics in psychology. For example, a seminar may be provided for trainees and/or staff on (a) psychosocial factors in the development, maintenance, and treatment of specific or general illnesses; (b) child development; (c) dealing with medical noncompliance; (d) lifestyle management change; and (e) ethics. Clinical psychologists may teach medical school classes on a host of topics such as health

Case Studies: Teaching in Academic Settings

Dr. I maintains a full-time private practice in psychotherapy. She also conducts workshops and provides guest lectures on emotional factors associated with chronic physical illnesses. She specializes in the treatment of both children and adults who experience emotional concerns associated with medical illnesses such as cancer, multiple sclerosis, diabetes, lupus, and heart disease. As a clinical faculty member of a local medical school in the department of psychiatry, she supervises two clinical psychology trainees (an intern and a postdoctoral fellow), providing one hour per week of individual supervision of their psychotherapy treatment cases. Her clinical and supervisory skills are useful in training these professionals. She often listens to audiotapes or watches videotapes of the trainees' work and offers suggestions and guidance about treating patients.

Like Dr. I, Dr. J is a clinical faculty member of a university medical school in the department of psychiatry. He is a psychologist who teaches an ethics course to psychology trainees and psychiatry residents on a weekly basis. He meets with a group of 10 students for one hour each week to discuss professional ethics. Students describe the ethical dilemmas they experience, and the group discusses ethical principles of behavior with Dr. J's guidance.

Dr. K is a psychologist working full time in a tenure-track position at a large university. She teaches two classes each semester (an undergraduate course in Abnormal Psychology and a graduate seminar in Psychological Testing). She also supervises the dissertation projects of several doctoral students in clinical psychology at the university. She conducts research as well and is working on a textbook in abnormal psychology. Dr. K also presents guest lectures to local hospitals and other groups on her area of specialization, depression among elderly persons.

psychology, pediatric psychology, and health behavior change.

Clinical psychologists are often asked to provide individual supervision and instruction to staff and trainees at hospital and medical schools. A nurse, a psychiatry or pediatric resident, or a medical student may regularly meet with a psychologist to discuss cases. Psychology interns, postdoctoral psychology fellows, and graduate students also receive individual supervision on their cases by a consulting psychologist. In this way, psychotherapy, psychological testing, and other psychological intervention skills are taught and supervised using a tutorial model (Hoffman, 1990; Norcross et al., 2008; Romans, Boswell, Carlozzi, & Ferguson, 1995; Russell & Petrie, 1994).

Students meet regularly with a supervisor to closely examine their clinical work. They may audio- or videotape sessions in order to review them in detail with the supervising psychologist. Videotaping is a popular method of conducting supervision sessions (Romans et al., 1995). Frequently supervision is provided in small groups of 3 to 5 trainees (Riva & Cornish, 1995). Supervision training can be general (i.e., emphasis on basic and global skills) or focused (i.e., emphasis on specific skill development) or a combination of both (Schindler & Talen, 1994). Effective clinical supervisors tend to be supportive, interested, and invested in the supervision process, and have solid clinical experience (Russell & Petrie, 1994). Clinical psychologists may be employed as staff members, as full-time or part-time faculty, or as guest lecturers at these medical schools and hospitals.

Teaching in Nonacademic Settings

Clinics: Clinical psychologists may teach seminars, provide guest lectures, or give presentations in outpatient community mental health clinics, group private practice clinics, nonprofit

Tension between Research and Practice for Teachers

Himelein and Putnam (2001) conducted a survey of 214 clinical psychologists teaching in universities and training programs across the United States to determine whether these psychologists "practice what they teach" (p. 537). The authors were interested in whether clinical psychologists who train undergraduate and graduate students in psychology actually do much clinical practice in addition to their teaching and research responsibilities. The comprehensive survey found that these professors and instructors spent on average twice as much time on their research activities as they did in any clinical practice, with almost half (44%) reporting no clinical practice at all. Comparing these survey findings to previous research indicates that, over time, clinical psychologists who teach undergraduate and graduate students tend to spend less and less time in actual clinical work. Stricker (2000) calls this trend the "SCIENTIST-practitioner model" (p. 254). A special issue of *Clinical Psychologist* (2003, Volume 56, Issue 1) focused on this issue by publishing a series of articles on the notion that academic clinical psychologists may tend to influence their students to "mirror" them by pursuing careers similar to ones chosen by their faculty mentors and instructors. This becomes problematic from a number of different perspectives. For example, while so many clinical psychology professors do not engage in clinical work, most of their students do anticipate pursuing clinical (rather than research) careers. Therefore, it is challenging for instructors who do little if any clinical work to teach students who want to learn to do clinical work.

institutes, day-care centers, and other nonacademic settings. Topics may include how to assess and treat patients experiencing certain disorders (e.g., anxiety, depression, panic, obesity) or how to work more effectively with certain patient populations (e.g., Asian Americans, young children, AIDS patients). Many clinics offer regularly scheduled guest lecture presentations for their staff and trainees so that these professionals can continue to stay up to date on new developments in their field.

Workshops: Many clinical psychologists conduct workshops for other psychologists or professionals (e.g., nurses, social workers, physicians). Workshops may last for a single day or for several days, and may offer continuing education credit. Psychologists may provide detailed information and training on specialized services or on how best to work with certain patient populations. Workshops may also incorporate individual case conferences, individual case supervision, and lectures. Almost all the national and regional psychology professional organizations offer yearly conventions that feature professional workshops.

Business and Industry: Clinical psychologists may teach in business and industry environments, focusing on stress management techniques, ways to improve employee morale, and strategies to improve interviewing and communication skills. Their presentations may involve ongoing classroom instruction or a one-time guest lecture.

General Public: Clinical psychologists are frequently asked to provide lectures and

Case Studies: Teaching in Nonacademic Locations

Dr. L conducts half-day workshops on stress management for various businesses. He provides information about strategies to maximize effective coping and uses his research on resiliency to help participants examine their lives and determine how they may change aspects that impair their ability to cope with stress. Dr. L also teaches several relaxation techniques, which are practiced during the workshop. He offers a follow-up seminar for those who participate in the workshop to review progress and discuss obstacles.

Dr. M conducts a daylong workshop for mental health professionals on group psychotherapy. She discusses relevant research and offers strategies for both inpatient and outpatient groups on how to deal with problems such as marital discord, eating disorders, panic attacks, and breast cancer. Dr.

M uses educational videos to demonstrate effective group therapy techniques and ends her workshop with participants role playing in hypothetical groups. She travels to several cities across the country to present her workshops.

Dr. O is a psychologist who specializes in problems of young children and parents. She offers parenting classes that meet weekly for two hours and are designed for new parents with children ages 0 to 3 months. She hires several students to help with babysitting while the classes meet. Dr. O discusses practical matters such as diapering and feeding babies as well as bonding and psychological development. She invites nurses and pediatricians as occasional guest speakers. Dr. O also offers parenting classes for parents of twins.

Photo: Bruce Ayres, Tony Stone Images, New York, Inc.

Figure 12.2

Business managers may wish to consult with a psychologist after layoffs.

presentations to the general public at schools, businesses, churches and synagogues, volunteer organizations, bookstores, coffeehouses, and other settings. For example,

an elementary school may wish to have a psychologist present a lecture on the effects of media violence on children or on how to help children deal with divorce. Many organizations ask psychologists to give lectures on stress management, intimate relationships, or how to deal more effectively with specific organizational problems (e.g., layoffs, downsizing, financial restraints; Figure 12.2).

Administration

According to Kilburg (1991), management involves "planning, organizing, leading or directing, decision making, and controlling" such that the manager is ultimately responsible for the "success or failure of (an) enterprise" (p. 38). Effective **administration** involves excellent leadership, decision-making, negotiating, and organizational skills. Although these skills may come naturally to some psychologists, they are generally not a specific part of the clinical psychology training process.

Many psychologists provide administrative services. In fact, 7% of all clinical psychologists report that their primary job is administration (Norcross et al., 1997a, b, 2005). Psychologists may work as unit chiefs of hospital psychiatric units, direct mental health services at community mental health clinics, chair psychology departments in colleges or universities, work as deans or provosts in universities, or manage support staff and other clinicians in large group private practices. Psychologists in these roles often have the responsibility of hiring and firing employees, designing and implementing programs and services, managing budgets, and supervising the activities of many other professionals.

Curiously, although many psychologists become administrators, very few have formal training in administration (Barton, 1991; Blouke, 1997; Grusky, Thompson, & Tillipman, 1991; Kelly, 1997). For example, it has been estimated that less than 25% of mental health administrators representing all mental health disciplines (e.g., psychiatry, psychology, and social work) have had formal training in administration (Barton, 1991). Unlike graduate programs in business administration, graduate programs in psychology rarely offer

courses or even guest lectures on administration. Almost no books or professional articles have been published that specifically deal with the issues of clinical psychology administrators. The qualities that make a psychologist a successful clinician, consultant, or researcher are not likely to be the same qualities that make a successful administrator. The ability to conduct high-quality research or to provide effective psychotherapy may involve skills that are very different from managing a budget, negotiating contracts, and dealing with employee conflicts and office politics. Many psychologists do not plan to become administrators but take on the role as their career progresses. Those who have good people skills, pay attention to detail, and manage systems and money well may be encouraged by colleagues and others to assume administrative responsibilities. Effective psychology administrators are organized, effective leaders, and good managers of both people and money (Barton, 1991; Kilburg, 1991; Shore, 1993). Katz (1980) reports that "human skill, the ability to work with others, is essential to effective administration at every level" (p. 82).

Barton (1991) proposed a model curriculum for mental health administration that would include both formal coursework and practicum experience. He suggests that a master's degree in Mental Health Administration or in Public Health be awarded to those who seek to become administrators in the mental health field. Since a large number of psychologists ultimately provide administrative services, it seems reasonable and prudent for graduate and postgraduate training programs to provide formal training in administration for those who elect this career path.

The following scenario illustrates how psychologists often become administrators. A psychologist may work as a clinician in a community mental health clinic. Over time, the psychologist develops a reputation as being a competent and professional colleague who is organized and effective in his responsibilities. The chief psychologist of the clinic takes another position out of state, and the clinician is invited to act as interim chief until

Case Studies: Administrators in Clinical Psychology

Dr. P is a training director of a clinical internship and postdoctoral fellowship program in clinical psychology. She is responsible for the selection, training, and supervision of 10 trainees in the program and also the management of the budget. She is also responsible for supplying the various service components of the hospital and affiliated agencies with capable trainees. She negotiates problems and conflicts that arise with trainees and secures consulting psychologists who can provide individual and group supervision as well as seminars on topics such as psychotherapy, assessment, and ethics. She organizes site visits from accreditation agencies (e.g., the American Psychological Association), develops advertising strategies, and conducts program evaluations in an effort to improve the training programs.

Dr. Q is chairman of a psychology department at a small liberal arts college. She is responsible for the psychology department budget; hiring new faculty; and managing 10 full-time faculty, 5 part-time adjunct faculty, and a department secretary. She represents the psychology department at university meetings and functions. She

also is currently working with university administrators, fund-development personnel, and an architect concerning plans to build a new sciences building that will house the psychology department. Dr. Q teaches several undergraduate courses per year and conducts research. She conducts department meetings and organizes program/curriculum evaluation projects.

Dr. R is the director of an inpatient psychiatric unit that specializes in the treatment of alcohol abuse and addiction. He manages a staff of 12 clinicians (i.e., several psychologists, social workers, nurses, occupational therapists, and a consulting physician), and a $2,000,000 budget; negotiates contracts with managed care and other insurance companies; and leads daily rounds to review patient admissions, discharges, and progress. He hires new staff and terminates those who are ineffective, and collaborates with the hospital public relations department to advertise services. Dr. R conducts program and treatment evaluation of the services provided by his unit. He also leads a family support group and follows several patients in treatment.

someone else is found for the job. The job search does not result in finding a superior candidate. The psychologist who is acting as chief psychologist takes to the job extremely well, and colleagues working in the agency generally feel that the acting chief of psychology should accept the permanent position. The psychologist agrees to continue in the role, begins to develop management skills, and enjoys the new career direction. Several years later, the executive director of the agency retires. The chief psychologist is asked to become the executive director by the agency's board of directors since he knows the agency so well and has done an excellent job in his administrative duties. This scenario occurs frequently among psychologists involved with

administration. Well-organized and well-liked professionals often move toward administrative and leadership responsibilities.

The Big Picture

Many psychologists thrive in the roles and activities associated with consultation, teaching, and administration. These activities allow the psychologist to positively impact the lives of many more people than generally possible through psychotherapy and psychological testing activities alone. As the mental health and health-care fields change, some professionals argue that consultation and teaching activities will be especially important and useful for psychologists to pursue in the future (Kovacs,

1996). Future contemporary clinical psychologists will likely be asked to consult on problems and issues in human behavior in many different areas both within and outside of the mental health field. Efforts to use our understanding of human behavior will be applied to perhaps all areas of personal and professional life, with clinical psychologists at the forefront of these consultative, administrative, and teaching experiences.

Key Points

1. In addition to research, assessment, and psychotherapy, clinical psychologists often spend a significant amount of time involved in other professional activities such as consultation, administration, and teaching.

2. Consultation in clinical psychology generally involves applying knowledge and theories regarding human behavior to specific questions and problems in various community settings such as hospitals, clinics, schools, businesses, and government agencies. Consultation involves offering professional advice to others concerning problems that exist in their setting.

3. Consultants may assume many different roles during the course of a consultation or between consultation assignments. Lippitt and Lippitt (1994) have suggested that the role of consultant is based on a continuum between being directive and nondirective.

4. Dougherty (1994) defines the following six common consultation roles for clinical psychologists: expert, trainer/educator, advocate, collaborator, fact finder, and process-specialist.

5. Several types of consultation are typically conducted by clinical psychologists in mental health settings. These include (a) client-centered case consultation, (b) program-centered administrative consultation, (c) consultee-centered case consultation, and (d) consultee-centered administrative consultation.

6. Clinical psychologists also frequently provide consultation to an enormous range of non–mental health agencies and organizations. Businesses, nonprofit agencies, and government organizations all employ people who must work cooperatively to achieve a common purpose and keep the organization running effectively and smoothly.

7. Many of the stages used to describe the psychotherapy process apply to consultation as well. These include (a) understanding the question, (b) assessment, (c) intervention, (d) termination, and (e) follow-up.

8. Clinical psychologists frequently provide advice and consultation to their peers. In addition to consultation with colleagues, many psychologists consult with professionals from other disciplines. Clinical psychologists frequently consult with schoolteachers and administrators, physicians and nurses, attorneys and judges, clergy, the military, and people working in business and industry.

9. A number of skills are needed to be an effective consultant. Most researchers and practitioners of consultation highlight the primary importance of competent interpersonal and communication skills. However, excellent group and problem-solving skills, talents working with organizations, and highly developed professional and ethical behavior are also a must.

10. Although consultants and consultees may readily agree on the need for and goals of a consultation relationship, several problems often typically emerge. Resistance to the consultant and to his or her suggestions is very common. Another common problem in consultation concerns whether the involved parties accept the consultation methods and recommendations. Additionally, the consultees expectations may be unreasonably high. Consultants themselves may contribute to problems. They may lack adequate knowledge, skill, experience, self-confidence, or

professional objectivity and integrity to be effective.

11. Teaching activities are at least a part of the professional duties of most psychologists. Although only about 30% of clinical psychologists work primarily in academic environments such as colleges, universities, and medical schools, most psychologists participate in some teaching activity even if they primarily work in clinical, administration, consulting, or other professional settings.

12. Clinical psychologists frequently teach in a wide variety of settings and to a wide variety of audiences. Teaching may involve formal college classroom instruction, individual supervision of a psychologist-in-training, or lecturing on stress management techniques in business firms or schools. Teaching may also be incorporated into psychotherapy and psychological testing activities.

13. Many psychologists provide administration services. Psychologists may work as unit chiefs of hospital psychiatric units, direct mental health services at community mental health clinics, chair psychology departments in colleges or universities, be on staff at elementary or secondary schools, work as deans or provosts in universities, or manage support staff and other clinicians in large group private practices. Although many psychologists become administrators, almost none of them have any formal training in administration.

Key Terms

Administration

Advocate

Client-centered case consultation

Collaborator

Consultation

Consultee-centered administrative consultation

Consultee-centered case consultation

Educator

Executive coaching

Expert

Fact finder

Process-specialist

Program-centered administrative consultation

Teacher

Trainer

For Reflection

1. Whom do psychologists consult with in both mental health and non–mental health fields?
2. What are the stages in consultation?
3. What roles are psychologists likely to use in consultation?
4. What are the typical problems associated with consultation?
5. What are the necessary skills needed to be an effective consultant?
6. What types of administrative positions are psychologists likely to hold?
7. In what environments do psychologists teach?
8. What types of lectures might psychologists present to the general public?
9. What is the training like for psychologist administrators?

Real Students, Real Questions

1. If administration is not what psychologists are trained in, how do they get administrative positions?
2. If a large portion of clinical psychologists participate in teaching activities, why don't the American Psychological Association and graduate programs incorporate more teaching training in their curriculums?
3. How does a psychologist become a consultant? Is this usually a career focus?
4. How much information does a psychologist reveal about a patient when receiving consultation from another professional?
5. Is it typical for a psychologist to get consultation from others on a regular basis? Is this difficult to do and schedule?

Web Resources

http://www.apa.org/journals/ccp/
Learn more about the *Journal of Consulting and Clinical Psychology* published by the American Psychological Association.

http://psych.hanover.edu/APS/teaching.html
Learn more about teaching resources from the American Psychological Society.

http://teachpsych.org/

Learn more about the teaching division of the American Psychological Association.

http://www-usr.rider.edu/~suler/tcp.html
Learn more about additional teaching resources.

http://psychcentral.com/resources/Psychology/
Learn more about additional teaching resources.

Ethical Standards

13

Chapter

How should clinical psychologists behave? What are the rules and guidelines for professional behavior among clinical psychologists? Should a psychologist have lunch with his or her patient? Should a psychologist date a current or former patient or student? Should a psychologist tell his or her friends at a cocktail party about a fascinating new patient he or she is treating in psychotherapy? Should a psychologist friend patients on Facebook?

Whether a psychologist is a researcher, teacher, therapist, or administrator, he or she is expected to maintain the highest professional ethics in all professional activities at all times. In fact, psychology is one of the few fields that has adopted ethical guidelines that hold members to a much higher standard than the law. The most current version of the **Ethics Code** published by the American Psychological Association (APA, 2002) is provided in the Appendix. Professional ethics form the cornerstone of professionalism in psychology. The APA formed an ethics committee in the

1930s, and developed its first set of ethical principles in 1953. It is especially important for the field of psychology to focus on professional ethics since psychologists generally have a high degree of responsibility that often significantly impacts the lives of others. For example, clinical psychologists who conduct psychotherapy are entrusted with the emotional and often physical vulnerabilities, confidences, and wellbeing of the people who seek their guidance. Clinical psychologists who are teachers or professors are called upon to provide objective, state-of-the-art, and unbiased information to and evaluation of their students. Clinical psychologists conducting research must design and conduct high-quality research, protect the rights of subjects, and carefully interpret and report their results in order to contribute meaningful information and knowledge about human behavior to the professional community in an unbiased manner. Thus, clinical psychologists must closely and carefully follow ethical principles to ensure that they behave in an appropriate, responsible, and professional manner, protecting the public as well as the profession.

Curiously, the preponderance of media portrayals of clinical psychologists and other mental health professionals in films and on television depict these professionals as engaging in highly unethical, unprofessional, self-serving, and often illegal behavior. Numerous feature-length films, such as *The Prince of Tides, Final Analysis, Mumford, Anger Management, Analyze This,* and *Analyze That,* as well as television shows such as *Frasier* and *In Treatment,* depict psychologists and other mental health professionals behaving inappropriately and unethically. Typically, the psychologists (and psychiatrists) portrayed in the media are involved in unethical dual relationships—rather than maintaining their professional relationships and boundaries, the psychologists fall in love with or befriend their patients. Using patients for personal gain or gratification, practicing outside of one's area of competence, and breaking **confidentiality** are also typical depictions. In a review of 207 films that included psychiatrists, 35% suggested that the mental health professional was more troubled than his or her patients, and 22% were involved in manipulative behavior with their patients for the benefit of the professionals themselves (Schneider, 1987). However, some films, such as *Ordinary People* and *Good Will Hunting,* provide fairly realistic portrayals of psychologists behaving in an ethical and professional manner. In real life, many of the mental health professionals depicted in the media would lose their license to practice and perhaps be prosecuted for engaging in the behaviors portrayed.

Psychologists in real life do commit ethical violations. Psychologists are human and suffer from the same vulnerabilities as the general public. They experience family conflicts, financial hardships, and stress and may behave in unbecoming and even illegal ways. It has been estimated that between 20% and 82% of psychologists experience relationship problems such as marital conflict, between 13% and 57% experience depression, and about 11% experience substance abuse problems (Deutsch, 1985; Norcross, Strausser-Kirtland,

& Missar, 1988). It also has been suggested that between 5% and 15% of psychologists are impaired (Laliotis & Grayson, 1985). They might, for example, inappropriately break confidentiality, become sexually involved with their patient(s), falsify research data, engage in sexual harassment, encourage their patients to do favors for them such as babysit their child or paint their house, provide ineffective or questionable treatment, or engage in financial mismanagement and fraud. They also make honest mistakes due to ignorance, inattention, or vulnerability. For example, a psychologist who is lonely might be tempted to initiate a friendship or romantic relationship with a highly appealing client. A psychologist with significant financial problems might be tempted to invest in a business deal with a wealthy and successful client.

Between 2004 and 2008, an average of 283 ethical complaints inquiries were received per year (APA, 2009). Many other ethical violations may not have been reported to the APA or to state ethics and licensing boards. Many of the ethical complaints filed are found to have little or no merit. Most of the complaints that result in action against the psychologist by the APA or local authorities involve breaking confidentiality, sexual misconduct (e.g., sexual relationship with a patient), nonsexual dual relationships (e.g., friendships or business partnerships with patients), and insurance/fee misbehavior (e.g., overbilling insurance, billing for services not rendered). Several authors have reported that the most common ethical violation involves patient confidentiality (Pope & Bajt, 1988; Pope & Vetter, 1992). While many of these violations involve breaking confidentiality without patient permission, a sizable number of cases involve psychologists refusing to break confidentiality when they are ethically and legally required, as in the case of reporting child abuse to the police or state child protective services. Fortunately, however, the vast majority of clinical psychologists do behave in an ethical and professional manner (APA, 2009; Bersoff, 2003; Koocher & Keith-Spiegel, 2008; Layman & McNamara,

1997). The unethical psychologist is certainly the exception rather than the rule.

What are the ethical guidelines for psychologists? How exactly should a psychologist behave? How can a psychologist be sure that he or she is behaving appropriately? While certain behaviors seem easy to recognize as unethical, such as sexual contact with current patients, falsifying research data or records, breaking patient confidentiality, and over-billing, many other behaviors may not be so clear. The Ethics Code has been updated nine times by the APA since the original 1953 document was published; the current version was published in December 2002. The most recent version of the Canadian Code of Ethics for Psychologists was published in 2000 and is more similar to than different from the American code (Canadian Psychological Association, 2000). Many of the principles outlined in these various versions were originally highlighted many centuries ago in the 2,500-year-old Hippocratic Oath. These include competence, respect, confidentiality, informed consent, social justice, and avoiding both harm and exploitation. The fundamental principles outlined several thousand years ago are still in use today. In addition to the Ethics Code, more specific specialty guidelines have also been developed to provide further instructions and expectations for professional conduct. For example, the APA has published the following specialty guidelines: *Specialty Guidelines for the Delivery of Services by Clinical Psychologists* (1981), *Guidelines for Computer Based Tests and Interpretations* (1987a), *Standards for Educational and Psychological Testing* (1985), and *Guidelines for Providers of Psychological Services to Ethnic, Linguistic, and Culturally Diverse Populations* (1990, 2003b). Additional guidelines are provided for school psychologists, counseling psychologists, forensic psychologists, and others.

Koocher and Keith-Spiegel (2008) outlined eight general principles for psychologists distilled from the Ethics Code, specialty guidelines, and additional sources. These include doing no harm, benefiting others, being just and faithful, according dignity, treating others with caring and compassion, pursuing excellence, respecting autonomy, and accepting accountability. These principles are found in the Hippocratic Oath as well. In this chapter, ethical principles for psychologists will be examined and case examples used to illustrate actual ethical violations. The case studies are based on actual cases but have been carefully edited and altered to protect the confidentiality of the parties involved. Before the ethical principles are outlined, it is important to understand how ethics differ from the law.

How Do Professional Ethics Differ from the Law?

Ethical principles are developed at the national level by the APA to protect the public and profession by providing guidelines for professional conduct among psychologists. These principles generally focus on how psychologists should behave. It is important to note that membership in the APA is voluntary but that adherence to the Ethics Code developed by the APA is *required* of APA members. Most laws involving the delivery of psychological services and conduct of psychologists are written and enforced at the state level. Because laws differ from state to state, certain unethical behaviors by a psychologist such as having sexual relationships with his or her patients may or may not be illegal, depending on the jurisdiction. Furthermore, laws and the Ethics Code may not be in agreement regarding a variety of situations. A judge may court-order a psychologist to release all records concerning a patient, whereas the Ethics Code prohibits the release of records without patient consent and prohibits releasing material such as psychological testing protocols to be examined and interpreted by unqualified persons such as lawyers and judges. In the case of conflicts between ethics and the law, psychologists are advised to follow the ethical principles and work toward solving the dilemma by making these issues known to relevant parties such as the police, attorneys, and judges. Ultimately, the psychologist must decide for him- or herself to follow ethical guidelines or the law if they are in an unworkable conflict. Generally, ethical standards represent a much higher standard of behavior than the law.

The Ethical Principles of Psychologists and Code of Conduct

The current version of the ethical principles for psychologists is divided into five general principles and ten ethical standards. The principles serve as aspirational goals while the ethical standards describe a variety of behaviors that define unethical acts. The complete version of the Ethics Code can be found in the Appendix.

Other ethical codes generally use similar ethical principles. For example, the Canadian code uses four principles, including (1) respect for the dignity of persons, (2) responsible caring, (3) integrity in relationships, and (4) responsibility to society (Canadian Psychological Association, 2000).

In the current version of the APA Ethics Code, five general aspirational ethical principles are highlighted. These include (1) beneficence and nonmaleficence, (2) fidelity and responsibility, (3) integrity, (4) justice, and (5) respect for people's rights and dignity. Beneficence and nonmaleficence means that "psychologists strive to benefit those with whom they work and take care to do no harm." Fidelity and responsibility means that "psychologists establish relationships of trust with those with whom they work ... (and) are aware of their professional and scientific responsibilities to society and to the specific communities in which they work." Integrity means that "psychologists seek to promote accuracy, honesty, and truthfulness in the science, teaching, and practice of psychology." Justice means that "psychologists recognize that fairness and justice entitles all persons to access and benefit from the contributions of psychology." Finally, respect for people's rights and dignity means that "psychologists respect the dignity and worth of all people, and the rights of individuals to privacy,

confidentiality, and self determination" (APA, 2002, pp. 1062–1063).

The 10 ethical standards outlined in the current version of the Ethics Code include (1) strategies to resolve ethical issues, (2) competence, (3) human relations (e.g., discrimination, harassment, multiple relationships, conflict of interest), (4) privacy and confidentiality, (5) advertising and other public statements, (6) recordkeeping and fees, (7) education and training, (8) research and publication, (9) assessment, and (10) therapy.

It is beyond the scope of this chapter to discuss in detail all of the ethical principles and standards outlined in this Ethics Code. However, some of the most salient principles and standards highlight some of the critical issues clinical psychologists must confront. This Ethics Code for psychologists has been updated nine times in the past 50+ years and will continue to be updated regularly in the future. However, regardless of the particulars of the Ethics Code, certain key issues are likely to be important for clinical psychologists to understand both now and in the future. These involve issues related to competence, integrity, respect, responsibility, and concern for others (Plante, 2004b). These principles will be discussed next.

Fundamental Ethical Principles

Competence: Psychologists must maintain competence in their area(s) of specialization. They must provide only services for which they have the appropriate training and experience and remain up-to-date regarding advances in the field to ensure that they maintain state-of-the-art skills.

It is important for psychologists to be well aware of their strengths and weaknesses, their skills and deficits, and most importantly, their limitations. Advances and new discoveries occur so frequently that regular continuing education is necessary and even mandated by law in most states. Psychologists must keep their skills sharp and current and be careful not to offer any service that is less than state-of-the-art. They also must ensure that their personal lives do not interfere with the provision of competent service. However, occasionally a psychologist may work while he or she is ill, tired, or preoccupied. A national survey of psychologists revealed that 60% acknowledged that they had worked when they were too distressed to be effective (Pope et al., 1987). It is troubling that the majority of psychologists in the survey felt that they were unable to be effective due to their personal needs at least at one point during their career.

It is not always obvious what constitutes competence and incompetence. Differences in opinion exist regarding the best ways to teach a class, conduct an assessment, provide psychotherapy for a particular problem, or design a research project to investigate a certain psychological phenomenon. For example, different theoretical orientations or integrative approaches may be employed to treat a particular psychiatric disorder. Some argue that interpersonal psychotherapy should be utilized in treating bulimia. Others believe that cognitive-behavioral psychotherapy is the approach of choice. Still others suggest a combination of the two approaches. Even when using empirically supported and evidence-based treatments, competent professionals may approach a given client differently due to a variety of reasons. Furthermore, because each person who seeks the services of a professional psychologist has unique needs, an individual personality, and a specific constellation of symptoms and biopsychosocial influences, many argue that treatment approaches must be highly individualized and tailored to each person. Competence, therefore, cannot usually be assessed in an absolute manner. While some interventions can be universally regarded as grossly incompetent (e.g., using leeches to treat depression or ECT to treat anorexia nervosa), most questionable professional behaviors are not so obvious. Often the community standard acts as the criterion for the assessment of professional competence. The *community standard* is defined as what several reasonable members of the professional psychological community would agree on as being an appropriate standard of care.

Why would a psychologist provide incompetent service? Why would someone skilled and intelligent enough to earn a doctorate in psychology and a license to practice engage in incompetent professional behavior? A variety of factors may lead a psychologist to provide incompetent service. First, a psychologist, like any human being, may develop a psychiatric disorder or psychological problem that impairs his or her judgment and behavior. For example, a psychologist might develop an alcohol or substance abuse problem that significantly impairs judgment. A psychologist could also develop severe depression and be unable to fully engage in his or her work. A psychologist might have a personality disorder that makes it very difficult for him or her to be trained or to accept corrective feedback and ultimately precludes competent service. The psychologist might miss patient appointments, fall asleep during sessions, inappropriately become irritable with patients or students, forget to arrive to teach a class, improperly recruit research subjects, or engage in a variety of other problematic behaviors that severely compromise his or her competence. Psychologists experience the full range of problems humans experience: divorce, illness, money troubles, anxiety, stress, and a host of ills such as greed, dishonesty, and the like. Thus, personal problems and weaknesses in integrity may lead a psychologist to falter.

A psychologist might become so burdened or "burned out" that he or she stops being effective. For example, a psychologist might work in a hospital or clinic deluged with a high volume of patients over the course of many years on the job. He or she may begin to feel less and less invested in his or her job and his or her patients. The psychologist might tune out during sessions and try to just get through the therapy hour with a minimum of investment. A psychologist who teaches the same courses year after year at a college or university may become bored and uninspired. The professor may fail to update his or her courses and show no interest in student learning. Burnout may result in incompetent professional activity.

A psychologist could be arrogant and narcissistic, feeling that he or she does not need to stay up-to-date or learn anything else following graduate school. The arrogant psychologist may feel that he or she can handle any problem, teach any class without preparation, publish any data collected, and provide clinical services to whomever seeks treatment and is willing to pay for services. The arrogant psychologist may feel above the professional literature and not alter his or her professional behavior to incorporate the latest research and clinical findings. The arrogant psychologist might enjoy providing a certain type of service and apply it to all of his or her patients whether it is appropriate or not. Thus, the arrogant psychologist is not open to new information and consultation from others to ensure professional competence.

A psychologist might behave in a selfish manner that contributes to incompetent professional behavior. For example, a psychologist might wish to fill his or her psychotherapy practice and agree to take any case that comes to his or her attention. The selfish psychologist might agree to treat someone experiencing a certain disorder despite a critical absence of training or experience with the particular disorder. The selfish psychologist might be more interested in earning money or promoting his career than providing quality clinical, teaching, research, or other professional services for the benefit of others. The selfish psychologist may put his or her own needs and wishes above those of patients, students, colleagues, and the public. Finally, the uninformed psychologist may provide incompetent services out of ignorance and misinformation. While he or she may be motivated to be competent, inexperience, lack of consultation, and ignorance may prevent competent performance.

Integrity: Psychologists must maintain professional and personal integrity and be respectful, fair, and honest in their dealings with others. They must be truthful in describing their services, their areas of expertise, their training, and what can be expected from their services. They must be well aware of their biases, needs, and values and how these may impact their work. Psychologists must make all efforts to avoid inappropriate dual relationships.

Unlike many sales and marketing tactics used in business and other areas, psychologists must be careful never to mislead, distort, misrepresent, or deceive. They must be honest and professional in their manner of advertisement and conscientious in their description of their professional services. For example, fees and what can be reasonably expected from an assessment or psychotherapy experience must be clearly delineated before services are provided. Importantly, psychologists must be willing to make a referral to another professional if it is in the best interest of the patient.

Psychologists must avoid conflicts of interest and dual relationships with their patients, clients, students, and others. Because psychologists often maintain a position of power in their professional relationships with patients and students, they must never exploit this power differential and never place their own interests and needs above those they serve. For instance, psychologists should not engage in sexual relationships with patients or students they supervise, no matter how consensual such a relationship may seem. While the issue of sexual relationships between psychologists and their patients and students will be discussed later in this chapter, other nonsexual dual relationships will be briefly discussed here.

Dual relationships are one of the most common ethical violations brought to the attention of ethics boards (APA, 1995c, 1996, 2009c; Zur, 2007). Dual relationships are commonly and casually portrayed in television and films involving psychologists, yet these relationships compromise the effectiveness of the psychologist's work and are often exploitive to the patient, client, or student. While it is common and often expected that business associates and clients have lunch, play golf, or attend social gatherings together, these situations must be avoided by psychologists in order

Case Study: Dr. A Treats a Patient Although He Has Inadequate Competence to Do So

Dr. A recently became licensed and opened a private practice. He was very excited about becoming independent and looked forward to developing a satisfying and profitable career. He became disappointed after several months when his practice did not fill up quickly. Furthermore, he was anxious about his financial status, feeling that he would be unable to pay his overhead expenses as well as his home mortgage. His wife was pregnant with their first child, and Dr. A was concerned about a significant increase in family expenses. An uninformed but well-meaning colleague referred to Dr. A a patient who suffered from panic attacks. The man was wealthy enough to be able to afford treatment and wanted to be seen in psychotherapy several times each week. Dr.

A happily agreed to treat the patient even though he had never treated a patient with panic disorder before and despite his own doubt that three sessions per week were necessary. He thought that he would search the web and read what he could find using a Google search on panic disorder to learn about it.

Without appropriate training, experience, and consultation in treating panic disorder, Dr. A unethically treated the patient. Dr. A should have referred the patient to a professional with adequate training or experience. He should have obtained appropriate training and supervision prior to treating a panic disorder patient. He also should have declined to see the patient more often than was clinically indicated.

Competence

to minimize compromising relationships. Unfortunately, dual relationships are somewhat common among psychologists. For example, a national survey conducted by Pope et al. (1987) revealed that 40% of psychologists had accepted a patient's invitation to a party, 16% had invited patients to a social event, and 28% had provided psychotherapy services to a friend. Furthermore, Pope et al. (1987) reported that 25% of psychology educators (e.g., college professors) had sold products such as cars to their students. No matter how challenging, the maintenance of clear and professional boundaries in all professional relationships is incumbent upon all psychologists.

Some psychologists effectively argue that occasional contact with patients outside of the office can be both ethical and helpful. For example, some psychologists will attend important special events in the life of a patient such as a Bar Mitzvah, confirmation, funeral, graduation, wedding, or other once-in-a-lifetime events (Borys & Pope, 1989). Other professionals argue that effective professional

service must sometimes occur in the patient's natural environment (Zur, 2007). For example, a psychologist might meet a patient at an airport to help treat the patient's plane phobia, or at someone's home to conduct clinical services for someone who is physically disabled. These situations can be effectively and ethically conducted if the psychologist is careful to maintain a professional relationship and not develop a potentially exploitive dual relationship.

Teachers and professors also occasionally socialize with their students. In fact, many campuses strongly encourage faculty and students to socialize together at various campus-sponsored events. These social contacts between faculty and students can certainly be ethical encounters as long as professional boundaries are maintained and the faculty members do not use their power or status to take advantage of their relationship with their students (e.g., ask students for personal favors, burden students with their personal problems, engage in sexual behavior). Sexual

Case Study: Dr. B Conducts Psychological Testing Less Than Rigorously   *competence*

Dr. B conducts psychological testing for a mental health clinic. She has been employed by the clinic for about five years and has routinely conducted several evaluations each week. At first, she enjoyed her work and found psychological testing exciting and rewarding. She felt like a detective trying to piece together a puzzle in order to determine exactly which diagnosis was warranted for each of her complex patients. After administering hundreds of evaluations, Dr. B became burned out and resented each additional evaluation she was assigned. She became less and less interested in her job and her patients. She joked with friends and colleagues that she could administer an IQ test in her sleep. Soon she started to take shortcuts in her testing administrations. She would give tests too quickly and would skip sections of her evaluation. Finally, her behavior resulted in a significant error that

severely impacted her patient. She had been asked to conduct psychological testing to determine if a child was learning disabled. Her testing was done in a sloppy manner and she made several significant calculation errors. She reported that the child was mentally retarded to the parents and the school. The child was placed in a special-education class based on Dr. B's evaluation. Six months later, the child was retested and found to function at a much higher level than indicated on Dr. B's evaluation. Her records were requested by the school district and the school psychologist found the errors. Dr. B allowed her boredom and burnout to impact her performance, resulting in significant harm to her patient and the patient's family.

What should Dr. B have done in this situation? What would you do if you were on the ethics board evaluating Dr. B?

---

intimacies between faculty and their students represent a serious ethical violation.

Some dual relationships are unavoidable (Bersoff, 2003; Stockman, 1990; Zur, 2007). For example, in very small communities a psychologist may be the only mental health professional in town and may need the services of his or her patient because the patient may be the only dentist, car dealer, or grocery store owner in town. A former patient may take a class with a professor who was also his or her therapist because he teaches the only section of a required course. These situations must be handled carefully by the psychologist to minimize any potential harm to others. Psychologists cannot always avoid a dual relationship but they can always be sensitive and thoughtful regarding this issue and proceed with caution in order to minimize any potential harm to those they serve.

Professional and Scientific Responsibility: Psychologists must be willing to consult with other professionals in order to best serve their patients or clients. For example, a psychologist may be treating a person from a different ethnic, cultural, or religious group and he or she may consult with a colleague who is more familiar and experienced with members of the particular group in order to offer the most effective and sensitive service possible. Psychologists may also feel stuck during the course of conducting psychotherapy or while completing an evaluation. They may feel that they are unclear about how to best help one of their patients. Consulting with a colleague often helps to develop a productive direction. Since there are often biological, psychological, and social factors that may influence a particular clinical problem, psychologists also must consult with non-psychologist professionals, such as physicians, in order to ensure

Case Study: Dr. C Misleads His Clients Regarding His Credentials

Dr. C received a doctorate in physics and was employed by a software company in a middle management position for 15 years. Dr. C became dissatisfied with his career choice and felt that he wanted to make a significant career change. He had been in psychotherapy for several years during and following his divorce and felt that becoming a therapist might be a satisfying career move. He enrolled in a local graduate program in psychology. Dr. C worked in several clinics during his graduate training. He introduced himself as "Dr. C" and had "Dr. C" printed on his business cards. Referring to himself as "Dr." is misleading. His doctorate in physics is not relevant to his new career path, and potential clients are likely to believe that his doctorate is in psychology or a closely related field. Patients have a right to know exactly what service and provider they are paying for.

integrity

that their patients obtain quality service. For example, a psychologist may wish to work closely with a physician while treating a patient who experiences anorexia nervosa to ensure that both medical and psychological services are coordinated. Of course, confidentiality must be maintained or permission of the patient obtained in order to discuss cases with others.

Psychologists conducting research, teaching, or other activities must also consult with others to maintain professional responsibility. For example, a psychologist conducting research may be confused about his or her research findings and the best means of data analysis. The psychologist may feel that consultation with a colleague who is more skilled in research design and statistical analysis would be helpful in order to best investigate the research question. A psychologist who teaches a college course may be unable to answer some questions asked by students, so

Case Study: Dr. D Participates in a Dual Relationship with Her Client

integrity

Dr. D is treating a patient who experiences obesity. Dr. D is providing a behavioral treatment program to help her patient decrease food consumption, increase exercise, and alter her lifestyle in order to minimize weight problems. Dr. D's patient happens to work in the printing business. Dr. D needs to order more stationery and business cards because she recently moved her office to a new location, so she asks her patient if she would produce the stationary and business cards for her at a discounted price. The patient agrees to produce the materials at a 30% discount. Dr. D felt that her patient did only a mediocre printing job and feels angry and resentful. Dr. D should have avoided the dual relationship of having her client also print her stationery and business cards. Dr. D tried to have both a therapeutic professional relationship and a separate business relationship with her patient. This dual relationship may have made it too difficult for the patient to say no to Dr. D, and Dr. D's dissatisfaction with the printing job may interfere with her ability to relate positively to the patient.

What should Dr. D do now?

Case Study: Dr. E Treats a Client Very Different from Those with Whom He Has Expertise   ~~Risa~~ P+S R

Dr. E is treating a Roman Catholic priest for depression. Dr. E is Jewish and knows very little about the Roman Catholic Church. Some aspects of the Church seem odd to Dr. E and very difficult to understand (e.g., vows of chastity, poverty, and obedience). Dr. E is unfamiliar with Church hierarchy and does not understand some of the issues the patient is interested in discussing. Dr. E made it clear to the patient that she was Jewish and that she was unfamiliar with many of the issues involved with being a Roman Catholic priest. The patient decided that he did not want to be treated by a Catholic because he wanted an "unbiased and fresh perspective." Dr. E decided to treat the patient but without consultation from someone who might provide appropriate professional guidance.

---

he or she may wish to consult a colleague in order to better answer the students' questions. In all of these examples, consultation with a colleague can assist the psychologist in providing the most effective and responsible service possible.

In addition to maintaining responsibility for professional behavior, psychologists must also assist in ensuring that colleagues maintain professional ethics. Psychologists must help stop and/or report unethical behavior engaged in by colleagues. Thus, if a psychologist witnesses irresponsible and unethical behavior on the part of a colleague, he or she has an ethical duty to intervene by speaking with the colleague or by reporting the violation to the appropriate authorities. Most cases of irresponsible and unethical behavior committed by colleagues can be rectified through informal and educative consultation. However, serious violations or conflicts that cannot be resolved through informal means must be reported to the appropriate ethics committee or board.

Respect for People's Rights and Dignity: Psychologists must be respectful of the rights and dignity of others. They must be sensitive to individual and cultural differences, and be aware of gaps in knowledge and areas of bias and prejudice. They must respect the right to freedom, privacy, and confidentiality. Psychologists must not discriminate against others based on sex, religion, ethnicity, sexual orientation, or other factors. Psychologists must be careful to not allow their personal biases and prejudices interfere with their work. Ageism, racism, and sexism have no place in the work of psychologists.

Confidentiality is the cornerstone of psychological services. Everything that is mentioned in the consultation room must be kept confidential. Without the assurance of confidentiality, many patients could not comfortably speak about what is on their minds and would be unable to obtain needed assistance. In fact, many psychologists feel that effective psychotherapy cannot be conducted without the assurance of confidentiality (e.g., Bersoff, 2003; Epstein, Steingarten, Weinstein, & Nashel, 1977; Koocher & Keith-Spiegal, 2008). However, there are several legal and ethical limits to confidentiality. These generally include serious and immediate danger to self or others, such as suicide and homicide, as well as information concerning the physical, sexual, and emotional abuse or neglect of a child, elderly person, or dependent adult (e.g., disabled adult). Persons seeking services of a psychologist have a right to know about these limits to confidentiality in order to make informed choices about the types of information they choose to disclose.

Patients may choose to waive their right to confidentiality in certain specific

Case Study: Dr. F Is Concerned about Unethical Behavior in a Colleague   P + S R

Dr. F is concerned about one of his colleagues. Dr. F works with Dr. G in a mental health clinic. Dr. G tends to be late for his appointments with his patients, speaks about his patients in derogatory terms, and never has his reports completed in a timely manner. Furthermore, Dr. G supervises several psychology interns and postdoctoral fellows. Several of these students report that Dr. G intimidates them and has them do personal favors for him. Dr. F is very concerned about Dr. G's behavior. Dr. F privately discussed his concerns with Dr. G. Dr. G became enraged and threatened Dr. F. Dr. F felt that although he should report his concerns to Dr. G's supervisor as well as to the ethics board, he didn't want to "make waves." Dr. F had a responsibility to report Dr. G's behavior since the situation could not be resolved informally and both patients and students were at risk due to Dr. G's unethical and unprofessional behavior.

circumstances. For example, they may wish to have their psychologist speak with their physician, school teacher, previous therapist, attorney, clergy, or other professional in order to obtain helpful background information or consultation. Patients may wish to bring others (e.g., spouse, child, parent, friend) to their sessions, which may potentially compromise their confidentiality. Psychologists must always obtain permission from their patients or clients prior to breaking confidentiality in these circumstances. Normally, written permission is necessary before a psychologist can discuss a patient with someone else.

Psychologists also must respect the rights of others to make their own decisions. They must not impose their wishes and opinions on the student, client, patient, or anyone else they serve even if the psychologist feels that a patient or student is making a poor decision (e.g., to quit school, marry someone who is abusive, use drugs). However, they can certainly provide guidance and discuss the pros and cons of these decisions.

Concern for Others' Welfare: Psychologists seek to improve the quality of life of those they serve and avoid harming their clients in any manner. Such concern for others' welfare includes the intention to never exploit their relationships with others. In all professional activities, psychologists work toward enhancing the welfare of clients, patients, and students. Research is conducted to help better understand human behavior as well as to develop methods of improving the human condition. Assessment and treatment are used to improve quality of life and teaching is conducted to enhance knowledge of students. As mentioned earlier in the chapter, psychologists must be highly sensitive to the power differential that exists between them and their clients, patients, and students and avoid misusing or exploiting these relationships (Bersoff, 2003; Borys & Pope, 1989; Koocher & Keith-Spiegel, 2008; Stockman, 1990).

Social Responsibility: Psychologists work to help others and to advance the science and knowledge of human behavior. They have a social responsibility to speak against causes and policies that contradict or exploit what is known about human behavior and psychological functioning (e.g., policies and causes that support discrimination). Psychologists are expected to contribute some professional time to causes that do not result in financial or other personal gains.

Psychologists are expected to contribute back to society in some professional way. For example, many psychologists agree to

Case Study: Dr. H Breaks Confidentiality with a Client

Dr. H is working with the children of a famous sports celebrity. She is conducting educational and intellectual testing to determine if one or both of his children have learning disabilities. Dr. H is a big sports fan and is extremely excited about meeting and having the opportunity to work with the family of the sports star. During the course of the evaluation, Dr. H learns a great deal about the family, including the fact that the sports celebrity has a learning disability and plans on retiring from sports very soon. Dr. H has difficulty keeping this information to herself. She decides to tell her husband as well as several close friends that she is working with the celebrity. She asks them not to tell anyone about his learning disability and upcoming retirement from sports. Dr. H had a responsibility to keep the identity of her client confidential. Breaking confidentiality was a serious ethical violation and should be reported.

rights + dignity

Case Study: Dr. I Does Not Report Child Abuse Due to Patient Pressure

Dr. I is conducting an interview with a woman and her two children. The woman is divorced and is concerned that both of her children seem anxious and upset after each visit with their father. The children, aged 7 and 9, report that their father makes them anxious because he drives too fast and erratically after drinking several beers. Furthermore, one of the children reports that their father touches her genitals after drinking. Dr. I informs the mother that he must report the sexual abuse and child endangerment to the county child protection services. The mother angrily states that she does not want Dr. I to break confidentiality and that she is afraid of what her former husband might do when he finds out that the children told someone about the sexual behavior and dangerous driving. They are fearful that it will "just make matters worse, not better." Dr. I capitulates, agreeing not to report the abuse if the father will agree to receive treatment. Dr. I had an obligation to report the abuse and should have informed the family of the limits of confidentiality prior to conducting the interview.

rights + dignity

Case Study: Dr. J Has Strong Personal Values That Impact His Work with Clients integrity, others welfare

Dr. J is working with a patient who is having an affair. Dr. J feels very strongly that marital affairs are wrong, sinful, and always a bad decision. Dr. J tells his patient that he strongly feels that marital affairs are immoral and destructive and that she would be well advised to stop the affair immediately. The patient, who feels that Dr. J is an excellent psychologist and highly values his opinion, feels upset with Dr. J's strong opinion. She doesn't want to disappoint Dr. J or do something that he feels is so terrible but she is also not willing to terminate the affair. Reluctantly, she decides to see another psychologist and never return to Dr. J for psychotherapy. Dr. J inappropriately imposed his strong views about marital affairs onto his client.

treat at least some patients who are unable to pay for services or can pay only a very small amount of money. Some psychologists agree to provide lectures to schools or civic organizations without financial compensation or the expectation that patient referrals will result from their talk. Some psychologists agree to treat graduate students in psychology for a reduced fee. Research psychologists may review manuscripts for publication without payment or other rewards. They also may serve on human subject or granting agency committees in order to contribute to the profession and society.

Ethical Standards

The ethical standards section of the Ethics Code uses the ethical principles already discussed and applies them to specific and typical professional activities associated with the psychology profession (e.g., teaching, research, psychotherapy, psychological testing). Other psychology ethics codes also generally use a list of ethical standards under the umbrella of ethical principles. The Canadian and British codes, for example, list a variety of similar ethical standards as they apply to informed consent, therapy, privacy, and care of animals among

Case Study: Dr. K Experiences Personal Prejudice That Impacts Her Work with Diverse Clients

Dr. K is Asian American and is treating a patient who is an African American male experiencing job dissatisfaction. Dr. K has little experience treating African American patients. Dr. K feels very uncomfortable with her patient and is hesitant to ask him to elaborate certain cultural issues that emerge (e.g., experience of discrimination at work, strong Christian faith and church ties). She also mistakenly attributes his unfamiliar urban dialect and speech and jargon to his "not being very bright." Dr. K's racism, ignorance, and discomfort prevent her from providing effective service and in fact have detrimental potential for the patient. Furthermore, it is inappropriate for her to fail to obtain consultation regarding a patient from a cultural group with whom she has no experience treating.

Study: Dr. L Takes Advantage of His Students for Personal Favors

Dr. L is a popular psychology professor on campus. He is an excellent teacher and involves many of his students in his research activities. He is generous with his students, ensuring them co-authorship on research papers and taking a great deal of time to train and mentor them. Dr. L and his wife just had a baby and need a nanny as well as general babysitting help. He invites his students to help him care for the baby. Many of the students feel honored that they were asked to care for Dr. L's baby and don't mind that they will not be paid for babysitting. They feel that it is the least they can do for Dr. L because he has been so generous with his time, attention, and effort. Dr. L not only is developing a dual relationship with his students but is also exploiting the power differential between himself and his students by asking them to babysit for him without pay. Dr. L should know that his young students would feel honored to be asked to babysit and he wrongly uses his allure to obtain free babysitting services.

Case Study: Dr. M Is Greedy and Unwilling to Give Back to Society soc., resp.

Dr. M has three children and lives in an expensive area of town. She wants to send her children to private school and build an addition to her house. Dr. M is interested in making as much money as possible in her private practice. She charges very high fees and bills by the minute for any telephone contact with her patients even if it is just to change an appointment time. She also bills colleagues whenever they contact her to obtain consultation. Because she is an expert in several important areas, she is often sought for consultations, lectures, and other professional activities. She refuses to participate in any professional activity without being paid and never donates time, money, or consultation for free or reduced prices. Dr. M feels that she owes nothing to society nor to others and feels that her practice is solely a way for her to have the kind of lifestyle she desires. Dr. M is not exercising social responsibility.

---

others (British Psychological Society, 1993; Canadian Psychological Association, 2000). The general standards section of the Ethics Code briefly reviews the ethical principles that must be applied to all professional activities. A review of some of these standards will be presented here, followed by the specific application to a number of professional psychology activities.

General Standards: Psychologists must be well aware of the limits and boundaries of their professional competence and never practice outside of their areas of expertise. They must be highly respectful of others and never engage in discrimination or sexual or other forms of harassment, or let their personal problems interfere with their professional work and obligations. They must avoid all dual relationships, such as business, friendship, or romantic relationships with patients, students, or other types of clients with whom they work in a professional capacity. They must base their judgments on scientific information and avoid any possible harm to others. Psychologists must adequately document their professional work and be careful with the storage and disposal of professional records. They should ensure that financial arrangements such as fees for service are understood and agreed on before providing services, and that the fees are

not exploitative or misleading. Psychologists must ensure that their employees are properly supervised and that consultations and referrals are made in the best interest of their clients.

Evaluation, Assessment, or Intervention: Psychologists must use assessment instruments only for the purposes for which they were developed and validated. They must also use only tests they are qualified to administer and interpret and not encourage unqualified persons to use these tests. It is necessary to provide assessment feedback to clients in an understandable manner and to protect the confidentiality of test results.

Psychologists are entrusted to use psychological testing instruments in an ethical manner at all times. Psychologists must know the strengths and weaknesses of each test they use as well as information regarding the reliability, validity, and standardization. They must ensure that they have adequate training and supervision in each test and be prepared to interpret results thoughtfully and carefully. Since new tests are developed frequently and new versions of tests become available on a regular basis, psychologists must stay up-to-date on the changes that impact their professional work in psychological testing.

Frequently, unqualified persons are interested in administering and/or interpreting

Staying Out of Legal and Ethical Trouble

It is not easy for psychologists or other health-care professionals to keep abreast of every new law and ethical nuance. However, there are a number of principles that can help psychologists and other professionals avoid legal and ethical problems (Plante, 1999c). Ten principles that are useful in avoiding ethical and legal problems are:

1. Always get written informed consent.
2. Secure regular professional consultation.
3. Work on maintaining professional competence.
4. Be familiar with the laws and Ethics Code.
5. Avoid high-risk patients and situations.
6. Avoid the use of collection agencies that anger customers.
7. Maintain good professional records.
8. Maintain confidentiality unless compelled to do otherwise by legal statutes.
9. Be hypervigilant with managed care and insurance companies, where patient information can be easily misused.
10. Get help when needed.

psychological tests. For example, school teachers and parents may wish to interpret the results of IQ tests given to children without the assistance of a psychologist. Sometimes psychiatrists, social workers, or other mental health professionals wish to administer or interpret psychological tests such as the Rorschach, the Thematic Apperception Test, Projective Drawings, or the Minnesota Multiphasic Personality Inventory-2 (MMPI-2) without appropriate training and supervision. Sometimes these professionals request that psychologists order testing materials for them to use. Most states do not prohibit non-psychologists such as psychiatrists from using psychological tests. However, psychologists have the ethical obligation to ensure that tests are used appropriately and only by those who have a proper level of training and experience.

Psychologists must protect the security of tests so that there is controlled access to sensitive testing materials. For example, IQ testing will be invalid if the person being tested has access to the test items prior to being formally administered the test. Just as tests such as the SAT, ACT, LSAT, MCAT, GMAT, and other standardized tests must be protected and used carefully, so, too, must psychological tests. Therefore, keeping testing supplies in an unlocked or easily accessible location or allowing clients, patients, or students to freely review testing materials would generally constitute an ethical violation. Many psychologists allow clients or patients to take the MMPI-2 home with them to complete since it generally takes about 1.5 hours to finish and it is a pencil-and-paper, self-report test. However, allowing the test to be taken home does not protect the security of the test nor does home-testing constitute standard testing procedures. Furthermore, patients could have someone else help them with answers or even complete the test for them. If the test is taken home by the client, reliability and validity as well as the security of the test are threatened.

Advertising and Other Public Statements: Psychologists should avoid any false or deceptive

Case Study: Dr. N Allows Unqualified Trainees to Give Psychological Tests   P + SR

Dr. N conducts a large number of neuropsychological evaluations at a local rehabilitation hospital. She has been conducting several evaluations each week for the past 10 years. Most of the patients at the hospital experience traumatic brain and/or spinal cord injuries. Dr. N is contacted by an undergraduate student majoring in psychology who is looking for summer work in the field. Following an interview, Dr. N decided to hire the student to conduct neuropsychological evaluations. Dr. N feels that she could use some help and that it would be an excellent training opportunity for the student to learn to administer neuropsychological tests. Dr. N spends several weeks training the student in testing administration, watches her perform several tests with actual patients, and then has her conduct the testing at the hospital. They meet at the end of each workday to review the testing given on that day, provide supervision, and address any questions that arise. Dr. N has committed an ethical violation by allowing an unqualified person to administer professional tests. With merely a few weeks of training, an undergraduate psychology student is not adequately trained to competently administer neuropsychological tests.

Case Study: Dr. O Uses Testing Materials for Purposes for Which They Were Not Developed   P + SR

Dr. O is approached by the board of a computer software company that is interested in hiring a company president. They are hoping that Dr. O will be able to conduct a psychological evaluation to determine which of the three top candidates would make the best company president. The board feels that all three candidates are excellent and that a better understanding of the psychological functioning, personality, and "character" of each person is needed to make the best decision. Dr. O decides to conduct a two-hour interview with each of the three candidates and then ask each to participate in psychological testing. Dr. O decides to use the Rorschach, the TAT, and projective drawings. Based on the testing results, Dr. O recommends one of the candidates as being the most promising company president. Dr. O unethically used testing materials for purposes for which they were not intended. These instruments were neither designed nor validated for personnel selection.

public statements misrepresenting themselves or their training, experience, degrees, and activities. Psychologists must make all efforts to correct misleading or deceptive statements made by others on their behalf. Psychologists must not solicit testimonials from current patients or others who are potentially vulnerable.

Psychologists must be very careful in how they represent themselves to the public. They must not mislead or deceive others by overstating or exaggerating their qualifications and abilities. Furthermore, they must ensure that those who represent them not mislead or misrepresent their skills and qualifications. Psychologists who conduct interviews for radio or television programming must be especially careful to prevent distortion of their statements and qualifications. Because the goal of

---

Case Study: Dr. P Does Not Protect Psychological Tests from Misuse   P+SR

Dr. P administered an IQ test to a 7-year-old girl who is applying to attend a school for gifted and talented children. An IQ score of 130 is needed to be admitted into the school. The child obtained a score of 126 on the WISC-IV. The child's mother feels that the test was an underestimate of her child's potential and suspects that the psychologist might have made an error in scoring the test. She demands that the psychologist give her a copy of the complete record form of the test so that she can have a school psychologist friend review the scoring. Dr. P feels intimidated by the child's mother and gives her the test. The mother has her

child study the test form provided by the psychologist and then take the test a second time with another psychologist who was unaware of the initial testing. She obtained a score of 139 on the second administration and was admitted to the school. Dr. P had an obligation to protect the security of the test materials and should not have given the mother a copy of the record form. While patients (or parents, if the patient is a minor) do have the legal right to review and copy their medical and other records in most states, they do not have the right to photocopy confidential and copyrighted psychological testing material.

---

such programming is often to entertain and to sensationalize a topic rather than simply to inform, psychologists must be vigilant in avoiding potential ethical dilemmas (McCall, 1988; McGrath, 1995). Furthermore, interviews may be edited so that careful and thoughtful comments made by a psychologist are removed while brief but potentially misleading soundbites are retained. Psychologists must be careful to avoid having their comments taken out of context or manipulated to make an inappropriate or misleading point.

Therapy: Psychologists must structure the therapeutic relationship in a professional manner. This includes clarifying from the outset what can be expected from psychotherapy, fees and confidentiality arrangements, and professional or training status. Psychologists must obtain informed consent prior to providing professional services. As mentioned previously, psychologists must never have sexual relationships with current clients and never begin therapy with someone with whom they have had a sexual relationship in the past. Psychologists must take precautions regarding any potential disruption in the service they

provide due to personal problems, illness, relocation, or death. Psychologists should not abandon clients or work toward termination of a professional relationship unless it is in the best interests of the client. Psychologists need to maintain client confidentiality unless a legal or ethical exception emerges such as serious and immediate danger to self and others, or suspected child abuse information that they are mandated to report. Psychologists should maintain professional records in a confidential manner and provide a method by which records remain confidential in the case of the psychologist's death, relocation, or termination at an employment position.

Although it may seem obvious that psychologists should not engage in sexual relationships with their patients, sexual indiscretion is one of the major ethical violations brought to the attention of ethics boards in psychology (APA, 1995c, 2009c). In fact, Pope (1998) reports that 7% of male therapists and 2% of female therapists have had sexual relationships with their patients. Other surveys suggest that between 3% and 12% of psychologists have had sexual contact with their patients (Pope, 1994; Rodolfa et al., 1994; Stake & Oliver,

Case Study: Dr. Q Uses His Work with a Client for His Own Advantage   *others' welfare*

Dr. Q successfully treated a wealthy celebrity for depression. Dr. Q feels that if the celebrity would publicly tell others about the treatment, he would become well-known and highly sought out by both new patients and the media. Dr. Q suggests that the celebrity patient and he both appear on a television talk show to discuss her treatment success. The patient reluctantly agrees, feeling that she owes Dr. Q a favor for providing such valuable and successful treatment. Dr. Q unethically used his influence to have his famous patient provide a testimonial for his work.

1991). Surveys have also supported the finding that male psychologists are much more likely to engage in sexual relationships with their patients than female psychologists (Baur, 1997; Holroyd & Brodsky, 1977; Pope, 1994, 1998; Rodolfa et al., 1994). Furthermore, about 80% of psychologists sexually involved with one patient have been sexually involved with other patients (Holroyd & Brofsky, 1977; Pope, 1998), including sexual involvement with children or adolescents (Bajt & Pope, 1989). One national survey found that the vast majority of psychologists have been sexually attracted to some of their clients (87%) with most experiencing guilt about these feelings (63%; Pope, 1998; Pope, Keith-Spiegel, & Tabachnick, 1986). Psychologists are even more likely to engage in sexual intimacies with their students or supervisees. One survey revealed that 17% of female psychologists had sexual relationships with a graduate school professor (Glaser & Thorpe, 1986), while about 12% of psychology teachers reported having sexual relationships with students (Pope et al., 1987).

The Ethics Code states that sexual intimacy between psychologist and patient is unethical during ongoing professional services such as psychotherapy as well as for at least two years following the termination of services (APA, 2002). Furthermore, sexual relationships that begin following the two-year post-termination

Case Study: Ms. R Allows Others to Misrepresent Her Credentials   *integrity*

Ms. R is a graduate student in clinical psychology completing her clinical internship at a local hospital. She has completed all of her coursework and even her dissertation toward her doctorate. As soon as she completes her internship program, she will be finished with her graduate program and will be awarded her degree. Ms. R's supervisor is a psychiatrist who works at the hospital on a full-time basis. He introduces Ms. R to patients at the hospital as "Dr. R." Ms. R informs her supervisor that she is not a "Dr." yet. The supervisor says that all students working at the hospital (including medical students) are referred to as "Dr." because it helps the patients have more confidence in their treatment. Because Ms. R feels that her supervisor, a licensed psychiatrist, must know what he is doing she drops the subject and introduces herself to patients as "Dr. R." Ms. R has committed an ethical violation by allowing her status to be misinterpreted by others, misleading patients and staff alike.

Case Study: Dr. S Misleads Others about His Training

Dr. S attended a six-week seminar at Harvard University during the summer months. Dr. S, who obtained his degrees at lesser-known universities, loved being at such a prestigious university for the six-week seminar. Following the seminar, Dr. S adds "Harvard University trained" to his resume, private practice stationery, and private practice brochures. He also mentions having been trained at Harvard University whenever he gives a public lecture. In fact, Dr. S appears to have developed a slight Boston accent and talks fondly about the Boston Red Sox! Dr. S behaves unethically in misrepresenting and exaggerating his training and experience at Harvard.

integrity

---

rule must demonstrate that they are not exploitive. A number of authors report being uncomfortable with any sexual relationships emerging between psychologist and patient even after two years following the termination of professional services (Gabbard, 1994). Although agreeing with the prohibition on sexual behavior between patients and therapists, some professionals feel that mutual attraction and love can be expected in many psychotherapy relationships and may even assist treatment (Baur, 1997; Zur, 2007).

Although confidentiality is critical to maintain in any psychotherapeutic relationship and every state has legal limitations on confidentiality (e.g., child abuse reporting laws), a sizeable number of psychologists do not warn their patients that there are limits to confidentiality. One survey revealed that 39% of psychologists reported that they did not discuss confidentiality arrangements with their patients and that 19% falsely inform their patients that everything that is mentioned in psychotherapy is confidential (Baird & Rupert, 1987).

Professional records must be maintained even following the termination of professional services. Many states have laws that determine how long professional records must be maintained. The APA (2007) suggests keeping full patient records for at least three years following the termination of professional services for adults and for three years past the age of maturity for minors but states that it is critical to be attentive to state and federal laws regarding recordkeeping guidelines and requirements.

California, for example, requires records to be kept for seven years for adults and seven years after the age of majority for children.

In the case of severe illness, a psychologist should make appropriate arrangements to ensure that client records are kept confidential yet are accessible to clients and their potential future psychologists or other mental health professionals with whom they choose to work. Psychologists should make arrangements for a colleague to handle the transition of records and services if such a crisis or situation unfolds.

Teaching, Training, Supervision, Research, and Publishing: Psychologists must be accurate and objective in their teaching activities and teach only in areas where they are qualified. Training or educational programs that they conduct must include accurate descriptions of course information, goals, and evaluation methods. Psychologists must provide timely and appropriate feedback to students they supervise or evaluate. They must obtain informed consent from research subjects and handle animals used in research in a humane manner. They must design and plan their research studies in a responsible manner, protecting the rights of others and reporting results in an honest and non-misleading manner. Psychologists must avoid deception in research, and, when unavoidable, take necessary precautions to debrief and minimize harm to subjects. Psychologists must never engage in plagiarism and must distribute publication credit based on the legitimate contributions made by each author. Accordingly,

Example of a Typical Psychological Services Consent Form

PSYCHOLOGIST–PATIENT SERVICES AGREEMENT [CALIFORNIA]

This document (the Agreement) contains important information about my professional services and business policies. It also contains summary information about the Health Insurance Portability and Accountability Act (HIPAA), a new federal law that provides new privacy protections and new patient rights with regard to the use and disclosure of your Protected Health Information (PHI) used for the purpose of treatment, payment, and health care operations. HIPAA requires that I provide you with a Notice of Privacy Practices (the Notice) for use and disclosure of PHI for treatment, payment and health care operations. The Notice, which is attached to this Agreement, explains HIPAA and its application to your personal health information in greater detail. The law requires that I obtain your signature acknowledging that I have provided you with this information at the end of this session. Although these documents are long and sometimes complex, it is very important that you read them carefully before our next session. We can discuss any questions you have about the procedures at that time. When you sign this document, it will also represent an agreement between us. You may revoke this Agreement in writing at any time. That revocation will be binding on me unless I have taken action in reliance on it; if there are obligations imposed on me by your health insurer in order to process or substantiate claims made under your policy; or if you have not satisfied any financial obligations you have incurred.

PSYCHOLOGICAL SERVICES
Psychotherapy is not easily described in general statements. It varies depending on the personalities of the psychologist and patient, and the particular problems you are experiencing. There are many different methods I may use to deal with the problems that you hope to address. Psychotherapy is not like a medical doctor visit. Instead, it calls for a very active effort on your part. In order for the therapy to be most successful, you will have to work on things we talk about both during our sessions and at home.

Psychotherapy and psychological evaluations can have benefits and risks. Since therapy and evaluation may often involve discussing unpleasant aspects of your life, you may experience uncomfortable feelings like sadness, guilt, anger, frustration, loneliness, and helplessness. On the other hand, psychotherapy and evaluation has also been shown to have many benefits. For example, therapy often leads to better relationships, solutions to specific problems, and significant reductions in feelings of distress. But there are no guarantees of what you will experience.

Our first session(s) will involve an evaluation of your needs. By the end of the evaluation, I will be able to offer you some first impressions of what our work will include and a treatment or evaluation plan to follow, if you decide to continue with therapy or evaluation. You should evaluate this information along with your own opinions of whether you feel comfortable working with me. Psychological services can involve a large commitment of time, money, and energy, so you should be very careful about the psychologist you select. If you have questions about my procedures, we should discuss them whenever they arise. If your doubts persist, I will be happy to help you set up a meeting with another mental health professional for a second opinion.

MEETINGS
I normally conduct an evaluation that will last from 1 to 2 sessions. During this time, we can both decide if I am the best person to provide the services that you need in order to meet your treatment or evaluation goals. If services are begun, I will usually schedule one 50-minute session (one appointment hour of 50 minutes duration) per meeting at a time we agree on, although some sessions could be longer or more frequent if we both agree on these arrangements in advance. **Once an appointment hour is scheduled, you will be expected to pay for it unless you provide 24 hours advance notice of cancellation. It is important to note that insurance companies do not provide reimbursement for cancelled or missed sessions.**

PROFESSIONAL FEES

My hourly fee is $200. In addition to face-to-face appointments ($400 per hour for psychological testing), I charge this amount for other professional services you may need, though I will break down the hourly cost if I work for periods of less than one hour. Other services include report writing, telephone conversations lasting longer than 15 minutes, consulting with other professionals with your permission, preparation of records or treatment summaries, and the time spent performing any other service you may request of me. If you become involved in legal proceedings that require my participation, you will be expected to pay for all of my professional time, including preparation and transportation costs, even if I am called to testify by another party. [Because of the difficulty of legal involvement, I charge $300 per hour for preparation and attendance at any legal proceeding.]

CONTACTING ME

Due to my work schedule, I am often not immediately available by telephone. When I am unavailable, my telephone is answered by voice mail that I monitor frequently. I will make every effort to return your call on the same day you make it or within 24 hours, with the exception of weekends, holidays, and vacations. If you are difficult to reach, please inform me of some times when you will be available. If you are unable to reach me and feel that you can't wait for me to return your call, contact your family physician or the nearest emergency room and ask for the psychologist [psychiatrist] on call. If I will be unavailable for an extended time, I will provide you with the name of a colleague to contact, if necessary and desired. You may also try to reach me via email.

LIMITS ON CONFIDENTIALITY

The law protects the privacy of all communications between a patient and a psychologist. In most situations, I can only release information about your treatment to others if you sign a written Authorization form that meets certain legal requirements imposed by state law and/or HIPAA. But, there are some situations where I am permitted or required to disclose information without either your consent or Authorization:

- I may occasionally find it helpful to consult other health and mental health professionals about a case. During a consultation, I make every effort to avoid revealing the identity of my patient. The other professionals are also legally bound to keep the information confidential. If you don't object, I will not tell you about these consultations unless I feel that it is important to our work together. I will note all consultations in your Clinical Record (which is called ''PHI'' in my Notice of Psychologist's Policies and Practices to Protect the Privacy of Your Health Information).
- Since I teach and publish both books and professional articles, aspects of treatment might appear in medical or scientific journals or be presented at professional conferences, lectures, or other presentations. All possible precautions will be taken to protect your anonymity.
- I also have contracts with several appropriate businesses. As required by HIPAA, I have a formal business associate contract with this/these business(es), in which it/they promise to maintain the confidentiality of this data except as specifically allowed in the contract or otherwise required by law. If you wish, I can provide you with the names of these organizations and/or a blank copy of this contract.
- Disclosures required by health insurers or to collect overdue fees are discussed elsewhere in this Agreement.
- If a patient threatens to harm himself/herself, I may be obligated to seek hospitalization for him/her, or to contact family members or others who can help provide protection.
- If you are involved in a court proceeding and a request is made for information about the professional services that I have provided you and/or the records thereof, such information is protected by psychologist-patient privilege law. I cannot provide any information without your (or your legally appointed representative's) written authorization, a court order, or compulsory process (a subpoena) or discovery request from another party to the court proceeding where that party has given you proper notice (when required) and has stated valid legal grounds for obtaining PHI, and I do not have grounds

(continued)

for objecting under state law (or you have instructed me not to object). If you are involved in or contemplating litigation, you should consult with your attorney to determine whether a court would be likely to order me to disclose information.

- If a government agency is requesting the information for health oversight activities pursuant to their legal authority, I may be required to provide it for them.
- If a patient files a complaint or lawsuit against me, I may disclose relevant information regarding that patient in order to defend myself.
- If a patient files a worker's compensation claim, I must, upon appropriate request, disclose information relevant to the claimant's condition, to the worker's compensation insurer. There are some situations in which I am legally obligated to take actions, which I believe are necessary to attempt to protect others from harm and I may have to reveal some information about a patient's treatment. These situations are unusual in my practice.
- If I have knowledge that a child under 18 or I reasonably suspect that a child under 18 that I have observed has been the victim of child abuse or neglect, the law requires that I file a report with the appropriate governmental agency, usually the county welfare department. I also may make a report if I know or reasonably suspect that mental suffering has been inflicted upon a child or that his or her emotional well-being is endangered in any other way (other than physical or sexual abuse, or neglect). Once such a report is filed, I may be required to provide additional information.
- If I observe or have knowledge of an incident that reasonably appears to be physical abuse, abandonment, abduction, isolation, financial abuse or neglect of an elder or dependent adult, or if an elder or dependent adult credibly reports that he or she has experienced behavior including an act or omission constituting physical abuse, abandonment, abduction, isolation, financial abuse, or neglect, or reasonably suspects that abuse, the law requires that I report to the appropriate government agency. Once such a report is filed, I may be required to provide additional information.
- If a patient communicates a serious threat of physical violence against an identifiable victim, I must take protective actions, including notifying the potential victim and contacting the police. I may also seek hospitalization of the patient, or contact others who can assist in protecting the victim.
- If I have reasonable cause to believe that the patient is in such mental or emotional condition as to be dangerous to him or herself, I may be obligated to take protective action, including seeking hospitalization or contacting family members or others who can help provide protection.

If such a situation arises, I will make every effort to fully discuss it with you before taking any action and I will limit my disclosure to what is necessary.

While this written summary of exceptions to confidentiality should prove helpful in informing you about potential problems, it is important that we discuss any questions or concerns that you may have now or in the future. The laws governing confidentiality can be quite complex, and I am not an attorney. In situations where specific advice is required, formal legal advice may be needed.

PROFESSIONAL RECORDS

The laws and standards of my profession require that I keep Protected Health Information about you in your Clinical Record. Except in unusual circumstances where disclosure would physically endanger you and/or others or makes reference to another person (unless such other person is a health care provider) and I believe that access is reasonably likely to cause substantial harm to such other person or where information has been supplied to me confidentially by others, you may examine and/or receive a copy of your Clinical Record, if you request it in writing. Because these are professional records, they can be misinterpreted and/or upsetting to untrained readers. For this reason, I recommend that you initially review them in my presence, or have them forwarded to another mental health professional so you can discuss the contents. There will be a copying fee of 25 cents per page. If I refuse your request for access to your records, you have a right of review (except for information supplied to me confidentially by others) which I will discuss with you upon request.

In addition, I may also keep a set of Psychotherapy Notes. These Notes are for my own use and are designed to assist me in providing you with the best treatment. While the contents of Psychotherapy

Notes vary from client to client, they can include the contents of our conversations, my analysis of those conversations, and how they impact on your therapy. They also contain particularly sensitive information that you may reveal to me that is not required to be included in your Clinical Record. [They also include information from others provided to me confidentially.] These Psychotherapy Notes are kept separate from your Clinical Record. Your Psychotherapy Notes are not available to you and cannot be sent to anyone else, including insurance companies without your written, signed Authorization. Insurance companies cannot require your authorization as a condition of coverage nor penalize you in any way for your refusal to provide it.

PATIENT RIGHTS

HIPAA provides you with several new or expanded rights with regard to your Clinical Records and disclosures of protected health information. These rights include requesting that I amend your record; requesting restrictions on what information from your Clinical Records is disclosed to others; requesting an accounting of most disclosures of protected health information that you have neither consented to nor authorized; determining the location to which protected information disclosures are sent; having any complaints you make about my policies and procedures recorded in your records; and the right to a paper copy of this Agreement, the attached Notice form, and my privacy policies and procedures. I am happy to discuss any of these rights with you.

MINORS AND PARENTS

Patients under 18 years of age who are not emancipated can consent to psychological services subject to the involvement of their parents or guardian *unless* the psychologist determines that their involvement would be inappropriate. A patient over age 12 may consent to psychological services if he or she is mature enough to participate intelligently in such services, *and* the minor patient either would present a danger of serious physical or mental harm to him- or herself or others, *or* is the alleged victim of incest or child abuse. In addition, patients over age 12 may consent to alcohol and drug treatment in some circumstances. However, unemancipated patients under 18 years of age and their parents should be aware that the law may allow parents to examine their child's treatment records unless I determine that access would have a detrimental effect on my professional relationship with the patient, or to his/her physical safety or psychological well-being. Because privacy in psychotherapy is often crucial to successful progress, particularly with teenagers, and parental involvement is also essential, it is usually my policy to request an agreement with minors [over age 12] and their parents about access to information. This agreement provides that during treatment I will provide parents with only general information about the progress of the treatment, and the patient's attendance at scheduled sessions. I will also provide parents with a summary of their child's treatment when it is complete. Any other communication will require the child's Authorization, unless I feel that the child is in danger or is a danger to someone else, in which case I will notify the parents of my concern. Before giving parents any information, I will discuss the matter with the child, if possible, and do my best to handle any objections he/she may have.

BILLING AND PAYMENTS

You will be expected to pay for each session at the time it is held, unless we agree otherwise or unless you have insurance coverage that requires another arrangement. Payment schedules for other professional services will be agreed to when they are requested. [In circumstances of unusual financial hardship, I may be willing to negotiate a payment installment plan.]

If your account has not been paid for more than 60 days and arrangements for payment have not been agreed upon, I have the option of using legal means to secure the payment. This may involve hiring a collection agency or going through small claims court which will require me to disclose otherwise confidential information. In most collection situations, the only information I release regarding a patient's treatment is his/her name, the nature of services provided, and the amount due. [If such legal action is necessary, its costs will be included in the claim.]

(continued)

INSURANCE REIMBURSEMENT

In order for us to set realistic treatment goals and priorities, it is important to evaluate what resources you have available to pay for your treatment. If you have a health insurance policy, it will usually provide some coverage for mental health treatment. I will fill out forms and provide you with whatever assistance I can in helping you receive the benefits to which you are entitled; however, you (not your insurance company) are responsible for full payment of my fees. It is very important that you find out exactly what mental health services your insurance policy covers.

You should carefully read the section in your insurance coverage booklet that describes mental health services. If you have questions about the coverage, call your plan administrator. Of course, I will provide you with whatever information I can based on my experience and will be happy to help you in understanding the information you receive from your insurance company. If it is necessary to clear confusion, I will be willing to call the company on your behalf.

Due to the rising costs of health care, insurance benefits have increasingly become more complex. It is sometimes difficult to determine exactly how much mental health coverage is available. "Managed Health Care" plans such as HMOs and PPOs often require authorization before they provide reimbursement for mental health services. These plans are often limited to short-term treatment approaches designed to work out specific problems that interfere with a person's usual level of functioning. It may be necessary to seek approval for more therapy after a certain number of sessions. While much can be accomplished in short-term therapy, some patients feel that they need more services after insurance benefits end. [Some managed-care plans will not allow me to provide services to you once your benefits end. If this is the case, I will do my best to find another provider who will help you continue your psychotherapy.]

You should also be aware that your contract with your health insurance company requires that I provide it with information relevant to the services that I provide to you. I am required to provide a clinical diagnosis. Sometimes I am required to provide additional clinical information such as treatment plans or summaries, or copies of your entire Clinical Record. Before I can disclose this information, both you and I must receive a written notification from the insurer stating what they are requesting, why they are requesting it, how long it will be kept and what will be done with the information when they are finished with it. In such situations, I will make every effort to release only the minimum information about you that is necessary for the purpose requested. This information will become part of the insurance company files and will probably be stored in a computer. Though all insurance companies claim to keep such information confidential, I have no control over what they do with it once it is in their hands. In some cases, they may share the information with a national medical information databank. I will provide you with a copy of any report I submit, if you request it. By signing this Agreement, you agree that I can provide requested information to your carrier.

Once we have all of the information about your insurance coverage, we will discuss what we can expect to accomplish with the benefits that are available and what will happen if they run out before you feel ready to end your sessions. It is important to remember that you always have the right to pay for my services yourself to avoid the problems described above [unless prohibited by contract]. Your signature below indicates that you have read the information in this document and agree to abide by its terms during our professional relationship.

YOUR SIGNATURE BELOW INDICATES THAT YOU HAVE READ THIS AGREEMENT AND AGREE TO ITS TERMS AND ALSO SERVES AS AN ACKNOWLEDGMENT THAT YOU HAVE RECEIVED THE HIPAA NOTICE FORM DESCRIBED ABOVE.

Signature_____ Date_____

Rev. 3/10

Case Study: Dr. T Dates a Relative of His Patient

Dr. T is a single psychologist looking for a mate. Dr. T conducts group psychotherapy and one of the group members mentions after a session that Dr. T should meet her niece. The patient feels that they would make a great couple. Dr. T agrees to go on a blind date with his patient's niece. They hit it off immediately and soon agree to marry. Dr. T continues seeing the patient in group psychotherapy but now also sees the patient at family events with his new wife. Dr. T developed a dual relationship with his patient by involving himself in the patient's family as well as dating and eventually marrying the patient's niece.

integrity

Case Study: Dr. U Abandons His Clients *other's welfare*

Dr. U decides to close his practice and move to Hawaii. He provides his patients with one week of notice and closes his practice. Dr. U, in a hurry to begin his new life, makes no arrangements for his patients to continue receiving therapy with colleagues. He feels that they are smart and resourceful enough to find someone else if they need therapy and gives them a list of all the psychologists who are members of the county psychological association. Dr. U has clearly abandoned his patients and has neither ethically nor thoughtfully made appropriate arrangements for their therapy needs.

Case Study: Dr. V Publishes Research in a Way to Help Her Career Rather Than Doing So More Responsibly *social resp.*

Dr. V is anxious about tenure. She feels that she is not a great researcher but really enjoys teaching and the academic lifestyle. She collected a great deal of data for her doctoral dissertation and decides to see how many professional articles she can publish based on this one study. She decides to write five different papers, each focusing on some small detail of her project. She later decides to publish a review article of her subject area primarily focusing on her five now-published articles. Dr. V exploits her data set to give the appearance that she has conducted five separate studies rather than one. Dr. V uses her research in an irresponsible and misleading manner to increase her chances of obtaining tenure.

psychologists do not duplicate the publication of their own or others' research data. They share data with colleagues when they wish to verify findings.

Forensic Activities: Psychologists who provide forensic or legal/court-related services must be careful to use assessment instruments for the purposes for which they were developed. They are careful to clarify their roles in forensic work and avoid misleading statements. Psychologists who work in forensic situations often provide expert testimony, consultation, and evaluation for legal cases involving, for example, child custody arrangements, workman's compensation, or criminal proceedings

Case Study: Dr. W Surprises His Students with Rejection without Any Warning P.52, others unsure

Dr. W is a professor who supervises several doctoral dissertation projects conducted by graduate students in his department. After working with students for many months and even years in some cases, Dr. W decides without warning to fail several of the students during their final dissertation oral defense. He informs them that their projects are unsatisfactory and not worthy of a dissertation. Dr. W 's actions were irresponsible and unethical because he never provided timely and appropriate feedback to his students during the course of conducting the projects and failed the students without warning or feedback.

to determine sanity. Often there are a number of different and opposing parties involved and invested in the work of the psychologist. These may include the judge, attorneys, defendants, and plaintiffs, among others. Psychologists working in forensic activities must make their role and limits clear to all parties involved to avoid misunderstandings and potential unethical or biased behavior. Furthermore, they must always be vigilant to testify within their areas of expertise and utilize data clearly supported by their evaluation results. The American Psychology-Law Society (Division 41 of the APA) has developed specific practice guidelines for psychologists working in legal settings (Committee on Ethical Guidelines for Forensic Psychologists, 1991).

Resolving Ethical Issues: Psychologists must be familiar with the Ethics Code and apply it to their professional work setting. They cooperate with ethics committees and try to resolve ethical dilemmas in an educative rather than punitive manner. If ethical conflicts cannot be resolved informally, psychologists must report ethical violations to the appropriate authority.

Highlight of a Contemporary Clinical Psychologist

Thomas G. Plante, PhD, ABPP

Photo: Courtesy
Thomas G. Plante

Dr. Plante combines a full-time academic career with a private practice and consultation with religious organizations.

Birth Date: January 23, 1960

College: Brown University (ScB, Psychology), 1982

Graduate Program: University of Kansas (MA, PhD, Clinical Psychology), 1987

Clinical Internship: Yale University School of Medicine (1986–1987)

Postdoctoral Fellowship: Yale University (1987–1988)

Current Jobs: Professor of Psychology, Santa Clara University; Adjunct Clinical Professor of Psychiatry and Behavioral Sciences, Stanford University School of Medicine; Private Practice

Pros and Cons of Being a Clinical Psychologist:

Pros: "There is nothing more interesting and compelling than human behavior. Why do people do the things they do or feel the way they feel? Helping people understand their emotional life and behavior as well as finding ways to improve the quality of their lives is very rewarding and meaningful. I can think of numerous times when an assessment, consultation, or treatment resulted in an important change for the better for someone. This also has ripple effects impacting family, friends, and co-workers, among others. Furthermore, there are numerous options and opportunities for teaching, research, practice, and consultation in clinical psychology and all of these activities can be very helpful to others. Finally, clinical psychology offers a great deal of autonomy and freedom with many opportunities in diverse areas of work."

Cons: "Many economic and political factors threaten the profession. Managed health care, turf battles with other disciplines such as psychiatry, and intra-profession conflicts between science- and practice-oriented psychologists cause distress. Clinical psychologists often have a great deal of responsibility, which can feel overwhelming at times. Salaries also generally tend to be low in comparison to many other professions that also require so many years of advanced training and advanced degrees."

Future of Clinical Psychology: "Clinical psychology will likely continue to specialize and subspecialize. Internal and external forces will also require the use of empirically supported and evidence-based assessment and treatments for clinical problems. Clinical psychology will also become more and more involved in general health behavior change such as treating lifestyle-related health problems. Most of the problems in society (e.g., terrorism, poverty, oppression of others, prejudice, conflicts among others, violence) can be altered with the help of clinical psychology. When you think about it, behavior is at the core of most troubles in the world and in the lives of people. Clinical psychology, perhaps more than any other field, offers useful reflection, research, and interventions on altering behavior, which can minimize so many troubles."

Typical Schedule:

8:30	Teach seminar on professional issues and ethics to psychology interns and postdoctoral fellows at Stanford University School of Medicine.
11:00	Teach clinical psychology class at Santa Clara University.
1:00	Meet with research lab group to discuss research projects involving the psychological benefits of exercise, faith and health research, and Catholic clergy research.
2:00	Meet individually with students for academic advising.
3:00–5:00	Teach ethics in psychology class at Santa Clara University for undergraduates.
5:00	Psychological evaluation of 24-year-old Vietnamese man interested in entering religious life as a Catholic priest. Conduct interview and administer several psychological tests.
6:00	Conference call with research subcommittee of the National Review Board for the Protection of Children and Youth for the U.S. Council of Catholic Bishops.

Why Would a Psychologist Behave in an Unethical Manner?

Psychologists are human beings, and they make mistakes in both judgment and behavior. While some psychologists are well aware that they are committing ethical violations, many others are not. Some allow their own needs to supersede those of their patients, students, colleagues, and the greater public. Some psychologists are emotionally disturbed,

---

Case Study: Dr. X Doesn't Provide Full Informed Consent to His Clients rights + dignity

Dr. X is conducting a psychological evaluation in a child custody lawsuit. He conducts an evaluation of the child and both parents who are fighting over custody of the child. He encourages each person to be as honest and open as possible and asserts that he will do whatever is in the best interest of each person. In a vulnerable moment, the father tells Dr. X that he really doesn't want to have custody but that he wants to get back at his wife for her infidelity. The father thinks that this information will be held in confi-

dence. The father is later infuriated that Dr. X included this statement in the evaluation report. Dr. X did not make clear to all of the parties involved what would and would not be communicated in the report and to the court. In fact, Dr. X also tape-recorded the evaluation without the knowledge or consent of the parties involved. Dr. X unethically failed to clarify his role in the evaluation, and failed to obtain informed consent and establish the boundaries of confidentiality prior to conducting the evaluations.

---

some are selfish, some are unaware of their missteps, some make errors in judgment, and some innocently fall into behavior that results in an ethical violation.

Many assume that those who commit ethical violations are incompetent or malicious. However, well-meaning psychologists striving to do what they believe is in the best interest of their patients, students, or others commit ethical violations as well. No one is immune from engaging in unethical behavior. Even well-trained, well-meaning, and thoughtful psychologists may commit ethical violations.

Being well informed of the Ethics Code and obtaining consultation when needed can greatly help to minimize the chances of making ethical violations. Furthermore, being attentive to ethical behavior in others can also assist in minimizing the chances that unethical behavior will continue once it has begun.

Sieber (1982) suggested that ethical violations tend to fall into one of six categories. The first category of common error includes inexperience or ignorance on the part of the psychologist leading to an unforeseen ethical dilemma. For example, a psychologist may not realize that photocopying the record form from an intelligence test and giving it

to the parents of a child violates the ethical requirement of protecting the security and confidentiality of testing materials.

A second common ethical category involves an underestimate by the psychologist regarding the potential for an ethical problem. For instance, a disorganized psychologist trying to save time may not take appropriate precautions to ensure that research subjects give informed consent prior to participating in a research study and are fully debriefed when the study is completed.

A third category outlined by Sieber includes ethical dilemmas that are unavoidable in the eyes of the psychologist. For example, a psychologist may feel it necessary to break confidentiality while working with an adolescent because of concerns about behaviors such as drunk driving.

A fourth category subsumes foreseen ethical dilemmas that arise out of a new procedure or approach. For instance, a new treatment may result in unforeseen harm to patients, which the clinician could not have predicted.

A fifth category includes ethical problems that emerge when no clear guidelines exist or guidelines are ambiguous in a particular situation. This can happen as new technology and different approaches develop (e.g., virtual reality therapy for phobia) that impact

Case Study: Dr. Y Fails to Help and Support Her Students

Dr. Y is a new assistant professor at a small college. Several of her students tell her about the classroom behavior of Dr. Z. They report that Dr. Z seems to run out of things to say in class and then routinely lets class out long before the time period ends. They also state that Dr. Z frequently talks about how much money he makes on a textbook he authored and offers strong opinions about other faculty members and their professional activities. He also frequently comments on the attire and attractiveness of the female students in his classes. Because Dr. Y does not have tenure, she refuses to get involved in any way. She tells her students that her hands are tied and that some professors are better than others. Dr. Y is not only insensitive to the needs and dilemmas faced by her students, but does nothing to assist in correcting the unethical behavior of Dr. Z.

P+SR , competence, integrity
respect + dignity

Case Study: Dr. AA Commits Insurance Fraud *soc. resp.*

Dr. AA is conducting an evaluation with an 8-year-old child to determine if the child has an attention deficit hyperactivity disorder (ADHD). The child's parents have few financial resources and hope that their health-care insurance will pay for most or all of the costs to complete the evaluation. Dr. AA completes the evaluation and determines that the child does not have ADHD. In fact, Dr. AA failed to find any diagnosable disorder (e.g., depression, oppositional defiant, anxiety). Because no diagnosis can be determined, the insurance provider will not pay for the evaluation. The child's parents feel that they cannot afford the evaluation and ask Dr. AA to list some diagnosis on the insurance forms so that the insurance company will pay for the evaluation. Dr. AA is concerned about his patient's financial problems and agrees to give the child a diagnosis of adjustment disorder with mixed emotional features. While Dr. AA is well meaning in trying to help his patient, he is committing not only an ethical violation but a legal one as well. Committing insurance fraud is a serious legal offense.

psychological services and are not addressed directly in the current Ethics Code.

Finally, ethical problems exist when the law contradicts ethical guidelines. For example, a judge may court order all of a patient's records from a psychologist. These records may include therapy notes and psychological testing data. Because the Ethics Code states that confidentiality cannot be broken without patient permission (or when someone is in immediate and serious danger) and that testing materials cannot be released to those not qualified to interpret them (e.g., non-psychologists), then the Ethics Code and legal demands are in conflict.

How Are Ethics Enforced?

All members of the APA are instructed to read and agree to follow the Ethics Code (APA, 2002). Members not only are expected to know and follow the code but are obligated to help correct unethical behavior by colleagues through education or by reporting them to local or national ethics boards. However, many are reluctant to do so, especially if the behavior is being conducted by their boss or a colleague with whom they work closely. All authors of articles published in journals published by the APA are asked to sign a statement prior to publication indicating that their research

Case Study: Dr. BB Enters a Dual Relationship with His Client

Dr. BB is treating a graduate student in psychology for anxiety and depressive concerns. The patient is having a very hard time completing his dissertation project. In fact, his graduate program has threatened to terminate his enrollment if he does not complete the project within several months. Dr. BB, wishing to help his patient, offers to give him a project he has been interested in completing and offers to be a member of his dissertation committee. Dr. BB agrees to deceive the graduate program so that they won't find out that Dr. BB is treating the student in psychotherapy. Dr. BB is willing to enter into an unethical dual relationship in an effort to try and help his patient complete his dissertation project.

Dr. BB is well meaning in his efforts to go the extra mile for his patient. His unethical behavior can actually result in advantages to his patient. However, his behavior compromises his therapeutic relationships and the integrity of the profession.

integrrity

was completed in keeping with the ethical guidelines. State licensing examinations and procedures include the Ethics Code in the examination process. Furthermore, a number of books are published by the APA to help psychologists more fully understand professional ethics (e.g., Bersoff, 2008; Campbell, Vasquez, Behnke, & Kinscherff, 2009; Canter, Bennett, Jones, & Nagy, 1994; Pope, 2007; Zur, 2007). Professional ethics are also generally taught during graduate school and internship/postdoctoral training (Plante, 1995). Therefore, all psychologists are expected to know and follow the ethical standards set forth by the APA. Ignorance of the Ethics Code is no excuse for unethical behavior.

Consumers of psychological services also help in enforcing ethical guidelines. Patients, students, clients, supervisors, colleagues, and others who complain about the professional conduct of a psychologist do so by contacting local professional associations or state boards of psychology. These complaints often are directed to local and national ethics boards associated with psychological associations such as the APA.

The APA maintains a committee to evaluate and monitor ethical violations. Complaints that the committee deem to have merit are investigated and acted upon. Depending on the results of the investigation, the committee may provide the psychologist with an educative advisory, warnings for minor violations or for ethical but unprofessional conduct, a reprimand or censure for more severe violations, or demand resignation or expulsion from the association for highly serious violations. Furthermore, the APA ethics committee works closely with state and local ethics committees and licensing boards to ensure that psychologists who are found to be guilty of ethical violations are appropriately dealt with at the local level (e.g., suspension or revocation of a state license to practice for serious violations).

Each state has independent licensing boards that assist in monitoring the practices of psychologists. The boards process applicants for licensure and assist in monitoring the professional conduct of psychologists once they are licensed. The licensing board can grant, deny, suspend, or revoke licenses to practice. For example, a license can be denied if the applicant does not meet minimum standards for training or has failed to pass the licensing examinations. Licenses can be suspended or revoked when a psychologist has been found to be engaging in unethical or illegal activity. The most common reasons that malpractice claims are filed result from inappropriate sexual behavior on the part of the psychologist, suicide of a patient, and inappropriate treatment conducted with a patient. Sexual dual relationships account for

Photo: Bruce Ayers, Tony Stone Images, New York, Inc.

Figure 13.1

When an ethical dilemma arises, a psychologist may consult with colleagues.

the majority of claims paid to plaintiffs by the APA's liability insurance carrier (Pope, 1991).

What Is the Process for Solving Ethical Dilemmas?

When ethical dilemmas arise, it is important to consult the Ethics Code to determine precisely what the written guidelines instruct. Second, consultation with colleagues concerning the conduct or issue in question can be extremely useful (Figure 13.1). If it has been determined that an ethical violation has or may have occurred, the psychologist discovering the violation has a duty to bring it to the attention of the offending psychologist. For minor violations committed by error or oversight, educating the person about the ethical principles involved is generally an adequate means of correcting the problematic conduct. If the collegial educative process does not result in ethical behavior, or if the violation is serious, the psychologist has the ethical responsibility to inform the ethics board at the state or national level. The ethics board then collects information and determines whether

the infraction is worthy of investigation and either action or dismissal.

Is Behaving in Accordance with Ethical Principles Always Clear Cut?

While it seems obvious that psychologists should maintain professional competence, never have sexual relationships with current or recent patients or students, and maintain patient confidentiality, numerous ethical dilemmas emerge that are more ambiguous and highly challenging to resolve. Pope and Vetter (1992) report several cases that surfaced from a national survey of 1,319 members of the APA. While easy answers to many cases cannot be found, careful analysis and professional consultation usually result in the soundest decision and professional judgment.

For example, Pope and Vetter (1992) describe the following case scenarios for consideration:

Case 1: A psychologist who has been treating a women for three years in psychotherapy coincidentally begins to date her best and closest friend.

Case 2: A psychologist in a rural community is active in his church group. Members of the church group wish to consult with him on a professional basis because they know and trust him and he is the only professional in the area who offers particular specialty services.

Case 3: A psychologist conducts psychotherapy with a child. Soon after the beginning of therapy, the child's mother and the therapist develop a strong mutual attraction. The psychologist considers referring the patient elsewhere but feels that therapeutic gains will be lost.

Case 4: A psychologist is providing psychotherapy to another psychologist. The patient reveals that he has committed a serious ethical violation. The patient states that due to patient confidentiality, the therapist cannot report the violation.

Case 5: The rules of a university medical center dictate that a psychologist must give Principal Investigator (PI) status on research grants to a physician even if the physician is not actually the PI on the project.

How should these actual cases be handled? None of the cases mentioned have simple and clear-cut answers. Careful review and consideration of the Ethics Code as well as appropriate consultation is generally required in order to make reasonable professional and ethical judgments.

The Big Picture

The Ethics Code provides useful guidelines for psychologists as well as the public concerning the standards of professional conduct. The APA has worked to ensure that a great deal of input from members of the organization occurs with each revision. The code is "living" in that it is frequently discussed in professional journals and circles and is updated often. Many professionals have suggested that the Ethics Code is a significant improvement over earlier versions, including greater detail and clarification regarding many of the principles. Furthermore, the APA spends more money on issues of professional ethics than any other professional organization (APA, 2009; Chalk, Frankel, & Chafer, 1980).

However, not everyone is satisfied with the Ethics Code (Koocher & Keith-Spiegal, 2008; Lakin, 1994; Payton, 1994; Sonne, 1994). Some have argued that the code does not go far enough in its emphasis on the declaration of respect for the worth and dignity of individuals. Payton (1994) reports that the code should go further in addressing issues of relevance to ethnic minority group members as well as women, gay men, and lesbians. Others are concerned that the code does not go far enough in protecting patients and students from sexual exploitation by psychologists (Koocher & Keith-Spiegal, 2008; Layman & McNamara, 1997). In fact, unlike previous versions of the Ethics Code, the current version allows for sexual relationships between psychologists and patients under special circumstances two years following the termination of services. Some argue that issues pertaining to multipatient therapies such as family therapy, couples therapy, and group therapy are not adequately addressed in the Ethics Code (Lakin, 1994). Some cynically state that the code is designed to protect psychologists more than the public (Payton, 1994). Finally, some argue that much of the code is too vague and does not provide specific guidelines in a number of important areas (Koocher & Keith-Spiegal, 2008).

However imperfect, the Ethics Code provides a working standard of conduct by which persons who receive psychological services can judge professional behavior. All psychologists are expected to both know and follow the Ethics Code. Professional ethical guidelines in psychology are not simply strict laws to follow or violate. Infractions are not generally met with a punitive response (unless the violation is very serious with potential significant harm to the public). Rather, professional ethics in psychology are meant to be educative and ethical dilemmas are generally resolved informally among colleagues. Diligent attention to ethical behavior upholds the stature, helpfulness, and humanitarian goals of the clinical psychology profession.

Although many future revisions of the Ethics Code are assured, the basic principles of ethical behavior outlined many years ago by Hippocrates are likely to be applicable indefinitely. Future clinical psychologists will always be expected to behave in a competent, professional, and ethical manner and maintain integrity and responsibility in their professional roles and responsibilities. It is unlikely that these basic tenets will ever change.

Key Points

1. Whether a psychologist is a researcher, teacher, therapist, or administrator, he or she is expected to maintain the highest professional ethics in all professional activities at all times.
2. Most complaints that result in action against psychologists by the APA involve breaking confidentiality, sexual misconduct (e.g., sexual relationship with a patient), nonsexual dual relationships (e.g., friendships or business partnerships with patients), and insurance/fee misbehavior (e.g., overbilling insurance, billing for services not rendered).
3. Since 1953, the APA has had an Ethics Code that specifically outlined the behavior expected of all psychologists. The Ethics Code has been updated nine times since 1953 and the current version was published in December 2002 (APA, 2002).
4. The current version of the ethical principles for psychologists is divided into five general principles and ten ethical standards. The general principles include (1) beneficence and nonmaleficence, (2) fidelity and responsibility, (3) integrity, (4) justice, and (5) respect for people's rights and dignity. The ethical standards include (1) resolving ethical issues, (2) competence, (3) human relations, (4) privacy and confidentiality, (5) advertising and other public statements, (6) recordkeeping and fees, (7) education and training, (8) research and publication, (9) assessment, and (10) therapy.

5. Psychologists must maintain competence in their area(s) of specialization and work. They must provide only services that they have the appropriate training and experience to legitimately offer to the public. They must also stay up-to-date on changes and advances in the field in order to ensure that they maintain state-of-the-art skills.
6. Psychologists must maintain professional and personal integrity and be respectful, fair, and honest in their dealings with others. They must be truthful in describing their services, their areas of expertise, and what can be expected from participation in their services. They must be well aware of their biases, needs, and values and how each of these impact their work.
7. Psychologists should make all efforts to avoid inappropriate dual relationships.
8. Psychologists must be willing to consult with others as indicated in order to best serve their patients or clients. They must also help to avoid unethical behavior engaged in by colleagues. Psychologists must be responsible for their own conduct and accept their obligations to the larger profession and public welfare.
9. Psychologists must be respectful of the rights and dignity of others. They must be sensitive to individual and cultural differences as well as vigilant in providing nondiscriminatory services. They must respect the rights to freedom, privacy, and confidentiality of their patients and clients.
10. Psychologists work to improve the quality of life and never incur harm through their work with others. Psychologists must never exploit their relationships with others.
11. Psychologists work to help others and advance the science and knowledge of human behavior. Psychologists are expected to contribute some professional time to

causes that do not result in financial or other personal gains.

12. Many assume that those who commit ethical violations are usually incompetent or malicious. However, well-meaning psychologists seeking to best serve the interests of their patients, students, or others commit ethical violations. No one is immune from engaging in unethical behavior. Even well-trained, well-meaning, and thoughtful psychologists are capable of committing an ethical violation.

13. Ethical principles are developed at the national level by the APA to protect the public and profession as well as to provide guidelines for conduct among psychologists. All psychologists are expected to know and follow the ethical standards set forth by the APA. Ignorance of the Ethics Code is no excuse for unethical behavior.

Key Terms

Confidentiality
Dual relationships
Ethics Code

For Reflection

1. What are the general principles and ethical standards of the APA Ethics Code?
2. Why bother having an Ethics Code?
3. What are the most common ethical violations?
4. Why would a psychologist make an ethical violation?
5. What is a dual relationship and why should it be avoided?
6. Why shouldn't psychologists have sexual relationships with patients or students following the termination of their professional relationship?
7. What are some of the pros and cons to the Ethics Code?

8. How are ethical dilemmas resolved?
9. How might the Ethics Code be changed in the future?
10. How do ethics and the law relate?

Real Students, Real Questions

1. What kind of screening do psychologists go through to find out if they have any psychological disorders before being licensed?
2. If membership in APA is optional for psychologists, then how can we really ensure ethical standards are upheld by all psychologists?
3. Can a psychologist counsel a friend? Is it ever beneficial or are there usually too many conflicts?
4. Is refusing to be socially responsible an ethical violation?
5. How can psychologists know if their colleagues are being ethical if their sessions are in private?
6. How often do psychologists "turn in" another psychologist for being unethical?

Web Resources

www.apa.org/ethics
Learn more about APA's Ethics Code and other ethical matters related to psychology.

www.scu.edu/ethics
The Markkula Center for Applied Ethics at Santa Clara University offers a variety of articles, web links, and other information about applied ethics.

http://commfaculty.fullerton.edu/lester/ethics/general.html
The School of Communications at California State University, Fullerton, offers this helpful web site with numerous links to ethics on the Web in many categories.

www.ethics.org.au
The St. James Ethics Center is a nonprofit organization that promotes ethics in daily life. It is not associated with any religious or political affiliations.

http://ethics.ubc.ca/resources/

This site offers useful links to a variety of applied ethics topics.

www.globalethics.org
The Institute for Global Ethics is an independent, nonprofit, nonsectarian, and nonpartisan organization that promotes ethics globally.

PART Three

WHERE IS CLINICAL PSYCHOLOGY GOING, AND SHOULD I GO WITH IT?

Photo: Courtesy Zach Plante.

Chapter Objective

To examine the contemporary trends and issues in clinical psychology.

Chapter Outline

Trends in Society
Highlight of a Contemporary Clinical Psychologist: Aisha Laureen Hamdan, PhD
Research Issues
Practice Issues
Reaching Beyond Mental Health in Contemporary Clinical Psychology
Training Issues

14

Chapter

Clinical psychology has evolved and changed rapidly during its 100+-year history. The influence of leaders in the field such as Sigmund Freud, B. F. Skinner, and Carl Rogers, and events such as the two world wars, the availability of National Institute of Mental Health (NIMH) training grants, cultural diversity among the population, the advent of managed health care, technological advances impacting our professional and personal lives, and the emphasis on empirically supported and evidence-based research and practice have expedited change and development. However, it is difficult to imagine a more rapidly changing period in clinical psychology than the present. Today, clinical psychology looks very different than it did, not only 50 or 40 years ago, but even 5 or 10 years ago. Changes in society as well as in many other professions have paralleled this evolution. Recent advances in science, technology, and information systems, as well as the innovation of managed health care and health-care reform, empirically supported treatments, and a growing sensitivity to multicultural and diversity issues, have all contributed to the evolution and advancement

of contemporary clinical psychology. Where is clinical psychology going? What is its future? What are some of the current hot topics in clinical psychology? What are its current and future challenges? These are some of the questions addressed in this chapter.

One of the best examples of a current hot topic in clinical psychology is managed health care and health-care reform. Many have suggested that managed health care and health-care reform will (and have) altered clinical psychology in a permanent and profound way (Anders, 1996; Benedict & Phelps, 1998; C. Chambless, 2000; Cummings, 1984, 1995; Fox, 1994; Kovacs, 1996; Rosenberg, Hickie, & Mendoza, 2009; Shi & Singh, 2007). Although managed health care will be addressed in more detail later, a brief introduction to this important issue demonstrates how quickly fundamental aspects of clinical psychology can change. Since the 1970s (and much earlier for physicians), someone who wanted to see a clinical psychologist for psychotherapy or other psychological service could choose to be treated by any licensed psychologist in his or her geographical area.

The psychologist would conduct as many sessions as necessary to best treat the patient, using whatever theoretical orientation(s) and techniques he or she deemed appropriate to provide competent and professional service. Insurance carriers such as Blue Cross/Blue Shield would rarely question the treatment plan, and would typically reimburse between 50% and 80% of the fees regardless of whether the treatment lasted for 3 sessions or 300. A similar scenario existed for physicians of all specialties.

However, over the past few decades (primarily during the late 1980s and 1990s), this scenario changed radically. Today, the patient typically contacts his or her insurance carrier to determine which therapists in the patient's area are part of the insurance company's preferred provider list. The patient then contacts the professional and is allowed a specific number of sessions authorized by the insurance carrier. The authorized number of sessions is usually just a few (e.g., 3 to 6). The patient pays nothing or a nominal fee (i.e., copayment) for the sessions. However, the provider accepts a steep discount or a reduction (usually about 30% and sometimes more than 50%) in his or her usual fee in order to be on the provider panel. Additional sessions or other treatment modalities (e.g., inpatient care, group psychotherapy, family psychotherapy) all must be authorized by the insurance company before these services can be provided. The insurance company representatives carefully examine the treatment plan offered by the provider and encourage very brief, problem-focused, and the least expensive services. In many ways, these changes in health care have permanently changed the science and practice of clinical psychology (e.g., emphasis on low-cost, brief crisis intervention) as well as the entire health-care system. These changes significantly impact all major areas of clinical psychology including research, training, and practice, as well as the larger cultural climate for public demand for psychological services. For example, since most managed care companies will not authorize treatment conducted by trainees, many hospitals and clinics cannot continue to train psychology trainees and expect to get insurance reimbursement for their services.

Trends in Society

Clinical psychology must change and adapt to a changing world just like any other field of study or practice. It would be foolish for clinical psychology to keep its "head in the sand" and try to resist societal changes (Benedict & Phelps, 1998; Cummings, 1995; Klein, 1996; Plante, 1996b). Rather, clinical psychology must grow and develop based on the issues and concerns of the world at large as well as respond to changes within the field as new research discoveries and clinical practice strategies emerge. In the words of Rachel Klein (1996), "psychology has to move with the times and should welcome the opportunity" (p. 216). Issues such as family changes, multicultural sensitivity, scientific advances, financial challenges, and gender shifts in professions will be highlighted here.

Contemporary Changes in the American Family

The American family has changed a great deal in recent years. The traditional image of a married couple living with two or more of their own children is no longer the norm. Today, almost 50% of first marriages end in divorce, less than half of all American households include a married couple, about 20% of adults over the age of 18 live alone, and approximately 55% of people report cohabitating together prior to marriage. Many households include single or remarried parents with blended families. Families today may include adopted or "test tube" children, children and parents of mixed ethnicity, race, and religious backgrounds, gay and lesbian parents, single parents, and unmarried parents. In fact, 10.5 million households are headed by single mothers (U.S. Census Bureau, 2006).

The changing face of the American family has implications for clinical psychology and related fields. Families who experience stress associated with, for example, being a single parent, integrating children in blended families under one roof, or dealing with discrimination associated with sexual orientation or interracial issues, have unique needs and concerns. Clinical psychologists must be sensitive to the issues associated with the changing American family and must be able to provide competent assessment, treatment, and consultation to these families (American Psychological Association [APA], 2002, 2003b).

Multicultural and Diversity Issues

The United States has quickly become an ethnically and culturally diverse nation. It has been estimated that over 25% of the American population consists of ethnic minorities, with about 50% in California (U.S. Census Bureau, 2008b). Of the approximately 300 million Americans in the United States, about 12% are African Americans; 15% are Latino Americans; and 5% are Asian Americans (U.S. Census Bureau, 2008b). The increase in numbers of ethnic minorities and immigrants has been dramatic. Some states have seen an increase of 34% within recent years (APA, 2003b; U.S. Census Bureau, 2008b). During the 1980s, the number of Asian Americans rose by over 100%, and now the majority of people living in California are ethnic minority group members. It is estimated that 50% of Americans will be ethnic minority members by the year 2050 (U.S. Census Bureau, 2008b). Increasing attention and interest have been focused in recent years on the role of **multicultural** and **diversity** issues in all aspects of society (APA, 2003; Hall, 1997; D. Sue & D. M. Sue, 2008; Trickett, Watts, & Birman, 1994). Psychologists, as well as professionals from other fields, have acquired greater insight into the role of culture and diversity in the development of behavior and behavioral problems (APA, 2003; Bernal & Castro, 1994; Cardemil & Battle, 2003; Fowers

& Richardson, 1996; Hall, 1997; Roysircar et al., 2003; D. Sue & D. M. Sue, 2008).

The roles of social context and culture are powerful influences on behavior. The understanding of culture is critical to the understanding of psychological and physical symptoms as well as in developing treatment interventions. For example, conversion disorders, which were rather common during Freud's time, are less common today in Western culture. The cultural context of the emotional and sexually repressive Victorian era along with the oppression of women have been associated with the frequency of conversion disorders 100 years ago (Shorter, 1994). Certain hypochondriacal and conversion disorders are found in some cultures but not others. For example, *koro* involves the belief that genitals are retracting into the stomach region and primarily occurs among Asian men (Rubin, 1982). Other culture-specific illnesses include *dhat*, anxiety about semen loss among men in India, hot sensations in the head among African individuals, and burning sensations in the hands and feet among Pakistanis (Ebigno, 1986). These symptoms tend to be culture related and all involve anxiety and depressive affect associated with bodily complaints that have no known physiological cause.

Even disorders that appear to be universally found among all cultures manifest differently depending on the specific culture. For example, schizophrenia seems to be found in all cultures. However, whereas schizophrenics from American and other industrialized Western countries generally experience auditory hallucinations, those from Latin American and African countries typically experience visual hallucinations (Ndetei & Singh, 1983). Although it is unclear what might contribute to these cultural differences in the manifestation of symptoms, psychologists and other mental health professionals must be sensitive to cultural issues in their patients (APA, 2002, 2003; Garb, 1997).

The APA (1990) has urged psychologists to "become familiar with indigenous beliefs and practices and respect them" (p. 3). Guidelines developed by the APA assert that both

Diversity: Working with Lesbian, Gay, Bisexual, and Transgender (LGBT) Clients

In 1973, the American Psychiatric Association removed homosexuality from its list of mental disorders and in 1975 the American Psychological Association adopted a resolution stating that "homosexuality per se implies no impairment in judgment, stability, reliability, or general social or vocational capabilities" (Conger, 1975, p. 633). Since then, other professional organizations such as the American Association for Marriage and Family Therapy, the National Association of Social Workers, the Canadian Psychological Association, and the British Psychological Society, among others, have made similar policy statements.

Over the years, the APA has offered a variety of guidelines for working with LGBT people that attempts to be respectful and helpful to their unique needs.

Most recent guidelines (e.g., APA Division 44, 2000) have provided suggestions and recommendations for psychologists regarding their attitudes toward homosexuality and bisexuality, issues regarding relationships and families of LGBT transgender individuals, diversity sensitivity issues, and education in research, practice, and resources relating to LGBT issues.

These guidelines underscore that although homosexuality is not indicative of mental illness, LGBT persons may be vulnerable to unique stresses and biases due to social stigmatization such as discrimination, violence, and prejudice as well as challenges with rejection from family of origin, neighbors, work associates, or significant others in their lives. They encourage psychologists to be familiar with both the research and clinical practice guidelines regarding homosexuality in order to best treat and work with those who experience LGBT-related issues.

One program that seeks to help psychologists as well as others to work more effectively and comfortably with homosexual clients and colleagues is entitled Safe Zone (Finkel, Ragnar, Bandele, & Schaefer, 2003). It was developed to "increase awareness and knowledge of, and sensitivity to, important issues affecting" (p. 555) this population. It has been used in numerous university, community, and business settings. Additionally, programs such as AFFIRM assist family members (as well as mental health professions) in accepting gay, lesbian, bisexual, and transgender family members and clients and offer numerous resources as well.

---

researchers and clinicians must develop and maintain a "socio-cultural framework" (p. 45) and "consider diversity of values, interactional styles, and cultural expectations in a systematic fashion" (p. 45) in their efforts to provide professional psychological service (APA, 1993a). The APA guidelines for 2003 (APA,

2003b) suggest that "psychologists use organizational change processes to support culturally informed organizational (policy) development and practices" (p. 392) and "apply culturally appropriate skills in clinical and other applied psychological practices" (p. 390). Graduate training programs now require coursework on multicultural issues (APA, 2003; Bernal & Castro, 1994; Norcross et al., 2008). Moreover, psychologists must "recognize ethnicity and culture as significant parameters in understanding psychological processes" (APA, 1990, p. 46). Thus, social factors such as ethnicity and culture are now highlighted as critical factors to consider and integrate in clinical psychology. Symptoms occur in the context of culture and thus culture must be understood to understand and treat problems.

Increasing attention and sensitivity toward various ethnic and cultural groups (e.g., African Americans, Mexican Americans, Asian Americans) have also generalized to other non-ethnic minority groups (e.g., gays and lesbians, women, persons with physical disabilities, various religious groups). This development has led to new strategies and methods for helping those with emotional and behavioral concerns among these groups. The traditional 50-minute hour of individual insight-oriented psychotherapy in the psychologist's office may be of limited value for many. Customary methods of conducting research as well as practice must be carefully examined and potentially altered to accommodate people from diverse backgrounds (APA, 1993a, 2003b; Brown, 1990; Cardemil & Battle, 2003; Garb, 1997; Greene, 1993; Hall, 1997; Lopez et al., 1989; D. Sue & D. M. Sue, 2008; Tharp, 1991). The vast majority of studies on psychotherapy outcome have used American, Canadian, or British subjects who tend to be fairly homogeneous in terms of race, income, and background. Since most therapies were developed from research and practice with middle- or upper-economic-level Caucasians, their generalizability to minority groups has been seriously and legitimately questioned (Cardemil & Battle, 2003; Hall, 1997; Landrine, 1992; Lopez et al., 1989; Trickett et al., 1994; D. Sue & D. M. Sue, 2008). For example, psychological treatment integrating traditional ethnic healing methods (e.g., the use of sweat lodges, talking circles) is now advised for many Native Americans (LaFromboise, 1988), and sensitivity to the role of family hierarchy and the "loss of face" (i.e., shamed among others) dynamic

is important for many Asian American clients (Murase, 1977; Sue et al., 1994; D. Sue & D. M. Sue, 2008). Furthermore, researchers and clinicians are more sensitive to the notion that tremendous diversity in perspectives, needs, and issues exists within each ethnic, minority, and religious group (Bernal & Castro, 1994; Fowers & Richardson, 1996; Landrine, 1992; Plante, 2009; Sue et al., 1994; D. Sue & D. Sue, 2008). Therefore, generalizing assessment, treatment, or research strategies to all ethnic or minority groups is inappropriate. Acculturation and assimilation factors as well as unique individual differences must be taken into consideration when working with members of diverse groups (APA, 2003b; Lopez et al., 1989; Roysircar et al., 2003).

More minority representation is needed within the field of psychology to provide better service to minority group members (APA, 2003b; Bernal & Castro, 1994; Hall, 1997; Landrine, 1992; Lopez et al., 1989; D. Sue & D. M. Sue, 2008). Although the United States has become a highly diverse nation, the vast majority of clinical psychologists are Caucasian. For example, fewer than 5% of the clinical psychology division of the APA (Division 12) is Asian, Hispanic, or African American. Of all the psychology doctorates awarded in 2001, fewer than 10% were awarded to ethnic minority group members (APA, 2003b). The APA has thus encouraged graduate training programs to increase minority group representation in graduate and postgraduate (e.g., internship and postdoctoral fellowship) admissions. As a result of these efforts, about 20% of incoming doctoral students in psychology are now ethnic minority group members (APA, 2000b, 2008; Norcross et al., 2008).

Advances in Science, Technology, and Medicine

Recent advances and significant discoveries in science, technology, and medicine have greatly impacted clinical psychology as well as many other fields. News outlets across the country and world report the latest developments in these areas. The enthusiasm generated by these reports typically reinforces the old medical model notion that the mind and body are separate and that biology is at the root of most human behavior. Thus, the biopsychosocial model is challenged by the seventeenth-century medical model even as current scientific advances unfold. The development of Prozac to treat depression, efforts to find the "fat gene" and other behavior-related genes, and medication treatments (e.g., Ritalin) to treat attention deficit disorders are excellent examples demonstrating how scientific advances influence attitudes about mind–body relationships.

Research conducted by pharmaceutical companies as well as by other investigators has resulted in the development of Prozac to treat depression. Prozac was introduced by Eli Lilly in 1986 and quickly became enormously popular. Within ten years of its availability, over 20 million people took Prozac worldwide (Horgan, 1996) and it became the topic of several best-sellers (Kramer, 1993; Wurtzel, 1995). Furthermore, other similar selective serotonin reuptake inhibitors (SSRIs) such as Zoloft and Paxil have also become enormously popular. Pfizer's sales of Zoloft alone are over a billion dollars each year (Valenstein, 2002). Improved medications to treat depression (such as Prozac) and other psychiatric symptoms (e.g., anxiety, bulimia) have fueled support for the biological foundation of many psychological problems. Advocates argue that if medication greatly reduces symptoms of depression or other psychiatric concerns, then biological factors such as chemical imbalances in the brain may be at the root of symptoms. This is faulty thinking. As discussed earlier, medications impacting behavior do not provide a causal link between biological causes of behavior. Contrary to research findings, many maintain the attitude that psychosocial interventions (such as psychotherapy) are of marginal value in comparison with these powerful new medications. The *remedicalization* of psychiatry with increasing emphasis on biological interventions (e.g., medication) and less emphasis on psychosocial treatments (e.g.,

psychotherapy) further diminishes adherence to a more comprehensive biopsychosocial framework (Borrell-Carrió et al., 2004; Fava & Sonino, 2008; Fleck, 1995; Glasser, 2003). Yet, research and new reports that suggest that many of the benefits of the SSRIs and other psychotropic medications are due to placebo effects (especially for mild-to-moderate symptom relief) often temper the enthusiasm for these medications and reinforce the biopsychosocial perspective.

The same trend is illustrated by the treatment of obesity. Scientific efforts to discover the fat gene as well as the development of fat substitutes and surgeries such as stomach stapling reinforce a strictly biological view of obesity and overeating, ignoring the role of psychosocial factors (Belluck, 2005; Bouchard, 1995; Brownell, 2002; Fairburn & Brownell, 2002; Gibbs, 1996; Hsu et al., 2008; Zhang, Proenca, Barone, Leopold, & Friedman, 1994). However, research continues to support the biopsychosocial perspective in obesity treatment (e.g., Belluck, 2005; Brownell, 1991a, 2002; Fairburn & Brownell, 2002; Hsu et al., 2008). The excitement and press attention associated with the Human Genome Project (Collins, 1999) further illustrates the interest in seeing how scientific discoveries impact our understanding of behavioral disease and mental health problems. These advances have many implications for clinical psychology (Masterpasqua, 2009; Plomin & Crabbe, 2000).

Medication treatment for attention deficit hyperactivity disorder (ADHD) provides yet another example of the impact of scientific advances on clinical psychology. Many parents and teachers show more interest in using medication to control the symptoms of ADHD (e.g., impulsivity, distractibility) than in using psychosocial interventions (e.g., parenting skill development, stimulus-control procedures). As in the previous examples, medication treatment for ADHD perpetuates the notion that these symptoms are due solely to biological issues and thus need biological solutions, whereas research continues to support the biopsychosocial perspective (e.g.,

Barkley, 1989, 1996, 2009; Castle et al., 2007; Glasser, 2003).

Technological advances (e.g., computer technology, fax machines, cellular phones, video, electronic mail, Internet, and virtual reality) also have an impact on clinical psychology. For instance, maintaining confidentiality when using computers to keep track of patient information is an important and controversial issue. Potential access to computer files containing sensitive and confidential patient information and the breaking of security codes are of great concern to many. In fact, technology-related confidentiality concerns led to a remarkable change in federal laws in 2003, called the Health Insurance Portability and Accountability Act (HIPAA). This sweeping federal legislation forced all health-care professionals and institutions to revamp the way they secure patient information and obtain patient consent. The use of the Internet (e.g., e-mail, Skype, Facebook) as well as the telephone to conduct psychotherapy or psychological consultation is also controversial (Bloom, 1992; Haas, Benedict, & Kobos, 1996; Jerome & Zaylor, 2000; Kessler, Lewis, Kaur, Wiles, King, Weich, et al., 2009; Maheu & Gordon, 2000; Markowitz, 2008; Roan, 1992; Sleek, 1997). Some argue that the telephone and the Internet may be acceptable avenues for conducting psychological services, while others feel it would be unethical to use these unsecured methods. Some say that telephone or Internet access to psychotherapy might have important advantages such as immediate access to services, privacy, and availability of services for more people, especially those in remote locations (Haas et al., 1996; Jerome & Zaylor, 2000; Kessler et al., 2008; Mermelstein & Holland, 1991; Tausig & Freeman, 1988; Tolmach, 1985). However, others have cautioned that these services may be counterproductive in crisis situations and therefore may be abused (Haas et al., 1996; Maheu & Gordon, 2000; Markowitz, 2008; Nagy, 1987).

Virtual reality has also been used to treat anxiety and other psychological disorders (Binik, Cantor, Ochs, & Meana, 1997;

Coelho, Waters, Hine, & Wallis, 2009; Glantz, Durlach, Barnett, & Aviles, 1996; Powers & Emmelkamp, 2008; Wallach, Safir, & Bar-Zvi, 2009). Patients and therapists can use virtual reality technology in exposure-style treatments. For example, a person with a phobic reaction can visualize the feared object in a realistic yet safe manner using this approach (see Figure 14.1).

Virtual reality has been used to help patients experiencing a variety of problems (most especially fears and phobias) to learn to cope more effectively with their concerns (Annesi, 2001; Coelho et al., 2009; Maltby, Kirsch, Mayers, & Allen, 2002; Powers & Emmelkamp, 2008; Wallach et al., 2009; Weiderhold & Weiderhold, 2000). Today, virtual reality environments have been incorporated into a variety of clinical and everyday settings to improve mental health and enhance wellbeing. For example, by simulating specific environments and images, therapists can use virtual exposure as an adjunct to cognitive-behavioral therapy to help their patients to cope better with phobias, such as airplane, driving, and spider phobias, as well as for posttraumatic stress with returning military veterans (Coelho et al., 2009; Maltby et al., 2002; Powers & Emmelkamp, 2008; Wallach et al., 2009; B. K. Weiderhold & M. D. Weiderhold, 2000). Virtual reality has also been used to help enhance exercise experiences so that people experiencing a virtual walk or bike ride experience positive mood effects with or without actual exercise (Plante, Aldridge, Bogden, & Hanelin, 2003a; Plante et al., 2003b).

Many technological advances have also increased the ability of clinical psychologists to obtain important information about issues of interest. For example, countless Web locations provide information on topics such as mental health resources, self-help newsletters, mental health legal issues, and family issues. The ease of accessing so much information using search engines such as Google can help psychologists maintain state-of-the-art services and use these sites to help their patients.

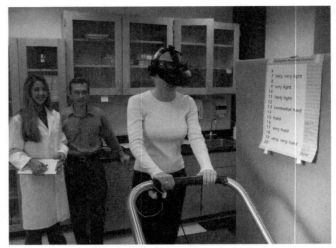

Photo: Courtesy Thomas G. Plante

Figure 14.1

Virtual reality and exercise.

Money

Photo: Courtesy Stockvault.net

During the economic boom of the 1960s and early 1970s, federal money from the NIMH and other government agencies was available to fund clinical psychology research, supplement the expense of training psychologists in graduate and postgraduate programs, and provide services for those in need (e.g., the community mental health movement). During more recent challenging economic times, efforts to reduce costs, to become more efficient, and to decrease services have affected many different segments of society and many different industries. Topics such as downsizing, layoffs, restructuring, and reduction in services have been highlighted on a daily basis across the country. This is especially true after the stock market losses starting in March 2000 and after the September 11, 2001 terrorist attacks on the United States that led to the Afghanistan and Iraq wars as well as the economic collapse in the United States and elsewhere beginning in 2008. Attempts to balance the federal deficit have also resulted in cuts in many programs affecting clinical psychology.

Money (or more specifically, the lack of money) is currently an important issue concerning research, practice, and training in clinical psychology. For over 30 years after World War II, the NIMH awarded generous research and training grants to clinical psychology graduate students, interns, and postdoctoral fellows in order to increase the number of qualified psychologists as well as to advance the science of psychology. In fact, most psychology graduate students in accredited training programs between the end of World War II and 1980 received a NIMH training grant to help pay for their education. Furthermore, generous research grants

Computer Therapy

Given the remarkable involvement of computer technology in so many aspects of contemporary life, can psychological services such as psychotherapy be offered by a computer? Curiously, much recent research has focused on web-based treatment interventions (WBTIs). Most of this research has used empirically supported and highly structured interventions such as smoking cessation, headache control, body image enhancement, diabetes management, and phobia treatment. Most have focused on clinical health psychology issues.

Ritterband and colleagues (2003) have offered a nine-step process in developing quality Internet interventions. These include:

1. Identifying the clinical problem of focus (e.g., anxiety, panic, compulsive behavior).
2. Determining the establishment of effective and established treatment such as empirically supported treatment manuals and protocols.
3. Operationalizing the treatment intervention.
4. Evaluating the potential legal and ethical issues and conflicts.
5. Altering the critical treatment components into engaging Internet components.
6. Personalizing treatment by identifying the aspects that can be individually tailored.
7. Including feedback as a measure of treatment success.
8. Constructing the web-based program.
9. Testing the program and adapting as needed.

Research generally supports the notion that web-based interventions can be effective for very specific symptoms using a step-by-step psychoeducational approach to intervention (Ritterband et al., 2003). The advantage to web-based interventions includes the ability to offer services to people who have access to the Internet anywhere in the world as well as the ability to offer services to those who do not have access or the ability to be treated in a face-to-face manner. For example, someone may be uncomfortable going to the office of a mental health professional or they may live in an isolated rural area too far from professional services. Furthermore, web-based interventions are much less costly than traditional services. Therefore, clients and insurance companies alike might find the low cost especially attractive. Finally, web-based treatment can be used as an adjunct to traditional services. Clients might use the web intervention between scheduled treatment sessions or as homework. Disadvantages or potential problems with computer therapy might include issues related to patient privacy and credentialing of professionals offering these services.

It is not always easy to manage confidentiality while using computers, and private information could find its way into the hands of those who do not have patient permission to see treatment or clinical records.

(continued)

Professionals offering these services may not be trained mental health professionals and thus they may be unqualified or unlicensed to offer mental health or health-care services to the public. Additionally, web-based treatments may not allow for the unique and individual approach that occurs in a face-to-face encounter with a client and a treating professional.

While computer therapy will unlikely replace the need and desire for the human connection that traditional psychotherapy offers, it clearly has a role in helping those who may need services but who would otherwise not get them due to access, costs, and other factors.

---

were awarded to psychologists in university and hospital settings to support research efforts. During the early years of the Reagan administration, when the government tried to cut federal spending, these grants were quickly decreased and ultimately eliminated. Federal grants to support behavioral science research have also dwindled significantly in recent years. Only about 15% of federal grant applications are funded (National Institutes of Health, 2004).

In 1995, the National Science Foundation (NSF) proposed that all behavioral science funding be eliminated. Reductions in financial support mean that the ability to conduct quality psychological research is much more challenging. Furthermore, reductions in federal money mean fewer jobs for psychologists and fewer clinical services in many settings such as VA hospitals, community mental health clinics, and state and county hospitals.

Financial constraints have also resulted in more debt among clinical psychology students. The median level of debt among new professionals with doctorates in applied psychology such as clinical psychology is $67,000 (APA, 2003b; Li, Wicherski, & Kohout, 2008). Federal grant support is available for only a minority of these new professionals; thus, they must use their own (or their family's) financial resources as well as student loans to pay for graduate training. In fact, 70% of all graduates report being in debt (APA, 2003b). The median starting salary for doctorates in clinical psychology is only about $50,000 (APA,

2001; Li et al., 2008). Modest starting salaries in combination with large educational debts can lead to a high degree of stress for many new psychologists.

Gender Shifts in Professions

Over the past several decades, more and more women have entered traditionally male professions such as law, psychology, business, and medicine (Denmark, 1994; Pion et al., 1996). This trend has been especially true in applied areas of psychology such as clinical psychology (Norcross et al., 2008; Pion et al., 1996; Snyder et al., 2000; Wicherski, Michalski, & Kohout, 2009). Whereas about 51% of APA members are men, the majority (about 75%) of new doctorates in clinical psychology are now awarded to women (Wicherski et al, 2009). Between 1973 and 1991, the number of men who entered the field of psychology rose by 130%, whereas the number of women choosing psychology as a career increased by 530% (APA, 1995c; NSF, 1994). Although most of the doctorates in clinical psychology were awarded to men in 1971 (74%) and 1981 (55%), the proportion dropped to only 36% by 1991 (Pion et al., 1996) and 30% in 1997 (APA, 1997) and is now under 25% (Wicherski et al, 2009). The percentage of female clinical psychologists has more than doubled between 1960 and 2008 (Norcross et al., 2008). These trends are also evident at the bachelor's degree level. In 1970, 43% of bachelor degrees in psychology were awarded

Highlight of a Contemporary Clinical Psychologist

Aisha Laureen Hamdan, PhD

Birth Date: September 14, 1964

College: Oklahoma State University (BS, Psychology), 1986; Minnesota State University (BS, Business Administration–International Business), 1987; American Open University (Bachelor's degree, Islamic Studies), 2005

Graduate Program: Minnesota State University (MA, Clinical Psychology), 1990; West Virginia University (PhD, Child Clinical Psychology), 1994

Clinical Internship: Meyer Rehabilitation Institute, University of Nebraska Medical Center and Boys Town, Omaha, Nebraska, 1993–1994

Current Job(s): Assistant Professor of Behavioral Sciences, Department of Family and Community Medicine and Behavioral Sciences, College of Medicine, University of Sharjah, United Arab Emirates

Pros and Cons of Being a Clinical Psychologist:

Pros: "Possessing a doctorate degree in clinical psychology opens up a world of opportunities, from teaching to clinical work to administration to consultancy. It offers the possibility of serving people, which is the primary reason that most people enter the field. The rewards are immense, whether they emerge from working with patients, students, other professionals, or communities. It truly is one of the most fulfilling fields to be in."

Cons: "The work can be very stressful at times, depending on the setting. At the university, there is a great deal of pressure to publish in quality journals in order to obtain promotion. Research takes time, which is not always available due to heavy course loads and administrative responsibilities. Stress management is an important component in coping."

Your Specialty and How You Chose It: "For some reason I was destined by Allah to be a clinical psychologist since I had some sort of premonition at the age of 13 years (I remember doing a career project in school and drawing pictures of work as a clinical psychologist). I was always interested in understanding how people think, feel, and act, particularly in relation to deviant or unusual behavior. I had originally planned to do clinical work, but later developed a love for teaching and mentoring students."

Future of Clinical Psychology: "In the United Arab Emirates, there is a strong future for clinical psychology. Although traditionally there has been stigma related to seeking professional help for personal problems, this seems to be changing to some degree. There also has been an increase in problems within families and communities due to the rapid economic transition that has occurred. This has led to some tension between traditional values and 'modern' expectations."

Typical Schedule:

9:00	Review session with year-one students.
10:00	Problem-based learning session with year-one students.
11:00	Problem-based learning session with year-one students.
12:00	Lecture preparation for year one.
1:00	Lunch.
2:00	Grant writing for research project.
3:00	Lecture for year two.
4:00	Meeting with students or faculty meeting.
5:00	Journal article writing/editorial review.

Note: A photo of Dr. Hamdan is absent due to religious reasons. It is forbidden in Islam to draw or make pictures of anything with a soul, unless for official or educational purposes. The photo presented here is of the university where she works.

---

to women; by 1991, about 75% of these degrees were awarded to women (NSF, 1994). By 2000, the number approached 80% (APA Research Office, 2000). Overall, women in clinical psychology outnumber men by about a 2.5-to-1 ratio (Snyder et al., 2000) and growing (Wicherski et al., 2009).

Many have suggested that the gender shift in psychology is a positive trend resulting in more professional sensitivity to women's issues (Denmark, 1994; Pion et al., 1996; Plante et al., 1998; Snyder et al., 2000). An increase in diversity adds new perspectives, awareness, and approaches to any field. Professions and services are enriched when people of gender, ethnicity, religious persuasion, and other differences enter the discipline. Furthermore, an increase in diversity allows more choice for those seeking psychological services as well as role models for students interested in the field (Denmark, 1994; Snyder et al., 2000). However, many people of both genders are concerned that the shift from a male-dominated to a female-dominated profession might mean that clinical psychology could be devalued in status and perceived importance, resulting in lower salaries (Goodheart & Markham, 1992; Snyder et al., 2000).

Research Issues

Research in clinical psychology has evolved beyond attempts to answer fairly simple and straightforward questions examining main effects. For example, research questions such as "Does psychotherapy work better than no treatment?" have been duly addressed. We know that psychotherapy does indeed work and that psychological interventions from a biopsychosocial perspective appear to be superior to no intervention or more limited interventions (e.g., medication alone). Therefore, more complicated and sophisticated research designs and questions are being implemented today. These research questions tend to look for interactions rather than main effects; for example, under which conditions, with which patients, treated by which therapists, and using which techniques will interventions work best.

As clinical psychology has evolved and matured, the need for newer research designs and methodologies has led to a move toward greater methodological pluralism. In addition to traditional research and statistical methods, qualitative, descriptive, and narrative approaches have been used in an attempt to better answer important research questions (Lambert et al., 2004; Prochaska, 2000). Investigating clinical rather than simply statistical significance has also been advanced as a more useful way to make sense of research data (Kazdin & Weisz, 2003). The use of effect size and meta-analysis techniques as well as more sophisticated statistical analysis aided by computer technology has increased the utility as well as the complexity of research methodologies and data analysis approaches (Kazdin, 1994; Kazdin & Weisz, 2003).

Cost containment concerns have also led many new research investigations to incorporate cost-effectiveness or cost-benefit analysis into their designs (Newman & Taylor, 1996; Lambert et al., 2004; Yates, 1994). Thus, it is important not only to determine what works and what doesn't work in clinical psychology but also to investigate the cost versus the benefits of assessment, treatment, consultation, and other clinical psychology activities. Recent research has focused on cost-effective, brief, empirically supported treatment, and evidence-based approaches (Barlow, 1996; Hawkins, 2001; Nathan & Gorman, 2007; Norcross, 2002; Rehm, 1997; Schmidt & Taylor, 2002; VandenBos, 1996).

Some authors criticize the historically narrow focus of psychological research, stating that "too many psychologists hug the intellectual shoreline and are content to paddle quietly in their own small ponds" (Bevan, 1991, p. 481) and that psychology is "a collection of studies rather than a coherent discipline" (Schneider, 1996, p. 715). Many authors have argued that psychology research of the future must work harder to answer the "big questions about [the world]" (Bevan, 1991, p. 481). Significant contemporary problems of society such as homelessness, violence, racism, terrorism, and the role of psychology and behavior in diseases such as AIDS and obesity must be better addressed with research. Calls for more creative, risky, and multidisciplinary research have been made by many as well. In the words of Stanley Schneider (1996), "There is almost universal agreement that multidisciplinary approaches are necessary to study contemporary scientific problems" (p. 718) and that "we should think about application, clinical relevance, and policy implications even if we are engaged in the most basic research" (p. 716).

Practice Issues

Managed Health Care and Health-Care Reform

Traditionally, physicians treated patients simply as they saw fit, and medical insurance paid for whatever procedures the doctors ordered. The physician decided what diagnostic and treatment approaches were in the best interest of the patient, and insurance companies supported and funded the physician's discretion in making professional judgments. Lacking medical degrees, clinical psychologists could

not be reimbursed by medical insurance companies. In the 1970s, however, psychologists lobbied state legislatures to pass "freedom-of-choice" laws that would allow anyone who held a license to practice in the mental health field (e.g., psychologists, social workers) to be eligible for medical insurance reimbursement. While physicians vigorously argued that only physicians (such as psychiatrists) should be allowed to treat patients in psychotherapy (and therefore be reimbursed by medical insurance), psychologists successfully argued that a mental health professional did not need to be a physician in order to conduct psychotherapy and other psychological services (e.g., psychological testing, consultation). Now all states and insurance carriers allow for psychologists to provide psychological and other services within the scope of their license and training.

Psychology enjoyed the advantages of freedom-of-choice legislation for about 10 to 20 years (although this timeframe varies significantly from state to state). Psychologists, like physicians, quickly became accustomed to treating patients as they saw fit and having insurance companies reimburse them and their patients for their professional services without question. Thus, psychologists could offer various types of psychotherapy (e.g., psychodynamic, cognitive-behavioral, humanistic, family systems, eclectic) and various types of modalities (e.g., individual, couple, family, group) for any diagnosable problem. Typically, insurance would reimburse 50% to 80% of the fees charged by the psychologist, and patients paid the remaining portion. With these arrangements, psychologists and patients decided on a treatment plan without input from or parameters from other parties such as insurance companies.

These private, fee-for-service insurance arrangements began to change radically during the latter part of the 1980s. Health-care costs rose steadily and dramatically during the 1970s and 1980s. Significant improvements in medical technology, newer and more expensive diagnostic tools such as CT, PET, and MRI scans, as well as newer and more expensive treatments resulted in enormous amounts of costly medical insurance claims. Furthermore, very ill patients could live longer using these newer technologies, so costs continued to escalate for the treatment of chronic and terminal conditions. Medical education and physician salaries continued to rise as well. In fact, health-care costs have increased about 3 times the rate of inflation in recent decades (Cummings, 1995; Resnick & DeLeon, 1995). Americans spend about $3 trillion per year on their health needs, representing over 16% of the gross national product (Centers for Medicare and Medicaid Services, 2009).

These escalating costs have clearly become unacceptable to insurance companies and other organizations (such as government agencies) that pay for medical services. Furthermore, it has been estimated that about $700 billion is wasted each year on unnecessary, ineffective, inappropriate, or fraudulent health care (Graham, 2008). In 1983, Congress passed legislation that initiated a new method of paying hospitals with a fixed and predetermined fee for treating Medicare patients. Under this plan, payment was determined by the patient diagnosis rather than by the actual total cost of treatment. Patients were categorized into diagnosis-related groups (DRGs), and the costs were calculated based on the average cost per patient for a given diagnosis. Thus, a hospital would receive a fixed fee for treating a patient with a particular diagnosis. If the hospital needed more time or money to treat the patient, monies would not be available for the additional services; or if the patient could be treated using less than the designated amount, hospitals would keep the difference to pay for other costs. Following the advent of DRGs in the early and mid-1980s, managed health-care plans such as **health maintenance organizations (HMOs)** and **preferred provider organizations (PPOs)** exploded onto the health-care scene during the late 1980s and the 1990s. The aim of these programs was to provide a more cost-effective way to pay for health services, including those services offered by mental health professionals such as clinical psychologists. While 96% of people

who had health-care insurance still had fee-for-service plans in 1984, only 37% still had these plans by 1990 (Weiner & de Lissovoy, 1993). The number of Americans with fee-for-service plans continues to diminish rapidly (Broskowski, 1995; Cummings, 1995; S. Taylor, 2009) and is almost nonexistent today. Over 75 million Americans belong to a health maintenance organization with about 175 million Americans covered by some form of **managed health care** (Cantor & Fuentes, 2008; Kongstvedt, 2008; Sanderson, 2004).

Contrary to the traditional fee-for-service plan outlined above, an HMO provides comprehensive health (and usually mental health) services within one organization. An employer (or employee) pays a monthly fee to belong to the HMO. Whenever health care is needed, members obtain all their care from the HMO for no additional cost above the monthly membership fee or a small copayment fee (e.g., $20 per office visit). Patients have little or no choice regarding which doctor or other health-care provider can treat them. Furthermore, they must obtain all their services (from flu shots to brain surgery) from health-care professionals working at the HMO. Unlike private practitioners, these providers are paid a yearly salary rather than a certain fee for each patient they treat. In order to be profitable, the HMO must control costs and minimize any unnecessary and expensive services (Kongstvedt, 2008). For example, Cummings (1995) reported that only 38 large HMOs "the size and efficiency of Kaiser-Permanente can treat 250 million Americans with only 290,000 physicians, half the present number, and with only 5% of the gross national product" (p. 13). Thus, it is theoretically possible for physicians and organizations to provide medical services at a fraction of the cost associated with traditional fee-for-service arrangements. The important concern is whether these more efficient services are of high quality and in the best interest of patient care.

A preferred provider organization (PPO) is a compromise between the traditional fee-for-service and the HMO style of health care. A PPO is a network of providers who agree to treat patients affiliated with the PPO network for discounted rates. Therefore, traditional private practice professionals in all medical specialties as well as clinical psychologists and other mental health professionals can choose to apply to be on the PPO network. A patient who is on a PPO plan must be treated by professionals in the community who have agreed to serve on the PPO panel of providers. Furthermore, large health organizations such as clinics and hospitals also may apply to be on the PPO network panel. The PPO network and the providers of professional services (including hospitals) agree to set fees for various types of professional services such as surgery, office visits, and psychotherapy. A patient who needs services may contact one of a number of hospitals, clinics, or private practice providers. Some of the services, however, still need to be authorized by the PPO network organization before they can be guaranteed payment. Thus, permission is needed by the insurance company before many major diagnostic or treatment services can be offered by any provider on the panel.

With the advent of HMOs and PPOs, spiraling health-care costs and some unnecessary procedures have been better contained. The HMO and PPO companies determine, along with the professional treating a patient, the most cost-effective and reasonable diagnostic or treatment plan to follow. Therefore, the insurance companies paying for physical and mental health-care services now have an important vote in the types of services that can be rendered. Some arguments have been made that ultimately these changes in managed health care do not save money (Fraser, 1996, Kongstvedt, 2008; S. Taylor, 2009). In fact, some argue that the monies going to health care have shifted from hospitals and providers to the managed care insurance industry. Evidence that the managed care insurance industry is one of the most profitable industries in the United States, with CEOs and other top executives enjoying salaries of over $6 million per year, supports this claim (Matthews, 1995). California HMOs made over $4 billion in profit in 2008 alone (California Medical Association, 2008).

Generally, providers and patients are not as satisfied with these managed care programs as are those very few who still can use fee-for-service professionals. While costs are theoretically contained in managed care models, freedom of choice for both patient and provider is strictly controlled. A survey of over 42,000 *Consumer Reports* readers found lukewarm satisfaction with their managed health-care plans, with an overall satisfaction score of 73 (out of 100), representing less satisfaction compared to their other insurance policies such as home and car (*Consumer Reports*, 2003). These survey results have raised concerns about the quality of service provided by managed health care. Managed care companies now routinely survey their members concerning client satisfaction and have done so for some time (Broskowski, 1995 Kongstvedt, 2008). The need for accountability has also resulted in the requirement that managed care organizations routinely report information on "9 quality of care indicators, over 60 usage indicators, measures of access to care and member satisfaction, and over 12 indicators of financial performance" (Broskowski, 1995 p. 160). This information is part of what is called the HEDIS Report (Corrigan & Nielson, 1993; National Committee for Quality Assurance, 2009).

Psychologists and other mental health professionals tend to be unhappy with managed health care (Anders, 1996; Cantor & Fuentes, 2008; Davenport & Woolley, 1997; Fox, 1994; Fraser, 1996; Karon, 1995; Murphy, DeBernardo, & Shoemaker, 1998; Newman & Taylor, 1996; Phelps, 1996; Phelps, Eisman, & Kohout, 1998; Saeman, 1996a, b) and have even formed special-interest groups to curtail its impact and abuses (e.g., the National Coalition of Mental Health Professionals and Consumers). A survey of over 14,000 members of the APA revealed that 78% of the group felt that managed care had a negative impact on their professional work, with only 10.4% reporting a positive impact (Phelps, 1996). A survey of over 200 diplomates in clinical

Clinical Psychology as a Primary Care Profession

During the past 100 years, clinical psychology has been seen as a mental health profession. This is changing with the notion that clinical psychology can actually be considered a primary care or general health-care profession that well integrates both mental health and physical health-care problems using the biopsychosocial model to guide assessment, treatment, and consultation (Cummings, O'Donohue, & Ferguson, 2003; Johnson, 2003). The APA mission statement recently was altered to reflect this new perspective on the role of psychology as a health-care profession (N. Johnson, 2003). As mentioned earlier, at least 50% of deaths are due to lifestyle and behavioral factors such as poor diet, lack of exercise, smoking cigarettes, drinking alcohol to excess, driving accidents, homicide, suicide, and so forth (Institute of Medicine, 2001; S. Taylor, 2009). Furthermore, the top medical complaints reported by patients seeking medical treatment include aches and pains, psychological and behavioral problems, and illnesses that have an important behavioral component to the etiology and maintenance (Cummings et al., 2003). Additionally, most patients seeking primary care attention have significant family, financial, school, or work stressors that impact their symptoms and illnesses (Cummings et al., 2003; S. Taylor, 2009). Therefore, many have called for a more active role of psychology to assist in primary health care. For example, a series of multidisciplinary conferences have been held at the University of Nevada, Reno, funded by the Nicholas and Dorothy Cummings Foundation, to help articulate how psychology can be put to better use in the primary care environment.

psychology from the American Board of Professional Psychology revealed that over 90% felt that managed health care was a negative and problematic trend (Plante, Boccaccini, & Andersen, 1998). In another national survey, 49% of 718 psychologists surveyed reported that their patients were negatively impacted by managed care that delayed or denied services while 90% reported that managed care reviewers interfered with appropriate treatment (Tucker & Lubin, 1994). Other surveys have demonstrated that psychologists generally feel that managed health care has requested that practitioners compromise professional ethics to contain costs (Murphy et al., 1998). Other surveys have found that dealing with managed care insurance leads to burnout and is the most stressful part of being a mental

health professional (Cantor & Fuentes, 2008; Rupert & Baird, 2004). The former president of the American Psychiatric Association, Harold Eist, has stated, ''We are under attack by a rapacious, dishonest, disruptive, greed-driven insurance-managed care big business combine that is in the process of decimating all health care in America, but most egregiously, the care of the mentally ill'' (Saeman, 1996a). The mental health professional's deep discontent with managed care stems from several concerns. First, all professional decisions (such as type and frequency of therapy services) must be authorized by the managed care insurance company. The cases must go through utilization review, which means that a representative of the insurance company reviews the services and plans of the professional before authorization for services can occur. Often the insurance agent with whom the psychologist works in this regard is not a licensed mental health professional and may not even have a college education. Therefore, many psychologists resent that they must "sell" their treatment plans to someone who is not as well trained in providing professional services. Furthermore, many feel that these reviewers are primarily interested in minimizing costs for the insurance company rather than being concerned about what is in the best interest of the patient (Anders, 1996; Kongstvedt, 2008; Rupert & Baird, 2004).

Second, concerns about patient confidentiality have arisen. Details about the patient must be disclosed in order to obtain authorization for services. Many mental health professionals (as well as patients) feel that their confidentiality is compromised by informing the insurance company about intimate details of the patient's life and problems. Many patients fear that this information might be misused or provided to their employer.

Third, many psychologists feel overwhelmed by the paperwork that is required of managed care providers. In addition to lengthy application forms for each separate panel to which the professional belongs (copies of malpractice insurance, license, transcripts from all professional training, updated curriculum vitae, documentation of medical staff affiliations), other lengthy forms often need to be completed after each session with a patient.

Fourth, many psychologists resent having to accept significant reductions in their typical fees for managed care patients. For example, a psychologist might charge $150 per hour for services, but in order to be admitted to a PPO panel, he or she might have to accept a $70-per-hour rate. Furthermore, the additional paperwork and time on the telephone for authorization and utilization review is not reimbursed.

Fifth, psychologists (and patients) often feel that too few sessions are authorized by the managed care company (Murphy et al.,

1998). For example, only 3 or 5 sessions might be authorized for services. Many psychologists feel that patients who truly need more services are being denied access to treatment (Phelps et al., 1998) and reimbursement for psychological testing is rarely available (Rupert & Baird, 2004). And finally, many psychologists resent having someone tell them how they should treat their patients. For example, a managed care company might urge the psychologist to have the patient enter group rather than individual therapy in order to save costs, given the typically lower fee for group as opposed to individual treatment.

Furthermore, many psychologists are concerned about the growing use of capitation methods by managed care companies. The capitation program is similar to the DRG program already outlined. In a capitation program, the insurance company will pay a set fee for the treatment of a given patient no matter what treatment or how many sessions are required. For example, when a managed care insurance company refers a patient to a practitioner, the company may pay $300 for whatever services are needed. If services can be provided within one to three sessions, the practitioner covers his or her costs. If many more services are needed (e.g., 20 sessions), the professional loses a good deal of time and income. Many managed care companies have thus transferred the risks of expensive services from the insurance company to the practitioner. In the words of Bertram Karon, "What started reasonably is becoming a national nightmare" (Karon, 1995, p. 5).

Some psychologists, however, have noted that managed care offers a variety of hidden benefits (Anonymous, 1995; Bobbitt, 2006; Chambless, 2000; Clement, 1996; Hayes, 1996). For example, justifying treatment plans to managed care companies encourages professionals to think clearly about how best to treat their patients in a cost-effective manner, keeping their clinical skills sharp and motivation for success high. Furthermore, managed care promotes interdisciplinary collaboration by forcing professionals to work with other professionals (such as physicians) also treating a given patient as well as with professionals representing the managed care company. Finally, managed health care demands that professionals be held more accountable for everything they do and for the price of their services. These changes have encouraged psychologists and other professionals to use empirically supported treatment and evidence-based approaches as well as brief, problem-focused treatments (APA, 2006; Barlow, 1996; Bickman, 1996; Bobbitt, 2006; Chambless, 2000; Clarke, Lynch, Spofford, & DeBar, 2006; Clement, 1996; Hayes, 1996; Lambert et al., 2004; Norcross et al., 2005; Rehm, 1997; Speer & Newman, 1996).

What is the future of managed health care and what will be the role of clinical psychology in the future marketplace? These are difficult questions to answer. However, it appears clear that clinical psychology must adjust to these rapid changes in the health-care delivery and reimbursement system or be excluded from them. However, many psychologists have decided to opt out of managed care altogether (Cantor & Fuentes, 2008). Kiesler and Morton (1988) predicted "declining provider autonomy, increasing integration of services, increasing emphasis on treatment outcomes, increasing management purview and control . . . and more consumer control via government and administrative decree" (Kiesler & Morton, 1988, p. 997). Many experts (Cantor & Fuentes, 2008; Cummings, 1984, 1995; Kiesler & Morton, 1987, 1988) predict that multidisciplinary group practices that focus on brief, problem-focused, and family-centered treatments with an emphasis on demonstrating effective treatment outcome and client satisfaction will be the future of clinical psychology practice. Others suggest that services will focus on self-help, will be delivered in primarycare environments, and will force providers to demonstrate quality improvement in order to get paid at all (Clarke et al., 2006). Some, however, have suggested that psychologists should no longer participate in the health-care and managed health-care systems and return to fee-for-service approaches such as those used by attorneys and accountants (Kovacs,

1996; Murphy et al., 1998). Kovacs (1996), for example, states that, "the best hope we confront as a group of professionals is for us to remain in traditional independent practice and to leave the health-care delivery system entirely" (p. 14). Clinical psychologists can likely expect an era of increased accountability along with many restrictions and limits on the types and length of services they provide (Cantor & Fuentes, 2008; Clarke et al., 2006).

Prescription Privileges

Historically, psychiatrists have been the only mental health professionals legally allowed to prescribe medication for their patients. Curiously, however, any physician from any specialty area (e.g., cardiology, urology, internal medicine) may legally prescribe psychotropic medications even if the physician lacks mental health training or experience. In fact, the majority (approximately 80%) of psychotropic medications prescribed to alleviate anxiety and depression are prescribed by general family practice or internal medicine physicians and not by psychiatrists (DeLeon & Wiggins, 1996). Although a number of psychologists actively conduct research on the neurobiology and psychopharmacology of behavior, and approximately two-thirds of graduate training programs in psychology offer psychopharmacology courses to their students (Popanz, 1991), psychologists have obtained legal permission to prescribe medications to the public in only a few locations (e.g., Guam, New Mexico, Louisiana).

A highly controversial issue facing clinical psychology is the possibility of obtaining the legal and professional ability to prescribe psychotropic medications in all states (Ax, Fagan, & Resnick, 2009; Fox, DeLeon, Newman, Sammons, Dunivin, & Baker, 2009). The APA, after careful study, has supported efforts to develop a curriculum to adequately train psychologists in psychopharmacology and to lobby state legislative groups across the country to pass laws allowing psychologists to prescribe medications (APA, 1992b; Cullen, 1998; DeLeon, Dunivin, & Newman, 2002; Fox et al., 2009; Martin, 1995; Resnick & Norcross, 2002; Smyer et al., 1993).

During the past several decades, there has been an explosion of research on the effects of various medications on psychiatric problems such as anxiety, depression, impulsivity, and thought disturbance. New and effective medications have become available to assist those experiencing a wide range of emotional and behavioral problems. For example, the development and popularity of Prozac, Zoloft, Paxil, and other SSRIs have led numerous people to become interested in using these drugs to combat depression and other problematic symptoms such as anxiety and bulimia. Additionally, the influence of alcohol, cocaine, nicotine, and other substances on behavior (such as substance abuse, domestic violence, and crime) continues to be a major issue for all health-care and mental health professionals. These substance abuse problems are often treated with medications such as antabuse for alcohol addiction and methadone for heroin addiction. Advances in the development and availability of psychotropic medication as well as the influence of substance use and abuse on behavior have set the stage for the controversial issue of prescription privileges for psychologists. Furthermore, as more integrative and biopsychosocial perspectives replace traditional one-dimensional theoretical models (e.g., psychodynamic, behavioral) of diagnosis and treatment, biological and medication issues become increasingly relevant for practicing psychologists.

Prescription privileges for psychologists is a hotly debated topic both within and outside the profession. For example, both the American Medical Association and the American Psychiatric Association are adamantly opposed to allowing psychologists the privilege of prescribing medication (American Medical Association, 1984; American Psychiatric Association, 2003; Klusman, 1998). A survey of approximately 400 family practice physicians revealed strong opposition to psychologists obtaining prescription privileges (Bell, Digman,

& McKenna, 1995). They claim that a medical degree is necessary to competently administer medications that deal with the complexities of mind–body interactions. Even many psychologists are opposed to having psychologists prescribe medication for their patients (DeNelsky, 1991, 1996; Hayes & Chang, 2002; Hayes & Heiby, 1996; Heiby, 2002). Some are concerned that allowing psychologists to prescribe medication would distract them from their traditional focus on non-biological emotional and behavioral interventions (e.g., psychotherapy, education; DeNelsky, 1996; Hayes & Chang, 2002; Hayes & Heiby, 1996). Some have argued that by obtaining prescription privileges psychology would lose its unique identity and psychologists would become "junior psychiatrists" (DeNelsky, 1996, p. 208; Lorion, 1996). Finally, many are concerned about the practical problems associated with prescription privileges such as sizable increases in the costs of malpractice insurance or the increased influence of pharmaceutical companies on the field of psychology (Hayes & Heiby, 1996).

On the other hand, many have argued for the development of prescription privileges for psychologists (Ax, Fagan, & Resnick, 2009; Brentar & McNamara, 1991; Cullen, 1998; Cullen & Newman, 1997; DeLeon, 1993; DeLeon et al., 2002; DeLeon, Fox, & Graham, 1991; DeLeon & Wiggins, 1996; Fox et al., 2009; Fox, Schwelitz, & Barclay, 1992; Klein, 1996; Welsh, 2003). Some of these outspoken supporters have been physicians (Victoroff, 2002). The majority of clinical psychologists support prescription privileges (Ax et al., 2009; Fox et al., 2009; Frederick/ Schneiders, 1990; Pimental, Stout, Hoover, & Kamen, 1997; Sammons, Gorny, Zinner, & Allen, 2000; Welsh, 2003). Furthermore, about half of all graduate students in clinical psychology wish to be able to prescribe medication, with the majority wanting the option available for the profession (Smith, 1992). Proponents argue that with appropriate and intensive training for those who wish to prescribe medications, psychologists would be excellent candidates to provide psychotropic medications for patients (Cullen &

Training for Psychologists Interested in Psychopharmacology

The APA's guidelines for training in psychopharmacology are divided into three levels depending on the level of involvement and independence a psychologist would like to have in potentially administering psychotropic medications (APA, 1996; DeLeon & Wiggins, 1996).

Level 1 is a basic psychopharmacology level of training to be provided to all clinical psychology graduate students. This level of training would help future psychologists learn about the issues in psychopharmacology but would not result in them securing prescription privileges. Even if they never prescribe medications, it is still important to have a good understanding of how and why they might work (or not work) in order to help those with whom they work. A biopsychosocial perspective demands an integrative level of understanding regardless of the ability to actually prescribe medicines.

Level 2 is focused on a collaborative practice with medical providers such as physicians so that psychologists would work closely with other medical professionals but, again, would not be prescribing medications on their own.

Finally, level 3 would provide education for the independent prescribing authority of medications. This training would be conducted at the postdoctoral level among those already licensed as a psychologist and who have five years of practice experience.

Therefore, not all psychologists would pursue this level of independence and thus complete the training process. Those who do would then be able to prescribe psychotropic medications in states that allow them to do so.

The psychopharmacology training would require both classroom and clinical practice training with instructors who have the appropriate training and experience in physiology, biochemistry, neuroscience, pharmacology, pharmacy, medicine, and psychology. The training would consist of a minimum of 300 contact hours of didactic classroom instruction, which would highlight five content areas:

1. Neuroscience
2. Clinical and research pharmacology and psychopharmacology
3. Physiology and pathophysiology
4. Physical and laboratory assessment
5. Clinical pharmacotherapeutics

The clinical practicum experience would involve treating (with very close supervision) at least 100 diverse inpatients and outpatients with at least two hours per week of individual supervision.

Following both the didactic and clinical training experiences, these psychologist trainees would also need to pass examinations developed by the APA College of Professional Psychology in 10 content areas (e.g., nervous system pathology, physiology, and pathophysiology).

The APA training model for prescription privileges is actually more extensive than those used for physicians in medical school. The number of classroom and practicum hours of specific training in pharmacology would be greater than for physicians.

Currently, level 3 training programs are offered in 12 states while 9 state licensing boards have formally endorsed the notion that consultation on psychopharmacologic drugs is within the scope of practice for psychologists.

The APA supports these initiatives and refers to the biopsychosocial model to justify the need to be more holistic in the manner in which psychologists conduct their work. In the words of APA president Robert Sternberg, ". . . the biopsychosocial model adopted by many psychologists is consistent with an integration of these kinds of treatments" (Sternberg, 2003, p. 5).

Newman, 1997; Lorion, 1996; Sammons et al., 2000; Smyer et al., 1993; Welsh, 2003), including the underserved populations (e.g., the elderly, the military, people with low-socioeconomic status, and people who live in rural areas) who have little opportunity to be treated by a psychiatrist (Brentar & McNamara, 1991; DeLeon, 2003; DeLeon & Wiggins, 1996; Smith, 1992). Many point out that other non-physicians (e.g., nurse practitioners, optometrists, podiatrists, dentists) already have the appropriate training and legal authority to prescribe a limited array of medications. Advanced nurse practitioners and optometrists have prescription privileges in all 50 states, while physician assistants can legally prescribe medication in 48 states (Holloway, 2004). Because medical schools in the United States typically spend only an average of 104 hours of classroom instruction on pharmacology (Holloway, 2004), psychologists have argued that obtaining a medical degree is not necessarily needed to prescribe medications if sufficient and specific training is available. Despite the advantage of no longer having to send patients to other professionals for medication, psychologists generally tend to have mixed feelings about obtaining prescription privileges and thus are not uniformly in favor of it (Boswell & Litwin, 1992; DeNelsky, 1996; Evans & Murphy, 1997; Hayes & Heiby, 1996; Heiby, 2003; Plante et al., 1997).

The Task Force on Psychopharmacology of the APA (Smyer et al., 1993) has outlined a curriculum for psychologists who are interested in being trained to prescribe medication. The program includes basic psychopharmacology education, collaborative practice, and, finally, prescription privilege. The basic psychopharmacology education would offer 26 graduate credits (390 lecture hours) of biochemistry, physiology, pharmacology, biological bases of behavior, and other relevant topics. Collaborative practice would follow a consultation-liaison model in which the psychologist would work closely with a skilled licensed professional in managing the integration of medications and psychosocial interventions for patients with a range of psychiatric problems. The prescription privilege endorsed by the Task Force would involve a limited-practitioner approach similar to that of dentists. Thus, psychologists would be able to prescribe medications for problems in which they specialize, such as anxiety, depression, and thought disorders. The Task Force also recommended mandatory postdoctoral supervised experience and training and continuing education training.

In 1991, the U.S. Department of Defense under the Civilian Health and Medical Program of the Uniformed Service (CHAMPUS) program developed a psychopharmacology training program for several psychologists at the postdoctoral level (Sammons & Brown, 1997). After several years of study, these psychologists have been allowed to prescribe medications for patients in the military. The success of this program has led to further enthusiasm for the development of prescription privileges for psychologists outside the military environment. By 1998, legislation for psychology prescription privileges was introduced in six states, including California, Florida, Hawaii, Louisiana, Missouri, and Tennessee (Cullen, 1998). In 2001, New Mexico became the first state to allow psychologists prescription privileges (Beutler, 2002; DeLeon et al., 2002). Louisiana became the second state to award these privileges to psychologists in 2004 (Holloway, 2004). Legislation is now pending in Georgia, Illinois, Hawaii, and Tennessee.

Medical Staff Privileges

Historically, only physicians were allowed to treat patients independently in a hospital setting and serve on the medical staff of a hospital. **Medical staff privileges** allowed a physician to admit and discharge patients as needed as well as organize or manage the treatment plan of patients while hospitalized. Therefore, if a psychologist was treating a patient in an outpatient environment (such as a community mental health clinic or in private practice) who then later required hospitalization, the psychologist would have to turn the hospital portion of the care over to a physician (such as a psychiatrist), who would admit, discharge, and direct treatment. The psychologist would be allowed to see the hospitalized patient only as a visitor (just like family members) and not as a professional. The psychologist also could not offer treatment services (such as psychotherapy) while the patient was in the hospital setting.

Psychologists have been interested in obtaining medical staff privileges to provide independent inpatient care for their patients. Many psychologists feel that physicians (such as psychiatrists) do not need to supervise their

work in hospital settings. Physicians, however, have generally opposed medical staff privileges for psychologists (American Medical Association, 1984). After years of legislative advocacy and activity, many clinical psychologists have obtained full medical staff privileges in the United States. Yet, many hospital-affiliated psychologists continue to struggle to maintain autonomous status within hospital settings (Rabasca, 1999). In 1978, legislation was passed allowing psychologists to be able to obtain medical staff privileges independently in California. However, many hospitals and physician groups fought the legislation. A past president of the American Psychiatric Association stated that it was a "dangerous trend" for psychologists to obtain hospital staff appointments (Fink, 1986, p. 816). The American Medical Association also passed a resolution stating that they must "fight incursions of nurse midwives, podiatrists, nurse practitioners, physician's assistants, psychologists . . . into medical practice via prescribing privileges, independent practice, mandated third-party reimbursement or other expansion of their scope of practice" (American Medical Association, 1984, p. 79). In 1990, the *CAPP v. Rank* lawsuit in California upheld the hospital privilege statute for psychologists. Since that time, many states have enacted similar legislation.

Private Practice

The number of clinical psychologists choosing to work in full-time or part-time **private practice** has grown steadily in the past several decades. Currently, about 35% to 40% of clinical psychologists primarily work in solo or group private practices (APA, 2000; Newman & Taylor, 1996; Norcross, Karg, & Prochaska, 1997a; Norcross et al., 2002, 2005, 2008; Phelps, 1996; U. S. Bureau of Labor Statistics, 2009). Over two-thirds of clinical psychologists maintain at least some part-time private practice activities (Kohout, Wicherski, Popanz, & Pion, 1990; Norcross et al., 1997a, 2002, 2005, 2008). This proportion represents a 47% increase since 1973 (Garfield & Kurtz, 1974;

Norcross et al., 1997a, 2002, 2005). While survey results have revealed a larger and larger percentage of clinical psychologists conducting at least part-time private practice activities, experts generally now predict that this trend might reverse itself owing to the changes in the health-care delivery and insurance reimbursement systems (Broskowski, 1995; Cummings, 1995; Fox, 1994). For example, a survey of over 15,000 members of the APA revealed that over 40% of practitioners who obtained their license prior to 1980 were working in solo independent practice, compared with only about 30% of those who obtained their license after 1990 (Newman & Taylor, 1996). Managed health care has made it increasingly difficult to develop and maintain an independent practice in clinical psychology. In the words of Russ Newman, former director of the Practice Directorate of the APA, "It is going to be very difficult to continue as a solo practitioner in the integrated marketplace of the future" (Nickelson, 1995, p. 367).

Managed care companies, in their efforts to provide cost-effective services, have looked to master's degree–trained counselors as a lower-cost alternative to clinical psychologists. Furthermore, the companies are less likely to pay for services that traditionally have been an integral part of a psychologist's independent practice (e.g., long-term insight-oriented psychotherapy). Managed care companies often find it more convenient and cost effective to work with large multidisciplinary health-care facilities rather than a host of independent practitioners. In fact, some authors have suggested that solo private practice might no longer exist within the next several years. In the words of Nicholas Cummings, "the golden era of clinical psychology is over" (Cummings, 1984, p. 19). Large multidisciplinary group practices offering a range of services that are solution-focused and based on solid treatment-outcome research are most likely to develop (Cummings, 1995), perhaps ushering in a different type of golden age that more efficiently addresses patient problems. However, others believe that there will always be room for private practitioners and that many of the pessimistic concerns about the end of private practice have not materialized (Norcross et al., 2005, 2008; U. S. Bureau of Labor Statistics, 2009).

Specialization

With advances in research and practice, the need for **specialization** in clinical psychology has become apparent. A general clinical psychologist, like a general practice physician, is likely to have significant limitations in terms of the depth the professional can provide in certain areas of practice and research. As clinical psychology has evolved and more and more information on human behavior has become available, practitioners have endeavored to specialize in areas such as neuropsychology, geropsychology, brief treatments, health psychology, infant psychology, and forensic psychology. Furthermore, efforts to subspecialize (e.g., pediatric neuropsychology versus geriatric neuropsychology) have begun. In fact the American Board of Professional Psychology (ABPP) has increased the number of specialization diplomate categories from four to nine within several years, reflecting the increased number of psychologists specializing in various areas. Some have expressed concern about overspecialization and loss of valuable general skills (Matarazzo, 1987; Plante, 1996b), arguing that it is important for psychologists to realize that there is only one psychology, with many different applications.

Specialization has also resulted in further certification requirements for psychologists. For example, Division 40 (Neuropsychology) and Division 38 (Health Psychology) have developed guidelines regarding the appropriate training and experience necessary to specialize in these areas. The potential access to prescription privileges in the future will create yet another new specialty area for psychologists. The APA has developed a "college" that educates and certifies psychologists in subspecialty areas such as alcohol and substance abuse. Thus, a generic psychologist license no longer allows someone to practice in all areas of professional practice.

Confidentiality and the New HIPAA Law

Confidentiality is at the cornerstone of clinical psychology regarding work with clients, patients, research subjects, consultees, and others. In order for psychologists to do the kind of work that they do in varied settings, they must be able to assure that what they hear will be kept confidential. Of course, there are several legal and ethical limits to confidentiality (e.g., issues of child abuse or neglect and serious and immediate danger to self and others). Maintaining confidentiality in an electronic world is often challenging because it is hard to control who has access to e-mail, faxes, telephone voice mail, and other methods of transmitting information. Health-care information is increasingly being shared between patients, doctors, health-care administrative staff (e.g., secretaries, accountants, and insurance representatives), financial professionals, attorneys, and so forth who use electronic methods (e.g., e-mail, web-based billing) for communication.

The federal government passed an important law in 1996 that addressed patient privacy and confidentiality for all health-care customers and practitioners. The Health Insurance Portability and Accountability Act (HIPAA) was a bipartisan piece of legislation that was sponsored by Democrats Edward Kennedy (MA) and Nancy Kassebaum (KS) and was signed into law during August 1996. The bill was initiated to protect people from losing their health insurance when they changed their jobs or residences. Congress was hoping to develop standard methods for the electronic transmission of protected health-care information. In order for this to be accomplished, it needed better protections for privacy and security. The Department of Health and Human Services then developed rules for securing the confidential information associated with patient health information.

This law took effect on April 14, 2003. HIPAA provides sweeping privacy protections and patient rights regarding the use and disclosure of patient protected health information (PHI). PHI, such as medical charts that include diagnoses and treatment plans and other relevant health-care information, is used for treatment, payment, and health-care operations. HIPAA requires that all health-care professionals (including clinical psychologists) provide their patients or clients with a Notice of Privacy Practices (the Notice) for use and disclosure of PHI for treatment, payment, and health-care operations. The Notice explains HIPAA and its application to health information in greater detail.

The purpose of the law is to help the public maintain confidential health and mental health information in an increasingly electronic age. Psychologists (and other health-care providers) must use mandated consent forms and follow very specific procedures about what can and what cannot be written in patient documents or charts. Furthermore, the law stipulates how information can be shared with insurance companies, managed care companies, and others who must have access to patient health-care information. The law forces all health-care professionals to be compliant with these guidelines or face severe financial and other penalties.

In addition to the privacy rules that became effective on April 14, 2003, new security rules that provide standards for health-care office access, use of files and computers, and managing patient information became effective during April 2005. These rules provide detailed guidelines about how patient information should be stored and secured and who may or may not have access to these records.

Empirically Supported Treatments and Evidence-Based Practice

Historically, psychologists and other providers of professional psychological services could evaluate and treat each patient as they saw fit. They could choose to use any treatment strategies, theoretical orientations, and methods that they felt were clinically indicated. Treatment could be short or long, insight oriented or behavior-change oriented, and conducted with or without research support. But the drastic changes in health care as well as advances in clinical research findings using randomized clinical trials have forced mental health professionals to examine more closely effective treatment outcome and client satisfaction, and have resulted in efforts to use only **empirically supported treatments,** that is, structured and manualized treatment approaches that have substantial empirical research support. Empirically supported treatments have received a great deal of attention and support from the APA and other professional organizations such as the American Psychiatric Association (1996; Duncan et al., 2009; Chambless et al., 1996; Chambless & Ollendick, 2001; Crits-Christoph et al., 1995; Hayes, Follette, Dawes, & Grady, 1995; Levant & Hasan, 2008; Nathan & Gorman, 2007; Rehm, 1997; Sanderson, 1994; Sanderson & Woody, 1995; Wilson, 1997). The clinical psychology division of the APA (Division 12) has been at the forefront in developing guidelines for both researchers and clinicians regarding research-supported empirically validated treatments (Chambless et al., 1996; Chambless & Ollendick, 2001;

Task Force on Promotion and Dissemination of Psychological Procedures, 1995). The APA clinical division was the first to establish a task force, develop criteria, and conduct an exhaustive review of the treatment outcome literature to develop these guidelines. Empirically supported treatment approaches have been developed for a variety of clinical problems (Nathan & Gorman, 2007) such as depression (Cornes & Frank, 1994), anxiety (Newman & Borkovec, 1995), obsessive-compulsive disorder (Foa, 1996), bulimia nervosa (Wilson, 1997), and conduct-disordered children (Feldman & Kazdin, 1995; Kazdin & Weise, 2003). The Appendix at the end of the chapter provides examples of empirically validated treatments for several disorders. Some professionals feel that because individuals are unique and have different personalities, symptoms, and coping resources, it is impossible to fit the same treatment approach to every patient based on empirical research support (Cooper, 2003; Fensterheim & Raw, 1996; Garfield, 1996; Ingram, Kendall, & Chen, 1991; Johnson & Remien, 2003; Nezu, 1996; Plante et al., 1998; Silverman, 1996). Therefore, many clinicians resist being instructed to provide treatments that they feel may not be useful to particular patients. Others, however, applaud the attempt to give treatment a more empirical and research-supported basis (Barlow, 1996; Beutler, 2009; Duncan et al., 2009; Chambless & Ollendick, 2001; Clement, 1996; Hayes, 1996; Kazdin & Weisz, 2003; Meehl, 1997; Nathan, 1996; Nathan & Gorman, 2002, 2007; Rehm, 1997; Wilson, 1996, 1997).

These tensions have resulted in the concept of **evidence-based practice**. The American Psychological Association convened a task force to examine the perspectives of researchers and clinicians and created a position that supports evidence-based practice (APA, 2006). Evidence-based practices utilize the findings of available high-quality research but leave room for the experience and judgment of clinicians working with complicated clients who often don't fit perfectly in the research protocols of clinical research experiments (Beutler, 2009; Duncan et al., 2009; Hunsley, 2009; Levant & Hasan, 2008; Wilson, Armoutliev, Yakunina, & Werth, 2009). For example, research on phobia may wish to use only those who suffer from a particular phobia without any evidence of additional problems or diagnoses such as alcoholism, personality disorders, and so forth. Clinicians working in the field cannot be as choosy and thus must work with clients who may be much more complicated, dealing with people who have multiple diagnoses at the same time, experiencing co-morbidity. Furthermore, each client has his or her own social context and resources that must be taken into consideration as well, such as family situation, insurance coverage, availability for treatment, cultural diversity issues, and so forth. Thus, evidence-based practice attempts to use the best that research has to offer with the realities of contemporary professional practice with actual diverse client populations (APA, 2006; Beutler, 2009; Duncan et al., 2009; Levant & Hasan, 2008; Nathan & Gorman, 2007; Wilson et al., 2009).

In addition to evidence-based practice, there have also been efforts to develop **clinical practice guidelines** for a wide variety of disorders and diagnoses. These have been developed by the Department of Health in the United Kingdom (2001) with attempts made in the United States and elsewhere to do the same (Institute of Medicine, 2008). Practice guidelines would offer unbiased reviews of mental health and health-care research findings by a variety of professionals and then outline specific guidelines for particular problems such as eating disorders, mood disorders, substance abuse problems, and so forth. For example, the National Institute for Health and Clinical Excellence (NICE) in the United Kingdom has done just this and has clear guidelines for a wide variety of clinical problems. For example, in the treatment of depression they offer a five-step process starting with screening in primary-care settings as step 1, treatment of moderate to severe depression. In primary-care settings as step 3, to inpatient care as step 5 (NICE, 2007).

Reaching Beyond Mental Health in Contemporary Clinical Psychology

Clinical psychology has been closely associated with the mental health field for many years. However, many psychologists feel that psychology is an important health-care discipline in itself, offering potentially useful services beyond mental health issues (Belar, 1995; Fox, 1994; Johnson, 2003; Kovacs, 1996; McDaniel, 1995; Resnick & DeLeon, 1995; S. Taylor, 2009; VandenBos, 1993). Because so many health problems are associated with behavior (e.g., alcohol, smoking, drug use, violence, sedentary lifestyles, risky sexual behavior), many psychologists have suggested that psychology can be helpful in altering high-risk behaviors in a wide variety of areas (Belar, 1995; Johnson, 2003; McDaniel, 1995; Resnick & DeLeon, 1995; S. Taylor, 2009). For example, unsafe sexual practices may lead to sexually transmitted diseases such as AIDS. Obesity, smoking, and sedentary lifestyles have been associated with cardiovascular diseases and cancer. Although approximately half of all traffic accidents are associated with alcohol consumption (Centers for Disease Control, 2009; National Center for Health Statistics, 2001; S. Taylor, 2009), an additional problem is that large numbers of Americans choose not to use seat-belts (McGinnis, 1984; Wald, 2001). Overall, it has been estimated that about half of all deaths are caused by lifestyle factors under behavioral control (Centers for

Disease Control, 2009; Institute for the Future, 2000; S. Taylor, 2009). In fact, a number of psychosocial factors (e.g., lack of trust, impulsivity, immature ego defenses) reliably predict premature death (Friedman et al., 1995). Psychologists, it is argued, are excellent candidates to assist in research, teaching, public policy, and clinical practice to improve health-promoting behaviors in the population and minimize health-damaging behaviors. Therefore, many have suggested that psychology be considered not only an independent mental health discipline but also an independent general health-care discipline (Belar, 1995; Fox, 1994; Johnson, 2003; McDaniel, 1995; Resnick & DeLeon, 1995; VandenBos, 1993). Clinical psychology may be useful for a variety of health-care behaviors, including those not generally associated with mental illness.

In 2001, the APA agreed with these arguments and altered their mission statement to include the goal of using psychology to promote "health, education, and human welfare" (Johnson, 2003). This and other policy statements have led to the endorsement of the biopsychosocial model by the APA (Johnson, 2003).

Training Issues

As outlined earlier, training models in clinical psychology include the scientist-practitioner, or Boulder, model; the scholar-practitioner, or Vail, model; the PhD or the PsyD degree programs; and the university or the freestanding professional school models. Today, within 35 years of the professional school movement, more than 50% of all doctorates awarded in clinical psychology are awarded from freestanding professional schools of psychology rather than through more traditional university psychology training programs. Therefore, the types of training models and contexts have changed tremendously during the past several decades. Which training models will survive and thrive and which will not has important implications for the future of clinical psychology. For instance, a recent APA president has suggested that the PsyD degree rather than the traditional PhD be awarded to all those who plan on being practitioners in clinical psychology (Shapiro & Wiggins, 1994). Although this suggestion is not likely to be embraced by both research- and practice-oriented psychologists who value the PhD degree, it does highlight the chasm between the science and practice of clinical psychology.

The proliferation of freestanding professional schools and now completely online schools of psychology has been controversial. Since admission standards (i.e., GPA, GRE scores, acceptance rates) at professional schools tend to be lower than those of university programs (Norcross et al., 2002, 2008), some surveys have found that many psychologists are concerned that professional standards have decreased with the advent of professional schools. For example, a survey of over 200 diplomates in clinical psychology found that over 70% believed that the advent of freestanding schools of psychology has been a negative influence on the profession (Plante et al., 1998). Many freestanding professional schools are unaccredited by the APA and several enroll any interested paying student without screening his or her academic or psychological readiness for graduate study.

With the explosion of graduate students attending freestanding professional schools of psychology and the emphasis on practitioner training (Shapiro & Wiggins, 1994), the proportion of psychologists conducting research and seeking academic careers relative to the total number of new psychologists has declined dramatically. Therefore, a smaller proportion of current and future psychologists will dedicate their careers to academic and research pursuits. Some have expressed concern that these shifts will result in a much more practice-oriented than science-oriented profession, thereby eroding the scientific base of clinical psychology (Rice, 1997). Such concerns have contributed to significant conflicts within the APA and the development of the more research-oriented American Psychological Society in 1988.

New discoveries, specializations, and the demands of society influence training as well. For example, efforts to obtain prescription privileges for psychologists mean that graduate and postgraduate training programs may need to provide comprehensive training in psychopharmacology and related areas (e.g., biochemistry) not typically or historically offered in clinical psychology training programs (APA, 1992b; DeLeon et al., 2002; DeLeon & Wiggins, 1996; Smyer et al., 1993). Society's focus on violence, ethnic diversity, technological advances, and cost-effective treatment all influence the training emphasis in clinical psychology. For instance, efforts to provide more training in brief and empirically supported and evidence-based treatments (Clement, 1996; Crits- Christoph et al., 1995; Garfield, 1996; Hayes, 1996; Hayes et al., 1995; Nathan, 1996; Norcross et al., 2003, 2008; Wilson, 1996) reflect managed care's emphasis on cost-effective treatment outcome.

Many psychologists have suggested that shifts in training models and focus must occur in order for clinical psychology to survive and thrive (Rice, 1997). Broskowski (1995) stated: "The dominant ideologies for training psychologists have not kept pace with contemporary realities. Training for clinical psychology is dominated either by a clinical practice model that stresses solo practice and traditional long-term therapy methods or a scientist-professional paradigm geared to forms of basic research but not health services research" (p. 161). Former APA president Ronald Fox (1994) has called for more uniform standards in professional education as well as an expansion of training away from the traditional mental health model to a more general health and wellbeing model. Many authors (Fox, 1994; McDaniel, 1995; Resnick & DeLeon, 1995; VandenBos, 1993) suggest that psychology educators, for example, should train students to offer preventive care, short-term acute care, rehabilitation services, and long-term care for those dealing with chronic illnesses. Thus, the shift to primary care in the health field as opposed to narrowly defined mental health roles has been advocated by many (Belar, 1995; Fox, 1994; Johnson, 2003; McDaniel, 1995; Resnick & DeLeon, 1995; VandenBos, 1993). This emphasis has important implications for training programs and career options for psychologists. Furthermore, as clinical psychology has developed more integrative and biopsychosocial perspectives that are evidence based and is evolving toward more involvement in general health care, training professionals in a one-dimensional theoretical orientation has become outdated. In the words of past APA presidents Robert Resnick and Patrick DeLeon (1995), "professional psychology must expand its traditional training boundaries or face being relegated to an unneeded and perhaps unnecessary discipline" (p. 4). Finally, Kovacs (1996) states, "There are many ways that young professionals can find and create careers for themselves . . . but they require shattering an identity that has constrained us" (p. 14).

Other trends in training include mandatory postdoctoral training and new joint degree programs. Most states now require postdoctoral supervisory experiences and training prior to obtaining a state license as a psychologist. These requirements, as well as the need for postdoctorate education, have resulted in efforts to develop accredited mandatory postdoctoral residency programs in psychology (Association of Psychology Postdoctoral and Internship Center [APPIC], 2009; Larsen et al., 1993). There have developed a number of joint degree programs that combine psychology training with other fields, such as business and law. For example, Widener University developed a PsyD/MBA degree program, and the University of Nebraska developed a PhD/JD program. As clinical psychology matures, more and more emphasis in research and practice will be placed on continuing education, specialization, and interdisciplinary training.

The Big Picture

Clinical psychology is changing and growing at a rapid pace. Some of these changes are very positive, some clearly negative. On the positive side, psychology has greatly contributed to a better understanding of human behavior and ways to improve the quality of life for many. Assessment, treatment, research, teaching, and consultation are all much more effective today than in the past. Psychology has also attained increasing independence as a discipline. Licensing laws, medical staff privileges, prescription privileges, and freedom of choice legislation have all contributed to the development of psychology as a respected independent profession. As the profession and field has matured, a more in-depth and sophisticated understanding of human behavior has unfolded. Unfortunately, however, the trend toward managed health care and further constraints in funding for research and practice potentially threaten the growth and types of services psychology can provide. In addition, sizable increases in the number of students being trained as psychologists, especially at large freestanding professional schools of psychology and online programs, may intensify competition for available job positions.

Despite the challenges confronting this as well as all related fields, clinical psychology as a profession remains a fascinating and exciting endeavor with a tremendous potential to help individuals, groups, and society in the course of a truly fulfilling professional career. Although the future of clinical psychology is uncertain, it is likely to continue to be a rewarding career for many. Future clinical psychologists must be flexible to adapt to changing needs and requirements as society and the discipline evolves and changes.

Key Points

1. Clinical psychology has evolved and changed rapidly during its 100+-year history. It is difficult to imagine a more rapidly changing period in clinical psychology than the present time. However, change was certainly rapid for clinical psychology both before World War I and between World Wars I and II. Today clinical psychology looks very different than it did, not only 30 or 40 years ago, but even 5 or 10 years ago.

2. The United States has quickly become an ethnically and culturally diverse nation. Increasing attention and interest have been focused in recent years on the role of multicultural and diversity issues in all aspects of society. Psychologists, as well as other professions, have acquired greater insight into the role of culture and diversity in the development of behavior and behavioral problems.

3. Recent advances and significant discoveries in science, technology, and medicine have greatly impacted clinical psychology as well as many other fields.

4. During recent years, efforts to reduce costs, to become more efficient, and to decrease services have affected many different industries and segments of society. Topics such as downsizing, layoffs, and reduction in services all have been highlighted on a daily basis in news outlets across the country. Attempts to save state and federal monies have also resulted in cuts in programs affecting clinical psychology.

5. Research in clinical psychology has evolved beyond attempts to answer fairly simple and straightforward questions examining main effects. As clinical psychology has evolved and matured, the need for newer research designs and methodologies has led to a move toward greater methodological pluralism.

6. One of the best examples of a current "hot topic" in clinical psychology involves the managed health care and health-care reform. Many have stated that managed health care has significantly altered the field of clinical psychology in a permanent way. With the advent of HMOs and PPOs, much of the spiraling health-care costs and unnecessary procedures are better contained. The HMO and PPO companies determine, along with the professional treating a patient, the most cost-effective and reasonable diagnostic or treatment plan that should be followed. Therefore,

the insurance companies paying for professional health and mental health-care services now have an important and often final say as to the types of services that can be rendered.

7. A highly controversial issue facing clinical psychology is the possibility of obtaining the legal and professional ability to prescribe psychotropic medications. The APA, after careful study, has supported efforts to develop a curriculum to adequately train psychologists in psychopharmacology and to lobby state legislative groups to pass laws allowing psychologists to prescribe medications. Legislation providing psychologists the ability to prescribe medication has passed in several states.

8. Psychologists in many states have obtained medical staff privileges in order to provide independent inpatient care for their patients. After several decades of legislative advocacy and activity, many clinical psychologists have obtained full medical staff privileges in the United States. Yet many hospital-affiliated psychologists continue to struggle to maintain autonomous status within hospital settings.

9. Whereas survey results have revealed a larger and larger percentage of clinical psychologists conducting at least part-time private practice activities, experts generally now predict that the private practice trend may reverse itself owing to the rapid changes in the health-care delivery and insurance reimbursement systems.

10. With advances in research and practice, the need for specialization in clinical psychology has become apparent. As clinical psychology has evolved and more information on human behavior has become available, practitioners have endeavored to specialize in areas such as neuropsychology, geropsychology, brief treatments, health psychology, infant psychology, and forensic psychology.

11. Psychologists, it is argued, are excellent candidates to assist in research, teaching, public policy, and clinical practice to improve health-promoting behaviors in the population and minimize health-damaging behaviors. Therefore, psychology is now considered not only an independent mental health discipline but also an independent general health-care discipline.

12. The types of training models have changed tremendously during the past several decades. Which training models will survive and thrive and which will not has important implications for the future of clinical psychology.

Key Terms

Clinical practice guidelines
Diversity
Empirically validated treatments
Evidence-based practice
Health maintenance organization (HMO)
Managed health care
Medical staff privileges
Multicultural
Preferred provider organization (PPO)
Prescription privileges
Private practice
Specialization

For Reflection

1. How do changes in society impact clinical psychology?
2. How do health-care reform and managed health care impact clinical psychology?
3. How are financial issues associated with the future of clinical psychology?
4. How do diversity issues affect clinical psychology?
5. What are medical staff privileges and why are they important to clinical psychologists?
6. What are prescription privileges and why are they important to clinical psychology?
7. What training issues affect the future of clinical psychology?

8. How might an interested student learn more about the field of clinical psychology?
9. What is likely to happen to private practice in clinical psychology in the future?
10. How is clinical psychology more than a mental health discipline?
11. What are empirically supported and evidence-based treatments?
12. What are some pros and cons to using empirically supported and evidence-based treatments?

Real Students, Real Questions

1. How does the future look for clinical psychologists who mainly want to counsel?

2. Why is there tension between researchers and practitioners? What is the point of researching people's behavior if the knowledge is not used to help those in need?
3. Given managed care, will the psychodynamic approach die out?
4. What additional training do psychologists need if they provide primary-care services?

Web Resources

www.psyfin.com
Learn about practical issues regarding psychology finances for psychology practitioners.

www.asppb.org
Learn more about state and provincial psychology boards.

Appendix Empirically Supported Treatment Manuals

Anxiety Disorders

Author/Year[a]	Title	Orientation	Patient Population	Modality	Strengths[b]
Barlow & Cerny (1988)	*Psychological Treatment of Panic*	CBT	Panic Disorder	Individual	1, 2, 3, 4
Beck, Emery, & Greenberg(1985)	*Anxiety Disorders and Phobias: A Cognitive Perspective*	Cognitive	Phobias	Individual	1, 2, 3
Bouman & Emmelkamp (1996)[e]	"Panic Disorder and Agoraphobia"	CBT	Agoraphobia	Individual	1, 2, 3
Brown, O'Leary, & Barlow (2001)[c]	"Generalized Anxiety Disorder"	Cognitive	GAD	Individual	1, 2, 3, 4
Clark & Salkovskis (1996)	*Treatment Manual for Focused Cognitive Therapy for Panic Disorder*	Cognitive	Panic Disorder	Individual	1, 2, 4
Craske & Barlow (2001)[c]	"Panic Disorder and Agoraphobia"	CBT	Panic Disorder & Agoraphobia	Individual, Group	1, 2, 3, 4, 6
Dugas (2002)[g]	"Generalized Anxiety Disorder"	Behavioral	GAD	Individual	3, 4
Falsetti & Resnick (2001)	*Posttraumatic Stress Disorder*	Cognitive	PTSD	Individual	1, 4
Foa & Franklin (2001)[c]	"Obsessive-Compulsive Disorder"	CBT	OCD	Individual	1, 2, 3, 4
Gaston (1995)	*Dynamic Therapy for Posttraumatic Stress Disorder*	Dynamic	Trauma	Individual	1, 2, 3
Harris (1998)	*Trauma Recovery and Empowerment: A Clinician's Guide for Working with Women in Groups*	Dynamic	Trauma Recovery, PTSD (mostly women)	Group	1, 2, 3, 4, 6
Kozak & Foa (1996)[e]	"Obsessive-Compulsive Disorder"	Behavioral	OCD	Individual	1, 2, 3
Resick & Calhoun (2001)[c]	"Posttraumatic Stress Disorder"	CBT	Rape victims w/PTSD	Individual	1, 2, 3, 4
Scholing, Emmelkamp, & Van Oppen (1996)[e]	"Cognitive-Behavioral Treatment of Social Phobia"	CBT	Social Phobia	Individual	1, 2, 3, 4

Reference	Title	Orientation	Population	Format	Notes
Smucker & Dancu (1999)	*Cognitive-Behavioral Treatment for Adult Survivors of Childhood Trauma: Imagery Rescripting and Reprocessing*	CBT	PTSD, Adult Survivors of Trauma	Individual	1, 2, 3, 4
Turk, Heimberg, & Hope (2001)[c]	"Social Anxiety Disorder"	CBT	Avoidant Personality Disorder, Social Anxiety	Group	1, 2, 3, 4
Turner & Beidel (1988)	*Treating Obsessive-Compulsive Disorder*	Behavioral	OCD	Individual	1, 2, 3, 4
White (2000)	*Treating Anxiety and Stress: A Group Psycho-Educational Approach Using Brief CBT*	CBT	Anxiety Disorders	Group	1, 2, 3, 4
Affective Disorders					
Beck, Rush, Shaw, & Emery (1979)	*Cognitive Therapy of Depression*	Cognitive	Depression	Individual	1, 2, 3, 4, 5
Becker, Heimberg, & Bellack (1987)	*Social Skills Training Treatment for Depression*	Behavioral	Depression	Individual, Group	1, 2, 3
Dick, Gallagher-Thompson, & Thompson (1996)	*Cognitive-Behavioral Therapy*	CBT	Depressed Older Adults	Individual	4
Eells (1995)[f]	"Relational Therapy for Grief Disorders"	Dynamic	Adjustment Difficulties	Individual	1, 2, 3, 4
Freeman & Reinecke (1993)	*Cognitive Therapy of Suicidal Behavior: A Manual for Treatment*	Cognitive	Suicide	Individual	1, 2, 3, 6
Gillies (2001)[c]	"Interpersonal Psychotherapy for Depression and Other Disorders"	Interpersonal	Depression: Postpartum, Adolescents, HIV-Seropositive, Late-Life	Individual	1, 2, 4
Klerman, Weissman, Rounsaville, & Chevron (1984)	*Interpersonal Psychotherapy of Depression*	Interpersonal	Depression	Individual	1, 2, 3, 4, 5

(continued)

441

Appendix *Continued*

Author/Year[a]	Title	Orientation	Patient Population	Modality	Strengths[b]
Lewinsohn, Antonuccio, Steinmetz, & Teri (1984)	*The Coping with Depression Course: A Psychoeducational Intervention for Unipolar Depression*	Behavioral	Depression	Group	1, 2, 3, 4
Luborsky, Mark, Hole, Popp, Goldsmith, & Cacciola (1995)[f]	"Supportive-Expressive Dynamic Psychotherapy of Depression: A Time-Limited Version"	Dynamic	Depression	Individual	1, 2, 3
Miklowitz (2001)[c]	"Bipolar Disorder"	Family Focused Treatment	Bipolar Disorder, Families of those with Bipolar Disorder	Individual, Family, Couple	1, 2, 3, 4
Otto & Reilly-Harrington (2002)[d]	"Cognitive-Behavioral Therapy for the Management of Bipolar Disorder"	CBT	Bipolar Disorder	Individual	2, 4
Rosselló & Bernal (1996)	*Adapting Cognitive-Behavioral and Interpersonal Treatments for Depressed Puerto Rican Adolescents*	CBT, Interpersonal	Depressed Puerto Rican Adolescents	Individual	1, 2, 4, 6
Swartz, Markowitz, & Frank (2002)[d]	"Interpersonal Psychotherapy for Unipolar and Bipolar Disorders"	Interpersonal	Bipolar Disorder, Depression	Individual	1, 2, 4
Thase (1996)[e]	"Cognitive Behavior Therapy Manual for Treatment of Depressed Inpatients"	CBT	Depressed Inpatients	Individual	1, 2, 3, 4
Affective Disorders					
Yost, Beutler, Corbishley, & Allender (1986)	*Group Cognitive Therapy: A Treatment Approach for Depressed Older Adults*	Cognitive	Depression	Group	1, 2, 3, 4
Young, Weinberger, & Beck (2001)[c]	"Cognitive Therapy for Depression"	Cognitive	Depression	Individual	1,2,3,4

Childhood/Adolescent Disorders

Anastopoulos (1998)[i]	"A Training Program for Parents of Children with Attention-Deficit/Hyperactivity Disorder"	Parent Training	Childhood ADHD	Parent(s)	1, 2, 3, 4
Barkley (1998)	Attention-Deficit Hyperactivity Disorder: A Handbook of Diagnosis and Treatment	CBT	ADHD	Individual, Family	1, 2, 3, 4
Bratton (1998)[i]	"Training Parents to Facilitate Their Child's Adjustment to Divorce Using Filial/Family Play Therapy Approach"	Parent Training	Adjustment Disorders, Children of Divorce	Parent(s)	1, 2, 3, 4
Camino (2000)	Treating Sexually Abused Boys	Empowerment	Sexually Abused Boys	Group, Individual	2, 3, 4
Eisen, Engler, & Geyer (1998)[i]	"Parent Training for Separation Anxiety Disorder"	Parent Training	Separation Anxiety Disorder	Parent(s)	1, 2, 3, 4
Everett & Everett (1999)	Family Therapy for ADHD: Treating Children, Adolescents, and Adults	Family Systems	ADHD	Family	3, 4
Fouse & Wheeler (1997)	A Treasure Chest of Behavioral Strategies for Individuals with Autism	Behavioral, Systems	Autistic Children	Individual, Group	1, 2, 3, 4
Franklin, Rynn, March, & Foa (2002)[g]	"Obsessive-Compulsive Disorder"	Behavioral	OCD	Individual/Systems	1, 2, 3
Landreth (1991)	Play Therapy: The Art of the Relationship	Dynamic	Children	Individual, Group	1, 2, 3, 4
March & Mulle (1996)[h]	"Banishing OCD: Cognitive-Behavioral Psychotherapy for Obsessive-Compulsive Disorders"	CBT	OCD	Individual	1, 3, 4
O'Connor (2000)	The Play Therapy Primer	Ecosystemic	Children	Individual, Group	1, 2, 3, 4
Reynolds (2002)[g]	"Childhood Depression"	Behavioral	Depression	Individual	3, 4

(continued)

Author/Year[a]	Title	Orientation	Patient Population	Modality	Strengths[b]
Roach & Gross (2002)[g]	"Conduct Disorder"	Behavioral	Conduct Disorder	Individual	3, 4
Rotheram-Borus, Goldstein, & Elkavich (2002)[d]	"Treatment of Suicidality: A Family Intervention for Adolescent Suicide Attempters"	CBT	Outpatient Families of Suicidal Adolescents	Family	3, 4
Sells (1998)	*Treating the Tough Adolescent: A Family-Based, Step-by-Step Guide*	Family Systems	Conduct Disorder, Oppositional Defiant Disorder	Family	1, 2, 3, 4
Weiss & Wolchik (1998)[i]	"New Beginnings: An Empirically-Based Intervention Program for Divorced Mothers to Help Their Children Adjust to Divorce"	Group Parent Training	Adjustment Disorders, Children of Divorce	Group	1, 2, 3, 4
Wolfson (1998)[i]	"Working with Parents on Developing Efficacious Sleep/Wake Habits for Infants and Young Children"	Parent Training	Infant/Childhood Sleep Disorders	Parent(s)	1, 2, 3, 4
Dissociative Identity Disorders					
Kluft (1995)[f]	"Psychodynamic Psychotherapy of Multiple Personality Disorder and Allied Forms of Dissociative Disorder Not Otherwise Specified"	Dynamic	Dissociative Disorder	Individual	1, 2, 3
Forensic					
Marshall & Eccles (1996)[e]	"Cognitive-Behavioral Treatments of Sex Offenders"	CBT	Sex Offenders	Group	1, 2, 3
Ward, Hudson, & Keenan (2001)	*The Assessment and Treatment of Sexual Offenders against Children*	CBT	Sex Offenders/Pedophiles and Ebeohiles	Group	2, 3, 4

Eating Disorders and Weight Management Treatments

Reference	Title	Orientation	Problem	Format	Ages
Cash & Grant (1996)[e]	"Cognitive-Behavioral Treatment of Body-Image Disturbances"	CBT	Eating Disorders, Body Dysmorphic Disorder	Individual	1, 2, 3, 4
Sansone & Johnson (1995)[f]	"Treating the Eating Disorder Patient with Borderline Personality Disorder: Theory and Technique"	Dynamic	Eating/Borderline	Individual	1, 2, 3
Williamson, Champagne, Jackman, & Varnado (1996)[e]	"Lifestyle Change: A Program for Long-Term Weight Management"	Behavioral	Obesity	Group (Closed)	2, 3, 4
Wilson & Pike (2001)[c]	"Eating Disorders"	CBT	Bulimia Nervosa, Anorexia Nervosa	Individual	2, 3, 4

Forensic

Reference	Title	Orientation	Problem	Format	Ages
Bricklin (1995)	*The Custody Evaluation Handbook: Research-Based Solutions and Applications*	Assessment	Divorce	Psychological Testing	2, 3
Ellis (2000)	*Rationale and Goals of the Custody Evaluation*	Assessment	Divorce	Psychological Testing	1, 2, 4
Ferguson & Mittenberg (1996)[e]	"Cognitive-Behavioral Treatment of Postconcussion Syndrome: A Therapist's Manual"	CBT	Brain Trauma	Individual	1, 2, 3, 4

Impulse Control Disorders

Reference	Title	Orientation	Problem	Format	Ages
Ciarrocchi (2002)	*Counseling for the Problem Gambler: A Self-Regulation Manual for Individual and Family Therapy*	Eclectic/Pragmatic	Adult Pathological Gamblers	Individual, Group, Family, Couple	1, 2, 3, 4
Larkin & Zayfert (1996)[e]	"Anger Management Training with Essential Hypertensive Patients"	Behavioral	Anger Management	Group	1, 2, 3, 4
Stanley & Mouton (1996)[e]	"Trichotillomania Treatment Manual"	Behavioral	Trichotillomania	Individual	1, 2, 3, 4

(continued)

Appendix *Continued*

Author/Year[a]	Title	Orientation	Patient Population	Modality	Strengths[b]
Outpatient Treatments					
Chethik, Morton (2000)	*Techniques for Child Therapy: Psychodynamic Strategies*	Dynamic	Outpatient Children	Individual	1, 2, 3, 4
Daldrup, Beutler, Engle, & Greenberg (1988)	*Focused Expressive Psychotherapy*	Experiential	Outpatient	Individual	1, 2, 3, 4
De Dominico (2000)	*Sand Tray World Play: A Comprehensive Guide to the Use of the Sand Tray in Psychotherapeutic and Transformational Settings*	Dynamic, Experiential	Outpatient Children, Adolescents, and Adults	Individual, Group, Family	1, 2, 3, 4
Gumaer (1984)	*Counseling and Therapy for Children*	Various	Outpatient Children	Individual, Group, Family	1, 2, 3, 4
Outpatient Treatments					
Hayes, Strosahl, & Wilson (1999)	*Acceptance and Commitment Therapy: An Experiential Approach to Behavior Change*	Behavioral, Experiential	Outpatient	Individual	1, 2, 3, 4
Hersen (2002)[g]	"Clinical Behavior Therapy: Adults & Children"	Behavioral	Outpatient	Individual	1, 2, 3, 4
Hibbs & Jensen (1996)[h]	"Psychosocial Treatments for Child and Adolescent Disorders: Empirically Based Strategies for Clinical Practice"	Various	Outpatient (Child and Adolescent)	Individual	1, 2, 3, 4
Padesky & Greenberger (1995)	*Clinician's Guide to Mind over Mood*	Cognitive	Outpatient	Individual	1, 2, 4, 6
Strupp & Binder (1984)	*Psychotherapy in a New Key*	Dynamic	Outpatient	Individual	1, 2, 3, 4
Wright & Wright (1987)	*Clinical Practice of Hypnotherapy*	Hypnotherapy	Outpatient	Individual	1, 2

Partner Relational Problems

N. Epstein & Baucom (2002)	Enhanced Cognitive-Behavioral Therapy for Couples: A Contextual Approach	CBT	Distressed Couples	Couples	1, 2, 3
Greenberg & Johnson (1988)	Emotionally Focused Therapy for Couples	Experiential	Distressed Couples	Couples	1, 2, 3, 4
Jacobson & Gurman (Eds.) (1995)	Clinical Handbook of Couple Therapy	Various	Distressed Couples	Couples	1, 2, 3, 4
Wheeler, Christensen, & Jacobson (2001)[c]	"Couple Distress"	Integrative, Behavioral	Distressed Couples	Couples	1, 2, 3, 4
M. Young & Long (1998)	Counseling and Therapy for Couples	Integrative	Infidelity, Divorce	Couples	1, 4, 6

Personality Disorders

Beck & Freeman (1990)	Cognitive Therapy of Personality Disorders	Cognitive	Personality Disorders	Individual	1, 2, 3
Benjamin (2002)	Interpersonal Diagnosis and Treatment of Personality Disorders	Interpersonal	Personality Disorders	Individual	1, 2, 3, 4
Linehan, Cochran, & Kehrer (2001)[c]	"Dialectical Behavior Therapy for Borderline Personality Disorder"	CBT, Dialectical Behavior Therapy	Borderline Personality Disorder (including those in substance abuse treatment settings)	Individual	1, 2, 3, 4
Piper, Rosie, Joyce, & Azim (1996)	Time-Limited Day Treatment for Personality Disorders: Integration of Research and Practice in a Group Program	Eclectic	Personality Disorders	Group	1, 2, 3, 4
Sperry (1999)	Cognitive Behavior Therapy of DSM-IV Personality Disorders: Highly Effective Interventions for the Most Common Personality Disorders	CBT	Avoidant, Borderline, Dependent, Narcissistic, OCPD, Histrionic	Individual	1, 2, 3, 4

(continued)

Appendix *Continued*

Author/Year[a]	Title	Orientation	Patient Population	Modality	Strengths[b]
Whitehurst, Ridolfi, & Gunderson (2002)[d]	"Multiple Family Group Treatment for Borderline Personality Disorder"	Psychoeducational	Borderlines	Family Educational Groups	1, 2, 3, 4
Schizophrenia					
Herz & Marder (2002)	*Schizophrenia: Comprehensive Treatment and Management*	Medical Model	Schizophrenia	Individual, Family	1, 2, 3, 4
Hogarty (2002)	*Personal Therapy for Schizophrenia and Related Disorders: A Guide to Individualized Treatment*	Systems	Schizophrenia	Individual, Group	1, 2, 3, 4
McFarlane (2002)	*Multifamily Groups in Treatment of Severe Psychiatric Disorders*	Systems	Schizophrenia	Group	1, 2, 3, 4
Pratt & Mueser (2002)[d]	"Social Skills Training for Schizophrenia"	Social Skills Training	Schizophrenia (Inpatient and Outpatient)	Group	1, 2, 3, 4 (template for Group)
Wong & Liberman (1996)[e]	"Biobehavioral Treatment and Rehabilitation for Persons with Schizophrenia"	Biobehavioral	Schizophrenia	Individual, Group	1, 2, 3
Sexual Disorders					
Bach, Wincze, & Barlow (2001)[c]	"Sexual Dysfunction"	CBT/Systems	Desire Disorders, Arousal Disorders, Orgasmic Disorders, Pain Disorders	Couple, Individual	1, 2, 3, 4
Jehu (1979)	*Sexual Dysfunction: A Behavioral Approach to Causation, Assessment, and Treatment*	Behavioral	Sexual Dysfunction	Individual, Couple	1, 2, 3
McConaghy (1996)[e]	"Treatment of Sexual Dysfunctions"	CBT	Sexual Dysfunction	Individual, Couple	1, 2, 3

Sleep Disorders					
Van Brunt, Riedel, & Lichstein (1996)[e]	"Insomnia"	Behavioral, Pharmacotherapy	Sleep Disturbance	Individual	1, 2, 3
Somatic Disorders					
P. Martin (1993)	*Psychological Management of Chronic Headaches*	CBT	Headaches	Individual	1, 2, 3, 4
Warwick & Salkovskis (2001)	*Cognitive-Behavioral Treatment of Hypochondriasis*	CBT	Hypochondriasis	Individual	1, 2, 3, 4
Substance Abuse Disorders					
Budney & Higgens (1998)	*A Community Reinforcement Approach: Treating Cocaine Addiction*	Behavioral, Relational	Cocaine Dependence	Individual	1, 2, 3, 4
Carroll (1998)	*A Cognitive-Behavioral Approach: Treating Cocaine Addiction*	CBT	Cocaine Dependence	Individual	1, 2, 3, 4
Daley, Mercer, & Carpenter (1997)	*Drug Counseling for Cocaine Addiction: The Collaborative Cocaine Treatment Study Model*	Behavioral	Inpatient/Outpatient Cocaine Addict	Group	1, 2, 3, 4
Handmaker & Walters (2002)[d]	"Motivational Interviewing for Initiating Change in Problem Drinking and Drug Use"	Client-Centered	Inpatient/Outpatient	Individual	1, 2, 4
Higgins, Budney, & Sigmon (2001)[c]	"Cocaine Dependence"	Community Reinforcement	Cocaine Addict	Individual	1, 2, 3
Luborsky, Woody, Hole, & Velleco (1995)[f]	"Supportive-Expressive Dynamic Psychotherapy for Treatment of Opiate Drug Dependence"	Dynamic	Opiate Dependence	Individual	1, 2, 3, 4
McCrady (2001)[c]	"Alcohol Disorders"	Relapse Prevention	Alcoholics and Spouses	Individual, Couple	1, 2, 3, 4

(continued)

449

Appendix   *Continued*

Author/Year[a]	Title	Orientation	Patient Population	Modality	Strengths[b]
D. Mercer & Woody (1998)	*An Individual Drug Counseling Approach to Treat Cocaine Addiction: The Collaborative Cocaine Treatment Study Model*	Behavioral	Outpatient Cocaine Addict	Individual	1, 2, 3, 4
Meyers, Dominguez, & Smith (1996)[e]	"Community Reinforcement Training with Concerned Others"	Behavioral	Families of Alcoholics	Individual/Family	1, 2, 3, 4
Paolantonio (1990)	*Relapse Prevention Training Manual*	CBT	Drug and Alcohol Relapse	Group	1, 2, 4
Stasiewicz & Bradizza (2002)[g]	"Alcohol Abuse"	Behavioral	Alcohol Disorders	Individual	3, 4
Wakefield, Williams, Yost, & Patterson (1996)	*Alcohol Disorders*	CBT	Alcoholics and Spouses	Couple	1, 2, 3, 4

Notes: [a]All references are located at the back of the book.

[b]Strengths of Manual Criteria: 1 = A presentation of the main principles behind the techniques of the form of psychotherapy; 2 = Concrete examples of each technical principle/treatment intervention; 3 = Description of etiology and/or assessment approaches; 4 = Specifically delineated description of treatment program (e.g., session-by-session, step-by-step, phases); 5 = Scales to guide independent judges in evaluating samples of sessions to determine the degree of conformity to the manual; 6 = Gives attention to cultural concerns that otherwise might interfere with treatment.

[c]From *Clinical Handbook of Psychological Disorders: A Step-by-Step Treatment Manual*, Third edition, D. H. Barlow (Ed.), 2001, New York: Guilford Press.

[d]From *Treating Chronic and Severe Mental Disorders: A Handbook of Empirically Supported Interventions*, S. G. Hofmann and M. C. Tompson (Eds.), 2002, New York: Guilford Press.

[e]From *Sourcebook of Psychological Treatment Manuals for Adult Disorders*, V. B. Van Hasselt and M. Hersen, 1996, New York: Plenum Press.

[f]From *Dynamic Therapies for Psychiatric Disorders (Axis I)*, J. P. Barber and P. Crits-Christoph (Eds.), 2000, New York: Basic Books.

[g]From *Clinical Behavior Therapy: Adults and Children*, Hersen (Ed.), 2002, New York: Wiley.

hFrom *Psychosocial Treatments for Child and Adolescent Disorders: Empirically Based Strategies for Clinical Practice*, M. Hersen (Ed.), 2002, New York: Wiley.
iFrom *Handbook of Parent Training: Parents as Co-Therapists for Children's Behavior Problems*, Second Edition, J. M. Breismeister and C. E. Schaefer (Eds.), 1998, New York: Wiley.

Publishers' Phone Numbers:
Basic Books
Phone: (800) 225-5945
Fax: (908) 302-2300

Plenum Press
Phone: (800) 221-9369
Fax: (212) 463-0742

John Wiley & Sons
Phone: (800) 225-5945
Fax: (908) 302-2300

Source: "Compendium of Current Psychotherapy Treatment Manuals," by M. J. Lambert, M. Bishop, T. Bybee, R. Houston, S. Rice, A. D. Sanders, and R. Wilkinson, in G. P. Koocher, J. C. Norcross, & S. S. Hill III (Eds.), *Psychologists' Desk Reference*, Second Edition, 2004, New York: Oxford.

Becoming a Clinical Psychologist: A Roadmap

15

Chapter

Students wishing to become clinical psychologists do so for a variety of reasons. Many are interested in being helpful to others, whereas others are fascinated by human behavior. Some are interested in the interface between psychology and biology as manifested in health issues. Others are sensitive to human suffering and the nuances of human relationships, feeling naturally drawn to clinical psychology as a field of study. Still others are primarily interested in contributing to improvements in society at large. Many are interested in all of these aspects of clinical psychology. Many people cynically believe that those who wish to become clinical psychologists are primarily interested in solving their own personal or family problems. Although some studies have indeed suggested that psychologists enter the field in order to help resolve personal or family conflicts or

problems (Elliott & Guy, 1993; Guy, 1987; Sussman, 1992), other studies have found little or no association between personal and family problems and choice of psychology as a profession (Murphy & Halgin, 1995; Norcross & Guy, 1989).

Although numerous terminal master's degree programs are available in clinical psychology, the American Psychological Association (APA) "recognizes the doctorate as the minimum educational requirement for entry into professional practice as a psychologist" (APA, 1987b, p. 3). Therefore, in this chapter, the stages toward the doctorate in clinical psychology and subsequent postdoctoral training and licensing will be discussed.

A career as a clinical psychologist is rife with both tremendous challenges and unanticipated rewards. The road to becoming a clinical psychologist is a long one divided into several distinct stages that include college, graduate

453

school, clinical internship, postdoctoral fellowship, licensure, and finally employment and advanced certification. In this chapter, each of these progressive stages will be reviewed. Although college students may not need details on postdoctoral training, licensing, employment, and board certification this early in their careers, this information is included in this chapter to provide a complete roadmap of the training process. If you are taking a long and involved road trip, you'll want to know exactly where you're going and what you can expect along the way.

College

Most college students who plan on becoming clinical psychologists will decide to major in psychology. However, while a psychology major is obviously advantageous, business, communications, biology, sociology, or any other major will not preclude a student from being accepted into graduate school in psychology. Prerequisite courses such as General Psychology, Statistics, Research Methods, Personality, Biopsychology, Learning, Cognition, and Abnormal Psychology are generally required or highly recommended to students who choose not to major in psychology as undergraduates (Lawson, 1995; Norcross, Sayette, & Mayne, 2008; Smith, 1985). Additional courses in math and science are also recommended. Overall, students interested in becoming clinical psychologists and gaining admission into high-quality graduate programs must take their college experience very seriously (Table 15.1). Solid grades and high-quality research and clinical experiences during the college years are important to acquire. Specifically, students must obtain a solid grade point average (GPA) and high scores on the Graduate Record Examination (GRE), obtain some clinical (e.g., working with patients or clients located at various social services agencies such as a homeless or battered women's shelter, suicide prevention hotline, school for developmentally disabled children, psychiatric unit of a local hospital)

Table 15.1 Important Goals during the College Experience

High grade point average
High Graduate Record Examination scores
Quality research experience
Quality clinical experience
Excellent verbal skills
Excellent interpersonal skills
Reliability and dependability
Excellent productivity
Excellent letters of recommendation
High motivation

and research experience (e.g., working with a professor or other researchers on psychology-related research), and receive excellent letters of recommendation. Each of these elements as well as other important aspects of the college experience will be highlighted in this chapter.

Grade Point Average

Whereas there are no absolute cutoffs, except for some set by the occasional graduate program, a 3.0 GPA should be generally viewed as a minimum while a 3.5 or higher is generally expected by graduate training programs. The mean GPA score for all clinical psychology graduate programs is about 3.5 (Norcross et al., 2008). While grade point average does not necessarily correlate strongly with graduate school performance in clinical psychology (Dollinger, 1989) or necessarily with intelligence, success as a psychologist, or with therapeutic skill, it does serve at least as an index of motivation and discipline. A high degree of motivation and determination are qualities found in successful graduate students. Ironically, once enrolled in a graduate program or employed as a psychologist, grades per se take on a relatively inconsequential role in later success (barring impressively poor grades). However, as an undergraduate, GPA is one way to be distinguished among the large number of graduate school applicants.

Graduate Record Exam

Students interested in applying to graduate school in psychology generally take the GRE during the fall term of their senior year. In fact, about 90% of all doctoral graduate programs in clinical psychology require that the GRE be taken in order to be considered for admission (Norcross et al., 2008; Steinpreis, Queen, & Tennen, 1992). The GRE is administered by the Educational Testing Service (Princeton, New Jersey) and yields four scores: Verbal, Quantitative, Analytic, and Psychology, the latter being administered in a separate testing session. The Verbal, Quantitative, and Analytical sections make up the GRE General Test while the Psychology portion is one of many GRE Subject Tests. The GRE General Test and Subject Tests are administered at different times. A total of 800 points is possible in each area. Each score has a mean of 500 and a standard deviation of 100.

Generally, graduate programs will focus on the combined Verbal/Quantitative total, looking for approximately 1,200 (e.g., 600 Verbal, 600 Quantitative) as a common cutoff. Higher scores on the Psychology section of the GRE are often expected by high-quality graduate programs (i.e., above 600). However, a recent study (Norcross et al., 2008) revealed that the mean GRE scores for graduate programs in clinical psychology are 581 ($SD = 46$) for the Quantitative measure, 580 ($SD = 48$) for the Verbal scale, 579 ($SD = 46$) for the Analytic scale, and 587 ($SD = 47$) for the Psychology subject test. According to this study, GRE scores tended to be higher among research-oriented PhD programs compared with, for example, practice-oriented PhD or PsyD graduate programs. Lawson (1995) reports mean GRE scores for incoming psychology doctoral students of 598 (Verbal), 612 (Quantitative), 633 (Analytic), and 616 (Psychology). The average combined Verbal and Quantitative score for doctoral programs in clinical psychology is 1,206. Most programs will rarely consider applicants with scores below 500 in each of the subject areas (Norcross et al., 2008). Many students obtain self-study GRE materials or enroll in GRE preparatory classes offered by several companies (such as Stanley Kaplan) in order to help maximize their performance. Students unable to afford the costs of these preparatory programs are well advised to discipline themselves to study and prepare on their own or with peers in order to maximize performance. There are many self-study preparation books available. Although the GRE is required by most doctoral programs in psychology, the test's ability to predict performance in graduate school is modest at best (Kuncel, Hezlett, & Ones, 2001; Sternberg, 2006; Sternberg & Williams, 1997).

Research Experience

Most high-quality graduate programs in clinical psychology expect applicants to have some research experience prior to admission to graduate school. In fact, survey research has indicated that quality research experience was the top-rated variable listed by graduate program directors as being important in graduate school admissions (Eddy, Lloyd, & Lubin, 1987). However, Lawson (1995) reported that work and clinical experience tend to be rated higher than research experience for clinical or counseling psychology programs. In general, any involvement in a quality research project or projects with college psychology professors or with other psychology professionals working in settings such as hospitals, clinics, and industry is valued. Quality research is not always easy to define. Professionals often disagree concerning the quality and value of various research projects. Generally, research that is conducted by well-trained professionals, is methodologically rigorous, and contributes to the professional community of scholars—evidenced by being presented at regional or national professional conferences and/or published in refereed professional journals—would be considered quality research.

Research experience at the undergraduate level typically occurs by working with a psychology faculty member who has undergraduate students help him or her as research assistants. It is not imperative that the research be clinically oriented. Rather, obtaining solid research experience with a professor who is productive and enjoyable to work with is important. Furthermore, having the opportunity to present research findings at professional or student research conferences and co-author manuscripts for publication in professional journals is also highly beneficial. Most areas of the country, for example, offer undergraduate psychology research conferences each spring (e.g., Greater Boston Undergraduate Psychology Research Conference, Western Undergraduate Psychology Research Conference), allowing undergraduates to present their research in paper or poster form to peers and faculty from a variety of schools. Often, college students working as research assistants may score questionnaires, run subjects through laboratory procedures, and conduct literature reviews as part of their work with the professor or other psychology professionals.

Closely associated with research experience, computer, data analysis, and statistical skills are also important to obtain during the college years. In addition to standard word processing skills, developing competence with statistical packages such as Statistical Package for the Social Sciences (SPSS) is extremely valuable. Although many students interested in clinical psychology careers may be uninterested in computer, mathematical, and statistical concepts and activities, these skills are generally extremely important to develop among all clinical psychologists. Even those who hope to conduct primarily psychotherapy in their professional career must use these skills to manage their finances, examine treatment outcome and client satisfaction, complete necessary paperwork, and be good consumers of research in order to maintain state-of-the-art service.

Clinical Experience

Most undergraduate psychology departments and colleges offer externships or field placements in clinical settings where students can gain exposure to the signs, symptoms, and language of clinical problems. In fact, over two-thirds of colleges and universities offer practicum experiences in psychology (Vande-Creek & Fleisher, 1984). Typical examples of volunteer placements include local hospitals, community mental health centers, drug and alcohol rehabilitation halfway houses, schools or summer camps for disabled children, homeless or battered women's shelters, and crisis or suicide hotlines. These experiences help students obtain experience with clinical populations as well as provide some important beginning skills and knowledge about clinical problems and interventions.

Students might ask their professors or fellow students about opportunities that are worthwhile. If a college does not have an organized internship or service-learning program, a student could still find appropriate and useful volunteer or even paid experiences by calling local social service agencies. Hospitals, crisis hotlines, schools for developmentally disabled children or adults, and shelters for battered women, homeless persons, or abused children are excellent starting points. Local United Way–funded agencies and church groups also may be helpful in finding appropriate positions for students.

Determining what is a quality clinical experience is sometimes difficult. Generally, a clinical experience that allows the student to observe a wide range of activities with a number of clients and allows the student to talk about his or her experiences with a professional in the clinical setting is more likely to be a quality experience. The best type of location is one that encourages and values student learning and is not merely interested in obtaining free labor. For example, observing and/or working directly with clients would be preferred relative to spending too much time doing clerical work such as filing and typing. Often the experiences of previous students who have worked in the particular clinical setting can assist in determining whether the experience would be worthwhile.

Verbal Skills

Beyond the confines of the GRE, the field of clinical psychology is highly dependent on a range of verbal skills. These include writing ability, public speaking ability, and the ongoing ability to verbally communicate with colleagues and clients in a direct, clear, and sensitive fashion. Often, professors will infer the intelligence and social skills of students largely on the basis of their ability to express themselves through written and oral communication. Thus, honing writing and speaking skills is an important element of the college experience. Additionally, being fluent in more than one language is always a plus.

Interpersonal Skills

Challenging to measure or quantify, this realm of social transaction is perhaps the most important quality to possess as a psychology student and eventual professional. Good interpersonal and social skills, empathy for others, and effective communication are critical to becoming an effective psychotherapist, consultant, teacher, and overall professional clinical psychologist. In clinical psychology, the ability to deal directly, sensitively, and in a reassuring manner is critical to success with both colleagues and clients. It is perhaps a well-kept secret that in addition to valuing competence, experience, and intellectual potential, graduate, intern, postdoctoral, and employment sites often give the edge to those whom they simply like and expect to be agreeable and engaging. Good interpersonal skills are important contributors to therapeutic alliance and effectiveness as well as appreciated among coworkers and supervisors.

Reliability and Dependability

The field of clinical psychology, like most professional careers, requires consistency and almost unerring reliability. Unreliability as manifested in lateness, tardy reports, inefficiency, sloppiness, and general "flakiness" is highly problematic at all stages in training and in employment as a clinical psychologist. Clinical, teaching, and research duties require an unselfish focus and conscientious levels of effort and dedication. Clinical psychologists as well as students in psychology must be able to be depended upon, for example, to finish what they say they will finish or arrive when agreed. A psychologist must earn the trust of others as someone capable of fulfilling a responsible, professional role. This point cannot be emphasized enough. Be responsible!

Productivity

In any competitive field, the ability to work efficiently and produce high-quality, thoughtful, accurate, and important work, and to do so fairly quickly, is a great advantage. For instance, research productivity is most apparent in one's list of publications and presentations; clinical and teaching experience are expressed in both variety and hours logged. However, even more than quantity, the quality of one's work is ultimately most compelling. A lot of quality work is even more impressive!

Letters of Recommendation

Much like interpersonal skills, a strong vote of support from a professor or supervisor can go a long and indefinable way toward enhancing one's appeal as a prospective graduate student. Not only does this necessitate quality work and positive relationships, but it involves establishing a mentor relationship with one or more professors or supervisors. The better an advisor knows, respects, and likes the person he or she is writing about, the better able he or she will be to strike both an informed professional and personal tone in a letter of recommendation. Letters of recommendation can figure in prominently, as they are the only part of an application (beyond a personal statement) that speaks of the applicant as a real live person in relation to others.

Motivation

Motivation is perhaps the key ingredient to a successful undergraduate record. Motivation helps to pull a student through aversive tasks such as studying for the GREs and adds enthusiasm and dedication to more enjoyable tasks. In other words, motivation helps to overcome the many obstacles posed by exams, papers, applications and the like, and is often apparent in graduate school applications through the depth and breadth of psychology experience pursued during college. Many highly motivated students have become successful psychologists despite significant weaknesses in academic or even interpersonal realms, utilizing their energy and drive to compensate for other relative shortcomings.

Applying to Graduate Programs in Clinical Psychology

Because quality graduate programs can be highly competitive, it is usually helpful to cast a wide net by applying to a fairly large number of programs in various parts of the country. Even schools that are not necessarily prestigious can be highly competitive. There are approximately 2,400 clinical psychology graduate school openings available each year, and the acceptance rate for all APA-accredited doctoral graduate programs in clinical psychology is about 10%. However, some programs are extremely competitive, accepting fewer than 2% of their applicants, whereas other programs are much less competitive, accepting greater than 60% of their applicants (APA, 2008; Norcross, 2009; Norcross et al., 2008). Generally, university-based programs are more competitive than freestanding professional schools and also tend to be significantly less expensive (Norcross, 2009).

In order to determine which schools to apply to, it is important to consider the type and quality of the programs as well as which geographic locations would be acceptable. Several resources, such as the *Insider's Guide to Graduate Programs in Clinical and Counseling Psychology* by Norcross and colleagues (2008) and *Graduate Study in Psychology* published by the APA (2009), may be helpful in creating a list of the programs most likely to be of

interest. Psychology faculty are also likely to be good sources of information. However, keep in mind that sometimes faculty and others who have been out of training for many years may not be up-to-date on all aspects of programs from across the country but rather only on those that they have regular and ongoing collaborations with. Once a list of 20 to 35 programs is developed, obtaining catalogs and application packets from these programs (usually available online) will help to further narrow the list. A final list of perhaps 13 to 16 schools should be developed and reviewed by professors or other professionals for final advice. A combination of competitive and less competitive "safety" schools should be considered. Although each applicant must decide to which programs he or she will apply, the national application average is about 13 (Norcross et al., 2008).

The application forms must be completed thoughtfully and correctly, avoiding typographical or grammatical errors. Because most programs request applicants to write a personal statement as well as submit a *curriculum vitae (CV)*, applicants must take these tasks very seriously. While there is generally no right or wrong way to complete the personal statement, revealing family secrets and personal problems is usually not advised. The focus of the statement should be more professional than personal, highlighting career, intellectual, and service interests and goals. The statement requires the applicant to discuss the reasons why he or she is interested in graduate school in clinical psychology as well as the particular factors leading him or her to apply to each specific graduate program. Furthermore, the personal statement generally requests that applicants outline their career and educational goals and specify how the specific program can help meet these goals. Sometimes they ask you to identify the professor you wish to work with in graduate school. This can be challenging unless you have inside information from current or former students of these professors to help make your selection.

The CV is an academic resume. The CV outlines the applicant's complete contact information, educational experiences (e.g., schools attended and degrees obtained), relevant work and volunteer experiences, and professional presentations and publications (if any). Unlike a resume, a CV is not confined to one page. While the CV of a college student, graduate student, or working professional differs a great deal, several general principles should be followed for all CVs. Preparation of a CV should include concise and honest descriptions of relevant work, educational, and other professional experiences (e.g., volunteer positions). Headings such as "Education, Honors and Awards, and Professional Activities" should be used (see Table 15.2). Asking a professor, career counselor, and several friends to review the completed personal statement and CV for feedback is generally beneficial. Retaining a copy of all application materials is wise in case any application materials get lost or destroyed. Using overnight delivery services or certified mail will help ensure that the application materials have indeed reached the intended destinations if web-based applications aren't required. Also, requests for transcripts and GRE scores are usually needed well in advance of the application deadlines. Excellent guidelines for preparing graduate school applications can be found in the guidebook by Norcross and colleagues (2008).

Once applications have been sent and received, the applicant must wait for responses. A telephone or in-person interview may be requested by interested schools. It is important to always be professional with all representatives of the graduate program. This includes faculty, secretaries, and current graduate students. Even during informal chats with students and secretarial staff, an applicant may be judged and evaluated by each and every interaction. Students are advised to avoid silly messages on their home answering machines. They should also be careful of what is on their web pages, blogs, Facebook, and other sources of information about them.

If you are fortunate enough to be invited for an onsite or telephone interview, you have passed the first critical cut of applicants. Graduate programs often interview only a small proportion of their applicants and thus the odds of getting an acceptance to the program increase substantially once an applicant reaches this stage of the process. In preparation for the interview, it is critical that the applicant be very familiar with the training program, interests of the faculty, and educational requirements and thus should read the brochures and course catalog carefully. Once onsite for an interview, applicants should be sure to dress in a professional manner as well as maintain a high level of interest, energy, and enthusiasm for the program throughout the day and with all interactions with faculty, graduate students, and staff. Be sure to remind yourself that you are never off-duty or speaking off the record during these interview experiences. Thoughtful questions for

Table 15.2   **General Headings and Subheadings for a Curriculum Vitae**

General information (i.e., name, address, telephone number, e-mail address, web site)

Education (i.e., university, degree, year of graduation, major field(s) of study)

Honors and awards

Professional memberships (e.g., American Psychological Association, Student Affiliate)

Professional activities (e.g., relevant work and volunteer positions with dates, location, supervisors' names, and brief description of activities)

Research (i.e., presentations at regional or national conferences, publications)

References (i.e., names, addresses, phone numbers, e-mail addresses of three or four professional references)

each interviewer should be prepared in advance. Additional guidelines for how to best prepare and participate in the interview process can be found in the guidebook by Norcross et al. (2008).

Graduate School in Clinical Psychology

Graduate training in psychology involves coursework, clinical training, research experience, and often teaching experience. There are approximately 180 accredited doctoral graduate programs in clinical psychology in the United States and Canada and many nonaccredited programs as well. About 1,200 doctorates in clinical psychology are awarded each year (APA, 2008). Graduate school in clinical psychology is designed to take five years to complete, including the required one-year clinical internship. However, the national average is closer to about six to eight years. This additional length of time is generally due to students taking longer than expected to complete their doctoral dissertations. In most graduate programs, the doctoral dissertation is a comprehensive and high-quality original research study that is supervised by a faculty committee of three to five professors with one professor acting as chairperson.

Students interested in graduate school in clinical psychology can choose between several different training models and types of programs to best suit their needs and interests. Each of the following choices and issues merit informed and careful consideration.

PhD or PsyD

A student interested in obtaining a doctorate in clinical psychology can choose between two types of doctorates: the traditional **PhD (Doctor of Philosophy)** or the newer **PsyD (Doctor of Psychology).** Historically, the PhD was awarded to graduate students training in psychology at the doctoral level. The most common model of training was and still is the scientist-practitioner model (Raimy, 1950), which encourages equal and integrated

training emphases on both research and clinical practice. The model seeks to train graduate students in becoming both competent practitioners of clinical psychology providing skilled psychotherapy, psychological assessment, and consultation services as well as competent researchers who are able to conduct rigorous scientific studies. Most universities with graduate training programs in clinical psychology award the PhD degree.

Several universities, such as the University of Denver, offer separate programs for PhD students and PsyD students. The PsyD degree was proposed as a viable alternative to the traditional PhD. Rather than a scientist-practitioner model that equally blends research and clinical practice in training graduate students, the PsyD model sought to train students in the scholar-practitioner model with much more emphasis on clinical practice and minimal emphasis on research skills. Thus, the goal of the PsyD training model is to spend most of the graduate training years preparing students to become practitioners of clinical psychology services (e.g., psychotherapy, psychological assessment, clinical consultation) with minimal focus on training professionals to become researchers. While research is generally valued in PsyD programs, the training model assumes that graduates will become practitioners and consumers of research rather than actually conducting research studies during their careers. The majority of graduate training programs currently award students the traditional PhD degree, yet more and more programs (especially freestanding professional schools that exist outside of the university environment) are offering the PsyD degree. The growth of the PsyD programs can be seen when you compare the number of accredited PsyD programs in 1973 (1) to the programs available by 2009 (63), awarding about half of all clinical psychology doctorates each per year (Norcross, 2009).

Currently, PsyD graduate programs tend to be larger than PhD programs and tend to be less competitive regarding admission. PhD program acceptance rates average about 10%, while PsyD programs accept about 40%

of their applicants (APA, 2008; Norcross, 2009; Norcross et al., 2008; Peterson, 2003). However, research has indicated that PhD and PsyD students perform equally well on graduate school qualifying examinations, on grades, and on clinical internships (Peterson, 2003). However, concerns about the quality of PsyD training programs remain (McFall, 1991, 2000; Strickland, 1985). These concerns generally highlight the very large number of students being admitted to these programs.

University versus Freestanding Professional Schools

Historically, graduate training in clinical psychology has been the domain of university programs throughout the United States and Canada. However, during the early 1970s, a number of freestanding professional schools opened to train graduate students in psychology. **Freestanding professional schools** are not university based or affiliated. These programs originally emerged and proliferated in California with the opening of the California School of Professional Psychology (CSPP). CSPP (now called Alliant University) operates many campuses in California (e.g., San Francisco, San Diego, Los Angeles, and Fresno), enrolling more than 5,000 students. These freestanding schools of psychology are not affiliated with any universities and maintain independent faculty, staff, and students. Today, freestanding professional schools can be found throughout the United States. Approximately 50% of all doctorates in clinical psychology are now awarded by these schools (Norcross, 2009; Peterson, 2003; Stricker & Cummings, 1992). The freestanding schools tend to have extremely large entry classes relative to university-based programs, older students, and tend to be less competitive regarding admission. Whereas many of these schools offer the PsyD degree, many offer a PhD degree or both. Furthermore, many of the freestanding schools admit older students who may look at psychology as a second career. Financial aid also tends to be less available in freestanding schools relative to university programs, and the expense is prohibitive for many students (Norcross, 2009; Norcross et al., 2008). Finally, students attending freestanding schools generally do not have the opportunity to be exposed to the entire field of psychology since nonclinical areas of psychology, such as cognitive, developmental, social, learning, physiological, and others, are not represented at these schools.

Accreditation

Since 1948, the APA has accredited graduate training programs in clinical psychology. They also accredit programs in other areas of applied psychology such as counseling, school, and industrial/organizational psychology. The APA lists specific criteria for **accreditation** and regularly (usually every three to five years) conducts onsite visitations to graduate training programs to ensure that all criteria for accreditation are met. It is assumed that any APA-accredited program would offer a high-quality graduate training experience.

However, not all graduate programs in psychology are accredited by the APA or even by local accreditation agencies such as the Western Association of Colleges and Schools (WASC). Accreditation by the APA as well as regional accreditation agencies is important to maximize the chances of obtaining quality graduate education, clinical internship, and postdoctoral training. APA accreditation increases the chance of obtaining a license to practice in any state as well as the ability to be employed in any appropriate work setting. In fact, obtaining training from an APA-accredited program is often a requirement for employment for many positions, including Veterans' Administration (VA) Hospitals. Furthermore, APA-accredited training is a requirement for obtaining board certification or the diploma from the American Board of Professional Psychology (ABPP) and for inclusion in the *National Register of Health Service Providers in Psychology*. The *National Register* is frequently used by insurance companies and others to determine which psychologists will be eligible to receive insurance reimbursement for professional services (Sheridan, Matarazzo, & Nelson, 1995). Finally, the APA has advised state licensing boards that only students from accredited programs should be allowed to obtain a license to practice psychology, stating that "by 1995 applicants for licensure shall have completed a doctoral program in psychology that is accredited by the American Psychological Association" (APA, 1987b, p. 3). However, 15 years after this suggested deadline, most states have ignored APA's advice.

Training Curriculum and Emphasis

Although the APA outlines a core curriculum for all accredited clinical psychology training programs, all accredited graduate training programs are not exactly alike. Each program maintains its own unique perspective and curriculum based on the faculty and traditions of the program. Not everyone is content with the way in which clinical psychologists are trained (R. Fox, 1994; Shapiro & Wiggins, 1994), because there is disagreement concerning how best to organize and structure graduate training in clinical psychology. These differences of opinion are thus reflected in the diversity of training programs available. While some programs heavily emphasize research skills and productivity (about 35% of programs), others may emphasize clinical training (about 25% of programs). Still other programs pride themselves on providing an equal balance between research and clinical training. Some programs focus their clinical training toward certain theoretical orientations such as cognitive-behavioral models, psychodynamic models, humanistic models, family systems models, or others, while many programs emphasize eclectic training in utilizing a variety of theoretical models and perspectives. For example, a survey of graduate school training directors found that 55% of training programs emphasize a cognitive-behavioral approach, 23% emphasize a psychodynamic

approach, and 10% focused on a humanistic-existential orientation (Wisocki, Grebstein, & Hunt, 1994). Another survey revealed that 49% emphasize a cognitive-behavioral approach, 28% emphasize a psychodynamic approach, and 19% emphasize a family systems approach (Norcross, Sayette, & Mayne, 2002). Some programs demand highly rigorous research dissertation projects while others allow theoretical papers or case studies to be written for dissertation projects. Some programs are primarily interested in training researchers, others are interested in training practitioners, while others maintain no specific agenda in the future employment of their students. Individual programs may offer specialty emphasis in areas such as health psychology, child clinical psychology, or multicultural psychology.

It is not always possible to determine the training emphasis of each program by reviewing its web site, course catalog, or application materials. Often one must have these questions answered by current graduate students, recent graduates of the training program, or by current faculty.

Graduate training programs generally offer the same core curriculum suggested by the APA (Table 15.3). This core curriculum has not changed significantly since it was proposed about 50 years ago (Shakow, 1947). This includes courses on the biological bases of behavior, the social bases of behavior, individual differences, and cognition and learning, as well as courses in professional ethics. Graduate courses in statistics, research methods, assessment, multiculturalism, and psychopathology are also required. In addition to coursework, graduate training usually includes practicum or field placements. These placements allow graduate students to work with clinical populations providing individual, couple, family, and group psychotherapy with a variety of patient populations (e.g., adults, children, inpatient, outpatient) as well as providing opportunities to acquire experience with psychological testing (e.g., intelligence, neuropsychological, personality). Graduate training also provides research training. Typically, a master's thesis

Table 15.3   **Typical Graduate School Program and Schedule**

First Year	
Fall Term	**Spring Term**
Statistics	Biological Basis of Abnormal Behavior
Psychopathology	Personality Testing
Research Methods	Interviewing Techniques
Intelligence Testing	History and Systems of Psychology
Multicultural Issues	Individual Differences
Master's Thesis Research	Master's Thesis Research

Second Year	
Fall Term	**Spring Term**
Psychological Testing	Development Psychology
Advanced Personality	Multivariate Statistics II
Multivariate Statistics	Social Psychology
Clinical Psychotherapy	Clinical Neuropsychology
Practicum	Practicum
Master's Thesis Research	Master's Thesis Research

Third Year	
Fall Term	**Spring Term**
Advanced Human Learning and Memory	Professional Ethics
Human Sexuality	Elective
Dissertation	Dissertation
Practicum	Practicum

Fourth Year	
Fall Term	**Spring Term**
Electives	Electives
Dissertation Research	Dissertation Research

Fifth Year
Full-Time Clinical Internship

Note: Although graduate programs may be completed in five years, a high degree of variability exists such that many students take longer than five years to complete their requirements.

as well as a doctoral dissertation are conducted, allowing the student to conduct a quality research project under the supervision and guidance of several graduate school faculty members. The master's thesis is typically completed by the end of the second year of graduate study while the dissertation is completed by the end of the fourth or fifth year. The dissertation project acts as a final capstone of research experience, where a student completes a comprehensive study under faculty supervision. The dissertation is often seen as the defining accomplishment of the doctoral degree. The student then defends the project in an oral examination among a group of faculty members. Finally, most graduate training programs require comprehensive qualifying examinations to determine the competence of their students in academic psychology, research, and clinical work prior to being allowed to complete their internships and doctoral degree. A typical graduate program in clinical psychology includes the courses and schedule listed in Table 15.3.

Clinical Internship

Almost all graduate training programs in clinical psychology require that students complete a one-year, full-time (or two-year, part-time)

clinical **internship** prior to being awarded the doctorate. As of 2009, there were 459 APA-accredited internship programs in the United States and Canada (Association of Psychology Postdoctoral and Internship Centers [APPIC], 2009). This training almost always occurs outside of the graduate training program in hospitals, clinics, and various clinical settings throughout the United States. Students apply for internship following the successful completion of all graduate coursework, practicum training (i.e., small, part-time local internship experiences), and research requirements of the graduate program. Therefore, the clinical internship generally serves as a capstone or final integrating experience prior to obtaining the doctorate.

Highlight of a Contemporary Clinical Psychologist

Martin M. Antony, PhD

Photo: Courtesy
Martin M. Antony

Birth Date: July 17, 1964

College: BSc (psychology), University of Toronto, 1987

Graduate Program: PhD (psychology), State University of New York at Albany, 1994

Current Job: Professor and Director of Graduate Program, Department of Psychology, Ryerson University, Toronto

Pros and Cons of Being a Clinical Psychologist:

Pros: "My work as a clinical psychologist is personally rewarding, in part because of the potential to impact people's lives in a meaningful way. In addition, a career in clinical psychology provides incredible flexibility with respect to work settings and day-to-day responsibilities. Clinical psychologists can work in a wide range of environments including hospitals, community agencies, universities, schools, prisons, private clinics, industry, and military bases, to name a few. The day-to-day activities of clinical psychologists can also vary greatly, often including clinical service (e.g., assessment, treatment), research, classroom teaching, supervision and training, administration, business, program development, writing, consulting, service to the profession, working with the media, and various other roles. Other advantages of a career in clinical psychology include the fact that there seems to be adequate demand for the services of psychologists, and psychologists are well paid for their work. In addition, clinical psychologists enjoy a great degree of autonomy, relative to many other careers."

Cons: "Actually, I don't see any big disadvantages of working as a clinical psychologist. For me, the main challenge is that it's impossible to do everything I want to do. With each year that passes, I seem to fall further behind on my to-do list, simply because exciting new opportunities keep coming up and it's hard to say 'no.' However, that probably says more about my willingness to set limits than about my decision to become a clinical psychology."

Your Specialty and How You Chose It: "My own work focuses primarily on anxiety disorders, though I have a secondary interest in the relationship between perfectionism and psychopathology. My interest in anxiety disorders came about by accident. After completing my undergraduate degree, I decided to take a year off school and work as a research assistant. I applied for two jobs—one involving work on a schizophrenia study and one in the area of anxiety disorders. At the time, I wanted the schizophrenia position but didn't get it. I ended up accepting a position in an anxiety disorders clinic, and found that the more I learned about anxiety disorders, the more interesting the area was to me. I was also struck by how dramatically people changed following cognitive and behavioral treatments. After my year as a research assistant, I decided to pursue graduate studies in universities that would provide me with the opportunity for further training in the area of anxiety disorders."

Advice for Students Interested in Becoming a Clinical Psychologist: "Most clinical psychology programs accept only a small percentage of applicants, so my best advice is to apply widely and make sure that your application is strong. Some of the factors that programs consider when making their decisions include the applicant's undergraduate grades, scores on the Graduate Record Exam (GRE), research experience, interpersonal skills (based on interviews and letters of recommendation), and the match between the applicant's research interests and those of the proposed supervisors. I recommend that anyone interested in applying to clinical psychology programs begin planning for the process early in their undergraduate training, to ensure that they have the experiences they need by the time they apply. There are a number of excellent books available on the application process, including the *Insider's Guide to Graduate Programs in Clinical and Counseling Psychology*, by Michael Sayette, Tracy Mayne, and John Norcross (published by Guilford Press). This book is updated every two years."

Future of Clinical Psychology: "Going forward, there are a number of issues that will likely influence the field of clinical psychology over the next decade. First, with the launch of numerous private, freestanding professional schools offering PsyD degrees in the United States, there has been a sharp increase in the number of doctoral-level psychologists graduating. Increasingly, those working in psychology worry that the supply of psychologists may start to exceed the demand for our services. Second, the world in which psychologists live is constantly changing—the population is aging and cultural diversity is increasing. Being trained to work with diverse populations is more important than ever, and must continue to be a top priority in psychology graduate programs. Third, health-care costs continue to increase, making it more difficult for people to afford the services of psychologists. There is a risk that psychologists will be seen as too expensive in the future, so it is important for psychologists to find ways to distinguish themselves from other less expensive mental health professions. Finally, there is still much variability in the extent to which clinical psychologists use evidence-based approaches to assessment and treatment. As health-care costs increase, there will be more pressure on psychologists (and other practitioners) to be more accountable for their services. Psychology training programs need to further emphasize evidence-based approaches in their curricula."

Typical Schedule: "Currently, I have a number of different roles. First, as president of the Canadian Psychological Association (2009–2010), I chair the CPA Board of Directors, which involves regular phone calls, e-mails, and travel to Board meetings. Second, as professor of Psychology, I teach courses in clinical psychology and supervise several MA and PhD students. Third, as Director of Graduate Training in the Department of Psychology at Ryerson University, I am responsible for ensuring that our training programs run smoothly. Fourth, as Director of Research at the Anxiety Treatment and Research Centre (St. Joseph's Healthcare, Hamilton, Ontario), I collaborate on clinical research, provide supervision to clinical psychology practicum students and residents, and see a small number of clients for psychotherapy. Finally, I travel regularly to provide training workshops and other presentations to professionals from across the United States, Canada, and overseas. On a typical day, I usually have several meetings with students I supervise, meetings related to my administrative responsibilities at Ryerson University, classes to teach, or meetings related to my work with the Canadian Psychological Association. I usually also receive over a hundred e-mails per day, which can take up to several hours to read and answer. I try to leave at least one or two days clear of meetings and classes, so I can devote uninterrupted time to writing books or scientific papers."

Many students are unable to complete their dissertation projects prior to attending their internship. These students often must return to their graduate training programs following the completion of internship in order to complete (and defend before a committee of faculty) their doctoral dissertations.

Many of the strategies and principles for applying to graduate school are applicable to clinical internship programs. Many training sites are very selective and seek graduate students who have outstanding academic credentials as well as excellent clinical training and experiences. The APA accredits about 450 internship programs as they do the approximately 180 graduate training programs. A complete list of accredited internship programs can be found in a yearly updated directory of internships published and provided by the APPIC. The

directory is available online (www.APPIC.org) through APPIC and all graduate programs and internship sites have a copy of the directory. Applications are obtained online and must be completed on or around December 1 of each year for those interested in the programs that begin the following July 1 or September 1. All internship programs maintain their own selection and interviewing process. However, internship programs are not allowed to make offers of admission until a set date in February of each year, which are conducted through a matching process.

Activities during the clinical internship usually focus specifically on clinical training. Psychotherapy, psychological testing, and consultation with a variety of patient populations are expected. Interns typically work in collaboration with a variety of professionals (e.g., physicians, nurses, social workers, counselors) in most settings. Interns also typically participate in seminars on topics such as psychotherapy, psychological testing, and professional ethics, among others. Some internship training sites specialize in certain patient populations (e.g., children, adolescents, college students, adults, the elderly) while certain sites specialize in particular types of professional services (e.g., testing, psychotherapy, consultation, acute hospital care). Research experience and training may also be a part of the internship experience. Following the successful completion of the clinical internship and all of the requirements of the graduate training program (including the doctoral dissertation), the doctorate is awarded.

Postdoctoral Fellowship

Contrary to what many assume, being awarded the doctorate is not the end of the organized training process for those wishing to become clinical psychologists. Most states require one to two years of postdoctoral training before one is eligible to take the licensing examination. However, nine states allow students who have already secured two years of supervised training to obtain their license without a postdoctoral fellowship training year. Anyone wishing to practice clinical psychology must obtain a license to practice from their state licensing board. Some psychologists who choose not to practice (e.g., full-time academics) do not necessarily need a license or a **postdoctoral fellowship** in order to teach and conduct their research in college or university settings. The criteria for postdoctoral training vary from state to state. The APA provides accreditation for some postdoctoral training sites. An organization affiliated with the APA (the APPIC) provides a list of member organizations that offer post-doctoral training meeting APPIC guidelines for quality training. This includes about 80 programs.

Postdoctoral training occurs in a wide variety of settings, including hospitals, clinics, counseling centers, universities, and even private practices. Postdoctoral training can include clinical work such as psychotherapy, psychological testing, and consultation as well as research, teaching, and many other professional activities. Some postdoctoral fellowships (especially research fellowships) can last three or four years. The APA as well as interested affiliated organizations such as APPIC are working toward more structured criteria, expectations, and accreditation procedures for postdoctoral training.

Finally, once postdoctoral training is successfully completed, one is now eligible to take the licensing examination in order to be fully licensed as a psychologist and eligible to practice and function as an independent professional. Four years of college followed by at least four years of graduate school, a year of clinical internship and finally one or more years of postdoctoral training have been completed before licensing as a psychologist is possible in most states.

Specialization

Clinical psychology offers many specialties. Various specialties and subspecialties (e.g., pediatric neuropsychology) have developed and become popular while others are popular for a while and fade in interest over time (Norcross et al., 2008; Plante, 1996b; Sayette & Mayne, 1990). For example, neuropsychology and health psychology have become very popular specialties in recent years (APA, 1995a, 2001, 2009). Postdoctoral training is generally the time when most of the intensive specialization training occurs. Some authors have warned that clinical psychology students often try to specialize too early in their careers and do not adequately obtain basic clinical psychology skills prior to specialization (Matarazzo, 1987; Plante, 1996b). Matarazzo (1987) warned that it is important to keep in mind that psychology is one field that has many applications rather than a set of numerous and distinct specialties. Each specialization, through its representative professional organization(s), typically offers guidelines for the specific training and educational requirements that are suggested to become competent in a specialty area. For instance, Division 38 (Health Psychology) and Division 40 (Neuropsychology) of the APA offer guidelines on training in these specialty areas. Furthermore, the board certification or ABPP diploma process (discussed later in this chapter) offers certification in a variety of specialty areas.

Certification and/or Licensure

Certification and **licensure** procedures are legally defined and regulated at the state level by state boards of psychology. The role of the psychology board is to set minimum standards for admission to the profession, conduct licensing examinations, and regulate the practice of psychology in order to protect the public from professional misconduct.

Certification laws control the use of the word *psychologist* such that only those who meet legal state standards are allowed to call themselves or represent themselves to the public as psychologists. While certification laws protect the title of psychologist from being misused, certification laws do not impact the practice of psychological services.

Licensing laws are more restrictive than certification laws. In addition to protection of the title of psychologist, licensing laws provide guidelines and restrictions in defining what constitutes the practice of psychological services. Almost all licensing laws provide a generic license for psychologists without acknowledgment of or restrictions on specialty or subspecialty (e.g., child clinical psychology, neuropsychology, clinical health psychology, counseling psychology). Therefore, contrary to what many believe, states do not generally recognize or have a specific license available for clinical psychologists separate from other practicing psychologists (e.g., counseling psychologists). In fact, in many states, such as California, it is not permissible to advertise to the public as a "clinical psychologist" or a "licensed clinical psychologist" because the state does not issue specialty licenses.

Since the certification and licensing processes are conducted at the state level, each state develops its own laws and procedures. However, since 1955, the APA has offered states a set of guidelines now called the "Model Act for State Licensure of Psychologists" (APA, 1955, 1967, 1987b), which outlines suggested rules and regulations for state licensing. The Model Act includes minimum educational requirements as well as guidelines concerning the suspension and revocation of licenses. While state licensing boards are not required to use the Model Act, the vast majority of states do in fact consider these and other APA documents in drafting state licensing laws and regulations.

Because most states maintain licensing laws rather than certification laws, licensing laws will be highlighted here. First, an application must be submitted to the state board of psychology in order to be allowed to take the licensing examination. While this procedure differs from state to state, all boards review applications to ensure that the state criteria for exam eligibility have been met. This includes ensuring that the applicant has an appropriate doctorate in psychology with the required amount of both predoctoral and, if required, postdoctoral supervisory experiences

and training. Once the state licensing board reviews the application and determines that it meets all of the necessary criteria, the applicant is allowed to take the written portion of the examination.

The Written Examination

All states administer the same national written examination for licensing (i.e., the **Examination for Professional Practice in Psychology [EPPP]**). This exam consists of 200 multiple choice items covering a variety of relevant areas within the field of psychology. The exam does not focus solely on the clinical practice of psychology as many people often assume. Questions about test construction, statistics, social psychology, experimental psychology, industrial/organizational psychology, developmental psychology, and other areas are all included in the written licensing examination. Many applicants choose to take structured preparatory courses provided by a few independent businesses such as the Association for Advanced Training in the Behavioral Sciences. These programs sell study materials including audiotape lectures, practice examinations, and detailed outlines of various domains likely to be addressed on the examination. For an additional charge, these companies also offer face-to-face classroom instruction to assist in concentrated preparation. Because these preparatory courses can be expensive, some applicants for licensure prefer to share the materials and thus the expense with a colleague who is also taking the examination at the same time. Others choose to borrow materials from a colleague who recently took the examination. While the national examination is renewed and updated each time it is given, certain areas of psychology such as statistics do not change radically between administrations. Some choose not to use any of these testing materials at all. With adequate preparation on their own, many successfully pass the written examination.

States do vary in designating what constitutes a passing score. Some states consider a fixed number of correct items such as 150 out of 200 as the criterion for passing, while others use the national median, which changes with each testing administration. Approximately 2,200 people take the examination across the United States each time it is given. An applicant may take the exam again if not passed on the first (or subsequent) attempt(s).

The Oral Examination

After successful completion of the written examination, many states then require an oral (or sometimes an essay) examination before obtaining the license. The oral examination differs from state to state. Typically, questions about legal and ethical issues pertaining to the practice of psychology (such as limits on confidentiality, treatment of minors, child abuse reporting laws, involuntary commitment) are discussed along with clinical questions regarding diagnosis and treatment of hypothetical patients. The examiners, typically licensed psychologists who volunteer to conduct the examinations, assess the applicant's understanding of the laws and ethics of professional practice as well as probing clinical skills, sensitivity to multicultural issues, and clinical judgment to determine if the applicant is competent enough to act as an independent and thus unsupervised professional.

Once an applicant successfully passes the state licensing requirements, he or she is issued a license number by the state and can finally represent him- or herself to the public as a psychologist capable of independent practice. In most states, the license must be renewed every year or two. To do so, the psychologist will typically need to document that he or she has not been convicted of any felony offenses, is not in trouble due to ethical violations, demonstrates successful completion of a certain number of continuing education credits (usually about 20 hours per year), and pays a licensing fee. The number of hours and the types of courses acceptable for continuing education vary from state to state. Topics for continuing education include the current understanding of the assessment and treatment of various psychiatric diagnoses, learning new assessment or treatment techniques, understanding specific concerns of diverse populations, and how to avoid legal and ethical dilemmas, among others.

Employment

The transition from student/trainee to an independent professional can be both exciting and challenging. Most professional training programs do surprisingly little to prepare students for this transition. Because graduate training programs tend to emphasize the academic, clinical, and research training of graduate students, they usually offer little if any attention to career development and professional issues (Plante, 1995, 1996b). Furthermore, the academic faculty at most graduate programs are often not involved with many of the professional issues that their students will typically experience during their nonacademic careers (e.g., developing a private or group practice, licensure and continuing education requirements, dealing with managed health care and hospital politics, working with a wide variety of clinicians from different professional disciplines). Therefore, many new clinical psychologists are unprepared for the transition to employment.

Olson, Downing, Heppner, and Pinkney (1986) reported a number of myths that afflict many early career psychologists:

> As soon as I unpack my bags, I'll be settled.
>
> My new associates will welcome me enthusiastically and accept me as one of them.
>
> I will never be an apprentice again.
>
> I will easily master the varied demands of my job.
>
> I must perform perfectly, lest someone discover that I am a fraud.
>
> Because I have worked so hard to get here, I will love my job.

One of the great advantages of being a clinical psychologist is that there are a wide variety of employment settings in which to work. Many psychologists wish to enter the academic world. Some look toward large research universities while others look toward small liberal arts colleges that emphasize teaching. Others wish for an academic career in a medical center environment while still other psychologists are interested in clinical practice. Some prefer medical centers, outpatient clinics, or solo or group private practice. Still others are interested in careers in administration and program development. Many new professionals wish to combine academic work with clinical practice. Median starting salaries vary depending on specialty area and job location. Private practitioners and consultants can earn much more. Strategies for finding a suitable first job vary significantly depending on which career direction the psychologist chooses (APA, 1997b, 2009; Kilburg, 1991; Sternberg, 2006). Strategies for academic and clinical positions will be highlighted next.

Academic Positions

Full-time tenure-track academic positions are a popular choice for many new psychologists. After being in school for so many years and being influenced by college and graduate school professors, academic careers are appealing to many. Although doctorates in clinical psychology can include the PhD or PsyD degrees, tenure-track academic positions in university settings generally prefer the PhD rather than the PsyD degree. Tenure-track academic positions are also very competitive and can be hard to find (Brems, Lampman, & Johnson, 1995). The American Psychological Association *Monitor on Psychology,* the *Chronicle of Higher Education,* and the *American Psychological Society Observer* are the most likely places to find these jobs advertised. Current professors may also provide an insider's view of good jobs that are available or at least imminent. After completing the application procedure (typically sending a curriculum vitae, reprints of published professional articles, a cover letter outlining teaching and research interests, and

having three letters of recommendation), the applicant must wait to be selected for a job interview. Typically, academic departments invite a very small number of top applicants (typically about three or four) for job interviews. The interview usually lasts a full day or two and includes individual meetings with the department chair, faculty members on the search committee, and sometimes the dean and student representatives. Additionally, most applicants are asked to present their research to a group of faculty and students during a one-hour "job talk." Applicants may be asked to give a guest lecture in a psychology course as well. Finally, lunch and dinner with faculty also can be expected during the interview.

Clinical Positions

If a psychologist is primarily seeking a clinical position in an outpatient clinic, hospital, or group private practice, the application and interview strategy will be very different from those for an academic position. Typically, these jobs will be advertised in the *APA Monitor on Psychology* only for organizations who wish to pursue a national search for a job candidate. Not all clinical settings are interested in interviewing people from all over the United States and therefore will not advertise in the *APA Monitor on Psychology* or other national publications. The costs for advertising in these national publications can be high, and many organizations may not be interested in the expense of having job candidates fly in from all over the country to interview for their job opening. Therefore, finding out about job openings can be challenging. Often, word of mouth is the best and most opportune way to find out about job openings (APA, 1997, 2003d, 2009). Also, contacting various hospitals, clinics, group practices, state and county psychological associations, postgraduate training institutes, and colleagues may help to determine whether positions are available. Positions are also often listed at local professional conferences (e.g., state psychological associations). Networking is the key to ultimately securing clinical jobs.

Clinical job applications usually require a curriculum vitae, cover letter outlining clinical interests and experiences, and three letters of recommendation. Often, a sample assessment or other clinical report (removed of all identifying patient information) is requested. All materials are reviewed and a small number of applicants are selected for interviews. The interview often includes individual (and sometimes) group interviews with staff and administrators. In some institutions, the applicant will be asked to present a clinical case in front of staff in a clinical case conference or treatment rounds format.

The American Board of Professional Psychology Diploma

After being awarded the doctorate, a clinical psychologist is eligible to become a **diplomate,** an advanced level of certification. The **American Board of Professional Psychology (ABPP)** diploma is a post-licensing certification that reflects advanced competency in a subspecialty of psychology. The American Board of Professional Psychology acts as the credentialing agency for psychology diplomas in a variety of specialty areas, including clinical psychology, neuropsychology, counseling psychology, health psychology, family psychology, behavior therapy, school psychology, industrial/organizational psychology, group therapy, psychoanalysis, rehabilitation psychology, and forensic psychology. The ABPP is an independent organization closely associated with the APA. It is modeled after medical boards in that following medical school and residency training, a physician may apply to be board certified in a specialty area (e.g., Child Psychiatry, Neurology). These board exams are very common in medicine and are now common for psychologists.

The ABPP diploma application and examination process is a challenging, time-consuming, and expensive endeavor. So, why

do it? First, board certification, modeled after medical boards, recognizes an advanced level of professional competence in a specialty area of practice. This certification process and demonstration of advanced competence are often helpful to the public and other consumers of psychological services such as hospitals, clinics, training programs, insurance companies, and courts by suggesting that very-high-quality skills and services can be expected from a diplomate. The ABPP diploma is becoming more strongly suggested and even required in some employment settings, such as university medical centers. For example, at Stanford University Medical School, clinical and medical staff faculty are required to be board certified in order to be promoted in the academic ranks. Therefore, for a Clinical Assistant Professor to be promoted to a Clinical Associate Professor or Clinical Professor position, the ABPP diploma is required. Higher salaries are offered for psychologists who are diplomates in some settings, such as in the military and VA Hospitals. Thus, several thousand dollars each year might be added to the salary of psychologists in these settings.

The ABPP diploma is also expected in a variety of professional circles in order to be considered an expert. For example, the diploma is almost a requisite in many neuropsychology and forensic psychology environments. Thus, credibility and effectiveness in court testimony, for example, is enhanced by having the ABPP diploma. The ABPP also allows for licensing reciprocity in many states. Therefore, psychologists who are diplomates often do not need to go through the licensing process of examinations if they move from state to state. Finally, distinguishing oneself professionally and attaining the satisfaction of such an accomplishment often serve as sufficient motivators for pursuing diplomate status. Approximately 3% of all members of the APA become diplomates, and about 10% of all eligible psychologists become diplomates (APA, 2009). Therefore, diplomates are a select group of psychologists. Although the numbers are growing, the majority of clinical psychologists choose not to become diplomates.

Professionals are eligible to apply for an ABPP diploma in one of several areas (e.g., Clinical, Counseling, School, Family, Health, Behavior Therapy, Neuropsychology, Forensic, Group) several years after completing their doctoral degree. The application process includes completing an application outlining training and employment background as well as providing the committee with letters of recommendation from three or more professionals who are either diplomates themselves or fellows of the APA. Once these materials are reviewed and deemed acceptable by the screening committee, the applicant is asked to provide work samples to submit to the committee.

The work samples typically include complete written transcripts and videotapes of a one-hour psychotherapy session and a one-hour diagnostic interview or testing session. Additionally, a written description of the patient background, diagnosis, treatment plan, and the role of the session example in the context of the overall assessment or treatment plan is required. The work samples are then reviewed by the committee.

The final step in the process is the oral examination. In 1997, the oral examination was changed from a full day to a half day. A committee of three diplomate examiners, including a nonvoting chairperson, conducts the examination. The examination includes: (1) a discussion of the applicant's theoretical orientation and professional activities, (2) a discussion and defense of the applicant's work samples, and (3) a discussion of ethical vignettes presented by the committee.

Is Clinical Psychology Right for Me?

What does it take to become a clinical psychologist? Is it right for me? Certainly drive and dedication are needed to complete the lengthy training process in order to become a psychologist. A natural curiosity and interest in human behavior and a desire to improve the quality of life for others are also important factors. Anyone interested in

Table 15.4   Some Pros and Cons of Becoming a Clinical Psychologist

Pros
Exciting range of employment settings
Exciting range of employment activities
Opportunity to play significant role in helping others
Opportunities for both personal and professional growth and satisfaction

Cons
Long training process
Moderate salaries
Increased competition for jobs
Reduced research and training funding

the field of clinical psychology as a career option must, of course, decide for himself or herself whether clinical psychology is a good career path to follow (Table 15.4). Decisions about types of training programs, specializations, and career emphasis (e.g., research, teaching, administration, practice) must be made as well. Generally, psychologists express a high degree of satisfaction with their career choice. In fact, 80% to 82% of clinical psychologists report high degrees of job satisfaction (Norcross et al., 1997b, 2005, 2008; Plante, Boccaccini, & Andersen, 1998). This book was written in the hope of providing enough background about the field for a student to make an informed decision.

How to Get More Information about Current Issues in Clinical Psychology

Where does a student obtain the most up-to-date information about clinical psychology?

Useful sources of information include books about the field (including this one), some focusing on admission to graduate school and other training experiences (e.g., Keith-Spiegal, 1991; Megargee, 1990; Norcross, Sayette,

Table 15.5   **Major Professional Associations in Clinical Psychology**

American Psychological Association (APA)
750 First Street, NW
Washington, DC 20002-4242
(202) 336-5500
www.apa.org

Society of Clinical Psychology
Division 12 Central Office
P.O. Box 1082
Niwot, CO 80544
(303) 652-3126
www.apa.org/divisions/div12

American Psychological Society (APS)
1133 15th Street, NW, Suite 1000
Washington, DC 20005
Phone: (202) 293-9300
Fax: (202) 293-9350

National Register of Health Service Providers in Psychology
1120 G Street, NW, Suite 330
Washington, DC 20005
(202) 783-7663
www.nationalregister.com

American Board of Professional Psychology (ABPP)
600 Market Street, Suite 300
Chapel Hill, NC 27516

Phone: (919) 537-8031
Fax: (919) 537-8034
E-mail: office@abpp.org

American Academy of Clinical Psychology
P.O. Box 700341
San Antonio, TX 78270-0341
Phone: 909-626-5579
Fax: 909-626-5579
E-mail: contact@aacpsy.org

Canadian Psychological Association
141 Laurier Avenue West, Suite 702
Ottawa, Ontario K1P 5J3
Phone: (613) 237-2144
Toll free: (888) 472-0657
Fax: (613) 237-1674
E-mail: cpa@cpa.ca
www.cpa.ca

British Psychological Society
The British Psychological Society
St Andrews House
48 Princess Road East
Leicester LE1 7DR
Phone: +44 (0)116 254 9568
Fax: +44 (0)116 227 1314
E-mail: enquiries@bps.org.uk
www.bps.org.uk

et al., 2008), and others on the roles and activities of clinical and other psychologists (e.g., Kilburg, 1991; Sternberg, 1997, 2006). A number of excellent professional journals, newsletters, and other periodicals also provide compelling and timely information. These include *Professional Psychology: Research and Practice,* the *Journal of Consulting and Clinical Psychology,* the *National Psychologist,* the *American Psychological Association Monitor on Psychology,* the *American Psychologist,* the *Clinical Psychologist,* and *Clinical Psychology: Science and Practice,* among others. The APA and appropriate divisions (e.g., Division 12—Clinical Psychology), and state and county psychological associations are additional resources. Students may also join the APA as student-affiliated members at a very low cost. Interested students

can contact APA (www.apa.org) and learn more. Students from Canada may wish to contact the Canadian Psychological Association (www.cpa.ca). Finally, individual clinical psychologists themselves may offer help to interested persons. Obtaining information from several different sources (e.g., professional organizations, books, journals, professionals in the field, students in various stages of training) is highly advised (Table 15.5).

The Big Picture

Such a detailed description of the step-by-step process toward becoming a clinical psychologist may seem long and daunting as delineated here. After completing college, it takes at least six years of full-time training to become a licensed psychologist. Such is the preparation required to ensure competency, if not excellence, in psychologists' contributions to patient care, diagnosis, teaching, and research. Becoming a clinical psychologist allows one to teach at the university level and elsewhere, conduct research, provide consultation to a wide variety of professionals and organizations, conduct psychotherapy and psychological testing with one's own patients, and work in numerous professional settings. While the process is lengthy, it is important not to lose sight of the fact that each step is ripe with new experiences, rewards, exciting skill development, and the ongoing satisfaction of moving toward a personal and professional goal in a field designed ultimately to contribute to the quality of human life.

How will the road to becoming a clinical psychologist change in the future? The application and training process likely will change. For example, the graduate curriculum must accommodate important changes in society such as multiculturalism. Postdoctoral training is likely to become mandatory while continuing education will become more rigorous in the future. The training process must adapt to the changing needs of both students and society for clinical psychology to remain both relevant and vibrant.

Key Points

1. The road to becoming a clinical psychologist is a long one divided by several distinct stages that include college, graduate school, clinical internship, postdoctoral fellowship, licensure, and finally employment and advanced certification (e.g., the diplomate).

2. Overall, students interested in becoming clinical psychologists and gaining admission into high-quality graduate programs must take their college experience very seriously. Solid grades and high-quality research and clinical experiences during the college years are important to acquire. Specifically, students must obtain a solid GPA, high scores on the GRE, obtain some clinical and research experience, and receive excellent letters of recommendation.

3. Graduate training in psychology involves coursework, clinical training, and research experiences. There are almost 200 accredited doctoral graduate programs in clinical psychology in the United States and Canada and many nonaccredited programs as well. Graduate school in clinical psychology generally takes five years to complete, including the required one-year clinical internship.

4. A student interested in obtaining a doctorate in clinical psychology can choose between two types of doctorates: the traditional PhD (or Doctor of Philosophy) or the newer PsyD (Doctor of Psychology). The most common model of training is the scientist-practitioner, or Boulder, model, which encourages equal training emphases on both research and clinical practice.

5. The PsyD degree seeks to train students in the scholar-practitioner, or Vail, model, with much more emphasis on clinical practice and minimal emphasis on research skills. While the majority of graduate training programs currently award students the traditional PhD degree, more and more programs (especially freestanding professional schools) are offering the PsyD degree.

6. Historically, graduate training in clinical psychology has been the domain of university programs throughout the United States and Canada. However, during the early 1970s, a number of freestanding professional schools opened to train graduate students in psychology. Approximately 50% of all doctorates in clinical psychology are now awarded by these schools. The freestanding schools tend to have large entry classes and older students, and tend to be less competitive regarding admission than university-based programs.

7. Since 1948, the APA has accredited graduate training programs in clinical psychology. Accreditation by the APA as well as

regional accreditation agencies is important to maximize the chances of obtaining quality graduate education, clinical internship, and postdoctoral training. APA accreditation also improves the odds of being able to obtain a license to practice in any state and to be employed in any appropriate setting.

8. All accredited graduate training programs are not alike. Each program maintains its own personality based on the faculty and traditions of the program.

9. Almost all graduate training programs in clinical psychology require that students complete a one-year, full-time (or two-year, part-time) clinical internship prior to being awarded the doctorate. There are about 400 APA-accredited internship programs in the United States and Canada. This training almost always occurs outside of the graduate training program in hospitals, clinics, and various clinical settings throughout the United States. The activities during the clinical internship focus specifically on clinical training such as psychotherapy, psychological testing, and consultation with a variety of patient populations.

10. Most states require one to two years of postdoctoral training before one is eligible to take the licensing examination. Postdoctoral training occurs in a wide variety of settings, including hospitals, clinics, counseling centers, universities, and even private practices. Postdoctoral training can include clinical work such as psychotherapy, psychological testing, and consultation as well as research, teaching, and many other professional activities. The APA and interested affiliated organizations such as APPIC are working toward more structured criteria, expectations, and accreditation for postdoctoral training.

11. Since the certification and licensing processes are conducted at the state level, each state develops its own laws and procedures. However, since 1955, the APA has offered states a set of guidelines called the Model Act, which outlines suggested rules and regulations for state licensing.

12. All states use the same national written examination for licensing (the EPPP). This exam consists of 200 multiple choice items covering a variety of relevant areas within the field of psychology. After successful completion of the written examination, many states then require an oral (or sometimes an essay) examination before granting the license.

13. One of the great advantages of being a clinical psychologist is that there are a wide variety of employment settings in which to work. Becoming a clinical psychologist allows one to teach at the university level, conduct research, provide consultation to a wide variety of professionals and organizations, conduct psychotherapy and psychological testing, and work in many different environments.

14. Several years after being awarded the doctorate, a clinical psychologist is eligible to become a diplomate, an advanced level of certification. The American Board of Professional Psychology (ABPP) diploma is a post-licensing certification that reflects advanced competency in a specialty area of psychology. The ABPP acts as the credentialing agency for psychology diplomates in a variety of specialty areas such as clinical psychology.

Key Terms

Accreditation
American Board of Professional Psychology (ABPP)
Certification
Diplomate
Doctor of Philosophy (PhD)
Doctor of Psychology (PsyD)
Examination for Professional Practice in Psychology (EPPP)
Freestanding professional school
Graduate Record Examination (GRE)
Internship
Licensure
Postdoctoral fellowship

For Reflection

1. What should a college student do during college to increase his or her chance of being admitted to a high-quality graduate program in clinical psychology?
2. What is the difference between a PhD and a PsyD degree?
3. What is the difference between university and freestanding professional schools for graduate training?
4. How long does it take from graduate school to licensure to become a clinical psychologist?
5. Why is accreditation important in selecting a graduate training program?
6. Which is the least regulated part of training for clinical psychology?
7. What is the ABPP diploma?
8. Why is licensure important?
9. What are the major training models in clinical psychology?
10. In general, how does the application process differ between academic and clinical positions?

Real Students, Real Questions

1. Is it frowned upon to take some time off before applying to graduate school?
2. If my GPA is low, do I have any chance of getting into graduate school?
3. Are there any differences in the jobs I could get if I get a PsyD rather than a PhD?
4. Why does it take so long to become a clinical psychologist?

Web Resources

www.ets.org
Learn more about the Graduate Record Examination.

www.psywww.com
Learn more about psychology; specifically designed for college and graduate students.

http://www.ncspp.info
Learn more about psychological training programs at professional schools.

Glossary

Academy of Psychological Clinical Science An organization of graduate training programs formed in 1994 to support the clinical-scientist model of graduate training.

Achenbach System of Empirically Based Assessment (ASEBA) The ASEBA is a group of symptom checklist assessment questionnaires used with children and adults of all ages to closely and empirically evaluate behavioral and psychiatric symptoms.

Accreditation Organizational review of curriculum to ensure training programs meet minimal standards of quality.

Acquired Immune Deficiency Syndrome (AIDS) Persons infected with one of several HIV viruses that may result in a serious and life-threatening disorder impacting the immune system.

Active listening Interviewing technique using a variety of methods to maximize understanding of what is being said.

Administration Clinical psychology activity involving management of people and organizations.

Advocate Consultation approach that seeks to convince a consultee to do something that the consultant believes is desirable.

Alcohol abuse The over use of alcohol to attempt to cope with stress, conflict, or other issues that interfer with occupational, relationship, social, and personal functioning.

Alzheimer's disease Degenerative disease involving memory loss, failure to recognize well-known people and objects, difficulty in organizing and planning, suspiciousness, and language problems.

American Board of Professional Psychology (ABPP) The credentialing agency for post-licensing psychology diplomas in a variety of specialty areas, including clinical psychology.

American Psychological Association (APA) Founded in 1892 and currently the largest organization of psychologists anywhere in the world, representing all specialties within psychology.

American Psychological Society (APS) Founded in 1988 and includes members primarily interested in research and scientific aspects of psychology.

Analogue Studies that use procedures, subjects, and measures that approximate a real-life clinical situations and are usually conducted in a laboratory where experimental conditions can be best controlled.

Anorexia nervosa A self-starvation problem that affects about 1% of the adolescent female population.

Assessment Clinical psychology activity involving various techniques, such as interviews and tests, to evaluate and answer clinical questions.

Attention Deficit Hyperactivity Disorder (ADHD) An inability to sustain attention and concentration, as well as problems with impulsivity, overactivity, irritability, and moodiness.

Beck Scales A series of inventories to assess depression, anxiety, hopelessness, and suicidal ideation developed by psychiatrist Aaron Beck.

Behavioral Applies theories of learning and conditioning to the understanding of human behavior and the treatment of behavioral and psychological problems.

Behavioral rehearsal Behavioral technique where someone practices how he or she might handle a given problem situation.

Between group Research designs that use two or more separate groups of subjects, each of which receives a different type of intervention or, in the case of a control condition, no intervention.

Bias Attempt to minimize potential error in research by controlling potentially influencing variables—also involves a point of view that is imposed on the patient or client.

Binet Scales Revised versions of the first standardized intelligence test developed by Alfred Binet in 1905. The current version, called the Stanford-Binet, was published in 1986.

Biofeedback Behavioral technique that provides physiological information such as heart rate and

477

blood pressure to patient in an attempt to learn to control these reactions to stress.

Biological vulnerability Genetic or other biological factors that put someone more at risk for the development of problems later.

Biopsychosocial An integrative perspective that suggests that biological, psychological, and social influences interact to contribute to both physical and mental health and illness.

Boston Process Approach Neuropsychological assessment approach developed by Edith Kaplan that uses a variety of tests to understand the process of brain–behavior functioning.

Boulder model Clinical psychology training model developed at a conference in Boulder, Colorado, that places equal weight on science and practice—also called the scientist-practitioner model.

Brain–behavior relationships The focus of the neuropsychology subspecialty that highlights the examination of how the brain impacts behavior and how behavior impacts the brain.

Brain injuries Trauma to the brain from vehicular accidents, falls, war wounds, sport injuries, gunshot wounds, violent assaults, and other tragic events that impact cognitive functioning.

Case studies Research approach that conducts an in-depth analysis of one person.

Certification Legal process that controls the word *psychologist* from being misused.

Child abuse and neglect Physical, sexual, or emotional misuse of children that puts them in danger or risk of physical or emotional injury.

Child Behavior Checklist (CBCL) Popular testing instrument used with children, parents, and teachers to assess behavioral problems among children ages 4 to 18.

Child clinical psychology Subspecialty area that focuses on the problems and concerns of children and their families.

Child custody The legal determination of who is the legal guardian of a minor following divorce, death, or mental disability.

Chronic pain Consistent discomfort or pain associated with a large range of medical and psychiatric conditions.

Clarification Interviewing technique where questions are asked to ensure that the message is being fully understood.

Classical conditioning Behavioral technique that maintains that learning occurs, and subsequently, behavior, through the association of conditioned and unconditioned stimuli

Client-centered Humanistic theoretical orientation that highlights nondirective techniques such as active listening, empathy, congruence, and unconditional positive regard to understand and help others.

Client-centered case consultation Involves consultation with a fellow professional such as another psychologist who is responsible for the treatment or care of a particular patient.

Client–therapist variation strategy Treatment outcome research approach that alters the types of therapists or patients to determine which combinations optimize treatment outcome.

Clinical practice guidelines Specific, generally accepted, and unbiased recommendations for ways to assess and treat particular disorders.

Clinical psychology Discipline that uses what is known about the principles of human behavior to help people with the numerous troubles and concerns they experience during the course of life in their relationships, emotions, and physical selves.

Clinical-scientist model A graduate training model that focuses on empirical and scientific approaches.

Cognitive-behavioral Approach that uses the principles of learning, conditioning, and information processing to understand, assess, and treat emotional and behavioral problems.

Collaborative multisite research projects Common and popular research strategy that uses researchers and subjects from a variety of locations.

Collaborator Consultant role that suggests that the consultant is an equal partner working with a consultee to achieve a common goal.

Common factors Elements of treatment that are curative and common in many different types of treatment approaches.

Community Mental Health Movement Attempt during the late 1950s and 1960s to develop outpatient community mental health services outside of the inpatient mental hospital setting.

Community-wide intervention Common and popular research approach that attempts to get large segments of entire communities to change behavior.

Comparative treatment strategy Treatment outcome research approach that generally compares different strategies (e.g., psychodynamic versus behavioral techniques) for producing change in a clinical problem.

Competence Ethical principle requiring that psychologists perform only the duties that they have appropriate levels of training and experience to perform.

Computerized Axial Tomography (CAT) Neuroimaging technique that provides multiple, computer-enhanced pictures of the brain from multiple angles.

Confidentiality Ethical and legal issue restraining a psychologist from disclosing information about a patient or research subject to a third party.

Congruence Or genuineness, refers to harmony between one's feelings and actions.

Constructive treatment strategies Strategies that attempt to answer the question, ''What might be added to an effective treatment to make it even more effective?'' The constructive treatment approach adds various components to the treatment to determine whether the additions will improve treatment outcome.

Consultation Clinical psychology activity that uses knowledge about human behavior to help individuals, groups, and organizations function better.

Consultee-centered administrative consultation Consultation model that involves working on administrative and personnel issues within an agency.

Consultee-centered case consultation Consultation model such that challenges experienced by the consultee rather than problems concerning an individual case or client are the focus.

Contingency management Behavioral technique that focuses on changing behavior by altering the consequences that follow behavior.

Controlled observation Behavioral technique that attempts to observe behavior in a prescribed manner by forcing the behavior of interest to occur in a simulated manner.

Correlational Research design that examines the degree of association between two or more variables.

Counseling psychologists Specialty of psychology similar to clinical psychology but generally with a historical focus on vocational and college counseling mostly free of major psychiatric disturbance.

Counterconditioning Behavioral technique that attempts to develop a more adaptive response to environmental stimuli.

Countertransference Psychodynamic concept where therapist responds to the transference of the patient through projecting his or her needs, wishes, and dynamics onto the patient.

Cross-sectional Research design that provides a snapshot view of behavior at a given moment in time.

Curative factors Elements of the psychotherapy experience that contribute to the cure or the significant reduction in symptoms.

Defense mechanisms Psychodynamic term that refers to strategies used to cope with anxiety and other uncomfortable emotions and impulses.

Dementia A particular neurological and psychiatric condition that results in a significant decrease in intellectual, memory, learning, and problem-solving functioning.

Dementia praecox Historical term referring to today's notion of schizophrenia.

Denial Defense mechanism such that person believes that problematic feelings, thoughts, or behaviors do not exist.

Diathesis-stress A causal perspective for illness or problems in that it suggests that a biological or other type of vulnerability in combination with psychosocial or environmental stress creates the necessary conditions for illness to occur.

Differentiation Family systems term to describe the need for family members to develop more adaptive separation and independence from other family members.

Diplomate Advanced level of certification awarded to eligible psychologists several years following training.

Disengagement Family systems term for a family member being uninterested or uninvolved with family members.

Dismantling Treatment outcome research approach that seeks to identify the active ingredient of a particular treatment strategy after the treatment has been determined effective.

Diversity Refers to differences in age, gender, ethnicity, sexual preference, socioeconomic, and religious orientations.

Doctor of Philosophy (PhD) Traditional doctorate that balances research and practice or focuses on research only.

Doctor of Psychology (PsyD) Newer doctoral degree that focuses on clinical practice.

Dualism Seventeenth-century notion that the mind and body are separate and do not significantly interact or influence each other.

Dual relationships Ethical term referring to psychologists maintaining outside relationships as friends, lovers, or business partners with their clients or patients.

Durham Rule 1954 law that added a "medical disease or defect" to the criteria for insanity.

Dyslexia Type of learning disability that involves difficulty reading.

Educator Type of consultation role such that the consultant has specialized information that is useful to the client and can be acquired through education.

Ego Psychodynamic term that refers to the rational and reasonable aspects of our personality helping us to adapt to a challenging world.

Electroencephalography (EEG) Technique that assesses electrical brain-wave activity.

Empathy Humanistic term conveying a sense of being heard and understood.

Empirically validated (supported) treatments Treatment approaches that have been found to be effective according to research studies and that use treatment manuals.

Enmeshment Family systems term that refers to maladaptive or over-involvement in the lives of family members.

Ephebophilia Adult sexual interest in post-pubescent minors.

Epilepsy Type of seizure disorder.

Ethics Code Ethical principles and standards published by the APA (and other psychological associations) to provide ethical guidelines for their members.

Evidence-based practice (EBP) Attempts to integrate the research findings with clinical expertise to provide effective assessment and treatment for clients.

Evoked potentials Electrical brain-wave readings.

Examination for Professional Practice in Psychology (EPPP) National 200-item examination used to license psychologists.

Executive coaching A fairly new field where professionals consult with executives to become better leaders and managers as well as develop strategies to improve interpersonal relationships, productivity, and efficiency. Executive coaches may consult with business leaders about stress management, goal setting, and other topics and services related to human behavior and business.

Experimental design Methods used to construct experiments to minimize error or bias in the results. Each design has unique advantages and disadvantages.

Experimental mortality Subject drops out from an experiment.

Expert consultation The expert consultant is an advisor who has the specialized skills, knowledge, or experience that the consultee needs to help solve a problem.

Exposure Behavioral term that refers to gradual or all-at-once approach to the feared situation or stimuli.

Fact finder Consultation role involves seeking information and relaying the results to consultees who lack the expertise, time, energy, or psychological sensitivities to do the task themselves.

Family systems Theoretical orientation that places a deemphasis on the problems of any one member of a family in favor of attention to the family system as a whole.

Flynn effect Higher IQ scores in recent generations relative to previous generations, likely due to improved health and nutrition, educational and technological advances, increased intellectual stimulation, and perhaps other factors.

Forensic psychology Clinical psychology subspecialty utilizing principles of human behavior to inform the judicial and legal systems.

Free association Psychodynamic term that refers to saying whatever is on one's mind without censoring.

Freestanding professional school Graduate training in clinical psychology not affiliated with a college or university.

Functional analysis Behavioral term for investigating the specific factors that precede and result from a behavior of interest.

Geropsychology Clinical psychology subspecialty utilizing principles of human behavior to assist elderly persons.

Gestalt Humanistic approach that focuses on being keenly aware of one's "here and now" or present experience.

Graduate Record Examination (GRE) Standardized examination for those interested in applying for graduate school.

Health maintenance organization (HMO) Provides comprehensive health, and usually mental health, services within one organization.

Health psychology Clinical psychology subspecialty utilizing principles of human behavior to prevent health problems from occurring or helping those with health problems cope better.

History Threat to validity of a research study and refers to events outside the experimental situation that could have a significant impact on the results of the study.

Humanistic A theoretical approach that emphasizes each individual's perception and experience of his or her world and tends to view people as being active, thinking, creative, and growth oriented.

Id Psychodynamic term that refers to all primitive impulses.

Insanity defense Legal term that suggests that people are not responsible for their criminal actions if they suffer from a disorder that renders them unaware of what they are doing or that what they are doing is wrong.

Insanity Defense Reform Act States that someone can be found innocent due to reasons of insanity if unable to understand that criminal behavior was wrong at the time of the crime due to a mental disease or mental retardation.

Insight Understanding of factors that contribute to problems or concerns.

Instrumentation Threat to validity of research that refers to the influences of the tests and measurement devices used to measure constructs in the study.

Integrative Combining two or more approaches to assessment, treatment, consultation, and other professional activities.

Integrity Ethical term and principle that focuses on honesty.

Intellectual testing Assessment approaches used to measure cognitive abilities.

Intelligence quotient (IQ) Term used to refer to score obtained on tests of intellectual functioning.

Interaction of selection biases A possible threat to research validity such that participants in one research group may have been differentially responsive to the experimental condition in some unique manner. For instance, subjects assigned to a relaxation group for test-taking anxiety may enjoy or respond differently than subjects assigned to another treatment condition such as exercise.

Internship Required one year of full-time clinical training prior to being awarded a doctorate in clinical psychology.

Involuntary commitment Being held in a hospital setting without agreeing to the hospitalization.

Joining Family systems term referring to the therapist's attempt to connect with the family and become part of the family unit rather than act in a detached observer manner in the sessions.

Joint custody Legal term for both divorced parents maintaining legal custody of their children.

Jury selection The use of principles of psychology to choose jury members who might maximize an advantage to one side of the legal case.

Kaufman Scales Cognitive tests that measure intellectual and achievement functioning.

Learning disorders Cognitive processing problems in reading, writing, math, and other skills important to success in school.

Licensure State document and registration that allows a psychologist to practice and offer services to the public.

Longitudinal Research method that follows the responses of subjects over time.

Magnetic resonance imaging (MRI) Neuroimaging technique that analyzes the nuclear magnetic movements of hydrogen in the water and fat of the body.

Malingering Faking an illness to obtain some desired gain.

Managed health care Organizational and insurance attempts to control the high cost of health care.

Marriage and family therapist Master's-level marriage, family, and child counseling discipline and license that focuses on counseling.

Maturation Threat to validity of study and refers to changes within subjects over the passage of time that may influence the experimental results.

Medical staff privileges Ability to admit, treat, and discharge patients in a hospital setting.

Mental status interview Series of screening questions to quickly assess a patient's cognitive functioning.

Meta-analysis Statistical technique that uses data from a variety of studies to determine overall effects.

Milan Approach Family systems approach that highly values neutrality as well as acceptance and respect for the family system.

Millon Clinical Multiaxial Inventory (MCMI) Popular personality test based on DSM-IV organization of personality disorders.

Minnesota Multiphasic Personality Inventory (MMPI) Popular personality test.

Mixed group Research design where experiments are constructed in such a way that different groups of subjects receive different treatment or experimental experiences (between group) while subject responses are assessed over time at different phases of the experiment (within group).

M'Naghten Rule Legal term that suggests that people are not responsible for their criminal actions if they suffer from a disorder that renders them unaware of what they are doing or that what they are doing is wrong.

Moral therapy Historical therapy sought to treat patients as humanely as possible and encourage the nurturance of interpersonal relationships. Multicultural attention and sensitivity to issues related to a variety of ethnic, racial, gender, sexual orientation, and religious issues and values.

Multiple-treatment interference Threat to validity of study and refers to exposing a subject to several treatment conditions or factors such that the experimenter cannot isolate any specific condition or factors.

Narrative Family systems approach that suggests that family members conceptualize their problems and concerns through a series of stories about their lives and various members of the family system.

Naturalistic observation Involves entering into the world of the patient in order to observe the person interacting with the environment in which problems occur.

Neuroimaging Techniques that involve obtaining a picture of internal brain and other bodily organs and structures.

Neuropsychological testing Assessment that measures brain–behavior relationship such as cognitive functioning, memory, visual motor skills, and language functioning.

Neuropsychology The subspecialty of clinical psychology that focuses on brain–behavior relationships.

Obesity Generally defined as being over 20% above expected weight.

Object relations A psychodynamic approach that views infants as being relationship seeking rather than pleasure seeking and believes that the early relationship with the mother provides the framework for the development of the sense of self and later psychological functioning.

Objective testing Highly structured tests that compare scores to national norms.

Oedipal complex Psychodynamic term referring to child's admiration and love of the parent of the opposite sex and disdain for parent of the same sex.

Operant perspective Behavioral approach that maintains that all behavior can be understood through a functional analysis of antecedents (the conditions present just before a target behavior occurs) and consequences of *behavior* (what occurs following the target behavior).

Paradoxical Family systems techniques that involve prescribing the symptom of concern in an exaggerated form, thus seeming to contradict the goals of intervention.

Parametric Treatment outcome research approach that changes a specific aspect of the treatment to determine whether the change can enhance treatment effectiveness.

Paraphrasing Interviewing technique that involves rephrasing the content of what is being said.

Peak experience Humanistic concept that refers to moments in life when self-actualization is actually reached.

Personality testing Assesses personality styles and psychological functioning.

Polygraph Machine that measures physiological activity such as heart rate and blood pressure.

Positron emission tomography (PET) S type of neuroimaging technique that uses radioactive isotopes injected into the bloodstream of a patient to create gamma rays in the body, allowing for views of internal structures.

Postdoctoral fellowship Training after the completion of the doctoral degree that is required prior to licensing in most states.

Preferred provider organization (PPO) Managed care organization that maintains a list of practitioners who will see patients on an insurance plan for reduced costs.

Prescription privileges Ability to prescribe psychotropic medication.

Private practice Providing professional services on one's own without being employed by an agency.

Process research strategy Attempts to answer the question, "How does the actual process of therapy impact treatment outcome?" This research approach seeks to determine which aspects of the psychotherapeutic process are associated with positive treatment outcome.

Process specialist A consultant who is an expert at focusing on process rather than outcome. They tend to help with strategies for dealing with problems and conflicts within organizations. An example might be how an organization could best deal with the press and public after a product recall.

Program-centered administrative consultation Consultation model that focuses on a program or system rather than on an individual case.

Projective drawings Technique that requires the subject or patient to draw pictures of objects or persons such as a tree, house, person, or family and is interpreted.

Projective testing Testing that provides unstructured or ambiguous stimuli such as inkblots or drawings.

Pseudoseizures Factitious seizures.

Psychiatric nurses Nursing that specializes in the care of psychiatric patients in both outpatient and inpatient settings.

Psychiatry Medical specialty that focuses on abnormal behavior.

Psychodynamic Theoretical approach that focuses on unconscious conflicts, defenses, early childhood experiences, dreams, impulses, and fantasies.

Psychological testing Assessment that examines personality, cognitive, mood, learning, and other skills.

Psychosexual stages Psychodynamic approach to development that examines where energy is directed during early childhood and adolescence.

Psychotherapy The informed and intentional application of clinical methods and interpersonal stances derived from established psychological principles for the purpose of assisting people to modify their behaviors, cognitions, emotions, and/or other personal characteristics in directions that the participants deem desirable.

Psychotherapy treatment outcome Results of psychological intervention to determine whether person(s) is (are) improved following treatment.

Psychotropic medication Medications used to alter psychological functioning and mood.

Quasi-experimental Research designs used when random assignment to experimental and control conditions is not possible because of ethical or other limitations.

Randomized clinical trials Research method that focuses on random assignment of clients into well-controlled and assessed treatment and control conditions with particular agreed-upon standards for the implementation and reporting of the research.

Rapport Term used to describe the comfortable working relationship that develops between the professional and the client.

Reactivity Threat to validity of study regarding the subject's potential response to participating in an experiment.

Reflection Rephrasing the sense of what is being said in order to encourage the person to express and better understand his or her feelings.

Reframing Family systems term involving reinterpretation of a behavior or issue in a new and different light.

Reliable Change Index A statistic that measures the clinical significance of therapeutic change.

Repression Psychodynamic term referring to the defense mechanism that keeps uncomfortable thoughts and feelings out of consciousness.

Research Clinical psychology activity involving use of the scientific method to answer questions of interest to researchers and society.

Research program A series of experiments or research studies that attempt to answer questions one step at a time.

Revisionists Psychodynamic theorists who altered or expanded upon Freud's theory.

Rorschach Projective inkblot test used to assess psychological functioning.

Scholar-practitioner model Graduate training model that focuses on training practitioners who are consumers of research but are not likely to conduct research—also known as the Vail model.

School psychologists Professionals who use knowledge about human behavior and apply that knowledge in a school setting.

Scientist-practitioner model Graduate training model that focuses on a balance between research and practice—also known as the Boulder model.

Seizures Intense muscle spasms, a complete or partial loss of consciousness, and sometimes unconscious purposeful behavior.

Selection bias Threat to validity of a study and refers to a differential and problematic selection procedure for choosing research subjects.

Self-actualization Humanistic term that refers to the forward movement in life toward greater growth, peace, and acceptance of self and others.

Self-efficacy Cognitive term that refers to the belief that one can accomplish a goal.

Self-monitoring Behavioral technique that includes maintaining a diary or log where one can record problematic behaviors as well as other important information such as feelings and thoughts associated with each behavioral occurrence.

Sentence completion Projective assessment where subjects are asked to complete an incomplete sentence with the first thing that comes to their mind.

Sixteen Personality Factors Questionnaire (16PF) Popular personality assessment questionnaire that assumes that the person does not experience significant psychiatric disturbance.

Social learning Cognitive-behavioral approach that suggests that behavior is learned by modeling others.

Social work Generally a master's-level discipline that has historically focused on patient case management, patient advocacy, and a liaison to optimal social service agencies and benefits.

Specialization A specific area of expertise.

Statistical regression Threat to validity of study and concerns the tendency of extreme scores on a measure to move toward the mean over time.

Strategic Family systems approach that utilizes direct involvement by the clinician to combat resistance by directing and altering the behavior of others.

Stress management A variety of techniques and strategies to cope more effectively with stress.

Structural Family systems approach that focuses on appropriate and adaptive levels of differentiation among family members.

Structured interview Interview techniques that involve highly specific questions and often scoring procedures.

Summarization Interviewing technique that involves both paraphrasing and reflection in attempting to pull together several points into a coherent, brief review of the message.

Superego Represents the internalization of familial, cultural, and societal norms and mores.

Symptom Checklist-90—Revised (SCL-90-R) A brief and multidimensional self-report measure to screen persons for major psychiatric symptoms.

Teaching Clinical psychology activity involving dispensing information to others and engaging them in learning.

Testing A potential threat to both internal and external validity of a research study. As a threat to internal validity, testing concerns the influence of the testing or evaluation process itself on research results, such as in the use of repeated measures obtained on the same subjects over time. As a threat to external validity, testing refers to the use of a questionnaire or other assessment device that may sensitize and alter the subject's response and, therefore, influence the dependent measure.

Thematic Apperception Test (TAT) Projective assessment that asks persons to examine pictures and tell a story about each one.

Theoretical orientation Philosophical perspectives used to approach assessment, treatment, consultation, and research.

Thought stopping Cognitive technique to eliminate problematic and maladaptive thoughts.

Threats to external validity Factors that decrease the generalizability of a research study.

Threats to internal validity Factors that decrease the experimental control and precision of a research study.

Trainer Consultation role that assumes that the consultant has specialized information that is useful to the client and can be acquired through education.

Transference Psychodynamic term that involves the projection of early relationship dynamics onto the therapist, who represents an authority figure similar to the patient's parents, for example.

Treatment Clinical psychology activity involving intervention strategies to help others improve their lives.

Treatment outcome research strategy approaches Various research methods to determine whether and how treatment works.

Treatment package strategy Approach that attempts to answer the basic question, "Does treatment work?" This approach seeks to determine whether a specific treatment is effective for a specific clinical problem or disorder.

Unconditional positive regard Humanistic term for allowing a client to discuss his or her concerns without judgment.

Vail model Graduate training model that suggests that clinical psychologists are generally practitioners and consumers of research—also referred to as the scholar-practitioner model.

Veterans Administration Government agency that manages numerous hospitals and clinics throughout the United States to assess and treat veterans.

Wechsler Scales A series of intellectual assessments for children and adults that are individually administered.

Within group Research approach that examines research effects within the same group of subjects.

Working through Psychodynamic term that refers to assimilating and incorporating new insights into daily life.

Ethical Principles of Psychologists and Code of Conduct 2002

Contents

Introduction and Applicability

The American Psychological Association's (APA's) Ethical Principles of Psychologists and Code of Conduct (hereinafter referred to as the Ethics Code) consists of an Introduction, a Preamble, five General Principles (A—E), and specific Ethical

Standards. The Introduction discusses the intent, organization, procedural considerations, and scope of application of the Ethics Code. The Preamble and General Principles are aspirational goals to guide psychologists toward the highest ideals of psychology. Although the Preamble and General Principles are not themselves enforceable rules, they should be considered by psychologists in arriving at an ethical course of action. The Ethical Standards set forth enforceable rules for conduct as psychologists. Most of the Ethical Standards are written broadly, in order to apply to psychologists in varied roles, although the application of an Ethical Standard may vary depending on the context. The Ethical Standards are not exhaustive. The fact that a given conduct is not specifically addressed by an Ethical Standard does not mean that it is necessarily either ethical or unethical.

This Ethics Code applies only to psychologists' activities that are part of their scientific, educational, or professional roles as psychologists. Areas covered include but are not limited to the clinical, counseling, and school practice of psychology; research; teaching; supervision of trainees; public service; policy development; social intervention; development of assessment instruments; conducting assessments; educational counseling; organizational consulting; forensic activities; program design and evaluation; and administration. This Ethics Code applies to these activities across a variety of contexts, such as in person, postal, telephone, Internet, and other electronic transmissions. These activities shall be distinguished from the purely private conduct of psychologists, which is not within the purview of the Ethics Code.

Membership in the APA commits members and student affiliates to comply with the standards of the APA Ethics Code and to the rules and procedures used to enforce them. Lack of awareness or misunderstanding of an Ethical Standard is not itself a defense to a charge of unethical conduct.

The procedures for filing, investigating, and resolving complaints of unethical conduct are described in the current Rules and Procedures of the APA Ethics Committee. APA may impose sanctions on its members for violations of the standards of the Ethics Code, including termination of APA membership, and may notify other bodies and individuals of its actions. Actions that violate the standards of the Ethics Code may also lead to the imposition of sanctions on psychologists or students whether or not they are APA members by bodies other than APA, including state psychological associations, other professional groups, psychology boards, other state or federal agencies, and payors for health services. In addition, APA may take action against a member after his or her conviction of a felony, expulsion or suspension from an affiliated state psychological association, or suspension or loss of licensure. When the sanction to be imposed by APA is less than expulsion, the 2001 Rules and Procedures do not guarantee an opportunity for an in-person hearing, but generally provide that complaints will be resolved only on the basis of a submitted record.

The Ethics Code is intended to provide guidance for psychologists and standards of professional conduct that can be applied by the APA and by other bodies that choose to adopt them. The Ethics Code is not intended to be a basis of civil liability. Whether a psychologist has violated the Ethics Code standards does not by itself determine whether the psychologist is legally liable in a court action, whether a contract is enforceable, or whether other legal consequences occur.

The modifiers used in some of the standards of this Ethics Code (e.g., reasonably, appropriate, potentially) are included in the standards when they would (1) allow professional judgment on the part of psychologists, (2) eliminate injustice or inequality that would occur without the modifier, (3) ensure applicability across the broad range of activities conducted by psychologists, or (4) guard against a set of rigid rules that might be quickly outdated. As used in this Ethics Code, the term reasonable means the prevailing professional judgment of psychologists engaged in similar activities in similar circumstances, given the knowledge the psychologist had or should have had at the time.

In the process of making decisions regarding their professional behavior, psychologists must consider this Ethics Code in addition to applicable laws and psychology board regulations. In applying the Ethics Code to their professional work, psychologists may consider other materials and guidelines that have been adopted or endorsed by scientific and professional psychological organizations and the dictates of their own conscience, as well as consult with others within the field. If this Ethics Code establishes a higher standard of conduct than is required by law, psychologists must meet the higher ethical standard. If psychologists' ethical responsibilities conflict with law, regulations, or other governing legal authority, psychologists make known their commitment to this Ethics Code and take steps to resolve the conflict in a responsible manner. If the conflict is unresolvable via such means, psychologists may adhere to the requirements of the law, regulations, or other governing authority in keeping with basic principles of human rights.

Preamble

Psychologists are committed to increasing scientific and professional knowledge of behavior and people's understanding of themselves and others and to the use of such knowledge to improve the condition of individuals, organizations, and society. Psychologists respect and protect civil and human rights and the central importance of freedom of inquiry and expression in research, teaching, and publication. They strive to help the public in developing informed judgments and choices concerning human behavior. In doing so, they perform many roles, such as researcher, educator, diagnostician, therapist, supervisor, consultant, administrator, social interventionist, and expert witness. This Ethics Code provides a common set of principles and standards upon which psychologists build their professional and scientific work.

This Ethics Code is intended to provide specific standards to cover most situations encountered by psychologists. It has as its goals the welfare and protection of the individuals and groups with whom psychologists work and the education of members, students, and the public regarding ethical standards of the discipline.

The development of a dynamic set of ethical standards for psychologists' work-related conduct requires a personal commitment and lifelong effort to act ethically; to encourage ethical behavior by students, supervisees, employees, and colleagues; and to consult with others concerning ethical problems.

General Principles

This section consists of General Principles. General Principles, as opposed to Ethical Standards, are aspirational in nature. Their intent is to guide and inspire psychologists toward the very highest ethical ideals of the profession. General Principles, in contrast to Ethical Standards, do not represent obligations and should not form the basis for imposing sanctions. Relying upon General Principles for either of these reasons distorts both their meaning and purpose.

Principle A: Beneficence and Nonmaleficence

Psychologists strive to benefit those with whom they work and take care to do no harm. In their professional actions, psychologists seek to safeguard the welfare and rights of those with whom they interact professionally and other affected persons, and the welfare of animal subjects of research. When conflicts occur among psychologists' obligations or concerns, they attempt to resolve these conflicts in a responsible fashion that avoids or minimizes harm. Because psychologists' scientific and professional judgments and actions may affect the lives of others, they are alert to and guard against personal, financial, social, organizational, or political factors that might lead to misuse of their influence. Psychologists strive to be aware of the possible effect of their own physical and mental health on their ability to help those with whom they work.

Principle B: Fidelity and Responsibility

Psychologists establish relationships of trust with those with whom they work. They are aware of their professional and scientific responsibilities to society and to the specific communities in which they work. Psychologists uphold professional standards of conduct, clarify their professional roles and obligations, accept appropriate responsibility for their behavior, and seek to manage conflicts of interest that could lead to exploitation or harm. Psychologists consult with, refer to, or cooperate with other professionals and institutions to the extent needed to serve the best interests of those with whom they work. They are concerned about the ethical compliance of their colleagues' scientific and professional conduct. Psychologists strive to contribute a portion of their professional time for little or no compensation or personal advantage.

Principle C: Integrity

Psychologists seek to promote accuracy, honesty, and truthfulness in the science, teaching, and practice of psychology. In these activities psychologists do not steal, cheat, or engage in fraud, subterfuge, or intentional misrepresentation of fact. Psychologists strive to keep their promises and to avoid unwise or unclear commitments. In situations in which deception may be ethically justifiable to maximize benefits and minimize harm, psychologists have a serious obligation to consider the need for, the possible consequences of, and their responsibility to correct any resulting mistrust or other harmful effects that arise from the use of such techniques.

Principle D: Justice

Psychologists recognize that fairness and justice entitle all persons to access to and benefit from the contributions of psychology and to equal quality in the processes, procedures, and services being conducted by psychologists. Psychologists exercise reasonable judgment and take precautions to ensure that their potential biases, the boundaries of their competence, and the limitations of their expertise do not lead to or condone unjust practices.

Principle E: Respect for People's Rights and Dignity

Psychologists respect the dignity and worth of all people, and the rights of individuals to privacy, confidentiality, and self-determination. Psychologists are aware that special safeguards may be necessary to protect the rights and welfare of persons or communities whose vulnerabilities impair autonomous decision making. Psychologists are aware of and respect cultural, individual, and role differences, including those based on age, gender, gender identity, race, ethnicity, culture, national origin, religion, sexual orientation, disability, language, and socioeconomic status and consider these factors when working with members of such groups. Psychologists try to eliminate the effect on their work of biases based on those factors, and they do not knowingly participate in or condone activities of others based upon such prejudices.

Ethical Standards

1. Resolving Ethical Issues

1.01 Misuse of Psychologists' Work

If psychologists learn of misuse or misrepresentation of their work, they take reasonable steps to correct or minimize the misuse or misrepresentation.

1.02 Conflicts Between Ethics and Law, Regulations, or Other Governing Legal Authority

If psychologists' ethical responsibilities conflict with law, regulations, or other governing legal authority,

psychologists make known their commitment to the Ethics Code and take steps to resolve the conflict. If the conflict is unresolvable via such means, psychologists may adhere to the requirements of the law, regulations, or other governing legal authority.

1.03 Conflicts Between Ethics and Organizational Demands

If the demands of an organization with which psychologists are affiliated or for whom they are working conflict with this Ethics Code, psychologists clarify the nature of the conflict, make known their commitment to the Ethics Code, and to the extent feasible, resolve the conflict in a way that permits adherence to the Ethics Code.

1.04 Informal Resolution of Ethical Violations

When psychologists believe that there may have been an ethical violation by another psychologist, they attempt to resolve the issue by bringing it to the attention of that individual, if an informal resolution appears appropriate and the intervention does not violate any confidentiality rights that may be involved. (See also Standards 1.02, Conflicts Between Ethics and Law, Regulations, or Other Governing Legal Authority, and 1.03, Conflicts Between Ethics and Organizational Demands.)

1.05 Reporting Ethical Violations

If an apparent ethical violation has substantially harmed or is likely to substantially harm a person or organization and is not appropriate for informal resolution under Standard 1.04, Informal Resolution of Ethical Violations, or is not resolved properly in that fashion, psychologists take further action appropriate to the situation. Such action might include referral to state or national committees on professional ethics, to state licensing boards, or to the appropriate institutional authorities. This standard does not apply when an intervention would violate confidentiality rights or when psychologists have been retained to review the work of another psychologist whose professional conduct is in question. (See also Standard 1.02, Conflicts Between Ethics and Law, Regulations, or Other Governing Legal Authority.)

1.06 Cooperating with Ethics Committees

Psychologists cooperate in ethics investigations, proceedings, and resulting requirements of the APA or any affiliated state psychological association to which they belong. In doing so, they address any confidentiality issues. Failure to cooperate is itself an ethics violation. However, making a request for deferment of adjudication of an ethics complaint pending the outcome of litigation does not alone constitute noncooperation.

1.07   Improper Complaints

Psychologists do not file or encourage the filing of ethics complaints that are made with reckless disregard for or willful ignorance of facts that would disprove the allegation.

1.08   Unfair Discrimination Against Complainants and Respondents

Psychologists do not deny persons employment, advancement, admissions to academic or other programs, tenure, or promotion, based solely upon their having made or their being the subject of an ethics complaint. This does not preclude taking action based upon the outcome of such proceedings or considering other appropriate information.

2.   Competence

2.01   Boundaries of Competence

(a) Psychologists provide services, teach, and conduct research with populations and in areas only within the boundaries of their competence, based on their education, training, supervised experience, consultation, study, or professional experience.

(b) Where scientific or professional knowledge in the discipline of psychology establishes that an understanding of factors associated with age, gender, gender identity, race, ethnicity, culture, national origin, religion, sexual orientation, disability, language, or socioeconomic status is essential for effective implementation of their services or research, psychologists have or obtain the training, experience, consultation, or supervision necessary to ensure the competence of their services, or they make appropriate referrals, except as provided in Standard 2.02, Providing Services in Emergencies.

(c) Psychologists planning to provide services, teach, or conduct research involving populations, areas, techniques, or technologies new to them undertake relevant education, training, supervised experience, consultation, or study.

(d) When psychologists are asked to provide services to individuals for whom appropriate mental health services are not available and for which psychologists have not obtained the competence necessary, psychologists with closely related prior training or experience may provide such services in order to ensure that services are not denied if they make a reasonable effort to obtain the competence required by using relevant research, training, consultation, or study.

(e) In those emerging areas in which generally recognized standards for preparatory training do not yet exist, psychologists nevertheless take reasonable steps to ensure the competence of their work and to protect clients/patients, students, supervisees, research participants, organizational clients, and others from harm.

(f) When assuming forensic roles, psychologists are or become reasonably familiar with the judicial or administrative rules governing their roles.

2.02   Providing Services in Emergencies

In emergencies, when psychologists provide services to individuals for whom other mental health services are not available and for which psychologists have not obtained the necessary training, psychologists may provide such services in order to ensure that services are not denied. The services are discontinued as soon as the emergency has ended or appropriate services are available.

2.03   Maintaining Competence

Psychologists undertake ongoing efforts to develop and maintain their competence.

2.04   Bases for Scientific and Professional Judgments

Psychologists' work is based upon established scientific and professional knowledge of the discipline. (See also Standards 2.01e, Boundaries of Competence, and 10.01b, Informed Consent to Therapy.)

2.05   Delegation of Work to Others

Psychologists who delegate work to employees, supervisees, or research or teaching assistants or who use the services of others, such as interpreters, take reasonable steps to (1) avoid delegating such work to persons who have a multiple relationship with those being served that would likely lead to exploitation or loss of objectivity; (2) authorize only those responsibilities that such persons can be expected to perform competently on the basis of their education, training, or experience, either independently or with the level of supervision being provided; and (3) see that such persons perform these services competently. (See also Standards 2.02, Providing Services in Emergencies; 3.05, Multiple Relationships; 4.01, Maintaining Confidentiality; 9.01, Bases for Assessments; 9.02, Use of Assessments; 9.03, Informed Consent in Assessments; and 9.07, Assessment by Unqualified Persons.)

2.06 *Personal Problems and Conflicts*

(a) Psychologists refrain from initiating an activity when they know or should know that there is a substantial likelihood that their personal problems will prevent them from performing their work-related activities in a competent manner.

(b) When psychologists become aware of personal problems that may interfere with their performing work-related duties adequately, they take appropriate measures, such as obtaining professional consultation or assistance, and determine whether they should limit, suspend, or terminate their work-related duties. (See also Standard 10.10, Terminating Therapy.)

3.   Human Relations

3.01 *Unfair Discrimination*

In their work-related activities, psychologists do not engage in unfair discrimination based on age, gender, gender identity, race, ethnicity, culture, national origin, religion, sexual orientation, disability, socioeconomic status, or any basis proscribed by law.

3.02 *Sexual Harassment*

Psychologists do not engage in sexual harassment. Sexual harassment is sexual solicitation, physical advances, or verbal or nonverbal conduct that is sexual in nature, that occurs in connection with the psychologist's activities or roles as a psychologist, and that either (1) is unwelcome, is offensive, or creates a hostile workplace or educational environment, and the psychologist knows or is told this or (2) is sufficiently severe or intense to be abusive to a reasonable person in the context. Sexual harassment can consist of a single intense

or severe act or of multiple persistent or pervasive acts. (See also Standard 1.08, Unfair Discrimination Against Complainants and Respondents.)

3.03 *Other Harassment*

Psychologists do not knowingly engage in behavior that is harassing or demeaning to persons with whom they interact in their work based on factors such as those persons' age, gender, gender identity, race, ethnicity, culture, national origin, religion, sexual orientation, disability, language, or socioeconomic status.

3.04 *Avoiding Harm*

Psychologists take reasonable steps to avoid harming their clients/patients, students, supervisees, research participants, organizational clients, and others with whom they work, and to minimize harm where it is foreseeable and unavoidable.

3.05 *Multiple Relationships*

(a) A multiple relationship occurs when a psychologist is in a professional role with a person and (1) at the same time is in another role with the same person, (2) at the same time is in a relationship with a person closely associated with or related to the person with whom the psychologist has the professional relationship, or (3) promises to enter into another relationship in the future with the person or a person closely associated with or related to the person.

A psychologist refrains from entering into a multiple relationship if the multiple relationship could reasonably be expected to impair the psychologist's objectivity, competence, or effectiveness in performing his or her functions as a psychologist, or otherwise risks exploitation or harm to the person with whom the professional relationship exists.

Multiple relationships that would not reasonably be expected to cause impairment or risk exploitation or harm are not unethical.

(b) If a psychologist finds that, due to unforeseen factors, a potentially harmful multiple relationship has arisen, the psychologist takes reasonable steps to resolve it with due regard for the best interests of the affected person and maximal compliance with the Ethics Code.

(c) When psychologists are required by law, institutional policy, or extraordinary circumstances to serve in more than one role in judicial or administrative proceedings, at the outset they clarify role expectations and the extent of confidentiality and thereafter as changes occur. (See also Standards 3.04, Avoiding Harm, and 3.07, Third-Party Requests for Services.)

3.06   Conflict of Interest

Psychologists refrain from taking on a professional role when personal, scientific, professional, legal, financial, or other interests or relationships could reasonably be expected to (1) impair their objectivity, competence, or effectiveness in performing their functions as psychologists or (2) expose the person or organization with whom the professional relationship exists to harm or exploitation.

3.07   Third-Party Requests for Services

When psychologists agree to provide services to a person or entity at the request of a third party, psychologists attempt to clarify at the outset of the service the nature of the relationship with all individuals or organizations involved. This clarification includes the role of the psychologist (e.g., therapist, consultant, diagnostician, or expert witness), an identification of who is the client, the probable uses of the services provided or the information obtained, and the fact that there may be limits to confidentiality. (See also Standards 3.05, Multiple Relationships, and 4.02, Discussing the Limits of Confidentiality.)

3.08   Exploitative Relationships

Psychologists do not exploit persons over whom they have supervisory, evaluative, or other authority such as clients/patients, students, supervisees, research participants, and employees. (See also Standards 3.05, Multiple Relationships; 6.04, Fees and Financial Arrangements; 6.05, Barter With Clients/Patients; 7.07, Sexual Relationships With Students and Supervisees; 10.05, Sexual Intimacies With Current Therapy Clients/Patients; 10.06, Sexual Intimacies With Relatives or Significant Others of Current Therapy Clients/Patients; 10.07, Therapy With Former Sexual Partners; and 10.08, Sexual Intimacies With Former Therapy Clients/Patients.)

3.09   Cooperation with Other Professionals

When indicated and professionally appropriate, psychologists cooperate with other professionals in order to serve their clients/patients effectively and appropriately. (See also Standard 4.05, Disclosures.)

3.10   Informed Consent

(a) When psychologists conduct research or provide assessment, therapy, counseling, or consulting services in person or via electronic transmission or other forms of communication, they obtain the informed consent of the individual or individuals using language that is reasonably understandable to that person or persons except when conducting such activities without consent is mandated by law or governmental regulation or as otherwise provided in this Ethics Code. (See also Standards 8.02, Informed Consent to Research; 9.03, Informed Consent in Assessments; and 10.01, Informed Consent to Therapy.)

(b) For persons who are legally incapable of giving informed consent, psychologists nevertheless (1) provide an appropriate explanation, (2) seek the individual's assent, (3) consider such persons' preferences and best interests, and (4) obtain appropriate permission from a legally authorized person, if such substitute consent is permitted or required by law. When consent by a legally authorized person is not permitted or required by law, psychologists take reasonable steps to protect the individual's rights and welfare.

(c) When psychological services are court ordered or otherwise mandated, psychologists inform the individual of the nature of the anticipated services, including whether the services are court ordered or mandated and any limits of confidentiality, before proceeding.

(d) Psychologists appropriately document written or oral consent, permission, and assent. (See also Standards 8.02, Informed Consent to Research; 9.03, Informed Consent in Assessments; and 10.01, Informed Consent to Therapy.)

3.11   Psychological Services Delivered To or Through Organizations

(a) Psychologists delivering services to or through organizations provide information beforehand to clients and when appropriate those directly affected by the services about (1) the nature and objectives of the services, (2) the intended recipients, (3) which of the individuals are clients, (4) the relationship the psychologist will have with each person and the organization, (5) the probable uses of services provided and information obtained, (6) who will have access to the information, and (7) limits of confidentiality. As soon as feasible, they provide information about the results and conclusions of such services to appropriate persons.

(b) If psychologists will be precluded by law or by organizational roles from providing such information to particular individuals or groups, they so inform those individuals or groups at the outset of the service.

3.12   Interruption of Psychological Services

Unless otherwise covered by contract, psychologists make reasonable efforts to plan for facilitating services in the event that psychological services are interrupted by factors such as the psychologist's illness, death, unavailability, relocation, or retirement or by the client's/patient's relocation or financial limitations. (See also Standard 6.02c, Maintenance, Dissemination, and Disposal of Confidential Records of Professional and Scientific Work.)

4.   Privacy and Confidentiality

4.01   Maintaining Confidentiality

Psychologists have a primary obligation and take reasonable precautions to protect confidential information obtained through or stored in any medium, recognizing that the extent and limits of confidentiality may be regulated by law or established by institutional rules or professional or scientific relationship. (See also Standard 2.05, Delegation of Work to Others.)

4.02   Discussing the Limits of Confidentiality

(a) Psychologists discuss with persons (including, to the extent feasible, persons who are legally incapable of giving informed consent and their legal representatives) and organizations with whom they establish a scientific or professional relationship (1) the relevant limits of confidentiality and (2) the foreseeable uses of the information generated through their psychological activities. (See also Standard 3.10, Informed Consent.)

(b) Unless it is not feasible or is contraindicated, the discussion of confidentiality occurs at the outset of the relationship and thereafter as new circumstances may warrant.

(c) Psychologists who offer services, products, or information via electronic transmission inform clients/patients of the risks to privacy and limits of confidentiality.

4.03   Recording

Before recording the voices or images of individuals to whom they provide services, psychologists obtain permission from all such persons or their legal representatives. (See also Standards 8.03, Informed Consent for Recording Voices and Images in Research; 8.05, Dispensing With Informed Consent for Research; and 8.07, Deception in Research.)

4.04   Minimizing Intrusions on Privacy

(a) Psychologists include in written and oral reports and consultations, only information germane to the purpose for which the communication is made.

(b) Psychologists discuss confidential information obtained in their work only for appropriate scientific or professional purposes and only with persons clearly concerned with such matters.

4.05   Disclosures

(a) Psychologists may disclose confidential information with the appropriate consent of the organizational client, the individual client/patient, or another legally authorized person on behalf of the client/patient unless prohibited by law.

(b) Psychologists disclose confidential information without the consent of the individual only as mandated by law, or where permitted by law for a valid purpose such as to (1) provide needed professional services; (2) obtain appropriate professional consultations; (3) protect the client/patient, psychologist, or others from harm; or (4) obtain payment for services from a client/patient, in which instance disclosure is limited to the minimum that is necessary to achieve the purpose. (See also Standard 6.04e, Fees and Financial Arrangements.)

4.06   Consultations

When consulting with colleagues, (1) psychologists do not disclose confidential information that reasonably could lead to the identification of a client/patient, research participant, or other person or organization with whom they have a confidential relationship unless they have obtained the prior consent of the person or organization or the disclosure cannot be avoided, and (2) they disclose information only to the extent necessary to achieve the purposes of the consultation. (See also Standard 4.01, Maintaining Confidentiality.)

4.07   Use of Confidential Information for Didactic or Other Purposes

Psychologists do not disclose in their writings, lectures, or other public media, confidential, personally identifiable information concerning their clients/patients, students, research participants, organizational clients, or other recipients of their services that they obtained during the course of their work, unless (1) they take reasonable steps to disguise the person or organization, (2) the person or organization has consented in writing, or (3) there is legal authorization for doing so.

5.   Advertising and Other Public Statements

5.01   Avoidance of False or Deceptive Statements

(a) Public statements include but are not limited to paid or unpaid advertising, product endorsements, grant applications, licensing applications, other credentialing applications, brochures, printed matter, directory listings, personal resumes or curricula vitae, or comments for use in media such as print or electronic transmission, statements in legal proceedings, lectures and public oral presentations, and published materials. Psychologists do not knowingly make public statements that are false, deceptive, or fraudulent concerning their research, practice, or other work activities or those of persons or organizations with which they are affiliated.

(b) Psychologists do not make false, deceptive, or fraudulent statements concerning (1) their training, experience, or competence; (2) their academic degrees; (3) their credentials; (4) their institutional or association affiliations; (5) their services; (6) the scientific or clinical basis for, or results or degree of success of, their services; (7) their fees; or (8) their publications or research findings.

(c) Psychologists claim degrees as credentials for their health services only if those degrees (1) were earned from a regionally accredited educational institution or (2) were the basis for psychology licensure by the state in which they practice.

5.02   Statements by Others

(a) Psychologists who engage others to create or place public statements that promote their professional practice, products, or activities retain professional responsibility for such statements.

(b) Psychologists do not compensate employees of press, radio, television, or other communication media in return for publicity in a news item. (See also Standard 1.01, Misuse of Psychologists' Work.)

(c) A paid advertisement relating to psychologists' activities must be identified or clearly recognizable as such.

5.03   Descriptions of Workshops and Non-Degree-Granting Educational Programs

To the degree to which they exercise control, psychologists responsible for announcements, catalogs, brochures, or advertisements describing workshops, seminars, or other non-degree-granting educational programs ensure that they accurately describe the audience for which the program is intended, the educational objectives, the presenters, and the fees involved.

5.04   Media Presentations

When psychologists provide public advice or comment via print, Internet, or other electronic transmission, they take precautions to ensure that statements (1) are based on their professional knowledge, training, or experience in accord with appropriate psychological literature and practice; (2) are otherwise consistent with this Ethics Code; and (3) do not indicate that a professional relationship has been established with the recipient. (See also Standard 2.04, Bases for Scientific and Professional Judgments.)

5.05   Testimonials

Psychologists do not solicit testimonials from current therapy clients/patients or other persons who because of their particular circumstances are vulnerable to undue influence.

5.06   In-Person Solicitation

Psychologists do not engage, directly or through agents, in uninvited in-person solicitation of business from actual or potential therapy clients/patients or other persons who because of their particular circumstances are vulnerable to undue influence. However, this prohibition does not preclude (1) attempting to implement appropriate collateral contacts for the purpose of benefiting an already engaged therapy client/patient or (2) providing disaster or community outreach services.

6. Record Keeping and Fees

6.01 Documentation of Professional and Scientific Work and Maintenance of Records

Psychologists create, and to the extent the records are under their control, maintain, disseminate, store, retain, and dispose of records and data relating to their professional and scientific work in order to (1) facilitate provision of services later by them or by other professionals, (2) allow for replication of research design and analyses, (3) meet institutional requirements, (4) ensure accuracy of billing and payments, and (5) ensure compliance with law. (See also Standard 4.01, Maintaining Confidentiality.)

6.02 Maintenance, Dissemination, and Disposal of Confidential Records of Professional and Scientific Work

(a) Psychologists maintain confidentiality in creating, storing, accessing, transferring, and disposing of records under their control, whether these are written, automated, or in any other medium. (See also Standards 4.01, Maintaining Confidentiality, and 6.01, Documentation of Professional and Scientific Work and Maintenance of Records.)

(b) If confidential information concerning recipients of psychological services is entered into databases or systems of records available to persons whose access has not been consented to by the recipient, psychologists use coding or other techniques to avoid the inclusion of personal identifiers.

(c) Psychologists make plans in advance to facilitate the appropriate transfer and to protect the confidentiality of records and data in the event of psychologists' withdrawal from positions or practice. (See also Standards 3.12, Interruption of Psychological Services, and 10.09, Interruption of Therapy.)

6.03 Withholding Records for Nonpayment

Psychologists may not withhold records under their control that are requested and needed for a client's/patient's emergency treatment solely because payment has not been received.

6.04 Fees and Financial Arrangements

(a) As early as is feasible in a professional or scientific relationship, psychologists and recipients of psychological services reach an agreement specifying compensation and billing arrangements.

(b) Psychologists' fee practices are consistent with law.

(c) Psychologists do not misrepresent their fees.

(d) If limitations to services can be anticipated because of limitations in financing, this is discussed with the recipient of services as early as is feasible. (See also Standards 10.09, Interruption of Therapy, and 10.10, Terminating Therapy.)

(e) If the recipient of services does not pay for services as agreed, and if psychologists intend to use collection agencies or legal measures to collect the fees, psychologists first inform the person that such measures will be taken and provide that person an opportunity to make prompt payment. (See also Standards 4.05, Disclosures; 6.03, Withholding Records for Nonpayment; and 10.01, Informed Consent to Therapy.)

6.05 Barter with Clients/Patients

Barter is the acceptance of goods, services, or other nonmonetary remuneration from clients/patients in return for psychological services. Psychologists may barter only if (1) it is not clinically contraindicated, and (2) the resulting arrangement is not exploitative. (See also Standards 3.05, Multiple Relationships, and 6.04, Fees and Financial Arrangements.)

6.06 Accuracy in Reports to Payors and Funding Sources

In their reports to payors for services or sources of research funding, psychologists take reasonable steps to ensure the accurate reporting of the nature of the service provided or research conducted, the fees, charges, or payments, and where applicable, the identity of the provider, the findings, and the diagnosis. (See also Standards 4.01, Maintaining Confidentiality; 4.04, Minimizing Intrusions on Privacy; and 4.05, Disclosures.)

6.07 Referrals and Fees

When psychologists pay, receive payment from, or divide fees with another professional, other than in an employer-employee relationship, the payment to each is based on the services provided (clinical, consultative, administrative, or other) and is not based on the referral itself. (See also Standard 3.09, Cooperation With Other Professionals.)

7.   Education and Training

7.01   Design of Education and Training Programs

Psychologists responsible for education and training programs take reasonable steps to ensure that the programs are designed to provide the appropriate knowledge and proper experiences, and to meet the requirements for licensure, certification, or other goals for which claims are made by the program. (See also Standard 5.03, Descriptions of Workshops and Non-Degree-Granting Educational Programs.)

7.02   Descriptions of Education and Training Programs

Psychologists responsible for education and training programs take reasonable steps to ensure that there is a current and accurate description of the program content (including participation in required course- or program-related counseling, psychotherapy, experiential groups, consulting projects, or community service), training goals and objectives, stipends and benefits, and requirements that must be met for satisfactory completion of the program. This information must be made readily available to all interested parties.

7.03   Accuracy in Teaching

(a) Psychologists take reasonable steps to ensure that course syllabi are accurate regarding the subject matter to be covered, bases for evaluating progress, and the nature of course experiences. This standard does not preclude an instructor from modifying course content or requirements when the instructor considers it pedagogically necessary or desirable, so long as students are made aware of these modifications in a manner that enables them to fulfill course requirements. (See also Standard 5.01, Avoidance of False or Deceptive Statements.)

(b) When engaged in teaching or training, psychologists present psychological information accurately. (See also Standard 2.03, Maintaining Competence.)

7.04   Student Disclosure of Personal Information

Psychologists do not require students or supervisees to disclose personal information in course- or program-related activities, either orally or in writing, regarding sexual history, history of abuse and neglect, psychological treatment, and relationships with parents, peers, and spouses or significant others except if (1) the program or training facility has clearly identified this requirement in its admissions and program materials or (2) the information is necessary to evaluate or obtain assistance for students whose personal problems could reasonably be judged to be preventing them from performing their training- or professionally-related activities in a competent manner or posing a threat to the students or others.

7.05   Mandatory Individual or Group Therapy

(a) When individual or group therapy is a program or course requirement, psychologists responsible for that program allow students in undergraduate and graduate programs the option of selecting such therapy from practitioners unaffiliated with the program. (See also Standard 7.02, Descriptions of Education and Training Programs.)

(b) Faculty who are or are likely to be responsible for evaluating students' academic performance do not themselves provide that therapy. (See also Standard 3.05, Multiple Relationships.)

7.06   Assessing Student and Supervisee Performance

(a) In academic and supervisory relationships, psychologists establish a timely and specific process for providing feedback to students and supervisees. Information regarding the process is provided to the student at the beginning of supervision.

(b) Psychologists evaluate students and supervisees on the basis of their actual performance on relevant and established program requirements.

7.07   Sexual Relationships with Students and Supervisees

Psychologists do not engage in sexual relationships with students or supervisees who are in their department, agency, or training center or over whom psychologists have or are likely to have evaluative authority. (See also Standard 3.05, Multiple Relationships.)

8.   Research and Publication

8.01   *Institutional Approval*

When institutional approval is required, psychologists provide accurate information about their research proposals and obtain approval prior to conducting the research. They conduct the research in accordance with the approved research protocol.

8.02   *Informed Consent to Research*

(a) When obtaining informed consent as required in Standard 3.10, Informed Consent, psychologists inform participants about (1) the purpose of the research, expected duration, and procedures; (2) their right to decline to participate and to withdraw from the research once participation has begun; (3) the foreseeable consequences of declining or withdrawing; (4) reasonably foreseeable factors that may be expected to influence their willingness to participate such as potential risks, discomfort, or adverse effects; (5) any prospective research benefits; (6) limits of confidentiality; (7) incentives for participation; and (8) whom to contact for questions about the research and research participants' rights. They provide opportunity for the prospective participants to ask questions and receive answers. (See also Standards 8.03, Informed Consent for Recording Voices and Images in Research; 8.05, Dispensing With Informed Consent for Research; and 8.07, Deception in Research.)

(b) Psychologists conducting intervention research involving the use of experimental treatments clarify to participants at the outset of the research (1) the experimental nature of the treatment; (2) the services that will or will not be available to the control group(s) if appropriate; (3) the means by which assignment to treatment and control groups will be made; (4) available treatment alternatives if an individual does not wish to participate in the research or wishes to withdraw once a study has begun; and (5) compensation for or monetary costs of participating including, if appropriate, whether reimbursement from the participant or a third-party payor will be sought. (See also Standard 8.02a, Informed Consent to Research.)

8.03   *Informed Consent for Recording Voices and Images in Research*

Psychologists obtain informed consent from research participants prior to recording their voices or images for data collection unless (1) the research consists solely of naturalistic observations in public places, and it is not anticipated that the recording will be used in a manner that could cause personal identification or harm, or (2) the research design includes deception, and consent for the use of the recording is obtained during debriefing. (See also Standard 8.07, Deception in Research.)

8.04   *Client/Patient, Student, and Subordinate Research Participants*

(a) When psychologists conduct research with clients/patients, students, or subordinates as participants, psychologists take steps to protect the prospective participants from adverse consequences of declining or withdrawing from participation.

(b) When research participation is a course requirement or an opportunity for extra credit, the prospective participant is given the choice of equitable alternative activities.

8.05   *Dispensing with Informed Consent for Research*

Psychologists may dispense with informed consent only (1) where research would not reasonably be assumed to create distress or harm and involves (a) the study of normal educational practices, curricula, or classroom management methods conducted in educational settings; (b) only anonymous questionnaires, naturalistic observations, or archival research for which disclosure of responses would not place participants at risk of criminal or civil liability or damage their financial standing, employability, or reputation, and confidentiality is protected; or (c) the study of factors related to job or organization effectiveness conducted in organizational settings for which there is no risk to participants' employability, and confidentiality is protected or (2) where otherwise permitted by law or federal or institutional regulations.

8.06   *Offering Inducements for Research Participation*

(a) Psychologists make reasonable efforts to avoid offering excessive or inappropriate financial or other inducements for research participation when such inducements are likely to coerce participation.

(b) When offering professional services as an inducement for research participation, psychologists clarify the nature of the services, as well as the risks, obligations, and limitations. (See also Standard 6.05, Barter With Clients/Patients.)

8.07 Deception in Research

(a) Psychologists do not conduct a study involving deception unless they have determined that the use of deceptive techniques is justified by the study's significant prospective scientific, educational, or applied value and that effective nondeceptive alternative procedures are not feasible.

(b) Psychologists do not deceive prospective participants about research that is reasonably expected to cause physical pain or severe emotional distress.

(c) Psychologists explain any deception that is an integral feature of the design and conduct of an experiment to participants as early as is feasible, preferably at the conclusion of their participation, but no later than at the conclusion of the data collection, and permit participants to withdraw their data. (See also Standard 8.08, Debriefing.)

8.08 Debriefing

(a) Psychologists provide a prompt opportunity for participants to obtain appropriate information about the nature, results, and conclusions of the research, and they take reasonable steps to correct any misconceptions that participants may have of which the psychologists are aware.

(b) If scientific or humane values justify delaying or withholding this information, psychologists take reasonable measures to reduce the risk of harm.

(c) When psychologists become aware that research procedures have harmed a participant, they take reasonable steps to minimize the harm.

8.09 Humane Care and Use of Animals in Research

(a) Psychologists acquire, care for, use, and dispose of animals in compliance with current federal, state, and local laws and regulations, and with professional standards.

(b) Psychologists trained in research methods and experienced in the care of laboratory animals supervise all procedures involving animals and are responsible for ensuring appropriate consideration of their comfort, health, and humane treatment.

(c) Psychologists ensure that all individuals under their supervision who are using animals have received instruction in research methods and in the care, maintenance, and handling of the species being used, to the extent appropriate to their role. (See also Standard 2.05, Delegation of Work to Others.)

(d) Psychologists make reasonable efforts to minimize the discomfort, infection, illness, and pain of animal subjects.

(e) Psychologists use a procedure subjecting animals to pain, stress, or privation only when an alternative procedure is unavailable and the goal is justified by its prospective scientific, educational, or applied value.

(f) Psychologists perform surgical procedures under appropriate anesthesia and follow techniques to avoid infection and minimize pain during and after surgery.

(g) When it is appropriate that an animal's life be terminated, psychologists proceed rapidly, with an effort to minimize pain and in accordance with accepted procedures.

8.10 Reporting Research Results

(a) Psychologists do not fabricate data. (See also Standard 5.01a, Avoidance of False or Deceptive Statements.)

(b) If psychologists discover significant errors in their published data, they take reasonable steps to correct such errors in a correction, retraction, erratum, or other appropriate publication means.

8.11 Plagiarism

Psychologists do not present portions of another's work or data as their own, even if the other work or data source is cited occasionally.

8.12 Publication Credit

(a) Psychologists take responsibility and credit, including authorship credit, only for work they have actually performed or to which they have substantially contributed. (See also Standard 8.12b, Publication Credit.)

(b) Principal authorship and other publication credits accurately reflect the relative scientific or professional contributions of the individuals involved, regardless of their relative status. Mere possession of an institutional position, such as department chair, does not justify authorship credit. Minor contributions to the research or to the writing for publications are acknowledged appropriately, such as in footnotes or in an introductory statement.

(c) Except under exceptional circumstances, a student is listed as principal author on any multiple-authored article that is substantially based on the student's doctoral dissertation. Faculty advisors discuss publication credit with students as early as feasible and throughout the research and publication process as appropriate. (See also Standard 8.12b, Publication Credit.)

8.13   Duplicate Publication of Data

Psychologists do not publish, as original data, data that have been previously published. This does not preclude republishing data when they are accompanied by proper acknowledgment.

8.14   Sharing Research Data for Verification

(a) After research results are published, psychologists do not withhold the data on which their conclusions are based from other competent professionals who seek to verify the substantive claims through reanalysis and who intend to use such data only for that purpose, provided that the confidentiality of the participants can be protected and unless legal rights concerning proprietary data preclude their release. This does not preclude psychologists from requiring that such individuals or groups be responsible for costs associated with the provision of such information.

(b) Psychologists who request data from other psychologists to verify the substantive claims through reanalysis may use shared data only for the declared purpose. Requesting psychologists obtain prior written agreement for all other uses of the data.

8.15   Reviewers

Psychologists who review material submitted for presentation, publication, grant, or research proposal review respect the confidentiality of and the proprietary rights in such information of those who submitted it.

9.   Assessment

9.01   Bases for Assessments

(a) Psychologists base the opinions contained in their recommendations, reports, and diagnostic or evaluative statements, including forensic testimony, on information and techniques sufficient to substantiate their findings. (See also Standard 2.04, Bases for Scientific and Professional Judgments.)

(b) Except as noted in 9.01c, psychologists provide opinions of the psychological characteristics of individuals only after they have conducted an examination of the individuals adequate to support their statements or conclusions. When, despite reasonable efforts, such an examination is not practical, psychologists document the efforts they made and the result of those efforts, clarify the probable impact of their limited information on the reliability and validity of their opinions, and appropriately limit the nature and extent of their conclusions or recommendations. (See also Standards 2.01, Boundaries of Competence, and 9.06, Interpreting Assessment Results.)

(c) When psychologists conduct a record review or provide consultation or supervision and an individual examination is not warranted or necessary for the opinion, psychologists explain this and the sources of information on which they based their conclusions and recommendations.

9.02   Use of Assessments

(a) Psychologists administer, adapt, score, interpret, or use assessment techniques, interviews, tests, or instruments in a manner and for purposes that are appropriate in light of the research on or evidence of the usefulness and proper application of the techniques.

(b) Psychologists use assessment instruments whose validity and reliability have been established for use with members of the population tested. When such validity or reliability has not been established, psychologists describe the strengths and limitations of test results and interpretation.

(c) Psychologists use assessment methods that are appropriate to an individual's language preference and competence, unless the use of an alternative language is relevant to the assessment issues.

9.03 Informed Consent in Assessments

(a) Psychologists obtain informed consent for assessments, evaluations, or diagnostic services, as described in Standard 3.10, Informed Consent, except when (1) testing is mandated by law or governmental regulations; (2) informed consent is implied because testing is conducted as a routine educational, institutional, or organizational activity (e.g., when participants voluntarily agree to assessment when applying for a job); or (3) one purpose of the testing is to evaluate decisional capacity. Informed consent includes an explanation of the nature and purpose of the assessment, fees, involvement of third parties, and limits of confidentiality and sufficient opportunity for the client/patient to ask questions and receive answers.

(b) Psychologists inform persons with questionable capacity to consent or for whom testing is mandated by law or governmental regulations about the nature and purpose of the proposed assessment services, using language that is reasonably understandable to the person being assessed.

(c) Psychologists using the services of an interpreter obtain informed consent from the client/patient to use that interpreter, ensure that confidentiality of test results and test security are maintained, and include in their recommendations, reports, and diagnostic or evaluative statements, including forensic testimony, discussion of any limitations on the data obtained. (See also Standards 2.05, Delegation of Work to Others; 4.01, Maintaining Confidentiality; 9.01, Bases for Assessments; 9.06, Interpreting Assessment Results; and 9.07, Assessment by Unqualified Persons.)

9.04 Release of Test Data

(a) The term test data refers to raw and scaled scores, client/patient responses to test questions or stimuli, and psychologists' notes and recordings concerning client/patient statements and behavior during an examination. Those portions of test materials that include client/patient responses are included in the definition of test data. Pursuant to a client/patient release, psychologists provide test data to the client/patient or other persons identified in the release. Psychologists may refrain from releasing test data to protect a client/patient or others from substantial harm or misuse or misrepresentation of the data or the test, recognizing that in many instances release of confidential information

under these circumstances is regulated by law. (See also Standard 9.11, Maintaining Test Security.)

(b) In the absence of a client/patient release, psychologists provide test data only as required by law or court order.

9.05 Test Construction

Psychologists who develop tests and other assessment techniques use appropriate psychometric procedures and current scientific or professional knowledge for test design, standardization, validation, reduction or elimination of bias, and recommendations for use.

9.06 Interpreting Assessment Results

When interpreting assessment results, including automated interpretations, psychologists take into account the purpose of the assessment as well as the various test factors, test-taking abilities, and other characteristics of the person being assessed, such as situational, personal, linguistic, and cultural differences, that might affect psychologists' judgments or reduce the accuracy of their interpretations. They indicate any significant limitations of their interpretations. (See also Standards 2.01b and c, Boundaries of Competence, and 3.01, Unfair Discrimination.)

9.07 Assessment by Unqualified Persons

Psychologists do not promote the use of psychological assessment techniques by unqualified persons, except when such use is conducted for training purposes with appropriate supervision. (See also Standard 2.05, Delegation of Work to Others.)

9.08 Obsolete Tests and Outdated Test Results

(a) Psychologists do not base their assessment or intervention decisions or recommendations on data or test results that are outdated for the current purpose.

(b) Psychologists do not base such decisions or recommendations on tests and measures that are obsolete and not useful for the current purpose.

9.09 Test Scoring and Interpretation Services

(a) Psychologists who offer assessment or scoring services to other professionals accurately describe the purpose, norms, validity, reliability, and applications of the procedures and any special qualifications applicable to their use.

(b) Psychologists select scoring and interpretation services (including automated services) on the basis of evidence of the validity of the program and procedures as well as on other appropriate considerations. (See also Standard 2.01b and c, Boundaries of Competence.)

(c) Psychologists retain responsibility for the appropriate application, interpretation, and use of assessment instruments, whether they score and interpret such tests themselves or use automated or other services.

9.10 Explaining Assessment Results

Regardless of whether the scoring and interpretation are done by psychologists, by employees or assistants, or by automated or other outside services, psychologists take reasonable steps to ensure that explanations of results are given to the individual or designated representative unless the nature of the relationship precludes provision of an explanation of results (such as in some organizational consulting, preemployment or security screenings, and forensic evaluations), and this fact has been clearly explained to the person being assessed in advance.

9.11 Maintaining Test Security

The term test materials refers to manuals, instruments, protocols, and test questions or stimuli and does not include test data as defined in Standard 9.04, Release of Test Data. Psychologists make reasonable efforts to maintain the integrity and security of test materials and other assessment techniques consistent with law and contractual obligations, and in a manner that permits adherence to this Ethics Code.

10. Therapy

10.01 Informed Consent to Therapy

(a) When obtaining informed consent to therapy as required in Standard 3.10, Informed Consent, psychologists inform clients/patients as early as is feasible in the therapeutic relationship about the nature and anticipated course of therapy, fees, involvement of third parties, and limits of confidentiality and provide sufficient opportunity for the client/patient to ask questions and receive answers. (See also Standards 4.02, Discussing the Limits of Confidentiality, and 6.04, Fees and Financial Arrangements.)

(b) When obtaining informed consent for treatment for which generally recognized techniques and procedures have not been established, psychologists inform their clients/patients of the developing nature of the treatment, the potential risks involved, alternative treatments that may be available, and the voluntary nature of their participation. (See also Standards 2.01e, Boundaries of Competence, and 3.10, Informed Consent.)

(c) When the therapist is a trainee and the legal responsibility for the treatment provided resides with the supervisor, the client/patient, as part of the informed consent procedure, is informed that the therapist is in training and is being supervised and is given the name of the supervisor.

10.02 Therapy Involving Couples or Families

(a) When psychologists agree to provide services to several persons who have a relationship (such as spouses, significant others, or parents and children), they take reasonable steps to clarify at the outset (1) which of the individuals are clients/patients and (2) the relationship the psychologist will have with each person. This clarification includes the psychologist's role and the probable uses of the services provided or the information obtained. (See also Standard 4.02, Discussing the Limits of Confidentiality.)

(b) If it becomes apparent that psychologists may be called on to perform potentially conflicting roles (such as family therapist and then witness for one party in divorce proceedings), psychologists take reasonable steps to clarify and modify, or withdraw from, roles appropriately. (See also Standard 3.05c, Multiple Relationships.)

10.03 Group Therapy

When psychologists provide services to several persons in a group setting, they describe at the outset the roles and responsibilities of all parties and the limits of confidentiality.

10.04   Providing Therapy to Those Served by Others

In deciding whether to offer or provide services to those already receiving mental health services elsewhere, psychologists carefully consider the treatment issues and the potential client's/patient's welfare. Psychologists discuss these issues with the client/patient or another legally authorized person on behalf of the client/patient in order to minimize the risk of confusion and conflict, consult with the other service providers when appropriate, and proceed with caution and sensitivity to the therapeutic issues.

10.05   Sexual Intimacies with Current Therapy Clients/Patients

Psychologists do not engage in sexual intimacies with current therapy clients/patients.

10.06   Sexual Intimacies with Relatives or Significant Others of Current Therapy Clients/Patients

Psychologists do not engage in sexual intimacies with individuals they know to be close relatives, guardians, or significant others of current clients/patients. Psychologists do not terminate therapy to circumvent this standard.

10.07   Therapy with Former Sexual Partners

Psychologists do not accept as therapy clients/patients persons with whom they have engaged in sexual intimacies.

10.08   Sexual Intimacies with Former Therapy Clients/Patients

(a) Psychologists do not engage in sexual intimacies with former clients/patients for at least two years after cessation or termination of therapy.

(b) Psychologists do not engage in sexual intimacies with former clients/patients even after a two-year interval except in the most unusual circumstances. Psychologists who engage in such activity after the two years following cessation or termination of therapy and of having no sexual contact with the former client/patient bear the burden of demonstrating that there has been no exploitation, in light of all relevant factors, including (1) the amount of time that has passed since therapy terminated; (2) the nature, duration, and intensity of the therapy; (3) the circumstances of termination; (4) the client's/patient's personal history; (5) the client's/patient's current mental status; (6) the likelihood of adverse impact on the client/patient; and (7) any statements or actions made by the therapist during the course of therapy suggesting or inviting the possibility of a posttermination sexual or romantic relationship with the client/patient. (See also Standard 3.05, Multiple Relationships.)

10.09   Interruption of Therapy

When entering into employment or contractual relationships, psychologists make reasonable efforts to provide for orderly and appropriate resolution of responsibility for client/patient care in the event that the employment or contractual relationship ends, with paramount consideration given to the welfare of the client/patient. (See also Standard 3.12, Interruption of Psychological Services.)

10.10   Terminating Therapy

(a) Psychologists terminate therapy when it becomes reasonably clear that the client/patient no longer needs the service, is not likely to benefit, or is being harmed by continued service.

(b) Psychologists may terminate therapy when threatened or otherwise endangered by the client/patient or another person with whom the client/patient has a relationship.

(c) Except where precluded by the actions of clients/patients or third-party payors, prior to termination psychologists provide pretermination counseling and suggest alternative service providers as appropriate.

History and Effective Date Footnote

This version of the APA Ethics Code was adopted by the American Psychological Association's Council of Representatives during its meeting, August 21, 2002, and is effective beginning June 1, 2003. Inquiries concerning the substance or interpretation of the APA Ethics Code should be addressed to the Director, Office of Ethics, American Psychological Association, 750 First Street, NE, Washington, DC 20002-4242. The Ethics Code and information regarding the Code can be found on the APA web site, http://www.apa.org/ethics. The standards in this Ethics Code will be used to adjudicate complaints brought concerning alleged conduct occurring on or after the effective date. Complaints regarding conduct occurring prior to the effective date will be adjudicated on the basis of the version of the Ethics Code that was in effect at the time the conduct occurred.

The APA has previously published its Ethics Code as follows:

American Psychological Association. (1953). Ethical standards of psychologists. Washington, DC: Author.

American Psychological Association. (1959). Ethical standards of psychologists. *American Psychologist, 14*, 279–282.

American Psychological Association. (1963). Ethical standards of psychologists. *American Psychologist, 18*, 56–60.

American Psychological Association. (1968). Ethical standards of psychologists. *American Psychologist, 23*, 357–361.

American Psychological Association. (1977, March). Ethical standards of psychologists. APA Monitor, 22–23.

American Psychological Association. (1979). Ethical standards of psychologists. Washington, DC: Author.

American Psychological Association. (1981). Ethical standards of psychologists. *American Psychologist, 36*, 633–638.

American Psychological Association. (1990). Ethical principles of psychologists (Amended June 2, 1989). *American Psychologist, 45*, 390–395.

American Psychological Association. (1992). Ethical principles of psychologists and code of conduct. *American Psychologist, 47*, 1597–1611.

Request copies of the APA's Ethical Principles of Psychologists and Code of Conduct from the APA Order Department, 750 First Street, NE, Washington, DC 20002-4242, or phone (202) 336-5510.

References

Abma, J. C., & Mott, F. L. (1991). Substance abuse and prenatal care during pregnancy among young women. *Family Planning Perspective, 23*, 117–122.

Academy of Psychological Clinical Science (2009). Mission statement. Retrieved on September 3, 2009, http://acadpsychclinicalscience.org.

Achenbach, T. M. (1991). *Manual for the Child Behavior Checklist/4-18 and 1991 Profile.* Burlington: University of Vermont Department of Psychiatry.

Achenbach, T. M. (1997). *Manual for the Young Adult Self-Report and Young Adult Behavior Checklist.* Burlington: University of Vermont, Department of Psychiatry.

Achenbach, T. M. (2009). *The Achenbach system of empirically based assessment (ASEBA): Development, findings, theory, and applications.* Burlington: University of Vermont, Research Center for Children, Youth, and Families.

Achenbach, T. M., & Rescorla, L. A. (2001). *Manual for ASEBA school-age forms and profiles.* Burlington: University of Vermont, Research Center for Children, Youth, and Families.

Achenbach, T. M., & Rescorla, L. A. (2003). *Manual for ASEBA adult forms & profiles.* Burlington: University of Vermont, Research Center for Children, Youth, & Families.

Achenbach, T. M., & Rescorla, L. A. (2007). *Multicultural supplement to the manual for ASEBA school-age forms & profiles.* Burlington: University of Vermont, Research Center for Children, Youth, & Families.

Addis, M. E. (1997). Evaluating the treatment manuals as a means of disseminating empirically validated psychotherapies. *Clinical Psychology: Science and Practice, 4*, 1–11.

Addis, M. E. (2002). Methods for disseminating research products and increasing evidence-based practice: Promises, obstacles, and future directions. *Clinical Psychology: Science and Practice, 9*, 367–378.

Ader, R., & Cohen, N. (1984). Behavior and the immune system. In W. D. Gentry (Ed.), *Handbook of behavioral medicine* (pp. 117–173). New York: Guilford Press.

Aegisdóttir, S., White, M. J., Spengler, P. M., Maugherman, A. S., Anderson, L. A., Cook, R. S. et al. (2006). The meta-analysis of clinical judgment project: Fifty-six years of accumulated research on clinical versus statistical prediction. *The Counseling Psychologist, 34*, 341–382.

Aglioni, G. (1982). *History and systems.* Berkeley, CA: Association for Advanced Training in the Behavioral Sciences.

Agras, W. S., & Berkowitz, R. (1980). Clinical research in behavior therapy: Halfway there? *Behavior Therapy, 11*, 472–488.

Agras, W. S., Berkowitz, R. I., Arnow, B. A., & Telch, C. F. (1996). Maintenance following a very-low calorie diet. *Journal of Consulting and Clinical Psychology, 64*, 610–613.

Agras, W. S., Telch, C. F., Arnow, B., Eldredge, K., Detzer, M. J., Henderson, J., et al. (1995). Does interpersonal therapy help patients with binge eating disorder who fail to respond to cognitive-behavioral therapy? *Journal of Consulting and Clinical Psychology, 63*, 356–360.

Albee, G. W., & Gullotta, T. P. (Eds.). (1997). *Primary prevention works.* Thousands Oaks, CA: Sage.

Albee, G. W., & Perry, M. (1996). Are we preventing diseases or promoting competencies? *Journal of Mental Health, 5*, 421–422.

Alcoholics Anonymous. (1990). *Comments on AA's triennial surveys.* New York: Alcoholics Anonymous World Services.

Alcoholics Anonymous. (2009). Welcome to Alcoholics Anonymous: Estimates of AA groups and members. New York: Alcoholics Anonymous World Services. Retrieved on September 27, 2009, http://www.aa.org/lang/en/subpage.cfm?page=74.

Allen, G. J., Nelson, W. J., & Sheckley, B. G. (1987). Continuing education activities of Connecticut psychologists. *Professional Psychology: Research and Practice, 18*, 78–80.

Allison, J., Blatt, S. J., & Zimet, C. N. (1968). *The interpretation of psychological tests.* New York: Harper & Row.

American Cancer Society. (1989). *Cancer facts and figures—1989.* Atlanta, GA: Author.

507

American Cancer Society. (1996). *Cancer facts and figures—1996.* Atlanta, GA: Author.

American Cancer Society. (1997). *Cancer facts and figures—1997.* Atlanta, GA: Author.

American Cancer Society. (2000). Cancer facts and figures—2000. Retrieved October 15, 2009, from www.cancer.org/downloads/STT/F&F00.pdf.

American Cancer Society (2009). *Cancer facts and figures—2009.* Washington, DC: Author.

American Heart Association. (2009). *Heart and stroke statistics—2009.* Dallas, TX: Author.

American Humane Association. (1984). *Highlights of official child abuse and neglect reporting—1982.* Denver, CO: Author.

American Medical Association. (1984). *Proceedings of the house of delegates of the American Medical Association.* Chicago: Author.

American Medical Association. (2001). *The Columbia encyclopedia* (6th ed.). New York: Author.

American Psychiatric Association. (2000). *Diagnostic and statistical manual of mental disorders* (4th ed., Text Rev.). Washington, DC: Author.

American Psychiatric Association. (2003). *APA scope of practice: Psychologists prescribing legislation.* Washington, DC: Author.

American Psychiatric Association. (2010). About the American Psychiatric Association. Retrieved on January 3, 2010, http://www.psych.org/.

American Psychiatric Nurses Association. (2009). *2009 annual report.* Arlington, VA: Author.

American Psychological Association. (1955). Joint report of the APA and CSPA (Conference of State Psychological Associations). *American Psychologist, 10,* 727–756.

American Psychological Association. (1967). A model for state legislation affecting the practice of psychology 1967: Report of the APA Committee on Legislation. *American Psychologist, 22,* 1095–1103.

American Psychological Association. (1981). Specialty guidelines for the delivery of services by clinical psychologists. *American Psychologist, 36,* 640–651.

American Psychological Association. (1985). *Standards for educational and psychological testing.* Washington, DC: Author.

American Psychological Association. (1987a). *Guidelines for computer based tests and interpretations.* Washington, DC: Author.

American Psychological Association. (1987b). Model act for state licensure of psychologists. *American Psychologist, 42,* 696–703.

American Psychological Association. (1990). *Guidelines for providers of psychological services to ethnic, linguistic, and culturally diverse populations.* Washington, DC: Author.

American Psychological Association. (1992a). Ethical principles of psychologists and code of conduct. *American Psychologist, 47,* 1597–1611.

American Psychological Association. (1992b). *Report of the ad hoc task force on psychopharmacology.* Washington, DC: Author.

American Psychological Association. (1993a). *Directory of the American Psychological Association,* 1993 edition. Washington, DC: Author.

American Psychological Association. (1993b). Guidelines for providers of psychological services to ethnic, linguistic, and culturally diverse populations. *American Psychologist, 48,* 45–48.

American Psychological Association. (1995a). *Current major field of APA members by employment status: 1995.* Unpublished manuscript.

American Psychological Association. (1995b). *Graduate study in psychology.* Washington, DC: Author.

American Psychological Association. (1995c). Report of the ethics committee, 1994. *American Psychologist, 50,* 706–713.

American Psychological Association. (1995d). *Report of the task force on the changing gender composition of psychology.* Washington, DC: Author.

American Psychological Association. (1995e). Training in and dissemination of empirically validated psychological treatments: Reports and recommendations. *Clinical Psychologist, 48,* 3–23.

American Psychological Association. (1996). *Recommended postdoctoral training in psychopharmacology for prescription privileges.* Washington, DC: Author.

American Psychological Association. (1997). *1997 doctorate employment survey.* Washington, DC: Author.

American Psychological Association. (1998). Appropriate therapeutic responses to sexual orientation in the proceedings of the American Psychological Association, Incorporated, for the legislative year 1997. *American Psychologist, 53,* 882–939.

American Psychological Association Research Office. (1999). *1999 doctorate employment survey.* Washington, DC: Author.

American Psychological Association. (2000a). *2000 APA directory survey.* Washington, DC: Author.

American Psychological Association Division 44/Committee on Lesbian, Gay, and Bisexual Concerns Joint Task Force on Guidelines for

Psychotherapy with Lesbian, Gay, and Bisexual Clients (2000b). Guidelines for psychotherapy with lesbian, gay, and bisexual clients. *American Psychologist, 55,* 1440–1451.

American Psychological Association. (2002). Report of the ethics committee, 2002. *American Psychologist, 58,* 650–659.

American Psychological Association. (2003a). *2003 doctorate employment survey.* Washington, DC: Author.

American Psychological Association. (2003b). Guidelines on multicultural education, training, research, practice, and organizational change for psychologists. *American Psychologist, 58,* 377–402.

American Psychological Association Presidential Task Force on Evidence-Based Practice. (2006). Evidence-based practice in psychology. *American Psychologist, 61,* 271–285.

American Psychological Association. (2007). Record keeping guidelines. *American Psychologist, 62,* 993–1004.

American Psychological Association. (2008). *2007 salaries in psychology.* Washington, DC: Author.

American Psychological Association. (2008). *Graduate study in psychology.* Washington, DC: Author.

American Psychological Association. (2009a). *Graduate study in psychology.* Washington, DC: Author.

American Psychological Association. (2009b). *2007 doctorate employment survey.* Washington, DC: Author.

American Psychological Association. (2009c). Report of the ethics committee, 2008. *American Psychologist, 64,* 464–473.

American Psychological Association. (2010a). *Directory of the American Psychological Association.* Washington, DC: Author.

American Psychological Association. (2010b). About APA. Retrieved on January 3, 2010, http://www.apa.org/about/.

Anastasi, A., & Urbina, S. (1997). *Psychology testing* (7th ed.). New York: Prentice-Hall.

Anastopoulos, A. D. (1998). A training program for parents of children with attention-deficit/hyperactivity disorder. In J. M. Breismeister & C. E. Schaefer (Eds.), *Handbook of parent training: Parents as co-therapists for children's behavior problems* (pp. 27–60). New York: Wiley.

Anders, G. (1996). *Health against wealth: HMOs and the breakdown of medical trust.* Boston: Houghton Mifflin.

Andersen, B. L. (1992). Psychological interventions for cancer patients to enhance the quality of life. *Journal of Consulting and Clinical Psychology, 60,* 552–568.

Andersen, B. L. (1996). Introduction to the featured section: Psychological and behavioral studies in cancer prevention and control. *Health Psychology, 15,* 411–412.

Andersen, B. L. (2002). Biobehavioral outcomes following psychological interventions for cancer patients. *Journal of Consulting and Clinical Psychology, 70,* 590–610.

Anderson, C. V., Bigler, E. D., & Blatter, D. D. (1995). Frontal lobe lesions, diffuse damage, and neuropsychological functioning in traumatic brain-injured patients. *Journal of Clinical and Experimental Neuropsychology, 17,* 900–908.

Anderson, E. M., & Lambert, M. J. (1995). Short-term dynamically oriented psychotherapy: A review and meta-analysis. *Clinical Psychology Review, 15,* 503–514.

Anderson, N. B., & Jackson, J. S. (1987). Race, ethnicity, and health psychology: The example of essential hypertension. In C. M. Stone, S. M. Weiss, J. D. Matarazzo, N. E. Miller, J. Rodin, C. D. Belar, et al. (Eds.), *Health psychology: A discipline and a profession* (pp. 264–283). Chicago: University of Chicago Press.

Andreasen, N. C. (Ed.). (1989). *Brain imaging: Applications in psychiatry.* Washington, DC: American Psychiatric Association.

Andreasen, N. C., & Black, D. W. (1995). *Introductory textbook of psychiatry* (2nd ed.). Washington, DC: American Psychiatric Association.

Andrews, G., & Harvey, R. (1981). Does psychotherapy benefit neurotic patients? A reanalysis of the Smith, Glass, and Miller data. *Archives of General Psychiatry, 38,* 1203–1208.

Andrews, J. (1991). *The active self in psychotherapy: An integration of therapeutic styles.* Boston: Allyn & Bacon.

Anisman, H. (1984). Vulnerability to depression: Contribution of stress. In R. Post & J. Ballenger (Eds.), *Neurobiology of mood disorders.* Baltimore: Williams & Wilkins.

Annesi, J. J. (2001). Effects of music, television, and combination entertainment system on distraction, exercise adherence, and physical output in adults. *Canadian Journal of Behavioural Science, 33,* 193–202.

Annis, H. M. (1990). Relapse to substance abuse: Empirical findings within a cognitive-social learning approach? *Journal of Psychoactive Drugs, 22,* 117–124.

Anonymous. (1995). Hidden benefits of managed care. *Professional Psychology: Research and Practice, 26*, 235–237.

Ansbacher, H. L. (1951). The history of the leaderless group discussion technique. *Psychological Bulletin, 48*, 383–391.

Antonova, E., Sharma, T., Morris, R., & Kumari, V. (2004). The relationship between brain structure and neurocognition in schizophrenia: A selective review. *Schizophrenia Research, 70*, 117–145.

Apfel, R. J., & Simon, B. (1985). Patient-therapist sexual contact: I. Psychodynamic perspectives on the causes and results. *Psychotherapy and Psychosomatics, 43*, 57–62.

Apple, R. F., & Agras, W. S. (1997). *Overcoming eating disorders: A cognitive-behavioral treatment for bulimia nervosa and binge-eating disorder.* San Antonio, TX: Psychological Corporation.

Arkowitz, H. (1989). The role of theory in psychotherapy integration. *Journal of Integrative and Eclectic Psychotherapy, 8*, 8–16.

Arkowitz, H. (1992). Integrative theories of therapy. In D. K. Freedheim (Ed.), *History of psychotherapy: A century of change* (pp. 261–303). Washington, DC: American Psychological Association.

Arkowitz, H., & Lilienfeld, S. O. (2007). The best medicine? How drugs stack up against talk therapy for the treatment of depression. *Scientific American Mind, 18*, 80–83.

Arling, G. (1976). The elderly widow and her family, neighbors, and friends. *Journal of Marriage and the Family, 38*, 757–768.

Arnkoff, D. B., & Glass, C. R. (1992). Cognitive therapy and psychotherapy integration. In D. K. Freedheim (Ed.), *History of psychotherapy: A century of change* (pp. 657–694). Washington, DC: American Psychological Association.

Aronne, L. J. (2001). Epidemiology, morbidity, and treatment of overweight and obesity. *Journal of Clinical Psychiatry, 62*(Suppl. 23), 13–22.

Asnis, G. M., Hameedi, F. A., Goddard, A. W., Potkin, S. G., Black, D., Jameel, M., et al. (2001). Fluvoxamine in the treatment of panic disorder: A multi-center, double-blind, placebo-controlled study in outpatients. *Psychiatry Research, 103*, 1–14.

Association for Medical School Pharmacology. (1990). *Knowledge objectives in medical pharmacology* (2nd ed.). Washington, DC: Author.

Association of Psychology Postdoctoral and Internship Centers (APPIC). (2009). *APPIC directory.* Washington, DC: Author.

Atkinson, D. R., & Hackett, G. (1998). *Counseling diverse populations* (2nd ed.). Boston: McGraw-Hill.

Auerbach, J. E. (2001). *Personal and executive coaching.* Los Angeles: Executive College Press.

Ax, R. K., Fagan, T. J., Resnick, R. J. (2009). Predoctoral prescriptive authority training: The rationale and a combined model. *Psychological Services. 6*, 85–95.

Bach, A. K., Wincze, J. P., & Barlow, D. H. (2001). Sexual dysfunction. In D. H. Barlow (Ed.), *Clinical handbook of psychological disorders: A step-by-step treatment manual* (3rd ed., pp. 562–608). New York: Guilford Press.

Baekeland, F., & Lundwall, L. (1975). Dropping out of treatment: A critical review. *Psychological Bulletin, 82*, 738–783.

Baird, K. A., & Rupert, P. A. (1987). Clinical management of confidentiality: A survey of psychologists in seven states. *Professional Psychology: Research and Practice, 18*, 347–352.

Bajt, T. R., & Pope, K. S. (1989). Therapist-patient sexual intimacy involving children and adolescents. *American Psychologist, 44*, 555.

Baker, R. W., & Trzepacz, P. T. (2005). Mental status examination. In G. P. Koocher, J. C. Norcross, & S. S. Hill, III (Eds.), *Psychologists' desk reference* (2nd ed., pp. 7–12). New York: Oxford University Press.

Bakker, A., van Balkom, A. J. L. M., Spinhoven, P., Blaauw, B. M. J. W., & van Dyck, R. (1998). Follow-up on the treatment of panic disorder with or without agoraphobia. *Journal of Nervous and Mental Diseases, 186*, 414–419.

Baldessarini, R. J., & Cole, J. O. (1988). Chemotherapy. In A. M. Nicholi, Jr. (Ed.), *The new Harvard guide to psychiatry.* Cambridge, MA: Harvard University Press.

Bandura, A. (1969). *Principles of behavior modification* New York: Holt, Rinehart & Winston.

Bandura, A. (1982). Self-efficacy mechanisms in human agency. *American Psychologist, 37*, 122–147.

Bandura, A. (1986). *Social foundations of thought and action: A social cognitive theory.* Englewood Cliffs, NJ: Prentice-Hall.

Bandura, A. (1989). Human agency in social cognitive theory. *American Psychologist, 33*, 344–358.

Banks, S. M., & Kerns, R. D. (1996). Explaining high rates of depression in chronic pain: A diathesis-stress framework. *Psychological Bulletin, 119*, 95–110.

Barber, J. P., & Crits-Christoph, P. (Eds.). (2000). *Dynamic therapies for psychiatric disorders (Axis I).* New York: Basic Books.

Barker, S. L., Funk, S. C., & Houston, B. K. (1988). Psychological treatment versus nonspecific factors: A meta-analysis of conditions that engender comparable expectations of improvement. *Clinical Psychology Review, 8,* 579–594.

Barkley, R. A. (1989). Attention deficit-hyperactivity disorder. In E. J. Mash & R. A. Barkley (Eds.), *Treatment of childhood disorders* (pp. 39–72). New York: Guilford Press.

Barkley, R. A. (1993). *Hyperactive children: A handbook for diagnosis and treatment.* New York: Guilford Press.

Barkley, R. A. (1996). Attention deficit/hyperactivity disorder. In E. J. Mash & R. A. Barkley (Eds.), *Child psychopathology* (pp. 63–112). New York: Guilford Press.

Barkley, R. A. (1998). *Attention-deficit hyperactivity disorder: A handbook for diagnosis and treatment.* New York: Guilford Press.

Barkley, R. A. (2000). *Taking charge of attention deficit hyperactivity disorder: The complete, authoritative guide for parents* (Rev. ed.). New York: Guilford Press.

Barkley, R. A. (2009). *Attention deficit/hyperactivity disorder in adults: The latest assessment and treatment strategies.* Sudbury, MA: Jones & Bartlett.

Barkley, R. A., Mash, E., Heffernan, K., & Fletcher, J. (2003). *Child psychopathology* (2nd ed.). New York: Guilford Press.

Barkow, J. H. (2006). *Missing the revolution: Darwinism for social scientists.* New York: Oxford University Press.

Barlow, D. H. (1996). Health care policy, psychotherapy research, and the future of psychotherapy. *American Psychologist, 51,* 1050–1058.

Barlow, D. H. (Ed.). (2001). *Clinical handbook of psychological disorders: A step-by-step treatment manual* (3rd ed.). New York: Guilford Press.

Barlow, D. H. (2002). *Anxiety and its disorders: The nature and treatment of anxiety and panic* (2nd ed.). New York: Guilford Press.

Barlow, D. H., & Cerny, J. A. (1988). *Psychological treatment of panic.* New York: Guilford Press.

Barlow, D. H., & Craske, M. G. (2000). *Mastery of your anxiety and panic* (3rd ed.). Albany, NY: Graywind.

Barlow, D. H., Hayes, S. C., & Nelson, R. O. (1984). *The scientist practitioner: Research and accountability in clinical and educational settings.* New York: Pergamon Press.

Barlow, D. H., & Rapee, R. M. (1991). *Mastering stress: A lifestyle approach.* Dallas, TX: American Health.

Barondes, S. H. (2005). *Better than Prozac: Creating the next generation of psychiatric drugs.* New York: Oxford University Press.

Barrett, P. M. Farrell, L., Pina, A. A., Peris. T. S., Piacentini, J. (2008). Evidence-based psychosocial treatments for child and adolescent obsessive–compulsive disorder. *Journal of Clinical Child & Adolescent Psychology, 37,* 131–155.

Barton, W. E. (1991). Toward a model curriculum in mental health administration. *Administration and Policy in Mental Health, 18,* 237–246.

Bateson, G., Jackson, D., Haley, J., & Weakland, J. (1956). Toward a theory of schizophrenia. *Behavioral Science, 1,* 251–264.

Baur, S. (1997). *The intimate hour: Love and sex in psychotherapy.* New York: Houghton Mifflin.

Baxter, L. R., Schwartz, J. M., Bergman, K. S., Szuba, M. P., Guze, B. H., Mazziotta, J. C., et al. (1992). Caudate glucose metabolic rate changes with both drug and behavior therapy for obsessive-compulsive disorder. *Archives of General Psychiatry, 49,* 681–689.

Bay-Hinitz, A. K., Peterson, R. F., & Quilitch, H. R. (1994). Cooperative games: A way to modify aggressive and cooperative behavior in young children. *Journal of Applied Behavior Analysis, 27,* 435–446.

Bayley, N. (1993). *Bayley Scale of Infant Development* (2nd ed.). San Antonio, TX: Psychological Corporation.

Beck, A. T. (1963). Thinking and depression. *Archives of General Psychiatry, 9,* 324–333.

Beck, A. T. (1976). *Cognitive therapy and emotional disorders.* New York: International Universities Press.

Beck, A. T. (1987). *Manual for the Beck Depression Inventory.* San Antonio, TX: Psychological Corporation.

Beck, A. T. (1988). *Manual for the Beck Hopelessness Scale.* San Antonio, TX: Psychological Corporation.

Beck, A. T. (1990). *Manual for the Beck Anxiety Inventory.* San Antonio, TX: Psychological Corporation.

Beck, A. T. (1991). *Manual for the Beck Scale for Suicide Ideation.* San Antonio, TX: Psychological Corporation.

Beck, A. T. (1993). *Manual for the Beck Anxiety Inventory* (2nd ed.). San Antonio, TX: Psychological Corporation.

Beck, A. T., & Alford, B. A. (2009). *Depression: Causes and treatments* (2nd ed.). Philadelphia: University of Pennsylvania Press.

Beck, A. T., Emery, G., & Greenberg, R. L. (1985). *Anxiety disorders and phobias: A cognitive perspective.* New York: Basic Books.

Beck, A. T., Emery, G., & Greenberg, R. L. (2000). *Anxiety disorders and phobias: A cognitive perspective.* New York: Guilford Press.

Beck, A. T., & Freeman, A. (1990). *Cognitive therapy of personality disorders.* New York: Guilford Press.

Beck, A. T., Rush, A. J., Shaw, B. E., & Emery, G. (1979). *Cognitive therapy of depression.* New York: Guilford Press.

Beck, A. T., Steer, R. A., & Brown, G. K. (1996). *Manual for the Beck Depression Inventory—II.* San Antonio, TX: Psychological Corporation.

Beck, J. S., Beck, A. T., & Jolly, J. B. (2005). *Manual for the Beck Youth Inventories* (2nd ed.). San Antonio, TX: Psychological Corporation.

Becker, C. B., Stice, E., Shaw, H., & Woda, S. (2009). Use of empirically supported interventions for psychopathology: Can the participatory approach move us beyond the research-to-practice gap? *Behaviour Research and Therapy, 47,* 265–274.

Becker, R. E., Heimberg, R. G., & Bellack, A. S. (1987). *Social skills training treatment for depression.* New York: Pergamon Press.

Beckham, E. E. (1990). Psychotherapy of depression at the crossroads: Directions for the 1990s. *Clinical Psychology Review, 10,* 207–228.

Beer, M., & Spector, B. (1993). Organizational diagnosis: Its role in organizational learning. *Journal of Counseling and Development, 71,* 642–650.

Beiderman, J., Faraone, S. V., Keenan, K., Bejamin, J., Krifcher, B., Moore, C., et al. (1992). Further evidence for family-genetic risk factors in attention deficit hyperactivity disorder: Patterns of comorbidity in probands and relative in psychiatrically and pediatrically referred samples. *Archives of General Psychiatry, 49,* 728–738.

Belar, C. D. (1995). Collaboration in capitated care: Challenges for psychology. *Professional Psychology: Research and Practice, 26,* 139–146.

Belar, C. D., Bieliauskas, L. A., Larsen, K. G., Mensh, I. N., Poey, K., & Roehike, H. J. (1989). National Conference on Internship Training in Psychology. *American Psychologist, 44,* 60–65.

Bell, C. J., & Nutt, D. J. (1998). Serotonin and panic. *British Journal of Psychiatry, 172,* 465–471.

Bell, J. E. (1961). *Family group therapy* (Public Health Monograph No. 64). Washington, DC: U.S. Government Printing Office.

Bell, P. F., Digman, R. H., & McKenna, J. P. (1995). Should psychologists obtain prescription privileges? A survey of family physicians. *Professional Psychology: Research and Practice, 26,* 371–376.

Bellack, A. S., & Herson, M. (Eds.). (1990). *Handbook of comparative treatments for adult disorders.* New York: Wiley.

Bellak, L. (1992). *The Thematic Apperception Test, the Children's Apperception Test, and the Senior Apperception Technique in Clinical Use* (5th ed.). Odessa, FL: Psychological Assessment Resources.

Belle, D., & Doucet, J. (2003). Poverty, inequality, and discrimination as sources of depression among United States women. *Psychology of Women Quarterly, 27,* 101–113.

Belluck, P. (2005, March 17). Children's life expectancy being cut short by obesity. *New York Times,* pp. A15.

Bem, D. J., & Funder, D. C. (1978). Predicting more of the people more of the time: Assessing the personality of situations. *Psychological Review, 85,* 485–501.

Ben-Porath, Y. S., & Tellegen, A. (2008). *Manual for the Minnesota Multiphasic Personality Inventory-2—Restructured Form (MMPI-2-RF).* Minneapolis, MN: Pearson.

Benedict, J. G., & Phelps, R. (1998). Introduction: Psychology's view of managed care. *Professional Psychology: Research and Practice, 29,* 29–30.

Benjamin, L. S. (2002). *Interpersonal diagnosis and treatment of personality disorders.* New York: Guilford Press.

Bennett-Johnson, S., & Millstein, S. G. (2003). Prevention opportunities in health care settings. *American Psychological Association, 58,* 475–481.

Benton, A. (1991). *Benton Visual Retention Test.* San Antonio, TX: Psychological Corporation.

Bentz, V. J. (1985). Research findings from personality assessment of executives. In H. J. Bernardin & D. A. Bownas (Eds.), *Personality assessment in organizations* (pp. 323–351). New York: Praeger.

Bergen, D. C. (2008). Diagnosing pseudoseizures: Don't hold your breath. *Epilepsy Currents, 8,* 154–155.

Bergin, A. E. (1971). The evaluation of therapeutic outcomes. In A. E. Bergin & S. L. Garfield (Eds.), *Handbook of psychotherapy and behavior change:*

An empirical analysis (pp. 217–270). New York: Wiley.

Bergin, A. E., & Garfield, S. L. (1994). Overview, trends, and future issues. In A. E. Bergin & S. L. Garfield (Eds.), *Handbook of psychotherapy and behavior change* (4th ed., pp. 818–824). New York: Wiley.

Bergin, A. E., & Lambert, M. J. (1978). The evaluation of therapeutic outcomes. In A. E. Bergin & S. L. Garfield (Eds.), *Handbook of psychotherapy and behavior change: An empirical analysis* (2nd ed., pp. 143–189). New York: Wiley.

Berk, M., & Parker, G. (2009). The elephant on the couch: Side-effects of psychotherapy. *Australian and New Zealand Journal of Psychiatry, 43*, 787–794.

Berkman, L. F., & Syme, S. L. (1979). Social networks, host resistance, and mortality: A nine-year follow-up study of Alameda County residents. *American Journal of Epidemiology, 109*, 186–204.

Berman, J. S., & Norton, N. C. (1985). Does professional training make a therapist more effective? *Psychological Bulletin, 98*, 401–406.

Bernal, M. E., & Castro, F. G. (1994). Are clinical psychologists prepared for service and research with ethnic minorities: Report of a decade of progress. *American Psychologist, 49*, 797–805.

Berrigan, L. P., & Garfield, S. L. (1981). Relationship of missed psychotherapy appointments to premature termination and social class. *British Journal of Clinical Psychology, 20*, 239–242.

Bersoff, D. N. (1995). *Ethical conflicts in psychology.* Washington, DC: American Psychological Association.

Bersoff, D. N. (2003). *Ethical conflicts in psychology* (3rd ed.). Washington, DC: American Psychological Association.

Bersoff, D. N. (2008). *Ethical conflicts in psychology* (4th ed.). Washington, DC: American Psychological Association.

Bertelsen, B., Harvald, B., & Hauge, M. (1977). A Danish twin study of manic-depressive disorders. *British Journal of Psychiatry, 130*, 330–351.

Bérubé, R. L., & Achenbach, T. M. (2007). *Bibliography of published studies using the ASEBA.* Burlington: University of Vermont, Research Center for Children, Youth, & Families.

Betz, N., & Shullman, S. (1979). Factors related to client return following intake. *Journal of Counseling Psychology, 26*, 542–545.

Beutler, L. E. (1986). Systematic eclectic psychotherapy. In J. C. Norcross (Ed.), *Handbook of eclectic psychotherapy* (pp. 94–131). New York: Brunner/Mazel.

Beutler, L. E. (2002). Proscriptive authority: Moving toward a new clinical psychology? *Clinical Psychologist, 55*, 1–3.

Beutler, L. E. (2009). Making science matter in clinical practice: Redefining psychotherapy. *Clinical Psychology: Science and Practice, 16*, 301–317.

Beutler, L. E., Bonger, B., & Shurkin, J. N. (1998). *A consumer's guide to psychotherapy.* New York: Oxford University Press.

Beutler, L. E., & Fisher, D. (1994). Combined specialty training in counseling, clinical, and school psychology: An idea whose time has returned. *Professional Psychology: Research and Practice, 25*, 62–69.

Beutler, L. E., & Groth-Marnat, G. (Eds.). (2003). *Integrative assessment of adult personality* (2nd ed.). New York: Guilford Press.

Beutler, L. E., & Malik, M. L. (Eds.). (2002). *Rethinking the DSM: A psychological perspective.* Washington, DC: American Psychological Association.

Beutler, L. E., Mohr, D. C., Grawe, K., Engle, D., & MacDonald, R. (1991). Looking for differential treatment effects: Cross-cultural predictions of differential therapeutic efficacy. *Journal of Psychotherapy Integration, 1*, 121–141.

Beutler, L. E., Moleiro, C., & Talebi, H. (2002). How practitioners can systematically use empirical evidence in treatment selection. *Journal of Clinical Psychology, 58*, 1199–1212.

Beutler, L. E., Williams, R. E., Wakefield, P. J., & Entwistle, S. R. (1995). Bridging scientist and practitioner perspectives in clinical psychology. *American Psychologist, 50*, 984–994.

Bevan, W. (1991). Contemporary psychology: A tour inside the onion. *American Psychologist, 46*, 475–483.

Bickman, L. (1987). Graduate education in psychology. *American Psychologist, 42*, 1041–1047.

Bickman, L. (1996). A continuum of care: More is not always better. *American Psychologist, 49*, 689–701.

Biglan, A., Mrazek, P. J., Carnine, D., & Flay, B. R. (2003). The integration of research and practice in the prevention of youth problem behaviors. *American Psychologist, 58*, 433–440.

Binik, Y. M., Cantor, J., Ochs, E., & Meana, M. (1997). From the couch to the keyboard: Psychotherapy in cyberspace. In S. Kiesler (Ed.), *Culture of the Internet* (pp. 71–100). Mahwah, NJ: Erlbaum.

Blackburn, I. M., & Moore, R. G. (1997). Controlled acute and follow up trial of cognitive and pharmacotherapy in outpatients with recurrent depression. *British Journal of Psychiatry, 171,* 328–334.

Blader, J., & Carlson, G. (2007). Increased rates of bipolar disorder diagnoses among U.S. child, adolescent, and adult inpatients, 1996–2004. *Biological Psychiatry, 62,* 107–114.

Blanchard, E. B. (1987). Long-term effects of behavioral treatment of chronic headaches. *Behavior Therapy, 18,* 375–385.

Blascovich, J., & Katkin, E. S. (1993). *Cardiovascular reactivity to psychological stress and disease.* Washington, DC: American Psychological Association.

Blatt, S. J. (1975). The validity of projective techniques and their research and clinical contribution. *Journal of Personality Assessment, 39,* 327–343.

Bloom, B. (1992). Computer-assisted intervention: A review and commentary. *Clinical Psychology Review, 128,* 169–198.

Bloom, B. L. (1981). Focused single-session therapy: Initial development and evaluation. In S. H. Budman (Ed.), *Forms of brief therapy* (pp. 167–216). New York: Guilford Press.

Blouke, P. S. (1997). Musings of a bureaucratic psychologist. *Professional Psychology: Research and Practice, 28,* 326–328.

Blount, A., Schoenbaum, M., Kathol, R., Rollman, B. L., Thomas, M., O'Donohue, W., & Peek, C. J. (2007). The economics of behavioral health services in medical settings: A summary of the evidence. *Professional Psychology: Research and Practice, 38,* 290–297.

Boananno, G. A., & Kaltman, S. (1999). Toward an integrative perspective on bereavement. *Psychological Bulletin, 125,* 760–776.

Bobbitt, B. L. (2006). The importance of managed care: A view of managed care. *Professional Psychology: Research and Practice, 37,* 590–597.

Bogerts, B. (1993). Images in psychiatry: Alois Alzheimer. *American Journal of Psychiatry, 160,* 1868.

Bohart, A. C. (1982). Similarities between cognitive and humanistic approaches in psychotherapy. *Cognitive Therapy and Research, 6,* 245–250.

Boice, R., & Myers, P. E. (1987). Which setting is healthier and happier, academe or private practice? *Professional Psychology: Research and Practice, 18,* 526–529.

Boisvert, C. M., & Faust, D. (2003). Leading researchers' consensus on psychotherapy research findings: Implications for the teaching and conduct of psychotherapy. *Professional Psychology: Research and Practice, 34,* 508–513.

Boll, T. (1981). The Halstead-Reitan Neuropsychological Battery. In S. B. Fisher & T. J. Boll (Eds.), *Handbook of clinical neuropsychology* (Vol. 1, pp. 577–607). New York: Wiley.

Bonica, J. J. (1992). Pain research and therapy: Past and current status and future goals. In C. E. Short & A. van Posnik (Eds.), *Animal pain. Proceedings of the Symposium on Animal Pain and Its Control,* Ithaca, NY, June 25–28, 1990.

Boras, N., & Holt, G. (Eds.) (2007). *Psychiatric and behavioural disorders in intellectual and developmental disabilities* (2nd ed.). New York: Cambridge University Press.

Boring, E. G. (1923, June 6). Intelligence as the tests test it. *New Republic,* 35–37.

Borrell-Carrió, F., Suchman, A. L., &. Epstein, R. M. (2004). The biopsychosocial model 25 years later: Principles, practice, and scientific inquiry. *Annals of Family Medicine, 2,* 576–582.

Borys, D. S., & Pope, K. S. (1989). Dual relationships between therapist and client: A national study of psychologists, psychiatrists, and social workers. *Professional Psychology: Research and Practice, 20,* 283–293.

Boscolo, L., Cecchin, G., Hoffman, L., & Penn, P. (1987). *Milan systemic family therapy: Conversations in theory and practice.* New York: Basic Books.

Boswell, D. L., & Litwin, W. J. (1992). Limited prescription privileges for psychologists: A 1 year follow-up. *Professional Psychology: Research and Practice, 23,* 108–113.

Bouchard, C. (1995). Genetics of obesity: An update on molecular markers. *International Journal of Obesity, 19,* S10–S13.

Bouchard, C., & Perusse, L. (1996). Current status of the human obesity gene map. *Obesity Research, 4,* 81–90.

Bouchard, T. J., Jr., & McGue, M. (1990). Genetic and environmental influences on adult personality: An analysis of adopted twins reared apart. *Journal of Personality, 58,* 263–295.

Bouman. T. K. & Emmelkamp, P. M. G. (1996). *Panic disorder and agoraphobia.* New York: Plenum Press.

Bowen, M. (1978). *Family therapy in clinical practice.* New York: Aronson.

Bowling, A. (2009). Predictors of mortality among a national sample of elderly widowed people:

Analysis of 28-year mortality rates. *Age and Ageing, 38,* 527–530.

Bradley, J. D. D., & Golden, C. J. (2001). Biological contributions to the presentation and understanding of attention-deficit/hyperactivity disorder: A review. *Clinical Psychology Review, 21,* 907–929.

Brady, J. P., Davison, G. C., DeWald, P. A., Egan, G., Fadiman, J., Frank, J. D., et al. (1980). Some views of effective principles of psychotherapy. *Cognitive Therapy and Research, 4,* 269–306.

Bratton, S. C. (1998). Training parents to facilitate their child's adjustment to divorce using filial/family of divorce play therapy approach. In J. M. Breismeister & C. E. Schaefer (Eds.), *Handbook of parent training: Parents as co-therapists for children's behavior problems* (pp. 549–572). New York: Wiley.

Bray, G. A. (2008). Lifestyle and pharmacological approaches to weight loss: Efficacy and safety *Journal of Clinical Endocrinology & Metabolism, 93,* 81–88.

Breggin, P. R. (1991). *Toxic psychiatry.* New York: St. Martin's Press.

Brehm, S. S., & Brehm, J. W. (1981). *Psychological reactance: A theory of freedom and control.* New York: Academic Press.

Breismeister, J. M., & Schaefer, C. E. (Eds.). (1998). *Handbook of parent training: Parents as cotherapists for children's behavior problems* (2nd ed.). New York: Wiley.

Breiter, H. C., Rauch, S. L., Kwong, K. K., & Baker, J. R. (1996). Functional magnetic resonance imaging of symptom provocation in obsessive-compulsive disorder. *Archives of General Psychiatry, 53,* 595–606.

Bremner, J. D. (2002). *Does stress damage the brain?* New York: Norton.

Brems, C., Johnson, M. E., & Gallucci, P. (1996). Publication productivity of clinical and counseling psychologists. *Journal of Clinical Psychology, 52,* 711–722.

Brems, C., Lampman, C., & Johnson, M. E. (1995). Preparation of applications for academic positions in psychology. *American Psychologist, 50,* 533–537.

Brennan, P. L., & Moos, R. H. (1990). Life stressor, social resources, and late-life problem drinking. *Psychology and Aging, 5,* 491–501.

Brentar, J., & McNamara, J. R. (1991). The right to prescribe medication: Considerations for professional psychology. *Professional Psychology: Research and Practice, 22,* 179–187.

Breuer, J., & Freud, S. (1957). *Studies in hysteria.* New York: Basic Books. (Original work published 1895.)

Bricklin, B. (1995). *The custody evaluation handbook: Research-based solutions and applications.* New York: Brunner/Mazel.

British Psychological Society. (1993). *Code of conduct for psychologists.* London: Author.

Brody, J. E. (1996, February 28). Good habits outweigh genes as key to a healthy old age. *New York Times,* p. B11.

Brody, N. (1983). Where are the emperor's clothes? *Behavioral and Brain Sciences, 6,* 303–308.

Brody, N. (1997). Intelligence, schooling and society. *American Psychologist, 52,* 1046–1050.

Brookmeyer, R. (1996). AIDS, epidemics, and statistics. *Biometrics, 52,* 781–796.

Brooks-Harris, J. E. (2008). *Integrative multi-theoretical psychotherapy.* Florence, KY: Cengage Learning.

Broskowski, A. T. (1995). The evolution of health care: Implications for the training and careers of psychologists. *Professional Psychology: Research and Practice, 26,* 156–162.

Brotemarkle, B. A. (1947). Fifty years of clinical psychology: Clinical psychology 1896–1946. *Journal of Consulting Psychology, 11,* 1–4.

Brous, J. F., & Olendzki, M. C. (1985). The offset effect of mental health treatment on ambulatory medical care utilization and charges. *Archives of General Psychiatry, 42,* 573–580.

Brown, D. (1985). The preservice training and supervision of consultants. *Counseling Psychologist, 13,* 410–425.

Brown, L. S. (1990). Taking account of gender in the clinical assessment interview. *Professional Psychology: Research and Practice, 21,* 12–17.

Brown, R. T. (2003). Introduction: Training in pediatric psychology [Special issue]. *Journal of Pediatric Psychology, 28,* 81–84.

Brown, S. L., Nesse, R. M., Vinokur, A. D., & Smith, D. M. (2003). Providing social support may be more beneficial than receiving it: Results from a prospective study of mortality. *Psychological Science, 14,* 320–327.

Brown, T. A., O'Leary, T. A., & Barlow, D. H. (2001). Cognitive-behavioral treatment of generalized anxiety disorder. In D. H. Barlow (Ed.), *Clinical handbook of psychological disorders: A step-by-step treatment manual (3rd ed., pp. 154–208).* New York: Guilford Press.

Brownell, K. D. (1991a). Dieting and the search for the perfect body: Where physiology and culture collide. *Behavior Therapy, 22,* 1–12.

Brownell, K. D. (1991b). Personal responsibility and control over our bodies: When expectations exceeds reality. *Health Psychology, 10,* 303–310.

Brownell, K. D. (1993). Whether obesity should be treated. *Health Psychology, 12,* 339–341.

Brownell, K. D. (2002). Public policy and the prevention of obesity. In C. G. Fairburn & K. D. Brownell (Eds.), *Eating disorders and obesity: A comprehensive handbook* (2nd ed., pp. 619–623). New York: Guilford Press.

Brownell, K. D., & Jeffery, R. W. (1987). Improving long-term weight loss: Pushing the limits of treatment. *Behavior Therapy, 18,* 353–374.

Brownell, K. D., & Wadden, T. A. (1992). Etiology and treatment of obesity: Understanding a serious, prevalent, and refractory disorder. *Journal of Consulting and Clinical Psychology, 55,* 139–144.

Bruce, M. L., & Kim, K. M. (1992). Differences in the effects of divorce on major depression in men and women. *American Journal of Psychiatry, 149,* 914–917.

Buck, J. N. (1948). The H-T-P technique: A qualitative and quantitative scoring manual. *Journal of Clinical Psychology, 4,* 319–396.

Budney, A. J., & Higgens, S. T. (1998). *A community reinforcement approach: Treating cocaine addiction.* Washington, DC: National Institute on Drug Abuse.

Bugental, J. T. F. (1987). *Psychotherapy and process: The fundamentals of an existential humanistic approach.* Reading, MA: Addison-Wesley.

Buhlungu, S., Daniel, J., Southall, R., & Lutchman, J. (2007). *State of the nation: South Africa 2007.* Capetown: Human Sciences Research Council Press.

Burish, T. G., & Trope, D. M. (1992). Psychological techniques for controlling the adverse side effects of cancer chemotherapy: Findings from a decade of research. *Journal of Pain and Symptom Management, 7,* 287–301.

Burton, R. (1977). *Anatomy of melancholy.* New York: Random House. (Original work published 1621.)

Bushman, B. J., & Anderson, C. A. (2001). Media violence and the American public: Scientific facts versus media misinformation. *American Psychologist, 56,* 477–489.

Buss, D. M. (2003). *The evolution of desire: Strategies of human mating.* New York: Basic Books.

Buss, D. M. (Ed.) (2005). *The handbook of evolutionary psychology.* New York: Wiley.

Butcher, J. N., Dahlstrom, W. G., Graham, J. R., Tellegen, A., & Kraemmer, B. (1989). *Minnesota Multiphasic Personality Inventory (MMPI-2): Manual for administration and scoring.* Minneapolis: University of Minnesota Press.

Butcher, J. N., Williams, C. L., Graham, J. R., Archer, R. P., Tellegen, A., Ben-Porath, Y. S., et al. (1992). *Minnesota Multiphasic Personality Inventory—Adolescent (MMPI-A): Manual for administration and scoring.* Minneapolis: University of Minnesota Press.

California Medical Association (2008, June 26). California HMO profits exceed $4B, study finds. *Medical News Today.* Author.

Callahan, R. J., McGreevy, M. A., Cirincione, C., & Stedman, H. J. (1992). Measuring the effects of the guilty but mentally ill (GBMI) verdict: Georgia's 1982 GBMI reform. *Law and Human Behavior, 16,* 447–462.

Camino, L. (2000). *Treating sexually abused boys: A practical guide for therapists and counselors.* San Francisco: Jossey-Bass.

Campbell, D. T., & Stanley, J. C. (2002). *Experimental and quasi-experimental designs for research.* New York: Houghton Mifflin.

Campbell, L., Vasquez, M., Behnke, S., & Kinscherff, R. (2009). *APA ethics code commentary and case illustrations.* Washington, DC: American Psychological Association.

Canadian Psychological Association. (2000). *Canadian code of ethics for psychologists.* Toronto, Ottawa, Canada: Author.

Canter, M. B., Bennett, B. E., Jones, S. E., & Nagy, T. F. (1994). *Ethics for psychologists: A commentary on the APA ethics code.* Washington, DC: American Psychological Association.

Cantor, D. W., & Fuentes, M. A. (2008). Psychology's response to managed care. *Professional Psychology: Research and Practice, 39,* 638–645.

Caplan, G. (1970). *The theory and practice of mental health consultation.* New York: Basic Books.

Caplan, G., & Caplan, R. B. (1993). *Mental health consultation and collaboration.* San Francisco: Jossey-Bass.

Caracci, G. (2006). Urban mental health: An international survey. *International Journal of Mental Health, 35,* 39–45.

Cardemil, E. V., & Battle, C. (2003). Guess who's coming to therapy? Getting comfortable with conversations about race and ethnicity in psychotherapy. *Professional Psychology: Research and Practice, 34,* 278–286.

Cardon, L. R., Smith, S. D., Fulker, D. W., Kimberling, W. J., Pennington, B. F., & DeFries, J. C.

(1994). Quantitative trait locus for reading disability on chromosome 6. *Science, 266,* 276–279.

Carmody, T. P., & Matarazzo, J. D. (1991). Health psychology. In M. Hersen, A. E. Kazdin, & A. S. Bellack (Eds.), *The clinical psychology handbook* (2nd ed.). New York: Pergamon Press.

Carpenter, P. J., & Range, L. M. (1982). Predicting psychotherapy duration from therapists' sex, professional affiliation, democratic values, and community mental health ideology. *Journal of Clinical Psychology, 38,* 90–91.

Carroll, K. M. (1998). *A cognitive-behavioral approach: Treating cocaine addiction.* Washington, DC: National Institute on Drug Abuse.

Carter, B. D., Bendell, D., & Matarazzo, J. D. (1985). Behavioral health: Focus on preventive child health behavior. In A. R. Zeiner, D. Bendell, & C. E. Walker (Eds.), *Health psychology: Treatment and research issues* (pp. 1–61). New York: Plenum Press.

Casey, R. J., & Berman, J. S. (1985). The outcome of psychotherapy with children. *Psychological Bulletin, 98,* 388–400.

Cash, T. F. & Grant, J. R. (1996). Cognitive-behavioral treatment of body-image disturbances. In V. B. Van Hasselt & M. Hersen (Eds.), *Sourcebook of psychological treatment manuals for adult disorders* (pp. 567–614), New York: Plenum Press.

Casswell, S., & Thamarangsi, T. (2009). Reducing harm from alcohol: Call to action. *The Lancet, 373,* 2247–2257.

Castle, L., Aubert, R. E., Verbrugge, R. R., Khalid, M., & Epstein, R. S. (2007). Trends in medication treatment for ADHD. *Journal of Attentional Disorders, 10,* 335–342.

Castonguay, L. G., & Beutler, L. E. (2006). *Principles of therapeutic change that work.* New York: Oxford University Press.

Castonguay, L. G., Reid, J. J., Jr., Halperin, G. S., & Goldfried, M. R. (2003). Psychotherapy integration. In G. Stricker & T. Widiger (Eds.), *Handbook of psychology: Clinical psychology* (pp. 327–366). New York: Wiley.

Cattell, R. B. (1963). Theory of fluid and crystallized intelligence: A critical experiment. *Journal of Educational Psychology, 54,* 1–22.

Cattell, R. B. (1971). *Abilities: Their structure, growth, and action.* Boston: Houghton Mifflin.

Cattell, R. B. (1979). Are culture-fair intelligence tests possible and necessary. *Journal of Research and Development in Education, 12,* 3–13.

Cattell, R. B., Cattell, A. K., & Cattell, H. E. P. (2002). *Sixteen Personality Factors Questionnaire* (5th ed.). Champaign, IL: Institute for Personality and Ability Testing.

Center for the Advancement of Health. (2001). *Targeting the at-risk drinker with screening and advice.* Washington, DC: Author.

Center for Disease Control. (2000). *11 leading causes of death, United States: 1998, all races, both sexes.* Washington, DC: Office of Statistics and Programming, National Center for Injury Prevention and Control.

Centers for Disease Control and Prevention. (2001). Statistics from the World Health Organization and the Centers for Disease Control. *AIDS, 6,* 1229–1233.

Centers for Disease Control and Prevention (2007). *HIV/AIDS: Basic statistics.* Washington, DC: Author.

Centers for Disease Control and Prevention (2008a). Smoking-attributable mortality: Years of potential life lost, and productivity losses—United States, 2000–2004. *Morbidity and Mortality Weekly Report, 57,* 1226–1228.

Centers for Disease Control and Prevention. (2008b). Youth Risk Behavior Surveillance—United States, 2007. *Morbidity and Mortality Surveillance Summary, 57,* 1–131.

Centers for Disease Control and Prevention (2009). *National vital statistics reports. Deaths: Final data for 2006.* Washington, DC: Author.

Centers for Medicare and Medicaid Services (2009). *2007 National Health Care Expenditures Data.* Author.

Cepeda-Benito, A. (1993). Meta-analytical review of the efficacy of nicotine chewing gum in smoking treatment programs. *Journal of Consulting and Clinical Psychology, 61,* 822–830.

Chafel, J. A., & Hadley, K. (2001). Poverty and the well being of children and families. In C. E. Walker & M. C. Roberts (Eds.), *Handbook of child clinical psychology* (pp. 48–71). New York: Wiley.

Chalk, R., Frankel, M. S., & Chafer, S. B. (1980). *AAAS professional ethics project.* Washington, DC: American Association for the Advancement of Science.

Chambless, C. H. (2000). *Psychology and managed care: Reconciling research and policy.* Boston: Allyn & Bacon.

Chambless, D. L. (1996). In defense of dissemination of empirically supported psychological interventions. *Clinical Psychology: Science and Practice, 3,* 230–235.

Chambless, D. L. (2002). Beware the dodo bird: The dangers of overgeneralization. *Clinical Psychology: Science and Practice, 9,* 13–16.

Chambless, D. L., & Hollon, S. D. (1998). Defining empirically supported therapies. *Journal of Consulting and Clinical Psychology, 66,* 7–18.

Chambless, D. L., & Ollendick, T. H. (2001). *Empirically supported psychological interventions, controversies and evidence: Annual review of psychology.* Washington, DC: American Psychological Association.

Chambless, D. L., Sanderson, W. C., Shoham, V., Johnson, S. B., Pope, K. S., Crits-Christoph, P., et al. (1996). An update on empirically validated therapies. *Clinical Psychologist, 49,* 5–18.

Champion, D. P., Kiel, D. H., & McLendon, J. A. (1990, February). Choosing a consulting role. *Training and Development Journal,* 66–69.

Charney, D. S., Nagy, L. M., Bremner, J. D., Goddard, A. W., Yehuda, R., & Southwick, S. M. (2000). Neurobiologic mechanisms of human anxiety. In B. S. Fogel (Ed.), *Synopsis of neuropsychiatry* (pp. 273–288). Philadelphia: Lippincott Williams & Wilkins.

Chassin, L., Presson, C. C., Rose, J. S., & Sherman, S. J. (1996). The natural history of cigarette smoking from adolescence to adulthood: Demographic predictors of continuity and change. *Health Psychology, 15,* 478–484.

Chesney, M. A. (1993). Health psychology in the 21st century: Acquired immunodeficiency syndrome as a harbinger of things to come. *Health Psychology, 12,* 259–268.

Chethik, M. (2000). *Techniques for child therapy: Psychodynamic strategies.* New York: Guilford Press.

Chida, Y., & Steptoe, A. (2009). The association of anger and hostility with future coronary heart disease: A meta-analytic review of prospective evidence. *Journal of the American College of Cardiology, 53,* 936–946.

Chorpita, B. F. (2002). Treatment manuals for the real world: Where do we build them? *Clinical Psychology: Science and Practice, 9,* 431–433.

Chou, R., & Huffman, L.H. (2007). Nonpharmacological therapies for acute and chronic low back pain: A review of the evidence for an American Pain Society/American College of Physicians clinical practice guideline. *Annals of Internal Medicine, 147,* 492–504.

Ciarrocchi, J. W. (2002). *Counseling for the problem gambler: A self-regulation manual for individual and family therapy.* San Diego: Academic Press.

Clark, D. M. (1988). A cognitive model of panic attacks. In S. Rachman & J. D. Maser (Eds.), *Panic: Psychological perspectives* (pp. 71–89). Hillsdale, NJ: Erlbaum.

Clark, D. M., & Salkovskis, P. M. (1996). *Treatment manual of focused cognitive therapy.* Unpublished manuscript, Oxford University.

Clarke, G., Lynch, F., Spofford, M., & DeBar, L. (2006). Trends influencing future delivery of mental health services in large healthcare systems. *Clinical Psychology: Science and Practice, 13,* 287–292.

Clarke, W. V. (1956). The construction of an industrial selection personality test. *Journal of Psychology, 41,* 379–394.

Clarkin, J. F., & Hull, J. W. (1991). The brief psychotherapies. In M. Hersen, A. E. Kazdin, & A. S. Bellack (Eds.), *The clinical psychology handbook* (2nd ed., pp. 780–796). New York: Pergamon Press.

Classen, C., Koopman, C., Angell, K., & Spiegel, D. (1996). Coping styles associated with psychological adjustment to advanced breast cancer. *Health Psychology, 15,* 434–437.

Clay, R. A. (2000). Psychotherapy is cost effective. *APA Monitor on Psychology, 31,* 12–13.

Clayton, S., & Bongar, B. (1994). The use of consultation in psychological practice: Ethical, legal, and clinical consideration. *Ethics and Behavior, 4,* 43–57.

Clement, P. W. (1996). Evaluation in private practice. *Clinical Psychology: Science and Practice, 3,* 146–159.

Coates, T. J., & Thoresen, C. E. (1981). Treating obesity in children and adolescents: Is there any hope. In J. M. Ferguson & C. B. Taylor (Eds.), *The comprehensive handbook of behavioral medicine* (Vol. 2, pp. 204–231). New York: Spectrum.

Coelho, C. M., Waters, A. M., Hine, T. J., & Wallis, G. (2009). The use of virtual reality in acrophobia research and treatment. *Journal of Anxiety Disorders, 23,* 563–574.

Cohen, R. (2009). Genetics of obesity syndromes. *Medicine & Science in Sports & Exercise, 41,* 736.

Cohen, R. Y., Stunkard, A., & Felix, M. R. J. (1986). Measuring community change in disease prevention and health promotion. *Preventive Medicine, 15,* 411–421.

Cohen, S. (1988). Psychosocial models of the role of social support in the etiology of physical disease. *Health Psychology, 7,* 269–297.

Cohen, S., Tyrrell, D. A. J., & Smith, A. P. (1993). Negative life events, perceived stress, negative affect, and susceptibility to the common cold. *Journal of Personality and Social Psychology, 64,* 131–140.

Coiro, M. J. (2001). Depression symptoms among women receiving welfare. *Women and Health, 32,* 1–23.

Cole, N. S. (1981). Bias in testing. *American Psychologist, 36,* 1067–1077.

Collins, F. S. (1999). Shattuck lecture: Medical and societal consequences of the human genome project. *New England Journal of Medicine, 341,* 28–37.

Colson, D., Lewis, L., & Horowitz, L. (1985). Negative outcome in psychotherapy and psychoanalysis. In D. T. Mays & C. M. Franks (Eds.), *Negative outcome in psychotherapy and what to do about it* (pp. 59–75). New York: Springer.

Committee on Environmental Health (2005). Lead exposure in children: Prevention, detection, and management. *Pediatrics, 116,* 1036–1046.

Committee on Ethical Guidelines for Forensic Psychologists. (1991). Specialty guidelines for forensic psychologists. *Law and Human Behavior, 15,* 655–665.

Conger, J. (1975). Proceedings of the American Psychological Association for the year 1974: Minutes of the annual meeting of the council of representatives. *American Psychologist, 30,* 620–651.

Conger, R. D., & Donnellan, M. B. (2007). An interactionist perspective on the socioeconomic context of human development. *Annual Review of Psychology, 58,* 175–199.

Conners, C. K. (2000). *Conners' Rating Scales— Revised: Technical manual.* North Tonawanda, NY: Multi-Health Systems.

Conners, C. K. (2007). *Conners' Rating Scales— Revised: Administration manual.* North Tonawanda, NY: Multi-Health Revised Systems.

Conoley, J. C., & Conoley, C. W. (1992). *School consultation: Practice and training* (2nd ed.). Boston: Allyn & Bacon.

Consumer Reports. (1998, November). Mental health: Does therapy help?, pp. 734–739.

Consumer Reports. (2003, October). HMO or PPO: Picking a managed health care plan. *pp. 658–670.*

Contrada, R. J., & Krantz, D. S. (1988). Stress, reactivity, and Type A behavior: Current status and future directions. *Annals of Behavioral Medicine, 10,* 64–70.

Conwell, Y., Pearson, L., & DeRenzo, E. G. (1996). Indirect self-destructive behavior among elderly patients in nursing homes: A research agenda. *American Journal of Geriatric Psychiatry, 4,* 152–163.

Conyne, R., & O'Neal, J. (1992). Closing the gap between consultation training and practice. In R. Conyne & J. O. O'Neal (Eds.), *Organizational consultation: A casebook* (pp. 1–16). Newbury Park, CA: Sage.

Cooke, G. (1984). Forensic psychology. In R. G. Corsini (Ed.), *Encyclopedia of psychology* (Vol. 2, pp. 898–910). New York: Wiley.

Cooper, B. (2003). Evidence-based mental health policy: A critical appraisal. *British Journal of Psychiatry, 183,* 105–113.

Cooper, N. A., & Clum, G. A. (1989). Imaginal flooding as a supplementary treatment for PTSD in combat veterans: A controlled study. *Behavior Therapy, 20,* 381–392.

Cooper, Z., & Fairburn, C. C. (2009). Management of bulimia nervosa and other binge eating problems. *Advances in Psychiatric Treatment, 15,* 129–136.

Corbet, J., Trimble, M., & Nicol, T. (1985). Behavioral and cognitive impairment in children with epilepsy: The long-term effects of anticonvulsant therapy. *Journal of the American Academy of Child Psychiatry, 24,* 17–23.

Corey, G., Corey, M. S., & Callanan, P. (1993). *Issues and ethics in the helping professions* (4th ed.). Pacific Grove, CA: Brooks/Cole.

Cormer, J. S., & Kendall, P. C. (2007). Terrorism: The psychological impact on youth. *Clinical Psychology: Research and Practice, 14,* 179–212.

Cormier, S., Nurius, P. S., & Osborn, C. J. (2008). *Interviewing and change strategies for helpers: Fundamental skills and cognitive behavioral interventions.* Pacific Grove, CA: Brooks/Cole.

Cornes, C. L., & Frank, E. (1994). Interpersonal psychotherapy for depression. *Clinical Psychologist, 47,* 9–10.

Corr, P. J., & Matthews, G. (Eds.). (2009). *The Cambridge handbook of personality psychology.* New York: Cambridge University Press.

Corrigan, N., & Nielson, D. (1993). Toward the development of uniform reporting standards for managed care organizations: The Health Plan Employer Data and Information Set (Version 2.0). *Journal of Quality Improvement, 19,* 566–575.

Costa, P., & McCrae, R. (1985). *NEO-Personality Inventory manual.* Odessa, FL: Psychological Assessment Resources.

Costa, P., & McCrae, R. (1989). *NEO-PI/NEO-FFI manual supplement.* Odessa, FL: Psychological Assessment Resources.

Costa, P., & McCrae, R. (1992). *Revised NEO-Personality Inventory (NEO-PI-R) and NEO Five Factor Inventory (NEO-FFI): Professional manual.* Odessa, FL: Psychological Assessment Resources.

Costa, P. T., Jr., & McCrae, R. R. (in press). The Revised NEO Personality Inventory. In S. R. Briggs, J. Cheek, & E. Donahue (Eds.), *Handbook of adult personality inventories.* New York: Plenum.

Craighead, L. W., Stunkard, A. J., & O'Brien, R. (1981). Behavior therapy and pharmacotherapy for obesity. *Archives of General Psychiatry, 38,* 763–768.

Craighead, W. E. (1990). There's a place for us: All of us. *Behavior Therapy, 21,* 3–23.

Cranston, C., Ulrey, G., Hansen, R., Hudler, M., Marshall, R., & Wuori, D. (1988). Interprofessional collaboration: Who is doing it? Who isn't? *Journal of Developmental and Behavioral Pediatrics, 9,* 134–139.

Craske, M. G., & Barlow, D. H. (2001). Panic disorder and agoraphobia. In D. H. Barlow (Ed.), *Clinical handbook of psychological disorders: A step-by-step treatment manual (3rd ed., p. 1–59).*

Crits-Christoph, P. (1996). The dissemination of efficacious psychological treatments. *Clinical Psychology: Science and Practice, 3,* 260–263.

Crits-Christoph, P., Baranackie, K., Kurcias, J. S., Beck, A. T., Carroll, K., Perry, K., et al. (1991). Meta-analysis of therapist effects in psychotherapy outcome studies. *Psychotherapy Research, 1,* 81–91.

Crits-Christoph, P., Chambless, D., Frank, E., Brody, C., & Karp, L. F. (1995). Training in empirically validated treatments: What are clinical psychology students learning? *Professional Psychology: Research and Practice, 26,* 514–522.

Crits-Christoph, P., & Mintz, J. (1991). Implications of therapist effects for the design and analysis of comparative studies of psychotherapies. *Journal of Consulting and Clinical Psychology, 59,* 20–26.

Cronbach, L. J. (1956). Assessment of individual differences. *Annual Review of Psychology, 7,* 173–196.

Crosby-Currie, C. A. (1996). Children's involvement in contested custody cases: Practices and experiences of legal and mental health professionals. *Law and Human Behavior, 20,* 289–311.

Cuellar, I., Arnold, B., & Maldonado, R. (1995). Acculturation Rating Scale for Mexican Americans: II. A revision of the original ARSMA scale. *Hispanic Journal of Behavioral Sciences, 17,* 275–304.

Cuipers, P., van Straten, A., & Warmerdam, L. (2007). Behavioral activation treatments of depression: A meta-analysis. *Clinical Psychology Review, 27,* 318–326.

Cullen, E. A. (1998). Legislative wrap-up: 1997 state prescription privilege activities. *California Psychologist, 31,* 8–9.

Cullen, E. A., & Newman, R. (1997). In pursuit of prescription privileges. *Professional Psychology: Research and Practice, 28,* 101–106.

Cummings, C., Gordon, J., & Marlatt, G. A. (1980). Relapse: Prevention and prediction. In W. Miller (Ed.), *The addictive behaviors* (pp. 203–218). Oxford, England: Pergamon Press.

Cummings, N. A. (1977). The anatomy of psychotherapy under national health insurance. *American Psychologist, 32,* 71–78.

Cummings, N. A. (1984). The future of clinical psychology in the United States. *Clinical Psychologist, 37,* 19–20.

Cummings, N. A. (1995). Impact of managed care on employment and training: A primer for survival. *Professional Psychology: Research and Practice, 26,* 10–15.

Cummings, N. A., O'Donohue, W. T., & Ferguson, K. E. (2003). *Behavioral health as primary care: Beyond efficacy to effectiveness.* Reno, NV: Context Press.

Daldrup, R. J., Beutler, L. E., Engle, D., & Greenberg, L. S. (1998). *Focused expressive psychotherapy: Freeing the overcontrolled patient.* New York: Guilford Press.

Daley, D. C., Mercer, D., & Carpenter, G. (1997). *Drug counseling for cocaine addiction: The collaborative cocaine treatment study model.* National Institute of Health publication. No. 02-4381, USA, 124 p.p. Available online at: http://www.drugabuse.gov/pdf/Manual4.pdf

Daley, D. C., Mercer, D. E., & Carpenter, G. (1998). *Drug counseling for cocaine addition: The collaborative cocaine treatment study model.* Washington, DC: National Institute on Drug Abuse.

Damsa, C., Kosel, M. Moussally, J. (2009). Current status of brain imaging in anxiety disorders. *Current Opinion in Psychiatry. 22,* 96–110.

Das, J. P., & Naglieri, J. A. (1997). *Manual for the cognitive assessment system.* New York: Riverside.

Davenport, D. S., & Woolley, K. K. (1997). Innovative brief pithy psychotherapy: A contribution from corporate managed mental health care. *Professional Psychology: Research and Practice, 28,* 197–200.

Davidson, R. J. (2000a). Affective style, psychopathology, and resilience: Brain mechanisms and plasticity. *American Psychologist, 55,* 1196–1214.

Davidson, R. J. (2000b). Award for distinguished scientific contributions. *American Psychologist, 55,* 1193–1196.

Davidson, K., & Scott, J. (2009). Does therapists competence matter in delivering psychological therapy? *Psychiatric Bulletin, 33,* 121–123.

Davison, G. C., & Lazarus, A. A. (1994). Clinical innovation and evaluation: Integrating practice with inquiry. *Clinical Psychology: Science and Practice, 1,* 157–168.

Dawes, R. M. (1979). The robust beauty of improper linear models in decision making. *American Psychologist, 34,* 571–582.

Dawes, R. M. (1994). *House of cards: Psychology and psychotherapy built on myth.* New York: Free Press.

Deakin, J. F. W., & Graeff, F. G. (1991). Critique: 5-HT and mechanisms of defense. *Journal of Psychopharmacology, 5,* 305–315.

De Angelis, T. (1989). Suit opens doors to analysis training. *APA Monitor, 20,* 16.

De Angelis, T. (1994). Experts see little impact from insanity plea ruling. *APA Monitor, 25,* 28.

Deary, I. J., Spinath, F. M., & Bates, T. C. (2006). Genetics of intelligence. *European Journal of Human Genetics, 14,* 690–700.

Deci, E. L., & Ryan, R. M. (Eds.). (2002). *Handbook of self-determination theory research.* Rochester, NY: University of Rochester Press.

De Dominico, G. S. (2000). *Sand tray world play: A comprehensive guide to the use of the sand tray in psychotherapeutic and transformational settings.* Oakland, CA: Vision Quest Images.

Deisz, R., Doueck, H. J., & George, N. (1996). Reasonable cause: A qualitative study of mandated reporting. *Child Abuse and Neglect, 20,* 275–287.

DeLeon, P. H. (1993). Legislative issues. *Independent Practitioner, 13,* 170–172.

DeLeon, P. H. (2003). What will the 21st century bring? *International Journal of Stress Management, 10,* 5–15.

DeLeon, P. H., Dunivin, D. L., & Newman, R. (2002). The tide rises. *Clinical Psychology: Science and Practice, 9,* 249–255.

DeLeon, P. H., Fox, R. E., & Graham, S. R. (1991). Prescription privileges: Psychology's next frontier? *American Psychologist, 46,* 384–393.

DeLeon, P. H., & Wiggins, J. G. (1996). Prescription privileges for psychologists. *American Psychologist, 51,* 225–229.

Delis, D. C., Kaplan, E., & Kramer, J. H. (2001). *Manual for the Delis-Kaplan executive function system (D-KEFS).* San Antonio, TX: Psychological Corporation.

Delis, D. C., Kramer, J., Kaplan, E., & Ober, B. A. (1987). *California Verbal Learning Test.* San Antonio, TX: Psychological Corporation.

Delis, D. C., Kramer, J., Kaplan, E., & Ober, B. A. (1994). *California Verbal Learning Test—Children's version.* San Antonio, TX: Psychological Corporation.

Delis, D. C., Kramer, J. H., Kaplan, E., & Ober, B. A. (2000). *Manual for the California Verbal Learning Test* (3rd ed.). San Antonio, TX: Psychological Corporation.

DeNelsky, G. Y. (1991). Prescription privileges for psychologists: The case against. *Professional Psychology: Research and Practice, 22,* 188–193.

DeNelsky, G. Y. (1996). The case against prescription privileges for psychologists. *American Psychologist, 51,* 207–212.

Denmark, F. L. (1994). Engendering psychology: 101st annual conference of the American Psychological Association distinguished contribution to psychology in the public interest award address. *American Psychologist, 49,* 329–334.

Derogatis, L. R. (1982). *Manual for the Brief Symptom Inventory.* Riderwood, MD: Clinical Psychometric Research.

Derogatis, L. R. (1994). *SCL-90-R administration, scoring and procedures manual—II for the revised version and other instruments of the psychopathology rating scale series* (2nd ed.). Riderwood, MD: Clinical Psychometric Research.

Desmond, D. W., & Tatemichi, T. K. (1998). Vascular dementia. In M. F. Folstein (Ed.), *Neurobiology of primary dementia* (pp. 167–190). Washington, DC: American Psychiatric Press.

Deutsch, C. J. (1985). A survey of therapists' personal problems and treatment. *Professional Psychology: Research and Practice, 16,* 305–315.

Devanand, D. P., Dwork, A. J., Hutchinson, E. R., Blowig, T. G., & Sackheim, H. A. (1994). Does ECT alter brain structure? *American Journal of Psychiatry, 151,* 957–970.

Devanand, D. P., & Sackheim, H. A. (1995). Does ECT alter brain structure?: Reply. *American Journal of Psychiatry, 152,* 1403.

Dick, L. P., Gallagher-Thompson, D., & Thompson, L. W. (1996). Cognitive-behavioral therapy. In R. T. Woods (Ed.), *Handbook of the clinical psychology of ageing* (pp. 509–544). New York: Wiley.

Digman, J. M. (1990). Personality structure: Emergence of the five-factor model. *Annual Review of Psychology, 41,* 417–470.

Diller, L. H., Tanner, J. L., & Weil, J. (1996). Etiology of ADHD: Nature or nurture? *American Journal of Psychiatry, 153,* 451–452.

Dimsdale, J. (2009). Psychological stress and cardiovascular disease. *Journal of the American College of Cardiology, 51,* 1237–1246.

DiNitto, D. M., Busch-Armendariz, N. B., Bender, K., Woo, H., Tackett-Gibson, M., Dyer, J. (2008). Testing telephone and web surveys for studying men's sexual assault perpetration behaviors. *Journal of Interpersonal Violence, 23,* 1483–1493.

Dishman, R. K. (1982). Compliance/adherence in health-related exercise? *Psychosomatic Medicine, 49,* 375–382.

Dittmann, M. (2003). Geropsychologists are badly needed. *APA Monitor on Psychology, 34,* 51.

Dleis, D. C., Kaplan, E., & Kramer, J. H. (2001). *Manual for the Delis-Kaplan Executive Function System (D-KEFS).* San Antonio, TX: Psychological Corporation.

Dobson, K. S., & Block, L. (1988). Historical and philosophical bases of cognitive-behavioral therapies. In K. S. Dobson (Ed.), *Handbook of cognitive-behavioral therapies* (pp. 3–38). New York: Guilford Press.

Dodd, J. A. (1970). A retrospective analysis of variables related to duration of treatment in a university psychiatric clinic. *Journal of Nervous and Mental Diseases, 151,* 75–85.

Dollard, J., & Miller, N. (1950). *Personality and psychotherapy: An analysis in terms of learning, thinking, and culture.* New York: McGraw- Hill.

Dollinger, S. J. (1989). Predictive validity of the Graduate Record Examination in a clinical psychology program. *Professional Psychology: Research and Practice, 20,* 56–58.

Dorgan, C., & Editue, A. (1995). *Statistical record of health and medicine: 1995.* Detroit, MI: Orale Research.

Dougherty, A. M. (1990). *Consultation: Practice and perspectives.* Pacific Grove, CA: Brooks/Cole.

Dougherty, A. M. (2004). *Consultation: Practice and perspectives in school and community settings* (4th ed.). Pacific Grove, CA: Brooks/Cole.

Dubin, S. S. (1972). Obsolescence or lifelong education: A choice for the professional. *American Psychologist, 27,* 486–496.

Dugas, M. J. (2002). Generalized anxiety disorder. In M. Hersen (Ed.), *Clinical behavior therapy: Adults and children* (pp. 125–143). New York: John Wiley & Sons.

Duncan, B. L., Miller, S. D., Wampold, B. E., & Hubble, M. A. (2009). *The heart and soul of change, second edition: Delivering what works in therapy.* Washington, DC: American Psychological Association.

Dunkin, J. J., & Anderson-Hanley, C. (1998). Dementia caregiver burden: A review of the literature and guidelines for assessment and intervention. *Neurology, 51,* S53–S60.

Dunn, L. M., & Dunn, L. M. (2007). *Peabody Picture Vocabulary Test—Fourth Edition: Manual.* Circles Pines, MN: American Guidance Service.

Dush, D. M., Hirt, M. L., & Schroeder, H. E. (1989). Self-statement modification in the treatment of child behavior disorders: A meta-analysis. *Psychological Bulletin, 106,* 97–106.

Dustin, D., & Ehly, S. (1984). Skills for effective consultation. *School Counselor, 32,* 23–29.

Dykens, E. M., & Hodapp, R. M. (1997). Treatment issues in genetic mental retardation syndromes. *Professional Psychology: Research and Practice, 28,* 263–270.

Eaker, E. D., Pinsky, J., & Castelli, W. P. (1992). Myocardial infarction and coronary death among women: Psychosocial predictors from a 20-year follow-up of women in the Framingham study. *American Journal of Epidemiology, 135,* 854–864.

Eamon, M. K., & Zuehl, R. M. (2001). Maternal depression and physical punishment as mediators of the effect of poverty on socioemotional problem of children in single-mother families. *American Journal of Orthopsychiatry, 71,* 218–226.

Eastwood, S., & Bisson, J. I. (2008). Management of factitious disorders: A systematic review. *Psychotherapy and Psychosomatics, 77,* 209–218.

Eaton, W. W., Holzer, C. E., Von Korff, M., Anthony, J. C., Helzer, J. E., George, L., et al. (1984). The design of the epidemiologic catchment area surveys. *Archives of General Psychiatry, 41,* 942–948.

Ebigno, P. O. (1986). A cross sectional study of somatic complaints of Nigerian females using the Enugu Somatization Scale. *Culture, Medicine, and Psychiatry, 10,* 167–186.

Economic Report of the President. (1998). *Economic report of the President: Transmitted to the congress February 1998 together with the annual report of the Council of Economic Development.* Washington, DC: U.S. Government Printing Office.

Eddy, B., Lloyd, P. J., & Lubin, B. (1987). Enhancing the application to doctoral professional programs: Suggestions from a national survey. *Teaching of Psychology, 14,* 160–163.

Edelbrock, H. P., & Costello, A. J. (1984). Structured psychiatric interviews for children and adolescents. In G. Goldstein & M. Herson (Eds.), *Handbook of psychological assessment* (pp. 276–290). Elmsford, NY: Pergamon Press.

Edelson, M. (1994). Can psychotherapy research answer this psychotherapist's questions. In P. F. Tally, H. H. Strupp, & S. F. Butler (Eds.), *Psychotherapy research and practice: Bridging the gap* (pp. 124–142). New York: Basic Books.

Edwards, A. J. (1994). *When memory fails: Helping the Alzheimer's and dementia patient.* New York: Plenum Press.

Edwards, A. L. (1959). *Edwards Personal Preference Schedule.* New York: Psychological Corporation.

Edwards, M. C., Schultz, E. G., & Long, N. (1995). The role of the family in the assessment of attention deficit hyperactivity disorder. *Clinical Psychology Review, 15,* 375–394.

Eells, T. D. (1995). Relational therapy for grief disorders. In J. P. Barber & P. Crits-Christoph (Eds.), *Dynamic therapies for psychiatric disorders (Axis I)* (pp. 386–xx). New York: Basic Books.

Eidelson, R. J., & Eidelson, J. I. (2003). Dangerous ideas: Five beliefs that propel groups toward conflict. *American Psychologist, 58,* 182–192.

Eisen, A. R., Engler, L. B., & Geyer, B. (1998). Parent training for separation anxiety. In J. M. Breismeister & C. E. Schaefer (Eds.), *Handbook of parent training: Parents as co-therapists for children's behavior problems* (pp. 205–224). New York: Wiley.

Eisenberg, L. (1968). The interaction of biological and experiential factors in schizophrenia. In D. Rosenthal & S. S. Kety (Eds.), *The transmission of schizophrenia* (pp. 403–409). Oxford, England: Pergamon Press.

Ekstrand, M. L., & Coates, T. J. (1990). Maintenance of safer sexual behaviors and predictors of risky sex: The San Francisco men's health study. *American Journal of Public Health, 80,* 973–977.

Elkin, I. (1994). The NIMH Treatment of depression collaborative research program: Where we began and where we are. In A. E. Bergin & S. L. Garfield (Eds.), *Handbook of psychotherapy and behavior change* (4th ed., pp. 114–139). New York: Wiley.

Elkin, I., Parloff, M. B., Hadley, S. W., & Autry, J. H. (1985). NIMH treatment of depression collaborative research program: Background and research plan. *Archives of General Psychiatry, 42,* 305–316.

Elkin, I., Shea, M. T., Watkins, J. T., Imber, S. D., Sotsky, S. M., Collins, J. F., et al. (1989). National Institute of Mental Health treatment of depression collaborative research program: General effectiveness of treatments. *Archives of General Psychiatry, 46,* 971–982.

Ellenberg, J., Hirtz, D., & Nelson, K. (1986). Do seizures in children cause intellectual deterioration? *New England Journal of Medicine, 314,* 1085–1088.

Elliott, D. M., & Guy, J. D. (1993). Mental health professionals versus non-mental-health professionals: Childhood trauma and adult functioning. *Professional Psychology: Research and Practice, 24,* 83–90.

Ellis, A. (1962). *Reason and emotion in psychotherapy.* New York: Stuart.

Ellis, A. (1977). *Sex without guilt.* Hollywood: Wilshire.

Ellis, A. (1980). Rational-emotive therapy and cognitive behavior therapy: Similarities and differences. *Cognitive Therapy and Research, 4,* 325–340.

Ellis, A., & Grieger, R. (Eds.). (1977). *Handbook of rational-emotive therapy.* New York: Springer.

Ellis, E. M. (2000). Rationale and goal of the custody evaluation. In E. M. Ellis (Ed.), *Divorce wars.* Washington, DC: American Psychological Association.

Ellison, P. T., & Gray, P. B. (Eds.) (2009). *Endocrinology of social relationships.* Boston: Harvard University Press.

Ellsworth, R. B. (1981). *CAAP Scale: The measurement of child and adolescent adjustment.* Palo Alto, CA: Consulting Psychologists Press.

Emery, R. E., & Laumann-Billings, L. (1998). An overview of the nature, causes, and consequences of abusive family relationships: Towards differentiating maltreatment and violence. *American Psychologist, 53,* 121–135.

Engel, G. L. (1977). The need for a new medical model: A challenge for biomedicine. *Science, 196,* 129–136.

Engel, G. L. (1980). The clinical application of the biopsychosocial model. *American Journal of Psychiatry, 137,* 535–544 .

Engel, J., & Pedley, T. A. (2007). *Epilepsy: A comprehensive textbook* (2nd ed.). Philadelphia: Lippincott, Williams, & Wilkins.

Enright, M. F., Resnick, R., DeLeon, P. H., Sciara, A. D., & Tanney, M. F. (1990). The practice of psychology in hospital settings. *American Psychologist, 45,* 1059–1065.

Epstein, G. N., Steingarten, J., Weinstein, H. D., & Nashel, H. M. (1977). Panel report: Impact of law on the practice of psychotherapy. *Journal of Psychiatry and Law, 5,* 7–40.

Epstein, N. B., & Baucom, D. H. (2002). *Enhanced cognitive-behavioral therapy for couples: A contextual approach*. Washington, DC: American Psychological Association.

Epstein, S. (1979). The stability of behavior: I. On predicting most of the people much of the time. *Journal of Personality and Social Psychology, 37,* 1097–1126.

Erikson, M. H. (1980). *The collected papers of Milton H. Erickson on hypnosis.* New York: Irvington.

Erickson, S. K., Lilienfeld, S. O., & Vitacco, M. J. (2007). Failing the burden of proof: The science and ethics of projective tests in custody evaluations. *Family Court Review, 45,* 185–192.

Evans, G. D., & Murphy, M. J. (1997). The practicality of predoctoral prescription training for psychologists: A survey of directors of clinical training. *Professional Psychology: Research and Practice, 28,* 113–117.

Everett, C. A., & Everett, S. V. (1999). *Family therapy for ADHD: Treating children, adolescents, and adults.* New York: Guilford Press.

Exner, J. E. (1974). *The Rorschach: A comprehensive system.* New York: Wiley.

Exner, J. E. (1976). Projective techniques. In I. B. Weiner (Ed.), *Clinical methods in psychology* (pp. 61–121). New York: Wiley.

Exner, J. E. (1986). *The Rorschach: A comprehensive system: Vol. 1. Basic foundations* (2nd ed.). New York: Wiley.

Exner, J. E. (1993). *The Rorschach: A comprehensive system: Vol. 1. Basic foundations* (3rd ed.). New York: Wiley.

Exner, J. E. (1997). The future of Rorschach in personality assessment. *Journal of Personality Assessment, 68,* 37–46.

Exner, J. E. (2003). *The Rorschach: A comprehensive system: Vol. 1. Basic foundations* (4th ed.). New York: Wiley.

Exner, J. E., & Erdberg, P. (2005). *The Rorschach: Advanced interpretation.* Hoboken, NJ: Wiley.

Exner, J. E., & Weiner, I. (1995). *The Rorschach: A comprehensive system: Assessment of children and adolescents* (Vol. 3, 2nd ed.). New York: Wiley.

Eysenck, H. J. (1952). The effects of psychotherapy: An evaluation. *Journal of Consulting Psychology, 16,* 319–324.

Eysenck, H. J. (1958). Personality tests: 1950–1955. In G. W. T. H. Fleming & A. Walk (Eds.), *Recent progress in psychiatry* (Vol. 3, pp. 118–159). New York: Grove Press.

Eysenck, H. J. (1960). *Handbook of abnormal psychology: An experimental approach.* London: Pitman.

Eysenck, H. J. (1970). A mish-mash of theories. *International Journal of Psychiatry, 9,* 140–146.

Eysenck, H. J. (1978). An exercise in meta-silliness. *American Psychologist, 33,* 517.

Eysenck, H. J. (1983). Special review by M. L. Smith, G. V. Glass, & T. I. Miller: The benefits of psychotherapy. *Behaviour Research and Therapy, 21,* 315–320.

Eysenck, H. J., & Eysenck, S. B. G. (1975). *Manual for the Eysenck Personality Questionnaire.* San Diego, CA: Educational and Individual Testing Service.

Fairbairn, W. R. D. (1954). *An object relations theory of the personality.* New York: Basic Books.

Fairburn, C. G., & Brownell, K. D. (Eds.). (2002). *Eating disorders and obesity: A comprehensive handbook* (2nd ed.). New York: Guilford Press.

Falsetti, S. A., & Resnick, H. S. (2001). Posttraumatic stress disorder. In W. J. Lyddon & J. V. Jones, Jr. (Eds.), *Empirically supported cognitive therapies: current and future applications.* New York: Springer.

Farrell, A. D., Complair, P. S., & McCullough, L. (1987). Identification of target complaints by computer interview: Evaluation of the computerized assessment system for psychotherapy evaluation and research. *Journal of Consulting and Clinical Psychology, 55,* 691–700.

Farrugia, D., & Fetter, H. (2009). Chronic pain: Biological understanding and treatment suggestions for mental health counselors. *Journal of Mental Health Counseling, 31,* 189–200.

Faust, D. (1986). Research on human judgment and its application to clinical practice. *Professional Psychology: Research and Practice, 17,* 420–430.

Faust, J., Runyon, M. K., & Kenny, M. C. (1995). Family variables associated with the onset and impact of intrafamilial childhood sexual abuse. *Clinical Psychology Review, 15,* 443–456.

Fava, G. A., Rafanelli, C., Remi, J., Yates, W. R., Troughton, E. P., & Steward, M. A. (1998). Prevention of recurrent depression with cognitive behavioral therapy: Preliminary findings. *Archive of General Psychiatry, 55,* 816–820.

Fava, G. A., & Sonino, N. (2008). The biopsychosocial model thirty years later. *Psychotherapy and Psychosomatics, 77,* 1–2.

Fava, L., & Morton, J. (2009). Causal models of panic disorder theories. *Clinical Psychology Reviews,* in press.

Feather, B. W., & Rhoads, J. M. (1972). Psychodynamic behavior therapy: I. Theory and rationale. *Archives of General Psychiatry, 26,* 496–502.

Federal Trade Commission. (2000). *Marketing violent entertainment to children: A review of self-regulation and industry practices in the motion picture, music* recording, and electronic game industries—*Appendix B*. Washington, DC: Author.

Feighner, J. P., Brown, S. L., & Oliver, J. E. (1973). Electrosleep therapy. *Journal of Nervous and Mental Disease, 157,* 121–128.

Feldman, J. M., & Kazdin, A. E. (1995). Parent management training for oppositional and conduct problem children. *Clinical Psychologist, 48,* 3–5.

Fensterheim, H., & Raw, S. D. (1996). Psychotherapy research is not psychotherapy practice. *Clinical Psychology: Science and Practice, 3,* 168–171.

Ferguson, R. J. & Mittenberg, W. (1996). Cognitive-behavioral treatment of postconcussion syndrome: A therapist's manual. In V. B. Van Hasselt & M. Hersen (Eds.), *Sourcebook of psychological treatment manuals for adult disorders* (pp. 615–656), New York: Plenum Press.

Feske, U., & Chambless, D. L. (1995). Cognitive behavioral versus exposure only treatment for social phobia: A meta-analysis. *Behavior Therapy, 26,* 695–720.

Fields, B. W., & Fristad, M. A. (2009). Assessment of childhood bipolar. *Clinical Psychology: Science and Practice, 16,* 166–181.

Fiester, A. R., & Rudestam, K. E. (1975). A multivariate analysis of the early dropout process. *Journal of Consulting and Clinical Psychology, 43,* 528–535.

Fink, P. J. (1986). Dealing with psychiatry's stigma. *Hospital and Community Psychiatry, 37,* 814–818.

Fink, P. J. (2003). A beautiful mind and insulin coma: Social constraints on psychiatric diagnosis and treatment. *Harvard Review of Psychiatry, 11,* 284–290.

Finkel, M. J., Ragnar, D. S., Bandele, A., & Schaefer, V. (2003). Diversity training in graduate school: An exploratory evaluation of the Safe Zone Project. *Professional Psychology: Research and Practice, 34,* 555–561.

Finkelhor, D., Hotaling, G., Lewis, I. A., & Smith, C. (1990). Sexual abuse in a national survey of adult men and women: Prevalence, characteristics, and risk factors. *Child Abuse and Neglect, 14,* 19–28.

Finney, J. W., & Moos, R. H. (1991). The long-term course of treated alcoholism: I. Mortality, relapse, and remission rates and comparisons with community controls. *Journal of Studies on Alcoholism, 52,* 44–54.

Fiore, T. A., Becker, E. A., & Nero, R. C. (1993). Educational interventions for students with attention deficit disorder. *Exceptional Children, 60,* 163–173.

First, M. B., Gibbon, M., Spitzer, R. L., Williams, J. B., & Benjamin, L. (1997). *Structured clinical interview for* DSM-IV *axis II personality disorders (SCID-II)*. Washington, DC: American Psychiatric Press.

First, M. B., Spitzer, R. L., Gibbon, M., & Williams, J. B. (1997). *Structured clinical interview for* DSM-IV *axis I disorders (SCID-I), clinical version*. Washington, DC: American Psychiatric Press.

First, M. B., Spitzer, R.L., Gibbon M., & Williams, J.B.W. (2002). Structured clinical interview for DSM-IV-TR axis I disorders, research version, patient edition. (SCID-I/P) New York: Biometrics Research.

Fischbach, G. D. (1992). Mind and brain. *Scientific American, 267,* 48–57.

Fisher, H. E. (1995). *Anatomy of love: A natural history of mating, marriage and why we stray*. New York: Ballantine Books.

Fisher, H. E. (2004). *Why we love: The nature of and chemistry of romance*. New York: Holt.

Fitzgibbon, M. L., Stolley, M. R., Avellone, M. E., Sugerman, S., & Chavez, N. (1996). Involving parents in cancer risk reduction: A program for Hispanic American families. *Health Psychology, 15,* 413–422.

Fleck, S. (1995). Dehumanizing developments in American psychiatry in recent decades. *Journal of Nervous and Mental Diseases, 183,* 195–203.

Flynn, J. R. (1984). The mean IQ of Americans: Massive gains 1932 to 1978. *Psychological Bulletin, 95,* 29–51.

Flynn, J. R. (1987). Massive IQ gains in 14 nations: What IQ tests really measure. *Psychological Bulletin, 101,* 171–191.

Flynn, J. R. (2007). *What is intelligence?: Beyond the Flynn Effect*. New York: Cambridge University Press.

Foa, E. B. (1996). The efficacy of behavioral therapy with obsessive-compulsives. *Clinical Psychologist, 49,* 19–22.

Foa, E. B., Dancu, C. V., Hembree, E. A., Jaycox, L. H., Meadows, E. A., & Street, G. P. (1999). A comparison of exposure therapy, stress inoculation training, and their combination for reducing posttraumatic stress disorder in female assault victims. *Journal of Consulting and Clinical Psychology, 67,* 194–200.

Foa, E. B., & Franklin, E. (2001). Obsessive-compulsive disorder. In D. H. Barlow (Ed.), *Clinical handbook of psychological disorders: A step-by-step treatment manual* (3rd ed., pp. 209–263). New York: Guilford Press.

Foa, E. B., & Steketee, G. (1977). Emergent fears during treatment of three obsessive compulsives: Symptom substitution or deconditioning? *Journal of Behaviour Therapy and Experimental Psychiatry, 8,* 353–358.

Fordyce, W. E. (1988). Pain and suffering: A reappraisal. *American Psychologist, 43,* 276–283.

Forer, B. R. (1957). *The Forer Structured Sentence Completion Test.* Los Angeles: Western Psychological Service.

Forsyth, D. R., & Corazzini, J. G. (2000). Groups as change agents. In C. R. Snyder & R. E. Ingram (Eds.), *Handbook of psychological change: Psychotherapy processes and practices for the 21st century* (pp. 309–336). New York: Wiley.

Fouse, B., & Wheeler, M. (1997). *A treasure chest of behavioral strategies for individuals with autism.* Arlington, TX: Future Horizons.

Fowers, B. J., & Richardson, F. C. (1996). Why is multiculturalism good? *American Psychologist, 51,* 609–621.

Fox, B. H. (1988). Psychogenic factors in cancer, especially its incidence. In S. Maes, D. Spielberger, P. B. Defares, & I. G. Sarason (Eds.), *Topics in health psychology* (pp. 37–55). New York: Wiley.

Fox, R. E. (1994). Training professional psychologists for the twenty-first century. *American Psychologist, 49,* 200–206.

Fox, R. E., DeLeon, P. H., Newman, R., Sammons, M. T., Dunivin, D. L., & Baker, D. C. (2009). Prescriptive authority and psychology: A status report. *American Psychologist. 64,* 257–268.

Fox, R. E., Schwelitz, F. D., & Barclay, A. G. (1992). A proposed curriculum for psychopharmacology training for professional psychologists. *Professional Psychology: Research and Practice, 23,* 216–219.

Frank, G. (1984). The Boulder model: History, rationale, and critique. *Professional Psychology: Research and Practice, 15,* 417–435.

Frank, J. D. (1961). *Persuasion and healing.* Baltimore: Johns Hopkins University Press.

Frank, J. D. (1982). Therapeutic components shared by all psychotherapies. In J. H. Harvey & M. M. Parks (Eds.), *The Master Lecture Series: Vol. 1. Psychotherapy research and behavior change* (pp. 5–38, 73–122). Washington, DC: American Psychological Association.

Frank, J. D. (1993). *Persuasion and healing* (3rd ed.). Baltimore: Johns Hopkins University Press.

Frank, L. K. (1948). *Projective methods.* Springfield, IL: Charles C Thomas.

Frankl, V. (1963). *Man's search for meaning.* New York: Washington Square Press.

Frankl, V. (1965). *The doctor and the soul.* New York: Knopf.

Franklin, M. E., & Foa, E. B. (2008). Obsessive-compulsive disorder. In D. H. Barlow (Ed). *Clinical handbook of psychological disorders: A step-by-step treatment manual* (4th ed., (pp. 164–215). New York: Guilford Press.

Franklin, M. E., Rynn, M., March, J. S., & Foa, E. B. (2002). Obsessive-compulsive disorder. In M. Hersen (Ed.), *Clinical behavior therapy: Adults and children* (pp. 276–303). New York: Wiley.

Fraser, J. S. (1996). All that glitters is not always gold: Medical offset effects and managed behavioral health care. *Professional Psychology: Research and Practice, 27,* 335–344.

Frederick/Schneiders, Inc. (1990, December). *Survey of American Psychological Association members.* Washington, DC: Author.

Fredrickson, M., & Matthews, K. A. (1990). Cardiovascular responses to behavioral stress and hypertension: A meta-analytic review. *Annals of Behavioral Medicine, 12,* 30–39.

Freedman, R. R. (1993). Raynaud's disease and phenomenon. In R. J. Gatchel & E. B. Blanchard (Eds.), *Psychophysiological disorders.* Washington, DC: American Psychological Association.

Freeman, A., & Reinecke, M. A. (1993). *Cognitive therapy of suicidal behavior: A manual for treatment.* New York: Springer.

French, S. A., Hennrikus, D. J., & Jeffery, R. W. (1996). Smoking status, dietary intake, and physical activity in a sample of working adults. *Health Psychology, 15,* 448–454.

Freud, S. (1959). The question of lay analysis. In J. Strachey (Ed. & Trans.), *The standard edition of the complete psychological works of Sigmund Freud* (Vol. 20, pp. 89–125). London: Hogarth Press. (Original work published 1926.)

Freud, S. (1963). Introductory lectures in psychoanalysis. In J. Strachey (Ed. & Trans.), *The standard edition of the complete psychological works of Sigmund Freud* (Vol. 16, pp. 241–489). London: Hogarth Press. (Original work published 1917.)

Freud, S. (1964). New introductory lectures on psychoanalysis. In J. Strachey (Ed. & Trans.), *The standard edition of the complete psychological works of Sigmund Freud* (Vol. 22, pp. 1–182). London: Hogarth Press. (Original work published 1933.)

Frick, P. J., Strauss, C. C., Lahey, B. B., & Christ, M. A. G. (1993). Behavior disorders of children. In P. B. Sutker & H. E. Adams (Eds.), *Comprehensive handbook of psychopathology* (2nd ed., pp. 765–789). New York: Plenum Press.

Friedman, H. S., Tucker, J. S., Schwartz, J. E., Tomlinson-Keasey, C., Martin, L. R., Wingard, D. L., et al. (1995). Psychosocial and behavioral predictors of longevity: The aging and death of the "termites." *American Psychologist, 50,* 69–78.

Fuqua, D., & Kupius, D. (1993). Conceptual models in organizational consultation. *Journal of Counseling and Development, 71,* 607–618.

Gabbard, G. O. (1994). Reconsidering the American Psychological Association's policy on sex with former patients: Is it justifiable? *Professional Psychology: Research and Practice, 25,* 329–335.

Gallagher-Thompson, D., Hanley-Peterson, P., & Thompson, L. W. (1990). Maintenance of gains versus relapse following brief psychotherapy for depression. *Journal of Consulting and Clinical Psychology, 58,* 371–374.

Gallessich, J. (1982). *The profession and practice of consultation.* San Francisco: Jossey-Bass.

Garb, H. N. (1988). Comment on "The study of clinical judgment: An ecological approach." *Clinical Psychology Review, 8,* 441–444.

Garb, H. N. (1989). Clinical judgment, clinical training, and professional experience. *Psychological Bulletin, 105,* 387–396.

Garb, H. N. (1997). Race bias, social class bias, and gender bias in clinical judgement. *Clinical Psychology: Science and Practice, 4,* 99–120.

Garbarino, J., & Stocking, S. H. (1980). *Protecting children from abuse and neglect.* San Francisco: Jossey-Bass.

Gardner, H. (1983). *Frames of mind: The theory of multiple intelligences.* New York: Basic Books.

Gardner, H. (1986). The waning of intelligence tests. In R. J. Sternberg & D. K. Detterman (Eds.), *What is intelligence?* Norwood, NJ: Ablex.

Gardner, H. (1994). *Creating minds.* New York: Basic Books.

Gardner, H. (2006). *Multiple intelligences: New horizons in theory and practice.* New York: Basic Books.

Garfield, S. L. (1986). Research on client variables in psychotherapy. In S. L. Garfield & A. E. Bergin (Eds.), *Handbook of psychotherapy and behavior change* (3rd ed., pp. 213–256). New York: Wiley.

Garfield, S. L. (1993). Methodological problems in clinical diagnosis. In P. B. Sutker & H. E. Adams (Eds.), *Comprehensive handbook of psychopathology* (2nd ed., pp. 27–46). New York: Plenum Press.

Garfield, S. L. (1994). Eclecticism and integration in psychotherapy: Developments and issues. *Clinical Psychology: Science and Practice, 1,* 123–137.

Garfield, S. L. (1996). Some problems associated with "validated" forms of psychotherapy. *Clinical Psychology: Science and Practice, 3,* 218–229.

Garfield, S. L. (1998). Some comments on empirically supported treatments. *Journal of Consulting and Clinical Psychology, 66,* 113–120.

Garfield, S. L., & Bergin, A. E. (Eds.). (1986). *Handbook of psychotherapy and behavior change* (3rd ed.). New York: Wiley.

Garfield, S. L., & Bergin, A. E. (1994). Introduction and historical overview. In A. E. Bergin & S. L. Garfield (Eds.), *Handbook of psychotherapy and behavior change* (4th ed.). New York: Wiley.

Garfield, S. L., & Kurtz, R. (1974). A survey of clinical psychologists: Characteristics, activities, and orientations. *Clinical Psychologist, 28,* 7–10.

Garfield, S. L., & Kurtz, R. (1976). Clinical psychologists in the 70s. *American Psychologist, 31,* 1–9.

Gaston, L. (1995). Dynamic therapy for post-traumatic stress disorder. In J. P. Barber and P. Crits-Christoph (Eds.), *Dynamic Therapies for psychiatric Disorders (Axis I)* (pp. 161–192). New York: Basic Books.

Gatchel, R. J., & Blanchard, E. B. (Eds.). (1993). *Psychophysiological disorders.* Washington, DC: American Psychological Association.

Gerrard, M., Gibbons, F. X., & Bushman, B. J. (1996). Relation between perceived vulnerability to HIV and precautionary sexual behavior. *Psychological Bulletin, 119,* 390–409.

Gershon, E. S. (1990). Genetics. In F. K. Goodwin & K. R. Jamison (Eds.), *Manic-depressive illness* (pp. 373–401). New York: Oxford University Press.

Gibbs, W. W. (1996). Gaining on fat. *Scientific American, 275,* 88–94.

Giecek, T. S. (2000). *Teaching economics as if people mattered: A high school curriculum guide to the new economy.* Boston: United for a Fair Economy.

Gill, M. M. (1984). Psychoanalytic, psychodynamic, cognitive behavior, and behavior therapies compared. In H. Arkowitz & S. B. Messer (Eds.), *Psychoanalytic therapy and behavior therapy: Is integration possible?* (pp. 179–188). New York: Plenum Press.

Gillies, L. A. (2001). Interpersonal psychotherapy for depression and other disorders. In D. H. Barlow (Ed.), *Clinical handbook of psychological disorders: A step-by-step treatment manual* (3rd ed., pp. 309–331). New York: Guilford Press.

Glantz, K., Durlach, N. I., Barnett, R. C., & Aviles, W. A. (1996). Virtual reality (VR) for psychotherapy: From the physical to the social environment. *Psychotherapy, 33*, 464–473.

Glaser, R., & Thorpe, J. (1986). Unethical intimacy: A survey of sexual contact and advances between psychology educators and female graduate students. *American Psychologist, 41*, 43–51.

Glasser, W. (2003). *Warning: Psychiatry can be hazardous to your mental health.* New York: Harper-Collins.

Goldberg, I. D., Krantz, G., & Locke, B. Z. (1970). Effect of a short-term outpatient psychiatric therapy benefit on the utilization of medical services in a prepaid group practice medical program. *Medical Care, 8*, 419–428.

Goldberg, P. A. (1965). A review of sentence completion methods in personality assessment. *Journal of Projective Techniques and Personality Assessment, 29*, 12–45.

Golden, C. J., Hammeke, T. A., & Purisch, A. D. (1980). *The Luria-Nebraska Neuropsychological Battery.* Los Angeles: Western Psychological Services.

Goldensohn, E., Glaser, G., & Goldberg, M. (1984). Epilepsy. In L. Rowland (Ed.), *Meritt's textbook of neurology* (pp. 629–649). Philadelphia: Lea & Febiger.

Goldfarb, L. A. (1987). Sexual abuse antecedent to anorexia nervosa, bulimia, and compulsive overeating: Three case reports. *International Journal of Eating Disorders, 6*, 675–680.

Goldfarb, L. A., Dykens, E., & Gerrard, M. (1985). The Goldfarb Fear of Fat Scale. *Journal of Personality Assessment, 49*, 329–332.

Goldfried, M. R. (1991). Research issues in psychotherapy integration. *Journal of Psychotherapy Integration, 1*, 5–25.

Goldfried, M. R. (1993). Commentary on how the field of psychopathology can facilitate psychotherapy integration: What can the field of psychotherapy offer to psychotherapy integration? [Special issue]. *Journal of Psychotherapy Integrations, 3*, 353–360.

Goldfried, M. R., Greenberg, L. S., & Marmar, C. (1990). Individual psychotherapy: Process and outcome. In M. R. Rosenzweig & L. W. Porter (Eds.), *Annual review of psychology.* Palo Alto, CA: Annual Reviews.

Goldfried, M. R., & Wolfe, B. E. (1996). Psychotherapy practice and research: Repairing a strained alliance. *American Psychologist, 51*, 1007–1016.

Goleman, D. (1995). *Emotional intelligence: Why it can matter more than IQ.* New York: Bantam Books.

Goleman, D. (2006). *Emotional intelligence: 10th anniversary edition: Why it can matter more than IQ.* New York: Bantam.

Goleman, D. (2007). *Social Intelligence: The new science of human relationships.* New York: Bantam.

Gonzalez, J. C. (1998). Measures of acculturation. In G. P. Koocher, J. C. Norcross, & S. S. Hill, III (Eds.), *Psychologists' desk reference* (pp. 70–73). New York: Oxford University Press.

Goodglass, H. (1986). The flexible battery in neuropsychological assessment. In T. Incagnoli, G. Goldstein, & C. J. Golden (Eds.), *Clinical applications of neuropsychological test batteries* (pp. 121–134). New York: Plenum Press.

Goodheart, C. D., & Markham, B. (1992). The feminization of psychology: Implications for psychotherapy. *Psychotherapy, 29*, 130–138.

Goodman, A. (2008). Neurobiology of addiction: An integrative review. *Biochemical Pharmacology, 75*, 266–322.

Goodwin, D. W. (1986). Heredity and alcoholism. *Annals of Behavioral Medicine, 8*, 3–6.

Goos, L., Ezzatian, P., & Schachar, R. (2007). Parent-of-origin effects in attention-deficit hyperactivity disorder. *Psychiatry Research, 149*, 1.

Gottesman, I. I. (1991). *Schizophrenia genesis: The origins of madness.* New York: Freeman.

Gottesman, I. I., & Erlenmeyer-Kimling, L. (2001). Family and twin strategies as a head start in defining prodromes and endophenotypes for hypothetical early-interventions in schizophrenia. *Schizophrenic Research, 51*, 93–102.

Gottesman, I. I., & Prescott, C. A. (1989). Abuses of the MacAndrew MMPI Alcoholism Scale: A critical review. *Clinical Psychology Review, 9*, 223–242.

Gough, H. G. (1962). Clinical versus statistical prediction in psychology. In L. Postman (Ed.), *Psychology in the making: Histories of selected research problems* (pp. 90–123). New York: Knopf.

Gough, H. G. (1984). A managerial potential scale for the California Psychological Inventory. *Journal of Applied Psychology, 69*, 233–240.

Graeff, F. G., & Del-Ben, C. M. (2008). Neurobiology of panic disorder: From animal models to brain neuroimaging. *Neuroscience & Biobehavioral Reviews, 32*, 1326–1335.

Graham, J. (2008, October 13). $700 billion: What we waste on health care every year. *Chicago Tribune*, A13.

Graham, J. R. (2006). *MMPI-2: Assessing personality and psychopathology* (4th ed.). New York: Oxford University Press.

Grant, D. A., & Berg, E. A. (1993). *Wisconsin Card Sorting Test.* Odessa, FL: Psychological Assessment Resources.

Grantham, R. J. (1973). Effects of counselor sex, race, and language style on black students in initial interviews. *Journal of Counseling Psychology, 20,* 553–559.

Gray, J. A. (1982). *The neuropsychology of anxiety.* New York: Oxford University Press.

Gray, J. A. (1991). Fear, panic, and anxiety: What's in a name? *Psychological Inquiry, 2,* 72–96.

Greenberg, L. S. & Johnson, S. M. (1988). *Emotionally focused therapy for couples.* New York: Guilford.

Greenberg, L. S., & Johnson, S. M. (1998). *Emotionally focused therapy for couples.* New York: Guilford Press.

Greenblatt, M. (1985). Mental health consultation. In H. I. Kaplan & B. J. Sadock (Eds.), *Comprehensive textbook of psychiatry* (4th ed., pp. 1897–1899). Baltimore: Williams & Wilkins.

Greene, B. (1993). Human diversity in clinical psychology: Lesbian and gay sexual orientations. *Clinical Psychologist, 46,* 74–82.

Greenfield, P. M. (1997). You can't take it with you: Why ability assessments don't cross cultures. *American Psychologist, 52,* 1115–1124.

Greenough, W. T., Withers, G. S., & Wallace, C. S. (1990). Morphological changes in the nervous system arising from behavioral experience: What is the evidence that they are involved in learning and memory. In L. R. Squire & E. Lindenlaub (Eds.), *The biology of memory, Symposia Medica Hoescht* (pp. 159–183). Stuttgart/New York: Schattauer Verlag.

Greist, J. H. (1990). Treatment of obsessive-compulsive disorder: Psychotherapies, drugs, and other somatic treatments. *Journal of Clinical Psychiatry, 51,* 44–50.

Grencavage, L. M., & Norcross, J. C. (1990). Where are the commonalities among the therapeutic common factors? *Professional Psychology: Research and Practice, 21,* 372–378.

Grisso, T., & Appelbaum, P. S. (1992). Is it unethical to offer predictions of future violence? *Law and Human Behavior, 16,* 621–633.

Grove, W. M., Zald, D. H., Lebow, B. S., Snitz, B. E., & Nelson, C. (2000). Clinical versus mechanical prediction: A meta-analysis. *Psychological Assessment, 12,* 19–30.

Grusky, O., Thompson, W. A., & Tillipman, H. (1991). Clinical versus administrative backgrounds for mental health administrators. *Administration and Policy in Mental Health, 18,* 271–278.

Guilford, J. P. (1967). *The nature of human intelligence.* New York: McGraw-Hill.

Guilford, J. P. (1979). Intelligence isn't what it used to be: What to do about it. *Journal of Research and Development in Education, 12,* 33–46.

Guilford, J. P. (1985). The structure-of-intellect model. In B. B. Wolman (Ed.), *Handbook of intelligence* (pp. 225–266). New York: Wiley.

Guion, R. M. (2008). Employment tests and discriminatory hiring. *Industrial Relations: A Journal of Economy and Society, 5,* 20–37.

Gumaer, J. (1984). *Counseling and therapy for children.* New York: Free Press.

Gump, B. B., Matthews, K. A., & Raikkonen, K. (1999). Modeling relationships among socioeconomic status, hostility, cardiovascular reactivity, and left ventricular mass in African American and White children. *Health Psychology, 18,* 140–150.

Gunn, W. B., & Blount, A. (2009). Primary care mental health: A new frontier for psychology. *Journal of Clinical Psychology, 65,* 235252.

Guy, J. D. (1987). *The personal life of the psychotherapist.* New York: Wiley.

Haas, L. J., Benedict, J. G., & Kobos, J. C. (1996). Psychotherapy by telephone: Risks and benefits for psychologists and consumers. *Professional Psychology: Research and Practice, 27,* 154–160.

Hale, R. L. (1991). Intellectual assessment. In M. Hersen, A. E. Kazdin, & A. S. Bellack (Eds.), *The clinical psychology handbook* (2nd ed.). New York: Pergamon Press.

Haley, J. (1973). *Uncommon therapy.* New York: Norton.

Haley, J. (1976). *Problem solving therapy: New strategies for effective family therapy.* San Francisco: Jossey-Bass.

Haley, J. (1987). *Problem-solving therapy* (3rd ed.). San Francisco: Jossey-Bass.

Hall, C. C. I. (1997). Cultural malpractice: The growing obsolescence of psychology with the changing U.S. population. *American Psychologist, 52,* 642–651.

Hall, S. M., Munoz, R. F., Reus, V. I., & Sees, K. L. (1993). Nicotine, negative affect, and depression. *Journal of Consulting and Clinical Psychology, 61,* 761–767.

Halpern, D. F. (2008). Careers in psychology: Combining work and family. *Educational Psychology Review, 20,* 57–64.

Halstead, W. C. (1947). *Brain and intelligence: A quantitative study of the frontal lobes.* Chicago: University of Chicago Press.

Ham, L. S., & Hope, D. A. (2003). College students and problematic drinking: A review of the literature. *Clinical Psychology Review, 23*, 719–759.

Hanesian, H., Paez, P., & Williams, D. T. (1988). The Neurologically impaired child and adolescent. In C. J. Kestenbaum & D. T. Williams (Eds.), *Handbook of clinical assessment of children and adolescents* (Vol. 1, pp. 415–445). New York: New York University Press.

Hanna, D. (1988). *Designing organizations for high performance*. Reading, MA: Addison-Wesley.

Hans, V. P. (1986). An analysis of public attitudes toward the insanity defense. *Criminology, 4*, 393–415.

Hansen, J., Himes, B., & Meier, S. (1990). *Consultation: Concepts and practices*. Englewood Cliffs, NJ: Prentice-Hall.

Hansen, M. J., Enright, R. D., Baskin, T. W., & Klatt, J. (2009). A palliative care intervention in forgiveness therapy for elderly terminally ill cancer patients. *Journal of Palliative Care, 25*, 51–60.

Harris, D. B. (1972). Review of the DAP. In O. K. Buros (Ed.), *The seventh mental measurement yearbook* (pp. 401–405). Highland Park, NJ: Gryphon Press.

Harris, M. (1998). *Trauma recovery and empowerment: A clinician's guide for working with women in groups*. New York: Free Press.

Hathaway, S. R. (1943). *The Minnesota Multiphasic Personality Inventory*. Minneapolis: University of Minnesota Press.

Hatsukami, D., Jensen, J., Allen, S., & Grillo, M. (1996). Effects of behavioral and pharmacological treatment on smokeless tobacco users. *Journal of Consulting and Clinical Psychology, 64*, 153–161.

Hattie, J. A., Sharpley, C. F., & Rogers, H. F. (1984). Comparative effectiveness of professional and paraprofessional helpers. *Psychological Bulletin, 95*, 534–541.

Hauser, W., Annegers, J., & Anderson, V. (1983). Epidemiology and genetics of epilepsy. *Research in Nervous and Mental Disorders, 61*, 267–294.

Havens, L. (1994). Some suggestions for making research more applicable to clinical practice. In P. F. Tally, H. H. Strupp, & S. F. Butler (Eds.), *Psychotherapy research and practice: Bridging the gap* (pp. 88–98). New York: Basic Books.

Havik, O. E., & VandenBos, G. R. (1996). Limitations of manualized psychotherapy for everyday clinical practice. *Clinical Psychology: Science and Practice, 3*, 264–267.

Hawkins, R. M. F. (2001). A systematic meta-review of hypnosis as an empirically supported treatment for pain. *Pain-Reviews, 8*, 47–73.

Hawkins, R. P. (1987). Selection of target behaviors. In R. O. Nelson & S. C. Hayes (Eds.), *Conceptual foundations of behavioral assessment* (pp. 311–385). New York: Guilford Press.

Hayes, S. (1996). Creating the empirical clinician. *Clinical Psychology: Science and Practice, 3*, 179–181.

Hayes, S. C. (2002). Getting to dissemination. *Clinical Psychology: Science and Practice, 9*, 410–415.

Hayes, S. C. (2008). Climbing our hills: A beginning conversation on the comparison of acceptance and commitment therapy and traditional cognitive behavioral therapy. *Clinical Psychology: Science and Practice, 15*, 286–295.

Hayes, S. C., & Chang, G. (2002). Invasion of the body snatchers: Prescription privileges, professional schools, and the drive to create a new behavioral health profession. *Clinical Psychology: Science and Practice, 9*, 264–269.

Hayes, S. C., Follette, W. C., Dawes, R. D., & Grady, K. (Eds.). (1995). *Scientific standards of psychological practice: Issues and recommendations*. Reno, NV: Context Press.

Hayes, S. C., & Heiby, E. (1996). Psychology's drug problem: Do we need a fix or should we just say no? *American Psychologist, 51*, 198–206.

Hayes, S. C., & Smith, S. (2005). *Get out of your mind and into your life: The new acceptance and commitment therapy*. Oakland, CA: New Harbinger.

Hayes, S. C., Strosahl, K. D., & Wilson, K. G. (1999). *Acceptance and commitment therapy: An experiential approach to behavior change*. New York: Guilford Press.

Haynes, S. G., Feinleib, M., & Kannel, W. B. (1980). The relationship of psychosocial factors to coronary heart disease in the Framingham study: III. Eight-year incidence of coronary heart disease. *American Journal of Epidemiology, 111*, 37–58.

Hays, K. F., & Brown, C. H. (2004). *You're on! Consulting for peak performance*. Washington, DC: APA Books.

Hayward, C., Gotlib, I. H., Schraedley, P. K., & Litt, I. F. (1999). Ethnic differences in the association between pubertal status and symptoms of depression in adolescent girls. *Journal of Adolescent Health, 25*, 143–149.

Hayward, P., Wardle, J., & Higgitt, A. (1989). Benzodiazepine research: Current findings and practical consequences. *British Journal of Psychiatry, 28,* 307–327.

Hazell, P. (2007). Pharmacological management of attention-deficit hyperactivity disorder in adolescents: Special considerations. *CNS Drugs, 21,* 37–46.

Heaton, R. K. (1988). Introduction to special series. *Journal of Consulting and Clinical Psychology, 56,* 787–788.

Heiby, E. M. (2002). It is time for a moratorium on legislation enabling prescription privileges for psychologists. *Clinical Psychology: Science and Practice, 9,* 256–258.

Helms, J. E. (1992). Why is there no study of cultural equivalence in standardized cognitive ability testing? *American Psychologist, 47,* 1083–1101.

Herbert, D. L., Nelson, R. O., & Herbert, J. D. (1988). Effects of psychodiagnostic labels, depression, severity, and instructions on assessment. *Professional Psychology: Research and Practice, 19,* 496–502.

Herrnstein, R. J., & Murray, C. (1994). *The bell curve: Intelligence and class structure in American life.* New York: Free Press.

Hersen, M. (Ed.). (2002). *Clinical behavior therapy: Adults and children.* New York: Wiley.

Hersen, M. (2003). *Comprehensive handbook of psychological assessment.* New York: Wiley.

Herz, M., & Marder, S. (2002). *Schizophrenia: Comprehensive treatment and management.* New York: Lippincott Williams & Wilkins.

Herzog, D. B. (1988). Eating disorders. In A. M. Nicoli, Jr. (Ed.), *The new Harvard guide to psychiatry* (pp. 434–445). Boston: Harvard University Press.

Hibbs, E. D., & Jensen, P. S. (Eds.). (1996). *Psychosocial treatments for child and adolescent disorders: Empirically based strategies for clinical practice.* Washington, DC: American Psychological Association.

Higgins, S. T., Budney, A. J., & Sigmon, S. C. (2001). Cocaine dependence. In D. H. Barlow (Ed.), *Clinical handbook of psychological disorders: A step-by-step treatment manual (3rd ed., pp. 434–469).* New York: Guilford Press.

Hildreth, C. J. (2009). Combat injuries in Iraq and Afghanistan help rewrite the book on war surgery. *Journal of the American Medical Association, 301,* 1866–1867.

Himelein, M. J., & Putnam, A. J. (2001). Work activities of clinical psychologists: Do they practice what they teach? *Professional Psychology: Practice and Research, 32,* 537–542.

Hinshaw, S. P. (2003). Attention deficit hyperactivity disorder. In J. J. Ponzetti (Ed.), *The encyclopedia of neurological sciences* (Vol. 2, pp. 393–412). San Diego, CA: Academic Press.

Hodapp, R. M., & Dykens, E. M. (2007). Behavioural phenotypes: Growing understanding of psychiatric disorders in individuals with intellectual disabilities. In N. Boras & G. Holt (Eds.), *Psychiatric and behavioural disorders in intellectual and developmental disabilities* (2nd ed., pp. 202–214). New York: Cambridge University Press.

Hoffman, L. W. (1990). *Old scapes, new maps: A training program for psychotherapy supervisors.* Cambridge, MA: Milusik Press.

Hoffman, B. M., Papas, R. K., Chatkoff, D. K., & Kerns, R. D. (2007). Meta-analysis of psychological interventions for chronic low back pain. *Health Psychology, 26,* 1–9.

Hofmann, S. G., & Tompson, M. C. (Eds.). (2002). *Treating chronic and severe mental disorders: A handbook of empirically supported interventions.* New York: Guilford Press.

Hogan, R., Hogan, J., & Roberts, B. W. (1996). Personality measurement and employment decisions: Questions and answers. *American Psychologist, 51,* 469–477.

Hogarty, G. E. (2002). *Personal therapy for schizophrenia and related disorders: A guide to individualized treatment.* New York: Guilford Press.

Holder, H. D., Saltz, R. F., Grube, J. W., Voas, R. B., Gruenewald, P. J., & Treno, A. J. (1997). A community prevention trial to reduce alcohol-involved accidental injury and death: Overview. *Addiction, 92*(Suppl. 2), S155–S171.

Hollon, S. D. (1996). The efficacy and effectiveness of psychotherapy relative to medications. *American Psychologist, 51,* 1025–1030.

Hollon, S. D. (2006). Randomized clinical trials. In J. C. Norcross, L. E. Beutler, & R. Levant (Eds.), *Evidence-based practice in mental health* (pp. 96–105). Washington, DC: American Psychological Association.

Hollon, S. D., & Beck, A. T. (1994). Cognitive and cognitive-behavioral therapies. In A. E. Bergin & S. L. Garfield (Eds.), *Handbook of psychotherapy and behavior change* (4th ed., pp. 428–466). New York: Wiley.

Holloway, L. D. (2004). Louisiana grants prescriptive authority. *Monitor on Psychology, 35,* 5.

Holroyd, J., & Brodsky, A. (1977). Psychologists' attitudes and practices regarding erotic and nonerotic physical contact with clients. *American Psychologist, 32,* 843–849.

Holtzman, W. H. (1975). New developments in Holtzman Inkblot Technique. In P. McReynolds (Ed.), *Advances in psychological assessment* (Vol. 3, pp. 243–260). San Francisco: Jossey-Bass.

Holtzman, W. H., Thorpe, J. W., Swartz, J. D., & Herron, E. W. (1961). *Inkblot perception and personality: Holzman Inkblot Technique.* Austin, TX: University of Texas Press.

Horgan, J. (1996). Why Freud isn't dead. *Scientific American, 275,* 106–111.

Horowitz, M. J. (1974). Microanalysis of working through in psychotherapy. *American Journal of Psychiatry, 131,* 1208–1212.

Horowitz, M. J. (1988). *Introduction to psychodynamics: A new synthesis.* New York: Basic Books.

Horowitz, M. J., Marmar, C., Krupnick, J., Wilner, N., Kaltreider, N., & Wallerstein, R. (1984). *Personality styles and brief psychotherapy.* New York: Basic Books.

Horvath, A. O., & Symonds, B. D. (1991). Relationship between working alliance and outcome in psychotherapy: A meta-analysis. *Journal of Counseling Psychology, 38,* 139–149.

Horvath, P. (1988). Placebos and common factors in two decades of psychotherapy research. *Psychological Bulletin, 104,* 214–225.

House, J. A., Robbins, C., & Metzner, H. L. (1982). The association of social relationships and activities with mortality: Prospective evidence from the Tecumseh Community Health Study. *American Journal of Epidemiology, 116,* 123–140.

House, J. S., Landis, K. R., & Umberson, D. (1988). Social relationships and health. *Science, 241,* 540–545.

Howard, K. I., Kopta, S. M., Krause, M. S., & Orlinsky, D. E. (1986). The dose-effect relationship in psychotherapy. *American Psychologist, 41,* 159–164.

Howard, K. I., Moras, K., Brill, P. L., & Martinovich, Z. (1996). Evaluation of psychotherapy: Efficacy, effectiveness, and patient progress. *American Psychologist, 51,* 1059–1064.

Howard, M., & McCabe, J. B. (1990). Helping teenagers postpone sexual involvement. *Family Planning Perspective, 22,* 21–26.

Hsu, C., Chou, P., Hwang, K., & Lin, S. (2008). Impact of obesity on young healthy male adults. *Nutrition, Metabolism and Cardiovascular Diseases, 18,* 19–20.

Hsu, L. K. G. (1990). *Eating disorders.* New York: Guilford Press.

Hubert, N., Wachs, T. D., Peters-Martin, P., & Gandour, M. (1982). The study of early temperament: Measurement and conceptual issues. *Child Development, 53,* 571–600.

Huesmann, L. R., Moise-Titus, J., Podolski, C. L., & Eron, L. D. (2003). Longitudinal relations between children's exposure to TV violence and their aggressive and violent behavior in young adulthood: 1977–1992. *Developmental Psychology, 39,* 201–221.

Hughes, J. R. (1993). Pharmacotherapy for smoking cessation: Unvalidated assumptions, anomalies, and suggestions for future research. *Journal of Consulting and Clinical Psychology, 61,* 751–760.

Humphreys, K., & Moos, R. H. (2007). Encouraging post-treatment self-help group involvement to reduce demand for continuing care services: Two-year clinical and utilization outcomes. *Focus, 5,* 193–198.

Hunsley, J. (2009). Advancing the role of assessment in evidence-based psychological practice. *Clinical Psychology: Science and Practice, 16,* 202–205.

Hynd, G. W., & Semrud-Clikeman, M. (1989). Dyslexia and brain morphology. *Psychological Bulletin, 106,* 447–482.

Iacono, W. G. (2008). Accuracy of polygraph techniques: Problems using confessions to determine ground truth. *Physiology & Behavior, 95,* 24–26.

Ikels, C. (1991). Aging and disability in China: Cultural issues in measurement and interpretation. *Social Science Medicine, 32,* 649–665.

In-Albon, T., & Schneider, S. (2007). Psychotherapy of childhood anxiety disorders: A meta-analysis department of clinical child and adolescent psychology. *Psychotherapy and Psychosomatics, 76,* 15–24.

Ingram, R. E., Hayes, A., & Scott, W. (2000). Empirically supported treatments: A critical analysis. In C. R. Snyder & R. E. Ingram (Eds.), *Handbook of psychological change: Psycho therapy processes, practices for the 21st century* (pp. 40–60). New York: Wiley.

Ingram, R. E., Kendall, P. C., & Chen, A. H. (1991). Cognitive-behavioral interventions. In C. R. Snyder & D. R. Forsyth (Eds.), *Handbook of social and clinical psychology: The health perspective* (pp. 509–522). New York: Pergamon Press.

Ingram, R. E., & Scott, W. D. (1990). Cognitive behavior therapy. In A. S. Bellack, M. Hersen, & A. E. Kazdin (Eds.), *International handbook of behavior modification and therapy* (2nd ed., pp. 53–65). New York: Plenum Press.

Insel, T. R. (Ed.). (1984). *New findings in obsessive-compulsive disorder.* Washington, DC: American Psychiatric Press.

Insel, T. R. (1992). Toward a neuroanatomy of obsessive-compulsive disorder. *Archives of General Psychiatry, 49,* 739–744.

Insel, T. R., Champoux, M., Scanlan, J. M., & Suomi, S. J. (1986, May). *Rearing condition and response to anxiogenic drug.* Paper presented at the annual meeting of the American Psychiatric Association, Washington, DC.

Institute for the Future. (2000). *Health and healthcare 2010: The forecast, the challenge.* San Francisco: Jossey-Bass.

Institute of Medicine. (2001). *Health and behavior: The interplay of biological, behavioral, and societal influences.* Washington, DC: National Academy Press.

Institute of Medicine. (2008). *Knowing what works in health care: A road map for the nation.* Washington, DC: National Academy Press.

International Human Genome Sequencing Consortium. (2001, February 15). Initial sequencing and analysis of the human genome. *Nature, 409,* 860–921.

Jablensky, A. (2000). Epidemiology of schizophrenia: The global burden of disease and disability. *European Archives of Psychiatry and Clinical Neuroscience, 250,* 274–285.

Jacobson, N. S. (1984). A component analysis of behavioral marital therapy: The relative effectiveness of behavior exchange and communication/problem-solving training. *Journal of Consulting and Clinical Psychology, 52,* 295–305.

Jacobson, N. S. (1985). Family therapy outcome research: Potential pitfalls and prospects. *Journal of Marital and Family Therapy, 11,* 149–158.

Jacobson, N. S., & Gurman, A. S. (Eds.). (1995). *Clinical handbook of couple therapy.* New York: Guilford Press.

Jacobson, N. S., & Margolin, G. (1979). *Marital therapy: Strategies based on social learning and behavior exchange principles.* New York: Brunner/Mazel.

Jacobson, N. S., & Revenstorf, D. (1988). Statistics for assessing the clinical significance of psychotherapy techniques: Issues, problems, and new developments. *Behavioral Assessment, 10,* 133–145.

Jacobson, N. S., & Truax, P. (1991). Clinical significance: A statistic approach to defining meaningful change in psychotherapy research. *Journal of Consulting and Clinical Psychology, 59,* 12–19.

James, W. (1890). *Principles of psychology.* New York: Holt.

Jamison, R. N., & Virts, K. L. (1990). The influence of family support on chronic pain. *Behaviour Research and Therapy, 28,* 283–287.

Jeffery, R. W. (1988). Dietary risk and their modification in cardiovascular disease. *Journal of Consulting and Clinical Psychology, 56,* 350–357.

Jehu, D. (1979). *Sexual dysfunction: A behavioural approach to causation, assessment, and treatment.* New York: Wiley.

Jenkins, C. D. (1988). Epidemiology of cardiovascular diseases. *Journal of Consulting and Clinical Psychology, 56,* 324–332.

Jerome, L. W., & Zaylor, C. (2000). Cyberspace: Creating a therapeutic environment for telehealth applications. *Professional Psychology: Research and Practice, 31,* 478–483.

Joëls, M. (2009). Stress, the hippocampus, and epilepsy. *Epilepsia, 50,* 586–597.

John Jay College of Criminal Justice (2004). *The nature and scope of the problem of sexual abuse of minors by Catholic priests and deacons in the United States.* New York: Author.

Johnson, M. O., & Remien, R. H. (2003). Adherence to research protocols in a clinical context: Challenges and recommendations from behavioral intervention trails. *American Journal of Psychotherapy, 57,* 348–360.

Johnson, N. G. (2003). Psychology and health research, practice, and policy. *American Psychologist, 58,* 670–677.

Joint statement on the impact of entertainment violence on children: Congressional public health summit. (2000, July 26). Washington, DC: U.S. Senate.

Jones, B. P., & Butters, N. (1991). Neuropsychological assessment. In M. Hersen, A. E. Kazdin, & A. S. Bellack (Eds.), *The clinical psychology handbook* (2nd ed., pp. 406–429). New York: Pergamon Press.

Jones, M. C. (1924). The elimination of children's fears. *Journal of Experimental Psychology, 7,* 383–390.

Jones, M. L., Ulicny, G. R., Czyzewski, M. J., & Plante, T. G. (1987). Employment in care-giving jobs for mentally disabled young adults: A feasibility study. *Journal of Employment Counseling, 24*(9), 122–129.

Jones, S. L. (1994). A constructive relationship for religion with the science and profession of psychology: Perhaps the boldest model yet. *American Psychologist, 49,* 184–199.

Jorgensen, R. S., Johnson, B. T., Kolodziej, M. E., & Schreer, G. E. (1996). Elevated blood pressure and personality: A meta-analytic review. *Psychological Bulletin, 120,* 293–320.

Jorm, A. F. (1989). Modifiability of trait anxiety and neuroticism: A meta-analysis of the literature. *Australian and New Zealand Journal of Psychiatry, 23,* 21–29.

Jucker, M., Beyreuther, K., Haass, C., Nitsch, R., & Christen, Y. (Eds.). (2006). *Alzheimer: 100 years and beyond.* Berlin: Springer.

Julien, R. M. (2007). *A primer of drug action* (11th ed.). New York: Worth.

Kagan, J., Reznick, J. S., & Snidman, N. (1988). Biological bases of childhood shyness. *Science, 240,* 167–171.

Kahn, M. W., & Heiman, E. (1978). Factors associated with length of treatment in a barrio-neighborhood mental health service. *International Journal of Social Psychiatry, 24,* 259–262.

Kaiser, J. (2008). DNA sequencing: A plan to capture human diversity in 1000 genomes. *Science, 319,* 395.

Kalat, J. W. (2008). *Biological psychology* (10th ed.). Belmont, CA: Wadsworth.

Kamps, D. M., Barbetta, P. M., Leonard, B. R., & Delquadri, J. (1994). Class-wide peer tutoring: An integration strategy to improve reading skills and promote peer interactions among students with autism and general education peers. *Journal of Applied Behavior Analysis, 27,* 49–61.

Kane, J. M. (2008). Relapse prevention in patients with schizophrenia. *Journal of Clinical Psychiatry, 69,* 11.

Kaplan, E., Fein, D. C., Kramer, J. H., Delis, D., & Morris, R. (1999). *Manual for the WISC-III as a process instrument (WISC-III PI).* San Antonio, TX: Psychological Corporation.

Kaplan, E., Fein, D., Morris, R., & Delis, D. C. (1991). *WAIS-R as a neuropsychological instrument.* San Antonio, TX: Psychological Corporation.

Kaplan, G. A., & Reynolds, P. (1988). Depression and cancer mortality and morbidity: Prospective evidence from the Alameda County study. *Journal of Behavioral Medicine, 11,* 1–13.

Karasu, T. B. (1986). Specificity versus nonspecificity. *American Journal of Psychiatry, 143,* 687–695.

Karg, R. S., & Wiens, A. N. (1998). Improving diagnostic and clinical interviewing. In G. P. Koocher, J. C. Norcross, & S. S. Hill, III (Eds.), *Psychologists' desk reference* (pp. 11–14). New York: Oxford University Press.

Karon, B. P. (1995). Provision of psychotherapy under managed health care: A growing crisis and national nightmare. *Professional Psychology: Research and Practice, 26,* 5–9.

Kaskutas, L. A. (2009). Alcoholics Anonymous effectiveness: Faith meets science. *Journal of Addictive Diseases, 28,* 145–157.

Katz, R. L. (1980). Human relations skills can be sharpened. In Paths towards personal progress: Leaders are made not born. *Harvard Business Review,* 82–93.

Katzman, R. (1993). Education and the prevalence of dementia and Alzheimer's disease. *Neurology, 43,* 13–20.

Katzman, R. (2008). Bottom of Form The prevalence and malignancy of Alzheimer disease: A major killer. *Alzheimer's & Dementia, 4,* 378–380

Kaufman, A. S., & Kaufman, N. L. (1990). *Kaufman Brief Intelligence Test (K-BIT): Administrative and scoring manual.* Circles Pines, MN: American Guidance Service.

Kaufman, A. S., & Kaufman, N. L. (1993). *Kaufman Adolescent and Adult Intelligence Test (KAIT): Administrative and scoring manual.* Circles Pines, MN: American Guidance Service.

Kaufman, A. S., & Kaufman, N. L. (1994). *Kaufman Short Neuropsychological Assessment Procedure (K-SNAP): Administrative and scoring manual.* Circles Pines, MN: American Guidance Service.

Kaufman, A. S., & Kaufman, N. L. (2004). *Kaufman Assessment Battery for Children (K-ABC): II. Administrative and scoring manual* (2nd ed.). Circles Pines, MN: American Guidance Service.

Kaye, W. H., Fudge, J. L., & Paulus, M. (2009). New insights into symptoms and neurocircuit function of anorexia nervosa. *Nature Reviews Neuroscience, 10,* 573–584.

Kazdin, A. E. (1991). Treatment research: The investigation and evaluation of psychotherapy. In M. Hersen, A. E. Kazdin, & A. S. Bellack (Eds.), *The clinical psychology handbook* (2nd ed.). New York: Pergamon Press.

Kazdin, A. E. (1994). Methodology, design, and evaluation in psychotherapy research. In A. E. Bergin & S. L. Garfield (Eds.), *Handbook of psychotherapy and behavior change* (4th ed.). New York: Wiley.

Kazdin, A. E., & Bass, D. (1989). Power to detect differences between alternative treatments in comparative psychotherapy outcome research. *Journal of Consulting and Clinical Psychology, 57,* 138–147.

Kazdin, A. E., & Weisz, J. R. (1998). Identifying and developing empirically supported child and adolescent treatments. *Journal of Consulting and Clinical Psychology, 66,* 19–36.

Kazdin, A. E., & Weisz, J. R. (Eds.). (2003). *Evidence-based psychotherapies for children and adolescents.* New York: Guilford Press.

Kazdin, A. E., & Wilson, G. T. (1978). *Evaluation of behavior therapy: Issues, evidence, and research strategies.* Cambridge, MA: Ballinger.

Keefe, F. J., Dunsmore, J., & Burnett, R. (1992). Behavioral and cognitive-behavioral approaches to chronic pain: Recent advances and future directions [Special issue]. *Journal of Consulting and Clinical Psychology, 60,* 528–536.

Keith-Spiegel, P. (1991). *The complete guide to graduate school admission: Psychology and related fields.* Hillsdale, NJ: Erlbaum.

Keith-Spiegel, P. (1994). The 1992 ethics: Boon or bane? *Professional Psychology: Research and Practice, 25,* 315–316.

Kelly, E. B. (2009). *The encyclopedia of attention deficit hyperactivity disorders.* New York: Macmillan.

Kelly, J. A., & Kalichman, S. C. (1995). Increased attention to human sexuality can improve HIV-AIDS prevention efforts: Key research issues and directions. *Journal of Consulting and Clinical Psychology, 63,* 907–918.

Kelly, J. A., St. Lawrence, J. S., Hood, H. V., & Brasfield, T. L. (1989). Behavioral intervention to reduce AIDS risk activities. *Journal of Consulting and Clinical Psychology, 57,* 60–67.

Kelly, J. F. (2003). Self-help for substance-use disorders: History, effectiveness, knowledge gaps, and research opportunities. *Clinical Psychology Review, 23,* 639–665.

Kelly, T. A. (1997). A wake-up call: The experience of a mental health commissioner in times of change. *Professional Psychology: Research and Practice, 28,* 317–322.

Kemp, S. (1990). *Medieval psychology.* New York: Greenwood Press.

Kendall, P. C., & Bemis, K. M. (1983). Thought and action in psychotherapy: The cognitive behavioral approaches. In M. Hersen, A. E. Kazdin, & A. S. Bellak (Eds.), *The clinical psychology handbook* (pp. 565–592). Elmsford, NY: Pergamon Press.

Kendall, P. C., & Braswell, L. (1985). *Cognitive behavioral therapy with impulsive children.* New York: Guilford Press.

Kendall, P. C., Holmbeck, G., & Verduin, T. (2004). Methodological, design, and evaluation in psychotherapy research. In M. J. Lambert (Ed.), *Bergin and Garfield's handbook of psychotherapy and behavior change* (5th ed., pp. 16–43). New York: Wiley.

Kendall, P. C., & Norton-Ford, J. D. (1982). Therapy outcome research methods. In P. C. Kendall & J. N. Butcher (Eds.), *Handbook of research methods in clinical psychology* (pp. 429–460). New York: Wiley.

Kendziora, K., & O'Leary, S. G. (1993). Dysfunctional parenting as a focus for prevention and treatment of child behavior problems. In H. Ollendick & R. J. Prinz (Eds.), *Advances in child clinical psychology* (Vol. 15, pp. 175–206). New York: Plenum Press.

Kenrick, D. T., & Funder, D. C. (1988). Profiting from controversy: Lessons from the person-situation debate. *American Psychologist, 43,* 23–34.

Kernberg, O. (1973). Summary and conclusion of "Psychotherapy and psychoanalysis: Final report of the Menninger Foundation's psychotherapy research project." *International Journal of Psychiatry, 11,* 62–77.

Kernberg, O. (1975). *Borderline conditions and pathological narcissism.* New York: Aronson.

Kernberg, O. (1976). *Object relations theory and clinical psychoanalysis.* New York: Aronson.

Kernberg, O. (1984). *Severe personality disorders: Psychotherapeutic strategies.* New Haven, CT: Yale University Press.

Kessler, D., Lewis, G., Kaur, S., Wiles, N., King, M., Weich, S., Sharp, D., Araya, R., Hollinghurst, S., & Peters, T. (2009). Therapist-delivered internet psychotherapy for depression in primary care: A randomised controlled trial. *The Lancet, 374,* 628–634.

Keys, C. L. M., & Haidt, J. (2003). *Flourishing: Positive psychology and the life well-lived.* Washington, DC: APA Books.

Kiecolt-Glaser, J. K., McGuire, L., Robles, T. F., & Glaser, R. (2002). Emotions, morbidity, and mortality: New perspectives from psychoneuroimmunology. *Annual Review of Psychology, 53,* 83–107.

Kiesler, C. A., & Morton, T. L. (1987). Responsible public policy in a rapidly changing world. *Clinical Psychologist, 40,* 28–31.

Kiesler, C. A., & Morton, T. L. (1988). Psychology and public policy in the "health care revolution." *American Psychologist, 43,* 993–1003.

Kiesler, C. A., & Zaro, J. (1981). The development of psychology as a profession in the United States. *International Review of Applied Psychology, 30,* 341–353.

Kilburg, R. R. (1991). *How to manage your career in psychology*. Washington, DC: American Psychological Association.

Kim-Cohen, J. (2007). Resilience and developmental psychopathology. *Child and Adolescent Psychiatric Clinics of North America, 16*, 271–283.

King, D. A., & Markus, H. E. (2000). Mood disorders in older adults. In S. K. Whitebourne (Ed.), *Psychopathology in later adulthood* (pp. 141–172). New York: Wiley.

Kirk, S. A., & Kutchins, H. (1992). *The selling of DSM: The rhetoric of science in psychiatry*. New York: Aldine de Gruyter.

Kirmayer, L. J. (2001). Cultural variations in the clinical presentation of depression and anxiety: Implications for diagnosis and treatment. *Journal of Clinical Psychiatry, 62*(Suppl. 13), 22–28.

Kirsch, I. (1990). *Changing expectations: A key to effective psychotherapy*. Pacific Grove, CA: Brooks/Cole.

Kirschner, D. A., & Kirschner, S. (1986). *Comprehensive family therapy: An integration of systemic and psychodynamic treatment models*. New York: Brunner/Mazel.

Kite, M. E., Russo, N. F., Brehm, S. S., Fouad, N. A., Iijima Hall, C. C., Hyde, J. S., et al. (2001). Women psychologists in academe: Mixed progress, unwarranted complacency. *American Psychologist, 56*, 1080–1098.

Klausner, R. D. (1998). Foreword. In K. Offit (Ed.), *Clinical cancer genetics: Risk counseling and management* (pp. ix–x). New York: Wiley-Liss.

Klein, M. (1952). Some theoretical conclusions regarding the emotional life of the infant. In M. Klein (Ed.), *Envy and gratitude and other works, 1946–1963* (pp. 61–93). New York: Delta.

Klein, R. G. (1995). The role of methylphenidate in psychiatry. *Archives of General Psychiatry, 52*, 429–433.

Klein, R. G. (1996). Comments on expanding the clinical role of psychologists. *American Psychologist, 51*, 216–218.

Kleinke, C. L. (1994). *Common principles of psychotherapy*. Pacific Grove, CA: Brooks/Cole.

Klerman, G. L., Weissman, M. M., Rounsaville, B. J., & Chevron, E. S. (1984). *Interpersonal psychotherapy of depression*. New York: Basic Books.

Klosko, J. S., Barlow, D. H., Tassinari, R., & Cerny, J. A. (1990). A comparison of alprazolam and behavior therapy in treatment of panic disorder. *Journal of Consulting and Clinical Psychology, 58*, 77–84.

Kluft, R. P. (1995). Psychodynamic psychotherapy of multiple personality disorder and allied forms of dissociative disorder not otherwise specified. In J. P. Barber & P. Crits-Christoph (Eds.), *Dynamic therapies for psychiatric disorders (Axis I)* (pp. 332–385). New York: Basic Books.

Klusman, L. E. (1998). Military health care providers' views on prescribing privileges for psychologists. *Professional Psychology: Research and Practice, 29*, 223–229.

Kobasa, S. C. (1982). The hardy personality: Toward a social psychology of stress and health. In G. S. Sanders & J. Suls (Eds.), *Social psychology of health and illness* (pp. 3–32). Hillsdale, NJ: Erlbaum.

Kohout, J. L., Wicherski, M. M., Popanz, T. J., & Pion, G. M. (1990). *1989 salaries in psychology: Report of the 1989 APA Salary Survey*. Washington, DC: American Psychological Association.

Kohut, H. (1971). *The analysis of the self*. New York: International Universities Press.

Kohut, H. (1977). *The restoration of the self*. New York: International Universities Press.

Kohut, H. (1984). *How does analysis cure?* Chicago: University of Chicago Press.

Kolb, B., & Whishaw, I. Q. (2008). *Fundamentals of human neuropsychology* (6th ed.). New York: Worth.

Kolko, D. J., Kazdin, A. E., & Meyer, E. C. (1985). Aggression and psychopathology in childhood fire-setters: Parent and child report. *Journal of Consulting and Clinical Psychology, 53*, 377–385.

Kombarakaran, F. A., Yang, J. A., Baker, M. N., & Fernandes, P. B. (2008). Executive coaching: It works! *Consulting Psychology Journal: Practice and Research, 60*, 78–90.

Kongstvedt, P. R. (2008). *Managed care: What it is and how it works* (3rd ed.). Sudbury, MA: Jones & Bartlett.

Koocher, G. P. (1994). The commerce of professional psychology and the new ethics code. *Professional Psychology: Research and Practice, 25*, 355–361.

Koocher, G. P., & Keith-Spiegal, P. (1998). *Ethics in psychology*. New York: Oxford University Press.

Koocher, G. P., & Keith-Spiegel, P. (2008). *Ethics in Psychology and the Mental Health Professions: Standards and Cases* (3rd Edition). NY: Oxford University Press.

Kopelman, P. G. (2000, April 6). Obesity as a medical problem. *Nature, 404*, 635–643.

Koran, L. M., Thienemann, M. L., & Davenport, R. (1996). Quality of life for patients with obsessive-compulsive disorder. *American Journal of Psychiatry, 153,* 783–788.

Korczyn, A. D., Kahana, E., & Galper, Y. (1991). Epidemiology of dementia in Ashkelon, Israel. *Neuroepidemiology, 10,* 100.

Koretz, G. (2001, January 15). Extra pounds, slimmer wages. *Business Week,* p. 28.

Korman, M. (Ed.). (1976). *Levels and patterns of professional training in psychology.* Washington, DC: American Psychological Association.

Kort, E. J., Paneth, N., & Vande Woude, G. F. (2009). The decline in U.S. cancer mortality in people born since 1925. *Cancer Research, 69,* 6500–6505.

Koss, M. P. (1993). Rape: Scope, impact, interventions, and public policy responses. *American Psychologist, 48,* 1062–1069.

Koss, M. P. (2000). Blame, shame, and community: Justice responses to violence against women. *American Psychologist, 55,* 1332–1343.

Kovacs, A. (1996, March/April). Advice to the new professional. *National Psychologist, 5,* 14.

Kovacs, M. (1985). The Children's Depression Inventory (CDI). *Psychopharmacology Bulletin, 21,* 995–998.

Kozak, M. J. & Foa, E. B. (1996). Obsessive-compulsive disorder. In V. B. Van Hasselt & M. Hersen (Eds.), *Sourcebook of psychological treatment manuals for adult disorders* (pp. 65–122), New York: Plenum Press.

Kramer, P. D. (1993). *Listening to Prozac.* New York: Viking Press.

Krantz, D. S., Contrada, R. J., Hill, D. R., & Friedler, E. (1988). Environmental stress and biobehavioral antecedents of coronary heart disease. *Journal of Consulting and Clinical Psychology, 56,* 333–341.

Krasner, L., & Ulmann, L. P. (Eds.). (1965). *Research in behavior modification: New developments and implications.* New York: Holt, Rinehart & Winston.

Krishman, K. R., Doraiswamy, P. M., Ventkataraman, S., Reed, D., & Richie, J. C. (1991). Current concepts in hypothalamic pituitary adrenal axis regulation. In J. A. McCubbin, P. G. Kaufmann, & C. B. Nemeroff (Eds.), *Stress, neuropeptides, and systemic disease* (pp. 19–35). San Diego, CA: Academic Press.

Kuncel, N. R., Hezlett, S. A., & Ones, D. S. (2001). A comprehensive meta-analysis of the predictive validity of the graduate record examinations: Implications for graduate student selection and performance. *Psychological Bulletin, 127,* 162–181.

Kurpius, D. (1985). Consultation interventions: Successes, failures, and proposals. *Counseling Psychologist, 13,* 368–389.

Kurpius, D., Fuqua, D., & Rozecki, T. (1993). The consulting process: A multidimensional approach. *Journal of Counseling and Development, 71,* 601–606.

Kurpius, D. J., & Lewis, J. E. (1988). Introduction to consultation: An intervention for advocacy and outreach. In D. J. Kurpius & D. Brown (Eds.), *Handbook of consultation: An intervention for advocacy and outreach* (pp. 1–4). Alexandria, VA: American Association for Counseling and Development.

Lafferty, P., Beutler, L. E., & Crago, M. (1991). Differences between more and less effective psychotherapists: A study of select therapist variables. *Journal of Consulting and Clinical Psychology, 57,* 76–80.

LaFromboise, T. D. (1988). American Indian mental health policy. *American Psychologist, 43,* 388–397.

La Greca, A. M. (2007). Understanding the psychological impact of terrorism on youth: Moving beyond posttraumatic stress disorder. *Clinical Psychology: Research and Practice, 14,* 219–223.

Lakin, M. (1994). Morality in group and family therapies: Multiperson therapies and the 1992 Ethics Code. *Professional Psychology: Research and Practice, 25,* 344–348.

Laliotis, D. A., & Grayson, J. H. (1985). Psychologist heal thyself: What is available for the impaired psychologist? *American Psychologist, 40,* 84–96.

Lally, S. J. (2003). What tests are acceptable for use in forensic evaluations? A survey of experts. *Professional Psychology: Research and Practice, 34,* 491–498.

Lam, D. J. (1991). The Tao of clinical psychology: Shifting from a medical to a biopsychosocial paradigm. *Bulletin of the Hong Kong Psychological Society, 26,* 107–113.

Lamb, H. R., & Weinberger, L. E. (Eds.). (2001). *Deinstitutionalization: Promise and problems.* San Francisco: Jossey-Bass.

Lamberg, L. (2008). Empirically supported treatments improve care of adolescents with depression *Journal of the American Medical Association, 300,* 269–270.

Lambert, K. G., & Kinsley, C. H. (2005). *Clinical neuroscience: Neurobiological foundations of mental health.* New York: Worth.

Lambert, L. E., & Wertheimer, M. (1988). Is diagnostic ability related to relevant training and experience? *Professional Psychology: Research and Practice, 19,* 50–52.

Lambert, M. J. (1986). Implications of psychotherapy outcome research for eclectic psychotherapy. In J. C. Norcross (Ed.), *Handbook of eclectic psychotherapy* (pp. 436–462). New York: Brunner/Mazel.

Lambert, M. J. (1992). Psychotherapy outcome research: Implications for integrative and eclectic therapists. In J. C. Norcross & M. R. Goldfried (Eds.), *Handbook of psychotherapy integration* (pp. 94–129). New York: Basic Books.

Lambert, M. J. (2005). Early response in psychotherapy: Further evidence for the importance of common factors rather than placebo effects. *Journal of Clinical Psychology, 61,* 855–869.

Lambert, M. J., & Bergin, A. E. (1994). The effectiveness of psychotherapy. In A. E. Bergin & S. L. Garfield (Eds.), *Handbook of psychotherapy and behavior change* (4th ed., pp. 143–189). New York: Wiley.

Lambert, M. J., Bergin, A. E., & Garfield, S. L. (2004). Introduction and historical overview. In M. J. Lambert (Ed.), *Bergin and Garfield's handbook of psychotherapy and behavior change* (5th ed., pp. 3–15). New York: Wiley.

Lambert, M. J., & Ogles, B. M. (1988). Treatment manuals: Problems and promise. *Journal of Integrative and Eclectic Psychotherapy, 7,* 187–205.

Lambert, M. J., & Ogles, B. M. (2004). The efficacy and effectiveness of psychotherapy. In M. J. Lambert (Ed.), *Bergin and Garfield's handbook of psychotherapy and behavior change* (5th ed., pp. 139–193). New York: Wiley.

Lambert, M. J., & Okishi, J. C. (1997). The effects of the individual psychotherapist and implications for future research. *Clinical Psychology: Science and Practice, 4,* 66–75.

Lambert, M. J., Shapiro, D. A., & Bergin, A. E. (1986). The effectiveness of psychotherapy. In S. L. Garfield & A. E. Bergin (Eds.), *Handbook of psychotherapy and behavior change* (3rd ed., pp. 157–211). New York: Wiley.

Lambert, M. J., Whipple, J. L., Hawkins, E. J., Vermeersch, D. A., Nielsen, S. L., & Smart, D. W. (2003). Is it time for clinicians to routinely track patient outcome? A meta-analysis. *Clinical Psychology: Science and Practice, 10,* 288–301.

Lambert, N., (1993). *AAMR Adaptive Behavior Scales—School* (2nd ed.). Monterey, CA: Publishers Test Service.

Landman, J. T., & Dawes, R. (1982). Psychotherapy outcome: Smith Glass's conclusions stand up under scrutiny. *American Psychologist, 37,* 504–516.

Landon, T. M., & Barlow, D. H. (2004). Cognitive-behavioral treatment for panic disorder: Current status. Journal of *Psychiatric Practice, 10,* 211–226.

Landreth, G. L. (1991). *Play therapy: The art of the relationship.* Muncie, IN: Accelerated Development.

Landrine, H. (1992). Clinical implications of cultural differences: The referential versus indexical self. *Clinical Psychology Review, 12,* 401–415.

Langlois, J. A., Rutland-Brown, W., & Thomas, K. E. (2006). Traumatic brain injury in the United States: Emergency department visits, hospitalizations, and deaths. Atlanta (GA): Centers for Disease Control and Prevention, National Center for Injury Prevention and Control.

Lanyon, B. P., & Lanyon, R. I. (1980). *Incomplete sentence task: Manual.* Chicago: Stoelting.

Laor, I. (2001). Brief psychoanalytic psychotherapy: The impact of its fundamentals on the therapeutic process. *British Journal of Psychotherapy, 18,* 169–183.

Larkin, K. T. & Zayfert, C. (1996). Anger management training with essential hypertensive patients. In V. B. Van Hasselt & M. Hersen (Eds.), *Sourcebook of psychological treatment manuals for adult disorders* (pp. 689–716), New York: Plenum Press.

La Roche, M., & Christopher, M. S. (2008). Culture and empirically supported treatments: On the road to a collision? *Culture & Psychology, 14,* 333–356.

Larsen, K. G., Belar, C. D., Bieliauskas, L. A., Klepac, R. K., Stigall, T. T., & Zimet, C. N. (1993). *Proceedings from the national conference on postdoctoral training in professional psychology.* Washington, DC: Association of Psychology Postdoctoral and Internship Centers.

La Rue, A. (1992). *Aging and neuropsychological assessment.* New York: Plenum Press.

Lawson, T. J. (1995). Gaining admission into graduate programs in psychology: An update. *Teaching of Psychology, 22,* 225–227.

Layman, M. J., & McNamara, J. R. (1997). Remediation for ethics violations: Focus on psychotherapists' sexual contact with clients. *Professional Psychology: Research and Practice, 28,* 281–292.

Lazarus, A. A. (1971). *Behavior therapy and beyond.* New York: McGraw-Hill.

Lazarus, A. A. (1981). *The practice of multimodal therapy.* New York: McGraw-Hill.

Lazarus, A. A. (Ed.). (1985). *Casebook of multimodal therapy*. New York: Guilford Press.

Lazarus, A. A. (1986). Multimodal therapy. In J. C. Norcross (Ed.), *Handbook of eclectic psychotherapy* (pp. 286–326). New York: Guilford Press.

Lazarus, A. A. (1989). *The practice of multimodal therapy*. Baltimore: Johns Hopkins University Press.

Lazarus, A. A. (1995). Integration and clinical verisimilitude. *Clinical Psychology: Science and Practice, 2*, 399–402.

Lazarus, A. A. (1996). The utility and futility of combining treatments in psychotherapy. *Clinical Psychology: Science and Practice, 3*, 59–68.

Lazarus, A. (2005). Multimodal therapy. In J. C. Norcross, & M. R. Goldfried (Eds.). *Handbook of psychotherapy integration* (2nd ed., pp. 105–120). New York: Oxford University Press.

Lebow, J. L. (1984). On the value of integrating approaches to family therapy. *Journal of Marital and Family Therapy, 10*, 127–138.

Lebow, J. L. (2008). *Twenty-first century psychotherapies: Contemporary approaches to theory and practice*. New York: Wiley.

Lechnyr, R. (1992). Cost savings and effectiveness of mental health services. *Journal of the Oregon Psychological Association, 38*, 8–12.

Lee, C. K. (1992). Alcoholism in Korea. In J. Helzer & G. Canino (Eds.), *Alcoholism—North America, Europe and Asia: A coordinated analysis of population data from ten regions* (pp. 247–262). London: Oxford University Press.

Leichsenring, F., & Rabung, S. (2008). Effectiveness of long-term psychodynamic psychotherapy: A meta-analysis. *Journal of the American Medical Association, 300*, 1551–1565.

Leichsenring, F., & Rabung, S. (2008). Effectiveness of long-term psychodynamic psychotherapy: A meta-analysis. *Journal of the American Medical Association, 300*, 1551–1565.

Levant, R. F., & Hasan, N. T. (2008). Evidence-based practice in psychology. *Professional Psychology: Research and Practice, 39*, 658–662.

Levine, M. (2003a). *A mind at a time: America's top learning expert shows how every child can succeed*. New York: Simon & Schuster.

Levine, M. (2003b). *The myth of laziness: America's top learning expert shows how kids—and parents—can become more productive*. New York: Simon & Schuster.

Levy, L. (1962). The skew in clinical psychology. *American Psychologist, 29*, 441–449.

Levy, L. H. (1984). The metamorphosis of clinical psychology: Towards a new charter as human services psychology. *American Psychologist, 39*, 486–494.

Levy, S. M. (1983). Host differences in neoplastic risk: Behavioral and social contributions to disease. *Health Psychology, 2*, 21–44.

Lewinsohn, P. M., Antonuccio, D. O., Steinmetz, J. L., & Teri, L. (1984). *The coping with depression course: A psychoeducational intervention for unipolar depression*. Eugene, OR: Castalia.

Lewinsohn, P. M., & Shaffer, M. (1971). Use of home observations as an integral part of the treatment of depression: Preliminary report and case studies. *Journal of Consulting and Clinical Psychology, 37*, 87–94.

Levinson, D. F. (2006). The genetics of depression: A review. *Biological Psychiatry, 60*, 84–92.

Lewis, G., David, A., Andreasson, S., & Allsbeck, P. (1992). Schizophrenia and city life. *Lancet, 340*, 137–140.

Lewis, J. F., & Mercer, J. R. (1978). The System of Multicultural Pluralistic Assessment (SOMPA). In W. A. Coulter & H. W. Morrow (Eds.), *Adaptive behavior: Concepts and measurement* (pp. 185–212). Orlando, FL: Grune & Stratton.

Lewis, O. (1969). A Puerto Rican boy. In J. C. Finney (Ed.), *Culture, change, mental health, and poverty*. New York: Simon & Schuster.

Lex, B. W. (1985). Alcohol problems in special populations. In J. H. Mendelson & N. K. Mello (Eds.), *The diagnosis and treatment of alcoholism* (2nd ed., pp. 89–187). New York: McGraw-Hill.

Lezak, M. D. (1995). *Neuropsychological assessment* (3rd ed.). New York: Oxford University Press.

Lezak, M. D., Howieson, D. B., & Loring, D. W. (2004). *Neuropsychological assessment* (4th ed.). New York: Oxford.

Li, X., Wicherski, M., & Kohout, J. L. (2008). *Salaries in Psychology 2007, Report of the 2007 APA Salary Survey*. Washington, DC: American Psychological Association.

Li, W., & Zinbarg, R. E. (2007). Anxiety sensitivity and panic attacks: A 1-year longitudinal study. *Behavior Modification, 31*, 145–161.

Liberman, B. L. (1978). The role of mastery in psychotherapy: Maintenance of improvement and prescriptive change. In J. D. Frank, R. Hoehn-Saric, S. D. Imber, B. L. Liberman, & A. A. Stone (Eds.), *Effective ingredients of successful psychotherapy* (pp. 1–34). New York: Brunner/Mazel.

Lilienfeld, S. (2007). Psychological treatments that cause harm. *Perspectives on Psychological Science, 2,* 53–70.

Lilienfeld, S. O., & Arkowitz, H. A., (2006). EMDR: Taking a closer look. *Scientific American Mind, 17,* 80–81.

Lilienfeld, S. O., Lynn, S. J., & Lohr, J. M. (Eds.). (2004). *Science and pseudoscience in clinical psychology.* New York: Guilford Press.

Lilienfeld, S. O., Wood, J. M., & Garb, H. N. (2000). The scientific status of protective techniques. *Psychological Science in the Public Interest, 1,* 27–66.

Linehan, M. M. (1993). *Cognitive-behavioral treatment of borderline personality disorder.* New York: Guilford Press.

Linehan, M. M., Cochran, B. N., & Kehrer, C. A. (2001). Dialectical behavior therapy for borderline personality disorder. In D. H. Barlow (Ed.), *Clinical handbook of psychological disorders: A step-by-step treatment manual (3rd ed., pp. 609–630).* New York: Guilford Press.

Linkins, R. W., & Comstock, G. W. (1988). Depressed mood and development of cancer. *American Journal of Epidemiology, 128,* 894.

Lippitt, G., & Lippitt, R. (1994). *The consulting process in action* (4th ed.). La Jolla, CA: University Associates.

Lipsey, M., & Wilson, D. (1993). The efficacy of psychological, educational, and behavioral treatment: Confirmation from meta-analysis. *American Psychologist, 48,* 1181–1209.

Lisansky-Gomberg, E. S. (2000). Substance abuse disorders. In S. K. Whitebourne (Ed.), *Psychotherapy in later adulthood* (pp. 277–289). New York: Wiley.

Litwin, W. J., Boswell, D. L., & Kraft, W. A. (1991). Medical staff membership and clinical privileges: A survey of hospital-affiliated psychologists. *Professional Psychology: Research and Practice, 22,* 322–327.

Loehlin, J. C. (1992). *Genes and environment in personality development.* Newbury Park, CA: Sage.

Loftus, E. F., & Pickrell, J. E. (1995). The information of false memories. *Psychiatric Annals, 25,* 720–725.

London, P. (1988). Metamorphosis in psychotherapy: Slouching toward integration. *Journal of Integrative and Eclectic Psychotherapy, 7,* 3–12.

Lopez, S. R., Grover, K. P., Holland, D., Johnson, M. J., Kain, C. D., Kanel, K., et al. (1989). Development of culturally sensitive psychotherapists. *Professional Psychology: Research and Practice, 20,* 369–376.

Lorion, R. P. (1996). Applying our medicine to the psychopharmacology debate. *American Psychologist, 51,* 219–224.

Lowe, J. R., & Widiger, T. A. (2009). Clinicians' judgments of clinical utility: A comparison of the DSM-IV with dimensional models of general personality. *Journal of Personality Disorders, 23,* 211–229.

Lubin, B., Larsen, R. M., Matarazzo, J. D., & Seever, M. (1985). Psychological test usage patterns in five professional settings. *American Psychologist, 40,* 857–861.

Luborsky, L., & Barber, J. P. (1993). Benefits of adherence to psychotherapy manuals and where to get them. In N. E. Miller, L. Luborsky, J. P. Barber, & J. P. Docherty (Eds.), *Psychodynamic treatment research.* New York: Basic Books.

Luborsky, L., & DeRubeis, R. J. (1984). The use of psychotherapy treatment manuals—a small revolution in psychotherapy research style. *Clinical Psychology Review, 4,* 5–14.

Luborsky, L., Mark, D., Hole, A. V., Popp, C., Goldsmith, B., & Cacciola, J. (1995). Supportive-expressive dynamic psychotherapy of depression: A time-limited version. In J. P. Barber & P. Crits-Christoph (Eds.), *Dynamic therapies for psychiatric disorders (Axis I)* (pp. 13–42). New York: Basic Books.

Luborsky, L., Rosenthal, R., Diguer, L., Andrusyna, T. P., Berman, J. S., Levitt, J. T., et al. (2002). The dodo bird verdict is alive and well—mostly. *Clinical Psychology: Science and Practice, 9,* 2–12.

Luborsky, L., Singer, B., & Luborsky, L. (1975). Comparative studies of psychotherapy. *Archives of General Psychiatry, 32,* 995–1008.

Luborsky, L., Woody, G. E., Hole, A. V., & Velleco, A. (1995). Supportive-expressive dynamic psychotherapy for treatment of opiate drug dependence. In J. P. Barber & P. Crits-Christoph (Eds.), *Dynamic therapies for psychiatric disorders (Axis I)* (pp. 294–331). New York: Basic Books.

Luskin, F. (2002). *Forgive for good.* San Francisco: HarperCollins.

Lykken, D. T. (1991). *Science, lies and controversy: An epitaph for the polygraph.* Invited address upon receipt of the Senior Career award for Distinguished Contribution to Psychology in the Public Interest, American Psychological Association.

Lyons, L. C., & Woods, P. J. (1991). The efficacy of rational-emotive therapy: A quantitative review of the outcome research. *Clinical Psychology Review, 11,* 357–369.

Maccoby, E. E. (2000). Parenting and its effects on children: On reading and misreading behavior genetics. *Annual Review of Psychology, 51,* 1–27.

MacDonald, G. (1996). Inferences in therapy: Processes and hazards. *Professional Psychology: Research and Practice, 27,* 600–603.

Machover, K. (1949). *Personality projection in the drawing of the human figure.* Springfield, IL: Charles C. Thomas.

MacKinnon, D. W. (1944). The structure of personality. In J. McVicker Hunt (Ed.), *Personality and the behavior disorders* (Vol. 1, pp. 3–48). New York: Ronald Press.

Magnusson, D. (1981). *Toward a psychology of situations: An interactional perspective.* Hillsdale, NJ: Erlbaum.

Maher, B. A., & Maher, W. B. (1985a). Psychopathology: I. From ancient times to the eighteenth century. In G. A. Kimble & K. Schlesinger (Eds.), *Topics in the history of psychology* (pp. 251–294). Hillsdale, NJ: Erlbaum.

Maher, B. A., & Maher, W. B. (1985b). Psychopathology: II. From the eighteenth century to modern times. In G. A. Kimble & K. Schlesinger (Eds.), *Topics in the history of psychology* (pp. 295–329). Hillsdale, NJ: Erlbaum.

Maheu, M. M., & Gordon, B. L. (2000). The Internet versus the telephone: What is telehealth anyway? *Professional Psychology: Research and Practice, 31,* 484–489.

Mahler, M. (1952). On child psychosis and schizophrenia: Autistic and symbiotic infantile psychoses. *Psychoanalytic Study of the Child, 7,* 206–305.

Mahoney, D. J., & Restak, R. M. (1998). *The longevity strategy: How to live to 100 using the brain-body connection.* New York: Wiley.

Mahoney, M. J. (1974). *Cognition and behavior modification.* Cambridge, MA: Ballinger.

Mahoney, M. J. (1988). The cognitive sciences and psychotherapy: Patterns in developing relationships. In K. S. Dobson (Ed.), *Handbook of cognitive-behavioral therapies* (pp. 357–386). New York: Guilford Press.

Malenfant, D., Catton, M., & Pope, J. E. (2009). The efficacy of complementary and alternative medicine in the treatment of Raynaud's phenomenon: A literature review and meta-analysis. *Rheumatology, 48,* 791–795.

Maltby, N., Kirsch, I., Mayers, M., & Allen, G. J. (2002). Virtual reality exposure therapy for the treatment of fear of flying: A controlled investigation. *Journal of Consulting and Clinical Psychology, 70,* 1112–1118.

Manne, S. L., & Glassman, M. (2000). Perceived control, coping efficacy, and avoidance coping as mediators between spouses' unsupportive behaviors and cancer patients' psychological distress. *Health Psychology, 19,* 155–164.

March, J. S. (2006). *Talking back to OCD: The program that helps kids and teens say ''no way''-- and parents say ''way to go.''* New York: Guilford Press.

March, J. S., & Mule, K. (1996). Banishing OCD: Cognitive-behavioral psychotherapy for obsessivecompulsive disorders. In E.D. Hibbs and P.S. Jensen (Eds.), ***Psychosocial treatments for child and adolescent disorders: Empirically based strategies for clinical practice*** (pp. 83–102). Washington, DC: American Psychological Association.

March, J. S., & Mulle, K. (1998). *OCD in children and adolescents: A cognitive-behavioral treatment manual.* New York: Guilford Press.

Mariotto, M. J., & Paul, G. L. (1974). A multimethod validation of the Inpatient Multidimensional Psychiatric Scale with chronically institutionalized patients. *Journal of Consulting and Clinical Psychology, 42,* 497–508.

Markowitz, J. C. (2008). How "supportive" is Internet-based supportive psychotherapy? *American Journal of Psychiatry, 165,* 534.

Marlatt, G. A., & Donovan, D. M. (Eds.). (2008). *Relapse prevention: Maintenance strategies in the treatment of addictive behaviors.* New York: Guilford Press.

Marlatt, G. A., & Gordon, J. R. (Eds.). (1985). *Relapse prevention: Maintenance strategies in the treatment of addictive behaviors.* New York: Guilford Press.

Marshall, W. L. & Eccles, A. (1996). Cognitive-behavioral treatments of sex offenders. In V. B. Van Hasselt & M. Hersen (Eds.), *Sourcebook of psychological treatment manuals for adult disorders* (pp. 295–332), New York: Plenum Press.

Martin, E. M., Lu, W. C., Helmick, K., French, L., Warden, D. L. (2008). Traumatic brain injuries sustained in the Afghanistan and Iraq wars. *Journal of Trauma Nursing, 15,* 94–99.

Martin, P. R. (1993). *Psychological management of chronic headaches.* New York: Guilford Press.

Martin, S. (1995, September). APA to pursue prescription privileges. *APA Monitor,* p. 6.

Mash, E. J., & Barkley, R. A. (Eds.). (1989). *Treatment of childhood disorders.* New York: Guilford Press.

Maslow, A. H. (1954). *Motivation and personality.* New York: Harper.

Maslow, A. H. (1971). *The farther reaches of human nature.* New York: Viking Press.

Masten, A. S. (2001). Ordinary magic: Resilience processes in development. *American Psychologist, 56,* 227–238.

Masterpasqua, F. (2009). Psychology and epigenetics. *Review of General Psychology, 13,* 194–201.

Masterson, J. L. (1981). *The narcissistic and borderline disorders: An integrated developmental approach.* New York: Brunner/Mazel.

Matarazzo, J. D. (1980). Behavioral health and behavioral medicine: Frontiers for a new health psychology. *American Psychologist, 35,* 807–817.

Matarazzo, J. D. (1982). Behavioral health's challenge to academic, scientific, and professional psychology. *American Psychologist, 37,* 1–14.

Matarazzo, J. D. (1984). Behavioral immunogens and pathogens in health and illness. In B. L. Hammonds & C. J. Scheirer (Eds.), *Psychology and health: The master lecture series* (Vol. 3, pp. 9–43). Washington, DC: American Psychological Association.

Matarazzo, J. D. (1987). There is only one psychology, no specialties, but many applications. *American Psychologist, 42,* 893–903.

Matarazzo, J. D. (1992). Psychological testing and assessment in the 21st century. *American Psychologist, 47,* 1007–1018.

Matt, G. E. (1989). Decision rules for selecting effect sizes in meta-analysis: A review and reanalysis of psychotherapy outcome studies. *Psychological Bulletin, 105,* 106–115.

Matthews, J. (1983). *The effective use of management consultants in higher education.* Boulder, CO: National Center for Higher Education Management Services.

Matthews, J. (1995, December 28). *CEOs feeling flush: HMO execs cut costs and salaries by not their own.* Washington, DC: Washington Post.

Matthews, K. A., Woodall, K. L., & Allen, M. T. (1993). Cardiovascular reactivity to stress predicts future blood pressure status. *Hypertension, 22*(4), 479–485.

Max, W. (1993). The economic impact of Alzheimer's disease. *Neurology, 43,* S6–S10.

May, R. (1977). *The meaning of anxiety.* New York: Norton.

May, R., Angel, E., & Ellenberger, H. (Eds.). (1958). *Existence: A new dimension in psychiatry and psychology.* New York: Basic Books.

Mays, D. T., & Frank, C. M. (1980). Getting worse: Psychotherapy or no treatment. The jury should still be out. *Professional Psychology, 11,* 78–92.

Mays, D. T., & Frank, C. M. (1985). *Negative outcome in psychotherapy and what to do about it.* New York: Springer.

Mazziotta, J. C. (1996). Mapping mental illness: A new era. *Archives of General Psychiatry, 53,* 574–576.

McArthur, D. S., & Roberts, G. E. (1982). *Roberts Apperception Test for Children: Manual.* Los Angeles: Western Psychological Services.

McCagh, J., Fisk, J., & Baker, G. (2009). Epilepsy, psychosocial and cognitive functioning *Epilepsy Research, 86,* 1–14.

McCall, R. B. (1988). Science and the press: Like oil and water? *American Psychologist, 43,* 87–94.

McCall, R. B., & Garriger, M. S. (1993). A meta-analysis of infant habituation and recognition memory performance as predictors of later IQ. *Child Development, 64,* 57–79.

McCaul, K. D., Branstetter, A. D., Schroeder, D. M., & Glasgow, R. E. (1996). What is the relationship between breast cancer risk and mammography screening? A meta-analytic review. *Health Psychology, 15,* 423–429.

McConaghy, N. (1996). Treatment of sexual dysfunctions. In V. B. Van Hasselt & M. Hersen (Eds.), *Sourcebook of psychological treatment manuals for adult disorders* (pp. 333–374), New York: Plenum Press.

McConnell, H. W., & Snyder, P. J. (Eds.). (1997). *Psychiatric comorbidity in epilepsy: Basic mechanisms, diagnosis, and treatment.* Washington, DC: American Psychiatric Press.

McCrady, B. S. (2001). Alcohol disorders. In D. H. Barlow (Ed.), *Clinical handbook of psychological disorders: A step-by-step treatment manual (3rd ed., pp. 376–433).* New York: Guilford Press.

McCrae, R. R., & Costa, P. T. (2003). *Personality in adulthood* (2nd ed.). New York: Guilford Press.

McDaniel, S. H. (1995). Collaboration between psychologists and family physicians: Implementing the biopsychosocial model. *Professional Psychology: Research and Practice, 26,* 117–122.

McDevitt, S. (1996). The impact of news media on child abuse reporting. *Child Abuse and Neglect, 20,* 261–274.

McFall, R. M. (1991). Manifesto for a science of clinical psychology. *Clinical Psychologist, 44,* 75–88.

McFall, R. M. (2000). Elaborate reflections on a simple manifesto. *Applied and Preventative Psychology, 9,* 5–21.

McFarlane, W. R. (2002). *Multifamily groups in the treatment of severe psychiatric disorders*. New York: Guilford Press.

McGinnis, J. M. (1984). Occupant protection as a priority in national efforts to promote health. *Health Education Quarterly, 11,* 127–131.

McGinnis, M., Richmond, J. B., Brandt, E. N., Windom, R. E., & Mason, J. O. (1992). Health progress in the United States: Results of the 1990 objectives for the nation. *Journal of the American Medical Association, 268,* 2545–2552.

McGlashan, T. H. (1986). The chestnut lodge follow-up study. *Archives of General Psychiatry, 43,* 20–30.

McGrath, E. (1995). Are we trading our souls for a sound bite? *APA Monitor, 24,* 5.

McGregor, B. A., & Antoni, M. H. (2009). Psychological intervention and health outcomes among women treated for breast cancer: A review of stress pathways and biological mediators. *Brain, Behavior, and Immunity, 23,* 159–166.

McGue, M., & Lykken, D. T. (1992). Genetic influence on risk of divorce. *Psychological Science, 3,* 368–373.

McGuffin, P., Katz, R., & Bebbington, P. (1988). The Camberwell Collaborative Depression Study: III. Depression and adversity in the relatives of depressed probands. *British Journal of Psychiatry, 152,* 775–782.

McKim, W. A. (1991). *Drugs and behavior: An introduction to behavioral pharmacology* (2nd ed.). Englewood Cliffs, NJ: Prentice-Hall.

McLeod, J. D., Kessler, R. C., & Landis, K. R. (1992). Speed of recovery from major depressive episodes in a community sample of married men and women. *Journal of Abnormal Psychology, 101,* 277–286.

McNally, R. J. (2001). The cognitive psychology of repressed and recovered memories of childhood sexual abuse: Clinical implications. *Psychiatric Annals, 31,* 509–514.

McNeill, B. W., May, R. J., & Lee, V. E. (1987). Perceptions of counselor source characteristics by premature and successful terminators. *Journal of Counseling Psychology, 34,* 86–89.

McReynolds, P. (1987). Lightner Witmer: Little-known founder of clinical psychology. *American Psychologist, 42,* 849–858.

Meehl, P. E. (1954). *Clinical versus statistical prediction*. Minneapolis: University of Minnesota Press.

Meehl, P. E. (1962). Schizotaxia, schizotypy, schizophrenia. *American Psychologist, 17,* 827–838.

Meehl, P. E. (1965). Seer over sign: The first good example. *Journal of Experimental Research in Personality, 1,* 27–32.

Meehl, P. E. (1997). Credentialed persons, credentialed knowledge. *Clinical Psychology: Science and Practice, 4,* 91–98.

Megargee, E. J. (1990). *A guide to obtaining a psychology internship*. Muncie, IN: Accelerated Development.

Meichenbaum, D. H. (1977). *Cognitive-behavior modification*. New York: Plenum Press.

Melchert, T. P. (2007). Strengthening the scientific foundations of professional psychology: Time for the next steps. *Professional Psychology: Research and Practice, 38,* 34–43.

Mercado, A. C., Carroll, L. J., Cassidy, J. D., & Cote, P. (2000). Coping with neck and low back pain in the general population. *Health Psychology, 19,* 333–338.

Mercer, D. E., & Woody, G. E. (1998). *An individual drug counseling approach to treat cocaine addiction: The collaborative cocaine treatment study model.* Washington, DC: National Institute on Drug Abuse.

Mercer, J. R., & Lewis, J. F. (1979). *System of multicultural pluralistic assessment*. Cleveland: Psychological Corporation.

Mermelstein, H. T., & Holland, J. C. (1991). Psychotherapy by telephone: A therapeutic tool for cancer patients. *Psychosomatics, 32,* 407–412.

Messer, S. B. (2001). Introduction to the special issue on assimilative integration. *Journal of Psychotherapy Integration, 11,* 1–4.

Messer, S. B. (2004). Evidence-based practice: Beyond empirically supported treatments. *Professional Psychology: Research and Practice, 35,* 580–588.

Messer, S. B. (2008). Unification in psychotherapy: A commentary. *Journal of Psychotherapy Integration, 18,* 363–366.

Messer, S. B., & Wampold, B. E. (2002). Let's face facts: Common factors are more potent than specific therapy ingredients. *Clinical Psychology: Science and Practice, 9,* 21–25.

Meyers, R. J., Dominguez, T. P., & Smith, J. E. (1996). Community reinforcement training with families of alcoholics. In V. B. Van Hasselt & M. Hersen (Eds.), *Sourcebook of psychological treatment manuals for adult disorders* (pp. 257–294), New York: Plenum Press.

Meyer, A. J., Maccoby, M., & Farquhar, J. W. (1980). Reply to Kasl and Levethal et al. *Journal of Consulting and Clinical Psychology, 48,* 159–163.

Meyer, A. J., Nash, J. D., McAlister, A. L., Maccoby, M., & Farquhar, J. W. (1980). Skills training in a cardiovascular health education campaign. *Journal of Consulting and Clinical Psychology, 2,* 129–142.

Micallef, J., & Blin, O. (2001). Neurobiology and clinical pharmacology of obsessive-compulsive disorder. *Clinical Neuropharmacology, 24,* 191–207.

Michels, R. (1995). Dehumanizing developments in American psychiatry. *Journal of Nervous and Mental Diseases, 183,* 204–205.

Miklowitz, D. J. (2001). Bipolar disorder. In D. H. Barlow (Ed.), *Clinical handbook of psychological disorders: A step-by-step treatment manual (3rd ed., pp. 1523–561).* New York: Guilford Press.

Milberg, W., Hebben, N., & Kaplan, E. (1986). The Boston process approach to neuropsychological assessment. In I. Grant & K. M. Adams (Eds.), *Neuropsychological assessment of neuropsychiatric disorders* (pp. 65–86). New York: Oxford University Press.

Miller, J. G. (1946). Clinical psychology in the Veterans Administration. *American Psychologist, 1,* 181–189.

Miller, J. G. (1978). *Living systems.* New York: McGraw-Hill.

Miller, N. E. (1969). Learning of visceral and glandular responses. *Science, 163,* 434–445.

Miller, N. E. (1987). Education for a lifetime of learning. In G. C. Stone, S. M. Weiss, J. D. Matarazzo, N. E. Miller, J. Rodin, C. D. Belar, et al. (Eds.), *Health psychology: A discipline and a profession* (pp. 3–14). Chicago: University of Chicago Press.

Miller, T., & Swartz, L. (1990). Clinical psychology in general hospital settings: Issues in interprofessional relationships. *Professional Psychology: Research and Practice, 21,* 48–53.

Miller, T. Q., Smith, T. W., Turner, C. W., Guijarro, M. L., & Hallet, A. J. (1996). A meta-analytic review of research on hostility and physical health. *Psychological Bulletin, 119,* 322–348.

Miller V. L., & Martin A.M. (2008). The Human Genome Project: Implications for families. *Health and Social Work, 33,* 73–76.

Miller, W. R., & DiPlato, M. (1983). Treatment of nightmares via relaxation and desensitization: A controlled evaluation. *Journal of Consulting and Clinical Psychology, 51,* 870–877.

Millon, T. (1981). *Disorders of personality: DSM-III, Axis II.* New York: Wiley.

Millon, T. (1987). *Manual for the Millon Clinical Multiaxial Inventory—II.* Minneapolis, MN: NCS Assessments.

Millon, T., Antoni, M., Millon, C., Minor, S., & Grossman, S. (2001). *Manual for the Millon Behavioral Medicine Diagnostic.* Minneapolis, MN: NCS Assessments.

Millon, T., Millon, C., & Davis, R. (1982). *Manual for the Millon Adolescent Personality Inventory.* Minneapolis, MN: NCS Assessments.

Millon, T., Millon, C., Davis, R., & Grossman, S. (1993). *Manual for the Millon Adolescent Clinical Inventory.* Minneapolis, MN: NCS Assessments.

Millon, T., Millon, C., Davis, R., & Grossman, S. (2001). *Manual for the Millon Pre-Adolescent Clinical Inventory.* Minneapolis, MN: NCS Assessments.

Millon, T., Millon, C., Davis, R., & Grossman, S. (2008). *Manual for the Millon Clinical Inventory-III.* Minneapolis, MN: Pearson.

Minuchin, S. (1974). *Families and family therapy.* Cambridge, MA: Harvard University Press.

Minuchin, S., & Fishman, H. C. (1981). *Family therapy techniques.* Cambridge, MA: Harvard University Press.

Mischel, W. (1968). *Personality and assessment.* New York: Wiley.

Mischel, W. (1973). Toward a cognitive social learning reconceptualization of personality. *Psychological Review, 80,* 252–283.

Mischel, W. (1986). *Introduction to personality* (4th ed.). New York: Holt, Rinehart and Winston.

Mjoseth, J. (1998, February). New diagnostic system could benefit psychologists. *APA Monitor, 29.*

Moghaddam, F. M., & Marsella, A. J. (2004). *Understanding terrorism: Psychosocial roots, consequences, and interventions.* Washington, DC: APA Books.

Mogul, K. M. (1982). Overview: The sex of the therapist. *American Journal of Psychiatry, 139,* 1–11.

Mohr, D. C. (1995). Negative outcome in psychotherapy: A critical review. *Clinical Psychology: Science and Practice, 2,* 1–27.

Mohr, D. C., Beutler, L. E., Engle, D., Shoham-Salomon, V., Bergan, J., Kaszniak, A. W., et al. (1990). Identification of patients at risk for nonresponse and negative outcome in psychotherapy. *Journal of Consulting and Clinical Psychology, 58,* 622–628.

Moleiro, C. & Beutler, L. (2009). Clinically significant change in psychotherapy for depressive disorders. *Journal of Affective Disorders, 115,* 220–224.

Molyneaux, D., & Lane, V. (1982). *Effective interviewing: Techniques and analysis*. Boston: Allyn & Bacon.

Mora, G. (1985). History of psychiatry. In H. Kaplan & B. J. Sadock (Eds.), *Comprehensive textbook of psychiatry* (Vol. 4, pp. 1034–2054). Baltimore: Williams & Wilkins.

Moras, K. (1993). The use of treatment manuals to train psychotherapists: Observations and recommendations. *Psychotherapy, 30*, 581–586.

Morris, D., & Turnbull, P. (2007). A survey-based exploration of the impact of dyslexia on career progression of UK registered nurses. *Journal of Nursing Management, 15*, 97–106.

Morrison, T., & Morrison, M. (1995). A meta-analytic assessment of the predictive validity of the quantitative and verbal components of the Graduate Record Examination with graduate grade point average representing the criterion of graduate success. *Educational and Psychological Measurement, 55*, 309–316.

Mukherjee, D., Levin, R. L., & Heller, W. (2006). The cognitive, emotional, and social sequelae of stroke: Psychological and ethical concerns in post-stroke adaptation. *Topics in Stroke Rehabilitation, 13*, 26–35.

Mungas, D., Reed, B. R., Crane, P.K.L., Haan, M. N., & Gonzalez, H. (2004). Spanish and English Neuropsychological Assessment Scales (SENAS): Further development and psychometric characteristics. *Psychological Assessment, 16*, 347–359.

Murase, K. (1977). Minorities: Asian-American. *Encyclopedia of Social Work, 2*, 953–960.

Murphy, K. (2000, May 8). An "epidemic" of sleeplessness. *BusinessWeek*, pp. 161–162.

Murphy, M. J., Cramer, D., & Lillie, F. J. (1984). The relationship between curative factors perceived by patients in their psychotherapy and treatment outcome: An exploratory study. *British Journal of Medical Psychology, 57*, 187–192.

Murphy, M. J., DeBernardo, C. R., & Shoemaker, W. E. (1998). Impact of managed care on independent practice and professional ethics: A survey of independent practitioners. *Professional Psychology: Research and Practice, 29*, 43–51.

Murphy, R. A., & Halgin, R. P. (1995). Influences on the career choice of psychotherapists. *Professional Psychology: Research and Practice, 26*, 422–426.

Murray, H. A. (1938). *Explorations in personality*. New York: Oxford University Press.

Murray, H. A. (1943). *Thematic Appreception Test*. Cambridge, MA: Harvard University Press.

Murray, H. A., & Bellak, L. (1942). *Thematic Apperception Test*. Cambridge, MA: Harvard University Press.

Murray, J. P. (2008). Media violence: The effects are both real and strong. *American Behavioral Scientist, 51*, 1212–1230.

Murphy, L., Parnass, P., Mitchell, D. L., Hallett, R., Cayley, P. & Seagram, S. (2009). Client satisfaction and outcome comparisons of online and face-to-face counselling methods. *British Journal of Social Work, 39*, 627–640.

Myers, D. (2000). *The American paradox: Spiritual hunger in a land of plenty*. New Haven, CT: Yale University Press.

Myers, P. I., & Hammil, D. D. (1990). *Learning disabilities: Basic concepts, assessment practices, and instructional strategies* (4th ed.). Austin, TX: ProEd.

Myles, B., Bock, S., & Simpson, R. (2001). *Manual for the Asperger Syndrome Diagnostic Scale*. Austin, TX: ProEd.

Naglieri, J. A., & Bardos, A. N. (1997). *Manual for the general ability measure for adults*. Minnetonka, MN: NCS Assessments.

Nagy, T. (1987, November). Electronic ethics. *APA Monitor*, p. 3.

Nash, J. M. (2003, August 25). Obesity goes global. *Time*, pp. 53–54.

Nathan, P. E. (1993). Alcoholism: Psychopathology, etiology, and treatment. In P. B. Sutker & H. E. Adams (Eds.), *Comprehensive handbook of psychopathology* (pp. 451–476). New York: Plenum Press.

Nathan, P. E. (1996). Validated forms of psychotherapy may lead to better-validated psychotherapy. *Clinical Psychology: Science and Practice, 3*, 251–255.

Nathan, P. E., & Gorman, J. M. (2002). *A guide to treatments that work* (2nd ed.). New York: Oxford University Press.

Nathan, P. E., & Gorman, J. M. (Eds.) (2007). *A guide to treatments that work* (3rd ed.). New York: Oxford.

Nation, M., Crusto, C., Wandersman, A., Kumpfer, K. L., Seybolt, D., Morrisey-Kane, E., et al. (2003). What works in prevention: Principles of effective prevention programs. *American Psychologist, 58*, 449–456.

National Advisory Mental Health Council. (1995). Basic behavioral science research for mental health: A national investment. *American Psychologist, 50*, 485–495.

National Association of Social Workers. (2010). *NASW membership demographics*. Washington, DC: National Association of Social Workers.

National Center for Education Statistics. (1993). *1993 national study of postsecondary faculty*. Washington, DC: Author.

National Center for Health Statistics. (1992). *Vital statistics of the United States, 1992*. Washington, DC: Government Printing Office.

National Center for Health Statistics. (1993). *Health U.S. 1992*. Hyattsville, MD: U.S. Public Health Service.

National Center for Health Statistics. (1996). *Health, United States, 1995*. Hyattsville, MD: U.S. Public Health Service.

National Center for Health Statistics. (1999). *Healthy People 2000 Review 1998–99*. Hyattsville, MD: U.S. Public Health Service.

National Center for Health Statistics. (2001). Health expenditures. Retrieved July 5, 2009, from http://www.cfc.gov/nchs/fastats/hexpense.htm.

National Center for Health Statistics. (2002). *Health United States, 2002, with urban and rural health chartbook*. Hyattsville, MD: Author.

National Center for Health Statistics. (2006). *Health, United States, 2006, with chartbook on trends in the health of Americans*. Hyattsville, MD: Author.

National Committee for Quality Assurance (2009). *HEDIS: Healthcare effectiveness data and information set*. Washington, DC: Author.

National Institute for Health and Clinical Excellence. (2007). *Depression: Management of depression in primary and secondary care. Quick reference guide (amended)*. London: Author.

National Institute on Alcohol Abuse and Alcoholism. (2000). 10th special report to the U.S. Congress on alcohol and health. Retrieved November 6, 2009, from http://silk.nih.gov/silk/niaaa1 /publication/10report/10-order.htm.

National Institute on Alcohol Abuse and Alcoholism. (2004). Estimated economic coats of alcohol abuse in the United States, 1992 and 1998. Retrieved October 11, 2009, from http://www.niaaa.nih.gov/resources/databaseresources/quickfacts/economic data/cost8.htm.

National Institute of Allergy and Infectious Diseases. (1999, December). HIV/AIDS statistics, NIAID FACT sheet. Retrieved November 6, 2009, from http://www.niaid.nih.gov/factsheets /aidsstat.htm.

National Institutes of Health. (1992). *Methods for voluntary weight loss and control* [Technology Assessment Conference Statement, March 30–April 1, 1992]. Bethesda, MD: National Institutes of Health.

National Institutes of Health. (2004). *Research funding: Grant application and review and funding policies*. Washington, DC: Author.

National Mental Health Association. (1986). *The prevention of mental-emotional disabilities: Report of the commission on prevention*. Alexandria, VA: Author.

National Organization on Disability. (1998). *Americans with disabilities still face sharp gaps in securing jobs, education, transportation, and in many areas of daily life* (Louis Harris Survey). Washington, DC: Author.

National Organization on Disability. (2009). Mission statement. Retrieved October 12, 2009, http://www.nod.org/index.cfm?fuseaction=Page.ViewPage&PageID=1580.

National Science Foundation. (1994). *Women, minorities, and persons with disabilities in science and engineering: 1994*(NSF 94-333). Arlington, VA: Author.

National Television Violence Study. (Vol. 3). (1998). Santa Barbara: University of California, Center for Communication and Social Policy.

Ndetei, D. M., & Singh, A. (1983). Hallucinations in Kenyan schizophrenic patients. *Acta Psychiatrica Scandinavica, 67*, 144–147.

Neisser, U., Boodoo, G., Bouchard, T. J., Boykin, A. W., Ceci, S. J., Halpern, D. F., et al. (1996). Intelligence: Knowns and unknowns. *American Psychologist, 51*, 77–101.

Nelson, G., Lord, J., & Ochocka, J. (2001). *Shifting the paradigm in community mental health: Towards empowerment and community*. Toronto, Ontario, Canada: University of Toronto Press.

Nemeroff, C. B., & Schatzberg, A. F. (2007). Pharmacological treatments for unipolar depression. In P. E. Nathan and J. M. Gorman (Eds.), *A guide to treatments that work* (3rd ed., pp. 271–288). New York: Oxford.

Newcombe, F. (1996). Very late outcome after focal wartime brain wounds. *Journal of Clinical and Experimental Neuropsychology, 18*, 1–23.

Newman, M. G., & Borkovec, T. D. (1995). Cognitive-behavioral treatment for generalized anxiety disorder. *Clinical Psychologist, 48*, 5–7.

Newman, R., & Taylor, G. (1996, June). Practitioner survey results offer comprehensive view of psychology practice. *Practitioner Update, 4*, 1–4.

Nezu, A. M. (1996). What are we doing to our patients and should we care if anyone else knows? *Clinical Psychology: Science and Practice, 3,* 160–163.

Ngo, K. (2009, January 12). How many people die from cancer each year? Retrieved September 10, 2009, from http://ezinearticles.com/?How-Many -People-Die-From-Cancer-Each-Year?&id=187 2925.

Nguyen, T. D., Attkisson, C. C., & Stegner, B. L. (1983). Assessment of patient satisfaction: Development and refinement of a Service Evaluation Questionnaire. *Evaluation and Program Planning, 6,* 299–313.

Nicholls, D., & Viner, R. (2009). Childhood risk factors for lifetime anorexia nervosa by age 30 years in a national birth cohort. *Journal of the American Academy of Child & Adolescent Psychiatry, 48,* 791–799.

Nicholson, H., Foote, C., & Grigerick, S. (2009). Deleterious effects of psychotherapy and counseling in the schools. *Psychology in the Schools, 46,* 232–237.

Nicholson, R. A., & Berman, J. S. (1983). Is follow-up necessary in evaluating psychotherapy? *Psychological Bulletin, 93,* 261–278.

Nickelson, D. W. (1995). The future of professional psychology in a changing health care marketplace: A conversation with Russ Newman. *Professional Psychology: Research and Practice, 26,* 366–370.

Nietzel, M. T., Berstein, D. A., & Milich, R. (1991). *Introduction to clinical psychology* (3rd ed.). Englewood Cliffs, NJ: Prentice-Hall.

Nietzel, M. T., Russell, R. L., Hemmings, K. A., & Gretter, M. L. (1987). Clinical significance of psychotherapy for unipolar depression: A meta-analytic approach to social comparison. *Journal of Consulting and Clinical Psychology, 55,* 156–161.

Nolen-Hoeksema, S. (2002). Gender differences in depression. In I. H. Gotlib & C. L. Hammen (Eds.), *Handbook of depression* (pp. 492–509). New York: Guilford Press.

Nolen-Hoeksema, S., & Hilt, L. (2008). Gender differences in depression. In I. H. Gotlib & C. L. Hammen (Eds.), *Handbook of depression* (2nd ed., pp. 386–404). New York: Guilford Press.

Nolen-Hoeksema, S., & Puryear Keita, G. (2003). Women and depression: Introduction. *Psychology of Women Quarterly, 27,* 89–90.

Norcross, J. C. (1990). An eclectic definition of psychotherapy. In J. K. Zeig & W. M. Munion (Eds.), *What is psychotherapy? Contemporary perspectives* (pp. 218–220). San Francisco, CA: Jossey-Bass.

Norcross, J. C. (1995). Dispelling the DoDo bird verdict and exclusivity myth in psychotherapy. *Psychotherapy, 32,* 500–504.

Norcross, J. C. (2001). Purposes, processes and products of the task force on empirically supported therapy relationships. *Psychotherapy: Theory, Research, Practice, Training. 38,* 345–356.

Norcross, J. C. (2002). *Psychotherapy relationships that work: Therapist contributions and responsiveness to patients.* London: Oxford University Press.

Norcross, J. C. (2009). The Integration of science and practice: The case of division 12 and PsyD psychologists. *The Clinical psychologist, 62,* 1–4.

Norcross, J. C., Beutler, L. E., & Levant R. (Eds.), (2006). *Evidence-based practice in mental health.* Washington, DC: American Psychological Association.

Norcross, J. C., & Goldfried, M. R. (Eds.). (1992). *Handbook of psychotherapy integration.* New York: Basic Books.

Norcross, J. C., & Goldfried, M. R. (Eds.). (2005). *Handbook of psychotherapy integration* (2nd ed.). New York: Oxford University Press.

Norcross, J. C., & Guy, J. D. (1989). Ten therapists: The process of becoming and being. In W. Dryden & L. Spurling (Eds.), *On becoming a psychotherapist* (pp. 215–239). London: Tavistock/Routledge.

Norcross, J. C., Hanych, J. M., & Terranova, R. D. (1996). Graduate study in psychology: 1992–1993. *American Psychologist, 51,* 631–643.

Norcross, J. C., Hedges, M., & Castle, P. H. (2002). Psychologists conducting psychotherapy in 2001: A study of the division 29 membership. *Psychotherapy: Theory, Research, Practice, Training, 39,* 97–102.

Norcross, J. C., Karg, R. S., & Prochaska, J. O. (1997a). Clinical psychologists in the 1990's: Part I. *Clinical Psychologist, 50,* 4–9.

Norcross, J. C., Karg, R. S., & Prochaska, J. O. (1997b). Clinical psychologists in the 1990's: Part II. *Clinical Psychologist, 50,* 4–11.

Norcross, J. C., Karpiak, C. P., & Santoro, S. M. (2005). Clinical psychologists across the years: The division of clinical psychology from 1960 to 2003. *Journal of Clinical Psychology, 61,* 1467–1483.

Norcross, J. C., & Prochaska, J. O. (1988). A study of eclectic (and integrative) views revisited. *Professional Psychology: Research and Practice, 19,* 170–174.

Norcross, J. C., Prochaska, J. O., & Gallagher, K. M. (1989). Clinical psychologists in the

1980s: I. Demographics, affiliations, and satisfactions. *Clinical Psychologist, 42*, 29–39.

Norcross, J. C., Sayette, M. A., & Mayne, T. J. (2002). *Insider's guide to graduate programs in clinical psychology: 2002/2003 edition.* New York: Guilford Press.

Norcross, J. C., Sayette, M. A., & Mayne, T. J. (2008). *Insider's guide to graduate programs in clinical psychology: 2008/2009 edition.* New York: Guilford Press.

Norcross, J. C., Strausser-Kirtland, D., & Missar, C. D. (1988). The processes and outcomes of psychotherapists' personal treatment experiences. *Psychotherapy, 25*, 36–43.

Nurnberger, J. I., & Gershon, E. S. (1992). Genetics. In E. S. Paykel (Ed.), *Handbook of affective disorders* (pp. 126–145). New York: Guilford Press.

Nuttall, J. (2002). Imperatives and perspectives of psychotherapy integration. *International Journal of Psychotherapy, 7*, 249–264.

O'Brien, M., & Houston, G. (2000). *Integrative therapy: A practitioner's guide.* Thousand Oaks, CA: Sage.

Ockene, J. K. (Ed.). (1986). *The pharmacologic treatment of tobacco dependence: Proceedings of the World Congress, November 4–5, 1985.* Cambridge, MA: Harvard University, Institute for the Study of Smoking Behavior and Policy.

Ockene, J. K., Emmoms, K. M., Mermelstein, R. J., Perkins, K. A., Bonollo, D. S., Voorhees, C. C., et al. (2000). Relapse and maintenance issues for smoking cessation. *Health Psychology, 19*, 17–31.

O'Connor, K. J. (2000). *The play therapy primer.* New York: Wiley.

Ogles, B. M., Lambert, M. J., & Sawyer, J. D. (1995). Clinical significance of the National Institute of Mental Health Treatment of Depression Collaborative Research Program data. *Journal of Consulting and Clinical Psychology, 63*, 321–326.

O'Leary, A. (1992). Self-efficacy and health: Behavioral and stress-physiological mediation. *Cognitive Therapy and Research, 16*, 229–245.

O'Leary, K. D., & Becker, W. C. (1967). Behavior modification of an adjustment class: A token reinforcement program. *Exceptional Children, 33*, 637–642.

O'Leary, K. D., & Wilson, G. T. (1987). *Behavior therapy: Application and outcome.* Englewood Cliffs, NJ: Prentice-Hall.

Olson, S. K., Downing, N. E., Heppner, P. P., & Pinkney, J. (1986). Is there life after graduate school? Coping with the transition to postdoctoral employment. *Professional Psychology: Research and Practice, 17*, 415–419.

Orlinsky, D. E., & Howard, K. I. (1986). Process and outcome in psychotherapy. In A. E. Bergin & S. L. Garfield (Eds.), *Handbook of psychotherapy and behavior change* (3rd ed., pp. 283–330). New York: Wiley.

Ornberg, B., & Zalewski, C. (1994). Assessment of adolescents with the Rorschach: A critical review. *Assessment, 1*, 209–217.

OSS Assessment Staff. (1948). *Assessment of men: Selection of personnel for the office of strategic services.* New York: Rinehart.

Otero, S. (2009). Psychopathology and psychological adjustment in children and adolescents with epilepsy. *World Journal of Pediatrics, 5*, 12–17.

Otto, M. W. & Reilly-Harrington, N. (2002). Cognitive-behavioral therapy for the management of bipolar disorder. In S. G. Hofmann & M. C. Tompson (Eds.), *Treating chronic and severe mental disorders: A handbook of empirically supported interventions,* (pp. 116–130). New York: Guilford Press.

Otto, R. K., & Heilbrun, K. (2002). The practice of forensic psychology: A look toward the future in the light of the past. *American Psychologist, 57*, 5–19.

Overall, J. E., & Pfefferbaum, B. (1962). The Brief Psychiatric Rating Scale for Children. *Psychopharmacology Bulletin, 18*, 10–16.

Padesky, C. A., & Greenberger, D. (1995). *The clinician's guide to mind over mood.* New York: Guilford Press.

Pandina, R. J. (1986). Methods, problems, and trends in studies of adolescent drinking practices. *Annals of Behavioral Medicine, 8*, 20–26.

Paolantonio, P. (1990). *Relapse prevention training manual.* Unpublished manuscript.

Papolos, D., & Papolos, J. (1999). *The bipolar child.* New York: Broadway Books.

Papolos, D., & Papolos, J. (2002). *The bipolar child* (2nd ed.). New York: Broadway Books.

Papolos, D., & Papolos, J. (2006). *The bipolar child* (3rd ed.). New York: Broadway Books.

Pargament, K. I., Falgout, K., Ensing, D. S., Reilly, B., Silverman, M., Van Haitsma, K., et al. (1991). The congregation development program: Data-based consultation with churches and synagogues. *Professional Psychology: Research and Practice, 22*, 393–404.

Parker, K. C. H. (1983). A meta-analysis of the reliability and validity of the Rorschach. *Journal of Personality Assessment, 47*, 227–231.

Parker, K. C. H., Hanson, R. K., & Hunsley, J. (1988). MMPI, Rorschach, and WAIS: A meta-analytic comparison of reliability, stability, and validity. *Psychological Bulletin, 103*, 367–373.

Pate, W. (2004). Survey reveals employment trends for medical school psychologists. *Monitor on Psychology, 35*, 11.

Patterson, G. R. (1977). Naturalistic observation in clinical assessment. *Journal of Abnormal Child Psychology, 5*, 307–322.

Pavuluri, M. N., Birmaher, B., & Naylor, M. W. (2005). Pediatric bipolar disorder: A review of the past 10 years. *Journal of the American Academy of Child & Adolescent Psychiatry, 44*, 846–871.

Payton, C. R. (1994). Implications of the 1992 Ethics Code for diverse groups. *Professional Psychology: Research and Practice, 25*, 317–320.

Peck, C. P., & Ash, E. (1964). Training in the Veterans Administration. In L. Blank & H. P. David (Eds.), *Sourcebook for training in clinical psychology* (pp. 61–81). New York: Springer.

Pelham, W. E. (1993). Pharmacotherapy for children with attention-deficit hyperactivity disorder. *School Psychology Review, 22*, 199–227.

Peltier, B. (2010). *The psychology of executive coaching: Theory and application* (2nd ed.). New York: Routledge.

Pennebaker, J. W. (1990). *Opening up: The healing power of confidence in others.* New York: Morrow.

Pennington, B. F., & Smith, S. D. (1988). Genetic influences on learning disabilities: An update. *Journal of Consulting and Clinical Psychology, 56*, 817–823.

Perls, F. S. (1947). *Ego, hunger and aggression: A revision of Freud's theory and method.* New York: Random House.

Perls, F. S. (1969). *Gestalt therapy verbatim.* Lafayette, CA: Real People Press.

Perucca, P., Gilliam, F. G., & Schmitz, B. (2009). Epilepsy treatment as a predeterminant of psychosocial ill health. *Epilepsy & Behavior, 15*, S46–S50.

Petegnief, V., Saura, J., De Gregorio-Rocasolano, N., & Paul, S. M. (2001). Neuronal injury-induced expression and release of apolipoprotein E in mixed neuron/GLIA co-cultures: Nuclear factor KB inhibitors reduce basal and lesion-induced secretion of apoplipoprotein E. *Neuroscience, 104*, 223–234.

Peterson, D. R. (1968). The doctor of psychology program at the University of Illinois. *American Psychologist, 23*, 511–516.

Peterson, D. R. (2003). Unintended consequences: Ventures and misadventures in the education of professional psychologists. *American Psychologist, 58*, 791–800.

Peterson, D. R., & Baron, A. (1975). Status of the University of Illinois doctor of psychology program, 1974. *Professional Psychology, 6*, 88–95.

Phelps, R. (1996, February). Preliminary practitioner survey results enhance APA's understanding of health care environment. *Practitioner Focus, 9*, 5.

Phelps, R., Eisman, E. J., & Kohout, J. (1998). Psychological practice and managed care: Results of the CAPP practitioner survey. *Professional Psychology: Research and Practice, 29*, 31–36.

Phillips, E. L., & Fagan, P. J. (1982, August). *Attrition: Focus on the intake and first therapy interviews.* Paper presented at the 90th annual convention of the American Psychological Association, Washington, DC.

Piaget, J. (1952). *The origins of intelligence in children.* New York: International Universities Press.

Piaget, J. (1970). *Science of education and the psychology of the child.* New York: Orion.

Piaget, J. (1972). Intellectual evolution from adolescence to adulthood. *Human Development, 15*, 1–12.

Pike, K. M., & Rodin, J. (1991). Mothers, daughters, and disordered eating. *Journal of Abnormal Psychology, 100*, 1–7.

Pilkonis, P. A., Imber, S. D., Lewis, P., & Rubinsky, P. (1984). A comparative outcome study of individual, group, and cojoint psychotherapy. *Archives of General Psychiatry, 41*, 431–437.

Pillay, A. L. (1990). The increasing demand for clinical psychological consultations in the smaller general hospital. *South African Journal of Psychology, 20*, 163–169.

Pimental, P. A., Stout, C. E., Hoover, M. C., & Kamen, G. B. (1997). Changing psychologists opinions about prescriptive authority: A little information goes a long way. *Professional Psychology: Research and Practice, 28*, 123–127.

Pinker, S. (2003). *The blank slate: The modern denial of human nature.* New York: Penguin Books.

Pion, G. M., Mednick, M. T., Astin, H. S., Hall, C. C. I., Kenkel, M. B., Keita, G. P., et al. (1996). The shifting gender composition of psychology: Trends and implications for the discipline. *American Psychologist, 51*, 509–528.

Piotrowski, C., & Keller, J. W. (1989). Psychological testing in outpatient mental health facilities: A national study. *Professional Psychology: Research and Practice, 20*, 423–425.

Piper, W. E., Rosie, J. S., Joyce, A. S., & Azim, H. F. A. (1996). *Time-limited day treatment for personality disorders: Integration of research and practice in a group program.* Washington, DC: American Psychological Association.

Plante, T. G. (1988). Postdoctoral training in clinical psychology: As amorphous as an inkblot. *Professional Psychology: Research and Practice, 19*, 251–253.

Plante, T. G. (1995). Training child clinical predoctoral interns and postdoctoral fellows in ethics and professional issues: An experiential model. *Professional Psychology: Research and Practice, 26*, 616–619.

Plante, T. G. (1996a). Catholic priests who sexually abuse minors: Why do we hear so much yet know so little? *Pastoral Psychology, 44*, 305–310.

Plante, T. G. (1996b). Ten principles of success for psychology trainees embarking on their careers. *Professional Psychology: Research and Practice, 27*, 304–307.

Plante, T. G. (1999). A collaborative relationship between professional psychology and the Roman Catholic Church: A case example and suggested principles for success. *Professional Psychology: Research and Practice, 30*, 541–546.

Plante, T. G. (2004a). *Do the right thing: Living ethically in an unethical world.* Oakland, CA: New Harbinger.

Plante, T. G. (2004b). *Sin against the innocents: Sexual abuse by priests and the role of the Catholic Church.* Westport, CT: Praeger.

Plante, T. G. (2009). *Spiritual practices in psychotherapy: Thirteen tools for enhancing psychological health.* Washington, DC: American Psychological Association.

Plante, T. G., Aldridge, A., Bogden, R., & Hanelin, C. (2003a). Might virtual reality promote the mood benefits of exercise? *Computers in Human Behavior, 19*, 495–509.

Plante, T. G., Aldridge, A., Su, D., Bogden, R., Khan, K., & Belo, M. (2003b). Mood improvements associated with virtual exercise. *International Journal of Stress Management*, 203–216.

Plante, T. G., Boccaccini, M., & Andersen, E. (1998). Attitudes concerning professional issues impacting psychotherapy practice among members of the American Board of Professional Psychology. *Psychotherapy, 35*, 34–42.

Plante, T. G., Couchman, C., & Diaz, A. (1995). Measuring mental health treatment outcome and client satisfaction among children and families. *Journal of Mental Health Administration, 22*, 261–269.

Plante, T. G., Couchman, C., & Hoffman, C. (1998). Measuring treatment outcome and client satisfaction among children and families: A case report. *Professional Psychology: Research and Practice, 29*, 52–55.

Plante, T. G., Goldfarb, L. P., & Wadley, V. (1993). Are stress and coping associated with aptitude and achievement testing performance among children? A preliminary investigation. *Journal of School Psychology, 31*, 259–266.

Plante, T. G., Lantis, A., & Checa, G. (1997). The influence of gender, hypertension risk, and aerobic fitness on cardiovascular responses to laboratory induced stress. *International Journal of Stress Management, 4*, 89–99.

Plante, T. G., Manual, G. M., & Bryant, C. (1996). Defensiveness and cognitive functioning among sexual offending Roman Catholic priests. *Pastoral Psychology, 45*, 129–139.

Plante, T. G., Pinder, S. L., & Howe, D. (1988). Introducing the living with illness group: A specialized treatment for patients with chronic schizophrenic conditions. *Group, 12*, 198–204.

Plante, T. G., & Sherman, A. S. (Eds.). (2001). *Faith and health: Psychological perspectives.* New York: Guilford Press.

Plante, T. G., & Sykora, C. (1994). Are stress and coping associated with WISC-III performance among children? *Journal of Clinical Psychology, 50*, 759–762.

Plante, T. G., & Thoresen, C. E. (Eds.) (2007). *Spirit, science and health: How the spiritual mind fuels physical wellness.* Westport, CT: Praeger/Greenwood.

Plaud, J. J., & Gaither, G. A. (1996). Behavioral momentum: Implications and development from reinforcement theories. *Behavior Modification, 20*, 183–201.

Plomin, R. (1990). The role of inheritance in behavior. *Science, 248*, 183–188.

Plomin, R., & Crabbe, J. (2000). DNA. *Psychological Bulletin, 126*, 806–828.

Plomin, R., DeFries, J. C., McClearn, G. E., & McGuffin, P. (2008). *Behavioral genetics.* NY: Worth.

Polivy, J., & Herman, C. P. (2002). Causes of eating disorders. *Annual Review of Psychology, 53*, 187–213.

Pomerleau, O. F., & Pomerleau, C. S. (1977). *Break the smoking habit.* Champaign, IL: Research Press.

Pomerleau, O. F., & Pomerleau, C. S. (Eds.). (1988). *Nicotine replacement: A critical evaluation*. New York: Alan, R. Liss.

Popanz, T. (1991). *Graduate training in psychopharmacology, substance abuse, and basic science: 1980–1990*. Washington, DC: American Psychological Association.

Pope, K. S. (1991). Ethical and legal issues in clinical practice. In M. Hersen, A. E. Kazdin, & A. S. Bellack (Eds.), *The clinical psychology handbook* (2nd ed., pp. 115–127). New York: Pergamon Press.

Pope, K. S. (1994). *Sexual involvement with therapists: Patient assessment, subsequent therapy, forensics*. Washington, DC: American Psychological Association.

Pope, K. S. (1998). Sexual feelings, actions, and dilemmas in psychotherapy. In G. P. Koocher, J. C. Norcross, & S. S. Hill, III (Eds.), *Psychologists' desk reference* (pp. 450–456). New York: Oxford University Press.

Pope, K. S. (2007). *Ethics in psychotherapy and counseling: A practical guide*. San Francisco: Jossey-Bass.

Pope, K. S., & Bajt, T. R. (1988). When laws and values conflict: A dilemma for psychologists. *American Psychologist, 43*, 828.

Pope, K. S., Keith-Spiegel, P., & Tabachnick, B. G. (1986). Sexual attraction to clients: The human therapist and the (sometimes) inhuman training system. *American Psychologist, 41*, 147–158.

Pope, K. S., Tabachnick, B. G., & Keith-Spiegel, P. (1987). Ethics of practice: The beliefs and behaviors of psychologists as therapists. *American Psychologist, 42*, 993–1006.

Pope, K. S., Vasquez, M. J. T. (2005). How to survive and thrive as a therapist: Information, ideas, and resources for psychologists in practice. Washington, DC: American Psychological Association.

Pope, K. S., & Vetter, V. A. (1992). Ethical dilemmas encountered by members of the APA: A national survey. *American Psychologist, 47*, 397–411.

Posner, M. I., & Rothbart, M. K. (2007). Temperament and learning. In M. I. Posner & M. K. Rothbart (Eds.). *Educating the human brain* (pp. 121–146). Washington, DC: American Psychological Association.

Post, J (2007). *The mind of the terrorist: The psychology of terrorism from the IRA to Al-Qaeda*. New York: Palgrave Macmillan.

Powers, M. B., & Emmelkamp, P. M. G. (2008). Virtual reality exposure therapy for anxiety disorders: A meta-analysis. *Journal of Anxiety Disorders, 22*, 561–569.

Powers, T. J., Shapiro, E. S., & DuPaul, G. J. (2003). Preparing psychologists to link systems of care in managing and preventing children's health problems. *Journal of Pediatric Psychology, 28*, 147–156.

Pratt, S. & Mueser, K. T. (2002). Social skills training for schizophrenia. In S. G. Hofmann & M. C. Tompson (Eds.), *Treating chronic and severe mental disorders: A handbook of empirically supported interventions*, (pp. 18–52). New York: Guilford Press.

Presley, C. A., & Meilman, P. W. (1992). *Alcohol and drugs on American college campuses: A report to college presidents*. Carbondale: Southern Illinois University Press.

Price, R. A. (1987). Genetics of human obesity. *Annals of Behavioral Medicine, 9*, 9–14.

Prochaska, J. O. (1984). *Systems of psychotherapy: A transtheoretical analysis* (2nd ed.). Homewood, IL: Dorsey.

Prochaska, J. O. (1995). Common problems: Common solutions. *Clinical Psychology: Science and Practice, 2*, 101–105.

Prochaska, J. O. (2000). Change at differing stages. In C. R. Snyder & R. E. Ingram (Eds.), *Handbook of psychological change: Psychotherapy processes and practices for the 21st century* (pp. 109–127). New York: Wiley.

Prochaska, J. O. (2008). Decision making in the transtheoretical model of behavior change. *Medical Decision Making, 28*, 845–849.

Prochaska, J. O., & Norcross, J. C. (2002). Stages of change. In J. C. Norcross (Ed.), *Psychotherapy relationships that work: Therapist contributions and responsiveness to patients* (pp. 303–313). London: Oxford University Press.

Prochaska, J. O., & Norcross, J. C. (2007). *Systems of psychotherapy: A transtheoretical analysis* (6th ed.). Belmont, CA: Brooks/Cole.

Prochaska, J. O., Velicer, W. F., DiClemente, C. C., & Fava, J. (1988). Measuring processes of change: Applications to the cessation of smoking. *Journal of Consulting and Clinical Psychology, 56*, 520–528.

Pyszczynski, T., Solomon, S., & Greenberg, J. (2003). *In the wake of 9/11: The psychology of terror*. Washington, DC: APA Books.

Rabasca, L. (1999). The role of psychologist at U.S. medical schools is being marginalized, study finds. *APA Monitor on Psychology 30*, 12–13.

Rabin, A. S., Kaslow, N. J., & Rehm, L. P. (1985). Factors influencing continuation in a behavioral therapy. *Behaviour Research and Therapy, 23,* 695–698.

Rachman, S. J., & Wilson, G. T. (1980). *The effects of psychological therapy* (2nd ed.). New York: Pergamon Press.

Raimy, V. C. (Ed.). (1950). *Training in clinical psychology.* New York: Prentice-Hall.

Rappoport, A. (2002). How psychotherapy works: The concepts of control-mastery theory. *Bulletin of the American Academy of Clinical Psychology, 8,* 10–14.

Raven, J. C. (1993). *Raven's progressive matrices.* Enberg, England: Author.

Raven, J., Raven, J. C., & Court, J. H. (2003). *Manual for Raven's Progressive Matrices and Vocabulary Scales. Section 1: General Overview.* San Antonio, TX: Harcourt Assessment.

Raymer, R., & Poppen, R. (1985). Behavioral relaxation training with hyperactive children. *Journal of Behavior Therapy and Experimental Psychiatry, 16,* 309–316.

Read, J. B., Larsen, C., & Robinson, C. J. (2009). Emerging models of psychological treatment: The path to prescriptive authority. *Journal of Contemporary Psychotherapy, 39,* 121–126.

Redmond, W. H. (1999). Trends in adolescent cigarette use: The diffusion of daily smoking. *Journal of Behavioral Medicine, 22,* 379–395.

Reed, T. E., & Jensen, A. R. (1991). Arm nerve conduction velocity (NCV), brain NCV, reaction time, and intelligence. *Intelligence, 15,* 33–47.

Regier, D. A., Myers, J. K., Kramer, M., Robins, L. N., Blazer, D. G., Hough, R. L., et al. (1984). The NIMH epidemiologic catchment area program. *Archives of General Psychiatry, 41,* 934–941.

Rehm, L. P. (1997). Continuing education for empirically supported treatments. *Clinical Psychologist, 50,* 2–3.

Reiman, E. M., Fusselman, M. J., Fox, P. T., & Raichle, M. E. (1989). Neuroanatomical correlates of anticipatory anxiety. *Science, 243,* 1071–1074.

Reisman, J. M. (1976). *A history of clinical psychology.* New York: Irvington.

Reisner, A. D. (2003). The electroconvulsive therapy controversy: Evidence and ethics. *Neuropsychology Review, 13,* 199–219.

Reitan, R. M., & Davison, L. A. (1974). *Clinical neuropsychology: Current status and applications* (pp. 19–46). Washington, DC: V. H. Winston & Sons.

Rende, R., & Plomin, R. (1992). Diathesis-stress models of psychopathology: A quantitative genetic perspective. *Applied & Preventive Psychology, 1,* 177–182.

Renzetti, C. M. (2008). Violence against women: Prevention, relationships, and coping behavior. *Violence Against Women, 14,* 867–869.

Report of the INS—Division 40 Task Force on Education, Accreditation, and Credentialing. (1987). *Clinical Neuropsychologist, 1,* 29–34.

Resick, P. A. & Calhoun, K. S. (2001). Posttraumatic stress disorder. In D. H. Barlow (Ed.), *Clinical handbook of psychological disorders: A step-by-step treatment manual (3rd ed., pp. 123–178).* New York: Guilford Press.

Resnick, R. J., & DeLeon, P. H. (1995). The future of health care reform: Implications of 1994 elections. *Professional Psychology: Research and Practice, 26,* 3–4.

Resnick, R. J., & Norcross, J. C. (2002). Prescription privileges for psychologists: Scared to death? *Clinical Psychologist: Science and Practice, 9,* 270–274.

Reynolds, C. R. (1982). The problem of bias in psychological assessment. In C. R. Reynolds & T. B. Gutkin (Eds.), *A handbook for school psychology* (pp. 178–208). New York: Wiley.

Reynolds, W. M. (2002). Childhood depression. In M. Hersen (Ed.). *Clinical behavior therapy: Adults and children* (pp. 256–275). New York: John Wiley.

Rice, C. E. (1997). Scenarios: The scientist-practitioner split and the future of psychology. *American Psychologist, 52,* 1173–1181.

Riggs, D. S., & Foa, E. B. (1993). Obsessive-compulsive disorder. In D. H. Barlow (Ed.), *Clinical handbook of psychological disorders* (2nd ed.). New York: Guilford Press.

Riley, K. P., Snowdon, D. A., Saunders, A. M., Roses, A. D., Mortimer, J. A., & Nanayakkara, N. (2000). Cognitive function and apolipoprotein in very old adults: Findings from the Nun Study. *Journal of Gerontology, 55B,* S69–S75.

Risch, N., Herrell, R., Lehner, T., Liang, K. Y., Eaves, L., Hoh, J., Griem, A., Kovacs, M., Ott, J., & Merikangas, J. R. (2009). Interaction between the serotonin transporter gene (*5-HTTLPR*), stressful life events, and risk of depression: A meta-analysis. *Journal of the American Medical Association, 301,* 2462–2471.

Ritterband, L. M., Gonder-Frederick, L. A., Cox, D. J., Clifton, A. D., West, R. W., & Borowitz, S. M. (2003). Internet interventions. In review, in use, and into the future. *Professional Psychology: Research and Practice, 34,* 527–534.

Riva, M. T., & Cornish, J. A. E. (1995). Group supervision practices at psychology predoctoral internship programs: A national survey. *Professional Psychology: Research and Practice, 26,* 523–525.

Rivas-Vazquez, R. A., Rice, J., & Kalman, D. (2003). Pharmacotherapy of obesity and eating disorders. *Professional Psychology: Research and Practice, 34,* 562–566.

Roach, C. N. & Gross, A. M. (2002). Conduct disorder. In M. Hersen (Ed.), *Clinical behavior therapy: Adults and children* (pp. 383–399). New York: Wiley.

Roan, S. (1992, November 24). Calling for help. *Los Angeles Times,* pp. E1, E6.

Robins, L. N., Helzer, J. E., Croughan, J., & Ratcliff, K. S. (1994). The National Institute of Mental Health Diagnostic Interview Schedule. In J. E. Mezzich, M. R. Jorge, & I. M. Salloum (Eds.), *Psychiatric epidemiology: Assessment concepts and methods* (pp. 227–248). Baltimore: Johns Hopkins University Press.

Roberts, G. E. (2005). *The Robert's Apperception test for Children* (2nd ed.). Los Angeles: Western Psychological Services.

Roberts, M. C., & Steele, R. G. (2009). *Handbook of pediatric psychology* (4th ed.). New York: Guilford Press.

Rodenburg, R., Benjamin, A., de Roos, C., Meijer, A. M., & Stams, G. J. (2009). Efficacy of EMDR in children: A meta-analysis. *Clinical Psychology Review, 29,* 599–606.

Rodnick, E. H. (1985). Clinical psychology. In H. I. Kaplan & B. J. Sadock. *Comprehensive textbook of psychiatry* (4th ed., pp. 1929–1935). Baltimore: Williams & Wilkins.

Rodolfa, E., Hall, T., Holms, V., Davena, A., Komatz, D., Antunez, M., et al. (1994). The management of sexual feelings in therapy. *Professional Psychology: Research and Practice, 25,* 168–172.

Rodrigue, J. R. (1994). Beyond the individual child: Innovative systems approaches to service delivery in pediatric psychology. *Journal of Child Clinical Psychology, 23,* 32–39.

Roe, A., Gustad, J. W., Moore, B. V., Ross, S., & Skodak, M. (Eds.). (1959). *Graduate education in psychology.* Washington, DC: American Psychological Association.

Rogers, C. R. (1951). *Client-centered therapy.* Boston: Houghton Mifflin.

Rogers, C. R. (1954). *Psychotherapy and personality change.* Chicago: University of Chicago Press.

Rogers, C. R. (1961). *On becoming a person.* Boston: Houghton Mifflin.

Rogler, L. H. (1999). Methodological sources of cultural insensitivity in mental health research. *American Psychologist, 54,* 424–433.

Roid, G.H. (2003). Stanford Binet Intelligence Scales 5th Edition: Examiner's Manual. Riverside Publishing, Itaska, Illinois

Romans, J. S. C., Boswell, D. L., Carlozzi, A. F., & Ferguson, D. B. (1995). Training and supervision practices in clinical, counseling, and school psychology programs. *Professional Psychology: Research and Practice, 26,* 407–412.

Rorschach, H. (1942). *Psychodiagnostics: A diagnostic test based on perception.* New York: Grune & Stratton. (Original work published 1921.)

Rorschach, H. (1951). *Rorschach technique.* New York: Grune & Stratton.

Rorschach, H. (1998). *Psychodiagnostics: A diagnostic test based on perception* (10th ed.). Cambridge, MA: Hogrefe.

Rosenberg, S., Hickie, I. B., & Mendoza, J. (2009). National mental health reform: Less talk, more action. *The Medical Journal of Australia, 190,* 193–195.

Rosenhan, D. L., & Seligman, M. E. (1989). *Abnormal psychology* (2nd ed.). New York: Norton.

Rosenthal, R. (1987). Pygmalion effects: Existence, magnitude, and social importance. *Educational Researcher, 16,* 37–41.

Rosowsky, E., Casciani, J. M., & Arnold, M. (Eds.) (2009). *Geropsychology and long term care: A practitioner's guide.* New York: Springer.

Rosselló & Bernal (1996). Adapting cognitive-behavioral and interpersonal treatments for depressed Puerto Rican adolescents. In E. Hibbs & P. Jensen (Eds.), *Psychosocial treatments for children and adolescent disorders: Empirically based approaches* (pp. 187–218). Washington, DC, USA: American Psychological Association.

Roth, M. (1996). The panic-agoraphobic syndrome: A paradigm of the activity group of disorders and its implications for psychiatric practice and theory. *American Journal of Psychiatry, 153,* 111–124.

Roth, A., & Fonagy, P. (2005). *What works for whom? A critical review of psychotherapy research* (2nd ed.). New York: Guilford Press.

Rotherman-Borus, M. J., Goldstein, A. M., & Elkavich, A. S. (2002). Treatment of suicidality: A family intervention for adolescent suicide attempters. In S. G. Hofmann & M. C. Tompson (Eds.), *Treating chronic and severe mental disorders: A handbook of empirically supported interventions,* (pp. 191–212). New York: Guilford Press.

Rotter, J. B. (1954). *Social learning and clinical psychology.* Englewood Cliffs, NJ: Prentice-Hall.

Rotter, J. B., & Rafferty, J. E. (1950). *The Rotter Incomplete Sentences Test.* New York: Psychological Corporation.

Rounsaville, B. J., O'Malley, S., Foley, S., & Weissman, M. W. (1988). Role of manual-guided training in the conduct and efficacy of interpersonal psychotherapy for depression. *Journal of Consulting and Clinical Psychology, 56,* 681–688.

Roy-Byrne, P. P., & Crowley, D. S. (2007). Pharmacological treatments for panic disorder, generalized anxiety disorder, specific phobia, and social anxiety disorder. In P. E. Nathan and J. M. Gorman (Eds.), *A guide to treatments that work* (3rd ed., pp. 395–430). New York: Oxford.

Roysircar, G., Sandhu, D. S., & Bibbins, V. E., Sr. (2003). *Multicultural competencies: A guidebook of practices.* Alexandria, VA: Association for Multicultural Counseling and Development.

Rubin, H. R., Gandek, B., Rogers, W. H., Kosinski, M., McHorney, C. A., & Ware, J. E. (1993). Patients' rating of outpatient visits in different practice settings: Results from the Medical Outcomes Study. *Journal of the American Medical Association, 270,* 835–840.

Rubin, R. T. (1982). Koro (Shook Yang): A culture-bound psychogenic syndrome. In C. T. H. Friedmann & R. A. Fauger (Eds.), *Extraordinary disorders of human behavior* (pp. 155–172). New York: Plenum Press.

Rudolph, K. D., Dennig, M. D., & Weisz, J. R. (1995). Determinants and consequences of children's coping in medical setting: Conceptualization, review, and critique. *Psychological Bulletin, 118,* 328–357.

Rupert, P. A., & Baird, K. A. (2004). Managed care and the independent practice of psychology. *Professional Psychology: Research and Practice, 35,* 18–193.

Russell, O. (Ed.). (1997). *Seminars in the psychiatry of learning disabilities.* Washington, DC: American Psychiatric Press.

Russell, R. K., & Petrie, T. A. (1994). Issues in training effective supervisors. *Applied and Preventive Psychology, 3,* 27–42.

Ryle, A. (2005). Cognitive analytic therapy. In J. C. Norcross, & M. R. Goldfried (Eds.). *Handbook of psychotherapy integration* (2nd ed.), pp. 196–220. New York: Oxford University Press.

Sackett, P. R. & Lievens, F. (2008). Personnel selection. *Annual Review of Psychology, 59,* 419–450.

Sachs, J. S. (1983). Negative factors in brief psychotherapy: An empirical assessment. *Journal of Consulting and Clinical Psychology, 51,* 557–564.

Sadock, B. J., Sadock, V. A., Ruiz, P. (2009). *Kaplan and Sadock's comprehensive textbook of psychiatry* (9th ed.). New York: Lippincott Williams & Wilkins.

Saeman, H. (1996a). Psychologists cheer as top psychiatrist jeers managed care. *National Psychologist, 5(3),* 1–4.

Saeman, H. (1996b). Psychologists frustrated with managed care, economic issues, but plan to "hang tough," survey reveals. *National Psychologist, 5(2),* 1–2.

Salvio, M., Beutler, L. E., Wood, J. M., & Engle, D. (1992). The strength of the therapeutic alliance in three treatments for depression. *Psychotherapy Research, 2,* 31–36.

Sammons, M. T., & Brown, A. B. (1997). The department of defense psychopharmacology demonstration project: An evolving program for postdoctoral education in psychology. *Professional Psychology: Research and Practice, 28,* 107–112.

Sammons, M. T., Gorny, S. W., Zinner, E. S., & Allen, R. P. (2000). Prescriptive authority for psychologists: A consensus of support. *Professional Psychology: Research and Practice, 31,* 604–609.

Sanchez, P. N., & Kahn, M. W. (1991). Differentiating medical from psychosocial disorders: How do medically and nonmedically trained clinicians differ? *Professional Psychology: Research and Practice, 22,* 124–126.

Sanders, M. J. (1995). Symptom coaching: Factitious disorder by proxy with older children. *Clinical Psychology Review, 15,* 423–442.

Sanderson, C. A. (2004). *Health psychology.* New York: Wiley.

Sanderson, W. C. (1994). Introduction to series on empirically validated psychological treatments. *Clinical Psychologist, 47,* 9.

Sanderson, W. C., & Woody, S. (1995). Manuals for empirically validated treatments. *Clinical Psychologist, 48,* 7–12.

Sandoval, J. (1989). The WISC-R and internal evidence of test bias with minority groups. *Journal of Counseling and Clinical Psychology, 47,* 919–927.

Sanford, N. (1953). Clinical method: Psychotherapy. *Annual Review of Psychology, 4,* 317–342.

Sansone, R. A. & Johnson, C. (1995). Treating the eating disorder patient with borderline personality disorder: Theory and technique. In J. P. Barber & P. Crits-Christoph (Eds.), *Dynamic therapies for psychiatric disorders (Axis I)* (pp. 230–266). New York: Basic Books.

Sapolsky, R. M. (1990, January). Stress in the wild. *Scientific American,* 116–123.

Sapolsky, R. M., & Meaney, M. J. (1986). Maturation of the adrenal stress response: Neuroendocrine control mechanisms and the stress hyporesponsive period. *Brain Research Review, 11,* 65–76.

Sapara, A., Cooke, M., Fannon, D., Francis, A., Buchanan, R., Anilkumar, A., Barkataki, I., Aasen, I., Kuipers, E., & Kumari, V. (2007). Prefrontal cortex and insight in schizophrenia: A volumetric MRI study. *Schizophrenia Research, 89,* 22–34.

Satir, V. (1967). *Conjoint family therapy.* Palo Alto, CA: Science and Behavior Books.

Satir, V. (1972). *Peoplemaking.* Palo Alto, CA: Science and Behavior Books.

Sattler, J. M. (1988). *Assessment of children* (3rd ed.). San Diego: Author.

Sattler, J. M. (1992). Assessment of children's intelligence. In C. E. Walker & M. C. Roberts (Eds.), *Handbook of clinical child psychology* (pp. 85–100). New York: Wiley.

Sattler, J. M. (2008). *Assessment of children, cognitive foundations* (5th ed.). San Diego, CA: Author.

Sayette, M. A., & Mayne, T. J. (1990). Survey of current clinical and research trends in clinical psychology. *American Psychologist, 45,* 1263–1266.

Schacter, D. L. (1999). The seven sins of memory. *American Psychologist, 54,* 182–203.

Schein, E. H. (1988). *Process consultation: Lessons for managers and consultants* (Vol. 2). Reading, MA: Addison-Wesley.

Scherg, H. (1987). Psychosocial factors and disease bias in breast cancer patients. *Psychosomatic Medicine, 49,* 302–312.

Scheufele, P. M. (2000). Effects of progressive relaxation and classical music on measurements of attention, relaxation, and stress responses. *Journal of Behavioral Medicine, 23,* 207–228.

Schiele, J. H. (1991). An epistemological perspective on intelligence assessment of African-American children. *Journal of Black Psychology, 17,* 23–36.

Schindler, N. J., & Talen, M. R. (1994). Focus supervision: Management format for supervision practices. *Professional Psychology: Research and Practice, 25,* 304–306.

Schindler-Rainman, E. (1985). Invited commentary: The modern consultant—a renaissance person. *Consultation, 4,* 264–267.

Schmidt, F., & Taylor, T. K. (2002). Putting empirically supported treatment into practice: Lessons learned in a children's mental health center. *Professional-Psychology: Research and Practice, 33,* 483–489.

Schenck-Gustafsson, K. (2009). Risk factors for cardiovascular disease in women. *Maturitas, 63,* 186–190.

Schneider, I. (1987). The theory and practice of movie psychiatry. *American Journal of Psychiatry, 144,* 996–1002.

Schneider, S. F. (1996). Random thoughts on leaving the fray. *American Psychologist, 51,* 715–721.

Schofield, W. (1952). Research in clinical psychology: 1951. *Journal of Clinical Psychology, 8,* 255–261.

Schofield, W. (1964). *Psychotherapy: The purchase of friendship.* Englewood Cliffs, NJ: Prentice-Hall.

Scholing, A., Emmelkamp, P. M. G., & Van Oppen, P. (1996). Cognitive-behavioral treatment of social phobia. In V. B. Van Hasselt & M. Hersen (Eds.), *Sourcebook of psychological treatment manuals for adult disorders* (pp. 123–178), New York: Plenum Press.

Schum, J. L., Jorgensen, R. S., Verhaeghen, P., Savro, M., & Thibodeau, R. (2003). Trait anger, anger expression, and ambulatory blood pressure: A meta analytic review. *Journal of Behavioral Medicine, 26,* 395–415.

Schwartz, G. E. (1982). Testing the biopsychosocial model: The ultimate challenge facing behavioral medicine? *Journal of Consulting and Clinical Psychology, 50,* 1040–1053.

Schwartz, G. E. (1984). Psychobiology of health: A new synthesis. In B. L. Hammonds & C. J. Scheirer (Eds.), *Psychology and health: The master lecture series* (Vol. 3, pp. 149–193). Washington, DC: American Psychological Association.

Schwartz, G. E. (1991). The data are always friendly: A systems approach to psychotherapy integration. *Journal of Psychotherapy Integration, 1,* 55–69.

Schwartz, G. E., & Beatty, J. (1977). *Biofeedback: Theory and research.* New York: Academic Press.

Schwartz, G. E., & Weiss, S. M. (1978a). Behavioral medicine revisited: An amended definition. *Journal of Behavioral Medicine, 1,* 249–251.

Schwartz, J. L. (1987). *Review and evaluation of smoking cessation methods: The United States and Canada, 1978–1985.* Washington, DC: Division of Cancer Prevention and Control, National Cancer Institute.

Schwartzman, J. B., & Glaus, K. D. (2000). Depression and coronary heart disease in women: Implications for clinical practice and research. *Professional Psychology: Research and Practice, 31,* 48–57.

Scogin, F., Floyd, M., & Forde, L. (2000). Anxiety in older adults. In S. K. Whitbourne (Ed.), *Psychopathology in later adulthood: Wiley series on adulthood and aging* (pp. 117–140). New York: Wiley.

Scott, A. I. F. (1995). Does ECT alter brain structure? *American Journal of Psychiatry, 152,* 1403.

Scriven, M. (1967). The methodology of evaluation. In R. Tyler, R. Gagne, & M. Scriven (Eds.), *Perspectives of curriculum evaluation* (American Educational Research Association Monograph Series on Curriculum Evaluation) (pp. 39–83). Chicago: Rand McNally.

Searles, J. S. (1985). A methodological and empirical critique of psychotherapy outcome meta-analysis. *Behaviour Research and Therapy, 23,* 453–463.

Seeman, M., Seeman, A. Z., & Budros, A. (1988). Powerlessness, work, and community: A longitudinal study of alienation and alcohol use. *Journal of Health and Social Behavior, 29,* 185–198.

Seeman, T. (2001). How do others get under our skin? Social relationships and health. In C. D. Ryff & B. H. Singer (Eds.), *Emotion, social relationships, and health: Series in affective science* (pp. 189–210). London: Oxford University Press.

Segal, Z. V., & Ingram, R. E. (1994). Mood priming and construct activation in tests of cognitive vulnerability to unipolar depression. *Clinical Psychology Review, 14,* 663–695.

Seligman, M. E. P. (1975). *Helplessness: On depression, development and death.* San Francisco: Freeman.

Seligman, M. E. P. (1994). *What you can change and what you can't.* New York: Knopf.

Seligman, M. E. P. (1995). The effectiveness of psychotherapy: The *Consumer Reports* study. *American Psychologist, 50,* 965–974.

Seligman, M. E. P. (1996). Science as an ally of practice. *American Psychologist, 51,* 1072–1079.

Seligman, M. E. P. (2006). *Learned happiness: How to change your mind and your life.* NY: Vintage.

Seligman, M. E. P., & Csikszentmihalyi, M. (2000). Positive psychology: An introduction. *American Psychologist, 55,* 5–14.

Seligman, M. E. P., Ernst, R. M., Gillham, J., Reivich, K., Linkins, M. (2009). Positive education: positive psychology and classroom interventions. *Oxford Review of Education, 35,* 293–311.

Seligman, M. E. P., Peterson, C., Kaslow, N. J., Tanenbaum, R. L., Alloy, L. B., & Abramson, L. Y. (1984). Explanatory style and depressive symptoms among school children. *Journal of Abnormal Psychology, 93,* 235–238.

Sells, S. P. (1998). *Treating the tough adolescent: A family-based, step-by-step guide.* New York: Guilford Press.

Selvini Palazzoli, M., Boscolo, L., Cecchin, G., & Prata, G. (1980). Hypothesizing-circularity-neutrality: Three guidelines for the conductor of the session. *Family Process, 19,* 73–85.

Settles, I. H., Cortina, L. M., Malley, J., & Stewart, A. J. (2006). The climate for women in academic science: The good, the bad, and the changeable. *Psychology of Women Quarterly, 30,* 47–58.

Shadish, W. R., Navarro, A. M., Matt, G. E., & Phillips, G. (2000). The effects of psychological therapies under clinically representative conditions: A meta-analysis. *Psychological Bulletin, 126,* 512–529.

Shakow, D. (1947). Recommended graduate training program in clinical psychology. *American Psychologist, 2,* 539–558.

Shakow, D. (1976). What is clinical psychology? *American Psychologist, 31,* 553–560.

Shakow, D. (1978). Clinical psychology seen some 50 years later. *American Psychologist, 33,* 148–158.

Shapiro, A. E., & Wiggins, J. G. (1994). A PsyD degree for every practitioner: Truth in labeling. *American Psychologist, 49,* 207–210.

Shapiro, D. L. (1984). *Psychological evaluation and expert testimony: A practical guide to forensic work.* New York: Van Nostrand Reinhold.

Shapiro, D. L., & Shapiro, D. (1982). Meta-analysis of comparative therapy outcome studies: A replication and refinement. *Psychological Bulletin, 92,* 581–604.

Shapiro, E. S., & Lentz, F. E. (1991). Vocational-technical programs: Follow-up of students with learning disabilities. *Exceptional Children, 58,* 47–59.

Shapiro, F. (1989). Efficacy of the eye movement desensitization procedure in the treatment of traumatic memories. *Journal of Traumatic Stress, 2,* 199–223.

Shapiro, F. (2001). *Eye movement desensitization and reprocessing: Basic principles, protocols, and procedures* (2nd ed.). New York: Guilford Press.

Shapiro, F. (2002). *EMDR as an integrative psychotherapy approach: Experts of diverse orientations explore the paradigm prism.* Washington, DC: American Psychological Association.

Sharif, Z., Bradford, D., Stroup, S., & Lieberman, J. (2007). Pharmacological treatment of schizophrenia In P. E. Nathan and J. M. Gorman (Eds.), *A guide to treatments that work* (3rd ed., pp. 203–242). New York: Oxford.

Sharow, D. (1947). Recommended graduate training program in clinical psychology. *American Psychologist, 2,* 539–558.

Sheldon, K. M., Joiner, T. E., Pettit, J. W., & Williams, G. (2003). Reconciling humanistic ideals and scientific clinical practice. *Clinical Psychology: Science and Practice, 10,* 302–315.

Sheldon, K. M., & King, L. (2001). Why positive psychology is necessary. *American Psychologist, 56,* 216–217.

Shell, E. R. (2002). *The hungry gene: The inside story of the obesity industry.* New York: Grove Press.

Shemberg, K. M., & Leventhal, D. B. (1981). Attitudes of internship directors toward preinternship training and clinical training models. *Professional Psychology, 12,* 639–646.

Sheridan, E. P., Matarazzo, J. D., & Nelson, P. D. (1995). Accreditation of psychology's graduate professional education and training programs: An historical perspective. *Professional Psychology: Research and Practice, 26,* 386–392.

Shi, L., & Singh, D. A. (2007). *Delivering health care in America: A systems approach* (4th ed.). Sudbury, MA: Jones & Bartlett.

Shipman, K., & Taussig, H. (2009). Mental health treatment of child abuse and neglect: The promise of evidence-based practice. *Pediatric Clinics of North America, 56,* 417–428.

Shneidman, E. S. (1951). *Thematic test analysis.* New York: Grune & Stratton.

Sholomskas, D. E., Barlow, D. H., Cohen, J., Gorman, J., Moras, K., Papp, L., et al. (1990). *Drug/behavior treatment of panic: Study design.* Paper presented at the annual meeting of the American Psychiatric Association, New York.

Shore, M. F. (1993). Thoughts on twenty years of mental health administration. *Administration and Policy in Mental Health, 21,* 117–121.

Shorter, E. A. (1994). *From the mind into the body: The cultural origins of psychosomatic symptoms.* New York: Free Press.

Shuster, E. A. (1996). Epilepsy in women. *Mayo Clinic Proceedings, 71,* 991–999.

Sieber, J. E. (1982). Ethical dilemmas in social research. In J. E. Sieber (Ed.), *The ethics of social research: Survey and experiments.* New York: Springer-Verlag.

Silverman, W. H. (1996). Cookbooks, manuals, and paint-by-numbers: Psychotherapy in the 90s. *Psychotherapy, 33,* 207–215.

Silverman, W. K., & Nelles, W. B. (1988). The Anxiety Disorders Interview Schedule for Children. *Journal of the American Academy of Child and Adolescent Psychiatry, 27,* 772–778.

Singer, M. T., & Lalich, J. (1996). *Crazy therapies: What are they? Do they work?* San Francisco: Jossey-Bass.

Skinner, B. F. (1948). *Walden two.* New York: Macmillan.

Skinner, B. F. (1953). *Science and human behavior.* New York: Macmillan.

Sklar, L. S., & Anisman, H. (1981). Stress and cancer. *Psychological Bulletin, 89,* 369–406.

Skrzypulec, V., Tobor, E., Drosdzol, A., & Nowosielski, K. (2009). Biopsychosocial functioning of women after mastectomy. *Journal of Clinical Nursing, 18,* 613–619.

Sleek, S. (1997, August). Providing therapy from a distance. *APA Monitor, 28,* 1, 38.

Sloane, R. B., Staples, F. R., Cristol, A. H., Yorkston, N. J., & Whipple, K. (1975). *Psychotherapy versus behavior therapy.* Cambridge, MA: Harvard University Press.

Smith, B. S. (1992). *Attitudes toward prescribing privileges among clinical graduate students.* Unpublished doctoral research project, Indiana State University.

Smith, M. L. (1982). What research says about the effectiveness of psychotherapy. *Hospital and Community Psychiatry, 33,* 457–461.

Smith, M. L., & Glass, G. V. (1977). Meta-analysis of psychotherapy outcome studies. *American Psychologist, 32,* 752–760.

Smith, M. L., Glass, G. V., & Miller, T. (1980). *The benefits of psychotherapy.* Baltimore: John Hopkins University Press.

Smith, R. A. (1985). Advising beginning psychology majors for graduate school. *Teaching of Psychology, 12,* 194–198.

Smith, T. W., Turner, C. W., Ford, M. H., Hunt, S. C., Barlow, G. K., Stults, B. M., et al. (1987). Blood pressure reactivity in adult male twins. *Health Psychology, 6,* 209–220.

Smith-Spark, J., & Fisk, J. (2007). Working memory functioning in developmental dyslexia. *Memory, 15,* 34–56.

Smucker, M. R., & Dancu, C. V. (1999). *Cognitive-behavioral treatment for adult survivors of childhood trauma: Imagery rescripting and reprocessing.* Northvale, NJ: Aronson.

Smyer, M. A., Balster, R. L., Egli, D., Johnson, D. L., Kilbey, M. M., Leith, N. J., et al. (1993). Summary of the report of the ad hoc task force on psychopharmacology of the American Psychological Association. *Professional Psychology: Research and Practice, 24,* 394–403.

Snepp, F. P., & Peterson, D. R. (1988). Evaluative comparison of PsyD and PhD students be clinical internship supervisors. *Professional Psychology: Research and Practice, 19,* 180–193.

Snow, D., & Amalu, J. (2009). Older adults and substance abuse. *Journal of Addictions Nursing, 20,* 153–157.

Snyder, C. R., & Ingram, R. E. (2000). Psychotherapy: Questions for an evolving field. In C. R. Snyder & R. E. Ingram (Eds.), *Handbook of psychological change: Psychotherapy processes and practices for the 21st century* (pp. 707–726). New York: Wiley.

Snyder, C. R., McDermott, D. S., Leibowitz, R. Q., & Cheavens, J. (2000). The role of female clinical psychologist in changing the field of psychotherapy. In C. R. Snyder & R. E. Ingram (Eds.), *Handbook of psychological change: Psychotherapy processes and practices for the 21st century* (pp. 640–659). New York: Wiley.

Sonne, J. L. (1994). Multiple relationships: Does the new ethics code answer the right questions? *Professional Psychology: Research and Practice, 25,* 336–343.

Sopchak, A. L., Sopchak, A. M., & Kohlbrenner, R. J. (1993). *Interpersonal relatedness from projective drawings: Applicability in diagnostic and therapeutic practice.* Springfield, IL: Charles C Thomas.

Sparrow, S. S., Balla, D. A., & Cicchetti, D. V. (2005). *Vineland Adaptive Behavior Scales, Second Edition: Manual.* Circles Pines, MN: American Guidance Service.

Spaulding, W. D., Johnson, D. L., & Coursey, R. D. (2001). Combined treatments and rehabilitation of schizophrenia. In M. T. Sammons & N. B. Schmidt (Eds.), *Combined treatment for mental disorders* (pp. 161–190). Washington, DC: American Psychological Association.

Spearman, C. (1927). *The abilities of man.* New York: Macmillan.

Speer, D. C., & Newman, F. L. (1996). Mental health services outcome evaluation. *Clinical Psychology: Science and Practice, 3,* 105–129.

Spengler, P. M., White, M. J., Aegisdottir, S., Maugherman, A. S., Anderson, L. A., Cook, R. S. et al. (2009). The meta-analysis of clinical judgment project: Effects of experience on judgment accuracy. *The Counseling Psychologist, 37,* 350–399.

Sperry, L. (1999). *Cognitive behavior therapy of DSM-IV personality disorders: Highly effective interventions for the most common personality disorders.* Edwards Brothers.

Spiegal, D. (1990). Can psychotherapy prolong cancer survival? *Psychosomatics, 31,* 361–366.

Spiegal, D. (1992). Effects of psychosocial support on patients with metastatic breast cancer. *Journal of Psychosocial Oncology, 10,* 113–120.

Spiegal, D. (1998). Efficacy studies of alprazolam in panic disorder. *Psychopharmacology Bulletin, 43,* 191–195.

Spiegal, D., Bloom, J. R., Kraemer, H. C., & Gottheil, E. (1989, October 14). Effects of psychosocial treatment on survival of patients with metastatic breast cancer. *Lancet,* 888–891.

Spitzer, R. L., Williams, J. B. W., Gibbon, M., & First, M. B. (1990). *Structured clinical interview for DSM-III-R (SCID).* Washington, DC: American Psychiatric Press.

Spoont, M. R. (1992). Modulatory role of serotonin in neural information processing: Implications for human psychopathology. *Psychological Bulletin, 112,* 330–350.

Spreen, O. (1988). Prognosis of learning disability. *Journal of Consulting and Clinical Psychology, 56,* 836–842.

Sprenkle, D. H., David, S. D., & Lebow, J. L. (2009). *Common factors in couple and family therapy: The overlooked foundation for effective practice.* New York: Guilford Press.

Stahl, S. M. (1998). Basic psychopharmacology of antidepressants: Part 1. Antidepressants have seven distinct mechanisms of action. *Journal of Clinical Psychiatry, 59*(Suppl. 4), 5–14.

Stahl, S. M. (2002). *Essential psychopharmacology of antipsychotics and mood stabilizers.* Cambridge: Cambridge University Press.

Stake, J. E., & Oliver, J. (1991). Sexual contact and touching between therapist and client: A survey of psychologists' attitudes and behavior. *Professional Psychology: Research and Practice, 22,* 297–307.

Stamps, R. F., & Barach, P. M. (2001). *The therapist's internet handbook: More than 1300 web sites and resources for mental health professionals*. New York: Norton.

Stanley, M. A. & Mouton, S. G. (1996). Trichotillomania treatment manual. In V. B. Van Hasselt & M. Hersen (Eds.), *Sourcebook of psychological treatment manuals for adult disorders* (pp. 657–688), New York: Plenum Press.

Stanley, M. A., & Novy, D. M. (2000). Cognitive-behavior therapy for generalized anxiety late in life: An evaluation overview. *Journal of Anxiety Disorders, 14*, 191–207.

Starkstein, S. E., & Robinson, R. G. (1988). Lateralized emotional response following stroke. In M. Kinsbourne (Ed.), *Cerebral hemisphere function in depression*. Washington, DC: American Psychiatric Press.

Stasiewicz, P. R. & Bradizza, C. M. (2002). Alcohol abuse. In M. Hersen (Ed.), *Clinical behavior therapy: Adults and children* (pp. 181–197). New York: Wiley.

Stears, J. C., & Spitz, M. C. (1996). The imaging of epilepsy. *Seminars in Ultrasound, 17*, 221–250.

Stein, D. M., & Lambert, M. J. (1984). On the relationship between therapist experience and psychotherapy outcome. *Clinical Psychology Review, 4*, 1–16.

Steinpreis, R., Queen, L., & Tennen, H. (1992). The education of clinical psychologists: A survey of training directors. *Clinical Psychologist, 45*, 87–94.

Stern, J. (2003). Integration in psychotherapy: Models and methods. *Psychoanalytic-Psychotherapy, 17*, 175–177.

Sternberg, R. J. (1996). *Successful intelligence: How practical and creative intelligence determines success in life*. New York: Simon & Schuster.

Sternberg, R. J. (1997). The concept of intelligence and its role in lifelong learning and success. *American Psychologist, 52*, 1030–1037.

Sternberg, R. J. (2003). It's time for prescription privileges. *APA Monitor on Psychology, 34*, 5.

Sternberg, R. J. (Ed.). (2006). *Career paths in psychology: Where your degree can take you* (2nd ed.). Washington, DC: American Psychological Association.

Sternberg, R. J. (2008). *Cognitive psychology* (5th ed.). Belmont, CA: Wadsworth.

Sternberg, R. J., & Kaye, D. B. (1982). Intelligence. In H. E. Mitzel, J. H. Best, & H. E. Rabinowitz (Eds.), *Encyclopedia of educational research* (5th ed., pp. 924–933). New York: Free Press.

Sternberg, R. J., & Williams, W. M. (1997). Does the Graduate Record Examination predict meaningful success in the graduate training of psychologists? A case study. *American Psychologist, 52*, 630–641.

Stewart, S. H. (1996). Alcohol abuse in individuals exposed to trauma: A critical review. *Psychological Bulletin, 120*, 83–112.

Stiles, W. B., Shapiro, D. A., & Elliott, R. (1986). Are all psychotherapies equivalent? *American Psychologist, 41*, 165–180.

Stith, S. M., Liu, T., Davies, L. C., Boykin, E. L., Alder, M. C., Harris, J. M., Som, A., McPherson, M., & Dees, J.E.M.E.G. (2009). Risk factors in child maltreatment: A meta-analytic review of the literature. *Aggression and Violent Behavior, 14*, 13–29.

Stockman, A. F. (1990). Dual relationships in rural mental health practice: An ethical dilemma. *Journal of Rural Community Psychology, 11*, 31–45.

Stoll, B. A. (1996). Obesity, social class and Western diet: A link to breast cancer prognosis. *European Journal of Cancer, 32A*, 1293–1295.

Stone, M. H. (1985). Negative outcome in borderline states. In D. T. Mays & C. M. Franks (Eds.), *Negative outcome in psychotherapy and what to do about it* (pp. 145–170). New York: Springer.

Stone, M. H. (1990). Treatment of borderline patients: A pragmatic approach. *Psychiatric Clinics of North America, 13*, 265–285.

Storandt, M (2008). Cognitive deficits in the early stages of Alzheimer's disease. *Current Directions in Psychological Science, 17*, 198–202.

Stricker, G. (2000). The scientist-practitioner model: Gandhi was right again. *American Psychologist, 55*, 253–254.

Stricker, G., & Cummings, N. A. (1992). The professional school movement. In D. K. Freedheim (Ed.), *History of psychotherapy* (pp. 801–828). Washington, DC: American Psychological Association.

Stricker, G., & Trierweiler, S. J. (1995). The local clinical scientist: A bridge between science and practice. *American Psychologist, 50*, 995–1002.

Strickland, B. R. (1985). Over the Boulder(s) and through the Vail. *Clinical Psychologist, 38*, 52–56.

Striegal-Moore, R. H. (2000). The epidemiology of eating disorders. *European Disorders Review, 8*, 344–346.

Striegal-Moore, R. H., Silberstein, L. R., & Rodin, J. (1986). Toward an understanding of risk factors for bulimia. *American Psychologist, 3*, 246–263.

Striegal-Moore, R. H., Silberstein, L. R., & Rodin, J. (1993). The social self in bulimia nervosa: Public self-consciousness, social anxiety, and perceived fraudulence. *Journal of Abnormal Psychology, 102,* 297–303.

Strober, M., & Humphrey, L. L. (1987). Familial contributions to the etiology and course of anorexia nervosa and bulimia: Eating disorders [Special issue]. *Journal of Consulting and Clinical Psychology, 55,* 654–659.

Strother, C. R. (1956). *Psychology and mental health.* Washington, DC: American Psychological Association.

Strupp, H. H. (1963). The outcome problem in psychotherapy revisited. *Psychotherapy: Theory, Research, and Practice, 1,* 1–13.

Strupp, H. H. (1980). Success and failure in time-limited psychotherapy: Further evidence (Comparison 4). *Archives of General Psychiatry, 37,* 947–954.

Strupp, H. H. (1992). The future of psychodynamic psychotherapy. *Psychotherapy, 29,* 21–27.

Strupp, H. H. (1995). The psychotherapist's skill revisited. *Clinical Psychology: Science and Practice, 2,* 70–74.

Strupp, H. H., & Anderson, T. (1997). On the limitations of therapy manuals. *Clinical Psychology: Science and Practice, 4,* 76–82.

Strupp, H. H., & Binder, J. L. (1984). *Psychotherapy in a new key: A guide to time-limited dynamic therapy.* New York: Basic Books.

Sue, D. W., & Sue, D. (2003). *Counseling the culturally diverse: Theory and practice* (4th ed.). New York: Wiley.

Sue, D., & Sue, D. M. (2008). *Foundations of counseling and psychotherapy: Evidence-based practices for a diverse society.* New York: Wiley.

Sue, S. (1983). Ethnic minority issues in psychology: A reexamination. *American Psychologist, 38,* 583–592.

Sue, S. (1988). Psychotherapeutic services for ethnic minorities. *American Psychologist, 43,* 301–308.

Sue, S., Fujino, D. C., Hu, L. T., Takeuchi, D. T., & Zane, N. W. S. (1991). Community mental health services for ethnic minority groups: A test of the cultural responsiveness hypothesis. *Journal of Counseling Psychology, 59,* 533–540.

Sue, S., McKinney, H. L., & Allen, D. B. (1976). Predictors of the duration of therapy for clients in the community mental health system. *Community Mental Health Journal, 12,* 365–375.

Sue, S., Zane, N., & Young, K. (1994). Research on psychotherapy with culturally diverse populations. In A. E. Bergin & S. L. Garfield (Eds.), *Handbook of psychotherapy and behavior change* (4th ed., pp. 783–817). New York: Wiley.

Suinn, R., Ahuna, C., & Khoo, G. (1992). The Suinn-Lew Asian Self-Identity Acculturation Scale: Concurrent and factorial validation. *Education and Psychological Measurement, 52,* 1041–1046.

Suinn, R. M., & Oskamp, S. (1969). *The predictive validity of projective measures: A fifteen-year evaluative review of the research.* Springfield, IL: Charles Thomas.

Sullivan, P. F., Neale, M. C., & Kendler, S. K. (2000). Genetic epidemiology of major depression: Review and meta-analysis. *American Journal of Psychiatry, 157,* 1552–1562.

Sultzer, D. L., Levin, H. S., Mahler, M. E., High, W. M., & Cummings, J. L. (1993). A comparison of psychiatric symptoms in vascular dementia and Alzheimer's disease. *American Journal of Psychiatry, 150,* 1806–1812.

Sussman, M. B. (1992). *A curious calling: Unconscious motivations for practicing psychotherapy.* Northvale, NJ: Aronson.

Suzuki, L. A., & Valencia, R. R. (1997). Race-ethnicity and measured intelligence: Educational implications. *American Psychologist, 52,* 1103–1114.

Svartberg, M., & Stiles, T. C. (1991). Comparative effects of short-term psychodynamic psychotherapy: A meta-analysis. *Journal of Consulting and Clinical Psychology, 59,* 704–714.

Swanson, J. M., McBurenett, K., Wigal, T., Pfiffner, L. J., Lerner, M. A., Williams, L., et al. (1993). Effect of stimulant medication on children with attention deficit disorder: A "review of reviews." *Exceptional Children, 60,* 154–162.

Swartz, J. D. (1978). Review of the TAT. In O. K. Buros (Ed.), *The eighth mental measurements handbook* (pp. 1127–1130). Highland Park, NJ: Gryphon Press.

Swartz, H. A., Markowitz, J. C., & Frank, E. (2002). Interpersonal psychotherapy for unipolar and bipolar disorders. In S. G. Hofmann & M. C. Tompson (Eds.), *Treating chronic and severe mental disorders: A handbook of empirically supported interventions,* (pp. 131–158). New York: Guilford Press.

Sweet, J. J., Rozensky, R. H., & Tovian, S. M. (Eds.). (1991). *Handbook of clinical psychology in medical settings.* New York: Plenum Press.

Szapocznik, J., Kurtines, W. M., & Fernandez, T. (1980). Bicultural involvement and adjustment in Hispanic-American youths. *International Journal of Intercultural Relations, 4*, 353–365.

Tageson, W. C. (1982). *Humanistic psychology: A synthesis.* Homewood, IL: Dorsey Press.

Talley, P. F., Strupp, H. H., & Butler, S. F. (Eds.). (1994). *Psychotherapy research and practice: Bridging the gap.* New York: Basic Books.

Tamaskar, P., & McGinnis, R. A. (2002). Declining student interest in psychiatry. *Journal of the American Medical Association, 287*, 1859.

Task Force on Promotion and Dissemination of Psychological Procedures. (1995). Training in and dissemination of empirically validated psychological treatments: Report and recommendations. *Clinical Psychologist, 48*, 3–23.

Taube, C. A., Burns, B. J., & Kessler, L. (1984). Patients of psychiatrists and psychologists in office-based practice: 1980. *American Psychologist, 39*, 1435–1447.

Tausig, J. E., & Freeman, E. W. (1988). The next best thing to being there: Conducting the clinical research interview by telephone. *American Journal of Orthopsychiatry, 58*, 418–427.

Taylor, C. B., Agras, W. S., Losch, M., Plante, T. G., & Burnett, K. (1991). Improving the effectiveness of computer-assisted weight loss. *Behavior Therapy, 22*, 229–236.

Taylor, J. E., & Harvey, S. T. (2009). Effects of psychotherapy with people who have been sexually assaulted: A meta-analysis. *Aggression and Violent Behavior, 14*, 273–285.

Taylor, S. E. (2009). *Health psychology* (7th ed.). New York: McGraw-Hill.

Taylor, S. E., & Stanton, A. L. (2007). Coping resources, coping processes, and mental health. *Annual Review of Clinical Psychology, 3*, 377–401.

Teachman, B. A., Woody, S. R. , & Magee, J. C. (2006). Implicit and explicit appraisals of the importance of intrusive thoughts. *Behavior Research and Therapy, 44*, 785–805.

Temoshok, L. (1987). Personality, coping style, emotion and cancer: Towards an integrative model. *Cancer Surveys, 6*, 545–567.

Teyber, E., & McClure, F. (2000). Therapist variables. In C. R. Snyder & R. E. Ingram (Eds.), *Handbook of psychological change: Psychotherapy processes and practices for the 21st century* (pp. 62–87). New York: Wiley.

Tharp, R. G. (1991). Cultural diversity and treatment of children. *Journal of Consulting and Clinical Psychology, 59*, 799–812.

Thase, M. (1996). Cognitive behavior therapy manual for depressed inpatients individual. In V. B. Van Hasselt & M. Hersen (Eds.), *Sourcebook of psychological treatment manuals for adult disorders* (pp. 201–232), New York: Plenum Press.

Thase, M. E (2009). Neurobiological aspects of depression. In I. H. Gotlib & C. L. Hammen (Eds.), *Handbook of depression* (2nd ed., pp. 187–217). New York: Guilford Press.

Thase, M. E., & Denko, T. (2008). Pharmacotherapy of mood disorders. *Annual Review of Clinical Psychology, 4*, 53–91.

Thomas, V. L., & Gostin, L. O. (2009). The Americans with Disabilities Act: Shattered aspirations and new hope. *Journal of the American Medical Association, 301*, 95–97.

Thoresen, C. E., & Powell, L. H. (1992). Type A behavior pattern: New perspectives on theory, assessment and intervention [Special issues: Behavioral medicine: An update for the 1990s]. *Journal of Consulting and Clinical Psychology, 60*, 595–604.

Thorndike, R. L., Hagen, E. P., & Sattler, J. M. (1986). *The Stanford-Binet Intelligence Scale: Technical manual* (4th ed.). Chicago: Riverside.

Thurstone, L. L. (1931). Multiple factor analysis. *Psychological Review, 38*, 406–427.

Thurstone, L. L. (1938). *Primary mental abilities.* Chicago: University of Chicago Press.

Tjaden, P., & Thoennes, N. (2000). Prevalence and consequences of male-to-female and female-to-male intimate partner violence as measured by the National Violence against Women Survey. *Violence and Victims, 15*, 427–441.

Tobias, L. L. (1990). *Psychological consultation to management: A clinician's perspective.* New York: Brunner/Mazel.

Tolmach, J. (1985). "There ain't nobody on my side": A new day treatment program for black urban youth. *Journal of Clinical Child Psychology, 14*, 214–219.

Tomkins, S. S. (1947). *The thematic apperception test.* New York: Grune & Stratton.

Trevisaw, M. S. (1996). Review of the Draw-a- Person: Screening procedures for emotional disturbance. *Measurement and Evaluation in Counseling and Development, 28*, 225–228.

Trickett, E. J., Watts, R. J., & Birman, D. (Eds.). (1994). *Human diversity: Perspectives on people in context.* San Francisco: Jossey-Boss.

Trimble, M. (1985). Psychosomatic aspects of epilepsy. *Advances in Psychosomatic Medicine, 13*, 133–150.

Truax, C. B., & Mitchell, K. M. (1971). Research on certain therapist interpersonal skills in relation to process and outcome. In A. E. Bergin & S. L. Garfield (Eds.), *Handbook of psychotherapy and behavior change* (pp. 299–344). New York: Wiley.

Trull, T. J., & Widiger, T. A. (1997). *Manual for the Structured Interview for the Five-Factor Model of Personality (SIFFM)*. Odessa, FL: Psychological Assessment Resources.

Tsai, J. L., & Chentsova-Dutton, Y. (2002). Understanding depression across cultures. In I. H. Gotlib & C. L. Hammen (Eds.), *Handbook of depression* (pp. 467–491). New York: Guilford Press.

Tucker, L., & Lubin, W. (1994). *National survey of psychologists. Report from Division 39, American Psychological Association*. Washington, DC: American Psychological Association.

Tuokko, H., Kristjansson, E., & Miller, J. (1995). Neuropsychological detection of dementia: An overview of the neuropsychological component of the Canadian Study of Health and Aging. *Journal of Clinical and Experimental Neuropsychology, 17,* 352–373.

Turk, D. C., & Fernandez, E. (1990). On the putative uniqueness of cancer pain: Do psychological principles apply? *Behavioural Research and Therapy, 28,* 1–13.

Turk, C. L., Heimberg, R. G., & Hope, D. A. (2001). Social anxiety disorder. In D. H. Barlow (Ed.), *Clinical handbook of psychological disorders: A step-by-step treatment manual (3rd ed., pp. 114–153).* New York: Guilford Press.

Turnbull, W. W. (1979). Intelligence testing in the year 2000. *Intelligence, 3,* 275–282.

Turner, S. M., & Beidel, D. C. (1988). *Treating obsessive-compulsive disorder.* New York: Pergamon Press.

Turner, S. M., DeMars, S. T., Fox, H. R., & Reed, G. M. (2001). APA's guidelines for test user qualifications: An executive summary. *American Psychologist, 56,* 1099–1113.

United Kingdom Department of Health. (2001). *Treatment choice in psychological therapies and counselling: Evidence based clinical practice guidelines.* London: Author.

U. S. Bureau of Labor Statistics. (2009). *Occupational outlook handbook, 2008–09 edition.* Washington, DC: Author.

U.S. Census Bureau. (1995). *Statistical abstract of the United States* (115th ed.). Washington, DC: Author.

U.S. Census Bureau. (2000). *Census of population and housing summary* (Tape File 1C, CD-ROM). Washington, DC: Government Printing Office.

U. S. Census Bureau. (2006). Current population survey (CPS) reports: Families and living arrangements. Retrieved on July 26, 2009, from http://www.census.gov/population/www/socde mo/hh-fam.html.

U.S. Census Bureau (2008a). Income, poverty, and health insurance coverage in the U. S.: 2007. Washington, DC: Author.

U.S. Census Bureau. (2008b). 2008 Population estimates. Retrieved October 23, 2009, http://factfinder.census.gov/servlet/GCTTable?_bm=y &-geo_id=01000US&-_box_head_nbr=GCT-T4 -R&-ds_name=PEP_2008_EST&-format=U-40Sc.

U.S. Census Bureau. (2010). U.S. POPclock Projection. Retrieved September 9, 2009, http://www .census.gov/population/www/popclockus.html.

U.S. Department of Health and Human Services. (1983). *The health consequences of smoking: Cardiovascular disease. A report to the Surgeon General* (DHHS Publication No. PHS 84-50204). Washington, DC: Office on Smoking and Health, Author.

U.S. Department of Health and Human Services. (1985a). *Health: United States, 1985* (DHHS Publication No. PHS 86-1232). Washington, DC: Author.

U.S. Department of Health and Human Services. (1985b). *Preventing lead poisoning in young children. Second revision of the statement by the Centers for Disease Control.* Washington, DC: U.S. Government Printing Office.

U.S. Department of Health and Human Services. (1990). *Healthy people 2000.* Washington, DC: Author.

U.S. Department of Health and Human Services (2007). *Federal Register.* Announcement of Establishment of the Secretary's Advisory Committee on National Health Promotion and Disease Prevention Objectives for 2020 and Solicitation of Nominations for Membership, 72, 161.

U.S. Department of Health and Human Services (2008). *Child Maltreatment 2007.* Washington, DC: Author.

U.S. Department of Health and Human Services, Health Resources and Services Administration, Maternal and Child Health Bureau. (2001). Child health USA, 2001. Washington, DC: U.S. Government Printing Office. Retrieved July 7, 2003, from http://www.mchirc.net/CH-USA.htm.

U.S. Surgeon General. (1994). *Preventing tobacco use among young people.* Washington, DC: U.S. Government Printing Office.

Valenstein, R. S. (2002). *Blaming the brain: The truth about drugs and mental health.* New York: Free Press.

Van Brunt, D. L., Riedel, B. W., & Lichstein, K. L. (1996). Insomnia. In V. B. Van Hasselt & M. Hersen (Eds.), *Sourcebook of psychological treatment manuals for adult disorders* (pp. 539–566), New York: Plenum Press.

van Dam, R. M., Li, T., Spiegelman, D., Franco, O. H., & Hu, F. B. (2008). Combined impact of lifestyle factors on mortality: prospective cohort study in US women. *British Medical Journal, 337,* 729–745.

VandeCreek, L., & Fleisher, M. (1984). The role of practicum in undergraduate psychology curriculum. *Teaching of Psychology, 11,* 9–14.

VandenBos, G. R. (1993). The U.S. mental health policy: Proactive evolution in the midst of health care reform. *American Psychologist, 48,* 283–290.

VandenBos, G. R. (1996). Outcome assessment of psychotherapy. *American Psychologist, 51,* 1005–1006.

VandenBos, G. R., & DeLeon, P. H. (1988). The use of psychotherapy to improve physical health. *Psychotherapy, 25,* 335–343.

Van Hasselt, V. B., & Hersen, M. (1996). *Sourcebook of psychological treatment manuals for adult disorders.* New York: Plenum Press.

van Os, J., Hanssen, M., Bijl, R. V., & Vollebergh, W. (2001). Prevalence of psychotic disorder and community level of psychotic symptoms. *Archives of General Psychiatry, 58,* 475–482.

Vasquez, M. J. T. (1994). Implications of the 1992 ethics code for the practice of individual psychotherapy. *Professional Psychology: Research and Practice, 25,* 321–328.

Vaugh, M., & Beech, H. R. (1985). Which obessionals fail to change. In D. T. Mays & C. M. Franks (Eds.), *Negative outcome in psychotherapy and what to do about it* (pp. 192–209). New York: Springer.

Vernon, P. E. (1950). The validation of civil service selection board procedures. *Occupational Psychology, 24,* 75–95.

Victoroff, M. S. (2002). Psychologists prescribing: Not such a crazy idea. *Managed Care Magazine, 12,* 3–4.

Vink, D., Aartsen, M., & Schoevers, R. (2008). Risk factors for anxiety and depression in the elderly: A review *Journal of Affective Disorders, 106,* 29–44.

Von Itallie, T. B. (1985). Health implications of overweight and obesity in the United States. *Annals of Internal Medicine, 103,* 983–988.

Voth, H. M., & Orth, M. H. (1973). *Psychotherapy and the role of the environment.* New York: Behavioral Press.

Wachtel, P. L. (1975). Behavior therapy and the facilitation of psychoanalytic exploration. *Psychotherapy: Theory, Research, and Practice, 12,* 68–72.

Wachtel, P. L. (1977). *Psychoanalysis and behavior therapy: Toward an integration.* New York: Basic Books.

Wachtel, P. L. (1982). What can dynamic therapies contribute to behavior therapy? *Behavior Therapy, 13,* 594–609.

Wachtel, P. L. (1984). On theory, practice, and the nature of integration. In H. Arkowitz & S. R. Messer (Eds.), *Psychoanalytic therapy and behavior therapy: Is integration possible?* (pp. 31–52). New York: Plenum Press.

Wachtel, P. L. (1987). *Action and insight.* New York: Guilford Press.

Wachtel, P. L. (2002). Termination of therapy: An effort at integration. *Journal of Psychotherapy Integration, 12,* 373–383.

Wachtel, P. L (2008). Psychotherapy and psychotherapy integration: An international perspective. *Journal of Psychotherapy Integration, 18,* 66–69.

Wadden, T. A., Sternberg, J. A., Letizia, K. A., Stunkard, A. J., & Foster, G. D. (1989). Treatment of obesity by very low calorie diet, behavior therapy, and their combination: A five-year perspective. *International Journal of Obesity, 13,* 39–46.

Wade, N. G., & Meyer, J. E. (2009). Comparison of brief group interventions to promote forgiveness: A pilot outcome study. *International Journal of Group Psychotherapy, 59,* 199–220.

Wagner, M. (1990, April). The school programs and school performance of secondary students classified as learning disabled: Findings from the National Longitudinal Transition study of special education students. Paper presented at *Division G, American Educational Research Association Annual Meeting,* Boston.

Wakefield, P. J., Williams, R. E., Yost, E. B., & Patterson, K. M. (1996). *Couple therapy for alcoholism: A cognitive-behavioral treatment manual.* New York: Guilford Press.

Wald, M. L. (2001). Low seat belt use linked to teenage death rates. *New York Times,* p. A12.

Wallace, W. A., & Hall, D. L. (1996). *Psychological consultation: Perspectives and applications*. Pacific Grove, CA: Brooks/Cole.

Wallach, H. S., Safir, M. P., & Bar-Zvi, M. (2009). Virtual reality cognitive behavior therapy for public speaking anxiety: A randomized clinical trial. *Behavior Modification, 33*, 314–338.

Walker, E. F. & Tessner, K. (2008). Schizophrenia. *Perspectives on Psychological Science, 3*, 30–37.

Wampold, B. E. (2001). *The great psychotherapy debate: Models, methods, and findings*. Mahwah, NJ: Erlbaum.

Wan, K. W. (2008). Mental health and poverty. *The Journal of the Royal Society for the Promotion of Health, 128*, 108–109.

Wandersman, A., Poppen, P. J., & Ricks, D. F. (Eds.). (1976). *Humanism and behaviorism: Dialogue and growth*. Elmsford, NY: Pergamon Press.

Wang, S. S., Wadden, T. A., Womble, L. G., & Noras, C. A. (2003). What consumers want to know about commercial weight-loss programs: A pilot investigation. *Obesity Research, 11*, 48–53.

Ward, T., Hudson, S. M., & Keenan, T. R. (2001). The assessment and treatment of sexual offenders against children. In C. R. Hollin (Ed.), *Handbook of offender assessment and treatment* (pp. 349–361). New York: Wiley.

Warwick, H. M. C., & Salkovskis, P. M. (2001). Cognitive-behavioral treatment of hypochondriasis. In V. Starcevic & D. R. Lipsitt (Eds.), *Hypochondriasis: Modern perspectives on an ancient malady* (pp. 314–328). Oxford, England: Oxford University Press.

Waschbusch, D. A. (2002). A meta-analytic examination of comorbid hyperactive-impulsive attention problems. *Psychological Bulletin, 128*, 118–150.

Watkins, C. E. (1992). Reflections on the preparation of psychotherapy supervisors. *Journal of Clinical Psychology, 48*, 145–147.

Watson, J. B., & Rayner, R. (1920). Conditioned emotional reactions. *Journal of Experimental Psychology, 3*, 1–14.

Watzlawick, P., Weakland, J., & Fisch, R. (1974). *Change: Principles of problem formation and problem resolution*. New York: Norton.

Wechsler, D. (1981). *Wechsler Adult Intelligence Scale—Revised*. San Antonio, TX: Psychological Corporation.

Wechsler, D. (1997a). *Wechsler Adult Intelligence Scale* (3rd ed.). San Antonio, TX: Psychological Corporation.

Wechsler, D. (1997b). *Wechsler Memory Scale* (3rd ed.). San Antonio, TX: Psychological Corporation.

Wechsler, D. (2002). *Wechsler Preschool and Primary Scale of Intelligence-III*. San Antonio, TX: Psychological Corporation.

Wechsler, D. (2003). *Wechsler Intelligence Scale for Children* (4th ed.). San Antonio, TX: Psychological Corporation.

Wechsler, D. (2008). *Wechsler Adult Intelligence Scale* (4th ed.). Minneapolis, MN: Pearson Assessments.

Wechsler, H., Seibring, M., Liu. I. C., & Ahl, M. (2004). Colleges respond to student binge drinking: Reducing student demand or limiting access. *Journal of American College Health, 52*, 159–168.

Weiderhold, B. K., & Weiderhold, M. D. (2000). Lessons learned from 600 virtual reality sessions. *CyberPsychology and Behavior, 3*, 393–400.

Weinberger, J. (1995). Common factors aren't so common: The common factors dilemma. *Clinical Psychology: Science and Practice, 2*, 45–69.

Weiner, I. B. (1975). *Principles of psychotherapy*. New York: Wiley.

Weiner, I. B. (1996). Some observations on the validity of the Rorschach Inkblot method. *Psychological Assessment, 8*, 206–213.

Weiner, I. B. (2003). *Principles of Rorschach interpretation*. Mahwah, N.J.: Lawrence Erlbaum.

Weiner, I. B., & Hess, A. K. (Eds.). (2006). *The handbook of forensic psychology* (3rd ed.). Hoboken, NJ: Wiley.

Weiner, J. P., & de Lissovoy, G. (1993). Razing a Tower of Babel: A taxonomy for managed care and health insurance plans. *Journal of Health, Politics, Policy, and Law, 18*, 75–103.

Weinhardt, L. S., Carey, M. P., Carey, K. B., Maisto, S. A., & Gordon, C. M. (2001). The relation of alcohol use to sexual HIV risk behavior among adults with a severe and persistent mental illness. *Journal of Consulting and Clinical Psychology, 69*, 77–84.

Weiss, L. & Wolchik, S. (1998). New beginnings: An empirically-based intervention program for divorced mothers to help their children adjust to divorce. In J. M. Breismeister & C. E. Schaefer (Eds.), *Handbook of parent training: Parents as co-therapists for children's behavior problems* (pp. 445–478). New York: Wiley.

Weissberg, R. P., Kumpfer, K. L., & Seligman, M. E. P. (2003). Prevention that works for children and youth: An introduction. *American Psychologist, 58,* 425–432.

Weisz, J. R., & Gray, J. S. (2008). Evidence-based psychotherapy for children and adolescents: Data from the present and a model for the future. *Child & Adolescent Mental Health, 13,* 54–65.

Weisz, J. R., Weiss, B., Alicke, M. D., & Klotz, M. L. (1987). Effectiveness of psychotherapy with children and adolescents: A meta-analysis for clinicians. *Journal of Consulting and Clinical Psychology, 55,* 542–549.

Welch, S. S. (2001). A review of the literature on the epidemiology of parasuicide in the general population. *Psychiatric Services, 52,* 368–375.

Weller, E. B., & Weller, R. A. (1988). Neuroendrocrine changes in affectively ill children and adolescents. *Endocrinology and Metabolism Clinics of North America, 17,* 41–53.

Wellner, A. S. (2001). Americans with disabilities. *Forecast, 21,* 1–2.

Welsh, R. S. (2003). Prescription privileges: Pro or con. *Clinical Psychology: Science and Practice, 10,* 371–372.

West, S. G., & Graziano, W. G. (1989). Long-term stability and change in personality: An introduction. *Journal of Personality, 57,* 175–193.

Weston, D. (2000). Integrative psychotherapy: Integrating psychological and cognitive-behavioral theory and technique. In C. R. Snyder & R. E. Ingram (Eds.), *Handbook of psychological change: Psychotherapy processes and practices for the 21st century* (pp. 217–242). New York: Wiley.

Whalen, C. K., Henker, B., & Hinshaw, S. P. (1985). Cognitive-behavioral therapies for hyperactive children: Premises, problems, and prospects. *Journal of Abnormal Child Psychology, 13,* 391–410.

Wheeler, J. G., Christensen, A., & Jacobson, N. S. (2001). Couple distress. In D. H. Barlow (Ed.), *Clinical handbook of psychological disorders: A step-by-step treatment manual (3rd ed., pp. 609–630).* New York: Guilford Press.

Whitaker, C., & Keith, D. (1981). Symbolic experiential family therapy. In A. Gurman & D. Kniskern (Eds.), *Handbook of family therapy* (pp. 187–225). New York: Brunner/Mazel.

White, J. (2000). *Treating anxiety and stress: A group psycho-educational approach using brief CBT.* New York: Wiley.

White, M. (1986). Negative explanation, restraint, and double description: A template for family therapy. *Family Process, 25,* 169–184.

White, M., & Epston, D. (1990). *Narrative means to therapeutic ends.* New York: Brunner/Mazel.

Whitehurst, T., Ridolfi, M. E., & Gunderson, J. (2002). Multiple family group treatment for borderline personality disorder. In S. G. Hofmann & M. C. Tompson (Eds.), *Treating chronic and severe mental disorders: A handbook of empirically supported interventions,* (pp. 343–363). New York: Guilford Press.

Wright, M. E., & Wright, B. A. (1987). *Clinical practice of hypnotherapy.* New York: Guilford Press.

Wicherski, M., Michalski, D., & Kohout, J. (2009). *2007 doctorate employment survey.* Washington, DC: American Psychological Association.

Widiger, T. A., & Clark, L. A. (2000). Toward *DSM-V* and the classification of psychopathology. *Psychological Bulletin, 126,* 946–963.

Wiens, A. N. (1989). Structured clinical interviews for adults. In G. Goldstein & M. Herson (Eds.), *Handbook of psychological assessment* (pp. 309–328). Elmsford, NY: Pergamon Press.

Wiggins, J. S., & Pincus, A. L. (1989). Conceptions of personality disorders and dimensions of personality. *Psychological Assessment, 1,* 305–316.

Wilens, T. E., Biederman, J., & Spencer, T. J. (2002). Attention deficit/hyperactivity disorder across the lifespan. *Annual Review of Medicine, 53,* 113–131.

Wilfley, D. E., Agras, W. S., Telch, C. F., Rossiter, E. M., Schneider, J. A., Cole, A. G., et al. (1993). Group cognitive-behavioral therapy and group interpersonal therapy for the nonpurging bulimic: A controlled comparison. *Journal of Consulting and Clinical Psychology, 61,* 296–305.

Wilkinson, G. S., & Robertson, G. J. (2006). *Wide Range Achievement Test 4 professional manual.* Lutz, FL: Psychological Assessment Resources.

Williams, D. (1982). The treatment of seizures: Special psychotherapeutic and psychobiological techniques. In H. Sands (Ed.), *Epilepsy: A handbook for the mental health professional* (pp. 58–74). New York: Brunner/Mazel.

Williams, D., & Mostofsky, D. (1982). Psychogenic seizures in childhood and adolescence. In T. Riley & A. Roy (Eds.), *Pseudoseizures* (pp. 169–184). Baltimore: Williams & Wilkins.

Williams, L. M. (1995). Recovered memories of abuse in women with documented child sexual victimization histories. *Journal of Traumatic Stress, 8,* 649–673.

Williams, P., & David, D. C. (2002). *Therapist as life coach: Transforming your practice.* New York: Norton.

Williamson, G. M. (2000). Extending the activity restriction model of depressed affect: Evidence from a sample of breast cancer patients. *Health Psychology, 19,* 339–347.

Williamson, D. A., Champagne, C. M., Jackman, L. P., & Varnado, P. J. (1996). Lifestyle Change: A Program for Long-Term Behavioral Weight Management. In V. B. Van Hasselt & M. Hersen (Eds.), *Sourcebook of psychological treatment manuals for adult disorders* (pp. 423–488), New York: Plenum Press.

Willis, D. (1995). Psychological impact of child abuse and neglect. *Journal of Clinical Child Psychology, 24,* 2–4.

Wilson, D. S., & Wilson, E. O. (2007). Rethinking the theoretical foundation of sociobiology. *The Quarterly Review of Biology, 82,* 327–348.

Wilson, E. O. (1978). *On human nature.* Cambridge, MA: Harvard University Press.

Wilson, E. O. (1983). Sociobiology and human beings. *Psychohistory Review, 11,* 5–14.

Wilson, E. O. (1991). Animal communication. In W. S. Y. Wang (Ed.), *The emergence of language: Development and evolution: Readings from Scientific American magazine* (pp. 3–15). New York: Freeman.

Wilson, E. O. (2003). *The future of life.* New York: Vintage.

Wilson, G. T. (1981). Some comments on clinical research. *Behavioral Assessment, 3,* 217–226.

Wilson, G. T. (1996). Empirically validated treatments: Reality and resistance. *Clinical Psychology: Science and Practice, 3,* 241–244.

Wilson, G. T. (1997). Cognitive behavioral treatment of bulimia nervosa. *Clinical Psychologist, 50,* 10–12.

Wilson, G. T., & Frank, C. M. (Eds.). (1982). *Contemporary behavior therapy: Conceptual and empirical foundations.* New York: Guilford Press.

Wilson, G. T., & Pike, K. M. (2001). Eating disorders. In D. H. Barlow (Ed.), *Clinical handbook of psychological disorders: A step-by-step treatment manual* (3rd ed., pp. 332–375). New York: Guilford.

Wilson, G. T., & Rachman, S. (1983). Meta-analysis and the evaluations of psychotherapy outcome: Limitations and liabilities. *Journal of Consulting and Clinical Psychology, 51,* 54–64.

Wilson, J. L., Armoutliev, E., Yakunina, E., & Werth, J. L. (2009). Practicing psychologists' reflections on evidence-based practice in psychology. *Professional Psychology: Research and Practice, 40,* 403–409.

Windle, C. (1952). Psychological tests in psychopathological prognosis. *Psychological Bulletin, 49,* 451–482.

Winker, M. A. (1994). Tacrine for Alzheimer's disease: Which patient, what dose? *Journal of the American Medical Association, 271,* 1023–1024.

Wisocki, P. A., Grebstein, L. C., & Hunt, J. B. (1994). Directors of clinical training: An insider's perspective. *Professional Psychology: Research and Practice, 25,* 482–488.

Wolfe, D. A., Aragona, J., Kaufman, K., & Sandler, J. (1980). The importance of adjudication in the treatment of child abuse: Some preliminary findings. *Child Abuse and Neglect, 4,* 127–135.

Wolff, E. N. (1998). Recent trends in the size distribution of household wealth. *Journal of Economic Perspectives, 12,* 3.

Wolfson (1998). Working with Parents on Developing Efficacious Sleep/Wake Habits for Infants and Young Children. In J. M. Breismeister & C. E. Schaefer (Eds.), *Handbook of parent training: Parents as co-therapists for children's behavior problems* (pp. 347–383). New York: Wiley.

Wolpe, J. (1958). *Psychotherapy by reciprocal inhibition.* Stanford, CA: Stanford University Press.

Wolpe, J., & Lazarus, A. A. (1966). *Behavior therapy techniques: A guide to treatment of neuroses.* New York: Pergamon Press.

Wong, S. E. & Liberman, R. P. (1996). Biobehavioral treatment and rehabilitation for persons with schizophrenia. In V. B. Van Hasselt & M. Hersen (Eds.), *Sourcebook of psychological treatment manuals for adult disorders* (pp. 233–256), New York: Plenum Press.

Wood, B. J., Klein, S., Cross, H. J., Lammers, C. J., & Elliott, J. K. (1985). Impaired practitioners: Psychologists' opinions about prevalence, and proposals for intervention. *Professional Psychology: Research and Practice, 16,* 843–850.

Wood, J. M., Lilienfeld, S. O., Garb, H. N., & Nezworski, M. T. (2000). The Rorschach test in clinical diagnosis: A critical review, with a backward look at Garfield (1947). *Journal of Clinical Psychology, 56,* 395–430.

Wood, J., Nezworski, M. T., Lilienfeld, S. O., Garb, H. N. (2003). *What's wrong with the Rorschach?* San Francisco: Jossey-Bass.

Woodcock, R. W., McGrew, K. S., & Mather, N (2001). *Manual for the Woodcock-Johnson Tests of Cognitive Abilities (WJ III).* Rolling Meadows, IL: Riverside.

World Health Organization (2006). *AIDS epidemic update.* Washington, DC: Author.

Wright, M. E. & Wright, B. A. (1987). *Clinical practice of hypnotherapy.* New York: Guilford.

Wrightsman, L. (2001). *Forensic psychology.* Belmont, CA: Wadsworth.

Wurtzel, E. (1995). *Prozac nation.* New York: Riverhead.

Yalom, I. D. (1980). *Existential psychotherapy.* New York: Basic Books.

Yalom, I. D. (1985). *The theory and practice of group psychotherapy* (3rd ed.). New York: Basic Books.

Yalom, I. D., & Lieberman, M. A. (1971). A study of encounter group casualties. *Archives of General Psychiatry, 25,* 16–30.

Yamamoto, J., Silva, A., Sasao, T., Wang, C., & Nguyen, L. (1993). Alcoholism in Peru. *American Journal of Psychiatry, 150,* 1059–1062.

Yates, B. T. (1994). Toward the incorporation of costs, cost-effectiveness analysis, and cost-benefit analysis into clinical research. *Journal of Consulting and Clinical Psychology, 62,* 729–736.

Yost, E. B., Beutler, L. E., Corbishley, M. A., & Allender, J. R. (1986). *Group cognitive therapy: A treatment approach for depressed older adults.* Elmsford, NY: Pergamon Press.

Young, J. E., Weinberger, A. D., & Beck, A. T. (2001). Cognitive therapy for depression. In D. H. Barlow (Ed.), *Clinical handbook of psychological disorders: A step-by-step treatment manual (3rd ed., pp. 264–308).* New York: Guilford Press.

Young, M. E., & Fristad, M. A. (2007). Evidence based treatments for bipolar disorder in children and adolescents. *Journal of Contemporary Psychotherapy, 37,* 157–164.

Young, M. E., & Long, L. L. (1998). *Counseling and therapy for couples.* Pacific Grove, CA: Brooks/Cole.

Young, S., Toone, B., & Tyson, C. (2003). Comorbidity and psychosocial profile of adults with attention deficit hyperactivity disorder. *Personality and Individual Differences, 35,* 743–755.

Zametkin, A. J., Nordahl, T., Gross, M., King, A. C., Semple, W. E., Rumsey, J., et al. (1990). Cerebral glucose metabolism in adults with hyperactivity of childhood onset. *New England Journal of Medicine, 323,* 1361–1366.

Zane, N., Nagayma Hall, G. C., Sue, S., Young, K., & Nunez, J. (2004). Research on psychotherapy with culturally diverse populations. In M. J. Lambert (Ed.), *Bergin and Garfield's handbook of psychotherapy and behavior change* (5th ed., pp. 767–804). New York: Wiley.

Zhang, L.-F., & Sternberg, R. J. (Eds.). (2009). *Perspectives on the nature of intellectual styles.* New York: Springer.

Zhang, X. R., Proenca, M., Barone, M., Leopold, L., & Friedman, J. M. (1994). Positional cloning of the mouse obese gene and its human homologue. *Nature, 372,* 425–432.

Zhu, S. H., Stretch, V., Balabanis, M., Rosbrook, B., Sadler, G., & Pierce, L. P. (1996). Telephone counseling for smoking cessation: Effects of single-session and multiple-session interventions. *Journal of Consulting and Clinical Psychology, 64,* 202–211.

Zimet, C. N., & Throne, F. M. (1965). *Preconference materials.* Conference on the Professional preparation of Clinical Psychologists. Washington, DC: American Psychological Association.

Ziskin, J., & Faust, D. (1988). *Coping with psychiatric and psychological testimony* (Vols. 1–3, 4th ed.). Marina Del Rey, CA: Law and Psychology Press.

Zubin, J. (1954). Failures of the Rorschach technique. *Journal of Projective Techniques, 18,* 303–315.

Zubin, J., & Spring, B. (1977). Vulnerability: A new view of schizophrenia. *Journal of Abnormal Psychology, 86,* 103–126.

Zucker, R. A., & Gomberg, E. S. L. (1986). Etiology of alcoholism reconsidered: The case for a biopsychosocial process. *American Psychologist, 41,* 783–793.

Zur, O. (2007). *Boundaries in psychotherapy: Ethical and clinical explorations.* Washington, DC: American Psychological Association.

Author Index

Subject Index